Beginning C
Third Edition

IVOR HORTON

Apress™

Beginning C, Third Edition
Copyright © 2004 by Ivor Horton

ISBN (pbk): 1-59059-253-0

Printed and bound in the United States of America 1098765321

Lead Editor: Gary Cornell

Editorial Board: Steve Anglin, Dan Appleman, Gary Cornell, James Cox, Tony Davis, John Franklin, Chris Mills, Steve Rycroft, Dominic Shakeshaft, Julian Skinner, Jim Sumser, Karen Watterson, Gavin Wray, John Zukowski

Project Manager: Nate McFadden

Copy Manager: Nicole LeClerc

Copy Editors: Nicole LeClerc and Damon Larson

Production Manager: Kari Brooks

Production Editor: Janet Vail

Compositor: Dina Quan

Proofreader: Elizabeth Welch

Indexer: Valerie Perry

Artist: Kinetic Publishing Services, LLC

Cover Designer: Kurt Krames

Manufacturing Manager: Tom Debolski

Distributed to the book trade in the United States by Springer-Verlag New York, Inc., 175 Fifth Avenue, New York, NY 10010 and outside the United States by Springer-Verlag GmbH & Co. KG, Tiergartenstr. 17, 69112 Heidelberg, Germany.

In the United States: phone 1-800-SPRINGER, e-mail orders@springer-ny.com, or visit http://www.springer-ny.com. Outside the United States: fax +49 6221 345229, e-mail orders@springer.de, or visit http://www.springer.de.

For information on translations, please contact Apress directly at 2560 Ninth Street, Suite 219, Berkeley, CA 94710. Phone 510-549-5930, fax 510-549-5939, e-mail info@apress.com, or visit http://www.apress.com.

The source code for this book is available to readers at http://www.apress.com in the Downloads section.

Dedicated to the memory of Max, our Abyssinian, who was part of the family for 19 years until July 2003. I still miss his intrusions when I was working, and his companionship and affection when I wasn't.

Contents

Chapter 10 Essential Input and Output Operations *419*

Chapter 11 Structuring Data *449*

About the Author

Ivor Horton started out as a mathematician, but after graduating, he was lured by a well-known manufacturer into messing around with computers. He has spent many happy years programming occasionally useful applications in a variety of languages as well as teaching scientists and engineers to do likewise. He has extensive experience in applying computers to problems in engineering design and manufacturing operations. He is the author of a number of tutorial books on programming in C, C++, and Java. When not writing programming books or providing advice to others, he leads a life of leisure.

Acknowledgments

I'D LIKE TO THANK Gary Cornell for his enthusiasm about my past efforts, and for encouraging me to produce this new updated edition of *Beginning C*. My thanks to all the people at Apress who have done their usual outstandingly professional job of converting my draft text with all its imperfections into this finished product. Any imperfections that remain are undoubtedly mine.

My sincere thanks also go to those readers of previous editions of this book who took the trouble to point out my mistakes and areas that could be better explained. They have contributed significantly to this edition. I also greatly appreciate all those who wrote or e-mailed just to say how much they enjoyed the book or how it helped them get started in programming.

Last but certainly not least I'd like to thank my wife, Eve, who provides limitless love, support, and encouragement for whatever I choose to do.

Introduction

WELCOME TO *Beginning C, Third Edition.* With this book you can become a competent
C programmer. In many ways, C is an ideal language with which to learn programming. C is a very compact language, so there isn't a lot of syntax to learn before you
can write real applications. In spite of its conciseness and ease, it's also an extremely
powerful language that's still widely used by professionals. The power of C is such that
it's used for programming at all levels, from device drivers and operating system components to large-scale applications. C compilers are available for virtually every kind of
computer, so when you've learned C, you'll be equipped to program in just about any
context. Finally, knowledge of C is also an excellent base from which you can build an
understanding of the object-oriented C++.

My objective in this book is to minimize what I think are the three main hurdles
the aspiring programmer must face: coming to grips with the jargon that pervades
every programming language, understanding how to *use* the language elements
(as opposed to merely knowing what they are), and appreciating how the language
is applied in a practical context.

Jargon is an invaluable and virtually indispensable means of communication for
the expert professional as well as the competent amateur, so it can't be avoided. My
approach is to ensure that you understand the jargon and get comfortable using it in
context. In this way, you'll be able to more effectively use the documentation that
comes along with most programming products, and also feel comfortable reading and
learning from the literature that surrounds most programming languages.

Comprehending the syntax and effects of the language elements is obviously an
essential part of learning a language, but appreciating *how* the language features work
and *how* they are used is equally important. Rather than just using code fragments, I
always provide you with practical working examples that show the relationship of each
language feature to specific problems. These examples can then provide a basis for you
to experiment and see the effects of changing the code in various ways.

Your understanding of programming in context needs to go beyond the mechanics
of applying individual language elements. To help you gain this understanding, I conclude each chapter with a more complex program that applies what you've learned in
the previous examples. These programs will help you gain the competence and confi-
dence to develop your own applications, and provide you with insight into how you
can apply language elements in combination and on a larger scale. Most important,
they'll give you an idea of what's involved in designing real programs and managing
real code.

It's important to realize three things that are true for learning any programming
language. First, there *is* quite a lot to learn, but this means you'll gain a greater sense of
satisfaction when you've mastered it. Second, it's great fun, so you really will enjoy it.
Third, it's much easier than you think, so you positively *will* make it.

How to Use This Book

Because I believe in the hands-on approach, you'll write your first programs almost immediately. Every chapter has several programs that put the theory into practice, and these examples are key to the book. I advise you to type in and run all the examples that appear in the text because the very act of typing in programs is a tremendous aid to remembering the language elements. You should also attempt all the exercises that appear at the end of each chapter. When you get a program to work for the first time—particularly when you're trying to solve your own problems—you'll find that the great sense of accomplishment and progress make it all worthwhile.

We will start off at a gentle pace, but we'll gain momentum as we get further into the subject. Each chapter will cover quite a lot of ground, so take your time and make sure you understand everything before moving on. Experimenting with the code and trying out your own ideas is an important part of the learning process. Try modifying the programs and see what else you can make them do—that's when it gets really interesting. And don't be afraid to try things out—if you don't understand how something works, just type in a few variations and see what happens. A good approach is to read each chapter through, get an idea of its scope, and then go back and work through all the examples.

You might find some of the end-of-chapter programs quite difficult. Don't worry if it's not all completely clear on the first try. There are bound to be bits that you find difficult to understand at first, because they often apply what you've learned to rather complicated problems. And if you really get stuck, you can skip the end-of-chapter programs, move on to the next chapter, and come back to them later. You can even go through the entire book without worrying about them. The point of these programs is that they're a useful resource for you—even after you've finished the book.

Who Is This Book For?

Beginning C is designed to teach you how to write useful programs as quickly and easily as possible. This is the tutorial for you, if

- You're a newcomer to programming but you want to plunge straight into the C language and learn about programming and writing C programs right from the start.

- You've done a little bit of programming before, so you understand the concepts behind it—maybe you've used BASIC or PASCAL. Now you're keen to learn C and develop your programming skills further.

This book doesn't assume any previous programming knowledge on your part, but it does move quickly from the basics to the real meat of the subject. By the end of *Beginning C*, you'll have a thorough grounding in programming the C language.

What You Need to Use This Book

To use this book, you'll need a computer with a C compiler and library installed so that you can execute the examples, and a program text editor for preparing your source code files. There are plenty of C compilers on the market to choose from, and there are shareware versions available over the Internet. Ideally, you should choose a compiler that conforms to the current American National Standards Institute (ANSI) standard for C. Most C++ compilers available today will also compile C, so you can use one of these if you wish.

You can use any plain text editor, such as Notepad or Vi, to create your source program files. However, you'll get along better if your editor is designed for editing C code. Don't use a word processor such as Microsoft Word—word processors typically embed formatting codes in the text that won't be understood by your compiler.

To get the most out of this book, you need the willingness to learn, the desire to succeed, and the determination to continue when things are unclear and you can't see the way ahead. Almost everyone gets a little lost somewhere along the way when learning programming for the first time. When you find you are struggling to grasp some aspect of C, just keep at it—the fog will surely disperse and you'll wonder why you didn't understand the topic in the first place. You might believe that doing all this is going to be difficult, but I think you'll be surprised by how much you can achieve in a relatively short time. I'll help you to start experimenting on your own and become a successful programmer.

Conventions Used

I use a number of different styles of text and layout in the book to help differentiate between the different kinds of information. For the most part, their meanings will be obvious. Program code will appear like this:

```
void main()
{
    cout << "Beginning C";
}
```

When code fragments have been modified from a previous instance, the altered lines are shown in bold type like this:

```
void main()
{
    cout << "Beginning C by Ivor Horton";
}
```

When code appears in the text, it has a different typestyle, which looks like this: cout.

I'll use different types of "brackets" in the program code. They aren't interchangeable, and their differences are very important. I'll refer to the symbols ( ) as parentheses, the symbols { } as braces, and the symbols [ ] as square brackets.

Important new words in the text are shown in **bold** type.

Code from the Book

All the code from the book and solutions to the exercises are available for download from the Apress website at http://www.apress.com.

CHAPTER 1

Programming in C

C IS A POWERFUL AND COMPACT computer language that allows you to write programs that specify exactly what you want your computer to do. You're in charge: you create a program, which is just a set of instructions, and your computer will follow those instructions.

Programming in C isn't difficult, as you're about to find out. I'm going to teach you all the fundamentals of C programming in an enjoyable and easy-to-understand way, and by the end of this chapter, you'll have written your first few C programs. It's as easy as that!

In this chapter you'll learn

- How to create C programs

- How C programs are organized

- How to write your own program to display text on the screen

Creating C Programs

There are four fundamental stages, or processes, in the creation of any C program:

- Editing

- Compiling

- Linking

- Executing

You'll soon know all these processes like the back of your hand (you'll be doing them so easily and so often), but first let's consider what each process is and how it contributes to the creation of a C program.

Editing

This is the process of creating and editing C **source code**—the name given to the program instructions you write. Some C compilers come with a specific editor that can provide a lot of assistance in managing your programs. In fact, an editor often provides a complete environment for writing, managing, developing, and testing your programs. This is sometimes called an **integrated development environment**, or **IDE**.

You can also use other editors to create your source files, but they must store the code as plain text without any extra formatting data embedded in it. In general, if you have a compiler system with an editor included, then it will provide a lot of features that make it easier to write and organize your source programs. There will usually be automatic facilities for laying out the program text appropriately and color highlighting for important language elements, which not only makes your code more readable, but also provides a clear indicator when you make errors in keying in such words.

If you're working in UNIX, then the most common text editor is the vi editor. Alternately, you might prefer to use the emacs editor.

From a PC, you could use one the many freeware and shareware programming editors. These will often provide a lot of help in ensuring your code is correct with syntax highlighting and autoindenting of your code. Don't use word processors such as Microsoft Word, as they aren't suitable for producing program code.

Compiling

The compiler converts your source code into machine language, and detects and reports errors in the compilation process. The input to this stage is the file you produced during your editing, which is usually referred to as a **source file**.

The compiler can detect a wide range of errors that are due to invalid or unrecognized program code, as well as structural errors where, for example, part of a program can never be executed. The output from the compiler is known as **object code** and is stored in files called **object files**, which usually have names with the extension .obj. The compiler can detect several different kinds of errors during the translation process, and most of these will prevent the object file from being created.

 NOTE *In UNIX, object files have the extension* .o.

The result of a successful compilation is a file with the same name that you used for the source file, but with the .obj extension.

If you're working in UNIX, then the standard command to compile your C programs will be cc. You can use it like this:

```
cc -c myprog.c
```

where myprog.c is the program you want to compile. Note that if you omit the -o flag, your program will automatically be linked as well. If you're using the GNU's Not UNIX (GNU) compiler, you should type

```
gcc -c myprog.c.
```

The result of a successful compilation will be an object file.

Most C compilers will have a standard compile option, whether it's from the command line (such as `cc myprog.c`) or a menu option from within an IDE (where you'll find a Compile menu option).

Linking

The linker combines the various modules generated by the compiler from source code files, adds required code modules from program libraries supplied as part of C, and welds everything into an executable whole. The linker can also detect and report errors—for example, if part of your program is missing or a nonexistent library component is referenced.

In practice, if your program is of any significant size, it will consist of several separate source code files, which can then be linked. A large program may be difficult to write in one session. By breaking it up into a number of smaller source files, you can make the development of the program a whole lot easier. The source files can be compiled separately, which makes eliminating simple typographical errors a bit easier. Furthermore, the whole program can usually be developed incrementally. Each source file will have its own file name, and the set of source files that make up the program will usually be integrated under a **project name**, which is used to refer to the whole program.

Program libraries support and extend the C language by providing routines to carry out operations that aren't part of the language. For example, libraries contain routines that support operations such as performing input and output, calculating a square root, comparing two character strings, or obtaining date and time information.

A failure during the linking phase means that, once again, you have to go back and edit your source code. Success, on the other hand, will produce an executable file. In a Microsoft Windows environment, this executable file will have the `.exe` extension; in UNIX, there will be no such extension, but the file will be of an executable type.

In UNIX, the modules that are to be linked are given together with the `cc` command, for example:

```
cc myprog.c mod1.c mod2.o
```

These three modules will be linked. Notice that the last module here has the extension `.o`. This is because it has previously been compiled: the `.o` extension tells the compiler that the module is waiting to be linked and doesn't need to be compiled again. The output of this stage is a file called `a.out`, which you should then rename to something more meaningful.

An alternative form to this is as follows:

```
cc -o myprog myprog.c mod.c mod2.o
```

This will compile and link the module `myprog.c` and create an executable file called `myprog` (defined straight after the `-o` flag).

Many C compilers also have a Build option, which will compile and link your program in one step. This option will usually be found, within an IDE, in the Compile menu; alternatively, it may have a menu of its own.

Executing

The execution stage is when you run your program, having completed all the previous processes successfully. Unfortunately, this stage can also generate a wide variety of error conditions, ranging from producing the wrong output to sitting there and doing nothing, perhaps crashing your computer for good measure. In all cases, it's back to the editing process to check your source code.

Now for the good news: this is the stage where, at last, you get to see your computer doing exactly what you told it to do!

In UNIX and DOS, to execute a program you just enter the name of the file that has been compiled and linked.

In most IDEs, you'll find an appropriate menu command that allows you to Run or Execute your compiled program. This option may have a menu of its own, or you may find it under the Compile menu option.

In Windows, you can use Windows Explorer to locate the .exe file of your program, and then you can double-click the file.

The processes of editing, compiling, linking, and executing are essentially the same for developing programs in any environment and with any compiled language. Figure 1-1 summarizes how you would typically pass through each of these processes as you create your own C programs.

Creating Your First Program

It's time to create your first program. Let's step through the processes of creating a simple C program, from entering the program itself to executing the program. Don't worry if what you type doesn't mean anything to you at this stage—I'll explain everything as we go along.

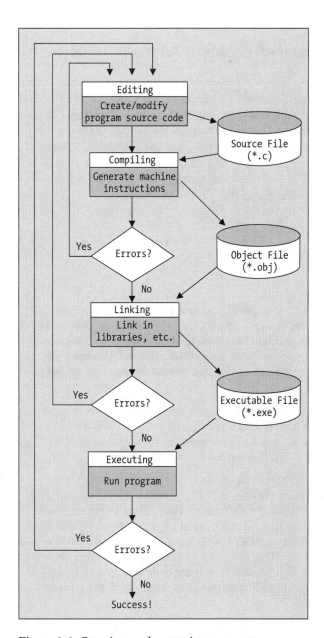

Figure 1-1. Creating and executing a program

....

Try It Out: An Example C Program

Run your editor and type in the following program exactly as it's written. Be careful to input the punctuation exactly as you see here. The brackets used on the fourth and last lines are braces—the curly ones {}, not the square ones [ ] or the round ones ()—it really does matter. Also, make sure you put the slashes the right way (/), as later you'll be using the backslash (\) as well. Don't forget the semicolon (;).

```
/* Program 1.1 Your Very First C Program - Displaying Hello World */
#include <stdio.h>

void main()
{
    printf("Hello world");
}
```

When you've entered the preceding source code, save the program as hello.c. You can use whatever name you like instead of hello, but the extension must be .c. This extension name is the common convention when you write C programs. The extension identifies the contents of the file as C source code. Most compilers will expect the source file to have the extension .c, and if it doesn't, the compiler may refuse to process it.

Now you're ready to compile your program. Exactly how you do this will depend upon which compiler you're using. If your C compiler allows you to work in an IDE, then you should easily be able to find your way to a menu where you can select the Compile option. In UNIX, the command you would use is cc.

Next, you'll link all the pieces necessary to create an executable program. This will add in code from the standard libraries that your program needs. Once again, the precise way to do this will depend upon which compiler system you're using. If you're using UNIX, then append any modules that you need to include at the end of your cc command. In an IDE, you'll find the Link option on one of the menus. Remember that many IDEs offer a Build option that will compile and link your program automatically. If you aren't working in an IDE, you should again consult your documentation to find out what the command is to run the linker.

Finally, you can execute your program. Remember that you can do this in several ways. There is the usual method of double-clicking the .exe file from Windows Explorer if you're using Windows. You could also run your program from the command line. To do so, just start a command-line session, change the current directory to the one that contains the .exe file for your program, and then enter the program name to run it. Within an IDE, you'll probably also have the option of running your program directly. Alternatively, there may be a Run menu that will compile, link, and execute the program in one go.

(Continued)

NOTE *If you're working in an IDE, you may need to use the Window menu to change to an Output window, where you can see the results of your program execution.*

If everything worked without producing any error messages, you've done it! This is your first program, and you should see the following message on the screen:

```
Hello world
```

Editing Your First Program

You could try altering the same program to display something else on the screen. For example, you might want to try editing the program to read like this:

```
/* Program 1.2 Your Second C Program */
#include<stdio.h>

void main()
{
   printf("If at first you don\'t succeed, try, try, try again!");
}
```

The \' sequence in the middle of the text to be displayed is called an **escape sequence**. Here it's a special way of including a single quote in the text. Because single quotes are used to indicate where a character constant begins and ends, you need a special way to indicate when you mean a single quote and not the start of a character constant. You'll learn more about escapes sequences very soon. You can try recompiling the program, relinking it, and running it again once you've altered the source. With a following wind, and a bit of luck, you've now edited your first program. You've written a program using the editor, edited it, and then compiled, linked, and executed it.

Dealing with Errors

To err is human, so there's no need to be embarrassed about making mistakes. Fortunately, computers don't generally make mistakes themselves and they're actually very good at indicating where we've slipped up. Sooner or later your compiler is going to present you with a list (and sometimes a list that's longer than you want) of the mistakes that are in your source code. You'll usually get an indication of the statements that are in error. When this happens, you must return to the editing stage, find out what's wrong with the incorrect code, and fix it. Keep in mind that one error can result in error messages for subsequent statements that may actually be correct. This usually happens with statements that refer to something that is supposed to be defined by a statement containing an error. Of course, if a statement that defines something has an error, then what was supposed to be defined won't be.

Let's step through what happens when your source code is incorrect by creating an error in a program. Edit your second program example, removing the semicolon (;) at the end of the line with printf() in it, as shown here:

```
/* Program 1.2 Your Second C Program */
#include<stdio.h>

void main()
{
   printf("If at first you don\'t succeed, try, try, try again!")
}
```

If you now try to compile this program, you'll see an error message that will vary slightly depending on which compiler you're using. A typical error message is as follows:

```
Syntax error : missing ';' before '}'
HELLO.C - 1 error(s), 0 warning(s)
```

Here, the compiler is able to determine precisely what the error is, and where. There really should be a semicolon at the end of that printf() line. As you start writing your own programs, you'll probably get lots of errors during compilation that are caused by simple punctuation mistakes. It's so easy to forget a comma or a bracket, or to just press the wrong key. Don't worry about this: lots of experienced programmers make exactly the same mistakes—even after years of practice.

As I said earlier, just one mistake can sometimes result in a whole stream of abuse from your compiler, as it throws you a multitude of different things that it doesn't like. Don't get put off by the number of errors reported. After you consider the messages carefully, the basic approach is to go back and edit your source code to fix what you can, ignoring the errors that you can't understand. Then try to compile the source file again. With luck, you'll get fewer errors the next time around.

To correct your example program, just go back to your editor and reenter the semicolon. Recompile and check for any other errors, and your program is fit to be run again.

Dissecting a Simple Program

Now that you've written and compiled your first program, let's go through another that's very similar and see what the individual lines of code do. Have a look at this program:

```
/* Program 1.3 Another Simple C Program - Displaying a Quotation */
#include <stdio.h>

void main()
{
   printf("Beware the Ides of March!");
}
```

This is virtually identical to your first program. Even so, you could do with the practice, so use your editor to enter this example and see what happens when you compile and run it. If you type it in accurately, compile it, and run it, you should get the following output:

```
Beware the Ides of March!
```

Comments

Look at the first line of code in the preceding example:

```
/* Program 1.3 Another Simple C Program - Displaying a Quotation */
```

This isn't actually part of the program code, in that it isn't telling the computer to do anything. It's simply a **comment**, and it's there to remind you, or someone else reading your code, what the program does. Anything between /* and */ is treated as a comment. As soon as your compiler finds /* in your source file, it will simply ignore anything that follows until it finds the matching */ that marks the end of the comment. This may be on the same line, or it can be several lines further on. Whatever is between /* and */ will be completely ignored by the compiler, even if it looks like program code.

You should try to get into the habit of documenting your programs, using comments as you go along. Your programs will, of course, work without comments, but when you write longer programs you may not remember what they do or how they work. Put in enough comments to ensure that, a month from now, you (and any other programmer) can understand the aim of the program and how it works.

As I said, comments don't have to be in a line of their own. A comment is everything between /* and */, wherever /* and */ are in your code. Let's add some more comments to the program:

```
/* Program 1.3 Another Simple C Program - Displaying a Quotation */
#include <stdio.h>                        /* This is a preprocessor directive    */

void main()                               /* This identifies the function main() */
{                                         /* This marks the beginning of main()  */
   printf("Beware the Ides of March!");   /* This line displays a quotation      */
}                                         /* This marks the end of main()        */
```

You can see that using comments can be a very useful way of explaining what's going on in the program. You can place comments wherever you want in your program, and you can use them to explain the general objectives of the code as well as the specifics of how the code works. You can also use comments to identify the author of the code and to assert your copyright if you wish.

Preprocessing Directives

Look at the following line of code:

```
#include <stdio.h>                /* This is a preprocessing directive */
```

This isn't strictly part of the executable program, but it is essential in this case—in fact, the program won't work without it. The symbol # indicates this is a **preprocessing directive**, which is an instruction to your compiler to do something before compiling the source code. The compiler handles these directives during an initial preprocessing phase before the compilation process starts. There are quite a few preprocessing directives, and they're usually placed at the beginning of the program source file.

In this case, the compiler is instructed to "include" in your program the contents of the file stdio.h. This file is called a **header file**, because it's usually included at the head of a program. It defines information about some of the functions that are provided by the standard C library. The header file will contain C source code and other preprocessor directives. In this case, as you're using the printf() function from the standard library, you have to include the stdio.h header file. This is because stdio.h contains the information that the compiler needs to understand what printf() means, as well as other functions that deal with input and output. All header files in C have file names with the extension .h. You'll use other C header files later in the book.

 NOTE *It's common practice to write the header file names in the* #include *directive in lowercase letters.*

Every C compiler that conforms to the American National Standards Institute (ANSI) standard for the language will have a set of standard header files supplied with it. Header files primarily contain definitions relating to standard library functions that are available with C. Although all ANSI standard C compilers will support the same set of standard library functions and will have the same set of standard header files available, there may be extra library functions provided with a particular compiler that may not be available with other compilers.

Defining the main() Function

The next four statements define the function main():

```
void main()                              /* This identifies the function main() */
{                                        /* This marks the beginning of main()  */
    printf("Beware the Ides of March!"); /* This line displays a quotation      */
}                                        /* This marks the end of main()         */
```

A **function** is just a named block of code between braces that carries out some specific set of operations. Every C program consists of one or more functions, and every C program must contain a function called main()—the reason being that a program will always start execution from the beginning of this function. So imagine that you've created, compiled, and linked a file called progname.exe. When you execute this program, it causes the function main() for the program to be called.

The first line of the definition for the function main() is as follows:

```
void main()                    /* This identifies the function main() */
```

This defines the start of the function main(). Notice that there is *no* semicolon at the end of the line. The first line identifying this as the function main() has the keyword void at the beginning. What appears here defines the type of value to be returned by the function. The keyword void signifies that the function main() returns no value.

There are circumstances in which you would want to return something from main() to the operating system—an error code, for example. In those situations, a keyword other than void would be used. I'll cover this in a later chapter.

The parentheses that immediately follow the name of the function, main, enclose a definition of what information is to be transferred to main() when it starts executing. In this example, however, you can see that there's nothing between the parentheses, so no information can be transferred. Later, you'll see how information is transferred to main() and to other functions in a program. In general, the function main() can call other functions that, in turn, may call further functions, and so on. For every function that's called, you have the opportunity to pass some information to it within the parentheses that follow its name.

Keywords

In C, a **keyword** is a word with special significance, so you shouldn't use keywords for any other purpose in your program. For this reason, keywords are also referred to as **reserved words**. In the preceding example, void is a keyword. C has several keywords, and you'll become familiar with more of them as you learn more of the language. You'll find a complete list of C keywords in Appendix C.

The Body of a Function

The general structure of the function main() is illustrated in Figure 1-2.

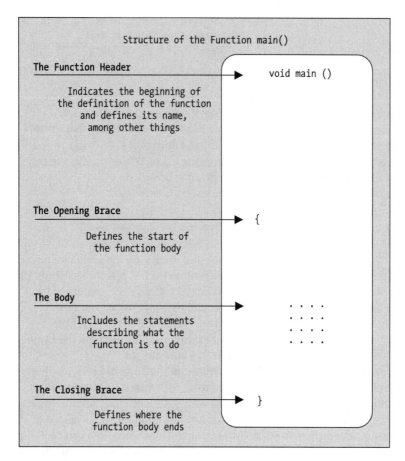

Figure 1-2. Structure of the function main()

The **function body** is the bit between the opening and closing braces that follow the line where the function name appears. The function body contains all the statements that define what the function does. The example's function main() has a very simple function body consisting of just one statement:

```
{                                       /* This marks the beginning of main() */
    printf("Beware the Ides of March!"); /* This line displays a quotation     */
}                                       /* This marks the end of main()       */
```

Every function must have a body, although the body can be empty and just consist of the two braces without any statements between them. In this case, the function will do nothing.

You may wonder where the use is for a function that does nothing. Actually, this can be very useful when you're developing a program that will have many functions. You can declare the set of (empty) functions that you think you'll need to write to solve the problem at hand, which should give you an idea of the programming that needs to be done, and then gradually create the program code for each function. This technique helps you to build your program in a logical and gradual manner.

> **NOTE** *You can see that I've aligned the braces one below the other. I've done this to make it clear where the block of statements that the braces enclose starts and finishes. Statements between braces are usually indented by a fixed amount—usually two or more spaces so that the braces stand out. This is good programming style, as the statements within a block can be readily identified.*

Outputting Information

The body of the example's function main() includes only one statement, which calls the printf() function:

```
printf("Beware the Ides of March!"); /* This line displays a quotation */
```

As I said, printf() is a standard library function, and it outputs information to the display screen based on what appears between the parentheses that immediately follow the function name. In this case, the call to the function displays a simple piece of Shakespearean advice that appears between the double quotes. Notice that this line *does* end with a semicolon.

Arguments

Items enclosed between the parentheses following a function name, as with the printf() function, are called **arguments**. When there is more than one argument to a function, they must be separated by commas.

If you don't like the quotation in this example's argument, you could display something else by simply including your own choice of words, within double quotes, between the parentheses. For instance, you might prefer a line from *Macbeth*:

```
printf("Out, damned Spot! Out I say!");
```

Try using this in the example. When you've modified the source code, you need to compile and link the program again before executing it.

> **NOTE** *As with all executable statements in C (as opposed to defining or directive statements) the* printf() *line must have a semicolon at the end. As you've seen, a very common error, particularly when you first start programming in C, is to forget the semicolon.*

Control Characters

You could alter the program to display two sentences on separate lines. Try typing in the following code:

```
/* Program 1.4 Another Simple C Program - Displaying a Quotation */
#include <stdio.h>

void main()
{
    printf("\nMy formula for success?\nRise early, work late, strike oil.");
}
```

The output from this program looks like this:

```
My formula for success?
Rise early, work late, strike oil.
```

Look at the printf() statement. At the beginning of the text and after the first sentence, you insert the characters \n. The combination \n actually represents one character: a newline character.

The backslash (\) is of special significance in a text string. It indicates the start of an **escape sequence**. Escape sequences are used to insert characters in a string that would otherwise be impossible to specify, such as tab and newline, or would confuse the compiler, such as a double quote that you use to delimit a string. The character following the backslash indicates what character the escape sequence represents. In this case, it's n for newline, but there are plenty of other possibilities. Obviously, if a backslash is of special significance, you need a way to specify a backslash in a text string. To do this, you simply use two backslashes: \\. Similarly, if you actually want to display a double quote character, you can use \".

Type in the following program:

```
/* Program 1.5 Another Simple C Program - Displaying Great Quotations */
#include <stdio.h>

void main()
{
    printf("\n\"It is a wise father that knows his own child.\"
                                                Shakespeare");
}
```

The output displays the following text:

```
"It is a wise father that knows his own child."  Shakespeare
```

You can use the \a escape sequence in an output string to sound a beep to signal something interesting or important. Enter and run the following program:

```
/* Program 1.6 A Simple C Program - Important */
#include <stdio.h>

void main()
{
   printf("\nBe careful!!\a");
}
```

The output of this program is sound and vision. Listen closely and you should hear a beep through the speaker in your computer.

```
Be careful!!
```

The \a sequence represents the "bell" character. Table 1-1 shows a summary of the escape sequences that you can use.

Table 1-1. Escape Sequences

Escape Sequence	Description
\n	Represents a newline character
\r	Represents a carriage return
\b	Represents a backspace
\f	Represents a form-feed character
\t	Represents a horizontal tab
\v	Represents a vertical tab
\a	Inserts a bell (alert) character
\"	Inserts a double quote (")
\'	Inserts a single quote (')
\\	Inserts a backslash (\)

Try displaying different lines of text on the screen and alter the spacing within that text. You can put words on different lines using \n, and you can use \t to space the text. You'll get lot more practice with these as you progress through the book.

Developing Programs in C

The process of developing programs in C may not be evident if you've never written a program before. However, it's very similar to many other situations in life in which, at the beginning, it just isn't clear how you're going to achieve your objective. Normally, you start with an idea of what you want to achieve, but you need to translate this into a more precise specification of what you want. Once you've reached this more precise specification, you can work out the series of steps that will lead to your final objective. So having an idea that you want to build a house just isn't enough. You need to know what kind of house you want, how large it's going to be, what kinds of materials you have to build it with, and where you want to build it. This kind of detailed planning is also necessary when you want to write a program.

Let's go through the basic steps that you need to follow when you're writing a program. The house analogy is a useful one, so we'll work with it for a while.

Understanding the Problem

The first step is to get a clear idea of what you want to do. It would be lunacy to start building your house before you had established what facilities it should provide: how many bedrooms, how many bathrooms, how big it's going to be, and so on. All these things affect the cost of the house in terms of materials and the work involved in building it. Generally, it comes down to a compromise that best meets your needs within the constraints of the money, the workforce, and the time that's available for you to complete the project.

It's the same with developing a program of any size. Even for a relatively straightforward problem, you need to know what kind of input to expect, how the input is to be processed, and what kind of output is required—and how it's going to look. The input could be entered with the keyboard, but it might also involve data from a disk file or information obtained over a telephone line or a network. The output could simply be displayed on the screen, or it could be printed; perhaps it might involve updating a data file on disk. For more complex programs, you'll need to look at many more aspects of what the program is going to do. A clear definition of the problem that your program is going to solve is an absolutely essential part of understanding the resources and effort needed for the creation of a finished product. Considering these details also forces you to establish whether or not the project is actually feasible.

Detailed Design

To get the house built, you'll need detailed plans. These plans enable the construction workers to do their job and the plans describe in detail how the house will go together—all the dimensions, the materials to use, and so on. You'll also need a plan of what is to be done and when. For example, you'll want the foundation dug before the walls are built, so the plan must involve segmenting the work into manageable units to be performed in a logical sequence.

It's the same with a program. You'll need to specify what the program does by dividing it into a set of well-defined and manageable chunks that are reasonably self-contained. You'll also need to detail the way in which these chunks connect, as well as what information each chunk will need when it executes. This will enable you to develop the logic of each chunk, relatively independently from the rest of the program. If you treat a large program as one huge process that you try to code as a single chunk, chances are that you'll never get it to work.

Implementation

Given the detailed design of a house, the work can start. Each group of construction workers will need to complete its part of the project at the right time. Each stage will need to be inspected to check that it's been done properly before the next stage begins. Omitting these checks could easily result in the whole house collapsing.

Of course, if a program is large, you'll write the source code one unit at a time. As one part is completed, you can write the code for the next. Each part will be based on the detailed design specifications, and you'll verify that each piece works, as far as you can, before proceeding to the next. In this way, you'll gradually progress to a fully working program that does everything you originally intended.

Testing

The house is complete, but there are a lot of things that need to be tested: the drainage, the water and electricity supplies, the heating, and so on. Any one of these areas can have problems that the contractors need to go back and fix. This is sometimes an iterative process, in which problems with one aspect of the house can be the cause of things going wrong somewhere else.

The mechanism with a program is similar. Each of your program **modules**—the pieces that make up your program—will need to be tested individually. When they don't work properly, you need to debug them. **Debugging** is the process of finding and correcting errors in your program. This term is said to have originated in the days when finding the errors in a program involved tracing where the information went and how it was processed by using the circuit diagram for the computer. The story goes that it was discovered how a computer program error was caused by an insect shorting part of the circuit in the computer. The problem was caused by a bug. Subsequently, the term **bug** was used to refer to any error in a program.

With a simple program, you can often find an error simply by inspecting the code. In general, though, the process of debugging usually involves adding extra program code to produce output that will enable you to check what the sequence of events is and what intermediate values are produced in a program. With a large program, you'll also need to test the program modules in combination because, although the individual modules may work, there's no guarantee that they'll work together! The jargon for this phase of program development is **integration testing**.

Functions and Modular Programming

The word "function" has appeared a few times so far in this chapter with reference to main(), printf(), function body, and so on. Let's explore in a little more depth what functions are and why they're important.

Most programming languages, including C, provide a way of breaking up a program into segments, each of which can be written more or less independently of the others. In C these segments are called **functions**. The program code in the body of one function is completely insulated from that of other functions. A function will have a specific interface to the outside world in terms of how information is transferred to it and how results generated by the function are transmitted back from it. This interface is specified in the first line of the function, where the function name appears.

Figure 1-3 shows a simple example of a program to analyze baseball scores that is composed of four modules.

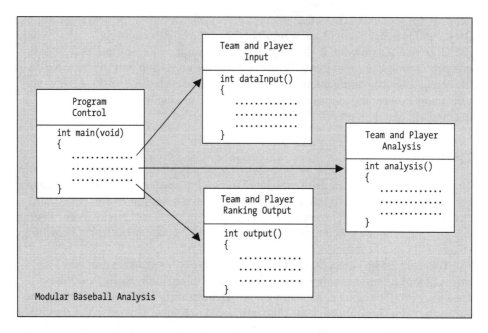

Figure 1-3. Modular programming

Each of the four modules does a specific, well-defined job. Overall control of the sequence of operations in the program is managed by one module, main(). There is a module to read and check the input data and another module to do the analysis. Once the data has been read in and analyzed, a fourth module has the task of outputting the team and player rankings.

Segmenting a program into manageable chunks is a very important aspect to programming, so let's go over the reasons for doing this:

- Dividing the program into a number of separate functions allows each function to be written and tested separately. This greatly simplifies the process of getting the total program to work.

- Several separate functions are easier to handle and understand than one huge function.

- Libraries are just sets of functions that people tend to use all the time. Because they've been prewritten and pretested, you know they'll work, so you can use them without worrying about their code details. This will accelerate your program development, by allowing you to concentrate on your own code, and it's a fundamental part of the philosophy of C. The richness of the libraries greatly amplifies the power of the language.

- You can accumulate your own libraries of functions that are applicable to the sorts of programs that you're interested in. If you find yourself writing a particular function frequently, you can write a generalized version of it to suit your needs and build this into your own library. Then, whenever you need to use that particular function, you can simply use your library version.

- In the development of very large programs, which can vary from a few thousand to millions of lines of code, development can be undertaken by teams of programmers, with each team working with a defined subgroup of the functions that make up the whole program.

You'll learn about C functions in greater detail in Chapter 8. Because the structure of a C program is inherently functional, you've already encountered one of the standard library functions in one of this chapter's earliest examples: the function printf().

Try It Out: Exercising What You Know

Let's now look at an example that puts into practice what you've learned so far. First, have a look at the following code and see whether you can understand what it does without running it. Then type it in; compile, link, and run it; and see what happens.

```
/* Program 1.7 A longer program   */
#include <stdio.h>     /* Include the header file for input and output */

void main()
{
   printf("Hi there!\n\n\nThis program is a bit");
   printf(" longer than the others.");
   printf("\nBut really it's only more text.\n\n\n\a\a");
   printf("Hey, wait a minute!! What was that???\n\n");
   printf("\t1.\tA bird?\n");
   printf("\t2.\tA plane?\n");
   printf("\t3.\tA control character?\n");
   printf("\n\t\t\b\bAnd how will this look when it prints out?\n\n");
}
```

The output will be as follows:

```
Hi there!


This program is a bit longer than the others.
But really it's only more text.


Hey, wait a minute!! What was that???
```

(Continued)

1.   A bird?
2.   A plane?
3.   A control character?

And how will this look when it prints out?

HOW IT WORKS

The program looks a little bit complicated, largely because the text strings between parentheses include a lot of escape sequences. Each text string is bounded by a pair of double quotation marks. However, the program is just a succession of calls to the printf() function, and it demonstrates that output to the screen is controlled by what you pass to the printf() function. Let's look at this program in detail.

You include the stdio.h file through the preprocessing directive:

```
#include <stdio.h>    /* Include the header file for input and output */
```

You can see that this is a preprocessing directive because it begins with #. The stdio.h file provides the definitions you need to be able to use the printf() function.

You then define the start of the function main() and specify that it doesn't return a value with this line:

```
void main()
```

The opening brace on the next line indicates that the body of the function follows:

```
{
```

The next statement calls the standard library function printf() to output Hi there! to your display screen, followed by two blank lines and the phrase This program is a bit.

```
  printf("Hi there!\n\n\nThis program is a bit");
```

The two blank lines are produced by the three \n escape sequences. Each of these starts a new line when the characters are written to the display. The first ends the line containing Hi there!, and the next two produce the two empty lines. The text This program is a bit appears on the fourth line of output. You can see that this one line of code produces a total of four lines of output on the screen.

The next line of output produced by the next printf() starts at the character position immediately following the last character in the previous output.

(Continued)

The next statement outputs the text longer than the others. with a space as the first character of the text:

```
printf(" longer than the others.");
```

This output will simply continue where the last line left off, following the t in bit. This means that you really do need the space at the beginning of the text, otherwise the computer will display This program is a bitlonger than the others, which isn't what you want.

The next statement starts its output on a new line, immediately following the previous line, because of the \n at the beginning of the text string between double quotation marks:

```
printf("\nBut really it's only more text.\n\n\n\a\a");
```

It then displays the text and adds two empty lines (because of the three \n escape sequences) and beeps twice. The next output to the screen will start at the beginning of the line that follows the second empty line produced here.

The next output is produced by the following statement:

```
printf("Hey, wait a minute!! What was that???\n\n");
```

This outputs the text and then leaves one empty line. The next output will be on the line following the empty line.

Each of the next three statements inserts a tab, displays a number, inserts another tab followed by some text, and ends with a new line. This is useful for making your output easier to read:

```
printf("\t1.\tA bird?\n");
printf("\t2.\tA plane?\n");
printf("\t3.\tA control character?\n");
```

This produces three numbered lines of output.

The last statement that produces output adds a new line, so that there will be an empty line after the previous output. Two tabs are then sent to the display, followed by two backspaces, which moves your cursor back two spaces from the last tab position. Lastly, the text is displayed, and two newline characters are sent to the display:

```
printf("\n\t\t\b\bAnd how will this look when it prints out?\n\n");
```

The closing brace marks the end of the function body:

```
}
```

Common Mistakes

Mistakes are a fact of life. When you write a computer program in C, the compiler must convert your source code to machine code, so there must be some very strict rules governing how you use the language. Leave out a comma where one is expected, or add a semicolon where you shouldn't, and the compiler won't be able to translate your program into machine code.

You'll be surprised just how easy it is to introduce typographical errors into a program, even after years of practice. If you're lucky, these errors will be picked up when you compile or link your program. If you're really unlucky, they can result in your program apparently working fine but producing some intermittent erratic behavior. You can end up spending a lot of time tracking these errors down.

Of course, it's not only typographical errors that cause problems. You'll often find that your detailed implementation is just not right. Where you're dealing with complicated decisions in your program, it's easy to get the logic wrong. Your program may be quite accurate from a language point of view, and it may compile and run without a problem, but it won't produce the right answers. These kinds of errors can be the most difficult to find.

Points to Remember

It would be a good idea to review what you've gleaned from your first program. You can do this by looking at the overview of the important points in Figure 1-4.

Summary

You've reached the end of the first chapter, and you've already written a few programs in C. You've covered quite a lot of ground, but at a fairly gentle pace. The aim of this chapter was to introduce a few basic ideas rather than teach you a lot about the C programming language. You should be confident about editing, compiling, and running your programs. You probably have only a vague idea about how to construct a C program at this point. It will become much clearer when you've learned a bit more about C and written some programs with more meat to them.

In the next chapter, you'll move on to more complicated things than just producing text output using the printf() function. You'll manipulate information and get some rather more interesting results. And by the way, the printf() function does a whole lot more than just display text strings—as you'll see soon.

Exercises

The following exercises enable you to try out what you've learned in this chapter. If you get stuck, look back over the chapter for help. If you're still stuck, you can download the solutions from the Downloads area of the Apress website (http://www.apress.com), but that really should be a last resort.

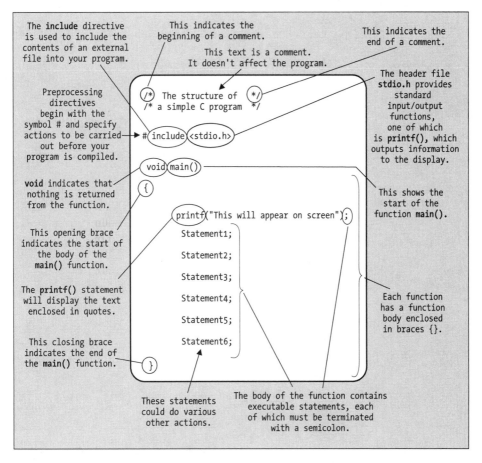

Figure 1-4. Elements of a simple program

Exercise 1-1. Write a program that will output your name and address using a separate printf() statement for each line of output.

Exercise 1-2. Modify your solution for the previous exercise so that it produces all the output using only one printf() statement.

Exercise 1-3. Write a program to output the following text, exactly as it appears here:

```
"It's freezing in here," he said coldly.
```

CHAPTER 2

First Steps in Programming

BY NOW YOU'RE PROBABLY EAGER to create programs that allow your computer to really interact with the outside world. You don't just want programs that work as glorified typewriters, displaying fixed information that you included in the program code, and indeed there's a whole world of programming that goes beyond that.

Ideally, you want to be able to enter data from the keyboard and have the program squirrel it away somewhere. This would make the program much more versatile. Your program would be able to access and manipulate this data, and it would be able to work with different data values each time you executed it. This idea of entering different information each time you run a program is key to the whole enterprise of programming. A place to store an item of data that varies in a program is, not altogether surprisingly, called a **variable**, and that is what this chapter covers.

This is quite a long chapter, and it covers a lot of ground. By the time you reach the end of it, you'll be able to write some really useful programs.

In this chapter you'll learn

- How memory is used and what variables are

- How you can calculate in C

- What different types of variables there are and what you use them for

- What casting is and when you need to use it

- How to write a program that calculates the height of a tree—any tree

Memory in Your Computer

First let's look at how the computer stores the data that's processed in your program. To understand this, you need to know a little bit about memory in your computer, so before you go into your first program, let's take a quick tour of your computer's memory.

The instructions that make up your program, and the data that it acts upon, have to be stored somewhere while your computer is executing that program. When your program is running, this storage place is the machine's memory. It's also referred to as **main memory**, or the **random access memory (RAM)** of the machine.

Your computer also contains another kind of memory called **read-only memory** (**ROM**). As its name suggests, you can't change ROM; you can only read its contents or have your machine execute instructions contained within it. The information contained in ROM was put there when the machine was manufactured. This information is mainly programs that control the operation of the various devices attached to your computer, such as the display, the hard disk drive, the keyboard, and the floppy disk drive. On a PC, these programs are called the **basic input/output system** (**BIOS**) of your computer. I don't need to refer to the BIOS in detail in this book. The interesting memory for your purposes is RAM: this is where your programs and data are stored when they execute. So let's understand a bit more about it.

You can think of your computer's RAM as an ordered sequence of boxes. Each of these boxes is in one of two states: either the box is full when it represents 1 or the box is empty when it represents 0. Therefore, each box represents one binary digit, either 0 or 1. The computer sometimes thinks of these in terms of **true** and **false**: 1 is true and 0 is false. Each of these boxes is called a **bit**, which is a contraction of "binary digit."

 NOTE *If you can't remember or have never learned about binary numbers, and you want to find out a little bit more, you'll find more detail in Appendix A. However, you needn't worry about these details if they don't appeal to you. The important point here is that the computer can only deal with 1s and 0s—it can't deal with decimal numbers directly. All the data that your program works with, including the program instructions themselves, will consist of binary numbers internally.*

For convenience, the boxes or bits in your computer are grouped into sets of eight, and each set of eight bits is called a **byte**. To allow you to refer to the contents of a particular byte, each byte has been labeled with a number, starting from 0 for the first byte, 1 for the second byte, and going up to whatever number of bytes you have in your computer's memory. This label for a byte is called its **address**. Thus, each byte will have an address that's different from that of all the other bytes in memory. Just as a street address identifies a particular house uniquely by its house number, the address of a byte uniquely references that byte in your computer's memory.

To summarize, you have your memory building blocks (called bits) that are in groups of eight (called bytes). A bit can only be either 1 or 0. This is illustrated in Figure 2-1.

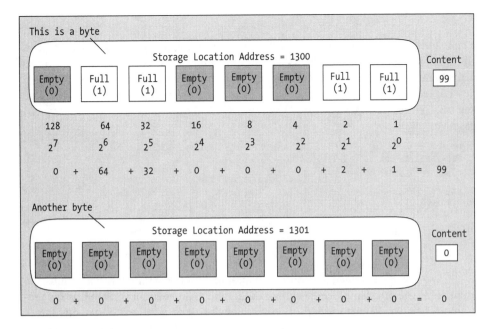

Figure 2-1. Bytes in memory

Memory is often expressed in terms of so many kilobytes, megabytes, or even gigabytes. Here's what those words mean:

- 1 kilobyte (or 1KB) is 1,024 bytes.

- 1 megabyte (or 1MB) is 1,024 kilobytes, which is 1,048,576 bytes.

- 1 gigabyte (or 1GB) is 1,024 megabytes, which is 1,073,741,841 bytes.

You might be wondering why you don't work with simpler, more rounded
numbers, such as a thousand, or a million, or a billion. The reason is that there are
1,024 numbers from 0 to 1,023, and 1,023 happens to be 10 bits that are all 1 in
binary: 11 1111 1111, which is a very convenient binary value. So while 1,000 is a very
convenient decimal value, it's actually rather inconvenient in a binary machine—it's
11 1110 1000, which is not exactly neat and tidy. The kilobyte (1,024 bytes) is therefore
defined in a manner that's convenient for your computer, rather than for you. Similarly,
for a megabyte, you need 20 bits, and for a gigabyte, you need 30 bits. One point of
confusion can arise here, particularly with disk drive capacities. Disk drive manufac-
turers often refer to a disk as having a capacity of 537 megabytes or 18.3 gigabytes,
when they really mean 537 million bytes and 18.3 billion bytes. Of course, 537 million
bytes is only 512 megabytes and 18.3 billion bytes is only 17 gigabytes.

Now that you know a bit about bytes, let's see how you can use this memory in
your programs.

What Is a Variable?

A **variable** is a specific piece of memory in your computer that consists of one or more contiguous bytes. Every variable has a name, and you can use that name to refer to that place in memory to retrieve what it contains or store a new data value there.

Let's start with a program that displays your salary using the printf() function that you saw in Chapter 1. Assuming your salary is $10,000, you can already write that program very easily:

```
/* Program 2.1 What is a Variable? */
#include <stdio.h>

void main()
{
   printf("My salary is $10000");
}
```

I'm sure you don't need any more explanation about how this works; it's almost identical to the programs you developed in Chapter 1. So how can you modify this program to allow you to customize the message depending on a value stored in memory? There are, as ever, several ways of doing this. What they all have in common, though, is that they use a variable.

In this case, you could allocate a piece of memory that you could call, say, salary, and store the value 10000 in it. When you want to display your salary, you could use the name you've given to the variable, which is salary, and the value that's stored in it (10000) would be displayed. Wherever you use a variable name in a program, the computer accesses the value that's stored there. You can access a variable however many times you need to in your program. And when your salary changes, you can simply change the value stored in the variable salary and the whole program will carry on working with the new value. Of course, all these values will be stored as binary numbers inside the computer.

You can have as many variables as you like in a program. The value that each variable contains, at any point during the execution of that program, is determined by the instructions contained in your program. The value of a variable isn't fixed, and it can change as many times as you need it to throughout a program.

Variables That Store Numbers

There are several different types of variables, and each type of variable is used for storing a particular kind of data. You'll start by looking at variables that you can use to store numbers. There are actually several ways in which you can store numbers in your program, so let's start with the simplest.

Integer Variables

Let's look first at variables that store integers. An **integer** is any whole number without a decimal point. Examples of integers are as follows:

1

10,999,000,000

−1

You'll recognize these values as integers, but what I've written here isn't quite correct so far as your program is concerned. You can't include commas in an integer, so the second value would actually be written in a program as 10999000000.

Here are some examples of numbers that are *not* integers:

1.234

999.9

2.0

−0.0005

Normally, 2.0 would be described as an integer because it's a whole number, but as far as your computer is concerned it isn't because it contains a decimal point. For your program, you must write the integer 2 as 2 with no decimal point. Integers are always written in a C program without a decimal point; if there's a decimal point, it isn't recognized an integer. Before I discuss variables in more detail (and believe me, there's a lot more detail!), let's look at a simple variable in action in a program, just so you can get a feel for how they're used.

....

Try It Out: Using a Variable

Let's go back to your salary. You can try writing the previous program using a variable:

```
/* Program 2.2 Using a variable  */
#include <stdio.h>

void main()
{
  int salary;            /* Declare a variable called salary          */
  salary = 10000;        /* A simple arithmetic assignment statement  */
  printf("My salary is %d.", salary);
}
```

(Continued)

Type in this example and compile, link, and execute it. You'll get the following output:

```
My salary is 10000.
```

The first three lines are exactly the same as in all the previous programs. Let's look at the new stuff.

The statement that identifies the memory that you're using to store your salary is as follows:

```
int salary;          /* Declare a variable called salary        */
```

This is called a **variable declaration** because it declares the name of the variable. The name, in this program, is salary.

 CAUTION *Notice that the variable declaration ends with a semicolon. If you omit the semicolon, your program will generate an error when you compile it.*

The variable declaration also specifies the type of data that the variable will store. You've used the keyword int to specify that the variable, salary, will be used to store an **int**eger value. The keyword int precedes the name of the variable. As you'll see later, declarations for variables that store other kinds of data consist of another keyword specifying a data type followed by a variable name in a similar manner.

 NOTE *Remember, keywords are special C words that mean something specific to the compiler. You must not use them as variable names or your compiler will get confused.*

The next statement is

```
salary = 10000;
```

This is a simple **arithmetic assignment statement**. It takes the value to the right of the equal sign and stores it in the variable on the left of the equal sign.

(Continued)

Here you're declaring that the variable salary will have the value 10000. You're storing the value on the right (10000) in the variable on the left (salary). The = symbol is called the **assignment operator** because it assigns the value on the right to the variable on the left.

You then have the familiar printf() statement, but it's a little different from how you've seen it in action before:

```
printf("My salary is %d.", salary);
```

There are now two **arguments** inside the parentheses, separated by a comma. An argument is an item of data that's passed to a function. In this program statement, the two arguments to the printf() function are as follows:

- *Argument 1* is a **control string**, so called because it controls how the output specified by the following argument (or arguments) is to be presented. This is the character string between the double quotes.

- *Argument 2* is the variable salary. How this variable will be displayed is determined by the first argument—the control string.

The control string is fairly similar to the previous example in that it contains some text to be displayed. However, if you look carefully, you'll see %d embedded in it. This is called a **conversion specifier** for the variable.

 NOTE *Conversion specifiers always start with a % character. Because a % in a control string always indicates the start of a conversion specifier, if you want to output a % character you must use the sequence %%.*

Conversion specifiers determine how variables are displayed on the screen. In this case, you use a d, which is a **d**ecimal specifier that applies to integer values (whole numbers). It just means that the second argument, salary, will be interpreted and output as a decimal (base 10) number.

Try It Out: Using More Variables

Let's try a slightly larger example:

```
/* Program 2.3 Using more variables */
#include <stdio.h>
```

(Continued)

```
void main()
{
    int brothers;              /* Declare a variable called brothers */
    int brides;                /* and a variable called brides       */

    brothers = 7;              /* Store 7 in the variable brothers   */
    brides = 7;                /* Store 7 in the variable brides      */

    /* Display some output */
    printf("%d brides for %d brothers", brides, brothers);
}
```

If you run this program you should get the following output:

```
7 brides for 7 brothers
```

HOW IT WORKS

This program works in a very similar way to the previous example. You first declare two variables, brothers and brides, with the following statements:

```
    int brothers;              /* Declare a variable called brothers */
    int brides;                /* and a variable called brides       */
```

Both of these variables are declared as type int so they both store integer values. Notice that they've been declared in separate statements. Because they're both of the same type, you could have saved a line of code and declared them together like this:

```
    int brothers, brides;
```

When you declare several variables in one statement, the variable names following the data type are separated by commas, and the whole line ends with a semicolon. This can be a convenient format, although there's a downside in that it isn't so obvious what each variable is for, because if they appear on a single line you can't add individual comments to describe each variable. However, you could write this single statement spread over two lines:

```
    int brothers,      /* Declare a variable called brothers */
        brides;        /* and a variable called brides       */
```

By spreading the statement out over two lines, you're able to put the comments back in. The comments will be ignored by the compiler, so it's still the exact equivalent of the original statement without the comments. Of course, you might as well write it as two statements.

(Continued)

Note that the declarations appear at the beginning of the executable code for the function. You should put all the declarations for variables that you intend to use at the beginning.

The next two statements initialize each of the variables with the same value, 7:

```
brothers = 7;        /* Store 7 in the variable brothers  */
brides = 7;          /* Store 7 in the variable brides    */
```

Note that the statements that declared these variables precede these statements. If one or the other of the declarations were missing or appeared later in the code, the program wouldn't compile.

In the next statement is a control string that will display a line of text. Within this text, the %d conversion specifiers will be replaced by the values currently stored in the variables that appear as the second and third arguments to the printf() function call—in this case, brides and brothers:

```
printf("%d brides for %d brothers", brides, brothers);
```

The conversion specifiers are replaced in order by the values of the variables that appear as the second and subsequent arguments to the printf() function, so the value of brides corresponds to the first specifier, and the value of brothers corresponds to the second. This would be clearer if you changed the statements that set the values of the variables as follows:

```
brothers = 8;        /* Store 8 in the variable brothers  */
brides = 4;          /* Store 4 in the variable brides    */
```

In this somewhat dubious scenario, the printf() statement would show clearly which variable corresponded to which conversion specifier, because the output would be

```
4 brides for 8 brothers
```

Naming Variables

The name that you give to a variable, conveniently referred to as a **variable name**, can be defined with some flexibility. A variable name is a string of one or more letters, digits, and underscore characters (_) that begins with a letter (incidentally, the underscore character counts as a letter). Examples of good variable names are as follows:

```
Radius

diameter
```

Auntie_May

Knotted_Wool

D666

Because a name can't begin with a digit, 8_Ball and 6_pack aren't legal names. A variable name can't include any other characters besides letters, underscores, and digits, so Hash! and Mary-Lou aren't allowed as names. This last example is a common mistake, but Mary_Lou would be quite acceptable. Because spaces aren't allowed in a name, Mary Lou would be interpreted as two variable names, Mary and Lou. Variables starting with one or two underscore characters are often used in the header files, so don't use the underscore as the first letter when naming your variables; otherwise, you run the risk of your name clashing with the name of a variable used in the standard library. For example, names such as _this and _that are best avoided.

Although you can call variables whatever you want within the preceding constraints, it's worth calling them something that gives you a clue to what they contain. Assigning the name x to a variable that stores a salary isn't very helpful. It would be far better to call it salary and leave no one in any doubt as to what it is.

 CAUTION *The number of characters that you can have in a variable name will depend upon your compiler. Up to 31 characters are generally supported, so you can always use names up to this length without any problems. I suggest that you don't make your variable names longer than this anyway, as they become cumbersome and make the code harder to follow. Some compilers will just truncate names that are too long.*

Another very important point to remember when naming your variables is that C is case sensitive, which means that the names Democrat and democrat are completely different. You can demonstrate this by changing the printf() statement so that one of the variable names starts with a capital letter, as follows:

```c
/* Program 2.3 Using more variables */
#include <stdio.h>

void main()
{
    int brothers;          /* Declare a variable called brothers */
    int brides;            /* and a variable called brides       */

    brothers = 7;          /* Store 7 in the variable brothers   */
    brides = 7;            /* Store 7 in the variable brides      */

    /* Display some output */
    printf("%d brides for %d brothers", Brides, brothers);
}
```

You'll get an error message when you try to compile this version of the program. The compiler interprets the two variable names brides and Brides as different, so it doesn't understand what Brides refers to. This is a common error. As I've said before, punctuation and spelling mistakes are one of the main causes of trivial errors.

Using Variables

You now know how to name and declare your variables, but so far this hasn't been much more useful than anything you learned in Chapter 1. Let's try another program in which you'll use the values in the variables before you produce the output.

....

Try It Out: Doing a Simple Calculation

This program does a simple calculation using the values of the variables:

```
/* Program 2.4 Simple calculations */
#include <stdio.h>

void main()
{
    int Total_Pets;            /* The total number of pets    */
    int Cats;                  /* The number of cats as pets   */
    int Dogs;                  /* The number of dogs as pets   */
    int Ponies;                /* The number of ponies as pets */
    int Others;                /* The number of other pets    */

    /* Set the number of each kind of pet */
    Cats = 2;
    Dogs = 1;
    Ponies = 1;
    Others = 46;

    /* Calculate the total number of pets */
    Total_Pets = Cats + Dogs + Ponies + Others;

    printf("We have %d pets in total", Total_Pets);  /* Output the result */
}
```

This example produces the output

```
We have 50 pets in total
```

(Continued)

As in the previous examples, all the statements between the braces are indented by the same amount. This makes it clear that all these statements belong together. You should always organize your programs the way you see here: indent a group of statements that lie between an opening and closing brace by the same amount. It makes your programs much easier to read.

You first define five variables of type `int`:

```
int Total_Pets;       /* The total number of pets    */
int Cats;             /* The number of cats as pets  */
int Dogs;             /* The number of dogs as pets  */
int Ponies;           /* The number of ponies as pets */
int Others;           /* The number of other pets    */
```

Because each of these variables will be used to store a count of a number of animals, it's definitely going to be a whole number. As you can see, they're all declared as type `int`.

Note that you could have declared all five variables in a single statement and included the comments, as follows:

```
int Total_Pets,       /* The total number of pets    */
    Cats,             /* The number of cats as pets  */
    Dogs,             /* The number of dogs as pets  */
    Ponies,           /* The number of ponies as pets */
    Others;           /* The number of other pets    */
```

The statement is spread over several lines so that you can add the comments in an orderly fashion. Notice that there are commas separating each of the variable names. Because the comments are ignored by the compiler, this is exactly the same as the following statement:

```
int Total_Pets, Cats, Dogs, Ponies, Others;
```

You can spread C statements over as many lines as you want. The semicolon determines the end of the statement, not the end of the line.

Now back to the program. The variables are given specific values in these four assignment statements:

```
Cats = 2;
Dogs = 1;
Ponies = 1;
Others = 46;
```

(Continued)

At this point the variable Total_Pets doesn't have an explicit value set. It will get its value as a result of the calculation using the other variables:

```
Total_Pets = Cats + Dogs + Ponies + Others;
```

In this arithmetic statement, you calculate the sum of all your pets on the right of the assignment operator by adding the values of each of the variables together. This total value is then stored in the variable Total_Pets that appears on the left of the assignment operator. The new value replaces any old value that was stored in the variable Total_Pets.

The printf() statement shows the result of the calculation by displaying the value of Total_Pets:

```
printf("We have %d pets in total", Total_Pets);
```

Try changing the numbers of some of the types of animals, or maybe add some more of your own. Remember to declare them, initialize their value, and include them in the Total_Pets statement.

Initializing Variables

In the previous example, you declared each variable with a statement such as this:

```
int Cats;                          /* The number of cats as pets    */
```

You set the value of the variable Cats using this statement:

```
Cats = 2;
```

This sets the value of the variable Cats to 2.

So what was the value before this statement was executed? Well, it could be anything. The first statement creates the variable called Cats, but its value will be whatever was left in memory from the last program that used this bit of memory. The assignment statement that appeared later set the value to 2, but it would be much better to initialize the variable when you declare it. You can do this with the following statement:

```
int Cats = 2;                      /* The number of cats as pets    */
```

This statement declares the variable Cats as type int *and* sets its initial value to 2.

Initializing variables as you declare them is a very good idea in general. It avoids any doubt about what the initial values are, and if the program doesn't work as it should, it can help you track down the errors. Avoiding leaving spurious values for variables when you create them also reduces the chances of your computer crashing when things do go wrong. Inadvertently working with junk values can cause all kinds of problems. From now on, you'll always initialize variables in the examples, even if it's just to 0.

Arithmetic Statements

The previous program was the first one that really *did* something. It was very simple—just adding a few numbers—but it *was* a significant step forward. This was an elementary example of using an arithmetic statement to perform a calculation. Now let's look at some more sophisticated calculations that you can do.

Basic Arithmetic Operations

In C, an arithmetic statement is of the following form:

```
Variable_Name = Arithmetic_Expression;
```

The arithmetic expression on the right of the = operator specifies a calculation using values stored in variables and/or explicit numbers that are combined using arithmetic operators such as addition (+), subtraction (-), multiplication (*), and division (/). There are also other operators, as you'll see.

In the previous example, the arithmetic statement was

```
Total_Pets = Cats + Dogs + Ponies + Others;
```

The effect of this statement is to calculate the value of the arithmetic expression to the right of the = and store that value in the variable specified on the left.

In C, the = symbol defines an action. It doesn't specify that the two sides are equal, as it does in mathematics. It specifies that the value resulting from the expression on the right is to be stored in the variable on the left. This means that you could have

```
Total_Pets = Total_Pets + 2;
```

This would be ridiculous as a mathematical equation, but in programming it's fine. Let's look at it in context. Imagine you'd rewritten the last part of the program to include the preceding statement. Here's a fragment of the program as it would appear with the statement added:

```
Total_Pets = Cats + Dogs + Ponies + Others;    /* Value stored is 50 */
Total_Pets = Total_Pets + 2;                    /* Value stored is 52 */
printf("The total number of pets is: %d", Total_Pets);
```

After executing the first statement here, `Total_Pets` contains the value 50. Then, in the second line, you add 2 to that value and store the result back in the variable `Total_Pets`. The final total that will be displayed is therefore 52.

 NOTE *In assignment operations, the expression on the right side of the = sign is evaluated first, and the result is then stored in the variable on the left. The new value replaces the value that was previously contained in the variable to the left of the assignment operator.*

Any expression that results in a numeric value is described as an **arithmetic expression**. The following are all arithmetic expressions:

```
3
```

```
1+2
```

```
Total_Pets
```

```
Cats + Dogs - Ponies
```

Evaluating any of these expressions produces a single numeric value. In a moment, you'll take a closer look at how an expression is made up, and you'll look into the rules governing its evaluation. First, though, you'll try some simple examples using the basic arithmetic operators that you have at your disposal. Table 2-1 shows these operators.

Table 2-1. Basic Arithmetic Operators

Operator	Action
+	Addition
-	Subtraction
*	Multiplication
/	Division
%	Modulus

You may not have come across the **modulus operator** before. It just calculates the remainder after dividing the value of the expression on the left of the operator by the value of the expression on the right. For this reason it's sometimes referred to as the **remainder operator**. The expression 12%5 would produce 2, because 12 divided by 5 leaves a remainder of 2. You'll look at this in more detail shortly. All these operators work as you'd expect with the exception of division, which has a slight aberration from the norm when applied to integers, as you'll see. Let's try some more arithmetic operations.

Try It Out: Subtraction and Multiplication

Let's look at a food-based program that demonstrates subtraction and multiplication:

```
/* Program 2.5 Calculations with cookies */
#include <stdio.h>

void main()
{
    int cookies = 5;
    int cookie_calories = 125;      /* Calories per cookie */
    int total_eaten = 0;            /* Total cookies eaten */

    int eaten = 2;                  /* Number to be eaten */
    cookies = cookies - eaten;      /* Subtract number eaten from cookies */
    total_eaten = total_eaten + eaten;
    printf("\nI have eaten %d cookies.  There are %d cookies left",
                                                    eaten, cookies);

    eaten = 3;                      /* New value for cookies to be eaten  */
    cookies = cookies - eaten;      /* Subtract number eaten from cookies */
    total_eaten = total_eaten + eaten;
    printf("\nI have eaten %d more.  Now there are %d cookies left\n",
                                                    eaten, cookies);
    printf("\nTotal energy consumed is %d calories.\n",
                                    total_eaten*cookie_calories);
}
```

This program produces the following output:

```
I have eaten 2 cookies.   There are 3 cookies left
I have eaten three more.   Now there are 0 cookies left

Total energy consumed is 625 calories.
```

HOW IT WORKS

You first declare and initialize three variables of type `int`:

```
    int cookies = 5;
    int cookie_calories = 125;      /* Calories per cookie */
    int total_eaten = 0;            /* Total cookies eaten */
```

(Continued)

You'll use the `total_eaten` variable to accumulate the total number of cookies eaten as execution of the program progresses, so you initialize it to 0.

The next variable that you declare and initialize holds the number of cookies to be eaten next:

```
int eaten = 2;                    /* Number to be eaten */
```

You use the subtraction operator to subtract `eaten` from the value of `cookies`:

```
cookies = cookies - eaten;       /* Subtract number eaten from cookies */
```

The result of the subtraction is stored back in the variable `cookies`, so the value of cookies will now be 5 – 2, which is 3.

Because you've eaten some cookies, you increment the count of the total eaten by the value of `eaten`:

```
total_eaten = total_eaten + eaten;
```

You add the current value of `eaten`, which is 2, to the current value of `total_eaten`, which is 0. The result, 2, is stored back in the variable `total_eaten`.

The `printf()` statement displays the number of cookies that are left:

```
printf("\nI have eaten %d cookies.  There are %d cookies left",
                                                eaten, cookies);
```

I couldn't fit the statement in the space available, so after the comma following the first argument to `printf()`, I put the rest of the statement on a new line. You can spread statements out like this to make them easier to read or fit within a given width on the screen.

Note that you could *not* split the string that is the first argument in this way. An explicit newline character isn't allowed in the middle of a string. When you need to split a string over two or more lines, each segment of the string on a line must have its own pair of double quotes delimiting it. For example, you could write the previous statement as follows:

```
printf("\nI have eaten %d cookies. "
                " There are %d cookies left",
                                                eaten, cookies);
```

Where there are two or more strings immediately following one another like this, the compiler will join them together to form a single string.

(Continued)

You display the values stored in eaten and cookies using the conversion specifier, %d, for integer values. The value of eaten will replace the first %d in the output string, and the value of cookies will replace the second. The string will be displayed starting on a new line because of the \n at the beginning.

The next statement sets the variable eaten to a new value:

```
eaten = 3;                          /* New value for cookies to be eaten  */
```

The new value, 3, replaces the previous value stored in eaten, which was 2. You then go through the same sequence of operations as you did before:

```
cookies = cookies - eaten;       /* Subtract number eaten from cookies */
total_eaten = total_eaten + eaten;
printf("\nI have eaten %d more.  Now there are %d cookies left\n",
                                                eaten, cookies);
```

Finally, you calculate and output the number of calories corresponding to the number of cookies eaten:

```
printf("\nTotal energy consumed is %d calories.\n",
                                total_eaten*cookie_calories);
```

Here the second argument to the printf() function is an arithmetic expression rather than just a variable. The compiler will arrange for the result of the expression total_eaten*cookie_calories to be stored in a temporary variable, and that value will be passed as the second argument to the printf() function. You can always use an expression for an argument to a function as long as it evaluates to a result of the required type.

Easy, isn't it? Let's take a look at division and the modulus operator.

Try It Out: Division and the Modulus Operator

Suppose you have a jar of 45 cookies and a group of 7 children. You'll share out the cookies equally among the children and work out how many each child has. Then you'll work out how many cookies are left over.

```
/* Program 2.6 Cookies and kids */
#include <stdio.h>

void main()
{
  int cookies = 45;                    /* Number of cookies in the jar */
```

(Continued)

```
int children = 7;                /* Number of children        */
int cookies_per_child = 0;       /* Number of cookies per child */
int cookies_left_over = 0;       /* Number of cookies left over */

/* Calculate how many cookies each child gets when they are divided up */
cookies_per_child = cookies/children;  /* Number of cookies per child */
printf("You have %d children and %d cookies", children, cookies);
printf("\nGive each child %d cookies.", cookies_per_child);

/* Calculate how many cookies are left over */
cookies_left_over = cookies%children;
printf("\nThere are %d cookies left over.\n", cookies_left_over);
}
```

When you run this program you'll get this output:

```
You have 7 children and 45 cookies
Give each child 6 cookies.
There are 3 cookies left over.
```

HOW IT WORKS

Let's go through this program step by step. Four integer variables, cookies, children, cookies_per_child, and cookies_left_over, are declared and initialized with the following statements:

```
int cookies = 45;                /* Number of cookies in the jar */
int children = 7;                /* Number of children        */
int cookies_per_child = 0;       /* Number of cookies per child */
int cookies_left_over = 0;       /* Number of cookies left over */
```

The number of cookies is divided by the number of children by using the division operator / to produce the number of cookies given to each child:

```
cookies_per_child = cookies/children;  /* Number of cookies per child */
```

The next two statements output what is happening, including the value stored in cookies_per_child:

```
printf("You have %d children and %d cookies", children, cookies);
printf("\nGive each child %d cookies.", cookies_per_child);
```

You can see from the output that cookies_per_child has the value 6. This is because the division operator always produces an integer result when the operands are integers. The result of dividing 45 by 7 is 6, with a remainder of 3.

(Continued)

You calculate the remainder in the next statement by using the modulus operator:

```
cookies_left_over = cookies%children;
```

The expression to the right of the assignment operator calculates the remainder that results when the value of cookies is divided by the value of children.

Finally, you output the reminder in the last statement:

```
printf("\nThere are %d cookies left over.\n", cookies_left_over);
```

....

More on Division with Integers

Let's look at the result of using the division and modulus operators where one or the other of the operands is negative. With division, if the operands have different signs, the result will be negative. Thus, the expression –45/7 produces the same result as the expression 45/–7, which is –6. If the operands in a division are of the same sign, then the result is positive. Thus, 45/7 produces the same result as –45/–7, which is 6.

With the modulus operator, the sign of the result is always the same as the sign of the left operand. Thus, 45%–7 results in the value 3, whereas –45%7 results in the value –3.

Unary Operators

The operators that you've dealt with so far have been **binary operators**. These operators are called **binary** operators because they operate on *two* data items. Incidentally, the items of data that an operator applies to are called **operands**. For example, the multiplication is a binary operator because it has two operands and the effect is to multiply one operand value by the other. However, there are some operators that are **unary**, meaning that they need only one operand. You'll see more examples later, but for now you'll just take a look at the single most common unary operator.

The Unary Minus Operator

You'll find the unary operator very useful in more complicated programs. It makes whatever is positive negative, and vice versa. You might not immediately realize when you would use this, but think about keeping track of your bank account. Say you have $200 in the bank. You record what happens to this money in a book with two columns, one for money that you pay out and another for money that you receive. One column is your expenditure (negative) and the other is your revenue (positive).

You decide to buy a CD for $50 and a book for $25. If all goes well, when you compare the initial value in the bank and subtract the expenditure ($75), you should end up with what's left. Table 2-2 shows how these entries could typically be recorded.

Table 2-2. Recording Revenues and Expenditures

Entry	Revenue	Expenditure	Bank Balance
Check received	$200	--	$200
CD	--	$50	$150
Book	--	$25	$125
Closing balance	$200	$75	$125

If these numbers were stored in variables, you could enter both the revenue and expenditure as positive values and only make the number negative when you wanted to calculate how much was left. You could do this by simply placing a minus sign (-) in front of the variable name.

To output the amount you had spent as a negative value, you could write

```
int expenditure = 75;
printf("Your balance has changed by %d.", -expenditure);
```

This would result in the output

```
Your balance has changed by -75.
```

The minus sign will remind you that you've spent this money rather than gained it. Note that the expression -expenditure doesn't change the value stored in expenditure—it's still 75. The value of the *expression* is –75.

The unary minus operator in the expression -expenditure specifies an action. Instructions must be executed in your program to evaluate this. This is subtly different from when you use the minus operator when you write a negative number such as –75 or –1.25. In this case, the minus doesn't result in an action and no instructions need to be executed when your program is running. It simply instructs the compiler to create the appropriate negative constant in your program.

Variables and Memory

So far you've only looked at integer variables without considering how much space they take up in memory. Each time you declare a variable, the computer allocates a space in memory big enough to store that particular type of variable. Every variable of a particular type will always occupy the same amount of memory—the same number of bytes—but different types of variables require different amounts of memory to be allocated.

NOTE *The amount of memory occupied by variables of a given type will always be the same on a particular machine. However, in some instances a variable of a given type on one computer may occupy more memory than it does on another.*

You saw at the beginning of this chapter how your computer's memory is organized into bytes. Each variable will occupy some number of bytes in memory, so how many bytes are needed to store an integer? Well, 1 byte can store an integer value from –128 to +127. This would be enough for the integer values that you've seen so far, but what if you wanted to store a count of the average number of stitches in a pair of knee-length socks? One byte wouldn't be anywhere near enough. Consequently, not only do you have variables of different types in C that store different types of numbers, one of which happens to be integers, but you also have several varieties of integer variables to provide for different ranges of integers to be stored.

As I describe each type of variable in the following sections, I'll include a table containing the range of values that can be stored and the memory the variable will occupy. I'll summarize all these in a complete table of all the variable types at the end of this chapter.

Integer Variable Types

You have three basic flavors of integer variables that you can declare. Each type is specified by a different keyword, as shown in Table 2-3.

Table 2-3. Keywords for Integer Variable Types

Keyword	Number of Bytes	Range of Values
int	2 or 4 (depending on your computer)	–32,768 to +32,767 or –2,147,438,648 to +2,147,438,647
short	2	–32,768 to +32,767
long	4	–2,147,438,648 to +2,147,438,647

The types short and long are really abbreviations for types short int and long int, but they're almost always written in their abbreviated forms. Table 2-3 reflects the typical size of each type of integer variable, although the amount of memory occupied by variables of these types depends on the particular compiler you're using. The only specific requirement is that type long won't occupy less memory than type int, and type int won't occupy less memory than type short. Outside of that, the compiler-writer has complete freedom to make the best use of the hardware arithmetic capabilities of the machine on which the compiler is executing.

Variables of type int should have the size most suited to the computer on which the code is executing. For example, consider the following statement:

```
int cookies = 0;
```

This statement declares a variable that will occupy 2 bytes on some machines and 4 bytes on others. You may also find that two different compilers on the same machine implement type int with different sizes. This variation may seem a little strange, but the int type is intended to correspond to the size of integer that the computer has been designed to deal with most efficiently, and this can vary not only between different types of machine, but also with the same machine architecture as the chip technology evolves over time. Ultimately, it's the compiler that determines what you get. Although at one time many C compilers for the PC created int variables as 2 bytes, with more recent C compilers on a PC, variables of type int occupy 4 bytes. This is because all modern processors move data around at least 4 bytes at a time. If your compiler is of an older vintage, it may still use 2 bytes for type int, even though 4 bytes would now be better on the hardware you're using.

NOTE *The sizes of all these types are compiler dependent. The ANSI standard for the C language requires only that the size of* short *variables should be less than or equal to the size of type* int, *which in turn should be less than or equal to the size of type* long.

If you use type short, you'll probably get 2-byte variables. The previous declaration could have been written as follows:

```
short cookies = 0;
```

Because the keyword short is actually an abbreviation for short int, you could write this as follows:

```
short int cookies = 0;
```

This is exactly the same as the previous statement. When you write just short in a variable declaration, the int is implied. Most people prefer to use this form—it's perfectly clear and it saves a bit of typing.

NOTE *Even though type* short *and type* int *may occupy the same amount of memory on some machines, they're still different types.*

If you need integers with a bigger range—to store the average number of hamburgers sold in one day, for instance—you can use the keyword long:

```
long Big_Number;
```

Type long defines an integer variable with a length of 4 bytes, which provides for a range of values from –2,147,438,648 to +2,147,438,647. As noted earlier, you can write long int if you wish instead of long, because it amounts to the same thing.

Integer Constants

Because you can have different kinds of integer variables, you might expect to have different kinds of integer constants, and you do. If you just write an integer value 100, for example, this will be of type int. If you want to make sure it is type long, you must append an upper- or lowercase letter L to the numeric value. So the integer 100 as a long value is written 100L. Although it's perfectly legal, a lowercase letter l is best avoided because it's easily confused with the digit 1.

To declare and initialize the variable Big_Number, you could write this:

```
long Big_Number = 1287600L;
```

An integer value will also be type long if it's outside the range of type int. Thus, if your compiler implementation uses 2 bytes to store type int values, the values 1000000 and 33000 will be of type long by default, because they won't fit into 2 bytes.

You write negative integer constants with a minus sign, for example:

```
int decrease = -4;
long  below_sea_level = -100000L;
```

You can also write integer values in hexadecimal form—that is, to base 16. The digits in a hexadecimal number are the equivalent of decimal values 0 to 15, and they're represented by 0 through 9 and A through F (or a through f). Because there needs to be a way to distinguish between 99_{10} and 99_{16}, hexadecimal numbers are written with the prefix 0x or 0X. You would therefore write 99_{16} in your program as 0x99 or as 0X99.

Hexadecimal constants are most often used to specify bit patterns because each hexadecimal digit corresponds to 4 binary bits. The bitwise operators that you'll see in the next chapter are usually used with hexadecimal constants that define masks. If you're unfamiliar with hexadecimal numbers, you can find a detailed discussion of them in Appendix A.

Floating-Point Values

Floating-point variables are used to store floating-point numbers. **Floating-point numbers** hold values that are written with a decimal point, so you can represent fractional as well as integral values. The following are examples of floating-point values:

1.6

0.00008

7655.899

Because of the way floating-point numbers are represented, they hold only a fixed number of decimal digits; however, they can represent a very wide range of values—much wider than integer types. Floating-point numbers are often expressed as a decimal value multiplied by some power of 10. For example, each of the previous examples of floating-point numbers could be expressed as shown in Table 2-4.

Table 2-4. Expressing Floating-Point Numbers

Value	With an Exponent	Can Also Be Written in C As
1.6	0.16×10^1	0.16E1
0.00008	0.8×10^{-4}	0.8E4
7655.899	0.7655899×10^4	0.7655899E4

The center column shows how the numbers in the left column could be represented with an exponent. This isn't how you write them in C; it's just an alternative way of representing the same value designed to link to the right column. The right column shows how the representation in the center column would be expressed in C. The E in each of the numbers is for exponent, and you could equally well use a lowercase e. Of course, you can write each of these numbers in your program without an exponent, just as they appear in the left column, but for very large or very small numbers, the exponent form is useful. I'm sure you'd rather write 0.5E-15 than 0.0000000000000005, wouldn't you?

Floating-Point Variables

There are three different types of floating-point variables, as shown in Table 2-5.

Table 2-5. Floating-Point Variable Types

Keyword	Number of Bytes	Range of Values
float	4	±3.4E38 (7 decimal digits precision)
double	8	±1.7E308 (15 decimal digits precision)
long double	10	±1.2E4932 (19 decimal digits precision)

These are typical values for the number of bytes occupied and the ranges of values that are supported. Like the integer types, the memory occupied and the range of values are dependent on the machine and the compiler. The type long double is sometimes exactly the same as type double with some compilers. Note that the number of decimal digits of precision is only an approximation because floating-point values will be stored internally in binary form.

A floating-point variable is declared in a similar way to an integer variable. You just use the keyword for the floating-point type that you want to use:

```
float Radius;
double Biggest;
```

If you need to store numbers with up to seven digits of accuracy (a range of 10^{-38} to 10^{+38}), then you should use variables of type float. Values of type float are known as **single precision** floating-point numbers. This type will occupy 4 bytes in memory, as you can see from the table. Using variables of type double will allow you to store **double precision** floating-point values. Each variable of type double will occupy 8 bytes in memory and give you 15-digit precision with a range of 10^{-308} to 10^{+308}. Variables of type double suffice for the majority of requirements, but some specialized applications require even more accuracy and range. The long double type provides the exceptional range and precision shown in the table.

To write a constant of type float, you append an f to the number to distinguish it from type double. You could have initialized the last two variables with these statements:

```
float Radius = 2.5f;
double Biggest = 123E30;
```

The variable Radius has the initial value 2.5, and the variable Biggest is initialized to the number that corresponds to 123 followed by 30 zeroes. Any number that you write containing a decimal point is of type double unless you append the F to make it type float. When you specify an exponent value with E or e, the constant need not contain a decimal point. For instance, 1E3f is of type float and 3E8 is of type double.

To specify a long double constant, you need to append an upper- or lowercase letter L to the number, for example:

```
long double huge = 1234567.89123L;
```

Division Using Floating-Point Values

As you've seen, division operations with integer operands always produce an integer result. Unless the left operand of a division is an exact multiple of the right operand, the result will be inherently inaccurate. Of course, the way integer division works is an advantage if you're distributing cookies to children, but it isn't particularly useful when you want to cut a 10-foot plank into four equal pieces. This is a job for floating-point values.

Division operations with floating-point values will give you an exact result—at least, a result that is as exact as it can be with a fixed number of digits of precision. The next example illustrates how division operations work with variables of type float.

....

Try It Out: Division with Values of Type float

Here's a simple example that just divides one floating-point value by another and displays the result:

(Continued)

```
/* Program 2.7 Division with float values */
#include <stdio.h>

void main()
{
    float plank_length = 10.0f;    /* In feet                 */
    float piece_count = 4.0f;      /* Number of equal pieces   */
    float piece_length = 0.0f;     /* Length of a piece in feet */

    piece_length = plank_length/piece_ccount;
    printf("A plank %f feet long can be cut into %f pieces %f feet long.",
                              plank_length, piece_count, piece_length);
}
```

This program should produce the following output:

```
A plank 10.000000 feet long can be cut into 4.000000 pieces 2.500000 feet long.
```

HOW IT WORKS

You shouldn't have any trouble understanding how you chop the plank into equal pieces. Note that you use a new format specifier for values of type float in the printf() statement:

```
printf("A plank %f feet long can be cut into %f pieces %f feet long.",
                          plank_length, piece_count, piece_length);
```

You use the format specifier %f to display floating-point values. In general, the format specifier that you use must correspond to the type of value that you're outputting. If you output a value of type float with the specifier %d that's intended for use with integer values, you'll get rubbish. This is because the float value will be interpreted as an integer, which it isn't. Similarly, if you use %f with a value of an integer type, then you'll also get rubbish as output.

More on Format Specifiers

In the last example, you got a lot of decimal places in the output that you really didn't need. You may be good with a rule and a saw, but you aren't going to be able to cut the plank with a length of 2.500000 feet rather than 2.500001 feet. You can specify the number of places that you want to see after the decimal point in the format specifier. To obtain the output to two decimal places, you would write the format specifier as %.2f. To get three decimal places, you would write %.3f.

You can change the `printf()` statement in the last example so that it will produce more suitable output:

```
printf("A plank %.2f feet long can be cut into %.0f pieces %.2f feet long.",
                                plank_length, piece_count, piece_length);
```

The first format specification corresponds to the `plank_length` variable and will produce output with two decimal places. The second specification will produce no decimal places—this makes sense here because the `piece_count` value is a whole number. The last specification is the same as the first. Thus, if you run the example with this version of the last statement, the output will be

```
A plank 10.00 feet long can be cut into 4 pieces 2.50 feet long.
```

This is much more appropriate and looks a lot better.

The field width for the output has been determined by default. The `printf()` function works out how many character positions will be required for a value, given the number of decimal places you specify. However, you may want to decide the field width yourself. This will be the case if you want to output a column of values so they line up. If you let the `printf()` function work out the field width, you're likely to get a ragged column of output. A more general form of the format specifier for floating-point values can be written like this:

```
%[width][.precision]f
```

The square brackets here aren't part of the specification. They enclose bits of the specification that are optional, so you can omit either the `width` or the `.precision`, or both. The `width` value is an integer specifying the total number of characters in the output: the field width. The `precision` value is an integer specifying the number of decimal places that are to appear after the decimal point.

You could rewrite `printf()` from the last example to specify the field width as well as the number of digits you want after the decimal point, for example:

```
printf("A %8.2f plank foot can be cut into %5.0f pieces %6.2f feet long.",
                                plank_length, piece_count, piece_length);
```

I changed the text a little to get it to fit across the page here. The first value now will have a field width of 8 and two decimal places after the decimal point. The second value, which is the count of the number of pieces, will have a field width of 5 characters and no decimal places. The third value will be presented in a field width of 6 with two decimal places.

When you specify the field width, the value will be right-aligned by default. If you want the value to be left-aligned in the field, you just put a minus sign following the `%`. For instance, the specification `%-10.4f` will output a floating-point value left-aligned in a field width of 10 characters with four digits following the decimal point.

Note that you can specify a field width and the alignment in the field with a specification for outputting an integer value. For example, %-15d specifies an integer value will be presented left-aligned in a field width of 15 characters.

There's more to format specifiers than I've introduced here, and you'll learn more about them later. Try some variations out using the previous example. In particular, see what happens when the field width is too small for the value.

More Complex Expressions

You know that arithmetic can get a lot more complicated than just dividing a couple of numbers. In fact, if that was all you were trying to do, then you may as well use paper and pencil. Now that you have the tools of addition, subtraction, multiplication, and division at your disposal, you can start to do some really heavy calculations.

For these more complicated calculations, you'll need more control over the sequence of operations when an expression is evaluated. Parentheses provide you with this capability. They can also help to make expressions clearer when they're getting intricate.

Parentheses in Arithmetic Expressions

You can use parentheses in arithmetic expressions, and they work much as you'd expect. Subexpressions contained within parentheses are evaluated in sequence from the innermost pair of parentheses to the outermost, with the normal rules that you're used to for operator precedence, where multiplication and division happen before addition or subtraction. Therefore, the expression 2 * (3 + 3 * (5 + 4)) evaluates to 60. You start with the expression 5 + 4, which produces 9. Then you multiply that by 3, which gives 27. Then you add 3 to that total (giving 30) and multiply the whole lot by 2.

You can also insert spaces to separate operands from operators to make your arithmetic statements more readable. If you're not quite sure of how an expression will be evaluated according to the precedence rules, you can always put in some parentheses to make sure it produces the result you want.

Try It Out: Arithmetic in Action

This time you'll have a go at calculating the circumference and area of a circular table from an input value for its diameter radius. You may remember from elementary math the equations to calculate the area and circumference of a circle using π or pi (circumference = $2\pi r$ and area = πr^2, where r is the radius). If you don't, then don't worry. This isn't a math book, so just look at how the program works.

```
/* Program 2.8 calculations on a table */
#include <stdio.h>
```

(Continued)

```
void main()
{
   float radius = 0.0f;              /* The radius of the table        */
   float diameter = 0.0f;            /* The diameter of the table      */
   float circumference = 0.0f;       /* The circumference of the table */
   float area = 0.0f;                /* The area of a circle           */
   float Pi = 3.14159265f;

   printf("Input the diameter of the table:");
   scanf("%f", &diameter);           /* Read the diameter from the keyboard */
   radius = diameter/2.0f;           /* Calculate the radius                */
   circumference = 2.0f*Pi*radius;   /* Calculate the circumference         */
   area = Pi*radius*radius;          /* Calculate the area                  */
   printf("\nThe circumference is %.2f", circumference);
   printf("nThe area is %.2f\n", area);
}
```

Here's some typical output from this example:

```
Input the diameter of the table: 6

The circumference is 18.85
The area is 28.27
```

HOW IT WORKS

Up to the first printf() the program looks much the same as those you've seen before:

```
   float radius = 0.0f;              /* The radius of the table        */
   float diameter = 0.0f;            /* The diameter of the table      */
   float circumference = 0.0f;       /* The circumference of the table */
   float area = 0.0f;                /* The area of a circle           */
   float Pi = 3.14159265f;
```

You declare and initialize five variables, where Pi has its usual value. Note how all the initial values have an f at the end because you're initializing values of type float. Without the f the values would be of type double. They would still work here, but you would be introducing some unnecessary conversion that the compiler would have to arrange, from type double to type float.

The following statement outputs a prompt for input from the keyboard:

```
   printf("Input the diameter of the table:");
```

(Continued)

The next statement deals with reading the value for the diameter of the table. You use a new standard library function, the scanf() function, to do this:

```
scanf("%f", &diameter);          /* Read the diameter from the keyboard */
```

The scanf() function is another function that requires the stdio.h header file to be included. This function handles input from the keyboard. In effect it takes what you enter through the keyboard and interprets it as specified by the first argument, which is a control string between double quotes. In this case the control string is "%f" because you're reading a value of type float. It stores the result in the variable specified by the second argument, diameter in this instance. The first argument is a control string similar to what you've used with the printf() function, except that here it controls input rather than output.

You've undoubtedly noticed something new here: the & preceding the variable name diameter. This is called the **address of** operator, and it's needed to allow the scanf() function to store the value that is read in your variable, diameter. The reason for this is bound up with the way argument values are passed to a function. For the moment, I won't go into a more detailed explanation of this; you'll see more on this in Chapter 11. The only thing to remember is to use the address of operator (the & sign) before a variable when you're using the scanf() function, and not to use it when you use the printf() function.

You'll see a lot more on how scanf() works later in the book, but for now the basic set of format specifiers you can use for reading data of various types are as follows:

To read a value of type short	%hd
To read a value of type int	%d
To read a value of type long	%ld
To read a value of type float	%f or %e
To read a value of type double	%lf or %le

In the %ld and %lf format specifiers, l is a lowercase L. Don't forget, you must *always* prefix the name of the variable that's receiving the input value with &. Also, if you use the wrong format specifier—if you read a value into a variable of type float with %d, for instance—the data value in your variable won't be correct, but you'll get no indication that a junk value has been stored.

Next, you have three statements that calculate the results you're interested in:

```
radius = diameter/2.0f;         /* Calculate the radius        */
circumference = 2.0f*Pi*radius; /* Calculate the circumference */
area = Pi*radius*radius;        /* Calculate the area          */
```

(Continued)

The first statement calculates the radius as half of the value of the diameter that was entered. The second statement computes the circumference of the table, using the value that was calculated for the radius. The third statement calculates the area. Note that if you forget the f in 2.0f, you'll probably get a warning message from your compiler. This is because without the f, the constant is of type double, and you would be mixing different types in the same expression. You'll see more about this later.

The next two statements output the values you've calculated:

```
printf("\nThe circumference is %.2f", circumference);
printf("\nThe area is %.2f\n", area);
```

These two printf() statements output the values of the variables circumference and area using the format specifier %.2f. As you've already seen, in both statements the format control string contains text to be displayed, as well as a format specifier for the variable to be output. The format specification outputs the values with two decimal places after the point. The default field width will be sufficient in each case to accommodate the value that is to be displayed.

Of course, you can run this program and enter whatever values you want for the diameter. You could experiment with different forms of floating-point input here, and you could try entering something like 1E1f, for example.

....

Defining Constants

Although you defined Pi as a variable in the previous example, it's really a constant value that you don't want to change. The value of π is always a fixed number. The only question is how many digits precision you use in its specification. It would be nice to make sure its value stayed fixed in a program so it couldn't be changed by mistake.

You actually have a couple of ways in which you can approach this. The first is to define Pi as a symbol that's to be replaced in the program by its value during compilation. In this case, Pi isn't a variable at all, but more a sort of alias for the value it represents. Let's try that out.

....

Try It Out: Defining a Constant

Let's look at specifying PI as an alias for its value:

```
/* Program 2.9 More round tables */
#include <stdio.h>
#define PI    3.14159f              /* Definition of the symbol PI */
```

(Continued)

```
void main()
{
    float radius = 0.0f;
    float diameter = 0.0f;
    float circumference = 0.0f;
    float area = 0.0f;

    printf("Input the diameter of a table:");
    scanf("%f", &diameter);
    radius = diameter/2.0f;
    circumference = 2.0f*PI*radius;
    area = PI*radius*radius;
    printf("\nThe circumference is %.2f", circumference);
    printf("\nThe area is %.2f", area);
}
```

This produces exactly the same output as the previous example.

HOW IT WORKS

After the comment and the #include directive for the header file, you have a pre-processing directive:

```
#definePI 3.14159f              /* Definition of the symbol PI */
```

You've now defined PI as a symbol that is to be replaced in the code by 3.14159f. You use PI rather than Pi, as it's a common convention in C to write identifiers that appear in a #define statement in capital letters. Wherever you reference PI within an expression in the program, the compiler will substitute the value you've specified for it in the #define directive. All the substitutions will be made before compiling the program. When the program is ready to be compiled, it will no longer contain references to PI, as all occurrences will have been replaced by the sequence of characters that you've specified in the #define directive. This all happens internally while your program is processed by the compiler. Your source program will not be changed: it will still contain the symbol PI.

....

The second possibility is to define Pi as a variable, but to tell the compiler that its value is fixed and must not be changed. You can fix the value of any variable by prefixing the type name with the keyword const when you declare the variable, for example:

```
const float Pi = 3.14159f;      /* Defines the value of Pi as fixed */
```

Adding the keyword const in the declaration for Pi will cause the compiler to check that the code doesn't attempt to change its value. Any code that does so will be flagged as an error and the compilation will fail. Let's see a working example of this.

Try It Out: Defining a Variable with a Fixed Value

You'll try using a constant in a variation of the previous example but shorten the code a little:

```
/* Program 2.10 Round tables again but shorter */
#include <stdio.h>

void main()
{
   float diameter = 0.0f;           /* The diameter of a table      */
   float radius = 0.0f;             /* The radius of a table        */
   const float Pi = 3.14159f;       /* Defines the value of Pi as fixed */

   printf("Input the diameter of the table:");
   scanf("%f", &diameter);
   float radius = diameter/2.0f;
   printf("\nThe circumference is %.2f", 2.0f*Pi*radius);
   printf("\nThe area is %.2f", Pi*radius*radius);
}
```

HOW IT WORKS

Following the declaration for the variable radius, you have this statement:

```
const float Pi = 3.14159f;         /* Defines the value of Pi as fixed */
```

This declares the variable Pi and defines a value for it; Pi is still a variable here, but the initial value you've given it can't be changed. The const modifier achieves this effect. It can be applied to any statement declaring a variable of any type to fix the value of that variable. Of course, the value must appear in the declaration in the same way as shown here: following an = sign after the variable name. The compiler will check your code for attempts to change variables that you've declared as const, and if it discovers that you've attempted to change a const variable it will complain. There are ways to trick the compiler to change const variables, but this defeats the whole point of using const in the first place.

The next two statements produce the output from the program:

```
printf("\nThe circumference is %.2f", 2.0f*Pi*radius);
printf("\nThe area is %.2f", Pi*radius*radius);
```

In this example, you've done away with the variables storing the circumference and area of the circle. The expressions for these now appear as arguments in the

(Continued)

`printf()` statements where they're evaluated, and their values are passed directly to the function.

As you've seen before, the value that you pass to a function can be the result of evaluating an expression rather than the value of a particular variable. The compiler will create a temporary variable to hold the value and that will be passed to the function. The temporary variable is subsequently discarded. This is fine, as long as you don't want to use these values elsewhere.

Choosing the Correct Type for the Job

You have to be careful when doing calculations as to the type of variable that you're using. If you use the wrong type, then you may find that errors creep into your programs that can be hard to detect. This is best shown with an example.

Try It Out: The Right Types of Variables

Here's an example of how things can go horribly wrong if you choose an unsuitable type for your variables:

```
/* Program 2.11 Choosing the correct type for the job  1*/
#include <stdio.h>

void main()
{
  const float Revenue_per_150 = 4.5f;
  short JanSold = 23500;                 /* Stock sold in January  */
  short FebSold = 19300;                 /* Stock sold in February */
  short MarSold = 21600;                 /* Stock sold in March    */
  float  RevQuarter = 0.0f;              /* Sales for the quarter  */

  short QuarterSold = JanSold+FebSold+MarSold; /* Calculate quarterly total */

  /* Output monthly sales and total for the quarter */
  printf("\nStock sold in\n Jan: %d\n Feb: %d\n Mar: %d",
                                        JanSold,FebSold,MarSold);
  printf("\nTotal stock sold in first quarter: %d",QuarterSold);

  /* Calculate the total revenue for the quarter and output it */
   RevQuarter = QuarterSold/150*Revenue_Per_150;
  printf("\nSales revenue this quarter is:$%.2f\n",RevQuarter);
}
```

(Continued)

These are fairly simple calculations, and you can see that the total stock sold in the quarter should be 64400. This is just the sum of each of the monthly totals, but if you run the program, the output you get is this:

```
Stock sold in
 Jan: 23500
 Feb: 19300
 Mar: 21600
Total stock sold in first quarter: -1136
Sales revenue this quarter is:$-31.50
```

Obviously, all is not right here. It doesn't take a genius or an accountant to tell you that adding three big, positive numbers together shouldn't give a negative result!

HOW IT WORKS

First you define a constant that will be used in the calculation:

```
const Revenue_per_150 = 4.5f;
```

This defines the revenue obtained for every 150 items sold. There's nothing wrong with that.

Next, you declare four variables and assign initial values to them:

```
short JanSold = 23500;                /* Stock sold in January  */
short FebSold = 19300;                /* Stock sold in February */
short MarSold = 21600;                /* Stock sold in March     */
float RevQuarter = 0.0f;              /* Sales for the quarter   */
```

The first three variables are of type `short`, which is quite adequate to store the initial value. The `RevQuarter` variable is of type `float` because you want two decimal places for the quarterly revenue.

The next statement declares the variable `QuarterSold` and stores the sum of the sales for each of the months:

```
short QuarterSold = JanSold+FebSold+MarSold; /* Calculate quarterly total */
```

Note that you're initializing this variable with the result of an expression. This is possible only because the values of these variables are known to the compiler, so this represents what is known as a **constant expression**. If any of the values in the expression were determined during execution of the program—from a calculation involving a value that was read in, for instance—then this wouldn't

(Continued)

compile. The compiler can only use initial values that are explicit or are produced by an expression that the compiler can evaluate.

In fact, the cause of the erroneous results is in the declaration of the QuarterSold variable. You've declared it to be of type short and given it the initial value of the sum of the three monthly figures. You know that their sum is 64400 and that the program outputs a negative number. The error must therefore be in this statement.

The problem arises because you've tried to store a number that's too large for type short. If you remember, the maximum value that a short variable can hold is 32,767. The computer can't interpret the value of QuarterSold correctly and happens to give a negative result. The solution to your problem is to use a variable of type long that will allow you to store much larger numbers.

SOLVING THE PROBLEM

Try changing the program and running it again. You need to change only two lines in the body of the function main(). The new and improved program is as follows:

```
/* Program 2.12 Choosing the correct type for the job  2 */
#include <stdio.h>

void main()
{
  const float Revenue_Per_150 = 4.5f;
  short JanSold =23500;            /* Stock sold in January  */
  short FebSold =19300;            /* Stock sold in February */
  short MarSold =21600;            /* Stock sold in March    */
  float  RevQuarter = 0.0f;        /* Sales for the quarter  */

  long QuarterSold = JanSold+FebSold+MarSold; /* Calculate quarterly total */

  /* Output monthly sales and total for the quarter */
  printf("Stock sold in\n Jan: %d\n Feb: %d\n Mar: %d\n",
                                    JanSold,FebSold,MarSold);
  printf("Total stock sold in first quarter: %ld\n",QuarterSold);

  /* Calculate the total revenue for the quarter and output it */
  RevQuarter = QuarterSold/150*Revenue_Per_150;
  printf("Sales revenue this quarter is:$%.2f\n",RevQuarter);
}
```

When you run this program, the output is more satisfactory:

(Continued)

```
Stock sold in
 Jan: 23500
 Feb: 19300
 Mar: 21600
Total stock sold in first quarter: 64400
Sales revenue this quarter is: $1930.50
```

The stock sold in the quarter is correct, and you have a reasonable result for revenue. Notice that you use %ld to output the total stock sold. This is to tell the compiler that it is to use a long conversion for the output of this value. Just to check the program, calculate the result of the revenue yourself with a calculator.

The result you should get is, in fact, $1,932. Somewhere you've lost a dollar and a half! Not such a great amount, but try saying that to an accountant! You need to find the lost $1.50. Consider what's happening when you calculate the value for revenue in the program:

```
RevQuarter = QuarterSold/150*Revenue_Per_150;
```

Here you're assigning a value to RevQuarter. The value is the result of the expression on the right of the = sign. The result of the expression will be calculated, step by step, according to the precedence rules you've already looked at in this chapter. Here you have quite a simple expression that's calculated from left to right, as division and multiplication have the same priority. Let's work through it:

QuarterSold/150 is calculated as 64400/150, which should produce the result 429.333.

This is where your problem arises. QuarterSold is an integer and so the computer truncates the result of the division to an integer, ignoring the .333. This means that when the next part of the calculation is evaluated, the result will be slightly off:

429*Revenue_Per_150 is calculated as 429 * 4.5 which is 1930.50.

You now know where the error has occurred, but what can you do about it? You could change all of your variables to floating-point types, but that would defeat the purpose of using integers in the first place. The numbers entered really are integers, so you'd like to store them as such. Is there an easy solution to this? In this case there is. You can rewrite the statement as follows:

```
RevQuarter = Revenue_Per_150*QuarterSold/150;
```

Now the multiplication will occur first, and because of the way arithmetic with mixed operands works, the result will be of type float. The compiler will automatically arrange for the integer operand to be converted to floating-point.

(Continued)

When you then divide by 150, that operation will execute with float values too, with 150 being converted to 150f. The net effect is that the result will now be correct.

However, there's more to it than that. Not only do you need to understand more about what happens with arithmetic between operands of different types, but also you need to understand how you can control conversions from one type to another. In C you have the ability to explicitly convert a value of one type to another type. This process is called **casting**.

Type Casting in Arithmetic Expressions

Let's look at the original expression to calculate the quarterly revenue again and see how you can control what goes on so that you end up with the correct result:

```
RevQuarter = QuarterSold/150*Revenue_Per_150;
```

You know that if the result is to be correct, this statement has to be amended so that the expression is calculated in floating-point form. If you cast the value of Quarter-Sold to type float, then the expression will be evaluated as floating-point and your problem will be solved. To convert the value of a variable to another type, you place the type that you want to cast the value to in parentheses in front of the variable. The statement to calculate the result correctly will thus be

```
RevQuarter = (float)QuarterSold/150.0f*Revenue_Per_150;
```

This is exactly what you require. You're using the right types of variables in the right places. You're also ensuring you don't use integer arithmetic when you want to keep the fractional part of the result of a division.

Automatic Casting

Look at the output from the second version of the program again:

```
Sales revenue this quarter is: $1930.50
```

Even without the explicit cast statement in the expression, the result was in floating-point form, even though it was still wrong. This is because the compiler automatically casts one or other of the operands when it's dealing with an operation that involves values of different types. Your computer can perform only binary arithmetic operations (add, subtract, multiply, divide, and remainder) when both operands are of the same type. When the operands that are involved in an operation are of different types, the compiler arranges for the value that is of a type with a more limited range to be converted to the type of the other variable. So, referring back to the expression to calculate revenue:

```
QuarterSold / 150 * Revenue_Per_150
```

This was evaluated as 64400 (int)/150 (int), which equals 429 (int). Then 429 (int converted to float) is multiplied by 4.5 (float), giving 1930.5 (float).

An automatic conversion applies when a binary operator applies operands of different types. With the first operation, the numbers are both of type int, so the result is of type int. With the second operation, the first value is type int and the second value is type float. Type int is more limited in its range than type float, so the value of type int is automatically cast to type float. Whenever there is a mixture of types in an arithmetic expression, C will use a set of specific rules to decide how the expression will be evaluated. Let's have a look at some of these conversion rules now.

Conversion Rules in Casting

As I've said, for each operation in an expression that involves operands of different types, your compiler will promote the operand with the type that has the more restricted range of values to be the same type as the other operand. The order of types in this context from highest to lowest is long double, then double, then float, followed by long, then int, then short, and finally the lowest, char. You haven't seen type char yet, but you'll be looking at it in a moment.

Let's see how these conversion rules apply in practice. Suppose you declare three variables: A as type double, B as type float, and C as type long. You can see how the expression A + B - C will be evaluated.

The operation A + B will be carried out first. Because A is type double and B is type long, B will be converted to type double and the result will therefore be type double. To subtract C from this result, C is first converted to double and you end up with the final result as type double.

Casts in Assignment Statements

You can also cause an implicit cast to be applied by assigning the value of one type to a variable of a different type. This can cause values to be truncated so information is lost.

For instance, if you assign a float or double value to a variable of type int or long, the fractional part of the float or double will be lost, and just the integer part will be stored. The following code fragment illustrates this situation:

```
int number = 0;
float value = 2.5f;
number = value;
```

The value stored in number will be 2. Because you've assigned the value of decimal (2.5) to the variable, number, which is of type int, the fractional part, .5, will be lost and only the 2 will be stored. Notice how I've used a specifier f at the end of 2.5f.

Note that an assignment statement that may lose information because an automatic cast has to be applied will usually result in a warning from the compiler. However, the code will still compile, so there's a risk that your program may be doing things that will result in incorrect results. Generally, it's better to put explicit casts in your code wherever conversions that may result in information being lost are necessary.

More Numeric Data Types

To complete the set of numeric data types, I'll now cover those that I haven't yet discussed. The first is one that I mentioned previously: type char. A variable of type char can store the code for a single character. Because it stores a character code, which is an integer, it's considered to be an integer type. Because it's an integer type, the value stored can be treated just as an integer and can participate in arithmetic calculations.

The Character Type

Values of type char occupy the least amount of memory of all the data types. They require just 1 byte. The integer that's stored in a variable of type char can be interpreted as a signed or unsigned value, depending on your compiler. An **unsigned** integer type is simply one that allows negative as well as positive integral values to be stored. As an unsigned type, the value stored in a variable of type char can range from 0 to 255. As a **signed** type, a variable of type char can store values from −128 to +127. Of course, both ranges correspond to the same set of bit patterns: from 0000 0000 to 1111 1111. With unsigned values, all 8 bits are data bits, so 0000 0000 corresponds to 0 and 1111 1111 corresponds to 255. With unsigned values, the leftmost bit is a sign bit, so −128 is the binary value 1000 0000, 0 is 0000 0000, and 127 is 0111 1111. The value 1111 1111 as a signed binary value is the decimal value −1.

Thus, from the point of view of representing character codes, which are bit patterns, it doesn't matter whether type char is regarded as signed or unsigned. Where it *does* matter is when you perform arithmetic operations on values of type char.

A char variable can hold any single character, so you can specify the initial value for a variable of type char by a character constant. A **character constant** is a character written between single quotes. Here are some examples:

```
char letter = 'A';
char digit = '9';
char exclamation = '!';
```

You can use escape sequences to specify character constants too:

```
char newline = '\n';
char tab = '\t';
char single_quote = '\'';
```

Of course, in every case the variable will be set to the code for the character between single quotes. The actual code value will depend on your computer environment, but by far the most common is American Standard Code for Information Interchange (ASCII). You can find the ASCII character set in Appendix B.

You can also initialize a variable of type char with an integer value, as long as the value fits into the range for type char with your compiler, for example:

```
char character = 74;    /* ASCII code for the letter J */
```

A variable of type char has a sort of dual personality: you can interpret it as a character or as an integer. Here's an example of an arithmetic operation with a value of type char:

```
char letter = 'C';      /* letter contains the decimal code value 67 */
letter = letter +3;     /* letter now contains 70, which is 'F'      */
```

Thus, you can perform arithmetic on a value of type char and still treat it as a character.

Character Input and Character Output

You can read a single character from the keyboard and store it in a variable of type char using the scanf() function with the format specifier %c:

```
char ch = 0;
scanf("%c", &ch);    /* Read one character */
```

To write a single character to the command line with the printf() function, you use the same format specifier, %c:

```
printf("The character is %c", ch);
```

Of course, you can output the numeric value of a character too:

```
printf("The character is %c and the code value is %d", ch, ch);
```

This statement will output ch as a character and as a numeric value.

....

Try It Out: Character Building

If you're completely new to programming, you may be wondering how on earth the computer knows whether it's dealing with a character or an integer. The reality is that it doesn't. It's a bit like in *Alice's Adventures in Wonderland* when Humpty Dumpty told Alice, "When *I* use a word, it means just what I choose it to mean—neither more nor less." An item of data in memory can mean whatever you choose it to mean. A byte containing the value 70 is a perfectly good integer. It's equally correct to regard as the code for the letter *J*.

(Continued)

Let's look at an example that should make it clear. Here, you'll use the conversion specifier %c, which indicates that you want to output a value of type char as a character rather than an integer:

```c
/* Program 2.13 Characters and numbers */
#include <stdio.h>

void main()
{
  char first = 'T';
  char second = 20;

  printf("\nThe first example as a letter looks like this - %c", first);
  printf("\nThe first example as a number looks like this - %d", first);
  printf("\nThe second example as a letter looks like this - %c", second);
  printf("\nThe second example as a number looks like this - %d\n", second);
}
```

The output from this program is

```
The first example as a letter looks like this - T
The first example as a number looks like this - 84
The second example as a letter looks like this - ¶
The second example as a number looks like this - 20
```

HOW IT WORKS

The program starts off by declaring two variables of type char:

```c
  char first = 'T';
  char second = 20;
```

One is initialized with a letter and the other with a number.

The next four statements output each of the variables in two ways:

```c
printf("\nThe first example as a letter looks like this - %c", first_example);
printf("\nThe first example as a number looks like this - %d", first_example);
printf("\nThe second example as a letter looks like this - %c", second_example);
printf("\nThe second example as a number looks like this - %d\n", second_example);
```

The %c conversion specifier interprets the contents of the variable as a single character, and the %d specifier interprets it as an integer. The numeric values that are output are the codes for the corresponding characters. These are ASCII codes in this instance, and will be in most instances, so that's what you'll assume throughout this book.

(Continued)

As I've noted, not all computers use the ASCII character set, so you may get different values than those shown previously. As long as you use the notation 'character' for a character constant, you'll get the character that you want regardless of the character coding in effect.

You could also output the integer values of the variables of type char as hexadecimal values by using the format specifier %x instead of %d. You might like to try that.

Try It Out: Arithmetic with Values of Type char

Let's look at another example in which you apply arithmetic operations to values of type char:

```
/* Program 2.14 Using type char  */
#include <stdio.h>

void main()
{
  char first = 'A';
  char second = 'B'';
  char last = 'Z';

  char number = 40;

  char ex1 = first + 2;        /* Add 2 to 'A'      */
  char ex2 = second - 1;       /* Subtract 1 from 'B' */
  char ex3 = last + 2;         /* Add 2 to 'Z'      */

  printf("Character values      %-5c%-5c%-5c", ex1, ex2, ex3);
  printf("\nNumerical equivalents %-5d%-5d%-5d", ex1, ex2, ex3);
  printf("\nThe number %d is the code for the character %c\n", number, number);
}
```

When you run the program you should get the following output:

```
Character values      C    A    \
Numerical equivalents 67   65   92
The number 40 is the code for the character (
```

(Continued)

HOW IT WORKS

This program demonstrates how you can happily perform arithmetic with char variables that you've initialized with characters. The first three statements in the body of main() are as follows:

```
char first = 'A';
char second = 'B';
char last = 'Z';
```

These initialize the variables first, second, and last to the character values you see. The numerical value of these variables will be the ASCII codes for the respective characters. Because you can treat them as numeric, as well as characters, you can perform arithmetic operations with them.

The next statement initializes a variable of type char with an integer value:

```
char number = 40;
```

The initializing value must be within the range of values that a 1-byte variable can store, so with my compiler where char is a signed type it must be between –128 and 127. Of course, you can interpret the contents of the variable as a character. In this case, it will be the character that has the ASCII code value 40, which happens to be a left parenthesis.

The next three statements declare three more variables of type char:

```
char ex1 = first + 2;       /* Add 2 to 'A'        */
char ex2 = second - 1;      /* Subtract 1 from 'B' */
char ex3 = last + 2;        /* Add 2 to 'Z'        */
```

These statements create new values and therefore new characters from the values stored in the variables first, second, and last; the results of these expressions are stored in the variables ex1, ex2, and ex3.

The next two statements output the three variables ex1, ex2, and ex3 in two different ways:

```
printf("Character values     %-5c%-5c%-5c", ex1, ex2, ex3);
printf("\nNumerical equivalents %-5d%-5d%-5d", ex1, ex2, ex3);
```

The first statement interprets the values stored as characters by using the %-5c conversion specifier. This specifies that the value should be output as a character left-aligned in a field width of 5. The second statement outputs the same variables again, but this time interprets the values as integers by using the %-5d specifier. The alignment and the field width are the same but d specifies the output is an integer. You can see that the two lines of output show the three characters with their ASCII codes aligned below on the next line.

(Continued)

The last line outputs the variable number as a character and as an integer:

```
printf("\nThe number %d is the code for the character %c\n", number, number);
```

To output the variable twice, you just write it twice—as the second and third arguments to the printf() function. It's output first as an integer value and then as a character.

This ability to perform arithmetic with characters can be very useful. For instance, to convert from uppercase to lowercase, you simply add the result of 'a'-'A' (which is 32 for ASCII) to the uppercase character. To achieve the reverse, just subtract 'a'-'A'. You can see how this works if you have a look at the decimal ASCII values for the alphabetic characters in Appendix B.

....

Unsigned Integers: Using Positive Integers

If you're sure that you'll be dealing with just positive integers, there's a way of increasing the maximum value that you can use. The unsigned modifier can be used with all of the basic integer types that I've covered, to define types that store only positive integers. This allows you to handle integers roughly twice as large as you otherwise might. You use the unsigned modifier as follows:

```
unsigned char a_value;          /* Can be from 0 to +255           */
unsigned int number;            /* Can be from 0 to +65,535        */
unsigned long big_number;       /* Can be from 0 to 4,294,967,295 */
```

You must be absolutely sure that you need only positive values if you want to use these. Unsigned variables can't store negative values at all.

When you want to specify an integer constant as unsigned, you append the letter U as upper- or lowercase to the numeric value. For example, you could write

```
number = 25U;
```

This sets the unsigned variable number of type int to 25.

If you want to define a constant that is of type unsigned long, you need a U and an L as a suffix to the numeric value. You can specify the letters in upper- or lowercase, for example:

```
big_number = 100000000UL;
```

This stores the value 100,000,000 in the variable big_number.

You use the format specifier %u to output an unsigned integer. You can also include a field width specification and a - for left alignment in the field if you wish.

For example, you could output the value of the unsigned integer variable called number with this statement:

```
printf("The value of number is %-12u", number);
```

The field width is 12 here and the value will be left-aligned in the field.

I've now covered all the numeric data types in C; Table 2-6 presents all of them.

Table 2-6. Numeric Data Types

Variable Type	Keyword	Number of Bytes	Range of Values
Character	char	1	−128 to +127 or 0 to 255
Unsigned character	unsigned char	1	0 to 255
Integer	int	2 or 4	−32,768 to +32,767 or −2,147,438,648 to +2,147,438,647
Unsigned integer	unsigned int	2 or 4	0 to 65,535 or 0 to 4,294,967,295
Short integer	short	2	−32,768 to +32,767
Unsigned short integer	unsigned short	2	0 to 65,535
Long integer	long	4	−2,147,438,648 to +2,147,438,647
Unsigned long integer	unsigned long	4	0 to 4,294,967,295
Single precision floating-point	float	4	±3.4E38 (6 digits)
Double precision floating-point	double	8	±1.7E308 (15 digits)
Extended double precision floating-point	long double	10	±1.2E4932 (19 digits)

Finding the Limits

I mentioned earlier and in various other places in this chapter how the limits for the range of values for some of these numerical types can vary from one system and/or compiler to another. This is obviously going to be a problem in some situations in which you really need to be able to determine within your program what the limits are in a particular instance. The C standard library includes header files that can provide you with this information. The limits.h header file provides information about integer types and the float.h header file does the same for floating-point types.

The limits.h header file contains definitions for symbols (not variables) such that define the upper and lower limits for each signed integer type. For instance, INT_MIN and INT_MAX are the symbols representing the upper and lower limits for type int, and CHAR_MIN and CHAR_MAX represent the limits for type char. For unsigned types only symbols for upper limits are defined because the lower limit is always zero. There are symbols with similarly formed names for each of the integer types in Table 2-6.

In the float.h header are symbols with the names FLT_MIN and FLT_MAX that represent the minimum and maximum positive values of type float. There are similar symbols such as DBL_MIN, DBL_MAX, LDBL_MIN, and LDBL_MAX for the double and long double types. If you look in the documentation for the library that comes with your compiler, you'll find many other symbols that represent values for other parameters relating to the implementation of the floating-point types on your system.

Let's see how you can access some of these with an example.

Try It Out: Finding the Limits

This program just outputs the values corresponding to the symbols defined in the header files:

```
/* Program 2.15 Finding the limits  */
#include <stdio.h>
#include < limits.h >   /* For limits on integer types       */
#include <float.h>      /* For limits on floating-point types */

void main()
{
  printf("Variables of type char store values from %d to %d",
                                          CHAR_MIN, CHAR_MAX);
  printf("\nVariables of type unsigned char store values from 0 to %u",
                                          UCHAR_MAX);
  printf("\nVariables of type short store values from %d to %d",
                                          SHRT_MIN, SHRT_MAX);
  printf("\nVariables of type unsigned short store values from 0 to %u",
                                          USHRT_MAX);
  printf("\nVariables of type int store values from %d to %d", INT_MIN, INT_MAX);
  printf("\nVariables of type unsigned int store values from 0 to %u", UINT_MAX);
  printf("\nVariables of type long store values from %d to %d",
                                          LONG_MIN, LONG_MAX);
  printf("\nVariables of type unsigned long store values from 0 to %u",
                                          ULONG_MAX);

  printf("\n\nThe size of the smallest non-zero value of type float is %.3e",
                                          FLT_MIN);
  printf("\nThe size of the largest value of type float is %.3e", FLT_MAX);
  printf("\nThe size of the smallest non-zero value of type double is %.3e",
                                          DBL_MIN);
  printf("\nThe size of the largest value of type double is %.3e", DBL_MAX);
  printf("\nThe size of the smallest non-zero value of type long double is %.3e",
                                          DBL_MIN);
```

(Continued)

```
    printf("\nThe size of the largest value of type long double is %.3e\n",
                                                       DBL_MAX);
}
```

You'll get output somewhat similar to the following:

```
Variables of type char store values from -128 to 127
Variables of type unsigned char store values from 0 to 255
Variables of type short store values from -32768 to 32767
Variables of type unsigned short store values from 0 to 65535
Variables of type int store values from -2147483648 to 2147483647
Variables of type unsigned int store values from 0 to 4294967295
Variables of type long store values from -2147483648 to 2147483647
Variables of type unsigned long store values from 0 to 4294967295

The magnitude of the smallest non-zero value of type float is 1.175e-038
The magnitude of the largest value of type float is 3.403e+038
The magnitude of the smallest non-zero value of type double is 2.225e-308
The magnitude of the largest value of type double is 1.798e+308
The magnitude of the smallest non-zero value of type long double is 2.225e-308
The magnitude of the largest value of type long double is 1.798e+308
```

HOW IT WORKS

You just output the values of the symbols in a series of printf() function calls. You have used the %u specifier to output the unsigned integer values. If you use %d for the maximum value of an unsigned type, values that have the leftmost bit (the sign bit for signed types) as 1 won't be interpreted correctly.

You use the %e specifier for the floating-point limits, which presents the values in exponential form. You also specify just three digits precision, as you don't need the full accuracy in the output. The %f specifier presents values without an exponent, so it's rather inconvenient for very large or very small values. If you try it in the example, you'll see what I mean.

Introducing the sizeof Operator

You can find out how many bytes are occupied by a given type by using the sizeof operator. Of course, sizeof is a keyword in C. The expression sizeof(int) will result in the number of bytes occupied by a variable of type int. The sizeof operator has other uses too, but for the moment let's just use it to find out how many bytes are occupied by each type.

....

Try It Out: Discovering the Number of Bytes Occupied by a Given Type

This program will output the number of bytes occupied by each numeric type:

```
/* Program 2.16 Finding the size of a type  */
#include <stdio.h>

void main()
{
  printf("\nVariables of type char occupy %d bytes", sizeof(char));
  printf("\nVariables of type short occupy %d bytes", sizeof(short));
  printf("\nVariables of type int occupy %d bytes", sizeof(int));
  printf("\nVariables of type long occupy %d bytes", sizeof(long));
  printf("\nVariables of type float occupy %d bytes", sizeof(float));
  printf("\nVariables of type double occupy %d bytes", sizeof(double));
  printf("\nVariables of type long double occupy %d bytes", sizeof(long double));
 }
```

On my system I get the following output:

```
Variables of type char occupy 1 bytes
Variables of type short occupy 2 bytes
Variables of type int occupy 4 bytes
Variables of type long occupy 4 bytes
Variables of type float occupy 4 bytes
Variables of type double occupy 8 bytes
Variables of type long double occupy 8 bytes
```

HOW IT WORKS

Because the sizeof operator results in an integer value, you can output it using the %d specifier. Note that you can also obtain the number of bytes occupied by a variable, var_name, with the expression sizeof var_name. Obviously, the space between the sizeof keyword and the variable name in the expression is essential.

Now you know the range limits and the number of bytes occupied by each numeric type with your compiler.

....

The op= Form of Assignment

C is fundamentally a very concise language, so it provides you with abbreviated short-cuts for some operations. Consider the following line of code:

```
number = number + 10;
```

This sort of assignment, in which you're incrementing or decrementing a variable by some amount, occurs very often, so there's a shorthand version:

```
number += 10;
```

The += operator after the variable name is one example of a family of op= operators. This statement has exactly the same effect as the previous one and it saves a bit of typing. The op in op= can be any of the following arithmetic operators:

```
+ - * / %
```

If you suppose number has the value 10, then you can write the following statements:

```
number *= 3;            /* number will be set to number*3 which is 30 */
number /= 3;            /* number will be set to number/3 which is 3  */
number %= 3;            /* number will be set to number%3 which is 1  */
```

The op in op= can also be a few other operators that you haven't encountered yet:

```
<< >> & ^ |
```

I'll defer discussion of these to Chapter 3, however.

The op= set of operators always works in the same way. If you have a statement of the form

```
lhs op= rhs;
```

then the effect is the same as a statement of the form

```
lhs = lhs op (rhs);
```

Note the parentheses around the rhs expression. This means that op applies to the value that results from evaluating the entire rhs expression, whatever it is. So just to reinforce your understanding of this, let's look at few more examples. The statement

```
variable *= 12;
```

is the same as

```
variable = variable * 12;
```

You now have two different ways of incrementing an integer variable by 1. Both of the following statements increment count by 1:

```
count = count+1;
count += 1;
```

You'll learn about yet another way of doing this in the next chapter. This amazing level of choice tends to make it virtually impossible for indecisive individuals to write programs in C.

Because the op in op= applies to the result of evaluating the rhs expression, the statement

```
a /= b+1;
```

is the same as

```
a = a/(b+1);
```

Your computational facilities have been somewhat constrained so far. You've been able to use only a very basic set of arithmetic operators. You can get more power to your calculating elbow using standard library facilities, so before you come to the final example in this chapter, you'll take a look at some of the mathematical functions that the standard library offers.

Mathematical Functions

The math.h header file includes declarations for a wide range of mathematical functions. To give you a feel for what's available, you'll take a look at those that are used most frequently. All the functions return a value of type double.

You have the set of functions shown in Table 2-7 available for numerical calculations of various kinds. These all require arguments to be of type double.

Table 2-7. Functions for Numerical Calculations

Function	Operation
floor(x)	Returns the largest integer that isn't greater than x as type double
ceil(x)	Returns the smallest integer that isn't less than x as type double
fabs(x)	Returns the absolute value of x
log(x)	Returns the natural logarithm (base e) of x
log10(x)	Returns the logarithm to base 10 of x
exp(x)	Returns the value of e^x
sqrt(x)	Returns the square root of x
pow(x, y)	Returns the value of x^y

Here are some examples of using these functions:

```
double x = 2.25;
double less = 0.0;
double more = 0.0;
double root = 0.0;
less = floor(x);    /* Result is 2.0 */
more = ceil(x);     /* Result is 3.0 */
root = sqrt(x);     /* Result is 1.5 */
```

You also have a range of trigonometric functions available, as shown in Table 2-8. Arguments and values returned are again of type double and angles are expressed in radians.

Table 2-8. Functions for Trigonometry

Function	Operation
sin(x)	Sine of x expressed in radians
cos(x)	Cosine of x
tan(x)	Tangent of x

If you're into trigonometry, the use of these functions will be fairly self-evident. Here are some examples:

```
double angle = 45.0;           /* Angle in degrees */
double pi = 3.14159265;
double sine = 0.0;
double cosine = 0.0;
sine = sin(pi*angle/180.0);    /* Angle converted to radians */
cosine = sin(pi*angle/180.0);  /* Angle converted to radians */
```

Because 180 degrees is the same angle as π radians, dividing an angle measured in degrees by 180 and multiplying by the value of π will produce the angle in radians, as required by these functions.

You also have the inverse trigonometric functions available: asin(), acos(), and atan(), as well as the hyperbolic functions sinh(), cosh(), and tanh(). Don't forget, you must include math.h into your program if you wish to use any of these functions. If this stuff is not your bag, you can safely ignore this section.

Designing a Program

Now it's time for the end-of-chapter real-life example. It would be a great idea to try out some of the numeric types in a new program. I'll take you through the basic elements of the process of writing a program from scratch. This involves receiving an initial specification of the problem, analyzing the problem, preparing a solution, writing the program and, of course, running the program and testing it to make sure it works. Each step in the process can introduce problems, beyond just the theory.

The Problem

The height of a tree is of great interest to many people. For one thing, if a tree is being cut down, knowing its height tells you how far away *safe* is. This is very important to those with a nervous disposition. Your problem is to find out the height of a tree without using a very long ladder, which itself would introduce risk to life and limb. To find the height of a tree, you're allowed the help of a friend—preferably a short friend. You should assume that the tree you're measuring is taller than both you and your friend. Trees that are shorter than you present little risk, unless they're of the spiky kind.

The Analysis

Real-world problems are rarely expressed in terms that are directly suitable for programming. Before you consider writing a line of code, you need to be sure that you have a complete understanding of the problem and how it's going to be solved. Only then can you estimate how much time and effort will be involved in creating the solution.

The analysis phase involves gaining a full understanding of the problem and determining the logical process for solving it. Typically this requires a significant amount of work. It involves teasing out any detail in the specification of the problem that is vague or missing. Only when you fully understand the problem can you begin to express the solution in a form that's suitable for programming.

You're going to determine the height of a tree using some simple geometry and the heights of two people: you and one other. Let's start by naming the tall person (you) Lofty and the shorter person (your friend) Shorty. If you're vertically challenged, the roles can be reversed. For more accurate results, the tall person should be significantly taller than the short person. Otherwise the tall person could consider standing on a box. The diagram in Figure 2-2 will give you an idea of what you're trying to do in this program.

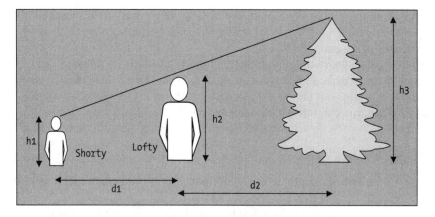

Figure 2-2. The height of a tree

Finding the height of the tree is actually quite simple. You can get the height of the tree, h_3, if you know the other dimensions shown in the illustration: h_1 and h_2, which are the heights of Shorty and Lofty, and d_1 and d_2, which are the distances between Lofty and Shorty, and from Lofty to the tree, respectively. You can use the technique of similar triangles to work out the height of the tree. You can see this in the simplified diagram in Figure 2-3.

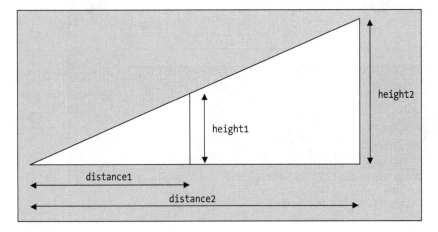

Figure 2-3. Similar triangles

Here, because the triangles are similar, `height1` divided by `distance1` is equal to `height2` divided by `distance2`. Using this relationship, you can get the height of the tree from the height of Shorty and Lofty and the distances to the tree as shown in Figure 2-4.

The triangles ADE and ABC are the same as those shown in the previous diagram. Using the fact that the triangles are similar, you can calculate the height of the tree as shown in the bottom equation in the diagram.

This means that you can calculate the height of the tree in your program from four values:

- The distance between Shorty and Lofty, d_1 in the diagram. You'll use the variable `shorty_to_lofty` to store this value.

- The distance between Lofty and the tree, d_2 in the diagram. You'll use the variable `lofty_to_tree` to store this value.

- The height of Lofty to the top of his head, h_2 in the diagram. You'll use the variable `lofty` to store this value.

- The height of Shorty, but only up to the eyes, h_1 in the diagram. You'll use the variable `shorty` to store this value.

You can then plug these values into the equation for the height of the tree.

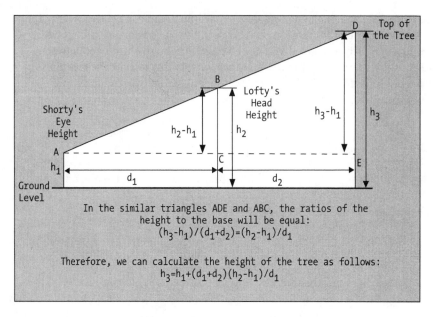

Figure 2-4. Calculating the tree height

Your first task is to get these four values into the computer. You can then use your ratios to find out the height of the tree, and finally output the answer. The steps are as follows:

1. Input the values you need.

2. Calculate the height of the tree using the equation in the diagram.

3. Display the answer.

The Solution

This section outlines the steps you'll take to solve the problem.

Step 1

Your first step is to get the values that you need to work out the height of the tree. This means that you have to include the stdio.h header file, because you need to use both printf() and scanf(). You then have to decide what variables you need to store these values in. After that, you can use printf() to prompt for the input and scanf() to read the values from the keyboard.

You'll provide for the heights of the participants to be entered in feet and inches for the convenience of the user. Inside the program, though, it will be easier to work with all heights and distances in the same units, so you'll convert all measurements to inches. You'll need two variables to store the heights of Shorty and Lofty in inches. You'll also need a variable to store the distance between Lofty and Shorty, and another to store the distance from Lofty to the tree—both distances in inches, of course.

In the input process, you'll first get Lofty's height as a number of whole feet and then as a number of inches, prompting for each value as you go along. You can use two more variables for this: one to store the feet value and the other to store the inches value. You'll then convert these into just inches and store the result in the variable you've reserved for Lofty's height. You'll do the same thing for Shorty's height (but only up to the height of his or her eyes) and finally the same for the distance between them. For the distance to the tree, you'll use only whole feet, because this will be accurate enough—and again you'll convert the distance to inches. You can reuse the same variables for each measurement in feet and inches that is entered. So here goes with the first part of the program:

```c
/* Program 2.17  Calculating the height of a tree */
#include <stdio.h>

void main()
{
  long shorty = 0L;             /* Shorty's height in inches               */
  long lofty = 0L;              /* Lofty's height in inches                */
  long feet = 0L;               /* A whole number of feet                  */
  long inches = 0L;             /* A whole number of inches                */
  long shorty_to_lofty = 0;     /* Distance from Shorty to Lofty in inches */
  long lofty_to_tree = 0;       /* Distance from Lofty to the tree in inches */
  const long inches_per_foot = 12L;

  /* Get Lofty's height */
  printf("Enter Lofty's height to the top of his/her head, in whole feet: ");
  scanf("%ld", &feet);
  printf("              ...and then inches: ");
  scanf("%ld", &inches);
  lofty = feet*inches_per_foot + inches;

  /* Get Shorty's height up to his/her eyes */
  printf("Enter Shorty's height up to his/her eyes, in whole feet: ");
  scanf("%ld", &feet);
  printf("                        ... and then inches: ");
  scanf("%ld", &inches);
  shorty = feet*inches_per_foot + inches;

  /* Get the distance from Shorty to Lofty */
  printf("Enter the distance between Shorty and Lofty, in whole feet: ");
  scanf("%ld", &feet);
  printf("                              ... and then inches: ");
  scanf("%ld", &inches);
  shorty_to_lofty = feet*inches_per_foot + inches;

  /* Get the distance from Lofty to the tree */
  printf("Finally enter the distance to the tree to the nearest foot: ");
```

```
        scanf("%ld", &feet);
        lofty_to_tree = feet*inches_per_foot;

        /* The code to calculate the height of the tree will go here */

        /* The code to display the result will go here                */
}
```

Notice how the program code is spaced out to make it easier to read. You don't have to do it this way, but if you decide to change the program next year, it will make it much easier to see how the program works if it's well laid out. You should always add comments to your programs to help with this. It's particularly important to at least make clear what the variables are used for and to document the basic logic of the program.

You use a variable that you've declared as const to convert from feet to inches. The variable name, inches_per_foot, makes it reasonably obvious what's happening when it's used in the code. This is much better than using the "magic number" 12 explicitly. Here you're dealing with feet and inches, and most people will be aware that there are 12 inches in a foot. In other circumstances, the significance of numeric constants may not be so obvious, though. If you're using the value 0.22 in a program calculating salaries, it's much less apparent what this might be; therefore, the calculation may seem rather obscure. If you create a const variable tax_rate that you've initialized to 0.22 and use that instead, then the mist clears.

Step 2

Now that you have all the data you need, you can calculate the height of the tree. All you need to do is implement the equation for the tree height in terms of your variables. You'll need to declare another variable to store the height of the tree.

You can now add the code that's shown here in bold type to do this:

```
/* Program 2.17  Calculating the height of a tree */
#include <stdio.h>

void main()
{
  long shorty = 0L;              /* Shorty's height in inches                 */
  long lofty = 0L;               /* Lofty's height in inches                  */
  long feet = 0L;                /* A whole number of feet                    */
  long inches = 0L;              /* A whole number of inches                  */
  long shorty_to_lofty = 0;      /* Distance from Shorty to Lofty in inches   */
  long lofty_to_tree = 0;        /* Distance from Lofty to the tree in inches */
  long tree_height = 0;          /* Height of the tree in inches              */
  const long inches_per_foot = 12L;

  /* Get Lofty's height */
  printf("Enter Lofty's height to the top of his/her head, in whole feet: ");
  scanf("%ld", &feet);
```

```
    printf("                 ...and then inches: ");
    scanf("%ld", &inches);
    lofty = feet*inches_per_foot + inches;

    /* Get Shorty's height up to his/her eyes */
    printf("Enter Shorty's height up to his/her eyes, in whole feet: ");
    scanf("%ld", &feet);
    printf("                       ... and then inches: ");
    scanf("%ld", &inches);
    shorty = feet*inches_per_foot + inches;

    /* Get the distance from Shorty to Lofty */
    printf("Enter the distance between Shorty and Lofty, in whole feet: ");
    scanf("%ld", &feet);
    printf("                         ... and then inches: ");
    scanf("%ld", &inches);
    shorty_to_lofty = feet*inches_per_foot + inches;

    /* Get the distance from Lofty to the tree */
    printf("Finally enter the distance to the tree to the nearest foot: ");
    scanf("%ld", &feet);
    lofty_to_tree = feet*inches_per_foot;

    /* Calculate the height of the tree in inches */
    tree_height = shorty + (shorty_to_lofty + lofty_to_tree)*(lofty-shorty)/
                                                       shorty_to_lofty;

    /* The code to display the result will go here          */
}
```

The statement to calculate the height is essentially the same as the equation in the diagram. It's a bit messy, but it translates directly to the statement in the program to calculate the height.

Step 3

Finally, you need to output the answer. To present the result in the most easily understandable form, you'll convert the result that you've stored in tree_height, which is in inches, back into feet and inches:

```
/* Program 2.17  Calculating the height of a tree */
#include <stdio.h>

void main()
{
    long shorty = 0L;            /* Shorty's height in inches           */
    long lofty = 0L;             /* Lofty's height in inches            */
    long feet = 0L;              /* A whole number of feet              */
    long inches = 0L;            /* A whole number of inches            */
    long shorty_to_lofty = 0;    /* Distance from Shorty to Lofty in inches  */
```

```
long lofty_to_tree = 0;        /* Distance from Lofty to the tree in inches */
long tree_height = 0;          /* Height of the tree in inches              */
const long inches_per_foot = 12L;

/* Get Lofty's height */
printf("Enter Lofty's height to the top of his/her head, in whole feet: ");
scanf("%ld", &feet);
printf("                                    ... and then inches: ");
scanf("%ld", &inches);
lofty = feet*inches_per_foot + inches;

/* Get Shorty's height up to his/her eyes */
printf("Enter Shorty's height up to his/her eyes, in whole feet: ");
scanf("%ld", &feet);
printf("                               ... and then inches: ");
scanf("%ld", &inches);
shorty = feet*inches_per_foot + inches;

/* Get the distance from Shorty to Lofty */
printf("Enter the distance between Shorty and Lofty, in whole feet: ");
scanf("%ld", &feet);
printf("                                ... and then inches: ");
scanf("%ld", &inches);
shorty_to_lofty = feet*inches_per_foot + inches;

/* Get the distance from Lofty to the tree */
printf("Finally enter the distance to the tree to the nearest foot: ");
scanf("%ld", &feet);
lofty_to_tree = feet*inches_per_foot;

/* Calculate the height of the tree in inches */
tree_height = shorty + (shorty_to_lofty + lofty_to_tree)*(lofty-shorty)/
                                                        shorty_to_lofty;

/* Display the result in feet and inches              */
printf("The height of the tree is %ld feet and %ld inches.\n",
                    tree_height/inches_per_foot, tree_height% inches_per_foot);
}
```

And there you have it. The output from the program looks something like this:

```
Enter Lofty's height to the top of his/her head, in whole feet first: 6
                                        ... and then inches: 2
Enter Shorty's height up to his/her eyes, in whole feet: 4
                        ... and then inches: 6
Enter the distance between Shorty and Lofty, in whole feet : 5
                        ... and then inches: 0
Finally enter the distance to the tree to the nearest foot: 20
The height of the tree is 12 feet and 10 inches.
```

Summary

This chapter covered quite a lot of ground. By now, you know how a C program is structured, and you should be fairly comfortable with any kind of arithmetic calculation. You should also be able to choose variable types to suit the job at hand. Aside from arithmetic, you've added quite a bit of input and output capability to your knowledge. You should now feel at ease with inputting values into variables via scanf(). You can output text and the values of character and numeric variables to the screen. You won't remember it all the first time around, but you can always look back over this chapter if you need to. Not bad for the first two chapters, is it?

In the next chapter, you'll start looking at how you can control the program by making decisions depending on the values you enter. As you can probably imagine, this is key to creating interesting and professional programs.

Table 2-9 summarizes the variable types and the format specifiers you've used so far. You can look back at these when you need a reminder as you continue through the book.

Table 2-9. Variable Types and Value Ranges

Type	Number of Bytes	Range of Values
char	1	–128 to +127 or 0 to 255
unsigned char	1	0 to 255
int	2 or 4	–32,768 to +32,767 or –2,147,438,648 to +2,147,438,647
unsigned int	2 or 4	0 to 65,535 or 0 to 4,294,967,295
short	2	–32,768 to +32,767
unsigned short	2	0 to 65,535
long	4	–2,147,438,648 to +2,147,438,647
unsigned long	4	0 to 4,294,967,295
float	4	±3.4E38 (6 digits)
double	8	±1.7E308 (15 digits)
long double	10	±1.2E4932 (19 digits)

The output format specifiers shown in Table 2-10 are used to control the form of output for values of variables of various types when you're using the printf() function.

Table 2-10. Output Format Specifiers

Output Format Specifier	Outputs
%[-][width]c	Character value
%[-][width]d	Signed decimal integer
%[width]x	Unsigned hexadecimal integer using "abcdef"
%[width]X	Unsigned hexadecimal integer using "ABCDEF"
%[-][width]ld	Long signed decimal integer

(Continued)

Table 2-10. Output Format Specifiers (Continued)

Output Format Specifier	Outputs
%[-][width]u	Unsigned decimal integer
%[-][width][.precision]f	Floating-point number without an exponent
%[-][width][.precision]e	Floating-point number with an exponent

The square brackets enclose optional elements in a format specification and aren't part of the specifier. The - specifies that the output is left-aligned in the field, the default being right-aligned. The width specifies the field width as an integral number of characters. .precision specifies the number of places that are to be displayed following the decimal point. Thus, %-15.6f is a specification for a left-aligned floating-point value in a field 15 characters wide with 6 digits following the decimal point.

The input format specifiers shown in Table 2-11 are used to control how data is interpreted when it's read from the keyboard by the scanf() function.

Table 2-11. Input Format Specifiers

Input Format Specifier	Reads
%c	A single character
%hd	A value of type short
%d	A value of type int
%ld	A value of type long
%f or %e	A value of type float
%lf or %le	A value of type double

You'll see more on scanf() input specifiers in later chapters.

Exercises

The following exercises enable you to try out what you've learned in this chapter. If you get stuck, look back over the chapter for help. If you're still stuck, you can download the solutions from the Downloads area of the Apress website (http://www.apress.com), but that really should be a last resort.

Exercise 2-1. Write a program that prompts the user to enter a distance in inches and then outputs that distance in yards, feet, and inches.

Exercise 2-2. Write a program that prompts for input of the length and width of a room in feet and inches, and then calculates and outputs the floor area in square yards with two decimal places after the decimal point.

Exercise 2-3. You're selling a product that's available in two versions: type 1 is a standard version priced at $3.50, and type 2 is a deluxe version priced at $5.50. Write a program using only what you've learned up to now that prompts for the user to enter the product type and a quantity, and then calculates and outputs the price for the quantity entered.

Exercise 2-4. Write a program that prompts for the user's weekly pay in dollars and the hours worked to be entered through the keyboard as floating-point values, and then calculate and output the average pay per hour in the following form:

```
Your average hourly pay rate is 7 dollars and 54 cents.
```

CHAPTER 3

Making Decisions

IN CHAPTER 2 YOU LEARNED HOW to do calculations in your programs. In this chapter, you'll take great leaps forward in the range of programs you can write and the flexibility you can build into them. You'll add one of the most powerful programming tools to your inventory: the ability to compare the values of expressions and, based on the outcome, choose to execute one set of statements or another.

What this means is that you'll be able to control the sequence in which statements are executed in a program. Up until now, all the statements in your programs have been executed strictly in sequence. In this chapter you're going to change all that.

In this chapter you'll learn

- How to make decisions based on arithmetic comparisons

- What logical operators are and how you can use them

- More about reading data from the keyboard

- How you can write a program that can be used as a calculator

The Decision-Making Process

You'll start with the essentials of decision making in a program. Decision making in a program is concerned with choosing to execute one set of program statements rather than another. In everyday life you do this kind of thing all the time. Each time you wake up you have to decide whether it's a good idea to go to work. You may go through these questions:

Do I feel well?

If the answer is no, stay in bed.

If the answer is yes, go to work.

You could rewrite this as follows:

If I feel well, I will go to work.

Otherwise, I will stay in bed.

That was a straightforward decision. Later, as you're having breakfast, you notice it's raining, so you think

If it is raining as hard as it did yesterday, I will take the bus. If it is raining harder than yesterday, I will drive to work. Otherwise, I will risk it and walk.

This is a more complex decision process. It's a decision based on several levels in the amount of rain falling, and it can have any of three different results.

As the day goes on, you're presented with more of these decisions. Without them you'd be stuck with only one course of action. Until now in this book, you've had exactly the same problem with your programs. All the programs will run a straight course to a defined end, without making any decisions. This is a severe constraint on what your programs can do and one that you'll relieve now. First, you'll set up some basic building blocks of knowledge that will enable you to do this.

Arithmetic Comparisons

To make a decision, you need a mechanism for comparing things. This involves some new operators. Because you're dealing with numbers, comparing numerical values is basic to decision making. You have three fundamental operators:

- < is less than.

- == is equal to.

- > is greater than.

NOTE *The equal to operator has **two** successive equal signs (==). You'll almost certainly use one equal sign on occasions by mistake. This will cause considerable confusion until you spot the problem. Look at the difference. If you type* my_weight = your_weight, *it's an assignment that puts the value from the variable* your_weight *into the variable* my_weight. *If you type the expression* my_weight == your_weight, *then you're comparing the two values: you're asking **whether** they're exactly the same—you're not making them the same.*

Logical Expressions

Have a look at these examples:

```
5 < 4     1 == 2     5 > 4
```

These expressions are called **logical expressions**, and each of them can result in just one of two values: either true or false. The value true is represented by 1, or more generally by any nonzero integer; false is represented by 0. The first expression is false because 5 is patently not less than 4. The second expression is also false because 1 is not equal to 2. The third expression is true because 5 is greater than 4.

The Basic if Statement

Now that you have some logical operators, you need a statement allowing you to make a decision. The simplest available to you is the `if` statement. If you want to compare weights and print a different sentence depending on the result, you can write the body of a program as follows:

```
if( your_weight > my_weight)
  printf("You are fatter than me.\n");

if(your_weight < my_weight)
  printf("I am fatter than you.\n");

if(your_weight == my_weight)
  printf("We are exactly the same weight.\n");
```

Note how the statement following each `if` is indented. This is to show that it's dependent on the result of the `if` test. Let's go through this and see how it works. The first `if` tests whether the value in `your_weight` is greater than the value in `my_weight`. The expression for the comparison appears between the parentheses that immediately follow the keyword `if`. If the result of the comparison is true, then the statement immediately after the `if` will be executed. This just outputs the following message:

```
You are fatter than me.
```

Execution will then continue with the next `if`. What if the expression between the parentheses in the first `if` is false? In this case, the statement immediately following the `if` will be skipped, so the message won't be displayed. It will be displayed only if `your_weight` is greater than `my_weight`.

The second `if` works in essentially the same way. If the expression between parentheses after the keyword `if` is true, then the following statement will be executed to output this message:

```
I am fatter than you.
```

This will be the case if `your_weight` is less than `my_weight`. If this isn't so, the statement will be skipped and the message won't display. The third `if` is again the same. The effect of these statements is to print one message that will depend on whether `your_weight` is greater than, less than, or equal to `my_weight`. Only one message will be displayed because only one of these can be true.

The general form or **syntax** of the if statement is as follows:

```
if(expression)
   Statement1;

Next_statement;
```

Notice that the expression that forms the test (the if) is enclosed between parentheses and that there is no semicolon at the end of the first line. This is because both the line with the if keyword and the following line are tied together. The second line could be written directly following the first, like this:

```
if(expression) Statement1;
```

but for the sake of clarity, people tend to put Statement1 on a new line.

The expression in parentheses can be any expression that results in a value of true or false. If the expression is true, then Statement1 is executed, after which the program continues with Next_statement. If the expression is false, then Statement1 is skipped and execution continues immediately with Next_statement. This is illustrated in Figure 3-1.

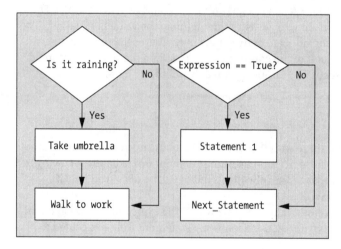

Figure 3-1. The operation of the if *statement*

You could have used the basic if statement to add some politically incorrect comments in the program that calculated the height of a tree at the end of the previous chapter. For example, you could have added the following code just after you calculated the height of the shortest person:

```
if(Shorty < 36)
   printf("\nMy, you really are on the short side, aren't you.");
```

Here, you use the if statement to add a gratuitously offensive remark, should the individual be less than 36 inches tall.

....

Try It Out: Checking Conditions

Let's see the if statement in action. This program gets the user to enter a number between 1 and 10 and then tells the user how big that number is:

```
/* Program 3.1 A simple example of the if statement */
#include <stdio.h>

void main()
{
   int number = 0;
   printf("\nEnter an integer between 1 and 10: ");
   scanf("%d",&number);

   if (number > 5)
     printf("You entered %d which is greater than 5\n", number);

   if (number < 6)
     printf("You entered %d which is less than 6\n", number);
}
```

Sample output from this program is as follows:

```
Enter an integer between 1 and 10: 7
You entered 7 which is greater than 5
```

or

```
Enter an integer between 1 and 10: 3
You entered 3 which is less than 6
```

HOW IT WORKS

As usual, you include a comment at the beginning as a reminder of what the program does. You include the stdio.h header file to allow you to use the printf() statement. You then have the beginning of the main() function of the program. This function doesn't return a value, as indicated by the keyword void.

(Continued)

```
/* Program 3.1 A simple example of the if statement*/
#include <stdio.h>

void main()
{
```

In the first three statements in the body of main(), you read an integer from the keyboard after prompting the user for the data:

```
int number = 0;
printf("\nEnter an integer between 1 and 10: \n");
scanf("%d",&number);
```

You declare an integer variable called number that you initialize to 0, and then you prompt the user to enter a number between 1 and 10. This value is then read using the scanf() function and stored in the variable number.

The next statement is an if that tests the value that was entered:

```
if (number > 5)
  printf("You entered %d which is greater than 5", number);
```

You compare the value in number with the value 5. If number is greater than 5, then you execute the next statement, which displays a message, and you go to the next part of the program. If number isn't greater than 5, then printf() is simply skipped. You use the %d conversion specifier for integer values to output the number the user typed in.

You then have another if statement:

```
if (number < 6)
  printf("You entered %d which is less than 6", number);
```

This compares the value entered with 6 and, if it's smaller, you execute the next statement to display a message. Otherwise, the printf() is skipped and the program ends. Only one of the two possible messages will be displayed because the number will always be less than 6 or greater than 5.

The if statement enables you to be selective about what input you accept and what you finally do with it. For instance, if you have a variable and you want to have its value specifically limited at some point, even though higher values may arise somehow in the program, you could write this:

```
if( x > 90)
  x = 90;
```

This would ensure that if anyone entered a value of x that was larger than 90, your program would automatically change it to 90. This would be invaluable if you had a program that could only specifically deal with values within a range.

(Continued)

You could also check whether a value was lower than a given number and, if not, set it to that number. In this way, you could ensure that the value was within the given range.

....

Extending the if Statement: if-else

You can extend the if statement with a small addition that gives you a lot more flexibility. Imagine it rained a little yesterday. You could write

If the rain today is worse than the rain yesterday, I will take my umbrella.

Else I will take my jacket.

Then I will go to work.

This is exactly the kind of decision making the if-else statement provides. The syntax of the if-else statement is as follows:

```
if(expression)
   Statement1;
else
   Statement2;

Next_statement;
```

Here, you have an either-or situation. You'll always execute either Statement1 or Statement2 depending on whether expression is true or false:

If expression is true, Statement1 is executed and the program continues with Next_statement.

If expression is false, then Statement2 following the else keyword is executed, and the program continues with Next_statement.

The sequence of operations involved here is shown in Figure 3-2.

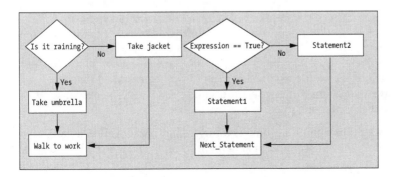

Figure 3-2. The operation of the if-else *statement*

Try It Out: Using if to Analyze Numbers

Let's suppose that you're selling a product at a single-unit price of $3.50, and for order quantities greater than ten you offer a 5 percent discount. You can use the if-else statement to calculate and output the price for a given quantity.

```
/* Program 3.2 Using ifs to decide on a discount         */
#include <stdio.h>

void main()
{
  const double unit_price = 3.50;                /* Unit price in dollars */
  int quantity = 0;
  printf("Enter the number that you want to buy:");   /* Prompt message */
   scanf(" %d", &quantity);                           /* Read the input */

   /* Test for order quantity qualifying for a discount */
   if( quantity>10)                                    /* 5% discount   */
     printf("The price for %d is $%.2f\n", quantity, quantity*unit_price*0.95);
   else                                               /* No discount   */
     printf("The price for %d is $%.2f\n", quantity, quantity*unit_price);
}
```

Typical output from this program is as follows:

```
Enter the number that you want to buy:20
The price for 20 is $66.50
```

HOW IT WORKS

Once your program has read the order quantity, the if-else statement does all the work:

```
  if( quantity>10)                               /* 5% discount */
    printf("\nThe price for %d is $%.2f\n", quantity, quantity*unit_price*0.95);
  else                                           /* No discount */
    printf("\nThe price for %d is $%.2f\n", quantity, quantity*unit_price);
```

If quantity is greater than ten, then the first printf() will be executed that applies a 5 percent discount. Otherwise, the second printf() will be executed that applies no discount to the price.

There a few more things I could say on this topic, though. First of all, you can also solve the problem with a simple if statement by replacing the if-else statement with the following code:

(Continued)

```
double discount = 0.0;                              /* Discount allowed */
if( quantity>10)
    discount = 0.05;                                /* 5% discount      */
printf("\nThe price for %d is $%.2f\n", quantity,
                              quantity*unit_price*(1.0-discount));
```

This considerably simplifies the code. You now have a single `printf()` call that applies the discount that is set, either 0 or 5 percent. With a variable storing the discount value, it's also clearer what is happening in the code.

The second point worth making is that floating-point variables aren't ideal for calculations involving money because of the potential rounding that can occur. Providing the amounts of money are reasonable, one alternative is to use integer values and just store cents, for example:

```
const long unit_price = 350L;                       /* Unit price in cents */
int quantity = 0;
printf("Enter the number that you want to buy:");   /* Prompt message      */
 scanf(" %d", &quantity);                            /* Read the input      */

long discount = 0L;                                 /* Discount allowed    */
if( quantity>10)
    discount = 5L;                                  /* 5% discount         */
long total_price = quantity*unit_price*(100-discount)/100;
long dollars = total_price/100;
long cents = total_price%100;
printf("\nThe price for %d is $%ld.%ld\n", quantity, dollars,cents);
```

Of course, you also have the possibility of storing the dollars and cents for each monetary value in separate integer variables. It gets a little more complicated because you then have to keep track of when the cents value reaches or exceeds 100 during arithmetic operations.

Using Blocks of Code in if Statements

You can also replace either Statement1 or Statement2, or even both, by a block of statements enclosed between braces {}. This means that you can supply many instructions to the computer after making a check of an expression, simply by placing these instructions together between braces.

The mechanics of this can be illustrated by a real-life situation:

If the weather is sunny

I will walk to the park, eat a picnic, and walk home

Else

I will stay in, watch football, and drink beer

The syntax for an `if` statement that involves statement blocks is as follows:

```
if(expression)
{
  StatementA1;
  StatementA2;
   ...
}
else
{
  StatementB1;
  StatementB2;
   ...
}
Next_statement;
```

All the statements that are in the block between the braces following the `if` condition will be executed if `expression` is `true`. If `expression` is `false`, all the statements between the braces following the `else` will be executed. In either case, execution continues with `Next_statement`. Have a look at the indentation. The braces aren't indented, but the statements between the braces are. This makes it clear that all the statements between an opening and a closing brace belong together.

NOTE *Although I've been talking about using a block of statements in place of a single statement in an `if` statement, this is just one example of a general rule. Wherever you can have a single statement, you can also have a block of statements between braces.*

Nested if Statements

It's also possible to have `if`s within `if`s. These are called **nested `if`s**. For example:

> If the weather is good, I will go out in the yard
>
> And if it's cool enough, I will sit in the sun
>
> Else I will sit in the shade
>
> Else I will stay indoors
>
> I will then drink some lemonade

In programming terms, this corresponds to the following:

```
if (expression1)            /* Weather is good?          */
{
   StatementA;              /* Yes - Go out in the yard  */
   if (expression2)         /* Cool enough?              */
      StatementB;           /* Yes - Sit in the sun      */
   else
      StatementC;           /* No - Sit in the shade     */
}
else
   StatementD;              /* Weather not good - stay in */
Statement E;                /* Drink lemonade in any event */
```

Here, the second `if` condition, `expression2`, is only checked if the first `if` condition, `expression1`, is true. The braces enclosing `StatementA` and the second `if` are necessary to make both of these statements a part of what is executed when `expression1` is true. Note how the `else` is aligned with the `if` it belongs to. The logic of this is illustrated in Figure 3-3.

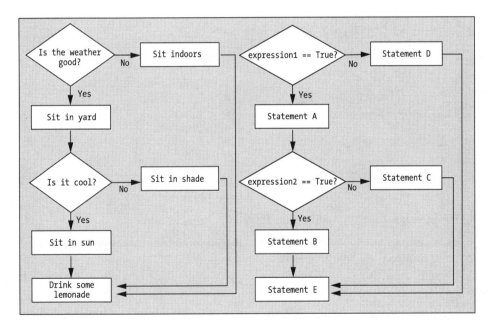

Figure 3-3. Nested `if` *statements*

Try It Out: Analyzing Numbers

You'll now exercise your if skills with a couple more examples. This program tests to see whether you enter an odd or an even number, and if the number is even, it then tests to see whether half that number is also even:

```c
/* Example 3.3 Using nested ifs to analyze numbers */
#include <stdio.h>
#include <limits.h>              /* For LONG_MAX                    */

void main()
{
  long test = 0L;               /* Stores the integer to be checked */

  printf("Enter an integer less than %ld:", LONG_MAX);
  scanf(" %ld", &test);

  /* Test for odd or even by checking the remainder after dividing by 2 */
  if( test % 2L == 0L)
  {
    printf("The number %ld is even", test);

    /* Now check whether half the number is also even */
    if ( (test/2L) % 2L == 0L)
    {
      printf("\nHalf of %ld is also even", test);
      printf("\nThat's interesting isn't it?\n");
    }
  }
  else
    printf("The number %ld is odd\n", test);
}
```

The output will look something like this:

```
Enter an integer less than 2147483647:20
The number 20 is even
Half of 20 is also even
That's interesting isn't it?
```

or this:

```
Enter an integer less than 2147483647:999
The number 999 is odd
```

(Continued)

HOW IT WORKS

The prompt for input makes use of the LONG_MAX symbol that's defined in the limits.h header file. This specifies the maximum value of type long. You can see from the output that on my system the upper limit for long values is 2147483647.

The first if condition tests for an even number:

```
if( test % 2L == 0L)
```

For any even number, the remainder after dividing by 2 will be 0. If the expression is true, then the block that follows will be executed:

```
{
  printf("The number %ld is even", test);

  /* Now check whether half the number is also even */
  if ( (test/2L) % 2L == 0L)
  {
    printf("\nHalf of %ld is also even", test);
    printf("\nThat's interesting isn't it?\n");
  }
}
```

After outputting a message that the value is even, you have another if statement. This is called a nested if because it's inside the first if. The nested if condition divides the original value by 2 and tests whether the result is even using the same mechanism as in the first if statement. There's an extra pair of parentheses in the nested if condition around the expression test/2L. These aren't strictly necessary, but they help to make what's going on clear. Making programs easier to follow is the essence of good programming style. If the result of the nested if condition is true, then the two further printf() statements in the block following the nested if will be executed.

Try adding code to make the nested if an if-else that will output "Half of %ld is odd".

If the original input value wasn't even, then the statement following the else keyword will be executed:

```
else
  printf("The number %ld is odd\n", test);
```

 NOTE *You can nest ifs anywhere inside another if, but I don't recommend this as a technique that you should use extensively. If you do, your program is likely to end up being very hard to follow.*

(Continued)

To make the nested `if` statement output a message when the condition is false, you would need to insert

```
else
    printf ("\nHalf of %ld is odd", test) ;
```

after the closing brace for the nested `if`.

Some Additional Comparison Operators

You can now add a few more numerical comparison operators that you can use in `if` statements. Three additional operators make up the complete set:

- `>=` is greater than or equal to.

- `<=` is less than or equal to.

- `!=` is not equal to.

These are fairly self-explanatory, but let's consider some examples anyway, starting with a few arithmetic examples:

```
6 >= 5     5 <= 5     4 <= 5     4 != 5     10 != 10
```

These are all true, except for the last one, which is false because 10 most definitely *is* equal to 10.

These operators can be applied to values of type char as well. If you remember, character types also have a numeric value associated with them. The ASCII table in Appendix B provides a full listing of all the standard characters and their numeric codes. Just to remind you for the next few examples, Table 3-1 is an extract from Appendix B.

Table 3-1. Characters and ASCII Codes

Character	ASCII Code (Decimal)
A	65
B	66
P	80
Q	81
Z	90
b	98

A char value may be expressed either as an integer or as a keyboard character between quotes, such as 'A'. Don't forget, numeric values stored as type char may be signed or unsigned, depending on how your compiler implements the type. When type char is unsigned, values can be from −128 to +127. When char is an unsigned type, values can be from 0 to 255. Here are a few examples of comparing values of type char:

```
'Z' >= 'A'        'Q' <= 'P'        'B' <= 'b'        'B' != 66
```

With the ASCII values of the characters in mind, the first expression is true, because 'Z', which has the code value 90, comes after 'A', which has the code value 65. The second is false, as 'Q' doesn't come before 'P'. The third is true. This is because, in ASCII code, lowercase letters are 32 higher than their uppercase equivalents. The last is false. The value 66 is indeed the decimal ASCII representation for the character 'B'.

Try It Out: Converting Uppercase to Lowercase

Let's exercise the new logical operators in an example. Here you have a program that will convert any uppercase letter that is entered to a lowercase letter:

```c
/* Program 3.4 Converting uppercase to lowercase */
#include <stdio.h>

void main()
{
  char letter = 0;                      /* Stores a character                  */

  printf("Enter an uppercase letter:"); /* Prompt for input                    */
  scanf("%c", &letter);                 /* Read a character                    */

  /* Check whether the input is uppercase */
  if(letter >= 'A')                     /* Is it A or greater?                 */
    if (letter <= 'Z')                  /* and is it Z or lower?               */
    {                                   /* It is uppercase                     */
      letter = letter - 'A'+ 'a';       /* Convert from upper- to lowercase */
      printf("You entered an uppercase %c\n", letter);
    }
    else                                /* It is not an uppercase letter    */
      printf("Try using the shift key, Bud! I want a capital letter.\n");
}
```

Sample output from this program might be

```
Enter an uppercase letter:G
You entered an uppercase g
```

(Continued)

or

```
Enter an uppercase letter:s
Try using the shift key, Bud! I want a capital letter.
```

HOW IT WORKS

In the first three statements, you declare a variable of type char called letter, you prompt the user to input a capital letter, and you store the character entered in the variable letter:

```c
char letter = 0;                          /* Stores a character        */

printf("Enter an uppercase letter:");     /* Prompt for input          */
scanf("%c", &letter);                     /* Read a character          */
```

If a capital letter was entered, the character in the letter variable must be between 'A' and 'Z', so the next if checks whether the character is greater than or equal to 'A':

```c
if(letter >= 'A')                         /* Is it A or greater?       */
```

If the expression is true, you continue with the nested if that tests whether letter is less than or equal to 'Z':

```c
if (letter <= 'Z')                        /* and is it Z or lower?     */
```

If this expression is true, then you convert the character to lowercase and output a message by executing the block of statements following the if:

```c
{                                         /* It is uppercase           */
  letter = letter - 'A'+ 'a';             /* Convert from upper- to lowercase */
  printf("You entered an uppercase %c\n", letter);
}
```

To convert to lowercase, you subtract the character code for 'A' from letter and add the character code for 'a'. If letter contained 'A', subtracting 'A' would produce 0, and adding 'a' would result in 'a'. If letter contained 'B', subtracting 'A' would produce 1, and adding 'a' would result in 'b'. You can see this conversion works for any uppercase letter. Note that although this works fine for ASCII, there are coding systems in which this won't work, because the letters don't have a contiguous sequence of codes. If you want to be sure that the conversion works for any code, you can use the standard library function tolower().

(Continued)

This converts the character passed as an argument to lowercase if it's an uppercase letter; otherwise, it returns the character code value unchanged. To use this function, you need to include the header file ctype.h in your program. This header file also declares the complementary function toupper(), which will convert lowercase letters to uppercase.

If the expression letter <= 'Z' is false, you go straight to the statement following else and display a different message:

```
    else                             /* It is not an uppercase letter    */
       printf("Try using the shift key, Bud! I want a capital letter.\n");
```

There's something wrong, though. What if the character that was entered was less than 'A'? There's no else clause for the first if, so the program just ends without outputting anything. To deal with this, you must add another else clause at the end of the program. The complete nested if would then become this:

```
  if(letter >= 'A')                  /* Is it A or greater?             */
    if (letter <= 'Z')               /* and is it Z or lower?           */
    {                                /* It is uppercase                 */
      letter = letter - 'A'+ 'a';    /* Convert from upper- to lowercase */
      printf("You entered an uppercase %c\n", letter);
    }
    else                             /* It is not an uppercase letter    */
       printf("Try using the shift key, Bud! I want a capital letter.\n");
  else
    printf("You didn't enter an uppercase letter\n");
```

Now you always get a message. Note the indentation to show which else belongs to which if. The indentation doesn't determine what belongs to what. It just provides a visual cue. An else always belongs to the if that immediately precedes it that isn't already spoken for by another else.

You used a nested if statement to check for two conditions in the preceding example but, as you can imagine, this could get very confusing when you have lots of different criteria that you need to check for. The good news is that C allows you to use logical operators to simplify the situation.

Logical Operations

Sometimes it just isn't enough to perform a single test for a decision. You may want to combine two or more checks on values and, if they're all true, then perform a certain action. Or you may want to perform a calculation if one or more of a set of conditions are true.

For example, you may only want to go to work if you're feeling well *and* it's a weekday. Just because you feel great doesn't mean you want to go in on a Saturday or a

Sunday. Alternatively, you could say that you'll stay at home if you feel ill *or* if it's a weekend day. These are exactly the sorts of circumstances for which the logical operators were intended.

The AND Operator &&

You can look first at the logical AND operator, &&. This is a **binary operator** because it operates on two items of data. The && operator combines two logical expressions; that is, two expressions that have a value true or false. The expression

```
Test1 && Test2
```

has the value true if both expressions Test1 and Test2 are true. If either or both of the operands are false, then the result of the operation is false.

The obvious place to use the && operator is in an if expression. Let's look at an example:

```
if( age > 12 && age < 20 )
  printf("You are officially a teenager.");
```

The printf() statement will be executed only if age has a value between 13 and 19 inclusive. Naturally, you can use more than one of these logical operators in an expression:

```
if( age > 12 && age < 20 && savings > 5000 )
  printf("You are a rich teenager.");
```

All three conditions must be true for the printf() to be executed. That is, the printf() will be executed only if the value of age is between 13 and 19 inclusive, and the value of savings is greater than 5000.

The OR Operator ||

The logical OR operator, ||, covers the situation in which you want to check for any of two or more conditions being true. Here's an example of using this operator:

```
if( a < 10 || b > c || c > 50 )
  printf("At least one of the conditions is true.");
```

The printf() will be executed only if *at least* one of the three conditions, a<10, b>c, or c<50, is true. When a, b, and c all have the value 9, for instance, this will be the case. Of course, the printf() will also be executed when two of the conditions are true, as well as all three.

You can also use the && and || logical operators in combination, as in the following code fragment:

```
if ((age > 12 && age <20) || savings>5000)
    printf ("Either you're a teenager, or you're rich, or possibly both.");
```

The printf() statement will be executed if the value of age is between 12 and 20, or the value of savings is greater than 5000, or both. As you can see, when you start to use more operators, things can get confusing.

The NOT Operator !

Last but not least is the logical NOT operator, represented by !. The ! operator is a unary operator, because it applies to just one operand. The logical NOT operator reverses the value of a logical expression: true becomes false, and false becomes true. Suppose you have two variables, a and b, with the values 5 and 2, respectively; then the expression a>b is true. If you use the logical NOT operator, the expression !(a>b) is false. I recommend that you avoid using this operator as much as possible—it tends to result in code that becomes difficult to follow. As an illustration of how not to use NOT, you can rewrite the previous example as follows:

```
if ((!(age >= 12) && !( age >= 20)) || !(savings <= 5000))
{
    printf("\nYou're either not a teenager and rich ");
    printf("or not rich and a teenager,\n");
    printf("or neither not a teenager nor not rich.");
}
```

As you can see, it becomes incredibly difficult to unravel the nots!

....

Try It Out: A Better Way to Convert Letters

Earlier in this chapter was a program in which the user was prompted to enter an uppercase character. You then used a nested if to ensure that the input was of the correct type, and then you printed the small letter equivalent or a remark indicating that the input was of the wrong type.

You can now see that all this was completely unnecessary, because you can achieve the same result like this:

```
/* Program 3.5   Testing letters the easy way */
#include <stdio.h>
void main()
{
    char letter =0;                       /* Stores an input character */

    printf("Enter an upper case letter:"); /* Prompt for input         */
    scanf(" %c", &letter);                /* Read the input character  */
```

(Continued)

```
            if ((letter >= 'A') && (letter <= 'Z')) /* Verify uppercase letter  */
            {
              letter += 'a'-'A';                     /* Convert to lowercase      */
              printf("You entered an uppercase %c.\n", letter);
            }
            else
              printf("You did not enter an uppercase letter.\n");
          }
```

The output will be similar to that from the earlier example.

HOW IT WORKS

The output is similar but not exactly the same as the original program. In the corrected version of the program, you generated a different message when the input was less than 'A'. This version is better, though. Compare the mechanism to test the input in the two programs and you'll see how much neater the second solution is. This is the original version:

```
if (letter >= 'A')
    if (letter <= 'Z')
```

This is the new version:

```
  if ((letter >= 'A') && (letter <= 'Z')) /* Verify uppercase letter  */
```

Rather than having confusing nested if statements, here you check that the character entered is greater than 'A' *and* less than 'Z' in one statement. Notice that you put extra parentheses around the two expressions to be checked. They aren't really needed in this case, but they don't hurt, and they leave you or any other programmer in no doubt as to the order of execution.

There's also a slightly simpler way of expressing the conversion to lowercase:

```
  letter += 'a'-'A';                       /* Convert to lowercase      */
```

Now you use the += operator to add the difference between 'a' and 'A' to the character code value stored in letter.

The Conditional Operator

There's another operator called the **conditional operator** that you can use to test data. It evaluates one of two expressions depending on whether a logical expression evaluates true or false.

Because three operands are involved—the logical expression plus two other expressions—this operator is also referred to as the **ternary operator**. The general representation of an expression using the conditional operator looks like this:

```
condition ? expression1 : expression2
```

Notice how the operator is arranged in relation to the operands. There is a ? following the logical expression, condition, to separate it from the next operand, expression1. This is separated from the third operand, expression2, by a colon. The resultant value will be produced by evaluating expression1 if condition evaluates to true, or by evaluating expression2 if condition evaluates to false. Note that only one of expression1 and expression2 will be evaluated. Normally this is of little significance, but sometimes this is important.

You can use the conditional operator in a statement such as this:

```
x = y>7 ? 25 : 50;
```

Executing this statement will result in x having the value 25 if y is greater than 7, or the value 50 otherwise. This is a nice shorthand way of producing the same effect as this:

```
if( y>7 )
  x = 25;
else
  x = 50;
```

The conditional operator enables you to express some things economically. An expression for the minimum of two variables can be written very simply using the conditional operator. For example, you can write an expression that compares two salaries and obtains the greater of the two like this:

```
your_salary > my_salary ? your_salary : my_salary
```

Of course, you can use the conditional operator in a more complex expression. Earlier in Program 3.2 you calculated a quantity price for a product using an if-else statement. The price was $3.50 per item with a discount of 5 percent for quantities over ten. You can do this sort of calculation in a single step with the conditional operator:

```
total_price = unit_price*quantity*(quantity>10 ? 1.0 : 0.95);
```

Try It Out: Using the Conditional Operator

This discount business could translate into a short example. Suppose you have the unit price of the product still at $3.50, but you now offer three levels of discount: 15 percent for more than 50, 10 percent for more than 20, and the original 5 percent for more than 10. Here's how you can handle that:

```
/* Program 3.6 Multiple discount levels */
#include <stdio.h>

void main()
{
  const double unit_price = 3.50; /* Unit price in dollars    */
  const double discount1 = 0.05;  /* Discount for more than 10 */
  const double discount2 = 0.1;   /* Discount for more than 20 */
  const double discount3 = 0.15;  /* Discount for more than 50 */
  double total_price = 0.0;
  int quantity = 0;

  printf("Enter the number that you want to buy:");   /* Prompt message */
  scanf(" %d", &quantity);                            /* Read the input */

  total_price = quantity*unit_price*(1.0 -
                  (quantity>50 ? discount3 : (
                        quantity>20 ? discount2 : (
                              quantity>10 ? discount1 : 0.0))));

  printf("The price for %d is $%.2f\n", quantity, total_price);
}
```

Some typical output from the program would be as follows:

```
Enter the number that you want to buy:60
The price for 60 is $178.50
```

HOW IT WORKS

The interesting bit is the statement that calculates the total price for the quantity that's entered. The statement uses three conditional operators, so it takes a little unraveling:

```
total_price = quantity*unit_price*(1.0 -
                (quantity>50 ? discount3 : (
                      quantity>20 ? discount2 : (
                            quantity>10 ? discount1 : 0.0))));
```

(Continued)

You can understand how this produces the correct result by breaking it into pieces. The basic price is produced by the expression `quantity*unit_price`, which simply multiplies the unit price by the quantity ordered. The result of this has to be multiplied by a factor that's determined by the quantity. If the quantity is over 50, then the basic price must be multiplied by (`1.0-discount3`). This is determined by the expression something like this:

```
(1.0 - quantity>50 ? discount3 : something_else)
```

If `quantity` is greater than 50 here, the expression will amount to (`1.0-discount3`), and the right side of the assignment is complete. Otherwise, it will be (`1.0-something_else`), where `something_else` is the result of another conditional operator.

Of course, if `quantity` isn't greater than 50, it may still be greater than 20, in which case you want `something_else` to be `discount2`. This is produced by the conditional operator that appears in the `something_else` position in the statement:

```
(quantity>20 ? discount2 : something_else_again)
```

This will result in `something_else` being `discount2` if the value of `quantity` is over 20, which is precisely what you want, and `something_else_again` if it isn't. You want `something_else_again` to be `discount1` if `quantity` is over 10, and 0 if it isn't. The last conditional operator that occupies the `something_else_again` position in the statement does this:

```
(quantity>10 ? discount1 : 0.0)
```

And that's it!

Using the Conditional Operator

In spite of its odd appearance, you'll see the conditional operator crop up quite frequently in C programs. A very handy application of this operator that you'll see in examples in this book and elsewhere is to vary the contents of a message or prompt depending on the value of an expression. For example, if you want to display a message indicating the number of pets that a person has, and you want the message to change between singular and plural, then you could write this:

```
printf("You have %d pet%s.", pets, pets == 1 ? "" : "s" );
```

You use the %s specifier when you want to output a string. If pets is equal to 1, an empty string will be output in place of the %s; otherwise, s will be output. Thus, if pets has the value 1, the statement will output this message:

```
You have 1 pet.
```

However, if the variable pets is 5, then you'll get this output:

```
You have 5 pets.
```

You can use this mechanism to vary an output message depending on the value of an expression in many different ways: she instead of he, wrong instead of right, and so on. You'll see this in action later in the chapter.

Operator Precedence: Who Goes First?

With all the parentheses you've used in the examples in this chapter, now is a good time to come back to **operator precedence**. Operator precedence determines the sequence in which operators in an expression are executed. You have the logical operators &&, ==, !=, and ||, plus the comparison operators and the arithmetic operators. When you have more than one operator in an expression, how do you know which ones are used first? This order of precedence can affect the result of an expression substantially.

For example, suppose you are to process job applications, and you want to accept only applicants who are 25 or older and have graduated from Harvard or Yale. Here's the age condition you can represent by this conditional expression:

```
Age >= 25
```

Suppose that you represent graduation by the variables Yale and Harvard, which may be true or false. Now you can write the condition as follows:

```
Age >= 25 && Harvard || Yale
```

Unfortunately, this will result in howls of protest because you'll now accept Yale graduates who are under 25. In fact, this statement will accept Yale graduates of any age. But if you're from Harvard, you must be 25 or over to be accepted! Because of operator precedence, this expression is effectively

```
( Age >= 25 && Harvard ) || Yale
```

So you take anybody at all from Yale. I'm sure those wearing a Y-front sweatshirt will claim that this is as it should be, but what you really meant was this:

```
Age >= 25 && ( Harvard || Yale )
```

Because of operator precedence, you must put the parentheses in to force the order of operations to be what you want.

Table 3-2 shows the order of precedence for the operators you've seen so far.

Table 3-2. Operator Order of Precedence

Operators	Associativity
( )	Left to right
! ~ unary+ unary-	Right to left
Type casts such as (int) or (double)	Right to left
* / %	Left to right
Binary+ binary-	Left to right
<< >>	Left to right
< <= > >=	Left to right
== !=	Left to right
&	Left to right
^	Left to right
|	Left to right
&&	Left to right
||	Left to right
?: (conditional operator)	Left to right
= op= (i.e., += -= etc.)	Right to left

You haven't encountered the ++ and – – operators yet, but you will in Chapter 4. You'll see the operators ~, <<, >>, &, ^, and | later in this chapter.

The operators are shown in Table 3-2 with the highest precedence operators (i.e., those to be executed first) at the top. All the operators that appear in the same row in the table are of equal precedence. The sequence of execution for operators of equal precedence is determined by their **associativity**, which determines whether they're selected from left to right or from right to left. Naturally, parentheses come at the very top of the list of operators because they're used to override the natural priorities defined.

As you can see, all the comparison operators are below the binary arithmetic operators, and the binary logical operators are below the comparison operators. As a result, arithmetic is done first, then comparisons, and then logical combinations. Assignments come last in this list, so they're performed only once everything else has been completed. The conditional operator squeezes in just above the assignment operators.

Note that the ! operator is highest, apart from parentheses. As a result, the parentheses around logical expressions are often essential.

....

Try It Out: Using Logical Operators Without Confusion

Suppose you want a program that will take applicant interviews for a large pharmaceutical corporation. The program should offer interviews to applicants who meet certain educational specifications. An applicant who meets any of the following criteria should be accepted for an interview:

1. Graduates over 25 who studied chemistry and who didn't graduate from Yale

2. Graduates from Yale who studied chemistry

3. Graduates from Harvard who studied economics and aren't older than 28

4. Graduates from Yale who are over 25 and who didn't study chemistry

One program to implement this policy is as follows:

```
/* Program 3.7 Confused recruiting policy */
#include <stdio.h>

void main()
{
    int age = 0;          /* Age of the applicant      */
    int college = 0;      /* Code for college attended */
    int subject = 0;      /* Code for subject studied  */
    int interview = 0;    /* 1 for accept, 0 for reject */

    /* Get data on the applicant */
    printf("\nWhat college? 1 for Harvard, 2 for Yale, 3 for other: ");
    scanf("%d",&college);
    printf("\nWhat subject? 1 for Chemistry, 2 for economics, 3 for other: ");
    scanf("%d", &subject);
    printf("\nHow old is the applicant? ");
    scanf("%d",&age);

    /* Check out the applicant */
    if((age>25 && subject==1) && (college==3 || college==1))
      interview = 1;
    if(college==2 &&subject ==1)
      interview = 1;
    if(college==1 && subject==2 && !(age>28))
      interview = 1;
    if(college==2 && (subject==2 || subject==3) && age>25)
      interview = 1;

    /* Output decision for interview */
    if(interview)
```

(Continued)

```
    printf("\n\nGive 'em an interview");
  else
    printf("\n\nReject 'em");
}
```

The output from this program should be something like this:

```
What college? 1 for Harvard, 2 for Yale, 3 for other: 2
What subject? 1 for Chemistry, 2 for Economics, 3 for other: 1
How old is the applicant? 24

Give 'em an interview
```

HOW IT WORKS

The program works in a fairly straightforward way. The only slight complication is with the number of operators and if statements needed to check a candidate out:

```
if((age>25 && subject==1) && (college==3 || college==1))
  interview =1;
if(college==2 &&subject ==1)
  interview =1;
if(college==1 && subject==2 && !(age>28))
  interview = 1;
if(college==2 && (subject==2 || subject==3) && age>25)
  interview =1;
```

The final if statement tells you whether to invite the applicant for an interview or not. It uses the variable interview.

```
if(interview)
  printf("\n\nGive 'em an interview");
else
  printf("\n\nReject 'em");
```

The variable interview is initialized to 0, but if any of the criteria is met, then you assign the value 1 to it. The if expression is just the variable interview, so the expression is false when interview is 0 and true when interview has any nonzero value.

This could be a lot simpler, though. Let's look at the conditions that result in an interview. You can specify each criterion with an expression.

(Continued)

115

Criterion	Expression
1. Graduates over 25 who studied chemistry and who didn't graduate from Yale	`age>25&&college!=2`
2. Graduates from Yale who studied chemistry	`college==2 && subject==1`
3. Graduates from Harvard who studied economics and aren't older than 28	`college==1 && subject==2 && age<=28`
4. Graduates from Yale who are over 25 and who didn't study chemistry	`college==2 && age>25 subject!=1`

The variable `interview` should be set to 1 if any of these four conditions is true, so you can now combine them using the `||` operator to set the value of the variable `interview`:

```
interview = (age>25&&college!=2)||( college==2 && subject==1)||
     (college==1 && subject==2 && age<=28)||( college==2 && age>25 subject!=1);
```

Now you don't need the `if` statements to check the conditions at all. You just store the logical value, 1 or 0, which arises from combining these expressions. If fact, you could dispense with the variable `interview` altogether, by just putting the combined expression for the checks into the last `if`:

```
if((age>25&&college!=2)||( college==2 && subject==1)||
     (college==1 && subject==2 && age<=28)||( college==2 && age>25 subject!=1))
  printf("\n\nGive 'em an interview");
else
  printf("\n\nReject 'em");
```

So you end up with a much shorter program.

Multiple-Choice Questions

Multiple-choice questions come up quite often in programming. One example is selecting a different course of action depending on whether a candidate is from one or the other of six different universities. Another example is when you want to choose to execute a particular set of statements depending on which day of the week it is. You have two ways to handle multiple-choice situations in C. One is a form of the `if` statement described as the `else-if` that provides the most general way to deal with multiple choices. The other is the `switch` statement, which is restricted in the way a particular choice is selected, but where it does apply it provides a very neat and easily understood solution. Let's look at the `else-if` statement first.

Using else-if Statements for Multiple Choices

The use of the else-if statement for selecting one of a set of choices looks like this:

```
if(choice1)
  /* Statement or block for choice 1 */
else if(choice2)
  /* Statement or block for choice 2 */
else if(choice3)
  /* Statement or block for choice 2 */

/* ... and so on ...   */
else
  /* Default statement or block  */
```

Each choicen expression can be anything as long as the result is true or false. If the first if expression, choice1, is false, then the next if is executed. If choice2 is false, then the next if is executed. This continues until an expression is found to be true, in which case the statement or block of statements for that if is executed. This ends the sequence, and the statement following the sequence of else-if statements is executed next.

If all of the if conditions are false, then the statement or block following the final else will be executed. You can omit this final else, in which case the sequence will do nothing if all the if conditions are false. Here's a simple illustration of this:

```
if(salary<5000)
  printf("Your pay is very poor.");     /* pay < 5000              */
else if(salary<15000)
  printf("Your pay is not good.");      /* 5000 <= pay < 15000     */
else if(salary<50000)
  printf("Your pay is not bad.");       /* 15000 <= pay < 50000    */
else if(salary<100000)
  printf("Your pay is very good.");     /* 50000 <= pay < 100000   */
else
  printf("Your pay is exceptional.");   /* pay > 100000            */
```

Note that you don't need to test for lower limits in the if conditions after the first. This is because if you reach a particular if, the previous test must have been false.

Because any logical expressions can be used as the if conditions, this statement is very flexible and allows you to express a selection from virtually any set of choices. The switch statement isn't as flexible, but it's simpler to use in many cases. Let's take a look at the switch statement.

The switch Statement

The switch statement enables you to choose one course of action from a set of possible actions, based on the result of an integer expression. Let's start with a simple illustration of how it works.

Imagine that you're running a raffle or a sweepstakes. Suppose ticket number 35 wins first prize, number 122 wins second prize, and number 78 wins third prize. You could use the switch statement to check for a winning ticket number as follows:

```
switch (ticket_number)
{
    case 35:
      printf("Congratulations! You win first prize!");
      break;
    case 122:
      printf("You are in luck - second prize.");
      break;
    case 78:
      printf("You are in luck - third prize.");
      break;
    default:
      printf("Too bad, you lose.");
}
```

The value of the expression in parentheses following the keyword switch, which is ticket_number in this case, determines which of the statements between the braces will be executed. If the value of ticket_number matches the value specified after one of the case keywords, then the following statements will be executed. If ticket_number has the value 122, for example, this message will be displayed:

```
You are in luck - second prize.
```

The effect of the break statement following the printf() is to skip over the other statements within that block and continue with whatever statement follows the closing brace. If you were to omit the break statement for a particular case, when the statements for that case are executed, execution would continue with the statements for the next case. If ticket_number has a value that doesn't correspond to any of the case values, the statements that follow the default keyword are executed, so you simply get the default message. Both default and break are keywords in C.

The general way of describing the switch statement is as follows:

```
switch (integer_expression)
{
    case constant_expression_1:
      statements_1;
      break;
      ....
    case constant_expression_n:
      statements_n;
      break;
    default:
      statements;
}
```

The test is based on the value of integer_expression. If that value corresponds to one of the case values defined by the associated constant_expression_n values, then the statements following that case value are executed. If the value of integer_expression differs from every one of the case values, then the statements following default are executed. Because you can't reasonably expect to select more than one case, all the case values must be different. If they aren't, you'll get an error message when you try to compile the program. The case values must all be constant expressions, which are expressions that can be evaluated at compile time. This means that a case value can't be dependent on a value that's determined when your program executes. Of course, the test expression integer_expression can be anything at all, as long as it evaluates to an integer.

You can leave out the default keyword and its associated statements. If none of the case values match, then nothing happens. Notice, however, that all of the case values for the associated constant_expression must be different. The break statement jumps to the statement after the closing brace.

Notice the punctuation and formatting. There's no semicolon at the end of the first switch expression. The body of the statement is enclosed within braces. The constant_expression value for a case is followed by a colon, and each subsequent statement ends with a semicolon, as usual.

You can associate several case values with one group of statements. You can also use an expression that results in a value of type char as the control expression for a switch. Suppose you read a character from the keyboard into a variable, ch, of type char. You can test this character in a switch like this:

```
switch (tolower(ch))
{
  case 'a': case 'e': case 'i': case 'o': case 'u':
    printf("The character is a vowel.");
    break;
  case 'b': case 'c': case 'd': case 'f': case 'g': case 'h': case 'j': case 'k':
  case 'l': case 'm': case 'n': case 'p': case 'q': case 'r': case 's': case 't':
  case 'v': case 'w': case 'x': case 'y': case 'z':
    printf("The character is a consonant.");
    break;
  default:
    printf("The character is not a letter.");
    break;
}
```

Because you use the function tolower() that is declared in the ctype.h header file to convert the value of ch to lowercase, you need test only for lowercase letters. In the case in which ch contains the character code for a vowel, you output a message to that effect because for the five case values corresponding to vowels you execute the same printf() statement. Similarly, you output a suitable message when ch contains a consonant. If ch contains a code that's neither a consonant nor a vowel, the default case is executed.

Note the break statement after the default case. This isn't necessary, but it does have a purpose. By always putting a break statement at the end of the last case, you ensure that the switch still works correctly if you later add a new case at the end.

You could simplify the switch by making use of another function that's declared in the ctype.h header. The isalpha() function will return a nonzero integer (thus true) if the character that's passed as the argument is an alphabetic character, and it will return 0 (false) if the character isn't an alphabetic character. You could therefore produce the same result as the previous switch with the following code:

```c
if(!isalpha(ch))
    printf("The character is not a letter.");
else
  switch (tolower(ch))
  {
    case 'a': case 'e': case 'i': case 'o': case 'u':
      printf("The character is a vowel.");
    break;
  default:
    printf("The character is a consonant.");
    break;
  }
```

The if statement tests for ch not being a letter, and if this is so, it outputs a message. If ch is a letter, the switch statement will sort out whether it is a vowel or a consonant. The five vowel case values produce one output, and the default case produces the other. Because you know that ch contains a letter when the switch statement executes, if ch isn't a vowel, it must be a consonant.

As well as the tolower(), toupper(), and isalpha() functions that I've mentioned, ctype.h also declares several other useful functions for testing a character, as shown in Table 3-3.

Table 3-3. Functions for Testing Characters

Function	Tests For
islower()	Lowercase letter
isupper()	Uppercase letter
isalnum()	Uppercase or lowercase letter
iscntrl()	Control character
isprint()	Any printing character including space
isgraph()	Any printing character except space
isdigit()	Decimal digit ('0' to '9')
isxdigit()	Hexadecimal digit ('0' to '9', 'A' to 'F', 'a' to 'f')
isspace()	Whitespace character (space, '\n', '\t', '\v', '\r', '\f')

In each case, the function returns a nonzero integer value (which is interpreted as true) if it finds what it's testing for and 0 (false) otherwise.

Let's look at the switch statement in action with an example.

....

Try It Out: Picking a Lucky Number

This example assumes that you're operating a lottery in which there are three winning numbers. Participants are required to guess a winning number, and the switch statement is designed to end the suspense and tell them about any valuable prizes they may have won:

```c
/* Example 3.8 Lucky Lotteries    */
#include <stdio.h>

void main()
{
   int choice = 0;                      /* The number chosen            */

   /* Get the choice input */
   printf("\nPick a number between 1 and 10 and you may win a prize! ");
   scanf("%d",&choice);

   /* Check for an invalid selection */
   if((choice>10) || (choice <1))
     choice = 11;                       /* Selects invalid choice message */

   switch(choice)
   {
     case 7:
       printf("\nCongratulations!");
       printf("\nYou win the collected works of Amos Gruntfuttock.");
       break;                      /* Jumps to the end of the block   */

     case 2:
       printf("\nYou win the folding thermometer-pen-watch-umbrella.");
       break;                      /* Jumps to the end of the block   */

     case 8:
       printf("\nYou win the lifetime supply of aspirin tablets.");
       break;                      /* Jumps to the end of the block   */

     case 11:
       printf("\nTry between 1 and 10. You wasted your guess.");
                    /* No break - so continue with the next statement */

     default:
       printf("\nSorry, you lose.\n");
       break;                   /* Defensive break - in case of new cases */
   }
}
```

(Continued)

Typical output from this program will be

```
Pick a number between 1 and 10 and you may win a prize! 3
Sorry, you lose.
```

or

```
Pick a number between 1 and 10 and you may win a prize! 7
Congratulations!
You win the collected works of Amos Gruntfuttock.
```

or, if you enter an invalid number

```
Pick a number between 1 and 10 and you may win a prize! 92
Try between 1 and 10. You wasted your guess.
Sorry, you lose.
```

HOW IT WORKS

You do the usual sort of thing to start with. You declare an integer variable
choice. Then you ask the user to enter a number between 1 and 10 and store the
value the user types in choice:

```
int choice = 0;                          /* The number chosen           */

/* Get the choice input */
printf("\nPick a number between 1 and 10 and you may win a prize! ");
scanf("%d",&choice);
```

Before you do anything else, you check that the user has really entered a number
between 1 and 10:

```
/* Check for an invalid selection */
if((choice>10) || (choice <1))
   choice = 11;                          /* Selects invalid choice message */
```

If the value is anything else, you automatically change it to 11. You don't have to
do this, but to ensure the user is advised of his or her mistake, you set the variable choice to 11, which produces the error message generated by the printf()
for that case value.

Next, you have the switch statement, which will select from the cases between
the braces that follow depending on the value of choice:

(Continued)

```
switch(choice)
{
  ...
}
```

If choice has the value 7, the case corresponding to that value will be executed:

```
case 7:
  printf("\nCongratulations!");
  printf("\nYou win the collected works of Amos Gruntfuttock.");
  break;                       /* Jumps to the end of the block  */
```

The two printf() calls are executed, and the break will jump to the statement following the closing brace for the block (which ends the program, in this case, because there isn't one).

The same goes for the next two cases:

```
case 2:
  printf("\nYou win the folding thermometer-pen-watch-umbrella.");
      break;                       /* Jumps to the end of the block  */

case 8:
  printf("\nYou win the lifetime supply of aspirin tablets.");
  break;                       /* Jumps to the end of the block  */
```

These correspond to values for the variable choice of 2 or 8.

The next case is a little different:

```
case 11:
  printf("\nTry between 1 and 10, you wasted your guess.");
                  /* No break - so continue with the next statement */
```

There's no break statement, so execution continues with the printf() for the default case after displaying the message. The upshot of this is that you get both lines of output if choice has been set to 11. This is entirely appropriate in this case, but usually you'll want to put a break statement at the end of each case. Remove the break statements from the program and try entering 7 to see why. You'll get all the output messages following any particular case.

The default case is as follows:

```
default:
  printf("\nSorry, you lose.\n");
  break;                     /* Defensive break - in case of new cases */
```

(Continued)

This will be selected if the value of choice doesn't correspond to any of the other case values. You also have a break statement here. Although it isn't strictly necessary, many programmers always put a break statement after the default case statements or whichever is the last case in the switch. This provides for the possibility of adding further case statements to the switch. The case statements can be in any order in a switch, and default doesn't have to be the last.

Try It Out: Yes or No

Let's see the switch statement in action controlled by a variable of type char where the value is entered by the user. You'll prompt the user to enter the value **y** or **Y** for one action and **n** or **N** for another. On its own this program may be fairly useless, but you've probably encountered many situations in which a program has asked just this question and then performed some action as a result (saving a file, for example).

```c
/* Program 3.9 Testing cases */
#include <stdio.h>

void main()
{
    char answer = 0;                    /* Stores an input character */

    printf("Enter Y or N: ");
    scanf(" %c", &answer);

    switch (answer)
    {
      case 'y': case 'Y':
        printf("\nYou responded in the affirmative.");
        break;

      case 'n': case 'N':
        printf("\nYou responded in the negative.");
        break;

      default:
        printf("\nYou did not respond correctly...");
        break;
    }
}
```

Typical output from this would be

(Continued)

```
Enter Y or N: y
You responded in the affirmative.
```

HOW IT WORKS

When you declare the variable answer as type char, you also take the opportunity to initialize it to 0. You then ask the user to type something in and store that value as usual:

```
char answer = 0;                    /* Stores an input character */

printf("Enter Y or N: ");
scanf(" %c", &answer);
```

The switch statement uses the character stored in letter to select a case:

```
switch ( answer )
{
  ...
}
```

The first case in the switch provides for the possibility of the user entering an uppercase or a lowercase letter Y:

```
case 'y': case 'Y':
  printf("\nYou responded in the affirmative.");
  break;
```

Both values 'y' and 'Y' will result in the same printf() being executed. In general, you can put as many cases together like this as you want. Notice the punctuation for this. The two cases just follow one another and each has a terminating colon after the case value.

The negative input is handled in a similar way:

```
case 'n': case 'N':
  printf("\nYou responded in the negative.");
  break;
```

If the character entered doesn't correspond with any of the case values, the default case is selected:

```
default:
  printf("\nYou did not respond correctly...");
  break;
```

(Continued)

Note the break statement after the printf() statements for the default case, as well as the legal case values. As before, this causes execution to break off at that point and continue after the end of the switch statement. Again, without it you'd get the statements for succeeding cases executed and, unless there's a break statement preceding the valid cases, you'd get the following statement (or statements), including the default statement, executed as well.

Of course, you could also use the toupper() or tolower() function to simplify the cases in the switch. By using one or the other you can nearly halve the number of cases:

```
switch (toupper(answer))
{
  case 'Y':
    printf("\nYou responded in the affirmative.");
    break;
  case 'N':
    printf("\nYou responded in the negative.");
    break;
  default:
    printf("\nYou did not respond correctly...");
    break;
}
```

Remember, you need an #include directive for ctype.h if you want to use the toupper() function.

The goto Statement

The if statement provides you with the ability to choose one or the other of two blocks of statements, depending on a test. This is a powerful tool that enables you to alter the naturally sequential nature of a program. You no longer have to go from A to B to C to D. You can go to A and then decide whether to skip B and C and go straight to D.

The goto statement, on the other hand, is a blunt instrument. It directs the flow of statements to change *unconditionally*—do not pass Go, do not collect $200, go directly to jail. When your program hits a goto, it does just that. It goes to the place you send it, without checking any values or asking the user whether that was really what he or she wanted.

I'm only going to mention the goto statement very briefly, because it isn't as great as it might at first seem. The problem with the goto statement is that it seems too easy. This might sound perverse, but the important word is *seems*. It feels so simple that you can be tempted into using it all over the place, where it would be better to use a different statement. This can result in heavily tangled code.

When you use the goto statement, the position in the code to be moved to is defined by a **statement label** at that point. A statement label is defined in exactly the same way as a variable name, which is a sequence of letters and digits, the first of which must be a letter. The statement label is followed by a colon (:) to separate it from the statement it labels. If you think this sounds like a case label in a switch, you would be right. Case labels are statement labels.

Like other statements, the goto statement ends with a semicolon:

```
goto there;
```

The destination statement must have the same label as appears in the goto statement, which is there in this case. As I said, the label is written preceding the statement it applies to, with a colon separating the label from the rest of the statement, for example:

```
there: x=10;                          /* A labeled statement */
```

The goto statement can be used in conjunction with an if statement, for example:

```
   ....
if (dice == 6)
   goto Waldorf;
else
   goto Jail;                         /* Go to the statement labeled Jail  */

Waldorf:
   comfort = high;
   ....
Jail:                    /* The label itself. Program control is sent here */
   comfort = low;
   ....
```

You roll the dice. If you get 6, then you go to the Waldorf; otherwise, you go to Jail. This might seem perfectly fine but, at the very least, it's confusing. To understand the sequence of execution you need to hunt for the destination labels. Imagine your code was littered with gotos. It would be very difficult to follow and perhaps even more difficult to fix when things go wrong. So it's best to avoid the goto statement as much as possible. In theory it's always possible to avoid using the goto statement, but there are one or two instances in which it's a useful option. You'll look into loops in Chapter 4, but for now know that exiting from the innermost loop of a deeply nested set of loops can be much simpler with a goto statement than with other mechanisms.

Bitwise Operators

Before you come to the big example for this chapter, you'll examine a group of operators that look a bit like the logical operators you saw earlier but in fact are quite different. These are called the **bitwise operators** because they operate on the bits in integer values. The six bitwise operators are shown in Table 3-4.

Table 3-4. Bitwise Operators

&	Bitwise AND operator
|	Bitwise OR operator
^	Bitwise Exclusive OR (EOR) operator
~	Bitwise NOT operator, also called the 1's complement operator
>>	Shift right operator
<<	Shift left operator

All of these operate only on integer types. The ~ operator is a unary operator—it applies to one operand—and the others are binary operators.

The bitwise AND operator, &, combines the corresponding bits of its operands in such a way that if both bits are 1, the resulting bit is 1; otherwise, the resulting bit is 0. Suppose you declare the following variables:

```
int x = 13;
int y = 6;
int z = x&y;                  /* AND the bits of x and y */
```

After the third statement, z will have the value 4 (binary 100). This is because the corresponding bits in x and y are combined as follows:

x	0	0	0	0	1	1	0	1
y	0	0	0	0	0	1	1	0
x&y	0	0	0	0	0	1	0	0

Obviously the variables would have more bits than I've shown here, but they would all be 0. With the values shown, only in the case of the third bit from the right in the two variables, x and y, are both bits 1, so this is the only case in which the result is 1.

CAUTION *It's important not to get the bitwise operators and the logical operators muddled. The expression* x&y *will produce quite different results from* x&&y *in general. Try it out and see.*

The bitwise OR operator, |, results in 1 if either or both of the corresponding bits are 1; otherwise, the result is 0. Let's look at a specific example. If you combine the same values using the | operator in a statement such as this:

```
int z = x|y;                  /* OR the bits of x and y */
```

the result would be as follows:

x	0	0	0	0	1	1	0	1
y	0	0	0	0	0	1	1	0
x|y	0	0	0	0	1	1	1	1

The value stored in z would therefore be 15 (binary 1111).

The bitwise EOR operator, ^, produces a 1 if both bits are different and 0 if they're the same. Again, using the same initial values, the statement

```
int z = x^y;               /*Exclusive OR the bits of x and y */
```

would result in z containing the value 11 (binary 1011), because the bits combine as follows:

x	0	0	0	0	1	1	0	1
y	0	0	0	0	0	1	1	0
x^y	0	0	0	0	1	0	1	1

The unary operator, ~, flips the bits of its operand, so 1 becomes 0 and 0 becomes 1. If you apply this operator to x with the value 13 as before, and you write

```
int z = ~x;                /* Store 1's complement of x */
```

then z will have the value –14. The bits are set as follows:

x	0	0	0	0	1	1	0	1
~x	1	1	1	1	0	0	1	0

The value 11110010 is –14 in 2's complement representation of negative integers. If you're not familiar with the 2's complement form, and you want to find out about it, I've described it in Appendix A.

The shift operators shift the bits in the left operand by the number of positions specified by the right operand. You could specify a shift-left operation with the following statements:

```
int value = 12;
int shiftcount = 3;            /* Number of positions to be shifted */
int result = value << shiftcount;   /* Shift left shiftcount positions   */
```

The variable result will contain the value 96. The binary number in value is 00001100. The bits are shifted to the left three positions, and 0s are introduced on the right, so the value of value << shiftcount, as a binary number, will be 01100000.

The right shift operator moves the bits to the right, but it's a little more complicated than left shift. For unsigned values, the bits that are introduced on the left (in the vacated positions as the bits are shifted right) are filled with 0s. Let's see how this works in practice. Suppose you declare a variable:

```
unsigned int value = 65372U;
```

As a binary value in a 2-byte variable, this is

1111	1111	0101	1100

Suppose you now execute the following statement:

```
unsigned int result = value >> 2;      /* Shift right two bits */
```

The bits in `value` will be shifted two places to the right, introducing 0s at the left end, and the resultant value will be stored in `result`. In binary this will be

0011	1111	1101	0111

which is the decimal value 16343.

For signed values that are negative, where the leftmost bit will be 1, the result depends on your system. In most cases, the sign bit is propagated, so the bits introduced on the right are 1 bits, but on some systems 0s are introduced in this case too. Let's see how this affects the result.

Suppose you define a variable with this statement:

```
int new_value = -164;
```

This happens to be the same bit pattern as the unsigned value that you used earlier; remember that this is the 2's complement representation of the value:

1111	1111	0101	1100

Suppose you now execute this statement:

```
int new_result = new_value >> 2;      /* Shift right two bits */
```

This will shift the value in `new_value` two bit positions to the right and the result will be stored in `new_result`. If, as is usually the case, the sign bit is propagated, 1s will be inserted on the left as the bits are shifted to the right, so `new_result` will end up as

1111	1111	1101	0111

This is the decimal value –41, which is what you might expect because it amounts to –164/4. If the sign bit isn't propagated, however, as can occur on some computers, the value in `new_result` will be

0011	1111	1101	0111

So shifting right two bits in this case has changed the value –164 to +16343—perhaps a rather unexpected result.

The op= use of Bitwise Operators

You can use all of the binary bitwise operators in the op= form of assignment. The exception is the operator ~, which is a unary operator. As you saw in the previous chapter, a statement of the form

```
lhs op= rhs;
```

is equivalent to the statement

```
lhs = lhs op (rhs);
```

This means that if you write

```
value <<= 4;
```

the effect is to shift the contents of the integer variable, `value`, left four bit positions. It's exactly the same as

```
value = value << 4;
```

You can do the same kind of thing with the other binary operators. For example, you could write the statement

```
value &= 0xFF;
```

where `value` is an integer variable. This is equivalent to

```
value = value & 0xFF;
```

The effect of this is to keep the rightmost eight bits unchanged and to set all the others to 0.

Using Bitwise Operators

The bitwise operators look interesting in an academic kind of way, but what use are they? They don't come up in everyday programs, but in some areas they become very useful. One major use of the bitwise AND, &, and the bitwise OR, |, is in operations to test and set individual bits in an integer variable. With this capability you can use individual bits to store data that involves one of two choices. For example, you could use a single integer variable to store several characteristics of a person. You could store whether the person is male or female with one bit, and you could use three other bits to specify whether the person can speak French, German, or Italian. You might use another bit to record whether the person's salary is $50,000 or more. So in just four bits you have a substantial set of data recorded. Let's see how this would work out.

The fact that you get only a 1 bit when both of the bits being combined are 1 means that you can use the & operator to select out a part of an integer variable or even just a single bit. You first define a value, usually called a **mask**, that you use to select the bit or bits that you want. It will contain a bit value of 1 for the bit positions you want to keep and a bit value of 0 for the bit positions you want to discard. You can then AND this mask with the value that you want to select from. Let's look at an example. You can define masks with the following statements:

```
unsigned int male      = 0x1;   /* Mask selecting first (rightmost) bit */
unsigned int french    = 0x2;   /* Mask selecting second bit            */
unsigned int german    = 0x4;   /* Mask selecting third bit             */
unsigned int italian   = 0x8;   /* Mask selecting fourth bit            */
unsigned int payBracket = 0x10; /* Mask selecting fifth bit             */
```

In each case, a 1 bit will indicate that the particular condition is true. These masks in binary each pick out an individual bit, so you could have an unsigned int variable, personal_data, which would store five items of information about a person. If the first bit is 1, the person is male, and if the first bit is 0, the person is female. If the second bit is 1, then the person speaks French, and if it is 0, the person doesn't speak French, and so on for all five bits at the right end of the data value.

You could therefore test the variable, personal_data, for a German speaker with the statement

```
if(personal_data & german)
  /* Do something because they speak German */
```

The expression personalData & german will be nonzero—that is, true—if the bit corresponding to the mask, german, is 1; otherwise, it will be 0.

Of course, there's nothing to prevent you from combining several expressions involving using masks to select individual bits with the logical operators. You could test whether someone was a female who spoke French or Italian with the following statement:

```
if(!(personal_data & male) && ((personal_data & french) ||
                                        (personal_data & italian)))
   /* We have a French or Italian speaking female */
```

As you can see, it's easy enough to test individual bits or combinations of bits. The only other thing you need to understand is how to set individual bits. The OR operator swings into action here.

You can use the OR operator set individual bits in a variable using the same mask as you use to test the bits. If you want to set the variable `personal_data` to record a person as speaking French, you can do it with this statement:

```
personal_data |= french;              /* Set second bit to 1 */
```

Just to remind you, the preceding statement is exactly the same as the following statement:

```
personal_data = personal_data|french;  /* Set second bit to 1 */
```

The second bit from the right in `personal_data` will be set to 1, and all the other bits will remain as they were.

Because of the way the | operator works, you can set multiple bits in a single statement:

```
personal_data |= french|german|male;
```

This sets the bits to record a French- and German-speaking male. If the variable `personalData` previously recorded that the person spoke Italian, that bit would still be set, so the OR operator is additive. If a bit was already set, it will stay set.

What about resetting a bit? Suppose you wanted to change the male bit to female. This amounts to resetting a 1 bit to 0, and it requires the use of the ! operator with the bitwise AND:

```
personal_data &= !male;              /* Reset male to female */
```

This works because `!male` will have a 0 bit set for the bit that indicates male, and all the other bits as 1. Thus, the bit corresponding to male will be set to 0: 0 ANDed with anything is 0, and all the other bits will be as they were. If another bit is 1, then 1&1 will still be 1. If another bit is 0, then 0&1 will still be 0.

I've used the example of using bits to record specific items of personal data. If you want to program a PC using the Windows application programming interface (API), you'll often use individual bits to record the status of various window parameters, so the bitwise operators can be very useful in this context.

··

Try It Out: Using Bitwise Operators

Let's exercise some of the bitwise operators in a slightly different example, but using the same principles discussed previously. This example illustrates how you can use a mask to select multiple bits from a variable. You'll write a program that sets a value in a variable and then uses the bitwise operators to reverse the sequence of hexadecimal digits. Here's the code:

```c
/* Program 3.10 Exercising bitwise operators */
#include <stdio.h>

void main()
{
   unsigned int original = 0xABC;
   unsigned int result = 0;
   unsigned int mask = 0xF;              /* Rightmost four bits              */

   printf("\n original = %X", original);

   /* Insert first digit in result */
   result |= original&mask;     /* Put right 4 bits from original in result */

   /* Get second digit */
   original >>= 4;              /* Shift original right four positions      */
   result <<= 4;               /* Make room for next digit                 */
   result |= original&mask;    /* Put right 4 bits from original in result */

   /* Get third digit */
   original >>= 4;              /* Shift original right four positions      */
   result <<= 4;               /* Make room for next digit                 */
   result |= original&mask;    /* Put right 4 bits from original in result */
   printf("\t result = %X\n", result);
}
```

This will produce the following output:

```
 original = ABC   result = CBA
```

HOW IT WORKS

This program uses the idea of masking that I just discussed. The rightmost hexadecimal digit in `original` is obtained by ANDing the value with `mask` in the expression `original&mask`. This sets all the other hexadecimal digits to 0. Because the value of `mask` as a binary number is

(Continued)

0000	0000	0000	1111

you can see that only the first four bits on the right are kept. Any of these four bits that is 1 in `original` will stay as 1 in the result, and any that are 0 will stay as 0. All the other bits will be 0 because 0 ANDed with anything is 0.

Once you've selected the rightmost four bits, you then store the result with the statement

```
result |= original&mask;    /* Put right 4 bits from original in result */
```

The content of `result` is ORed with the hexadecimal digit that's produced by the expression on the right side.

To get at the second digit in `original`, you need to move it to where the first digit was. You do this by shifting `original` right by four bit positions:

```
original >>= 4;             /* Shift original right four positions     */
```

The first digit is shifted out and is lost.

To make room for the next digit from `original`, you shift the contents of `result` left by four bit positions with this statement:

```
result <<= 4;               /* Make room for next digit                */
```

Now you want to insert the second digit from `original`, which is now in the first digit position, into `result`. You do this with the following statement:

```
result |= original&mask;    /* Put right 4 bits from original in result */
```

To get the third digit you just repeat the process. Clearly, you could repeat this for as many digits as you want.

Designing a Program

You've almost reached the end of Chapter 3. Now you'll apply what you've learned so far to build a useful program.

The Problem

The problem is to write a simple calculator that can add, subtract, multiply, divide, and find the remainder when one number is divided by another. The program must allow the calculation that is to be performed to be keyed in a natural way, such as 5.6 * 27 or 3 + 6.

The Analysis

All the math involved is simple, but the processing of the input adds a little complexity. You need to make checks on the input to make sure that the user hasn't asked the computer to do something impossible. You must allow the user to input a calculation in one attempt, for example:

```
34.87 + 5
```

or

```
9 * 6.5
```

The steps involved in writing this program are as follows:

1. Get the user's input for the calculation that the user wants the computer to perform.

2. Check that input to make sure that it's understandable.

3. Perform the calculation.

4. Display the result.

The Solution

This section outlines the steps you'll take to solve the problem.

Step 1

Getting the user input is quite easy. You'll be using printf() and scanf(), so you need the stdio.h header file. The only new thing I'll introduce is in the way in which you'll get the input. As I said earlier, rather than asking the user for each number individually and then asking for the operation to be performed, you'll get the user to type it in more naturally. You can do this because of the way scanf() works, but I'll discuss the details of that after you've seen the first part of the program. Let's kick off the program with the code to read the input:

```
/* Example 3.11 A calculator */
#include <stdio.h>

void main()
{
   double number1 = 0.0;          /* First operand value a decimal number  */
   double number2 = 0.0;          /* Second operand value a decimal number */
   char operation = 0;            /* Operation - must be +, -, *, /, or %  */

   printf("\nEnter the calculation\n");
   scanf("%lf %c %lf", &number1, &operation, &number2);

   /* Plus the rest of the code for the program */
}
```

The scanf() function is fairly clever when it comes to reading data. You don't actu-ally need to enter each input data item on a separate line. All that's required is one or more whitespace characters between each item of input. (You create a whitespace character by pressing the spacebar, the Tab key, or the Enter key.)

Step 2

Next, you must check to make sure that the input is correct. The most obvious check to perform is that the operation to be performed is valid. You've already decided that the valid operations are +, -, /, *, and %, so you need to check that the operation is one of these.

You also need to check the second number to see if it's 0 if the operation is either / or %. If the right operand is 0, then these operations are invalid. You could do all these checks using if statements, but a switch statement provides a far better way of doing this:

```
/* Example 3.11 A calculator */
#include <stdio.h>

void main()
{
   double number1 = 0.0;          /* First operand value a decimal number  */
   double number2 = 0.0;          /* Second operand value a decimal number */
   char operation = 0;            /* Operation - must be +, -, *, /, or %  */

   printf("\nEnter the calculation\n");
   scanf("%lf %c %lf", &number1, &operation, &number2);

   /* Code to check the input goes here */
   switch(operation)
   {
     case '+':                    /* No checks necessary for add        */
       break;
```

```
       case '-':                        /* No checks necessary for subtract */
         break;

       case '*':                        /* No checks necessary for multiply */
         break;

       case '/':
         if(number2 == 0)          /* Check second operand for zero     */
           printf("\n\n\aDivision by zero error!\n");
           break;

       case '%':                        /* Check second operand for zero     */
         if((long)number2 == 0)
           printf("\n\n\aDivision by zero error!\n");
           break;

      default:                          /* Operation is invalid if we get to here */
        printf("\n\n\aIllegal operation!\n");
    }

   /* Plus the rest of the code for the program */
}
```

Because you're casting the second operand to an integer when the operator is %, it isn't sufficient to just check the second operand against 0—you must check that number2 doesn't have a value that will result in 0 when it's cast to type long.

Steps 3 and 4

So now that you've checked the input, you can calculate the result. You have a choice here. You could calculate each result in the switch and store it to be output after the switch, or you could simply output the result for each case. Let's go for the latter approach. The code you need to add is as follows:

```
/* Example 3.11 A calculator */
#include <stdio.h>

void main()
{
   double number1 = 0.0;          /* First operand value a decimal number  */
   double number2 = 0.0;          /* Second operand value a decimal number */
   char operation = 0;            /* Operation - must be +, -, *, /, or %  */

   printf("\nEnter the calculation\n");
   scanf("%lf %c %lf", &number1, &operation, &number2);

   /* Code to check the input goes here */
   switch(operation)
   {
```

```
  case '+':                    /* No checks necessary for add      */
    printf("= %lf\n", number1 + number2);
    break;

  case '-':                    /* No checks necessary for subtract */
    printf("= %lf\n", number1 - number2);
    break;

  case '*':                    /* No checks necessary for multiply */
    printf("= %lf\n", number1 * number2);
    break;

  case '/':
    if(number2 == 0)           /* Check second operand for zero    */
      printf("\n\n\aDivision by zero error!\n");
    else
      printf("= %lf\n", number1 / number2);
    break;

  case '%':                    /* Check second operand for zero    */
    if((long)number2 == 0)
      printf("\n\n\aDivision by zero error!\n");
    else
      printf("= %ld\n", (long)number1 % (long)number2);
    break;

  default:                     /* Operation is invalid if we get to here */
    printf("\n\n\aIllegal operation!\n");
  }
}
```

Notice how you cast the two numbers from double to long when you calculate the modulus. This is because the % operator works only with integers in C. All that's left is to try it out! Don't forget the spaces between the operands and the operator. You'll get an error message if you don't include these spaces. Here's some typical output:

```
Enter the calculation
56 * 75
= 4200.000000
```

Here's another output sample:

```
Enter the calculation
7 % 0

Division by zero error!
```

Summary

This chapter ended with quite a complicated example. In the first two chapters, you really just looked at the groundwork for C programs. You could do some reasonably useful things, but you couldn't control the sequence of operations in a program once it had started. In this chapter, you've started to feel the power of the language and how you can use data entered by the user or results calculated during execution to determine what happens next.

You've learned how to compare variables and then use if, if-else, else-if, and switch statements to affect the outcome. You also know how to use logical operators to combine comparisons between your variables. You should now understand a lot more about making decisions and taking different paths through your program code.

In the next chapter, you'll learn how to write even more powerful programs: programs that can repeat a set of statements until some condition is met. By the end of Chapter 4, you'll think your calculator is small fry.

Exercises

The following exercises enable you to try out what you've learned in this chapter. If you get stuck, look back over the chapter for help. If you're still stuck, you can download the solutions from the Downloads area of the Apress website (http://www.apress.com), but that really should be a last resort.

Exercise 3-1. Write a program that will first allow a user to choose one of two options:

1. Convert a temperature from degrees Celsius to degrees Fahrenheit.

2. Convert a temperature from degrees Fahrenheit to degrees Celsius.

The program should then prompt for the temperature value to be entered, and output the new value that results from the conversion. To convert from Celsius to Fahrenheit you can multiply the value by 1.8 and then add 32. To convert from Fahrenheit to Celsius, you can subtract 32 from the value, then multiply by 5, and divide the result by 9.

Exercise 3-2. Write a program that prompts the user to enter the date as three integer values for the month, the day in the month, and the year. The program should then output the date in the form 31st December 2003 when the user enters **12 31 2003**, for example.

You'll need to work out when "th," "nd," "st," and "rd" need to be appended to the day value. Don't forget: 1st, 2nd, 3rd, 4th; but 11th, 12th, 13th, 14th; and 21st, 22nd, 23rd, and 24th.

Exercise 3-3. Write a program that will calculate the price for a quantity entered from the keyboard, given that the unit price is $5, and there is a discount of 10 percent for quantities over 30 and 15 percent discount for quantities over 50.

Exercise 3-4. Modify the last example in the chapter that implemented a calculator so that the user is given the option to enter **y** or **Y** to carry out another calculation, and **n** or **N** to end the program. (Note: You'll have to use a goto statement for this at this time, but you'll learn a better way of doing this in the next chapter.)

CHAPTER 4

Loops

IN THE LAST CHAPTER YOU LEARNED how to compare items and base your decisions on the result. You were able to choose how the computer reacted based on the input to a program. In this chapter you'll learn how you can repeat a block of statements until some condition is met. This is called a **loop**.

The number of times that a loop is repeated can be controlled simply by a count—repeating the statement block a given number of times—or it can be more complex—repeating a block until the user enters **n** or **N**, for instance. The latter would enable you to program the calculator example in the previous chapter to repeat as many times as required, without having to use a goto statement.

In this chapter you'll learn

- How you can repeat a statement or a block of statements as many times as you want

- How you can repeat a statement or a block of statements until a particular condition is fulfilled

- How you use the for, while, and do-while loops

- What the increment and decrement operators do, and how you can use them

- How you can write a program that plays a Simple Simon game

Loops

As I said, the programming mechanism that executes a series of statements repeatedly a given number of times, or until a particular condition is fulfilled, is called a **loop**. The loop is a fundamental programming tool, along with the ability to compare items. Once you can compare data values and repeat a block of statements, you can combine these capabilities to control how many times the block of statements is executed. For example, you can keep performing a particular action until two items that you're comparing are the same. Once they *are* the same, you can go on to perform a different action.

In the lottery example, you could give the user exactly three guesses—in other words, let him continue to guess until a variable called number_of_guesses, for instance, equals 3. Alternatively, you could set up a specific number (0, for example) so that when the user types in the number, the program ends. The user will then be able to continue entering guesses as long as he wants. When he's had enough, he just needs to type in **0**.

Figure 4-1 illustrates the way a typical loop works.

Figure 4-1. The logic of a typical loop

More often than not, you'll find that you want to apply the same calculation to different sets of data values. Without loops, you would need to write out the instructions to be performed as many times as there were sets of data values to be processed, which wouldn't be very satisfactory. A loop allows you to use the same program code for any number of sets of data to be entered.

Before I discuss the various types of loops that you have available in C, I'll first introduce two new arithmetic operators that you'll encounter frequently in C programs: the **increment operator** and the **decrement operator**. These operators are often used with loops, which is why I'll discuss them here. I'll start with the briefest of introductions to the increment and decrement operators and then go straight into an example of how you can use them in the context of a loop. Once you're comfortable with how loops work, you'll return to the increment and decrement operators to investigate some of their idiosyncrasies. By then, you'll be a confident exponent of loops, and you'll be ready to use them in your own programs.

Introducing the Increment and Decrement Operators

The **increment operator** (++) and the **decrement operator** (--) will increment or decrement the value stored in the integer variable that they apply to by 1. Suppose you've defined an integer variable, number, that currently has the value 6. You can increment it by 1 with the following statement:

```
++number;                       /* Increase the value by 1 */
```

After executing this statement, number will contain the value 7. Similarly, you could decrease the value of number by 1 with the following statement:

```
--number;                       /* Decrease the value by 1 */
```

These operators are different from the other arithmetic operators you've encountered. When you use any of the other arithmetic operators, you create an expression that will result in a value, which may be stored in a variable or used as part of a more complex expression. They don't directly modify the value stored in a variable. When you write the expression -number, for instance, the result of evaluating this expression is -6 if number has the value +6, but the value stored in number is unchanged. On the other hand, the expression --number *does* modify the value in number. This expression will decrement the value in number by 1, so number will end up as 5 if it was originally 6.

There's much more you'll need to know about the increment and decrement operators, but you can defer that until later. Right now, let's get back to the main discussion and take a look at the simplest form of loop, the for loop. There are other types of loops as you'll see later, but you'll give the for loop a larger slice of time because once you understand this one, the others will be easy.

The for Loop

You can use the for loop in its basic form to execute a block of statements a given number of times. Suppose you want to display the numbers from 1 to 10. Instead of writing ten printf() statements, you could write this:

```
int count = 0;
for(count = 1 ; count <= 10 ; ++count)
  printf("\n%d", count);
```

The for loop operation is controlled by the contents of the parentheses that follow the keyword for. This is illustrated in Figure 4-1. The action that you want to repeat each time the loop repeats is the statement immediately following the first line that contains the keyword for. Although you have just a single statement here, this could equally well be a block of statements between braces.

Figure 4-2 shows the three expressions that are separated by semicolons and that control the loop.

Figure 4-2. Control expressions in a for *loop*

The effect of each of the statements in Figure 4-2 is shown in the diagram, but let's take a closer look at exactly what's going on:

- The first control expression is executed only once, when the loop starts. In the example, the first expression sets a variable, count, to 1. This is the expression count = 1.

- The second control expression must be a logical expression that produces a result of true or false; in this case, it's the expression count <= 10. The second expression is evaluated before each loop iteration starts. If the expression evaluates to true, the loop continues; if it's false, the loop ends and execution of the program continues with the first statement following the loop block or loop statement. Remember that false is a zero value, and any nonzero value is true. Thus, the example loop will execute the printf() statement as long as count is less than or equal to 10. The loop will end when count reaches 11.

- The third control expression, ++count in this case, is executed at the end of each iteration. Here, you use the increment operator to add 1 to the value of count. On the first iteration, count will be 1, so the printf() will output 1. On the second iteration, count will have been incremented to 2, so the printf() will output the value 2. This will continue until the value 10 has been displayed. At the start of the next iteration, count will be incremented to 11, and because the second control expression will then be false, the loop will end.

Notice the punctuation. The for loop parameters are contained within parentheses, and each expression is separated from the next by a semicolon. You can omit any of the control expressions, but if you do then you must still include the semicolon. For example, you could declare and initialize the variable count to 1 outside the loop:

```
int count = 1;
```

Now you wouldn't need to specify the first control expression at all, and the for loop could look like this:

```
for( ; count <= 10 ; ++count)
  printf("\n%d", count);
```

As a trivial example, you could make this into a real program simply by adding a few lines of code:

```
/* Program 4.1 List ten integers */
#include <stdio.h>

void main()
{
   int count = 1;
   for( ; count <= 10 ; ++count)
     printf("\n%d", count);
   printf("\nWe have finished.\n");
}
```

This program will list the numbers from 1 to 10 on separate lines and then output this message:

```
We have finished.
```

The flowchart in Figure 4-3 illustrates the logic of this program.

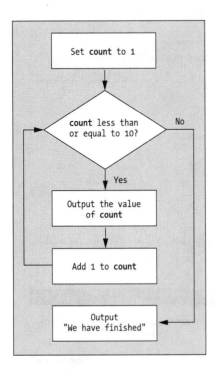

Figure 4-3. The logic of Program 4.1

In this example, it's easy to see what the variable count starts out as, so this code is quite OK. In general, though, unless the variable controlling the loop is initialized very close to the loop statement itself, it's better to initialize it in the first control expression. That way, there's less potential for error.

Let's try a slightly different example.

....

Try It Out: Drawing a Box

Suppose that you want to draw a box on the screen using * characters. You could just use the printf() statement lots of times, but the typing would be exhausting. You can use a for loop to draw a box much more easily. Let's try it:

```
/* Program 4.2 Drawing a box */
#include <stdio.h>

void main()
{
    int count = 0;
    printf("\n*************");          /* Draw the top of the box    */

    for(count = 1 ; count <= 8 ; ++count)
        printf("\n*           *");      /* Draw the sides of the box  */

    printf("\n*************\n");         /* Draw the bottom of the box */
}
```

No prizes for guessing, but the output for this program looks like this:

```
*************
*           *
*           *
*           *
*           *
*           *
*           *
*           *
*           *
*************
```

HOW IT WORKS

The program itself is really very simple. The first statement declares the variable count:

(Continued)

```
int count = 0;
```

The first `printf()` statement is then used to output the top of the box to the screen:

```
printf("\n**************");    /* Draw the top of the box    */
```

The next statement is the `for` loop:

```
for(count = 1 ; count <= 8 ; ++count)
   printf("\n*            *");   /* Draw the sides of the box  */
```

This repeats the `printf()` statement eight times to output the sides of the box. You probably understand this, but let's look again at how it works and pick up a bit more jargon. The loop control is

```
for(count = 1 ; count <= 8 ; ++count )
```

The operation of the loop is controlled by the three expressions that appear between the parentheses following the keyword, `for`. The first expression is

```
count = 1
```

This initializes the **loop control variable**, or **loop counter**, which in this case is the integer variable `count`, which you set to 1. You could use other types of variables for this, but integers are convenient for the job. The next expression is

```
count <= 8
```

This is the **continuation condition** for the loop. This is checked *before* each loop iteration, to see whether the loop should continue. If the expression is true, the loop continues. If it's false, the loop ends and execution continues with the statement following the loop. In this example, the loop continues as long as the variable `count` is less than or equal to 8. The last expression is

```
count++
```

This statement increments the loop counter at the end of each loop iteration. The loop statement that outputs the sides of the box will therefore be executed eight times. After the eighth iteration, `count` will be incremented to 9 and the continuation condition will be false, so the loop will end.

Program execution will then continue by executing the statement that follows the loop:

```
printf("\n**************\n");    /* Draw the bottom of the box */
```

(Continued)

This outputs the bottom of the box on the screen.

 TIP *Whenever you find yourself repeating something more than a couple of times, it's worth considering a loop. They'll usually save you time and memory.*

General Syntax of the for Loop

The general pattern of the for loop is as follows:

```
for(starting_condition ; continuation_condition ; action_per_iteration)
   Statement;

Next_statement;
```

The statement to be repeated is represented by Statement. In general, this could equally well be a block of statements (a group of statements) enclosed between a pair of braces.

The starting_condition usually (but not always) sets an initial value to a loop control variable. The loop control variable is typically, but not necessarily, a counter of some kind that tracks how often the loop has been repeated.

The continuation_condition is a logical expression evaluating to true or false. This determines whether or not the loop should continue to be executed. As long as this condition has the value true, the loop continues. It typically checks the value of the loop control variable, but any logical expression can be placed here, as long as you know what you're doing.

As you've already seen, the continuation_condition is tested at the beginning of the loop rather than the end. This obviously makes it possible to have a for loop whose statements aren't executed at all if the continuation_condition starts out as false.

The action_per_iteration is executed at the end of each loop iteration and is usually (but again, not necessarily) an increment of the loop control variable. At each iteration of the loop, the statement or block of statements immediately following the for statement is executed. The loop is terminated, and execution continues with Next_statement as soon as the continuation_condition is false.

More on the Increment and Decrement Operators

Now that you've seen an increment operator in action, let's delve a little deeper and find out what else these increment and decrement operators can do. They're both unary operators, which means that they're used with only one operand. You know they're used to increment (increase) or decrement (decrease) a value stored in a variable of one of the integer types by 1.

The Increment Operator

Let's start with the increment operator. It takes the form ++ and adds 1 to the variable it acts on. For example, assuming your variables are of type int, the following three statements have exactly the same effect:

```
count = count + 1;
count += 1;
++count;
```

Each of these statements increments the variable count by 1. The last form is clearly the most concise.

Thus, if you declare a variable count and initialize it to 1:

```
int count = 1;
```

and then you repeat the following statement six times in a loop:

```
++count;
```

by the end of the loop, count will have a value of 7. Each time you execute ++count you add 1 to the value stored in the variable. At the outset count has the value 1 stored in it. After the first cycle count will equal 2. Then, before the second iteration starts, count is equal to 2; after the second iteration count will equal 3; and so on up to 7.

You can also use the increment operator in an expression. The action of this operator in an expression is to increment the value of the variable and then use the incremented value in the expression. For example, suppose count has the value 5 and you execute the statement

```
total = ++count + 6;
```

The variable count will be incremented to 6 and the variable total will be assigned the value 12, so the one statement modifies two variables. The variable count, with the value 5, has 1 added to it, making it 6, and then 6 is added to this value to produce 12 for the expression on the right side of the assignment operator. This value is stored in total.

The Prefix and Postfix Forms of the Increment Operator

Up to now you've written the operator ++ in front of the variable to which it applies. This is called the **prefix form**. The operator can also be written *after* the variable to which it applies, and this is referred to as the **postfix form**. In this case, the effect is significantly different from the prefix form when it's used in an expression. If you write count++ in an expression, the incrementing of the variable count occurs *after* its value has been used. This sounds more complicated than it is.

Let's look at a variation on the earlier example:

```
total = 6 + count++;
```

With the same initial value of 5 for count, total is assigned the value 11. This is because the initial value of count is used to evaluate the expression on the right of the assignment (6 + 5). The variable count is incremented by 1 after its value has been used in the expression. The preceding statement is therefore equivalent to these two statements:

```
total = 6 + count;
++count;
```

Note, however, that when you use the increment operator in a statement by itself (as in the preceding second statement, which increments count), it doesn't matter whether you write the prefix or the postfix version of the operator. They both have the same effect.

Where you have an expression such as a++ + b—or worse, a+++b—it's less than obvious what is meant to happen or what the compiler will achieve. The expressions are actually the same, but in the second case you might really have meant a + ++b, which is different because it evaluates to one more than the other two expressions.

For example, if a = 10 and b = 5, then in the statement

```
x = a++ + b;
```

x will have the value 15 (from 10 + 5) because a is incremented after the expression is evaluated. The next time you use the variable a, however, it will have the value 11.

On the other hand, if you execute the following statement, with the same initial values for a and b

```
y = a + ++b;
```

y will have the value 16 (from 10 + 6) because b is incremented before the statement is evaluated.

It's a good idea to use parentheses in all these cases to make sure there's no confusion. So you should write these statements as follows:

```
x = (a++) + b;
y = a + (++b);
```

The Decrement Operator

The decrement operator works in much the same way as the increment operator. It takes the form -- and subtracts 1 from the variable it acts on. It's used in exactly the same way as ++. For example, assuming the variables are of type int, the following three statements all have the same effect:

```
count = count - 1;
count -= 1;
--count;
```

They each decrement the variable count by 1. For example, if count has the value 10, then the statement

```
total = --count + 6;
```

results in the variable total being assigned the value 15 (from 9 + 6). The variable count, with the initial value of 10, has 1 subtracted from it so that its value is 9. Then 6 is added to the new value, making the value of the expression on the right of the assignment operator 15.

Exactly the same rules that I discussed in relation to the prefix and postfix forms of the increment operator apply to the decrement operator. For example, if count has the initial value 5, then the statement

```
total = --count + 6;
```

results in total having the value 10 (from 4 + 6) assigned, whereas

```
total = 6 + count-- ;
```

sets the value of total to 11 (from 6 + 5). Both operators are usually applied to integers, but you'll also see, in later chapters, how they can be applied to certain other data types in C.

The for Loop Revisited

Now that you understand a bit more about ++ and --, let's move on with another example that uses a loop.

....

Try It Out: Summing Numbers

This is a more useful and interesting program than the one that draws a box with asterisks (unless what you really need is, of course, a box drawn with asterisks). Have you ever wanted to know what all the house numbers on your street totaled? Here, you're going to read in an integer value and then use a for loop to sum all the integers from 1 to the value that was entered.

```c
/* Program 4.3    Sum the integers from 1 to a user-specified number */
#include <stdio.h>

void main()
{
   long sum = OL;                     /* Stores the sum of the integers      */
   int count = 0;                     /* The number of integers to be summed */
   int i = 0;                         /* The loop counter                    */

   /* Read the number of integers to be summed */
   printf("\nEnter the number of integers you want to sum: ");
   scanf(" %d", &count);

   /* Sum integers from 1 to count */
   for(i = 1 ; i <= count ; i++)
     sum += i;

   printf("\nTotal of the first %d numbers is %ld\n", count, sum);
}
```

The typical output you should get from this program is as follows:

```
Enter the number of integers you want to sum: 10

Total of the first 10 integers is 55
```

HOW IT WORKS

You start by declaring and initializing three variables that you'll need during the calculation:

```c
   long sum = OL;                     /* Stores the sum of the integers      */
   int count = 0;                     /* The number of integers to be summed */
   int i = 0;                         /* The loop counter                    */
```

(Continued)

You use sum to hold the final value of your calculations. You declare it as type long to allow the maximum total you can deal with to be as large an integer as possible. The variable count will store the integer that's entered as the number of integers to be summed, and you'll use this value to control the number of iterations in the for loop. The variable i is the loop counter.

You deal with the input by means of the following statements:

```
printf("\nEnter the number of integers you want to sum: ");
scanf(" %d", &count);
```

After the prompt, you read in the integer that will define the sum required. If the user enters **4**, for instance, then the program will compute the sum of 1, 2, 3, and 4.

The sum is calculated in the following loop:

```
for(i = 1 ; i <= count ; i++)
   sum += i;
```

The loop variable i is initialized to 1 by the starting condition in the for loop. On each iteration, the value of i is added to sum, and then i is incremented, so the values 1, 2, 3, and so on up to the value stored in count will be added to sum. The loop ends when the value of i exceeds the value of count.

....

As I've hinted with the occasional "not necessarily" in my description of how the for loop is controlled, you have a lot of flexibility about what you can use as control expressions. The next program demonstrates how this flexibility might be applied to shortening the previous example slightly.

....

Try It Out: The Flexible for Loop

This example demonstrates how you can carry out a calculation within the third control expression in a for loop:

```
/* Program 4.4 Summing integers - compact version */
#include <stdio.h>

void main()
{
   long sum = 0L;            /* Stores the sum of the integers      */
   int count = 0;            /* The number of integers to be summed */
   int i = 0;               /* The loop counter                    */
```

(Continued)

```
  /* Read the number of integers to be summed */
  printf("\nEnter the number of integers you want to sum: ");
  scanf(" %d", &count);

  /* Sum integers from 1 to count */
  for (i = 1 ; i<= count ; sum += i++ );
    printf("\nTotal of the first %d numbers is %ld\n", count, sum);
}
```

Typical output would be as follows:

```
Enter the number of integers you want to sum: 6

Total of the first 6 numbers is 21
```

HOW IT WORKS

This program will execute exactly the same as the previous program. The only difference is that you place the operation that accumulates the sum in the third control expression for the loop:

```
  for (i = 1 ; i<= count ; sum += i++ );
```

The loop statement is empty: it's just the semicolon after the closing parenthesis. This expression adds the value of i to sum and then increments i ready for the next iteration. It works this way because you've used the postfix form of the increment operator. If you use the prefix form here, then you'll get the wrong answer, because the total in sum will include the number count+1 from the first iteration of the loop, instead of just count.

Modifying the for Loop Variable

Of course, you aren't limited to incrementing the loop control variable by 1. You can change it by any value, positive or negative. You could have summed the first *n* integers backward if you wished, as in the following example:

```
/* Program 4.5 Summing integers backward */
#include <stdio.h>
void main()
{
  long sum = 0L;                 /* Stores the sum of the integers      */
  int count = 0;                 /* The number of integers to be summed */
  int i = 0;                     /* The loop counter                    */
```

```
/* Read the number of integers to be summed */
printf("\nEnter the number of integers you want to sum: ");
scanf(" %d", &count);

/* Sum integers from count to 1 */
for (i = count ; i >= 1 ; sum += i-- );
  printf("\nTotal of the first %d numbers is %ld\n", count, sum);
}
```

This produces the same output as the previous example. The only change is in the loop control expressions. The loop counter is initialized to count, rather than to 1, and it's *decremented* on each iteration. The effect is to add the values count, count-1, count-2, and so on down to 1. Again, if you used the prefix form, then the answer would be wrong, because you would start with adding count-1 instead of just count.

Just to keep any mathematically inclined readers happy, I should mention that it's quite unnecessary to use a loop to sum the first *n* integers. The following tidy little formula will do the trick much more efficiently:

```
n*(n+1)/2
```

However, it wouldn't teach you much about loops, would it?

A for Loop with No Parameters

As I've already mentioned, you have no obligation to put any parameters in the for loop statement at all. The minimal for loop looks like this:

```
for ( ;; )
  statement;
```

Here, as previously, statement could also be a block of statements enclosed between braces, and in this case it usually will be. Because the condition for continuing the loop is absent, as is the initial condition and the loop increment, the loop will continue indefinitely. As a result, unless you want your computer to be indefinitely doing nothing, statement must contain the means of exiting from the loop. To stop repeating the loop, the loop body must contain two things: a test of some kind to determine whether the condition for ending the loop has been reached, and a statement that will end the current loop iteration and continue execution with the statement following the loop.

The break Statement in a Loop

You encountered the break statement in the context of the switch statement. Its effect there was to stop executing the code within the switch block and continue with the first statement following the `switch`. The `break` statement works in essentially the same way within the body of a loop—any kind of loop. For instance:

```
char answer = 0;
for( ;; )
{
    /* Code to read and process some data */
  printf("Do you want  to enter some more(y/n): ");
  scanf("%c", &answer);
  if(tolower(answer) == 'n')
    break;                          /* Go to statement after the loop */
}
/* Statement after the loop */
```

Here you have a loop that will execute indefinitely. The `scanf()` statement reads a character into `answer`, and if the character entered was **n** or **N**, the `break` statement will be executed. The effect is to stop executing the loop and to continue with the first statement following the loop. Let's see this in action in another example.

....

Try It Out: A Minimal for Loop

This example computes the average of an arbitrary number of values:

```
/* Program 4.6 The almost indefinite loop - computing an average */
#include <stdio.h>
#include <ctype.h>             /* For tolower() function */

void main()
{
    char answer = 'N';       /* Records yes or no to continue the loop */
    double total = 0.0;      /* Total of values entered            */
    double value = 0.0;      /* Value entered                      */
    int count = 0;           /* Number of values entered           */

    printf("\nThis program calculates the average of"
                            " any number of values.");

    for( ;; )                         /* Indefinite loop */
    {
      printf ("\nEnter a value: ");   /* Prompt for the next value */
      scanf(" %lf", &value);          /* Read the next value       */
      total += value;                 /* Add value to total        */
      ++count;                        /* Increment count of values */

      /* check for more input */
      printf("Do you want to enter another value? (Y or N): ");
      scanf(" %c", &answer );         /* Read response Y or N   */
```

(Continued)

```
    if( tolower(answer) == 'n' )    /* look for any sign of no */
      break;                        /* Exit from the loop      */
  }
  /* output the average to 2 decimal places */
  printf ("\nThe average is %.2lf\n", total/count );
}
```

Typical output from this program is as follows:

```
This program calculates the average of any number of values.
Enter a value: 2.5
Do you want to enter another value? (Y or N): y

Enter a value: 3.5
Do you want to enter another value? (Y or N): y

Enter a value: 6
Do you want to enter another value? (Y or N): n

The average is 4.00
```

HOW IT WORKS

The general logic of the program is illustrated in Figure 4-4.

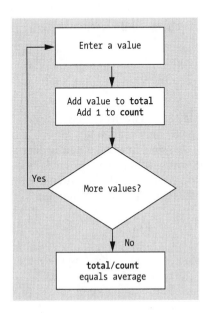

Figure 4-4. The basic logic of Program 4.6

(Continued)

You've set up the loop to continue indefinitely because the for loop has no end condition specified—or indeed any loop control expressions:

```
for( ;; )                          /* Indefinite loop */
```

Therefore, as far as the loop control is concerned, the block of statements enclosed between the braces will be repeated indefinitely.

You display a prompt and read an input value in the loop with these statements:

```
printf ("\nEnter a value: ");     /* Prompt for the next value */
scanf(" %lf", &value);            /* Read the next value       */
```

Next, you add the value entered to your variable total:

```
total += value;                   /* Add value to total        */
```

You then increment the count of the number of values:

```
++count;                          /* Increment count of values */
```

Having read a value and added it to the total, you check with the user to see if more input is to be entered:

```
/* check for more input */
printf("Do you want to enter another value? (Y or N): ");
scanf(" %c", &answer );           /* Read response Y or N    */
```

This prompts the user to enter either **Y** or **N**. The character the user enters is checked in the if statement:

```
if( tolower(answer) == 'n' )      /* look for any sign of no */
   break;                         /* Exit from the loop      */
```

The character stored in answer is converted to lowercase by the tolower() function that's declared in the ctype.h header file, so you only need to test for 'n'. If the user enters the character **N** or **n** to indicate that she's finished entering data, the break statement will be executed. Executing break within a loop has the effect of immediately ending the loop so that execution continues with the statement following the closing brace for the loop block. This is the following statement:

```
printf ("\nThe average is %.2lf\n", total/count );
```

This statement calculates the average of the values entered by dividing the value in total by the count of the number of values. The result is then displayed.

Limiting Input Using a for Loop

You can use a for loop to limit the amount of input from the user. Each iteration of the loop will permit some input to be entered. When the loop has completed a given number of iterations, the loop ends, so no more data can be entered. You can write a simple program to demonstrate how this can work. The program will implement a guessing game.

......

Try It Out: A Guessing Game

This program asks the user to guess the number that the program has picked as the lucky number. It uses one for loop and plenty of if statements. I've also thrown in a conditional operator, just to make sure you haven't forgotten how to use it!

```
/* Program 4.7  A Guessing Game */
#include <stdio.h>

void main()
{
   long chosen = 15;               /* The lucky number           */
   int guess = 0;                  /* Stores a guess             */
   int count = 3;                  /* The maximum number of tries */

   printf("\nThis is a guessing game.");
   printf("\nI have chosen a number between 1 and 20"
                            " which you must guess.\n");

   for( ; count>0 ; --count)
   {
     printf("\nYou have %d tr%s left.", count, count == 1 ? "y" : "ies");
     printf("\nEnter a guess: ");      /* Prompt for a guess  */
     scanf("%d", &guess);              /* Read in a guess      */

     /* Check for a correct guess */
     if (guess == chosen)
     {
       printf("\nYou guessed it!\n");
       return;                    /* End the program      */
     }

     /* Check for an invalid guess */
     if(guess<1 || guess > 20)
       printf("I said between 1 and 20.\n ");
     else
       printf("Sorry. %d is wrong.\n", guess);
```

(Continued)

```
    }
    printf("\nYou have had three tries and failed. The number was %ld\n",
                                                        chosen);
}
```

Here's some sample output:

```
This is a guessing game.
I have chosen a number between 1 and 20 which you must guess.

You have 3 tries left.
Enter a guess: 5
Sorry. 5 is wrong.

You have 2 tries left.
Enter a guess: 18
Sorry. 18 is wrong.

You have 1 try left.
Enter a guess: 7
Sorry. 7 is wrong.

You have had three tries and failed. The number was 15
```

HOW IT WORKS

You first declare and initialize three variables of type int: chosen, guess, and count:

```
    long chosen = 15;          /* The lucky number            */
    int guess = 0;             /* Stores a guess              */
    int count = 3;             /* The maximum number of tries */
```

These variables are to store, respectively, the number that's to be guessed, the number that's the user's guess, and the number of guesses the user is permitted. Notice that you've created a variable to store the chosen number. You could have just used the number 15 in the program, but doing it this way makes it much easier to alter the value of the number that the user must guess. It also makes obvious what's happening in the code when you use the variable chosen.

You provide the user with an initial explanation of the program:

```
    printf("\nThis is a guessing game.");
    printf("\nI have chosen a number between 1 and 20"
                                " which you must guess.\n");
```

(Continued)

The number of guesses that can be entered is controlled by this loop:

```
for( ; count>0 ; --count)
{
   ...
}
```

All the operational details of the game are within this loop, which will continue as long as count is positive, so the loop will repeat count times.

There's a prompt for a guess to be entered, and the guess itself is read by these statements:

```
printf("\nYou have %d tr%s left.", count, count == 1 ? "y" : "ies");
printf("\nEnter a guess: ");        /* Prompt for a guess */
scanf("%d", &guess);                /* Read in a guess    */
```

The first printf() looks a little complicated, but all it does is insert "y" after "tr" in the output when count is 1, and "ies" after "tr" in the output in all other cases. You must, after all, get your plurals right.

After reading a guess value using scanf(), you check whether it's correct with these statements:

```
/* Check for a correct guess */
if (guess == chosen)
{
  printf("\nYou guessed it!");
  return;                          /* End the program    */
}
```

If the guess is correct, you display a suitable message and execute the return statement. The return statement ends the function main(), and so the program ends. You'll learn more about the return statement when I discuss functions in greater detail in Chapter 8.

The program will reach the last check in the loop only if the guess is incorrect:

```
/* Check for an invalid guess */
if(guess<1 || guess > 20)
  printf("I said between 1 and 20.\n ");
else
  printf("Sorry. %d is wrong.\n", guess);
```

This group of statements tests whether the value entered is within the prescribed limits. If it isn't, a message is displayed reiterating the limits. If it's a valid guess, a message is displayed to the effect that it's incorrect.

(Continued)

The loop ends after three iterations and thus three guesses. The statement after the loop is

```
printf("\nYou have had three tries and failed. The number was %ld\n",
                                                        chosen);
```

This will be executed only if all three guesses were wrong. It displays an appropriate message, revealing the number to be guessed, and then the program ends.

This program is designed so that you can easily change the value of the variable chosen and have endless fun. Well, endless fun for a short while, anyway.

Generating Pseudo-Random Integers

The previous example would have been much more entertaining if the number to be guessed could have been generated within the program so that it was different each time the program executed. Well, you can do that using the rand() function that's declared in the stdlib.h header file:

```
int chosen = 0;
chosen = rand();                /* Set to a random integer */
```

Each time you call the rand() function, it will return a random integer. The value will be from 0 to a maximum of RAND_MAX, the value of which is defined in stdlib.h. The integers generated by the rand() function are described as **pseudo-random** numbers because truly random numbers can arise only in natural processes and can't be generated algorithmically.

The sequence of numbers that's generated by the rand() function uses a starting seed number, and for a given seed the sequence will always be the same. If you use the function with the default seed value, you'll always get exactly the same sequence, which won't make the game very challenging. However, C provides another standard function, srand(), that you can call to initialize the sequence with a particular seed that you pass as an argument to the function. This function is also declared in the stdlib.h header. At first sight, this doesn't seem to get you much further with the guessing game, as you now need to generate a different seed each time the program executes. Yet another library function can help with this: the time() function that's declared in the time.h header file. The time() function returns the number of seconds that have elapsed since January 1, 1970, as an integer, and because time always marches on, you can get a different value returned by the time() function each time the program executes. The time() function requires an argument to be specified that you'll specify as NULL. NULL is a symbol that's defined in stdlib.h, but I'll defer further discussion of it until Chapter 7.

Thus, to get a different sequence of pseudo-random numbers each time a program is run, you can use the following statements:

```
srand(time(NULL));                  /* Use clock value as starting seed */
int chosen = 0;
chosen = rand();                    /* Set to a random integer 0 to RAND_MAX */
```

The value of the upper limit, RAND_MAX, is likely to be quite large—often the maximum value that can be stored as type int. When you need a more limited range of values, you can scale the value returned by rand() to provide values within the range that you want. Suppose you want to obtain values in a range from 0 up to, but not including, limit. The simplest approach to obtaining values in this range is like this:

```
srand(time(NULL));                  /* Use clock value as starting seed     */
int limit = 20.0;                   /* Upper limit for pseudo-random values */
int chosen = 0;
chosen = rand()%limit;              /* 0 to limit-1 inclusive               */
```

Of course, if you want numbers from 1 to limit, you can write this:

```
chosen = 1+rand()%limit;            /* 1 to limit   inclusive               */
```

This works reasonably well with the implementation of rand() in my compiler and library. However, this isn't a good way in general of limiting the range of numbers produced by a pseudo-random number generator. This is because you're essentially chopping off the high-order bits in the value that's returned and implicitly assuming that the bits that are left will also represent random values. This isn't necessarily the case.

You could try using rand() in a variation of the previous example:

```
/*  Program 4.7A  A More Interesting Guessing Game */
#include <stdio.h>
#include <stdlib.h>                 /* For rand() and srand() */
#include <time.h>                   /* For time() function    */

void main()
{
    int chosen = 0;                 /* The lucky number                     */
    int guess = 0;                  /* Stores a guess                       */
    int count = 3;                  /* The maximum number of tries          */
    int limit = 20;                 /* Upper limit for pseudo-random values */


    srand(time(NULL));              /* Use clock value as starting seed     */
    chosen = 1 + rand()%limit;      /* Random int 1 to limit                */

    printf("\nThis is a guessing game.");
    printf("\nI have chosen a number between 1 and 20"
                            " which you must guess.\n");

    for( ; count>0 ; --count)
    {
```

```
  printf("\nYou have %d tr%s left.", count, count == 1 ? "y" : "ies");
  printf("\nEnter a guess: ");        /* Prompt for a guess  */
  scanf("%d", &guess);                /* Read in a guess     */

  /* Check for a correct guess */
  if (guess == chosen)
  {
    printf("\nYou guessed it!\n");
    return;                           /* End the program */
  }

  /* Check for an invalid guess */
  if(guess<1 || guess > 20)
    printf("I said between 1 and 20.\n ");
  else
    printf("Sorry. %d is wrong.\n", guess);
}
printf("\nYou have had three tries and failed. The number was %ld\n",
                                                   chosen);
}
```

Now you should get a different number to guess most of the time.

More for Loop Control Options

You've seen how you can increment or decrement the loop counter by 1 using the ++ and -- operators. You can increment or decrement the loop counter by any amount that you wish. Here's an example of how you can do this:

```
int n = 0;
long sum = 0L;
for(n = 1 ; n<20 ; n += 2 )
  sum += n;
printf("Sum is %ld", sum);
```

The loop in the preceding code fragment sums all the odd integers from 1 to 20. The third control expression increments the loop variable n by 2 on each iteration. You can write any expression here, including any assignment. For instance, to sum every seventh integer from 1 to 1,000, you could write the loop

```
for(n = 1 ; n<1000 ; n = n+7 )
  sum += n;
```

Now the third loop control expression increments n by 7 at the end of each iteration, so you'll get the sum 1 + 8 + 15 + 22 + and so on up to 1,000.

You aren't limited to a single loop control expression. You could rewrite the loop in the first code fragment, summing the odd numbers from 1 to 20, like this:

```
for(n = 1 ; n<20 ; sum += n, n += 2 )
  ;
```

Now the third control expression consists of two expressions separated by a comma. These will execute in sequence at the end of each loop iteration, so first the expression

```
sum +=n
```

will add the current value of n to sum. Next, the second expression

```
n += 2
```

will increment n by 2. Because these expressions execute in sequence from left to right, you must write them in the sequence shown. If you reverse the sequence, the result will be incorrect.

You aren't limited to just two expressions either. You can have as many expressions here as you like, as long as they're separated by commas. Of course, you should make use of this only when there's a distinct advantage in doing so. Too much of this can make your code hard to understand.

The first and second control expressions can also consist of several expressions separated by commas, but the need for this is quite rare.

Floating-Point Loop Control Variables

The loop control variable can also be a floating-point variable. Here's a loop to sum the fractions from 1/1 to 1/10:

```
double sum = 0.0;
double x = 0.0;
for(x = 1.0 ; x<11 ; x += 1.0)
  sum += 1.0/x;
```

You'll find this sort of thing isn't required very often. It's important to remember that fractional values often don't have an exact representation in floating-point form, so it's unwise to rely on equality as the condition for ending a loop, for example:

```
double x = 0.0;
for(x = 0.0 ; x != 2.0 ; x+= 0.2)        /* Indefinite loop!!! */
  printf("\nx = %.2lf",x);
```

This loop is supposed to output the values of x from 0.0 to 2.0 in steps of 0.2, so there should be 11 lines of output. Because 0.2 doesn't have an exact representation as a binary floating-point value, x never has the value 2.0, so this loop will take over your computer and run indefinitely (until you stop it; use Ctrl+C under Microsoft Windows).

The while Loop

That's enough of the for loop. Now that you've seen several examples of for loops, let's look at a different kind of loop: the while loop. With a while loop, the mechanism for repeating a set of statements allows execution to continue for as long as a specified logical expression is true. In English, this could be represented as follows:

While this condition is true

   Keep on doing this;

Alternatively, it could be represented like this:

While you are hungry

   Eat sandwiches

This means that you ask yourself "Am I hungry?" before eating the next sandwich. If the answer is yes, then you eat a sandwich and ask yourself "Am I still hungry?" You keep eating sandwiches until the answer is no, at which point you go on to do something else—drink some coffee, maybe.

The general syntax for the while loop is as follows:

```
while( expression )
  Statement1;

  Statement2;
```

As always, "Statement1" could be a block of statements.

The logic of the while loop is shown in Figure 4-5.

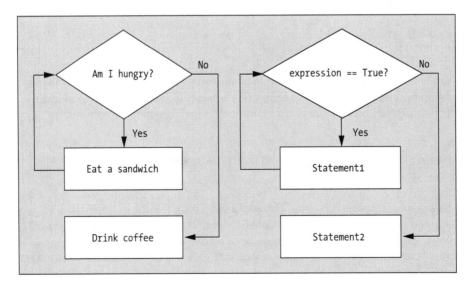

Figure 4-5. The logic of the while *loop*

Just like the for loop, the condition for continuation of the while loop is tested at the start, so if expression starts out false, none of the loop statements will be executed. If you answer the first question "No, I'm not hungry," then you don't get to eat any sandwiches at all, and you move straight on to the coffee.

Try It Out: Using the while Loop

The while loop looks fairly straightforward, so let's go straight into applying it in that old favorite, humming and summing house numbers:

```c
/*  Example 4.8 While programming and summing integers */
#include <stdio.h>

void main()
{
   long sum = 0L;                  /* The sum of the integers           */
   int i = 1;                      /* Indexes through the integers      */
   int count = 0;                  /* The count of integers to be summed */

   /* Get the count of the number of integers to sum */
   printf("\nEnter the number of integers you want to sum: ");
   scanf(" %d", &count);

   /* Sum the integers from 1 to count */
   while(i <= count)
     sum += i++;

   printf("Total of the first %d numbers is %ld\n", count, sum);
}
```

Typical output from this program is

```
Enter the number of integers you want to sum: 7
Total of the first 7 numbers is 28
```

HOW IT WORKS

Well, really this works pretty much the same as when you used the for loop. The only aspect of this example worth discussing is the while loop:

```c
while(i <= count)
  sum += i++;
```

(Continued)

The loop contains a single statement action that accumulates the total in sum. This continues to be executed with i values up to and including the value stored in count. Because you have the postfix increment operator here (the ++ comes after the variable), i is incremented *after* its value is used to compute sum on each iteration. What the statement really means is this:

```
sum += i;
i++;
```

So the value of sum isn't affected by the increment of i until the next loop iteration.

I'll try to explain this in relatively plain English, so that you understand what's really happening.

- *Entering the* while *loop*: When you enter the while loop, i is 1 and count has the value corresponding to whatever you've typed in (let's say **3**). When the loop starts, you first check whether i <= count is true. In this case, it amounts to 1<=3, which is true, so you execute the loop statement:

  ```
  sum += i++;
  ```

- *First time through the* while *loop*: First, the value of i (which is 1) is added to the variable sum. The variable sum was equal to 0, so it's now equal to 1. Because you've used the postfix increment operator, the variable i is incremented after the value to be stored in sum has been calculated. So i is now 2, and you return to the beginning of the loop. You check the while expression and see whether the value in i is still less than or equal to count. Because i is now 2, which is indeed less than 3, you execute the loop statement again.

- *Second time through the* while *loop*: In the second loop iteration, you add the new value of i (which is now 2) to the old value of sum (which is 1) and store the result in sum. The variable sum now equals 3. You add 1 to i so i now has the value 3, and you go back to the beginning of the loop to check whether the control expression is still true.

- *Third time through the* while *loop*: At this point i is equal to count, so you can still continue the loop. You add the new value of i (which is 3) to the old value of sum (which is also 3) and store the result in sum, which now has the value 6. You add 1 to i, so i now has the value 4, and you go back to check the loop expression once more.

- *Last time through the* while *loop*: Now i, which has the value 4, is greater than count, which has the value 3, so the expression i <= count is false, and you leave the loop.

This example used the postfix increment operator as postfix. How could you change the preceding program to use the prefix form of the ++ operator? Have a try and see whether you can work it out. You'll find the answer in the next section.

(Continued)

USING ++ AS A PREFIX OPERATOR

The obvious bit of code that will change is the `while` loop:

```
sum += ++i;
```

Try just changing this. If you run the program now you get the wrong answer:

```
Enter the number of integers you want to sum: 3
Total of the first 3 numbers is 9
```

This is because the ++ operator is adding 1 to the value of i *before* it stores the value in `sum`. The variable i starts at 1 and is increased to 2 on the first iteration, whereupon that value is added to `sum`.

To make the first loop iteration work correctly, you need to start i off as 0. This means that the first increment would set the value of i to 1, which is what you want. So you must change the declaration of i to

```
int i = 0;
```

However, the program still doesn't work properly, because it continues doing the calculation until the value in i is greater than `count`, so you get one more iteration than you need. The alteration you need to fix this is to change the control expression so that the loop continues while i is less than but not equal to `count`:

```
while(i < count)
```

Now the program will produce the correct answer. This example should help you really understand postfixing and prefixing these operators.

Nested Loops

Sometimes you may want to place one loop inside another. For each house on a street, you might want to count the number of occupants. You step from house to house, and for each house you count the number of occupants. Going through all the houses could be an outer loop, and for each iteration of the outer loop you could have an inner loop that counted the occupants.

The best way to understand how a nested loop works is to look at a simple example.

Try It Out: Using Nested Loops

To demonstrate a nested loop, you'll use a simple example based on the summing integers program. Originally, you produced the sums of all the integers from 1 up to the value entered. Now for every house, you'll produce the sum of all the numbers from the first house, 1, up to the current house. If you look at the program output, it will become clearer.

```
/* Program 4.9 Sums of integers step-by-step */
#include <stdio.h>

void main()
{
    long sum = OL;                    /* Stores the sum of integers     */
    int i = 1;                        /* Outer loop control variable     */
    int j = 1;                        /* Inner loop control variable     */
    int count = 0;                    /* Number of sums to be calculated */

    /* Prompt for, and read the input count */
    printf("\nEnter the number of integers you want to sum: ");
    scanf(" %d", &count);

    for( i = 1 ; i <= count ; i++ )
    {
      sum = OL;                       /* Initialize sum for the inner loop */

      /* Calculate sum of integers from 1 to i */
      for(j = 1 ; j <= i ; j++ )
        sum += j;

      printf("\n%d\t%ld", i, sum);    /* Output sum of 1 to i */
    }
}
```

You should see some output like this:

```
Enter the number of integers you want to sum: 5

1               1
2               3
3               6
4               10
5               15
```

As you can see, if you enter **5**, then the program calculates the sums of the integers from 1 to 1, from 1 to 2, from 1 to 3, from 1 to 4, and from 1 to 5.

(Continued)

The program calculates the sum from 1 to each integer value, for all values from 1 up to the value of count that you enter. The important thing to grasp about this nested loop is that the inner loop completes all its iterations *for each iteration* of the outer loop. Thus, the outer loop sets up the value of i that determines how many times the inner loop will repeat:

```
for( i = 1 ; i <= count ; i++ )
{
  sum = OL;                     /* Initialize sum for the inner loop */

  /* Calculate sum of integers from 1 to i */
  for(j = 1 ; j <= i ; j++ )
    sum += j;

  printf("\n%d\t%ld", i, sum);  /* Output sum of 1 to i */
}
```

The outer loop starts off by setting i to 1, and the loop is repeated for successive values of i up to count. For each iteration of the outer loop, and therefore for each value of i, sum is initialized to 0, the inner loop is executed, and the result displayed by the printf() statement. The inner loop accumulates the sum of all the integers from 1 to the current value of i:

```
/* Calculate sum of integers from 1 to i */
for(j = 1 ; j <= i ; j++ )
  sum += j;
```

Each time the inner loop finishes, the printf() to output the value of sum is executed. Control then goes back to the beginning of the outer loop for the next iteration.

Look at the output again to see the action of the nested loop. The first loop simply sets the variable sum to 0 each time around, and the inner loop adds up all the numbers from 1 to the current value of i. You could modify the nested loop to use a while loop for the inner loop and to produce output that would show what the program is doing a little more explicitly.

Try It Out: Nesting a while Loop Within a for Loop

In the previous example you nested a for loop inside a for loop. In this example you'll nest a while loop inside a for loop.

(Continued)

```
/* Example 4.10 Sums of integers with a while loop nested in a for loop */
#include <stdio.h>

void main()
{
    long sum = 1L;                    /* Stores the sum of integers      */
    int i = 1;                        /* Outer loop control variable     */
    int j = 1;                        /* Inner loop control variable     */
    int count = 0;                    /* Number of sums to be calculated */

    /* Prompt for, and read the input count */
    printf("\nEnter the number of integers you want to sum: ");
    scanf(" %d", &count);

    for( i = 1 ; i <= count ; i++ )
    {
      sum = 1L;                       /* Initialize sum for the inner loop */
      j=1;                            /* Initialize integer to be added     */
      printf("\n1");

      /* Calculate sum of integers from 1 to i */
      while(j < i)
      {
        sum += ++j;
        printf("+%d", j);             /* Output +j – on the same line */
      }
      printf(" = %ld\n", sum);        /* Output  = sum  */
    }
}
```

This program produces the following output:

```
Enter the number of integers you want to sum: 5

1 = 1

1+2 = 3

1+2+3 = 6

1+2+3+4 = 10

1+2+3+4+5 = 15
```

(Continued)

The differences are inside the outer loop:

```
for( i = 1 ; i <= count ; i++ )
{
    sum = 1L;                           /* Initialize sum for the inner loop */
    j=1;                                /* Initialize integer to be added    */
    printf("\n1");

    /* Calculate sum of integers from 1 to i */
    while(j < i)
    {
        sum += ++j;
        printf("+%d", j);               /* Output +j - on the same line */
    }
    printf(" = %ld\n", sum);            /* Output  = sum */
}
```

The outer loop control is exactly the same as before. The difference is what occurs during each iteration. The variable sum is initialized to 1 within the outer loop, because the while loop will add values to sum starting with 2. The integer to be added is stored in j, which is also initialized to 1. The first printf() in the outer loop just outputs a newline character followed by 1, the first integer in the set to be summed. The inner loop adds the integers from 2 up to the value of i. For each integer value in j that's added to sum, the printf() in the inner loop outputs +j on the same line as the 1 that was output first. Thus, the inner loop will output +2, then +3, and so on for as long as j is less than i. Of course, for the first iteration of the outer loop i is 1, so the inner loop won't execute at all, because j<i (1 < 1) is false from the beginning.

When the inner loop ends, the last printf() statement is executed. This outputs an equal sign followed by the value of sum. Control then returns to the beginning of the outer loop for the next iteration.

Nested Loops and the goto Statement

You've learned how you can nest one loop inside another, but it doesn't end there. You can nest as many loops one inside another as you want, for instance:

```
int i = 0, j = 0, k = 0;
for(i = 0 ; i<10 ; ++i)
    for(j = 0 ; j<20 ; ++k)         /* Loop executed 10 times          */
        for(k = 0 ; k<30 ; ++k)     /* Loop executed 10x20 times       */
        {                           /* Loop body executed 10x20x30 times */
            /* Do something useful */
        }
```

The inner loop controlled by j will execute once for each iteration of the outer loop controlled by i. The innermost loop controlled by k will execute once for each iteration of the loop controlled by j. Thus, the body of the innermost loop will be executed 6,000 times.

Occasionally with deeply nested loops like this, you'll want to break out of all the nested loops from the innermost loop and then continue with the statement following the outermost loop. A break statement in the innermost loop will only break out of that loop and execution will continue with the loop controlled by j. To escape the nested loops completely using break statements therefore requires quite complicated logic to break out of each level until you escape the outermost loop. This is one situation in which the goto statement can be very useful because it provides a way to avoid all the complicated logic. For example:

```c
int i = 0, j = 0, k = 0;
for(i = 0 ; i<10 ; ++i)
  for(j = 0 ; j<20 ; ++k)              /* Loop executed 10 times              */
    for(k = 0 ; k<30 ; ++k)           /* Loop executed 10x20 times           */
    {                                 /* Loop body executed 10x20x30 times */
        if(must_escape)
          goto out;
        /* Do something useful */
    }
out: /*Statement following the nested loops */
```

If the variable must_escape is true (nonzero), then you execute the goto statement to branch directly to the statement with the label out. So you have a direct exit from the complete nest of loops without any complicated decision making in the outer loop levels.

The do-while Loop

The third type of loop is the do-while loop. Now, you may be asking why you need this when you already have the for loop and the while loop. Well, there's actually a very subtle difference between the do-while loop and the other two. The test for whether the loop should continue is at the *end* of the loop, so the loop statement or statement block always executes at least once.

The while loop tests at the beginning of the loop. So before any action takes place, you check the expression. Look at this fragment of code:

```c
int number = 4;

while(number < 4)
{
  printf("\nNumber = %d", number);
  number++;
}
```

Here, you would never output anything. The control expression number < 4 is false from the start, so the loop block is never executed.

The do-while loop, however, works differently. You can see this if you replace the preceding while loop with a do-while loop and leave the rest of the statements the same:

```
int number = 4;

do
{
  printf("\nNumber = %d", number);
  number++;
}
while(number < 4);
```

Now when you execute this loop, you get Number = 4 displayed. This is because the expression number < 4 is only checked at the end of the first iteration of the loop.

The general representation of the do-while loop is as follows:

```
do
  Statement;
while (expression);
```

Notice the semicolon after the while statement in a do-while loop. There isn't one in the while loop. As always, a block of statements between braces can be in place of Statement. In a do-while loop, if the value of expression is true (nonzero), the loop continues. The loop will exit only when the value of expression becomes false (zero). You can see how this works more clearly in Figure 4-6.

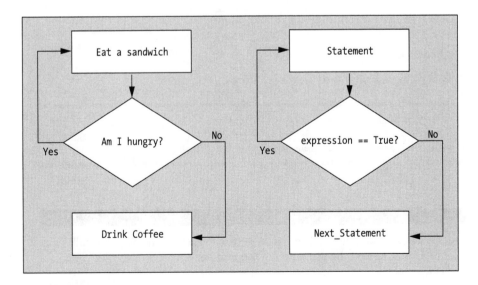

Figure 4-6. Operation of the do-while *loop*

Here, you can see that you eat a sandwich *before* you check whether you're hungry or not. You'll always eat at least one sandwich.

....

Try It Out: Using a do-while Loop

You can try out the do-while loop with a little program that reverses the digits of a positive number:

```
/* Program 4.11 Reversing the digits */
#include <stdio.h>
void main()
{
   int number = 0;                     /* The number to be reversed */
   int rebmun = 0;                     /* The reversed number       */
   int temp = 0;                       /* Working storage           */

   /* Get the value to be reversed */
   printf("\nEnter a positive integer: ");
   scanf(" %d", &number);

   temp = number;                      /* Copy to working storage   */

   /* Reverse the number stored in temp */
   do
   {
     rebmun = 10*rebmun + temp % 10;   /* Add the rightmost digit     */
     temp = temp/10;                   /* Remove the rightmost digit */
   } while (temp);                     /* Continue while temp>0       */

   printf ("\nThe number %d reversed is  %d rebmun ehT\n",
                                     number, rebmun );
}
```

The following is a sample of the output from this program:

```
Enter a positive integer: 43

The number 43 reversed is 34 rebmun ehT
```

HOW IT WORKS

The best way to explain what's going on here is to take you through a small example. Assume that the user entered the number **43**.

(Continued)

After reading the input integer and storing it in the variable number, the program copies the value in number to the variable temp:

```
temp = number;                      /* Copy to working storage  */
```

This is necessary, because the process of reversing the digits destroys the original value, and you want to output the original integer along with the reversed version.

The reversal of the digits is done in the do-while loop:

```
do
{
  rebmun = 10*rebmun + temp % 10;   /* Add the rightmost digit    */
  temp = temp/10;                   /* Remove the rightmost digit */
} while (temp);                     /* Continue while temp>0      */
```

The do-while loop is most appropriate here because any number will have at least one digit. You get the rightmost digit from the value stored in temp by using the modulus operator, %, to get the remainder after dividing by 10. Because temp originally contains 43, temp%10 will be 3. You assign the value of 10*rebmun + temp%10 to rebmun. Initially, the value of the variable rebmun is 0, so on the first iteration 3 is stored in rebmun.

You've now stored the rightmost digit of your input in rebmun, and so you now remove it from temp by dividing temp by 10. Because temp contained 43, temp/10 will be rounded down to 4.

At the end of the loop, the while(temp) condition is checked, and because temp contains the value 4, it is true. Therefore, you go back to the top of the loop to begin another iteration.

NOTE *Remember, any nonzero integer is true. False is represented by zero.*

This time, the value stored in rebmun will be 10 times rebmun, which is 30, plus the remainder when temp is divided by 10, which is 4, so the result is that rebmun becomes 34. You again divide temp by 10, so it will contain 0. Now when you arrive at the end of the loop iteration, temp is 0, which is false, so the loop finishes and you've reversed the number. You can see how this would work with numbers with more digits. An example of the output from the program running with a longer number entered is as follows:

```
Enter a positive integer: 1234

The number 1234 reversed is 4321 rebmun ehT
```

(Continued)

This form of loop is used relatively rarely, compared with the other two forms. Keep it in the back of your mind, though: when you need a loop that always executes at least once, the do-while loop delivers the goods.

....

The continue Statement

Sometimes a situation will arise in which you don't want to end a loop, but you want to skip the current iteration and continue with the next. The continue statement in the body of a loop does this and is written simply as follows:

```
continue;
```

Of course, continue is a keyword, so you must not use it for other purposes. Here's an example of how the continue statement works:

```
int day = 0;
for(day = 1; day<=7 ; ++day)
{
  if(day == 3)
    continue;
  /* Do something useful with day */
}
```

This loop will execute with values of day from 1 to 7. When day has the value 3, however, the continue statement will execute, and the rest of the current iteration is skipped and the loop continues with the next iteration when day will be 4.

You'll see more examples of using continue later in the book.

Designing a Program

It's time to try your skills on a bigger programming problem and to apply some of what you've learned in this chapter and the previous chapters. You'll also see a few new standard library functions that you're sure to find useful.

The Problem

The problem that you're going to solve is to write a game of Simple Simon. Simple Simon is a memory-test game. The computer displays a sequence of digits on the screen for a short period of time. The player then has to memorize them, and when the digits disappear from the screen, the player must enter exactly the same sequence of digits. Each time the player succeeds, he can repeat the process to get a longer list of digits to try. The objective is to continue the process for as long as possible.

The Analysis

The program must generate a sequence of integers between 0 and 9, and display the sequence on the screen for 1 second before erasing it. The player then has to try to enter the identical sequence of digits. The sequences gradually get longer until the player gets a sequence wrong. A score is then calculated based on the number of successful tries and the time taken, and the player is asked if he would like to play again.

The logic of the program is quite straightforward. You could express it in general terms in the flowchart shown in Figure 4-7.

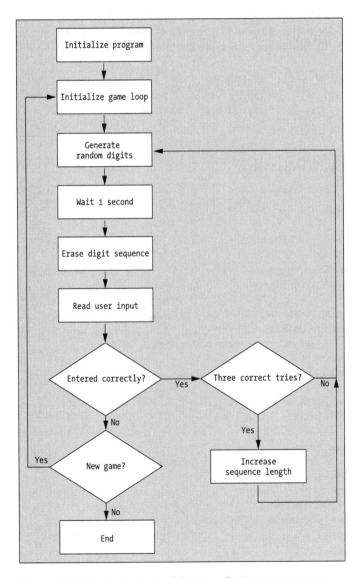

Figure 4-7. The basic logic of the Simple Simon program

Each box describes an action in the program, and the diamond shapes represent decisions. Let's use the flowchart as the basis for coding the program.

The Solution

This section outlines the steps you'll take to solve the problem.

Step 1

You can start by putting in the main loop for a game. The player will always want to have at least one game, so the loop check should go at the end of the loop. The do-while loop fits the bill very nicely. The initial program code will be this:

```
/* Program 4.12 Simple Simon */
#include <stdio.h>                      /* For input and output   */
#include <ctype.h>                      /* For toupper() function */

void main()
{
    /* Records if another game is to be played */
    char another_game = 'Y';

    /* Rest of the declarations for the program */

    /* Describe how the game is played */
    printf("\nTo play Simple Simon, ");
    printf("watch the screen for a sequence of digits.");
    printf("\nWatch carefully, as the digits are only displayed"
                                          " for a second! ");
    printf("\nThe computer will remove them, and then prompt you ");
    printf("to enter the same sequence.");
    printf("\nWhen you do, you must put spaces between the digits. \n");
    printf("\nGood Luck!\nPress Enter to play\n");
    scanf("%c", &another_game);

    /* One outer loop iteration is one game */
    do
    {
        /* Code to play the game */

        /* Output the score when the game is finished */

        /* Check if a new game is required */
        printf("\nDo you want to play again (y/n)? ");
        scanf("%c", &another_game);
    }while(toupper(another_game) == 'Y');
}
```

As long as the player enters **y** or **Y** at the end of a game, she will be able to play again. Note how you can automatically concatenate two strings in the `printf()` statement:

```
printf("\nWatch carefully, as the digits are only displayed"
                                    " for a second! ");
```

This is a convenient way of splitting a long string over two or more lines. You just put each piece of the string between its own pair of double-quote characters and the compiler will take care of assembling them into a single string.

Step 2

Next, you can add a declaration for another variable, called `correct`, that you'll need in the program to record whether or not the entry from the player is correct. You can make this of type `int`, but define the symbols TRUE and FALSE by using #define pre-processor directives, and then use these to set the value of `correct`. You'll use this variable to control the loop that plays a single game.

```
/* Program 4.12 Simple Simon */
#include <stdio.h>              /* For input and output    */
#include <ctype.h>             /* For toupper() function */

#define TRUE  1                 /* Defines the symbol TRUE  */
#define FALSE 0                 /* Defines the symbol FALSE */

void main()
{
   /* Records if another game is to be played */
   char another_game = 'Y';

   /* TRUE if correct sequence entered, FALSE otherwise */
   int correct = TRUE;

   /* Rest of the declarations for the program */

   /* Describe how the game is played */
   printf("\nTo play Simple Simon, ");
   printf("watch the screen for a sequence of digits.");
   printf("\nWatch carefully, as the digits are only displayed"
                                       " for a second! ");
   printf("\nThe computer will remove them, and then prompt you ");
   printf("to enter the same sequence.");
   printf("\nWhen you do, you must put spaces between the digits. \n");
   printf("\nGood Luck!\nPress Enter to play\n");
   scanf("%c", &another_game);

   /* One outer loop iteration is one game */
   do
```

```
{
   correct = TRUE;          /* By default indicates correct sequence entered  */

   /* Other code to initialize the game */

   /* Inner loop continues as long as sequences are entered correctly */
   while(correct)
   {
     /* Play the game */
   }

   /* Output the score when the game is finished */

   /* Check if new game required*/
   printf("\nDo you want to play again (y/n)? ");
   scanf("%c", &another_game);
}while(toupper(another_game) == 'Y');
}
```

Defining symbols for TRUE and FALSE as you've done here is a very useful mechanism for making a program more readable. Instead of using 1 and 0 in the program for values of correct, you have TRUE or FALSE, which makes it quite clear that you're treating correct as a logical variable. Defining symbols in this way is also useful when you want to change a value in a program that's used many times. By defining a symbol for the value at the beginning of the program using a #define directive, you make it possible to change the value throughout the program just by modifying the #define directive.

 CAUTION *The code will compile as it is, and you should compile it to check it out, but you shouldn't run it yet! As you develop your own programs, you'll want to make sure that the code will at least compile along each step of the way. If you write all the program code in one attempt, then you could end up with hundreds of errors to correct, and as you correct one problem, more may appear. This can be very frustrating. By checking out the program incrementally, you can minimize this issue, and the problems will be easier to manage. This brings us back to the current program. If you run this program, then your computer will be completely taken over by the program because it contains an indefinite loop. The reason for this is the inner* while *loop. The condition for this loop is always true because the loop doesn't do anything to change the value of* correct. *However, you'll be adding that bit of the program shortly.*

Step 3

Now you have a slightly more difficult task to do: you need to generate the sequence of random digits. There are two problems to be tackled here. The first is to generate the sequence of random digits. The second is to check the player's input against the computer-generated sequence.

The main difficulty with generating the sequence of digits is that the numbers have to be random. You've already seen that you have a standard function, rand(), available that returns a random integer each time you call it. You can get a random digit by just getting the remainder after dividing by 10, by using the % operator.

To ensure that you get a different sequence each time the program is executed, you'll also need to call srand() to initialize the sequence with the value returned by the time() function in the way you've already seen. Both the rand() and srand() functions require that you include the stdlib.h header file into the program, and the time() function requires an #include directive for time.h.

Now let's think about this a bit more. You'll need the sequence of random digits twice: once to display it initially before you erase it and the second time to check against the player's input. You could consider saving the sequence of digits as an integer value of type unsigned long. The problem with this is that the sequence could get very long if the player is good, and it could exceed the upper limit for integer values of type unsigned long. There is another possible approach. The rand() function can produce the same sequence of numbers twice. All you need to do is to start the sequence each time with the same seed by calling srand(). This means that you won't need to store the sequence of numbers. You can just generate the same sequence twice.

Now let's add some more code to the program that will generate the sequence of random digits and check them against what the player enters:

```
/* Program 4.12 Simple Simon */
#include <stdio.h>              /* For input and output    */
#include <ctype.h>             /* For toupper() function */
#include <stdlib.h>            /* For rand() and srand() functions */
#include <time.h>              /* For time() function     */

#define TRUE  1                /* Defines the symbol TRUE  */
#define FALSE 0                /* Defines the symbol FALSE */

void main()
{
  /* Records if another game is to be played */
  char another_game = 'Y';

  /* TRUE if correct sequence entered, FALSE otherwise */
  int correct = TRUE;

  /* Number of sequences entered successfully */
  int counter = 0;

  int sequence_length = 0;   /* Number of digits in a sequence     */
  int i = 0;                 /* Loop counter                       */
  long seed = 0;             /* Seed value for random number sequence */
  int number = 0;            /* Stores an input digit              */

  /* Rest of the declarations for the program */

  /* Describe how the game is played */
```

```
printf("\nTo play Simple Simon, ");
printf("watch the screen for a sequence of digits.");
printf("\nWatch carefully, as the digits are only displayed"
                                      " for a second! ");
printf("\nThe computer will remove them, and then prompt you ");
printf("to enter the same sequence.");
printf("\nWhen you do, you must put spaces between the digits. \n");
printf("\nGood Luck!\nPress Enter to play\n");
scanf("%c", &another_game);

/* One outer loop iteration is one game */
do
{
  correct = TRUE;        /* By default indicates correct sequence entered  */
  counter = 0;           /* Initialize count of number of successful tries */
  sequence_length = 2;   /* Initial length of a digit sequence             */

  /* Other code to initialize the game */

  /* Inner loop continues as long as sequences are entered correctly */
  while(correct)
  {
    /* On every third successful try, increase the sequence length */
    sequence_length += counter++%3 == 0;

    /* Set seed to be the number of seconds since Jan 1, 1970      */
    seed = time(NULL);

    /* Generate a sequence of numbers and display the number       */
    srand((int)seed);               /* Initialize the random sequence */
    for(i = 1; i <= sequence_length; i++)
      printf("%d ", rand() % 10); /* Output a random digit */

    /* Wait one second */

    /* Now overwrite the digit sequence */

    /* Prompt for the input sequence */

    /* Check the input sequence of digits against the original  */
    srand((int)seed);               /* Restart the random sequence  */
    for(i = 1; i <= sequence_length; i++)
    {
      scanf("%d", &number);           /* Read an input number        */
      if(number != rand() % 10)     /* Compare against random digit */
      {
        correct = FALSE;            /* Incorrect entry             */
        break;                      /* No need to check further... */
      }
    }
    printf("%s\n", correct? "Correct!" : "Wrong!");
```

```
    }

    /* Output the score when the game is finished */

    /* Check if new game required*/
    printf("\nDo you want to play again (y/n)? ");
    scanf("%c", &another_game);
  }while(toupper(another_game) == 'Y');
}
```

You've declared five new variables that you need to implement the while loop that will continue to execute as long as the player is successful. Each iteration of this loop displays a sequence that the player must repeat. The variable counter records the number of times that the player is successful, and sequence_length records the current length of a sequence of digits. Although you initialize these variables when you declare them, you must also initialize their values in the do-while loop to ensure that the initial conditions are set for every game. The variable i is used as a control variable. You also declare a variable, seed, of type long, that you'll pass as an argument to srand() to initialize the random number sequence returned by the function rand(). The value for seed is obtained in the while loop by calling the standard library function time().

At the beginning of the while loop, you can see that you increase the value stored in sequence_length by adding the value of the expression counter++%3 == 0 to it. This expression will be 1 when the value of counter is a multiple of 3, and 0 otherwise. This will increment the sequence length by 1 after every third successful try. The expression also increments the value in counter by 1 after the expression has been evaluated.

There are some other things to notice about the code. The first is the conversion of seed from type long to type int when you pass it to the srand() function. This is because srand() requires that you use type int, but you have the value returned from time() stored as type long. Because the number of seconds since January 1, 1970, is in excess of 800,000,000, you need a 4-byte variable to store it. By casting it to type int, you're using the low-order 2 bytes of the number, but this should still give you a unique seed for each game. Second, you obtain a digit between 0 and 9 by taking the reminder when you divide the random integer returned by rand() by 10. This isn't the best way of obtaining random digits in the range 0 to 9, but it's a very easy way.

The sequence of digits is displayed by the for loop. The loop just outputs the low-order decimal digit of the value returned by rand(). You then have some comments indicating the other code that you still have to add that will delay the program for 1 second and then erase the sequence from the screen. This is followed by the code to check the sequence that was entered by the player. This reinitializes the random number–generating process by calling srand() with the same seed value that was used at the outset. Each digit entered is compared with the low-order digit of the value returned by the function rand(). If there's a discrepancy, correct is set to FALSE so the while loop will end.

Of course, if you try to run this code as it is, the sequence won't be erased, so it isn't usable yet. The next step is to add the code to complete the while loop.

Step 4

You must now erase the sequence after a delay of 1 second. How can you get the program to wait? One way is to use another standard library function. The library function clock() returns the time since the program started, in units of clock ticks. The header file time.h defines a symbol CLOCKS_PER_SEC that's the number of clock ticks in 1 second. All you have to do is wait until the value returned by the function clock() has increased by CLOCKS_PER_SEC, whereupon 1 second will have passed. You can do this by storing the value returned by the function clock() and then checking, in a loop, when the value returned by clock() is CLOCKS_PER_SEC more than the value that you saved. With a variable now to store the current time, the code for the loop would be as follows:

```
for( ;clock() - now < CLOCKS_PER_SEC; );          /* Wait one second */
```

You also need to decide how you can erase the sequence of computer-generated digits. This is actually quite easy. You can move to the beginning of the line by outputting the escape character '\r', which is a carriage return. All you then need to do is output a sufficient number of spaces to overwrite the sequence of digits. Let's fill out the code you need in the while loop:

```
/* Program 4.12 Simple Simon */
#include <stdio.h>                 /* For input and output   */
#include <ctype.h>                 /* For toupper() function */
#include <stdlib.h>                /* For rand() and srand() functions */
#include <time.h>                  /* For time() and clock() functions */

#define TRUE  1                    /* Defines the symbol TRUE  */
#define FALSE 0                    /* Defines the symbol False */

void main()
{
   /* Records if another game is to be played */
   char another_game = 'Y';

   /* TRUE if correct sequence entered, FALSE otherwise */
   int correct = TRUE;

   /* Number of sequences entered successfully        */
   int counter = 0;

   int sequence_length = 0;    /* Number of digits in a sequence       */
   int i = 0;                  /* Loop counter                         */
   long seed = 0;              /* Seed value for random number sequence */
   int number = 0;             /* Stores an input digit                */

   /* Stores current time - seed for random values */
   long now = 0;
   /* Rest of the declarations for the program */
```

```
/* Describe how the game is played */
printf("\nTo play Simple Simon, ");
printf("watch the screen for a sequence of digits.");
printf("\nWatch carefully, as the digits are only displayed"
                                      " for a second! ");
printf("\nThe computer will remove them, and then prompt you ");
printf("to enter the same sequence.");
printf("\nWhen you do, you must put spaces between the digits. \n");
printf("\nGood Luck!\nPress Enter to play\n");
scanf("%c", &another_game);

/* One outer loop iteration is one game */
do
{
  correct = TRUE;        /* By default indicates correct sequence entered   */
  counter = 0;           /* Initialize count of number of successful tries  */
  sequence_length = 2;   /* Initial length of a digit sequence              */

  /* Other code to initialize the game */

  /* Inner loop continues as long as sequences are entered correctly */
  while(correct)
  {
    /* On every third successful try, increase the sequence length */
    sequence_length += counter++%3 == 0;

    /* Set seed to be the number of seconds since Jan 1, 1970    */
    seed = time(NULL);

    now = clock();                    /* record start time for sequence  */

    /* Generate a sequence of numbers and display the number */
    srand((int)seed);                 /* Initialize the random sequence  */
    for(i = 1; i <= sequence_length; i++)
      printf("%d ", rand() % 10);    /* Output a random digit           */

    /* Wait one second */
    for( ;clock() - now < CLOCKS_PER_SEC; );

    /* Now overwrite the digit sequence */
    printf("\r");                     /* go to beginning of the line     */
    for(i = 1; i <= sequence_length; i++)
      printf("  ");                   /* Output two spaces               */

    if(counter == 1)         /* Only output message for the first try */
      printf("\nNow you enter the sequence  - don't forget"
                                      " the spaces\n");
    else
      printf("\r");                   /* Back to the beginning of the line   */

    /* Check the input sequence of digits against the original  */
```

```
        srand((int)seed);                     /* Restart the random sequence   */
        for(i = 1; i <= sequence_length; i++)
        {
          scanf("%d", &number);               /* Read an input number          */
          if(number != rand() % 10)           /* Compare against random digit */
          {
            correct = FALSE;                  /* Incorrect entry               */
            break;                            /* No need to check further...   */
          }
        }
        printf("%s\n", correct? "Correct!" : "Wrong!");
      }

      /* Output the score when the game is finished */

      /* Check if new game required*/
      printf("\nDo you want to play again (y/n)? ");
      scanf("%c", &another_game);
    }while(toupper(another_game) == 'Y');
}
```

You record the time returned by clock() before you output the sequence. The for loop that's executed when the sequence has been displayed continues until the value returned by clock() exceeds the time recorded in now by CLOCKS_PER_SEC, which of course will be 1 second.

Because you haven't written a newline character to the screen at any point when you displayed the sequence, you're still on the same line when you complete the output of the sequence. You can move the cursor back to the start of the line by executing a carriage return without a linefeed, and outputting '\r' does just that. You then output two spaces for each digit that was displayed, thus overwriting each of them with blanks. Immediately following that, you have a prompt for the player to enter the sequence that was displayed. You output this message only the first time around; otherwise, it gets rather tedious. On the second and subsequent tries, you just back up to the beginning of the now blank line, ready for the user's input.

Step 5

All that remains is to generate a score to display, once the player has gotten a sequence wrong. You'll use the number of sequences completed, and how many seconds it took to complete them, to calculate this score. You can arbitrarily assign 100 points to each digit correctly entered and divide this by the number of seconds taken for the game. This means that the faster the player is, the higher the score, and the more sequences the player enters correctly, the higher the score.

Actually, there's also one more problem with this program that you need to address. If one of the numbers typed by the player is wrong, then the loop exits and the player is asked if she wants to play again. However, if the digit in error isn't the last digit, then you could end up with the next digit entered as the answer to the question "Do you want to play again (y/n)?" because these digits will still be in the keyboard buffer. What you need to do is remove any information that's still in the keyboard buffer. So there are two problems: first, how to address the keyboard buffer, and second, how to clean out the buffer.

 NOTE *The **keyboard buffer** is memory that's used to store input from the keyboard. The* scanf() *function looks in the keyboard buffer for input rather than getting it directly from the keyboard itself.*

With standard input and output—that is, from the keyboard and to the screen—there are actually two buffers: one for input called stdin and one for output called stdout. Now that you know what the buffer is called, how do you remove the information in it? Well, there's a standard library function for clearing out buffers. Although this function tends to be used for files, which I'll cover later in the book, it will actually work for any buffer at all. You simply tell the function which buffer you mean. The function you need is fflush(). So to clean out the contents of the input buffer, you simply use this statement:

```
fflush(stdin);                    /* Flush the stdin buffer */
```

Here's the complete program, which includes calculating the scores and flushing the input buffer:

```
/* Program 4.12 Simple Simon */
#include <stdio.h>                /* For input and output        */
#include <ctype.h>               /* For toupper() function */
#include <stdlib.h>              /* For rand() and srand() functions */
#include <time.h>                /* For time() and clock() functions */

#define TRUE  1                  /* Defines the symbol TRUE     */
#define FALSE 0                  /* Defines the symbol False    */

void main()
{
   /* Records if another game is to be played */
   char another_game = 'Y';

   /* TRUE if correct sequence entered, FALSE otherwise */
   int correct = FALSE;

   /* Number of sequences entered successfully        */
   int counter = 0;

   int sequence_length = 0;   /* Number of digits in a sequence    */
   int i = 0;                 /* Loop counter                      */
   long seed = 0;             /* Seed value for random number sequence */
   int number = 0;            /* Stores an input digit             */
```

```
long now = 0;              /* Stores current time - seed for random values  */
long time_taken = 0;       /* Time taken for game in seconds                 */

/* Describe how the game is played */
printf("\nTo play Simple Simon, ");
printf("watch the screen for a sequence of digits.");
printf("\nWatch carefully, as the digits are only displayed"
                                            " for a second! ");
printf("\nThe computer will remove them, and then prompt you ");
printf("to enter the same sequence.");
printf("\nWhen you do, you must put spaces between the digits. \n");
printf("\nGood Luck!\nPress Enter to play\n");
scanf("%c", &another_game);

/* One outer loop iteration is one game */
do
{
  correct = TRUE;          /* By default indicates correct sequence entered */
  counter = 0;             /* Initialize count of number of successful tries*/
  sequence_length = 2;     /* Initial length of a digit sequence            */
  time_taken = clock();    /* Record current time at start of game          */

  /* Inner loop continues as long as sequences are entered correctly */
  while(correct)
  {
    /* On every third successful try, increase the sequence length */
    sequence_length += counter++%3 == 0;

    /* Set seed to be the number of seconds since Jan 1, 1970  */
    seed = time(NULL);

    now = clock();                  /* record start time for sequence  */

    /* Generate a sequence of numbers and display the number */
    srand((int)seed);               /* Initialize the random sequence */
    for(i = 1; i <= sequence_length; i++)
      printf("%d ", rand() % 10);   /* Output a random digit          */

    /* Wait one second */
    for( ;clock() - now < CLOCKS_PER_SEC; );

    /* Now overwrite the digit sequence */
    printf("\r");                   /* go to beginning of the line */
    for(i = 1; i <= sequence_length; i++)
      printf("  ");                 /* Output two spaces */

    if(counter == 1)          /* Only output message for the first try */
      printf("\nNow you enter the sequence  - don't forget"
                                     " the spaces\n");
    else
      printf("\r");                 /* Back to the beginning of the line */
```

```
      /* Check the input sequence of digits against the original */
      srand((int)seed);                /* Restart the random sequence    */
      for(i = 1; i <= sequence_length; i++)
      {
        scanf("%d", &number);          /* Read an input number           */
        if(number != rand() % 10)      /* Compare against random digit   */
        {
          correct = FALSE;             /* Incorrect entry                */
          break;                       /* No need to check further...     */
        }
      }
      printf("%s\n", correct? "Correct!" : "Wrong!");
    }

    /* Calculate total time to play the game in seconds)*/
    time_taken = (clock() - time_taken) / CLOCKS_PER_SEC;

    /* Output the game score */
    printf("\n\n Your score is %d", --counter * 100 / time_taken);

    fflush(stdin);

    /* Check if new game required*/
    printf("\nDo you want to play again (y/n)? ");
    scanf("%c", &another_game);

  }while(toupper(another_game) == 'Y');
}
```

The declaration required for the function fflush() is in the header file stdio.h for which you already have an #include directive. Now you just need to see what happens when you actually play:

```
To play Simple Simon, watch the screen for a sequence of digits.
Watch carefully, as the digits are only displayed for a second!
The computer will remove them, and then prompt you to enter the same sequence.
When you do, you must put spaces between the digits.

Good Luck!
Press Enter to play


Now you enter the sequence  - don't forget the spaces
2 1 4
Correct!
8 7 1
Correct!
4 1 6
Correct!
```

```
7 9 6 6
Correct!
7 5 4 6
Wrong!


Your score is 16
Do you want to play again (y/n)? n
```

Summary

In this chapter you learned all you need to know about repeating actions using loops. With the powerful set of programming tools you've learned up to now, you should be able to create quite complex programs of your own.

In keeping with this chapter's topic, I'll now repeat myself and reiterate some of the rules and recommendations I've presented so far:

- Before you start programming, work out the logic of the process and computations you want to perform, and write it down—preferably in the form of a flowchart. Try to think of lateral approaches to a problem—there may be a better way than the obvious approach.

- Use parentheses to ensure expressions do what you want and are readily understood.

- Comment your programs to explain all aspects of their operation and use. Assume the comments are for the benefit of someone else reading your program with a view to extend or modify it. Explain the purpose of each variable as you declare it.

- Program with readability foremost in your mind. Go for the simple, easy-to-understand programming style, rather than the flashy, convoluted, and opaque use of the language facilities.

- In complicated logical expressions, avoid using the operator !.

- Use indentation to visually indicate the structure of your program.

Prepared with this advice, you can now move on to the next chapter—after you've completed all the exercises, of course!

Exercises

The following exercises enable you to try out what you've learned in this chapter. If you get stuck, look back over the chapter for help. If you're still stuck, you can download the solutions from the Downloads area of the Apress website (http://www.apress.com), but that really should be a last resort.

Exercise 4-1. Write a program that will generate a multiplication table of a size entered by the user. A table of size 4, for instance, would have four rows and four columns. The rows and columns would be labeled from 1 to 4. Each cell in the table contains the product of the corresponding row and column numbers, so the value in the position corresponding to the third row and the fourth column would contain 12.

Exercise 4-2. Write a program that will output the printable characters for character code values from 0 to 127. Output each character code along with its symbol with two characters to a line. Make sure the columns are aligned. (Hint: You can use the isgraph() function that's declared in ctype.h to determine when a character is printable.)

Exercise 4-3. Extend the previous program to output the appropriate name, such as "newline," "space," "tab," and so on, for each whitespace character.

Exercise 4-4. Use nested loops to output a box bounded by asterisks as in Program 4.2, but with a width and height that's entered by the user. For example, a box ten characters wide and seven characters high would display as follows:

```
*********
*       *
*       *
*       *
*       *
*       *
*********
```

Exercise 4-5. Modify the guessing game implemented in Program 4.7 so that the program will continue with an option to play another game when the player fails to guess the number correctly and will allow as many games as the player requires.

CHAPTER 5

Arrays

YOU'LL OFTEN NEED TO STORE MANY DATA values of a particular kind in your programs. For example, if you were writing a program to track the performance of a basketball team, then you might want to store the scores for a season of games and the scores for individual players. You could then output the scores for a particular player over the season or work out an ongoing average as the season progressed. Armed with what you've learned so far, you could write a program that does this using a different variable for each score. However, if there are a lot of games in the season, this will be rather tedious because you'll need as many variables for each player as there are games. All your basketball scores are really the same kind of thing. The values are different, but they're all basketball scores. Ideally, you would want to group these values together under a single name—perhaps the name of the player—so that you wouldn't have to define separate variables for each item of data.

In this chapter I'll show you how to do just that using arrays in C. I'll then show you how powerful this can be when you write programs that process arrays.

In this chapter you'll learn

- What arrays are

- How to use arrays in your programs

- How memory is used by an array

- What a multidimensional array is

- How to write a program to work out your hat size

- How to write a game of tic-tac-toe

An Introduction to Arrays

The best way to show you what an array is and how powerful it can be is to go through an example in which you can see how much easier a program becomes when you use an array. For this example, you'll look at ways in which you can find the average score of the students in a class.

Programming Without Arrays

To find the average score of a class of students, assume that there are only ten students in the class (mainly to avoid having to type in a lot of numbers). To work out the average of a set of numbers, you add them all together and then divide by how many you have (in this case, by 10):

```
/* Program 5.1 Averaging ten numbers without storing the numbers */
#include <stdio.h>

void main()
{
    int number = 0;                    /* Stores a number            */
    int count = 10;                    /* Number of values to be read */
    long sum = 0L;                     /* Sum of the numbers         */
    float average = 0.0f;              /* Average of the numbers     */
    int i = 0;                         /* Loop counter               */

    /* Read the ten numbers to be averaged */
    for(i = 0; i < count; i ++)
    {
      printf("Enter grade: ");
      scanf("%d", &number);            /* Read a number */
      sum += number;                   /* Add it to sum */
    }

    average = (float)sum/count;        /* Calculate the average */

    printf("\nAverage of the ten numbers entered is: %f\n", average);
}
```

If you're interested only in the average, then you don't have to remember what the previous grades were. All you're interested in is the sum of them all, which you then divide by count, which has the value 10. This simple program uses a single variable, number, to store each grade as it's entered within the loop. The loop repeats for values of i of 1, 2, 3, and so on up to 9, so there are ten iterations. You've done this sort of thing before, so the program should be clear.

But let's assume that you want to develop this into a longer program in which you'll need the values you enter later. Perhaps you want to print out each person's grade, with the average grade next to it. In the previous program, you had only one variable. Each time you add a grade, the old value is overwritten, and you can't get it back.

So how do you store the results? You could do this by declaring ten integers to store the grades in, but then you can't use a for loop to enter the values. Instead, you have to include code that will read the values individually. This would work, but it's quite tiresome:

```
/* Program 5.2 Averaging ten numbers - storing the numbers the hard way */
#include <stdio.h>

void main()
{
    int number0 = 0, number1 = 0, number2 = 0, number3 = 0, number4 = 0;
```

```
    int number5 = 0, number6 = 0, number7 = 0, number8 = 0, number9 = 0;

    long sum = 0L;          /* Sum of the numbers     */
    float average = 0.0f;   /* Average of the numbers */

    /* Read the ten numbers to be averaged */
    printf("Enter the first five numbers,\n");
    printf("use a space or press Enter between each number.\n");
    scanf("%d%d%d%d%d", &number0, &number1, &number2, &number3, &number4);
    printf("Enter the last five numbers,\n");
    printf("use a space or press Enter between each number.\n");
    scanf("%d%d%d%d%d", &number5, &number6, &number7, &number8, &number9);

    /* Now we have the ten numbers, we can calculate the average */
    sum = number0 + number1+ number2 + number3 + number4+
            number5 + number6 + number7 + number8 + number9;
    average = (float)sum/10.0f;

    printf("\nAverage of the ten numbers entered is: %f\n", average);
}
```

This is OK for ten students, but what if your class has 30 students, or 100, or 1,000? How can you do it then? Well, this is when this approach becomes wholly impractical and arrays become essential.

What Is an Array?

An **array** is a collection of data items, referred to as **elements**, that are all of the same type. This is an important feature of an array—the elements of each array are all of type int, or of type long, or of type whatever. So you can have arrays of elements of type int, arrays of elements of type float, arrays of elements of type long, and so on. To declare an array in which you can store ten items of data of type long, you would write the following:

```
long numbers[10];
```

This is very similar to how you would declare a normal variable that contains a single value, except that you've placed a number between square brackets [ ] following the name. This defines how many elements you want to store in your array and is called the array **dimension**. The important feature here is that each of the data items stored in the array is accessed by the same name—in this case, numbers.

If you have only one variable name but are storing ten values, how do you differentiate between them? Each individual value in the array is identified by what is called an **index value**. An index value is an integer that's written after the array name between square brackets [ ]. Each element in an array has a different index value, and index values are sequential integers starting from 0. The index values for the elements in the preceding numbers array would run from 0 to 9. The index value 0 refers to the first element and the index value 9 refers to the last element. To access a particular element, you just write the appropriate index value between square brackets immediately following the array name. Therefore, the array elements would be referred to as numbers[0], numbers[1], numbers[2], and so on up to numbers[9]. You can see this in Figure 5-1.

Figure 5-1. Accessing the elements of an array

Don't forget, index values start from 0, not 1. It's a common mistake to assume that they start from 1 when you're working with arrays for the first time. In a ten-element array, the index value for the last element is 9. To access the fourth value in your array, you use the expression numbers[3]. You can think of the index value for an array element as the offset from the first element. The first element is the first element, so it has an offset of 0. The second element has an offset of 1 from the first element, the third element has an offset of 2 from the first element, and so on.

To access the value of an element in the numbers array, you could also place an expression in the square brackets following the array name. The expression would have to result in an integer value that corresponded to one of the possible index values. For example, you could write numbers[i-2]. If i had the value 3, this would access numbers[1], the second element in the array. Thus, there are two ways to specify an index to access a particular element of an array. You can use a simple integer to explicitly reference the element that you want to access. Alternatively, you can use an integer expression that's evaluated during the execution of the program.

Note that if you use an index value in your program that's outside the legal range for an array, the program won't work properly. The compiler can't check for this, so your program will still compile perfectly well, but execution is likely to be less than satisfactory. At best you'll just pick up a junk value from somewhere so that the results are incorrect and may vary from one run to the next. At worst the program may overwrite something important and lock up your computer so a reboot becomes necessary.

Using Arrays

That's a lot of theory, but you still need to solve your average score problem. Let's put what you've just learned about arrays into practice in that context.

Try It Out: Averages with Arrays

Now that you understand arrays, you can use an array to store all the scores you want to average. This means that all the values will be saved, and you'll be able to reuse them. You can now rewrite the program to average ten scores:

```
/* Program 5.3 Averaging ten numbers - storing the numbers the easy way */
#include <stdio.h>

void main()
{
    int numbers[10];                /* Array storing 10 values     */
    int count = 10;                 /* Number of values to be read */
    long sum = 0L;                  /* Sum of the numbers          */
    float average = 0.0f;           /* Average of the numbers      */
    int i = 0;                      /* Loop counter                */

    printf("\nEnter the 10 numbers:\n");        /* Prompt for the input */

    /* Read the ten numbers to be averaged */
    for(i = 0; i < count; i ++)
    {
      printf("%2d> ",i+1);
      scanf("%d", &numbers[i]);      /* Read a number */
      sum += numbers[i];             /* Add it to sum */
    }

    average = (float)sum/count;       /* Calculate the average */

    printf("\nAverage of the ten numbers entered is: %f\n", average);
}
```

The output from the program looks something like this:

```
Enter the ten numbers:
 1> 450
 2> 765
 3> 562
 4> 700
 5> 598
 6> 635
 7> 501
 8> 720
 9> 689
10> 527

Average of the ten numbers entered is: 614.700000
```

(Continued)

HOW IT WORKS

You start off the program with the ubiquitous #include directive for stdio.h because you want to use printf() and scanf(). At the beginning of main(), you declare an array of ten integers and then the other variables that you'll need for calculation:

```
int numbers[10];            /* Array storing 10 values     */
int count = 10;             /* Number of values to be read */
long sum = 0L;              /* Sum of the numbers          */
float average = 0.0f;       /* Average of the numbers      */
int i = 0;                  /* Loop counter                */
```

You then prompt for the input to be entered with this statement:

```
printf("\nEnter the 10 numbers:\n");  /* Prompt for the input */
```

Next, you have a loop to read the values and accumulate the sum:

```
for(i = 0; i < count; i ++)
{
  printf("%2d> ",i+1);
  scanf("%d", &numbers[i]);         /* Read a number */
  sum += numbers[i];                /* Add it to sum */
}
```

Because the loop counts from 0 to 9, rather than from 1 to 10, you can use the loop variable i directly to reference each of the members of the array. The printf() call outputs the current value of i+1 followed by >, so it has the effect you see in the output. By using %2d as the format specifier, you ensure that each value is output in a two-character field, so the numbers are aligned. If you had used %d instead, the output for the tenth value would have been out of alignment.

You read each value entered into element i of the array using the scanf() function; the first value will be stored in number[0], the second number entered will be stored in number[1], and so on up to the tenth value entered, which will be stored in number[9]. For each iteration of the loop, the value that was read is added to sum.

When the loop ends, you calculate the average and display it with these statements:

```
average = (float)sum/count;       /* Calculate the average */

printf("\nAverage of the ten numbers entered is: %f\n", average);
```

(Continued)

You've calculated the average by dividing the sum by count, which has the value 10. Notice how, in the call to printf(), you've told the compiler to convert sum (which is declared as type long) into type float. This is to ensure that the division is done using floating-point values, so you don't discard any fractional part of the result.

....

....

Try It Out: Retrieving the Numbers Stored

This example, in itself, doesn't show how useful the array is, but you can expand it a little to demonstrate one of the advantages. I've made only a minor change to the original program (highlighted in the following code in bold), but now the program displays all the values that were typed in. Having the values stored in an array means that you can access those values whenever you want and process them in many different ways.

```c
/* Program 5.4 Reusing the numbers stored */
#include <stdio.h>

void main()
{
    int numbers[10];                /* Array storing 10 values      */
    int count = 10;                 /* Number of values to be read */
    long sum = 0L;                  /* Sum of the numbers           */
    float average = 0.0f;           /* Average of the numbers       */
    int i = 0;                      /* Loop counter                 */

    printf("\nEnter the 10 numbers:\n");        /* Prompt for the input */

    /* Read the ten numbers to be averaged */
    for(i = 0; i < count; i++)
    {
        printf("%2d> ",i+1);
        scanf("%d", &numbers[i]);   /* Read a number */
        sum += numbers[i];          /* Add it to sum */
    }

    average = (float)sum/count;     /* Calculate the average */

    for(i = 0; i < count; i++)
        printf("\nGrade Number %d was %d", i + 1, numbers[i]);

    printf("\nAverage of the ten numbers entered is: %f\n", average);
}
```

(Continued)

Typical output from this program is as follows:

```
Enter the ten numbers:
 1> 56
 2> 64
 3> 34
 4> 51
 5> 52
 6> 78
 7> 62
 8> 51
 9> 47
10> 32

Grade No 1 was 56
Grade No 2 was 64
Grade No 3 was 34
Grade No 4 was 51
Grade No 5 was 52
Grade No 6 was 78
Grade No 7 was 62
Grade No 8 was 51
Grade No 9 was 47
Grade No 10 was 32
Average of the ten numbers entered is: 52.700001
```

HOW IT WORKS

I'll just explain the new bit where you reuse the elements of the array in a loop:

```
for(i = 0; i < count; i++)
   printf("\nGrade Number %d was %d", i + 1, number[i]);
```

You simply add another for loop to step through the elements in the array and output each value. You use the loop control variable to produce the sequence number for the value of the number of the element and to access the corresponding array element. These values obviously correspond to the numbers you typed in. To get the grade numbers starting from 1, you use the expression i+1 in the output statement so you get grades numbers from 1 to 10 as i runs from 0 to 9.

Before you go any further with arrays, you need to look into how your variables are stored in the computer's memory. You also need to understand how an array is different from the variables you've seen up to now.

A Reminder About Memory

Let's quickly recap what you learned about memory in Chapter 2. You can think of the memory of your computer as an ordered line of boxes, as shown in Figure 5-2. Each box is in one of two states: either the box is full (let's call this state 1) or the box is empty (this is state 0). Each box holds one binary digit and is referred to as a **bit**.

Figure 5-2. Bytes in memory

For convenience, you group your boxes into sets of eight, which you call a **byte**. To identify each byte so that its contents may be accessed, the byte is labeled with a number starting from 0 for the first byte in memory and going up to whatever number of bytes there are in memory. This label for a byte is called its address.

You've already been using the **address of** operator, &, extensively with the scanf() function. You've been using this as a prefix to the variable name, because the function needs to store data that is entered from the keyboard into the variable. Just using the variable name by itself as an argument to a function makes the value stored in the variable available to the function. Prefixing the variable name with the address of operator and using that as the argument to the function makes the address of the variable available to the function. This enables the function to store information at this address and thus modify the value that's stored in the variable. The best way to get a feel for the address of operator is to use it a bit more, so let's do that.

Try It Out: Using the Address Of Operator

Each variable that you use in a program takes up a certain amount of memory, measured in bytes, and the exact amount of memory is dependent on the type of the variable. Let's try finding the address of some variables of different types with the following program:

```
/* Program 5.5 Using the & operator */
#include<stdio.h>

void main()
{
   /* declare some integer variables */
   long a = 1L;
   long b = 2L;
   long c = 3L;

   /* declare some floating-point variables */
   double d = 4.0;
   double e = 5.0;
   double f = 6.0;

   printf("A variable of type long occupies %d bytes.", sizeof(long));
   printf("\nHere are the addresses of some variables of type long:");
   printf("\nThe address of a is: %p   The address of b is: %p", &a, &b);
   printf("\nThe address of c is: %p", &c);
   printf("\n\nA variable of type double occupies %d bytes.", sizeof(double));
   printf("\nHere are the addresses of some variables of type double:");
   printf("\nThe address of d is: %p   The address of e is: %p", &d, &e);
   printf("\nThe address of f is: %p\n", &f);
}
```

Output from this program will be something like this:

```
A variable of type long occupies 4 bytes.
Here are the addresses of some variables of type long:
The address of a is: 0064FDF4   The address of b is: 0064FDF0
The address of c is: 0064FDEC

A variable of type double occupies 8 bytes.
Here are the addresses of some variables of type double:
The address of d is: 0064FDE4   The address of e is: 0064FDDC
The address of f is: 0064FDD4
```

(Continued)

The addresses that you get will almost certainly be different from these. What you get depends on the operating system you're using and the other programs running at the time.

HOW IT WORKS

You declare three variables of type `long` and three of type `double`:

```
/* declare some integer variables */
long a = 1L;
long b = 2L;
long c = 3L;

/* declare some floating-point variables */
double d = 4.0;
double e = 5.0;
double f = 6.0;
```

Next, you output the size of variables of type `long`, followed by the addresses of the three variables of that type that you created:

```
printf("A variable of type long occupies %d bytes.", sizeof(long));
printf("\nHere are the addresses of some variables of type long:");
printf("\nThe address of a is: %p  The Address of b is: %p", &a, &b);
printf("\nThe address of c is: %p", &c);
```

The address of operator is the & that precedes the name of each variable. You also use a new format specifier, %p, to output the address of the variables. This format specifier is for outputting a memory address, and the value is presented in hexadecimal format. A memory address on my computer is eight hexadecimal digits; on your machine it may be different.

You then output the size of variables of type `double`, followed by the addresses of the three variables of that type that you also created:

```
printf("\n\nA variable of type double occupies %d bytes.", sizeof(double));
printf("\nHere are the addresses of some variables of type double:");
printf("\nThe address of d is: %p  The address of e is: %p", &d, &e);
printf("\nThe address of f is: %p\n", &f);
```

In fact, the interesting part isn't the program itself so much as the output. Look at the addresses that have been displayed. You can see that the value of the address gets steadily lower, in a regular pattern, as shown in Figure 5-3. On my computer, the address of b is 4 lower than that of a, and c is lower than b also by 4. This is because each variable of type `long` occupies 4 bytes. There's a similar situation with the variables d, e, and f, except that the difference is 8. This is because 8 bytes are used to store a value of type `double`.

(Continued)

Figure 5-3. Addresses of variables in memory

 CAUTION *If the addresses for the variables are separated by greater amounts than the size value, this is most likely because you've compiled the program as a debug version. In debug mode your compiler may allocate extra space to store additional information about the variable that will be used when you're executing the program in debug mode.*

Arrays and Addresses

With arrays, the method of addressing individual elements is slightly different from a simple variable. Suppose you have an array called number with the capacity to store ten values:

```
long number[10];
```

The array name, number, identifies the address of the area of memory where your data is stored, and the specific location of each element is found by combining this with the index value, because the index value represents an offset from the beginning of the array.

When you declare an array, you give the compiler all the information it needs to allocate the memory for the array. You tell it the type of value, which will determine the number of bytes that each element will require, and how many elements there will be. The array name identifies where in memory the array begins. An index value specifies how many elements from the beginning you have to go to address the element you want. The address of an array element is going to be the address where the array starts, plus the index value for the element multiplied by the number of bytes required to store each element of the type stored in the array. Figure 5-4 represents the way that array variables are held in memory.

Figure 5-4. The organization of an array in memory

You can obtain the address of an array element in a similar fashion to ordinary variables. For an integer variable called value, you would use the following statement to print its address:

```
printf("\n%p", &value);
```

To output the address of the third element of an array called number, you could write the following:

```
printf("\n%p", &number[2]);
```

Remember that you use the value 2, in the brackets, to reach the third element. Here, you've obtained the address of the element with the address of operator. If you used the same statement without the &, you would display the actual value stored in the third element of the array, not its address.

Initializing an Array

Of course, you may want to assign initial values for the elements of your array, even if it's only for safety's sake. To do this, you just specify the list of initial values, between braces, and separated by commas in the declaration, for example:

```
double values[5] = { 1.5, 2.5, 3.5, 4.5, 5.5 };
```

This declares the array values with five elements. The elements are initialized with values[0] having the value 1.5, value[1] having the initial value 2.5, and so on.

To initialize the whole array, there should be one value for each element. If there are fewer initializing values than elements, the elements without initializing values will be set to 0. Thus, if you write

```
double values[5] = { 1.5, 2.5, 3.5 };
```

the first three elements will be initialized with the values between braces, and the last two elements will be initialized with 0.

If you put in more initializing values than there are array elements, you'll get an error message from the compiler.

Finding the Size of an Array

You've already seen that the sizeof operator computes the number of bytes that a variable of a given type occupies. You can apply the sizeof operator to a type name like this:

```
printf("\nThe size of a variable of type long is %d bytes.", sizeof(long));
```

The parentheses around the type name following the sizeof operator are required. If you leave them out, the code won't compile.

You can also apply the sizeof operator to a variable, and it will compute the number of bytes occupied by that variable. For example, suppose you declare the variable value with the following statement:

```
double value = 1.0;
```

You can now output the number of bytes occupied by value with this statement:

```
printf("\nThe size of value is %d bytes.", sizeof value);
```

Note that no parentheses around the operand for sizeof are necessary in this case, but you can include them if you wish. This statement will output the line

```
The size of value is 8 bytes.
```

This is because a variable of type double occupies 8 bytes in memory. Of course, you can store the size value you get from applying sizeof if you want:

```
int value_size = sizeof value;
```

The sizeof operator works with arrays too. You can declare an array with the statement

```
double values[5] = { 1.5, 2.5, 3.5, 4.5, 5.5 };
```

Now you can output the number of bytes that the array occupies with the statement

```
printf("\nThe size of the array, values, is %d bytes.", sizeof values);
```

This will produce the output

```
The size of the array, values, is 40 bytes.
```

You can also obtain the number of bytes occupied by a single element of the array with the expression `sizeof values[0]`. This expression will have the value 8. Of course, any legal index value for an element could be used to produce the same result. You can therefore use the `sizeof` operator to calculate the number of elements in an array:

```
int element_count = sizeof values/sizeof values[0];
```

After executing this statement, the variable `element_count` will contain the number of elements in the array `values`.

Because you can apply the `sizeof` operator to a data type, you could have written the previous statement to calculate the number of array elements as follows:

```
int element_count = sizeof values/sizeof(double);
```

This would produce the same result as before because the array is of type `double` and `sizeof(double)` would have produced the number of bytes occupied by a `double` value. Because there's a risk that you might accidentally use the wrong type, it's probably better to use the former statement in practice.

Although the `sizeof` operator doesn't require the use of parentheses when applied to a variable, it's common practice to use them anyway, so the earlier example could be written as follows:

```
int ElementCount = sizeof(values)/sizeof(values[0]);
```

Multidimensional Arrays

So far you've been dealing with arrays with one index value to reference an element. These are called **one-dimensional** arrays. You're not limited to just one index dimension for an array, though. You can declare arrays of two, three, or more dimensions to suit your application needs. If you grow carrots in a field in 25 rows of 50 plants, you could use a two-dimensional array to record how big each carrot turned out to be. If you have ten fields of carrots on your farm, you could use a three-dimensional array to record your carrot data. One dimension would identify the field, another dimension would identify a particular row in the field, and the third dimension would select a particular carrot in the row. Of course, if you have several farms . . . well, you get the idea.

Let's stick to two dimensions for the moment and work our way up. A two-dimensional array can be declared as follows:

```
float carrots[25][50];
```

This declares an array, `carrots`, containing 25 rows of 50 floating-point elements. Similarly, you can declare another two-dimensional array of floating-point numbers with this statement:

```
float numbers[3][5];
```

Like the vegetables in the field, you tend to visualize these arrays as rectangular arrangements because it's convenient to do so. They're actually stored in memory sequentially by row, as shown in Figure 5-5.

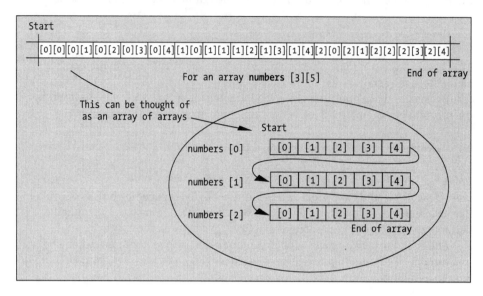

Figure 5-5. Organization of a 3×5 element array in memory

It's easy to see that the rightmost index varies most rapidly. Figure 5-5 also illustrates how you can envisage a two-dimensional array as a one-dimensional array of elements, in which each element is itself a one-dimensional array. You can view the numbers array as a one-dimensional array of three arrays, in which each array contains five elements. The first row of five elements of type float is located in memory at an address labeled numbers[0], the next row at numbers[1], and the last row of five elements at numbers[2].

The amount of memory allocated to each element is, of course, dependent on the type of variables that the array contains. An array of type double will need more memory to store each element than an array of type float or type int. Figure 5-6 illustrates how the array numbers[4][10] with four rows of ten elements of type float is stored.

Because the array elements are of type float, which on my machine occupy 4 bytes, the total memory occupied by this array on my computer will be 4×10×4 bytes, which amounts to a total of 160 bytes.

Figure 5-6. Memory occupied by a 4×10 array

Initializing Multidimensional Arrays

Let's first consider how you initialize a two-dimensional array. The basic structure of the declaration, with initialization, is the same as you've seen before, except that you need to put all the initial values for each row between braces {}, for example:

```
int numbers[3][4] = {
                      { 10, 20, 30, 40 },      /* Values for first row  */
                      { 15, 25, 35, 45 },      /* Values for second row */
                      { 47, 48, 49, 50 }       /* Values for third row  */
                    };
```

Each set of values for a row is between braces, and the whole lot goes between another pair of braces. The values for a row are separated by commas, and each set of values for a row is separated from the next set by a comma.

If you specify fewer initializing values than there are elements in a row, the values will be assigned to elements in sequence, starting with the first in the row. The remaining elements in a row that are left when the initial values have all been assigned will be initialized to 0.

For arrays of three or more dimensions, the process is extended. A three-dimensional array, for example, will have three levels of nested braces, with the inner level containing sets of initializing values for a row, for example:

```
int numbers[2][3][4] = {
                         {                          /* First block of 3 rows  */
                           { 10, 20, 30, 40 },
                           { 15, 25, 35, 45 },
                           { 47, 48, 49, 50 }
                         },
                         {                          /* Second block of 3 rows */
                           { 10, 20, 30, 40 },
```

```
                            { 15, 25, 35, 45 },
                            { 47, 48, 49, 50 }
                   }
              };
```

As you can see, the initializing values are between an outer pair of braces that enclose two blocks of three rows, each between braces. Each row is also between braces, so you have three levels of nested braces for a three-dimensional array. This is true generally; for instance, a six-dimensional array will have six levels of nested braces enclosing the initial values for the elements.

....

Try It Out: Multidimensional Arrays

Let's move away from vegetables and turn to more practical applications. You could use arrays in a program to help you to work out your hat size. With this program, you just enter the circumference of your head in inches, and your hat size will be displayed.

```c
/* Program 5.6 Know your hat size - if you dare... */
#include <stdio.h>
#define TRUE  1
#define FALSE 0

void main()

{
   /* The size array stores hat sizes from 6 1/2 to 7 7/8 */
   /* Each row defines one character of a size value so    */
   /* a size is selected by using the same index for each */
   /* the three rows. e.g. Index 2 selects 6 3/4.         */
   char size[3][12] = {               /* Hat sizes as characters */
      {'6', '6', '6', '6', '7', '7', '7', '7', '7', '7', '7', '7'},
      {'1', '5', '3', '7', ' ', '1', '1', '3', '1', '5', '3', '7'},
      {'2', '8', '4', '8', ' ', '8', '4', '8', '2', '8', '4', '8'}
                     };

   int headsize[12] =                 /* Values in 1/8 inches    */
      {164,166,169,172,175,178,181,184,188,191,194,197};

   float cranium = 0.0;            /* Head circumference in decimal inches */
   int your_head = 0;              /* Headsize in whole eighths            */
   int i = 0;                      /* Loop counter                         */
   int hat_found = FALSE;          /* Indicates when a hat is found to fit */
   int too_small = FALSE;          /* Indicates headsize is too small      */

   /* Get the circumference of the head */
   printf("\nEnter the circumference of your head above your eyebrows "
```

(Continued)

```
        "in inches as a decimal value: ");
    scanf(" %f", &cranium);

    /* Convert to whole eighths of an inch */
    your_head = (int)(8.0*cranium);

    /* Search for a hat size */
    for (i = 0 ; i < 12 ; i++)
    {
      /* Find head size in the headsize array */
      if(your_head > headsize[i])
        continue;

      /* If it is the first element and the head size */
      /* is more than 1/8 smaller then the head is    */
      /* too small for a hat.                         */
      if(( i == 0) && (your_head < headsize[0]-1))
      {
        printf("\nYou are the proverbial pinhead. No hat for"
                                        " you I'm afraid.\n");
        too_small = TRUE;
          break;                       /* Exit the loop */
      }

      /* If head size is more than 1/8 smaller than the */
      /* current element in headsize array, take the    */
      /* next element down as the head size             */
      if( your_head < headsize[i]-1 )
        i--;

      printf("\nYour hat size is %c %c%c%c\n",
               size[0][i], size[1][i], (size[1][i]==' ')?' ' : '/', size[2][i]);
      hat_found = TRUE;
      break;                           /* Exit the loop */
    }

    /* Check for no hat found and head not too small */
    if (!hat_found && !too_small)
      printf("\nYou, in technical parlance, are a fathead."
                                " No hat for you, I'm afraid.\n");
}
```

Typical output from this program could be this:

```
Enter the circumference of your head above your eyebrows in inches as a decimal
 value: 22.5
Your hat size is 7 1/4
```

(Continued)

or possibly this:

```
Enter the circumference of your head above your eyebrows in inches as a decimal
  value: 29
You, in technical parlance, are a fathead. No hat for you I'm afraid.
```

HOW IT WORKS

Before I start discussing this example, I should give you a word of caution. Don't use it to assist large football players to determine their hat size unless they're known for their sense of humor.

The example is here to illustrate using arrays rather than programming elegance, so it looks a bit complicated. Let's go through what's happening.

After the #include directive for stdio.h, you use two preprocessor directives to define the symbols TRUE and FALSE for use in the program:

```
#define TRUE  1
#define FALSE 0
```

The first declaration in the body of main() is as follows:

```
    char size[3][12] = {                    /* Hat sizes as characters */
      {'6', '6', '6', '6', '7', '7', '7', '7', '7', '7', '7', '7'},
      {'1', '5', '3', '7', ' ', '1', '1', '3', '1', '5', '3', '7'},
      {'2', '8', '4', '8', ' ', '8', '4', '8', '2', '8', '4', '8'}
                       };
```

This array corresponds to 12 possible hat sizes, each of which is made up of three values. For each size you store three characters, making it more convenient to output the fractional sizes. The smallest hat size is 6 1/2, so the first three characters corresponding to the first size are in size[0][0], size[1][0], and size[2][0]. They contain the characters '6', '1', and '2', representing the size 6 1/2. The biggest hat size is 7 7/8, and it's stored in size[0][11], size[1][11], size[2][11].

You then declare the array headsize, which provides the reference head dimensions in this declaration:

```
    int Headsize[12] =       /* Values in 1/8 inches   */
      {164,166,169,172,175,178,181,184,188,191,194,197};
```

The values in the array are all whole eighths of an inch. They correspond to the values in the size array containing the hat sizes. This means that a head size of 164 eighths of an inch (about 20.5 inches) will give a hat size of 6 1/2.

(Continued)

Notice that the head sizes don't run consecutively. You could get a head size of 171, for example, which doesn't fall into a definite hat size. You need to be aware of this later in the program so that you can decide which is the closest hat size for the head size.

After declaring your arrays, you then declare all the variables you're going to need:

```
float cranium = 0.0;          /* Head circumference in decimal inches */
int your_head = 0;            /* Headsize in whole eighths            */
int i = 0;                    /* Loop counter                         */
int hat_found = FALSE;        /* Indicates when a hat is found to fit */
int too_small = FALSE;        /* Indicates headsize is too small      */
```

Notice that cranium is declared as type float, but the rest are all type int. This becomes important later. You use the variables hat_found and too_small as logical values, so you use the symbol FALSE to initialize these.

Next, you prompt for your head size to be entered in inches, and the value is stored in the variable cranium (remember it's type float, so you can store values that aren't whole numbers):

```
printf("\nEnter the circumference of your head above your eyebrows "
    "in inches as a decimal value: ");
scanf(" %f", &cranium);
```

The value stored in cranium is then converted into eighths of an inch with this statement:

```
your_head = (int)(8.0*cranium);
```

The value stored in your_head will then be in the same units as the values stored in the array headsize. Note that you need the cast to type int here to avoid a warning message from the compiler. The parentheses around the expression (8.0*cranium) are also necessary: without them, you would only cast the value 8.0 to type int, not the whole expression.

You use the value stored in your_head to find the closest value in the array headsize that isn't less than that value:

```
for (i = 0 ; i < 12 ; i++)
{
  /* Find head size in the headsize array */
  if(your_head > headsize[i])
    continue;
  ...
}
```

(Continued)

The process is a simple one and is carried out in this for loop. On each loop iteration, you compare your head size with a value stored in the array headsize to find the first value that is less than or equal to your input size. The if compares the size you entered with the current headsize element, and as long as your_head is greater, the continue is executed to go to the next iteration.

You encountered the continue statement in the previous chapter—didn't you just know that it would turn up again sooner or later? When the continue statement is executed, the rest of the current loop iteration is skipped and the loop continues with the next iteration after incrementing the loop variable i and checking that the loop condition i<12 is true.

Once the value in the ith element of headsize is greater than your_head, you should be able find your hat size, so the continue statement isn't executed and you proceed with the rest of the loop iteration.

It's possible that someone could enter a value that was too small for your hats, so you first check for a small head:

```
/* If it is the first element and the head size */
/* is more than 1/8 smaller then the head is    */
/* too small for a hat.                          */
if(( i == 0) && (your_head < headsize[0]-1))
{
  printf("\nYou are the proverbial pinhead. No hat for"
                                  " you I'm afraid.\n");
  too_small = TRUE;
  break;                        /* Exit the loop */
}
```

This if statement checks whether the value of your_head happens to be less than the first value in the headsize array. To be precise, it checks whether your_head is more than one-eighth of an inch less with the expression (your_head < headsize[0]-1). If so, then you know that the value entered must be smaller than that for the size 6 1/2 (the smallest size), and you output the pinhead message. You also assign the value TRUE to too_small. You then execute the break statement to break out of the loop, because there's no point in checking against any of the larger sizes.

If you didn't exit the loop as a result of the previous if statement, you can definitely find a suitable hat size. You first check whether the value in your_head is more than 1 unit away from the current headsize array element and, if so, you adjust the index value i to select the previous element as the size:

```
if( your_head < headsize[i]-1 )
  i--;
```

You could have achieved the same result with a single statement:

```
i -= your_head < headsize[i]-1;
```

(Continued)

The logical expression on the right side of the assignment will have the value 1 or 0. When it is 1, i will be decremented, which is the result you want.

You now use the value of the loop counter, i, to select the size of the hat for the given head size. You then set hat_found to TRUE so you can determine later what happened in the loop, and you exit the loop:

```
printf("\nYour hat size is %c %c%c%c\n",
        size[0][i], size[1][i], (size[1][i]==' ')?' ' : '/', size[2][i]);
hat_found = TRUE;
break;                          /* Exit the loop */
```

As I said, the hat sizes are stored in the array size as characters to simplify the outputting of fractions. The printf() here uses the conditional operator to decide when to print a blank and when to print a slash (/) for the fractional output value. The fifth element of the headsize array corresponds to a hat size of exactly 7. You don't want it to print 7 /; you just want 7. Therefore, you customize the printf() depending on whether or not the element size[1][i] contains ' '. In this way, you omit the slash for any size where the numerator of the fractional part is a space, so this will still work even if you add new sizes to the array.

There are three possible situations with the head size that you enter. It may be too small, in which case the output will be dealt with inside the loop. It may be just right for a hat size, in which case the output will be produced as I've just described. The third possibility is that the head size is too large for a hat, and this will be dealt with after the loop, because all the elements of headsize must be checked. This situation will result in both too_small and hat_found having the value FALSE after the loop has completed; so you test for this with the following statements:

```
if (!hat_found && !too_small)
  printf("\nYou, in technical parlance, are a fathead."
                        " No hat for you, I'm afraid.\n");
```

The printf() will be executed only if the size stored in your_head is greater than all the values in the headsize array.

Remember, when you use this program, if you lie about the size of your head, your hat won't fit. The more mathematically astute, and any hatters reading this book, will appreciate that the hat size is simply the diameter of a notionally circular head. Therefore, if you have the circumference of your head in inches, you can produce your hat size by dividing this value by π.

Designing a Program

Now that you've learned about arrays, let's see how you can apply them in a bigger problem. Let's try writing another game.

The Problem

The problem you're set is to write a program that allows two people to play tic-tac-toe (also known as noughts and crosses) on the computer.

The Analysis

Tic-tac-toe is played on a 3×3 grid of squares. Two players take turns entering either an **X** or an **O** in the grid. The player that first manages to get three of her symbols in a line horizontally, vertically, or diagonally is the winner. You know how the game works, but how does that translate into designing your program? You'll need the following:

- *A 3×3 grid in which to store the turns of the two players.* That's easy. You can just use a two-dimensional array with three rows of three elements.

- *A way for a square to be selected when a player takes his turn.* You can label the nine squares with digits from 1 to 9. A player will just need to enter the number of the square to select it.

- *A way to get the two players to take alternate turns.* You can identify the two players as 1 and 2, with player 1 going first. You can then determine the player number by the number of the turn. On odd-numbered turns it's player 1. On even-numbered turns it's player 2.

- *Some way of specifying where to place the player symbol on the grid and checking to see if it's a valid selection.* A valid selection is a digit from 1 to 9. If you label the first row of squares with 1, 2, and 3, the second row with 4, 5, and 6, and the third row with 7, 8, and 9, you can calculate a row index and a column index from the square number. If you subtract 1 from the player's choice of square number, the square numbers are effectively 0 through 8:

Original

1	2	3
4	5	6
7	8	9

Subtract 1

0	1	2
3	4	5
6	7	8

Then the expression choice/3 gives the row number, as you can see here:

Original Less 1

0	1	2
3	4	5
6	7	8

Divide by 3

0	0	0
1	1	1
2	2	2

The expression choice%3 will give the column number:

Original Less 1

0	1	2
3	4	5
6	7	8

Remainder After Divide by 3

0	1	2
0	1	2
0	1	2

- *A method of finding out if one of the players has won.* After each turn, you'll need to check to see if any row, column, or diagonal in the board grid contains identical symbols. If it does, the last player has won.

- *A way to detect the end of the game.* Because the board has nine squares, a game consists of up to nine turns. The game ends when a winner is discovered or after nine turns.

The Solution

This section outlines the steps you'll take to solve the problem.

Step 1

You can first add the code for the main game loop and the code to display the board:

```c
/* Program 5.7 Tic-Tac-Toe */
#include <stdio.h>

void main()
{
```

```
    int i = 0;                      /* Loop counter            */
    int player = 0;                 /* Player number - 1 or 2 */
    int winner = 0;                 /* The winning player      */

    char board[3][3] = {            /* The board */
            {'1','2','3'},          /* Initial values are reference numbers */
            {'4','5','6'},          /* used to select a vacant square for   */
            {'7','8','9'}           /* a turn.                              */
                    };

    /* The main game loop. The game continues for up to 9 turns */
    /* As long as there is no winner                            */
    for( i = 0; i<9 && winner==0; i++)
    {
      /* Display the board */
      printf("\n\n");
      printf(" %c | %c | %c\n", board[0][0], board[0][1], board[0][2]);
      printf("--+--+--\n");
      printf(" %c | %c | %c\n", board[1][0], board[1][1], board[1][2]);
      printf("--+--+--\n");
      printf(" %c | %c | %c\n", board[2][0], board[2][1], board[2][2]);

      player = i%2 + 1; /* Select player */

      /* Code to play the game */
    }
    /* Code to output the result */
}
```

Here, you've declared the following variables: i, for the loop variable; player, which stores the identifier for the current player, 1 or 2; winner, which contains the identifier for the winning player; and the array board, which is of type char. The array is of type char because you want to place the symbols 'X' or 'O' in the squares. The array is initialized with the characters for the digits that identify the squares. The main game loop continues for as long as the loop condition is true. It will be false if winner contains a value other than 0 (which indicates that a winner has been found) or the loop counter is equal to or greater than 9 (which will be the case when all nine squares on the board have been filled).

When you display the grid in the loop, you use vertical bars and underline characters to delineate the squares. When a player selects a square, the symbol for that player will replace the digit character.

Step 2

Next, you can implement the code for the player to select a square and to ensure that the square is valid:

```
/* Program 5.7 Tic-Tac-Toe */
#include <stdio.h>
```

```
void main()
{
    int i = 0;                      /* Loop counter                      */
    int player = 0;                 /* Player number - 1 or 2            */
    int winner = 0;                 /* The winning player                */
    int choice = 0;                 /* Square selection number for turn  */
    int row = 0;                    /* Row index for a square            */
    int column = 0;                 /* Column index for a square         */

    char board[3][3] = {            /* The board */
                {'1','2','3'},       /* Initial values are reference numbers */
                {'4','5','6'},       /* used to select a vacant square for   */
                {'7','8','9'}        /* a turn.                              */
                    };

    /* The main game loop. The game continues for up to 9 turns */
    /* As long as there is no winner                           */
    for( i = 0; i<9 && winner==0; i++)
    {
      /* Display the board */
      printf("\n\n");
      printf(" %c | %c | %c\n", board[0][0], board[0][1], board[0][2]);
      printf("--+--+--\n");
      printf(" %c | %c | %c\n", board[1][0], board[1][1], board[1][2]);
      printf("--+--+--\n");
      printf(" %c | %c | %c\n", board[2][0], board[2][1], board[2][2]);

      player = i%2 + 1; /* Select player   */

      /* Get valid player square selection */
      do
      {
        printf("\nPlayer %d, please enter the number of the square "
               "where you want to place your %c: ",
               player,(player==1)?'X':'O');
        scanf("%d", &choice);

        row = --choice/3;              /* Get row index of square    */
        column = choice%3;             /* Get column index of square */
      }while(choice<0 || choice>9 || board[row][column]>'9');

      /* Insert player symbol */
      board[row][column] = (player == 1) ? 'X' : 'O';

      /* Code to check for a winner */
    }
    /* Code to output the result */
}
```

You prompt the current player for input in the do-while loop and read the square number into the variable choice that you declared as type int. You'll use this value to compute the row and column index values in the array; the value therefore needs to be numeric rather than of type char. The row and column index values are stored in the integer variables row and column, and you compute these values using the expressions you saw earlier. The do-while loop condition verifies that the square selected is valid. There are three possible ways that an invalid choice could be made: the integer entered for the square number could be less than the minimum, 1, or greater than the maximum, 9,or it could select a square that already contains 'X' or 'O'. In the latter case, the contents of the square will have a value greater than the character '9', because the character codes for 'X' and 'O' are greater than the character code for '9'. If the choice that was entered fails on any of these conditions, you just repeat the request to select a square.

Step 3

You can add the code to check for a winning line next. This needs to be executed after every turn:

```
/* Program 5.7 Tic-Tac-Toe */
#include <stdio.h>

void main()
{
    int i = 0;                      /* Loop counter                        */
    int player = 0;                 /* Player number - 1 or 2              */
    int winner = 0;                 /* The winning player                  */
    int choice = 0;                 /* Square selection number for turn    */
    int row = 0;                    /* Row index for a square              */
    int column = 0;                 /* Column index for a square           */
    int line=0;                     /* Row or column index in checking loop */

    char board[3][3] = {            /* The board */
            {'1','2','3'},          /* Initial values are reference numbers */
            {'4','5','6'},          /* used to select a vacant square for   */
            {'7','8','9'}           /* a turn.                              */
                    };

    /* The main game loop. The game continues for up to 9 turns */
    /* As long as there is no winner                            */
    for( i = 0; i<9 && winner==0; i++)
    {
        /* Display the board */
        printf("\n\n");
        printf(" %c | %c | %c\n", board[0][0], board[0][1], board[0][2]);
        printf("--+--+--\n");
        printf(" %c | %c | %c\n", board[1][0], board[1][1], board[1][2]);
        printf("--+--+--\n");
        printf(" %c | %c | %c\n", board[2][0], board[2][1], board[2][2]);
```

```
    player = i%2 + 1;                    /* Select player    */

    /* Get valid player square selection           */
    do
    {
      printf("\nPlayer %d, please enter the number of the square "
              "where you want to place your %c: ",
              player,(player==1)?'X':'0');
      scanf("%d", &choice);

      row = --choice/3;                   /* Get row index of square    */
      column = choice%3;                  /* Get column index of square */
    }while(choice<0 || choice>9 || board[row][column]>'9');

    /* Insert player symbol */
    board[row][column] = (player == 1) ? 'X' : '0';

    /* Check for a winning line - diagonals first */
    if((board[0][0]==board[1][1] && board[0][0]==board[2][2]) ||
       (board[0][2]==board[1][1] && board[0][2]==board[2][0]))
      winner = player;
    else
      /* Check rows and columns for a winning line */
      for(line = 0; line <= 2; line ++)
        if((board[line][0]==board[line][1] &&
            board[line][0]==board[line][2])||
           (board[0][line]==board[1][line] &&
            board[0][line]==board[2][line]))
          winner = player;
    }
    /* Code to output the result */
}
```

To check for a winning line, you can compare one element in the line with the other two to test for equality. If all three are identical, then you have a winning line. You check both diagonals in the board array with the if expression, and if either diagonal has identical symbols in all three elements, you set winner to the current player. The current player, identified in player, must be the winner because he or she was the last to place a symbol on a square. If neither diagonal has identical symbols, you check the rows and the columns in the else clause, using a for loop. The for loop contains one statement, an if statement that checks both a row and a column for identical elements. If either is found, winner is set to the current player. Each value of the loop variable line is used to index a row and a column. Thus the for loop will check the row and column corresponding to index value 0, which is the first row and column, then the second row and column, and finally the third row and column corresponding to line having the value 2. Of course, if winner is set to a value here, the main loop condition will be false, so the loop will end and you'll continue with the code following the main loop.

Step 4

The final task is to display the grid with the final position and to display a message for the result. If winner is 0, the game is a draw; otherwise, winner contains the player number of the winner.

```c
/* Program 5.7 Tic-Tac-Toe */
#include <stdio.h>

void main()
{
    int i = 0;                      /* Loop counter                      */
    int player = 0;                 /* Player number - 1 or 2            */
    int winner = 0;                 /* The winning player                */
    int choice = 0;                 /* Square selection number for turn  */
    int row = 0;                    /* Row index for a square            */
    int column = 0;                 /* Column index for a square         */
    int line=0;                     /* Row or column index in checking loop */

    char board[3][3] = {            /* The board */
                {'1','2','3'},       /* Initial values are reference numbers */
                {'4','5','6'},       /* used to select a vacant square for   */
                {'7','8','9'}        /* a turn.                              */
                        };

    /* The main game loop. The game continues for up to 9 turns */
    /* As long as there is no winner                            */
    for( i = 0; i<9 && winner==0; i++)
    {
      /* Display the board */
      printf("\n\n");
      printf(" %c | %c | %c\n", board[0][0], board[0][1], board[0][2]);
      printf("--+--+--\n");
      printf(" %c | %c | %c\n", board[1][0], board[1][1], board[1][2]);
      printf("--+--+--\n");
      printf(" %c | %c | %c\n", board[2][0], board[2][1], board[2][2]);

      player = i%2 + 1;             /* Select player */

      /* Get valid player square selection */
      do
      {
        printf("\nPlayer %d, please enter the number of the square "
               "where you want to place your %c: ",
               player,(player==1)?'X':'O');
        scanf("%d", &choice);

        row = --choice/3;           /* Get row index of square   */
        column = choice%3;          /* Get column index of square */
      }while(choice<0 || choice>9 || board[row][column]>'9');
```

```
    /* Insert player symbol */
    board[row][column] = (player == 1) ? 'X' : '0';

    /* Check for a winning line - diagonals first */
    if((board[0][0]==board[1][1] && board[0][0]==board[2][2]) ||
       (board[0][2]==board[1][1] && board[0][2]==board[2][0]))
      winner = player;
    else
      /* Check rows and columns for a winning line */
      for(line = 0; line <= 2; line ++)
        if((board[line][0]==board[line][1] &&
            board[line][0]==board[line][2])||
           (board[0][line]==board[1][line] &&
            board[0][line]==board[2][line]))
          winner = player;
  }
  /* Game is over so display the final board */
  printf("\n\n");
  printf(" %c | %c | %c\n", board[0][0], board[0][1], board[0][2]);
  printf("--+--+--\n");
  printf(" %c | %c | %c\n", board[1][0], board[1][1], board[1][2]);
  printf("--+--+--\n");
  printf(" %c | %c | %c\n", board[2][0], board[2][1], board[2][2]);

  /* Display result message */
  if(winner == 0)
    printf("\nHow boring, it is a draw\n");
  else
    printf("\nCongratulations, player %d, YOU ARE THE WINNER!\n",
                                                  winner);
}
```

Typical output from this program and a very bad player number 2 would be as follows:

```
1 | 2 | 3
---+---+---
4 | 5 | 6
---+---+---
7 | 8 | 9

Player 1, please enter your go: 1

X | 2 | 3
---+---+---
4 | 5 | 6
---+---+---
7 | 8 | 9
```

```
Player 2, please enter your go: 2

X | O | 3
---+---+---
4 | 5 | 6
---+---+---
7 | 8 | 9

Player 1, please enter your go: 5


X | O | 3
---+---+---
4 | X | 6
---+---+---
7 | 8 | 9

Player 2, please enter your go: 3


X | O | O
---+---+---
4 | X | 6
---+---+---
7 | 8 | 9

Player 1, please enter your go: 9

X | O | O
---+---+---
4 | X | 6
---+---+---
7 | 8 | X

Congratulations, player 1, YOU ARE THE WINNER!
```

Summary

In this chapter, I explained what arrays are and how to use them. I covered a bit more about memory in your computer to help you understand how your computer works with the information you give it. I also covered one-dimensional and multidimensional arrays and presented examples of how these work in practice in the context of the implementation of a game of tic-tac-toe.

This chapter explored some ideas that extend your ability to deal with much more complicated programming problems. Once you start dealing with arrays, particularly multidimensional arrays, you're dealing with a lot more information. The possibilities for your programs increase immensely, although you do have to invest more time in planning and designing your programs.

Up until now, you've mainly concentrated on processing numbers. The examples haven't really dealt with text to any great extent. You're going to change that in the next chapter, where you'll write programs that can process and analyze strings of characters.

Exercises

The following exercises enable you to try out what you've learned in this chapter. If you get stuck, look back over the chapter for help. If you're still stuck, you can download the solutions from the Downloads area of the Apress website (http://www.apress.com), but that really should be a last resort.

Exercise 5-1. Write a program that will read five values of type double from the keyboard and store them in an array. Calculate the reciprocal of each value (the reciprocal of a value x is 1.0/x) and store it in a separate array. Output the values of the reciprocals, and calculate and output the sum of the reciprocals.

Exercise 5-2. Define an array, data, with 100 elements of type double. Write a loop that will store the following sequence of values in corresponding elements of the array:

```
1/(2*3*4) 1/(4*5*6) 1/(6*7*8) … up to 1/(200*201*202)
```

Write another loop that will calculate the following:

```
data[0]-data[1]+data[2]-data[3]+… -data[99]
```

Multiply the result of this by 4.0, add 3.0, and output the final result.

Exercise 5-3. Write a program that will read five values from the keyboard and store them in an array of type float with the name amounts. Create two arrays of five elements of type long with the names dollars and cents. Store the whole number part of each value in the amounts array in the corresponding element of dollars and the fractional part of the amount as a two-digit integer in cents (e.g., 2.75 in amounts[1] would result in 2 being stored in dollars[1] and 75 being stored in cents[1]). Output the values from the two arrays of type long as monetary amounts (e.g., $2.75).

Exercise 5-4. Define a two-dimensional array, data[12][5], of type double. Initialize the elements in the first column with values from 2.0 to 3.0 inclusive in steps of 0.1. If the first element in a row has the value x, populate the remaining elements in each row with the values $1/x$, x^2, x^3, and x^4. Output the values in the array with each row on a separate line and with a heading for each column.

Applications with Strings and Text

IN THE LAST CHAPTER YOU WERE INTRODUCED to arrays, and you saw how using arrays of numerical values could make many programming tasks much easier. In this chapter you'll extend your knowledge of arrays by exploring how you can use arrays of characters. You'll frequently have a need to work with a text string as a single entity. As you'll see, C doesn't provide you with a string data type, as some other languages do. Instead, C uses an array of elements of type char to store a string.

In this chapter I'll show you how you can create and work with variables that store strings, and how the standard library functions can greatly simplify the processing of strings.

In this chapter you'll learn

- How you can create string variables

- How to join one or more strings together to form a single string

- How you compare strings

- How to use arrays of strings

- What library functions are available to handle strings and how you can apply them

- How to write a simple password-protection program

What Is a String?

You've already seen examples of **string constants**—quite frequently in fact. A string constant is a sequence of characters or symbols between a pair of double quote characters. Anything between a pair of double quotes is interpreted by the compiler as a string, including any special characters and embedded spaces. Every time you've displayed a message using printf(), you've defined the message as a string constant. Examples of strings used in this way appear in the following statements:

```
printf("This is a string.");
printf("This is quite a long string.");
printf("AAA");
```

These three example strings are shown in Figure 6-1. The decimal value of the character codes that will be stored in memory are shown below the characters.

```
"This is a string."
┌─┬─┬─┬─┬─┬─┬─┬─┬─┬─┬─┬─┬─┬─┬─┬─┬─┬─┬──┐
│T│h│i│s│ │i│s│ │a│ │s│t│r│i│n│g│.│\0│
└─┴─┴─┴─┴─┴─┴─┴─┴─┴─┴─┴─┴─┴─┴─┴─┴─┴──┘
84 104 105 115 32 105 115 32 97 32 115 116 114 105 110 103 46  00

"This is quite a long string."
┌─┬─┬─┬─┬─┬─┬─┬─┬─┬─┬─┬─┬─┬─┬─┬─┬─┬─┬─┬─┬─┬─┬─┬─┬─┬─┬─┬──┐
│T│h│i│s│ │i│s│ │q│u│i│t│e│ │a│ │l│o│n│g│ │s│t│r│i│n│g│.│\0│
└─┴─┴─┴─┴─┴─┴─┴─┴─┴─┴─┴─┴─┴─┴─┴─┴─┴─┴─┴─┴─┴─┴─┴─┴─┴─┴─┴──┘
84 104 105 115 32 105 115 32 113 117 105 116 101 32 97 32 108 111 110 103 32 115 116 114 105 110 103 46 00

"AAA"
┌─┬─┬─┬──┐
│A│A│A│\0│
└─┴─┴─┴──┘
65 65 65 00
```

Figure 6-1. Examples of strings in memory

As Figure 6-1 shows, a special character with the code value 0 is added to the end of each string to mark where it ends. This character is known as the **null character** (not to be confused with NULL, which you'll see later), and you write it as \0.

 NOTE *Because a string in C is always terminated by a \0 character, the length of a string is always one greater than the number of characters in the string.*

There's nothing to prevent you from adding a \0 character to the end of a string yourself, but if you do, you'll simply end up with two of them. You can see how the null character \0 works with a simple example. Have a look at the following program:

```
/* Program 6.1 Displaying a string */
#include <stdio.h>

void main()
{
  printf("The character \0 is used to terminate a string");
}
```

If you compile and run this program, you'll get this output:

```
The character
```

It's probably not quite what you expected: only the first part of the string has been displayed. The output ends after the first two words because the printf() function stops outputting the string when it reaches the first null character, \0. Even though there's another \0 at the end of string, it will never be reached. The first \0 that's found always marks the end of the string.

String- and Text-Handling Methods

Unlike some other programming languages, C has no specific provision within its syntax for variables that store strings, and it has no special operators for processing strings. This isn't a problem, though, because you're quite well equipped to handle strings with the tools already at your disposal.

Declaring Variables That Store Strings

As I said at the beginning of this chapter, you can use an array of type char to hold strings. This is the simplest form of string variable. You could declare a char array variable as follows:

```
char saying[20];
```

The variable saying that you declare in this statement can store a string that has up to 19 characters, because you must allow one element for the termination character. Of course, you can also use this array to store 20 characters that aren't a string.

CAUTION *Remember that you must always declare the dimension of an array that you intend to use to store a string as at least one greater than the number of characters that you want to allow the string to have because the compiler will automatically add \0 to the end of a string constant.*

You could also initialize the preceding string variable in the following declaration:

```
char saying[] = "This is a string.";
```

Here you haven't explicitly defined the array dimension. The compiler will assign a value to the dimension sufficient to hold the initializing string constant. In this case it will be 18: 17 elements for the characters in the string plus an extra one for the terminating \0. You could, of course, have put a value for the dimension yourself, but if you leave it for the compiler to do, you can be sure it will be correct.

You could also initialize just part of an array of elements of type char with a string, for example:

```
char str[40] = "To be";
```

Here, the compiler will initialize the first five elements from str[0] to str[4] with the characters of the specified string in the sequence, and str[5] will contain the null value

'\0'. Of course, space is allocated for all 40 elements of the array, and they're all available to use in any way you want.

Initializing a char array and declaring it as constant is a good way of handling standard messages:

```
const char message[] = "The end of the world is nigh";
```

Because you've declared message as const, it's protected from being modified explicitly within the program. Any attempt to do so will result in an error message from the compiler. This technique for defining standard messages is particularly useful if they're used in various places within a program. It prevents accidental modification of such constants in other parts of your program. Of course, if you do need to be able to change the message, then you shouldn't specify the array as const.

When you want to refer to the string stored in an array, you just use the array name by itself. For instance, if you want to output the string stored in message using the printf() function, you could write this:

```
printf("\nThe message is: %s", message);
```

The %s specification is for outputting a null-terminating string. At the position where the %s appears in the first argument, the printf() function will output successive characters from the message array until it finds the '\0' character.

The main disadvantage of using char arrays to hold a variety of different strings is the potentially wasted memory. Because arrays are, by definition, of a fixed length, you have to declare each array that you intend to use to store strings with its dimension set to accommodate the maximum string length you're likely to want to process. In most circumstances, your typical string length will be somewhat less than the maximum, so you end up wasting memory. Because you normally use your arrays here to store strings of different lengths, getting the length of a string is important, especially if you want to add to it. Let's look at how you do this using an example.

Try It Out: Finding Out the Length of a String

In this example, you're going to initialize two strings and then find out how many characters there are in each, excluding the null character:

```
/* Program 6.2 Lengths of strings   */
#include <stdio.h>
void main()
{
  char str1[40] = "To be or not to be";
  char str2[40] = ",that is the question";
  int count = 0;                 /* Stores the string length          */
  while (str1[count] != '\0')    /* Increment count till we reach the string */
```

(Continued)

```
     count++;                        /* terminating character.          */
  printf("\nThe length of the string \"%s\" is %d characters.", str1, count);

  count = 0;                    /* Reset to zero for next string        */
  while (str2[count] != '\0')   /* Count characters in second string    */
     count++;
  printf("\nThe length of the string \"%s\" is %d characters.\n", str2, count);
}
```

The output you'll get from this program is

```
The length of the string "To be or not to be" is 18 characters.
The length of the string ",that is the question" is 21 characters.
```

First you have the inevitable declarations for the variables that you'll be using:

```
char str1[40] = "To be or not to be";
char str2[40] = ",that is the question";
int count = 0;                    /* Stores the string length           */
```

You declare two arrays of type char that are each initialized with a string with a length considerably less than the length of the array. You also declare and initialize a counter, count, to use in the loops in the program. Of course, you could have omitted the dimension for each array and left the compiler to figure out what is required, as you saw earlier.

Next, you have a while loop that determines the length of the first string:

```
while (str1[count] != '\0')      /* Increment count till we reach the string */
   count++;                       /* terminating character.          */
```

Using a loop in the way you do here is very common in programming with strings. To find the length, you simply keep incrementing a counter in the while loop as long as you haven't reached the end of string character. You can see how the condition for the continuation of the loop is whether the terminating '\0' has been reached. At the end of the loop, the variable count will contain the number of characters in the string, excluding the terminating null.

It would also be possible to put the incrementing of count in the while condition with a statement such as this:

```
while (str1[count++] != '\0');   /* Increment count till we reach \0 */
```

(Continued)

However, you would then have to decrement count by 1 after the loop finished, as count would have been incremented one more time in the loop condition when the '\0' is detected. This would be fine if you wanted the length to include the termination character. However, with the loop as written in the example, you come out with the correct value because count is incremented in the loop proper, rather than in the exit condition. It doesn't get incremented when the '\0' is found.

Another possibility is to initialize the counter to –1 and use the prefix form of the increment operator:

```
int count = -1;                  /* Stores the string length      */
while (str1[++count] != '\0');   /* Increment count till we reach \0 */
```

Now the value in count will be incremented before it's used to index the array. The result is that on the first iteration count will be 0, and on the last iteration when the '\0' is found it will correspond to the index position of the element containing the '\0' character. This means that on exit from the loop, the value stored in count will also correspond to the number of characters in the string, excluding the '\0' character.

Although it didn't quite suit this example's purposes, this alternative approach, in which everything is done in the loop condition, crops up quite frequently in C.

Now that you've determined the length, you display the string with the following statement:

```
printf("\nThe length of the string \"%s\" is %d characters.", str1, count);
```

This also displays the count of the number of characters that the string contains, excluding the terminating null. Notice that you use the new format specifier, %s, that I introduced earlier. This outputs characters from the string until it reaches the terminating null. If there was no terminating character, it would continue to output characters until it found one somewhere in memory. In some cases, that can mean a *lot* of output. You also use the escape character, \", to include a double quote in the string. If you didn't precede the double quote character with the backslash, the compiler would think it marked the end of the string that is the first argument to the printf() function, and the statement would cause an error message to be produced.

You find the length of the second string and display the result in exactly the same way as the first string.

Operations with Strings

So, now that you know how to find the lengths of strings, how can you manipulate them?

Unfortunately, you can't use the assignment operator to copy a string in the way you do with int or double variables. To achieve the equivalent of an arithmetic assignment with strings, one string has to be copied element by element to the other. In fact, performing any operation on string variables is very different from the arithmetic operations with numeric variables you've seen so far. Let's look at some common operations that you might want to perform with strings and how you would achieve them.

Appending a String

Joining one string to the end of another is a common requirement. For instance, you might want to assemble a single message from two or more strings. You might define the error messages in a program as a few basic text strings to which you append one of a variety of strings to make the message specific to a particular error. Let's see how this works in the context of an example.

Try It Out: Joining Strings

You could rework the last example to append the second string to the first:

```
/* Program 6.3 Joining strings */
#include <stdio.h>
void main()
{
  char str1[40] = "To be or not to be";
  char str2[40] = ",that is the question";
  int count1 = 0;                  /* Length of str1 */
  int count2 = 0;                  /* Length of str2 */

  /* find the length of the first string */
  while (str1[count1] != '\0')   /* Increment count till we reach the string */
     count1++;                    /* terminating character.                   */


  /* Find the length of the second string */
  while (str2[count2] != '\0')   /* Count characters in second string      */
     count2++;

  /* Check that we have enough space for both strings  */
  if(sizeof str1 < count1 + count2 + 1)
     printf("\nYou can't put a quart into a pint pot.");
  else
  { /* Copy 2nd string to end of the first */
     count2 = 0;                     /* Reset index for str2 to 0   */
     while(str2[count2] != '\0')  /* Copy up to null from str2   */
       str1[count1++] = str2[count2++];

     str1[count1] = '\0';         /* Make sure we add terminator */
```

(Continued)

```
        printf("\n%s\n", str1 );      /* Output combined string      */
    }
}
```

The output from this program will be

To be or not to be,that is the question

This program first finds the lengths of the two strings exactly as before. It then checks that str1 has enough elements to hold both strings plus the terminating null character:

```
if(sizeof str1 < count1 + count2 + 1)
  printf("\nYou can't put a quart into a pint pot.");
```

Notice how you use the sizeof operator to get the total number of bytes in the array by just using the array name as an argument. The value that results from the expression sizeof str1 is the number of characters that the array will hold, because each character occupies 1 byte.

If you discover that the array is too small to hold the contents of both strings, then you display a message. The program will then end as you fall through the closing brace in main(). It's essential that you do not try to place more characters in the array than it can hold, as this will overwrite some memory that may contain important data or even machine instructions. This is likely to crash your program. You should never append characters to a string without first checking that there is sufficient space in the array to accommodate them.

You reach the else block only if you're sure that both strings will fit in the first array. Here, you reset the variable count2 to 0 and copy the second string to the first array with the following statements:

```
  else
  { /* Copy 2nd string to end of the first  */
    count2 = 0;                    /* Reset index for str2 to 0   */
    while(str2[count2] != '\0')  /* Copy up to null from str2   */
      str1[count1++] = str2[count2++];

    str1[count1] = '\0';          /* Make sure we add terminator */
    printf("\n%s\n", str1 );      /* Output combined string      */
  }
```

(Continued)

The variable count1 starts from the value that was left by the loop that determined the length of the first string, str1. This is why you use two separate variables to count the number of characters in each of the two strings. Because the array is indexed from 0, the value that's stored in count1 will point to the element containing '\0' at the end of the first string. So, when you use count1 to index the array str1, you know that you're starting at the end of the message proper and that you'll overwrite the null character with the first character of the second string.

You then copy characters from str2 to str1 until you find the '\0' in str2. You still have to add a terminating '\0' to str1 because it isn't copied from str2. The end result of the operation is that you've added the contents of str2 to the end of str1, overwriting the terminating null character for str1 and adding a terminating null to the end of the combined string.

You could replace the three lines of code that did the copying with a more concise alternative:

```
while ((str1[count1++] = str2[count2++]) != '\0');
```

This would replace the loop you have in the program as well as the statement to put a '\0' at the end of str1. This statement would copy the '\0' from str2 to str1, because the copying occurs in the loop continuation condition. This works because of the precedence of the operators. Let's consider what happens at each stage.

The parentheses around the assignment ensure that this is done before the result is compared with '\0'. The parentheses have the highest order of precedence, so you carry out all the operations contained within them first. This means the sequence of events is as follows:

1. Assign the value of str2[count2] to str1[count1]. An assignment expression has a value that is the value that was stored in the left operand of the assignment operator. In this case it is the character that was copied into str1[count1].

2. Increment each of the counters by 1, using the postfix form of the ++ operator.

3. Compare the value of the assignment expression—which will be the last character stored in str1—for inequality with '\0'. The loop ends after the '\0' has been copied to str1, which will result in the comparison being false.

Arrays of Strings

It may have occurred to you by now that you could use a two-dimensional array of elements of type char to store strings, where each row is used to hold a separate string. In this way you could arrange to store a whole bunch of strings and refer to any of them through a single variable name, for example:

```
char sayings[3][32] = {
                  "Manners maketh man.",
                  "Many hands make light work.",
                  "Too many cooks spoil the broth."
             };
```

This creates an array of three rows of 32 characters. The strings between the braces will be assigned in sequence to the three rows of the array, sayings[0], sayings[1], and sayings[2]. Note that you don't need braces around each string. The compiler can deduce that each string is intended to initialize one row of the array. The last dimension is specified to be 32, which is just sufficient to accommodate the longest string, including its terminating \0 character. The first dimension specifies the number of strings.

When you're referring to an element of the array—sayings[i][j], for instance—the first index, i, identifies a row in the array, and the second index, j, identifies a character within a row. When you want to refer to a complete row containing one of the strings, you just use a single index value between square brackets. For instance, sayings[1] refers to the second string in the array, "Many hands make light work.".

Although you must specify the last dimension in an array of strings, you can leave it to the compiler to figure out how many strings there are:

```
char sayings[][32] = {
                  "Manners maketh man.",
                  "Many hands make light work.",
                  "Too many cooks spoil the broth."
             };
```

I've omitted the value for the size of the first dimension in the array here so the compiler will deduce this from the initializers between braces. Because you have three initializing strings, the compiler will make the first array dimension 3. Of course, you must still make sure that the last dimension is large enough to accommodate the longest string, including its terminating null character.

You could output the three sayings with the following code:

```
int i = 0;
for(i = 0 ; i<3 ; i++)
  printf("\n%s", sayings[i]);
```

You reference a row of the array using a single index in the expression sayings[i]. This effectively accesses the one-dimensional array that is at index position i in the sayings array.

You could change the last example to use a two-dimensional array.

....

Try It Out: Arrays of Strings

You'll change the previous example so that it stores the two initial strings in a single array:

```
/* Example 6.4 Arrays of strings */
#include <stdio.h>
void main()
{
  char str[][40] = {
                      "To be or not to be"   ,
                      ",that is the question"
                   };
  int count1 = 0;               /* Length of first string */
  int count2 = 0;               /* Length of second string */

  /* find the length of the first string */
  while (str[0][count1] != '\0')
    count1++;

  /* Find the length of the second string */
  while (str[1][count2] != '\0')
    count2++;

  /* Check that we have enough space for both strings  */
  if(sizeof str[0] < count1 + count2 + 1)
    printf("\nYou can't put a quart into a pint pot.");
  else
  { /* Copy 2nd string to first */
    count2 = 0;
    while((str[0][count1++] = str[1][count2++]) != '\0');

    printf("\n%s\n", str[0]);    /* Output combined string */
  }
}
```

Typical output from this program would be

```
To be or not to be,that is the question
```

(Continued)

━━━━━━━━━━━━━━━━━━━━━━━━━━━━━━━━━━━━
HOW IT WORKS

Well, I have to admit, it isn't a great improvement on the previous version. However, it does demonstrate an array of strings in action. You declare a single two-dimensional char array instead of the two one-dimensional arrays you had before:

```
char str[][40] = {
                   "To be or not to be",
                   ",that is the question"
                 };
```

The first initializing string is stored with the first index value as 0, and the second initializing string is stored with the first index value as 1. Of course, you could add as many initializing strings as you want between the braces and the compiler would adjust the first array dimension to accommodate them.

To access any particular string, you just use an index to the first array dimension, 0 for the first string and 1 for the second. Otherwise, it's the same as the previous example. You would probably come out much further ahead if you had 20 strings instead of 2. And, of course, if you needed to cope with a variable number of strings, you couldn't make it in practice with naming them individually. A disadvantage of this approach is that if your strings are significantly less than 40 characters long, you waste quite a bit of memory in the array.

....

String Library Functions

Now that you've struggled through the previous examples, laboriously copying strings from one variable to another, it's time to reveal that there's a standard library for string functions that can take care of all these little chores. Still, at least you know what's going on when you use the library functions.

The string functions are declared in the string.h header file, so you'll need to put

```
#include <string.h>
```

at the beginning of your program if you want to use them. The library actually contains quite a lot of functions, and your compiler may provide an even more extensive range of string library capabilities than is required by the ANSI C standard. I'll discuss just a few of the essential functions to demonstrate the basic idea and leave you to explore the rest on your own.

Copying Strings Using a Library Function

First, let's return to the process of copying the string stored in one array to another, which is the string equivalent of an assignment operation. The while loop mechanism you carefully created to do this must still be fresh in your mind. Well, you can do the same thing with this statement:

```
strcpy(string1, string2);
```

The arguments to the strcpy() function are char array names. What the function actually does is copy the string specified by the second argument to the string specified by the first argument, so in the preceding example string2 will be copied to string1, replacing what was previously stored in string1. The copy operation will include the terminating '\0'. It's your responsibility to ensure that the array string1 has sufficient space to accommodate string2. The function strcpy() has no way of checking the sizes of the arrays, so if it goes wrong it's all your fault. Obviously, the sizeof operator is important in this because you'll most likely check that everything is as it should be like this:

```
if(sizeof string2 <= sizeof string1)
  strcpy(string1, string2);
```

You execute the strcpy() operation only if the length of the string2 array is less than or equal to the length of the string1 array.

You have another function available, strncpy(), that will copy the first n characters of one string to another. The first argument is the destination string, the second argument is the source string, and the third argument is the number of characters to be copied. Here's an example of how this works:

```
char destination[] = "This string will be replaced";
char source[] = "This string will be copied in part";
int n = 26;                     /* Number of characters to be copied */
strncpy(destination, source, n);
```

After executing these statements, destination will contain the string "This string will be copied", because that corresponds to the first 26 characters from source. A '\0' character will be appended after the last character copied. If source has fewer than 26 characters, the function will add '\0' characters to make up the count to 26.

Determining String Length Using a Library Function

To find out the length of a string you have the function strlen(), which returns the length of a string as an unsigned integer. To find the length of a string in the example you wrote this:

```
while (str2[count2] != '\0')
  count2++;
```

Instead of this rigmarole, you could simply write this:

```
count2 = strlen(str2);
```

All the counting and searching that's necessary to find the end of the string is performed by the function, so you no longer have to worry about it. Note that it returns the length of the string *excluding* the '\0', which is generally the most convenient result. It also returns the value as unsigned, so you may want to declare the variable to hold the result as unsigned as well. If you don't, you may get warning messages from your compiler.

To be precise, the strlen() function returns a value of type size_t, which is a type defined in the standard library header file stddef.h. This is also the type returned by the operator sizeof. The type size_t will be defined to be one of the unsigned integer types you have seen, typically unsigned int. The reason for implementing things this way is code portability. The type returned by sizeof and the strlen() function, among others, can vary from one C implementation to another. It's up to the compiler writer to decide what it should be. Defining the type to be size_t and defining size_t in a header file enables you to accommodate such implementation dependencies in your code very easily. As long as you define count2 in the preceding example as type size_t, you have code that will work in every ANSI C implementation, even though the definition of size_t may vary from one implementation to another.

So for the most portable code, you should write the following:

```
size_t count2 = 0;
count2 = strlen(str2);
```

As long as you have #include directives for string.h and stddef.h, this code will compile with the ANSI standard C compiler.

Joining Strings Using a Library Function

In Program 6.3, you copied the second string onto the end of the first using the following rather complicated-looking code:

```
count2 = 0;
while(str2[count2] != '\0')
  str1[count1++] = str2[count2++];
str1[count1] = '\0';
```

Well, the string library gives a slight simplification here, too. You could use a function that joins one string to the end of another. You could achieve the same result as the preceding fragment with the following exceedingly simple statement:

```
strcat(str1, str2);          /* Copy str2 to the end of str1 */
```

This function finds the end of str1 and copies str2 to the end of str1. The strcat() function is so called because it performs **string cat**enation. As well as appending str2 to str1, the strcat() function also returns str1.

If you only want to append part of the source string to the destination string, you can use the strncat() function. This requires a third argument to be specified that indicates the number of characters to be copied, for instance:

```
strcat(str1, str2, 5);    /* Copy 1st 5 characters of str2 to the end of str1 */
```

As with all the operations that involve copying one string to another, it's up to you to ensure that the destination array is sufficiently large to accommodate what's being copied to it. This function and others will happily overwrite whatever lies beyond the end of your destination array if you get it wrong.

All these string functions return the destination string. This allows you to use the value returned in another string operation, for example:

```
size_t length = 0;
length = strlen(strcat(str1, str2, 5));
```

Here the strcat() function copies five characters from str2 to the end of str1. The function returns the array str1, so this is passed as an argument to the strlen() function. This will then return the length of the new version of str1 with the five characters from str2 appended.

....

Try It Out: Using the String Library

You now have enough tools to do a good job of rewriting Program 6.3:

```
/* Program 6.5 Joining strings - revitalized */
#include <stdio.h>
#include <string.h>
#define STR_LENGTH 40

void main()
{
  char str1[STR_LENGTH] = "To be or not to be";
  char str2[STR_LENGTH] = ",that is the question";

  if(STR_LENGTH > strlen(str1) + strlen(str2)) /* Enough space ?            */
    printf("\n%s\n", strcat(str1, str2));   /* yes, so display joined string */
  else
    printf("\nYou can't put a quart into a pint pot.");
}
```

This program will produce exactly the same output as before.

(Continued)

Well, what a difference a library makes. It actually makes the problem trivial, doesn't it? You defined a symbol for the size of the arrays using a #define directive. If you want to change the array sizes in the program later, you can just modify the definition for STR_LENGTH. You simply check that you have enough space in your array by means of the if statement:

```
if(STR_LENGTH > strlen(str1) + strlen(str2)) /* Enough space ?          */
  printf("\n%s\n", strcat(str1, str2));   /* yes, so display joined string  */
else
  printf("\nYou can't put a quart into a pint pot.");
```

If you do have enough space, you join the strings using the strcat() function within the argument to the printf(). Because the strcat() functions returns str1, the printf() displays the result of joining the strings. If str1 is too short, you just display a message. Note that the comparison uses the > operator—this is because the array length must be at least one greater than the sum of the two string lengths to allow for the terminating '\0' character.

Comparing Strings

The string library also provides the facility for comparing strings and deciding whether one string is greater than or less than another. It may sound a bit odd applying such terms as "greater than" and "less than" to strings, but the result is produced quite simply. Successive corresponding characters of the two strings are compared based on the numerical value of their character codes. This mechanism is illustrated in Figure 6-2, in which the character codes are shown as hexadecimal values.

Figure 6-2. Comparing two strings

If two strings are identical, then of course they're equal. The first pair of corresponding characters that are different in two strings determines whether the first string is less than or greater than the second. So, for example, if the character code for the character in the first string is less than the character code for the character in the second string, then the first string is less than the second. This mechanism for comparison generally corresponds to what you expect when you're arranging strings in alphabetical order.

The function strcmp(str1, str2) compares two strings. It returns a value of type int that is less than, equal to, or greater than 0, corresponding to whether str1 is less than, equal to, or greater than str2. You can express the comparison illustrated in Figure 6-2 in the following code fragment:

```c
char str1[] = "The quick brown fox";
char str2[] = "The quick black fox";
if(strcmp(str1 , str2) < 0)
  printf("str1 is less than str2");
```

The printf() statement will execute only if the strcmp() function returns a negative integer. This will be when for the first pair of corresponding characters in the two strings that are different, the character code in str1 is less than the character code in str2.

The strncmp() function compares up to n characters of the two strings. The first two arguments are the same as for the strcmp() function and the number of characters to be compared is specified by a third argument that's an integer of type size_t. This function would be useful if you were processing strings with a prefix of ten characters, say, that represented a part number or a sequence number. You could use the strncmp() function to compare just the first ten characters of two strings to determine which should come first, for instance:

```c
if(strncmp(str1, str2, 10) <= 0)
  printf("\n%s\n%s", str1, str2);
else
  printf("\n%s\n%s", str2, str1);
```

These statements output strings str1 and str2 arranged in ascending sequence according to the first ten characters in the strings.

Let's try comparing strings in a working example.

....

Try It Out: Comparing Strings

You can demonstrate the use of comparing strings in an example that compares just two words that you enter from the keyboard:

```c
/* Program 6.6 Comparing strings */
#include <stdio.h>
#include <string.h>
```

(Continued)

```
void main()
{
  char word1[20];                /* Stores the first word  */
  char word2[20];                /* Stores the second word */

  printf("\nType in the first word:\n1: ");
  scanf("%s', word1);            /* Read the first word    */
  printf("Type in the second word:\n 2: ");
  scanf("%s", word2);            /* Read the second word   */

  /* Compare the two words */
  if(strcmp(word1,word2) == 0)
    printf("You have entered identical words");
  else
    printf("%s precedes %s",
                  (strcmp(word1, word2) < 0) ? word1 : word2,
                  (strcmp(word1, word2) < 0) ? word2 : word1);
}
```

The program will read in two words and then tell you which word comes before the other alphabetically. The output looks something like this:

```
Type in two words:
1: apple
2: banana
apple comes before banana
```

HOW IT WORKS

You start the program with the #include directives for the header files for the standard input and output library, and the string handling library:

```
#include <stdio.h>
#include <string.h>
```

In the body of main(), you first declare two character arrays to store the words that you'll read in from the keyboard:

```
char word1[20];                /* Stores the first word  */
char word2[20];                /* Stores the second word */
```

You set the size of the arrays to 20. This should be enough for an example, but there's a risk that this may not be sufficient. As with the strcpy() function, it's *your* responsibility to allocate enough space for what the user may key in. The function scanf() has no way to tell when it runs out of space, and it will happily

(Continued)

overwrite things it shouldn't. With just 20 characters allowed for in each array, you have an opportunity to see what can happen when it isn't enough.

The next task is to get two words from the user, so after a prompt, you use scanf() twice to read a couple of words from the keyboard:

```
printf("\nType in the first word:\n1: ");
scanf("%s", word1);                    /* Read the first word    */
printf("Type in the second word:\n 2: ");
scanf("%s", word2);                    /* Read the second word   */
```

Notice how in this example you haven't used an & before the variables. This is because the name of an array by itself is an address. It corresponds to the address of the first element in the array. You could have written this explicitly using the & operator like this:

```
scanf("%s", &word1[0]);
```

Therefore, &word1[0] is equal to word1! I'll go into more detail on this in the next chapter.

Finally, you use the strcmp() function to compare the two words that were entered:

```
if(strcmp(word1,word2) == 0)
  printf("You have entered identical words");
else
  printf("%s precedes %s",
                (strcmp(word1, word2) < 0) ? word1 : word2,
                (strcmp(word1, word2) < 0) ? word2 : word1);
```

If the value returned by the strcmp() function is 0, then the two strings are equal and you display a message to this effect. If not, then you print out a message specifying which word precedes the other. You do this using the conditional operator to specify which word you want to print first and which you want to print second.

....

Searching a String

The string.h header file declares several string searching functions, but before I get into these, please take a peek at the subject of the next chapter. You'll need an appreciation of the basics of this in order to understand how to use the string searching functions.

The Idea of a Pointer

As you'll learn in detail in the next chapter, C provides a remarkably useful type of variable called a **pointer**. A pointer is a variable that contains an address—that is, it contains a reference to another location in memory that can contain a value. You've already used an address when you've used the function scanf(). A pointer is described very simply in Figure 6-3.

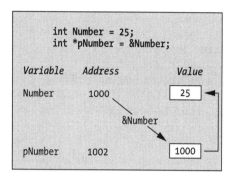

Figure 6-3. An example of a pointer

You declare a variable, Number, with the value 25, and a pointer, pNumber, which contains the address of Number. You can now use the variable pNumber in the expression *pNumber to obtain the value contained in Number.

The main reason for introducing this idea early is that the functions I'll now discuss return pointers, so you could be a bit confused by them if there was no explanation here at all. If you end up confused anyway, don't worry—all will be illuminated in the next chapter.

Searching a String for a Character

The strchr() function searches a given string for a specified character. The first argument to the function is the string to be searched (which will be the address of a char array), and the second argument is the character that you're looking for. The function will search the string starting at the beginning and return a pointer to the first position in the string where the character is found. This is the address of this position in memory, so to store the value that's returned you must create a variable that can store an address of a character. If the character isn't found, the function will return NULL, which is the equivalent of 0 for a pointer and represents a pointer that doesn't point to anything.

You can use the strchr() function like this:

```
char str[] = "The quick brown fox";  /* The string to be searched      */
char c = 'q';                         /* The character we are looking for */
char* pGot_char = NULL;               /* Pointer initialized to zero    */
pGot_char = strchr(str, c);           /* Stores address where c is found */
```

You define the character that you're looking for by the variable c of type char. Because the strchr() function expects the second argument to be of type int, the compiler will convert the value of c to this type before passing it to the function.

You could just as well define c as type int like this:

```
int c = 'q';   /* Initialize with character code for q */
```

Functions are often implemented so that a character is passed as an argument of type int because it's simpler to work with type int than type char.

Figure 6-4 illustrates the result of this search using the strchr() function.

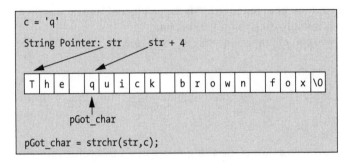

Figure 6-4. Searching for a character

The address of the first character in the string is given by the array name str. Because 'q' appears as the fifth character in the string, its address will be str+4, an offset of 4 bytes from the first character. Thus, the variable pGot_char will contain the address str+4.

Using the variable name pGot_char in an expression will access the address. If you want to access the character that's stored at that address too, then you must dereference the pointer. To do this, you precede the point variable name with the dereference operator *, for example:

```
printf("Character found was %c.", *pGot_char);
```

I'll detail using the dereferencing operator further in the next chapter.

Of course, in general it's always possible that the character you're searching for might not be found in the string, so you should take care that you don't attempt to dereference a NULL pointer. If you do try to dereference a NULL pointer, your program will crash. This is very easy to avoid with an if statement, like this:

```
if(pGot_char != NULL)
  printf("Character found was %c.", *pGot_char);
```

Now you only execute the printf() statement when the variable pGot_char isn't NULL.

The strrchr() function is very similar in operation to the strchr() function, except that it searches for the character starting from the end of the string. Thus, it will return the address of the *last* occurrence of the character in the string or NULL if it isn't found.

Searching a String for a Substring

The strstr() function is probably the most useful of all the searching functions declared in string.h. It searches one string for the first occurrence of a substring and returns a pointer to the position in the first string where the substring is found. If it doesn't find a match, it returns NULL. So if the value returned here isn't NULL, you can be sure that the searching function that you're using has found an occurrence of what it was searching for. The first argument to the function is the string that is to be searched, and the second argument is the substring you're looking for.

Here's an example of how you might use the strstr() function:

```
char text[] = "Every dog has his day";
char word[] = "dog";
char* pFound = NULL;
pFound = strstr(text, word);
```

This searches text for the first occurrence of the string stored in word. Because the string "dog" appears starting at the seventh character in text, pFound will be set to the address text+6. The search is case sensitive, so if you search the text string for "Dog", it won't be found.

....

Try It Out: Searching a String

Here's some of what I've been talking about in action:

```
/* Program 6.7 A demonstration of seeking and finding   */
#include <stdio.h>
#include <string.h>
void main()
{
  char str1[] = "This string contains the holy grail.";
  char str2[] = "the holy grail";
  char str3[] = "the holy grill";

  /* Search str1 for the occurrence of str2 */
  if(strstr(str1, str2) == NULL)
    printf("\n\"%s\" was not found.", str2);
  else
    printf("\n\"%s\" was found in \"%s\"",str2, str1);

  /* Search str1 for the occurrence of str3 */
```

(Continued)

```
  if(strstr(str1, str3) == NULL)
    printf("\n\"%s\" was not found.", str3);
  else
    printf("\nWe shouldn't get to here!");
}
```

This program produces the following output:

```
"the holy grail" was found in "This string contains the holy grail."
"the holy grill" was not found.
```

HOW IT WORKS

Note the #include directive for string.h. This is necessary when you want to use any of the string processing functions.

You have three strings defined: str1, str2, and str3:

```
char str1[] = "This string contains the holy grail.";
char str2[] = "the holy grail";
char str3[] = "the holy grill";
```

In the first if statement, you use the library function strstr() to search for the occurrence of the second string in the first:

```
if(strstr(str1, str2) == NULL)
  printf("\n\"%s\" was not found.", str2);
else
  printf("\n\"%s\" was found in \"%s\"",str2, str1);
```

You display a message corresponding to the result by testing the returned value of strstr() against NULL. If the value returned is equal to NULL, this indicates the second string wasn't found in the first, so a message is displayed to that effect. If the second string *is* found, the else is executed. In this case, a message is displayed indicating that the string was found.

You then repeat the process in the second if statement and check for the occurrence of the third string in the first:

```
if(strstr(str1, str3) == NULL)
  printf("\n\"%s\" was not found.", str3);
else
  printf("\nWe shouldn't get to here!");
```

If you get output from the first or the last printf() in the program, something is seriously wrong.

Analyzing and Transforming Strings

If you need to examine the internal contents of a string, you can use the set of standard library functions that are declared the header file `ctype.h` and that I introduced in Chapter 3. These provide you with a very flexible range of analytical functions that enable you to test what kind of character you have. They also have the advantage that they're independent of the character code in use on the computer you're using. Just to remind you, Table 6-1 shows the functions that will test for various categories of characters.

Table 6-1. Character Classification Functions

Function	Tests For
`islower()`	Lowercase letter
`isupper()`	Uppercase letter
`isalnum()`	Uppercase or lowercase letter
`iscntrl()`	Control character
`isprint()`	Any printing character including space
`isgraph()`	Any printing character except space
`isdigit()`	Decimal digit ('0' to '9')
`isxdigit()`	Hexadecimal digit ('0' to '9', 'A' to 'F', 'a' to 'f')
`isspace()`	Whitespace character (space, '\n', '\t', '\v', '\r', '\f')

The argument to a function is the character to be tested. All these functions return a nonzero value of type `int` if the character is within the set that's being tested for; otherwise, they return 0. Let's see how you can use these functions for testing the characters in a string.

Try It Out: Using the Character Classification Functions

The following example determines how many digits and letters there are in a string that's entered from the keyboard:

```
/* Program 6.8 Testing characters in a string */
#include <stdio.h>
#include <ctype.h>
void main()
{
  char buffer[80];              /* Input buffer            */
  int i = 0;                    /* Buffer index            */
  int num_letters = 0;          /* Number of letters in input */
  int num_digits = 0;           /* Number of digits in input  */
```

(Continued)

```
   printf("\nEnter an interesting string of less than 80 characters:\n");
   gets(buffer);                    /* Read a string into buffer  */


   while(buffer[i] != '\0')
   {
     if(isalpha(buffer[i]))
       num_letters++;               /* Increment letter count    */
     if(isdigit(buffer[i++]))
       num_digits++;                /* Increment digit count     */
   }
   printf("\nYour string contained %d letters and %d digits.\n",
                                          num_letters, num_digits);
}
```

Typical output from this program is

```
Enter an interesting string of less than 80 characters:
I was born on the 3rd of October 1895

Your string contained 24 letters and 5 digits.
```

HOW IT WORKS

This example is quite straightforward. You read the string into the array, buffer, with the following statement:

```
gets(buffer);
```

The string that you enter is read into the array buffer using a new standard library function, gets(). So far, you've used only scanf() to accept input from the keyboard, but it's not very useful for reading strings because it interprets a space as the end of an input value. The gets() function has the advantage that it will read all the characters entered from the keyboard, including blanks, up to when you press the Enter key. This is then stored as a string into the area specified by its argument, which in this case is the buffer array. A '\0' will be appended to the string automatically.

As with any input or output operation, things can go wrong. If an error of some kind prevents the gets() function from reading the input successfully, it will return NULL (normally, it returns the address that was passed as the argument; buffer in this case). You could therefore check that the read operation was successful like this:

```
if(gets(buffer) == NULL)
{
```

(Continued)

```
    printf("Error reading input.");
    return;                        /* End the program */
}
```

This will output a message and end the program if the read operation failed for any reason. Errors on keyboard input are relatively rare, so you won't include this testing when you're reading from the keyboard in your examples, but if you were reading from a file, then verifying that the read was successful is essential.

The statements that analyze the string are as follows:

```
while(buffer[i] != '\0')
{
  if(isalpha(buffer[i]))
    num_letters++;                 /* Increment letter count    */
  if(isdigit(Buffer[i++]))
    num_digits++;                  /* Increment digit count     */
}
```

The input string is tested character by character in the while loop. Checks are made for alphabetic characters and digits in turn in the two if statements. When either is found, the appropriate counter is incremented. Note that you increment the index to the buffer array in the second if. Remember, because you're using the postfix form of the increment operator, the check is made using the current value of i, and then i is incremented.

You could implement this without using if statements:

```
while(buffer[i] != '\0')
{
  num_letters += isalpha(buffer[i]) != 0;
  num_digits += isdigit(buffer[i++]) != 0;
}
```

The test functions return a nonzero value (not necessarily 1, though) if the argument belongs to the group of characters being tested for. The value of the logical expressions to the right of the assignment operators will be 1 if the character does belong to the category you're testing for; otherwise, it will be 0.

The way the example is coded isn't a particularly efficient way of doing things, because you test for a digit even if you've already discovered the current character is alphabetic. You could try to improve on this if the TV is really bad one night.

Converting Characters

You've already seen that the standard library also includes two conversion functions that you get access to through `ctype.h`. The `toupper()` function converts from lowercase to uppercase, and the `tolower()` function does the reverse. Both functions return either the converted character or the same character for characters that are already in the case being converted to. You can therefore convert a string to uppercase using these statements:

```
int i = 0;
for(i = 0 ; (buffer[i] = toupper(buffer[i])) != '\0' ; i++);
```

This loop will convert the entire string to uppercase by stepping through the string one character at a time, converting lowercase to uppercase and leaving uppercase characters unchanged. The loop stops when it reaches the string termination character '\0'. This sort of pattern in which everything is done inside the loop control expressions is quite common in C.

Let's try a working example that applies these functions to a string.

··

Try It Out: Converting Characters

You can use the function `toupper()` in combination with the `strstr()` function to find out whether one string occurs in another, ignoring case. Look at the following example:

```
/* Program 6.9 Finding occurrences of one string in another  */
#include <stdio.h>
#include <string.h>
#include <ctype.h>

void main()
{
  char text[100];           /* Input buffer for string to be searched */
  char substring[40];       /* Input buffer for string sought          */
  int i = 0;                /* Index to string characters              */

  printf("\nEnter the string to be searched(less than 100 characters):\n");
  gets(text);
  printf("\nEnter the string sought (less than 40 characters ):\n");
  gets(substring);

  /* Convert both strings to uppercase. */
  for(i = 0 ; (text[i] = toupper(text[i])) != '\0' ; i++);
  for(i = 0 ; (substring[i] = toupper(substring[i])) != '\0' ; i++);
```

(Continued)

```
    printf("\nThe second string %s found in the first.",
            ((strstr(text, substring) == NULL) ? "was not" : "was"));
}
```

Typical operation of this example will produce the following:

```
Enter the string to be searched(less than 100 characters):
Cry havoc, and let slip the dogs of war.

Enter the string sought (less than 40 characters ):
The Dogs of War

The second string was found in the first.
```

HOW IT WORKS

This program has three distinct phases: getting the input strings, converting both strings to uppercase, and searching the first string for an occurrence of the second.

First of all, you use printf() to prompt the user for the input, and you use the gets() function introduced in the previous example to read the input into text and substring:

```
printf("\nEnter the string to be searched(less than 100 characters):\n");
gets(text);
printf("\nEnter the string sought (less than 40 characters ):\n");
gets(substring);
```

You use the gets() function here because it will read in any string from the keyboard, including spaces, the input being terminated when the Enter key is pressed.

The conversion of both strings to uppercase is accomplished using the following statements:

```
for(i = 0 ; (text[i] = toupper(text[i])) != '\0' ; i++);
for(i = 0 ; (substring[i] = toupper(substring[i])) != '\0' ; i++);
```

These statements use for loops to do the conversion. The first for loop initializes i to 0, and then converts the ith character of text to uppercase in the loop condition and stores that result back in the same position in text. The loop condition also checks whether the character that was stored is equal to '\0', and if it is the loop ends. The index, i, is incremented in the third loop control expression. This ensures that there's no confusion as to when the incrementing of i takes place. The second loop works in exactly the same way to convert substring to uppercase.

(Continued)

With both strings in uppercase, you can test for the occurrence of substring in text, regardless of the case of the original strings. The test is done inside the output statement that reports the result:

```
printf("\nThe second string %s found in the first.",
            ((strstr(text, substring) == NULL) ? "was not" : "was"));
```

The conditional operator chooses either "was not" or "was" to be part of the output string, depending on whether or not the strstr() function returns NULL. You saw earlier that the strstr() function returns NULL when the string specified by the second argument isn't found in the first. Otherwise, it returns the address where the string was found.

Converting Strings to Numerical Values

The stdlib.h header file declares functions that you can use to convert a string to a numerical value. Each of the functions in Table 6-2 requires an argument that's a pointer to a string or an array of type char that contains a string that's a representation of a numerical value.

Table 6-2. Functions That Convert Strings to Numerical Values

Function	Returns
atof()	A value of type double that is produced from the string argument
atoi()	A value of type int that is produced from the string argument
atol()	A value of type long that is produced from the string argument

These functions are very easy to use, for example:

```
char value_str[] = "98.4";
double value = 0;
value = atof(value_str);        /* Convert string to floating-point */
```

The value_str array contains a string representation of a value of type double. You pass the array name as the argument to the atof() function to convert it to type double. You use the other two functions in a similar way.

These functions are particularly useful when you need to read numerical input in the format of a string. This can happen when the sequence of the data input is uncertain, so you need to analyze the string in order to determine what it contains. Once you've figured out what kind of numerical value the string represents, you can use the appropriate library function to convert it.

Designing a Program

You've almost come to the end of this chapter. All that remains is to go through a larger program to use some of what you've learned so far.

The Problem

The program you're going to write will lock your computer until someone types in a password. It isn't a realistic solution for preventing access to your computer in general, but you could use this code as a model for when you want to prevent unauthorized access to other programs that you write. The program will remain locked until the correct password is entered.

The Analysis

You're not going to store the password as a normal string, as this would make it possible to discover the password by looking at the program. You'll store the password internally in an encrypted form, so that even if you find the encrypted password, you won't be able to determine the original password entry too easily.

You'll implement this program in two distinct parts. The first part will generate an encrypted password according to an algorithm that you'll define—this is the password entry process. The second part will prompt for a password entry to gain access to a program, and then encrypt the entry and compare it with the original encrypted version. If they're equal, then access is granted.

Therefore, the steps are as follows:

1. Define and implement the encryption scheme and use this to encrypt the password to be used in the program.

2. Use the preceding program as a basis for the final protection program. This works by

    *   Getting the password from the user

    *   Encrypting the password using the scheme devised for step 1

    *   Comparing the encrypted entry to the previously encrypted password

The Solution

This section outlines the steps you'll take to solve the problem.

Step 1

The trickiest part of this program is implementing the encryption scheme. You'll provide for a password of up to 20 characters long but, of course, a shorter password can be entered. You'll have a default string of 20 different characters, and the password entered will replace the default string, starting with the first default character. In this way, you ensure that you don't have a sequence of identical characters at the end, unless of course the user enters them. When you actually encrypt the password, you'll apply the encryption scheme to all 20 characters, regardless of how many characters were entered. This way, no one will know the true length of the original password.

This encryption scheme will generate a final encrypted string containing only alphabetic characters. You'll encrypt the password by generating an encrypted character from each character in the original. The process will involve using one encrypted character in the process of encrypting the next. So you'll take each character in turn, encrypt it, and then use the result to encrypt the next character.

So how will you encrypt the first character? A simple approach is to calculate the sum of the character codes of all the characters in the password, and then calculate the remainder after dividing by 52. This will produce a value from 0 to 51 that you can use to generate a letter. For values between 0 and 25, you'll select the corresponding capital letter between 'A' and 'Z'. For values from 26 to 51, you'll select from 'a' to 'z'.

How will you encrypt the second and subsequent characters in the password? For that, you can take the character code for the previous encrypted character, multiply it by the character code for the current character to be encrypted, and then calculate the remainder after dividing by 52. This produces a value from 0 to 51, which you'll use as you did for the first character in the password to select from 'A' to 'Z' and 'a' to 'z'. Figure 6-5 illustrates this process.

Let's start to write the code that will put this into action. First, you need to set up the variables your program is going to use and get the password from the user:

```
/* Program 6.10 Encrypting a password */
#include <stdio.h>

void main()
{
  char unencrypted[] = "abcdefghijklmnopqrst";  /* Default password */
  char encrypted[21];             /* Stores encrypted password  */
  char password[80];              /* Input buffer               */

  printf("\nEnter your password of up to 20 characters(no spaces):\n");
  scanf("%s", password);          /* Read the password          */

  /* Plus the rest of the code */
}
```

You set the default, unencrypted password to "abcdefghijklmnopqrst" so that all the default characters that follow the password as entered will be different. You store the encrypted password in the array encrypted. You read the user's password into the array password. This has a dimension of 80 to allow for overzealousness on the part of the user when typing the entry. It's easy to enter 21 characters instead of 20, but you'll use only the first 20 in any event.

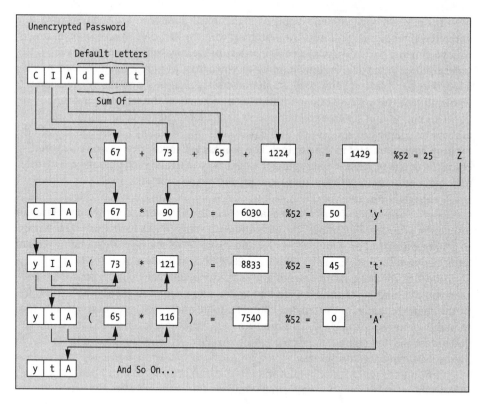

Figure 6-5. How the encryption scheme works

The next step in the encryption process is to copy password into unencrypted, leaving off the terminating '\0' from the end of the string when you copy it:

```
/* Program 6.10 Encrypting a password */
#include <stdio.h>

void main()
{
  char unencrypted[] = "abcdefghijklmnopqrst";    /* Default password */
  char encrypted[21];          /* Stores encrypted password  */
  char password[80];           /* Input buffer               */
  int i = 0;                   /* Loop counter               */

  printf("\nEnter your password of up to 20 characters(no spaces):\n");
  scanf("%s", password);       /* Read the password          */

  /* Copy the input to the unencrypted array */
   for(i = 0; i < 20 && password[i] != '\0'; i++)
      unencrypted[i] = password[i];

  /* Plus the rest of the code */
}
```

By putting the extra expression i<20 in the loop condition expression, you ensure that you don't copy more than 20 characters from the input. The loop will continue only as long as i is less than 20 *and* the current character isn't '\0'. Thus, reaching '\0' or copying 20 characters will end the loop.

Now let's add the code to encrypt the password and display it in its encrypted form:

```
/* Program 6.10 Encrypting a password */
#include <stdio.h>

void main()
{
  char unencrypted[] = "abcdefghijklmnopqrst";    /* Default password */
  char encrypted[21];                 /* Stores encrypted password */
  char password[80];                  /* Input buffer            */
  int i = 0;                          /* Loop counter            */
  long code = 0L;                     /* Stores encrypted character */

  printf("\nEnter your password of up to 20 characters(no spaces):\n");
  scanf("%s", password);              /* Read the password       */

  /* Copy the input to the unencrypted array */
   for(i = 0; i < 20 && password[i] != '\0'; i++)
      unencrypted[i] = password[i];

  /* Set up multiplier for first character encryption */
  code = 0;
  for (i = 0; i < 20; code += unencrypted[i++]);  /* Sum the characters */
  code %= 52;                              /* Get the remainder   */
  code += code < 26 ? 'A' : ('a' – 26);        /* select a letter    */

  /* Encrypt the password string */
  for (i = 0; i < 20; i++)
  {
     code *= unencrypted[i];                  /* multiply character to encrypt */
     code %= 52;                              /* Get remainder      */
     code += (code < 26) ? 'A' : ('a' – 26);  /* Select character   */
     encrypted[i] = (char)code;               /* Store character    */
  }
  encrypted[i] = '\0';                         /* Append terminator */

  printf("\nEncrypted password is: %s", encrypted);
}
```

You now have the complete encryption program. There are two steps in the encryption process. The first is to set up the multiplier that will be used to encrypt the first character in the password. To do this, you sum all the character codes and store the total in the variable, code, and then obtain the remainder after dividing by 52. You use this value to select a letter using the conditional operator. To understand how this works, let's consider a couple of examples.

Suppose the remainder in code is 3. The condition code<26 will be true, so you'll add 'A' to the current value of code, which will produce 'D'. You should be able to see that values of code from 0 to 25 will produce 'A' to 'Z'.

Now suppose the remainder in code was 26. The condition code<26 will be false, so you'll add 'a'-26 to code, which will result in 'a'. Thus, values 26 to 51 will produce 'a' to 'z', which is what you want.

All 20 characters in the string are encrypted in the for loop. The initial value of code that you produced will be applied to the first character, and for subsequent characters the encrypted version of the previous character, which is left in code, will be used. The process for selecting the encrypted letter after multiplying code by the character to be encrypted is the same as for the initial value of code. Once all 20 characters have been encrypted, you must not forget to add the '\0' at the end; otherwise, you may get some strange output.

Here's an example of the output from the encryption program:

```
Enter your password of up to 20 characters(no spaces):
ApressPublishing


Encrypted password is: AAaVKtYNAANaANAnCunU
```

Step 2

Now that you have your encrypting program, with a few changes you can convert it into the checking program. The checking program will continue to loop, asking for the password to be entered and checking it until the encrypted entry matches the saved version. It's important when you type in your own encrypted word that you get it right; otherwise you won't get control of your computer back unless you power it off!

Actually, this isn't entirely true, as you have no way of disabling the Break key. This means that anyone can break your program using the Break key and gain access to the computer. Another flaw you need to be aware of is that the password attempt appears on the screen as you type and remains there. There are ways around both of these problems, but they're a little beyond the scope of this book.

```c
/* Program 6.11 Checking a password */
#include <stdio.h>
#include <string.h>

void main()
{
  /* Enter your own encrypted password here. */
  /* If you want to use this one the password is ApressPublishing */
  char encrypted[] = "AAaVKtYNAANaANAnCunU";
  char password[80];              /* Input buffer             */
  char unencrypted[21];           /* Unencrypted password     */
```

```
   int i = 0;                      /* Loop counter             */
   long code = 0;                  /* Stores encrypted character */

   for( ;; )
   {
     strcpy(unencrypted, "abcdefghijklmnopqrst");  /* Initialize unencrypted */

     printf("\nEnter your password of up to 20 characters(no spaces):\n");
     scanf("%s", password);        /* Read the password        */

     /* Copy the input to the unencrypted array */
     for(i = 0; i < 20 && password[i] != '\0'; i++)
       unencrypted[i] = password[i];

     /* Set up multiplier for first character encryption */
     code = 0;
     for (i = 0; i < 20; code += unencrypted[i++]);/* Sum the characters */

     code %= 52;                             /* Get the remainder */
     code += code < 26 ? 'A' : ('a' - 26);    /* select a letter   */

     for (i = 0; i < 20; i++)
     {
       code *= unencrypted[i];       /* multiply character to encrypt */
       code %= 52;                   /* Get remainder                 */
       code += (code < 26) ? 'A' : ('a' - 26);  /* Select character */
       password[i] = (char)code;   /* Store character             */
     }
     password[i] = '\0';
     if(!strcmp(password, encrypted))
     {
       printf("\nPassword OK.\n");
       break;
     }
     else
       printf("\nIncorrect password.\n");
   }
}
```

Here's some sample output from the program:

```
Enter your password of up to 20 characters(no spaces):
ApressPublications#

Incorrect password.

Enter your password of up to 20 characters(no spaces):
Apresspublishing
```

```
Incorrect password.

Enter your password of up to 20 characters(no spaces):
ApressPublishing

Password OK.
```

The code here implements essentially the same mechanism as in the program to encrypt the password. The only difference is that the encryption of the password that is entered is done in an indefinite `for` loop. The loop repeats as long as the password in entered incorrectly. When the correct password is entered, a message is displayed and the loop is exited using a `break` statement.

Summary

In this chapter, you applied the techniques you learned in earlier chapters to the general problem of dealing with character strings. Strings present a different, and perhaps more difficult, problem than numeric data types.

Most of the chapter dealt with handling strings using arrays, but I also mentioned pointers. These will provide you with even more flexibility in dealing with strings, and many other things besides, as you'll discover as soon as you move on to the next chapter.

Exercises

The following exercises enable you to try out what you've learned in this chapter. If you get stuck, look back over the chapter for help. If you're still stuck, you can download the solutions from the Downloads area of the Apress website (http://www.apress.com), but that really should be a last resort.

Exercise 6-1. Write a program that will prompt for and read a positive integer less than 1,000 from the keyboard, and then create and output a string that is the value of the integer in words. For example, if **941** is entered, the program will create the string "Nine hundred and forty one".

Exercise 6-2. Write a program that will allow a list of words to be entered separated by commas, and then extract the words and output them one to a line, having removed any leading or trailing spaces. For example, if the input is

```
John  , Jack ,   Jill
```

then the output will be

```
John
Jack
Jill
```

Exercise 6-3. Write a program that will output a randomly chosen thought for the day from a set of at least five thoughts of your own choosing.

Exercise 6-4. A **palindrome** is a phrase that reads the same backward as forward, ignoring whitespace and punctuation. For example, "Madam, I'm Adam" and "Are we not drawn onward, we few? Drawn onward to new era?" are palindromes. Write a program that will determine whether or not a string entered from the keyboard is a palindrome.

CHAPTER 7

Pointers

YOU HAD A GLIMPSE OF POINTERS in the last chapter and just a small hint at what you can use them for. Here, you'll delve a lot deeper into the subject of pointers and see what else you can do with them.

I'll cover a lot of new concepts here, so you may need to repeat some things a few times. This is a long chapter, so spend some time on it and experiment with the examples. Remember that the basic ideas are very simple, but you can apply them to solving complicated problems. By the end of this chapter, you'll be equipped with an essential element for effective C programming.

In this chapter you'll learn

- What a pointer is and how it's used

- What the relationship between pointers and arrays is

- How to use pointers with strings

- How you can declare and use arrays of pointers

- How to write an improved calculator program

A First Look at Pointers

You now come to one of the most extraordinarily powerful tools in the C language. It's also potentially the most confusing, so it's important you get the ideas straight in your mind at the outset and maintain a clear idea of what's happening as you dig deeper.

Back in Chapters 2 and 5 I discussed memory. I talked about how your computer allocates an area of memory when you declare a variable. You refer to this area in memory using the variable name in your program, but once your program is compiled and running, your computer references it by the address of the memory location. This is the number that the computer uses to refer to the "box" in which the value of the variable is stored.

Look at the following statement:

```
int number = 5L;
```

Here an area of memory is allocated to store an integer, and it's called number. The value 5 is stored in this area. The computer references the area using an address. The specific address where this data will be stored depends on your computer and what operating system and compiler you're using. Even though the variable name is fixed in the source program, the address is likely to be different on different systems.

Variables that can store addresses are called **pointers**, and the address that's stored in a pointer is usually that of another variable, as illustrated in Figure 7-1. You have a pointer P that contains the address of another variable, called number, which is an integer variable containing the value 5.

Figure 7-1. How a pointer works

The first thing to appreciate is that it's not enough to know that a particular variable, such as P, is a pointer. You, and more important, the compiler, must know the type of variable to which it points. Without this information it's virtually impossible to know how to handle the contents of the memory to which it points. A pointer to a value of type char is pointing to a value occupying 1 byte, whereas a pointer to a value of type long is usually pointing to a value occupying 4 bytes. This means that every pointer will be associated with a specific variable type, and it can be used only to point to variables of that type. So pointers of type "pointer to int" can point only to variables of type int, pointers of type "pointer to float" can point only to variables of type float, and so on.

Declaring Pointers

You can declare a pointer to a variable of type int with the following statement:

```
int *pointer;
```

This statement creates the pointer but doesn't initialize it. Uninitialized pointers are particularly hazardous, so you should always initialize a pointer when you declare it. You can initialize pointer so that it doesn't point to anything by rewriting the declaration like this:

```
int *pointer = NULL;
```

NULL is a constant that's defined in the standard library and is the equivalent of 0 for a pointer. NULL is a value that's guaranteed not to point to any location in memory. This means that it implicitly prevents the accidental overwriting of memory by using a pointer that doesn't point to anything specific.

If you want to initialize your variable pointer with the address of a variable that you've already declared, you use the address of operator, &, for example:

```
int number = 10;
int *pointer = &number;
```

Now the initial value of pointer is the address of the variable number. Note that the declaration of number must precede the declaration of the pointer. If this isn't the case, your code won't compile. The compiler needs to have already allocated space and thus an address for number to use it to initialize the pointer variable.

There's nothing special about the declaration of a pointer. You can declare regular variables and pointers in the same statement, for example:

```
double value, *pVal, fnum;
```

This statement declares two double-precision floating-point variables, value and fnum, and a variable, pVal, of type "pointer to double".

Accessing a Value Through a Pointer

You use the **indirection operator**, *, to access the value of the variable pointed to by a pointer. This operator is also referred to as the **dereference operator** because you use it to "dereference" a pointer. Suppose you declare the following variables:

```
int number = 15;
int *pointer = &number;
int result = 0;
```

The pointer variable contains the address of the variable number, so you can use this in an expression to calculate a new value for the total, like this:

```
result = *pointer +5;
```

The expression *pointer will evaluate to the value stored at the address contained in the pointer. This is the value stored in number, 15, so result will be set to 15 + 5, which is 20.

So much for the theory. Let's look at a small program that will highlight some of the characteristics of this special kind of variable.

Try It Out: Declaring Pointers

In this example, you're simply going to declare a variable and a pointer. You'll then see how you can output their addresses and the values they contain.

```
/* Program 7.1 A simple program using pointers */
#include <stdio.h>

void main()
{
    int number = 0;              /* A variable of type int initialized to 0  */
    int *pointer = NULL;         /* A pointer that can point to type int      */

    number = 10;
    printf("\nnumber's address: %p", &number);              /* Output the address */
    printf("\nnumber's value: %d\n\n", number);             /* Output the value    */

    pointer = &number;           /* Store the address of number in pointer    */

    printf("pointer's address: %p", &pointer);              /* Output the address */
    printf("\npointer's size: %d bytes", sizeof(pointer));  /* Output the size     */
    printf("\npointer's value: %p", pointer);  /* Output the value (an address) */
    printf("\nvalue pointed to: %d\n", *pointer);           /* Value at the address */
}
```

The output from the program will look something like the following. Remember, the actual address is likely to be different on your machine.

```
number's address: 0012FEE4
number's value: 10

pointer's address: 0012FEE0
pointer's size: 4 bytes
pointer's value: 0012FEE4
value pointed to: 10
```

HOW IT WORKS

You first declare a variable and a pointer:

```
    int number = 0;              /* A variable of type int initialized to 0  */
    int *pointer = NULL;         /* A pointer that can point to type int      */
```

(Continued)

The variable called number is of type int, and the pointer called pointer is of type "pointer to int". Pointers need to be declared just like any other variable. To declare the pointer called pointer, you put an asterisk (*) in front of the variable name in the declaration. The asterisk defines pointer as a pointer, and the type, int, fixes it as a pointer to integer variables. The initial value, NULL, is the equivalent of 0 for a pointer—it doesn't point to anything.

After the declarations, you store the value 10 in the variable called number and then output its address and its value with these statements:

```
number = 10;
printf("\nnumber's address: %p", &number);          /* Output the address */
printf("\nnumber's value: %d\n\n", number);          /* Output the value   */
```

To output the address of the variable called number, you use the output format specifier %p. This outputs the value as a memory address in hexadecimal form.

You use the address of operator, &, to store an address in pointer:

```
pointer = &number;                  /* Store the address of number in pointer   */
```

This statement obtains the address of the variable number and stores that address in pointer. Remember, the only kind of value that you should store in pointer is an address.

Next, you have four printf() statements that output, respectively, the address of pointer (which is the memory location that pointer occupies), the number of bytes that the pointer occupies, the value stored in pointer (which is the address of number), and the value stored at the address that pointer contains (which is the value stored in number).

Just to make sure you're clear about this, let's go through these line by line. The first output statement is as follows:

```
printf("pointer's address: %p", &pointer);
```

Here, you output the address of the pointer. Remember, the pointer itself has an address, just like any other variable. You use %p as the conversion specifier to display an address, and you use the & (address of) operator to reference the address that the variable occupies.

Next you output the size of the pointer:

```
printf("\npointer's size: %d bytes", sizeof(pointer)); /* Output the size   */
```

You can use the sizeof operator to obtain the number of bytes a pointer occupies, just like any other variable, and the output on my machine shows that a pointer occupies 4 bytes, so a memory address on my machine is 32 bits.

(Continued)

The next statement outputs the value stored in pointer:

```
printf("\npointer's value: %p", pointer);
```

The value stored in pointer is the address of number. Because this is an address, you use %p to display it and you use the variable name, pointer, to access the address value.

The last output statement is as follows:

```
printf("\nvalue pointed to: %d", *pointer);
```

Here, you use the pointer to access the value stored in number. The effect of the * operator is to access the data contained in the address stored at pointer. You use %d because you know it's an integer value. The variable pointer stores the address of number, so you can use that address to access the value stored in number. As I said, the * operator is called the **indirection operator**, or sometimes the **dereferencing operator**.

The addresses shown will be different on different computers, and they'll often be different at different times on the same computer. The latter is due to the fact that your program won't always be loaded at the same place in memory. The addresses of number and pointer are where in the computer the variables are stored. Their values are what's actually stored at that address. For the variable called number, it's an actual integer value (10), but for the variable called pointer, it's the address of number. Using *pointer actually gives you access to the value of number. You're accessing the value of the variable, number, indirectly.

You'll certainly have noticed that your indirection operator, *, is also the symbol for multiplication. Fortunately, there's no risk of confusion for the compiler. Depending on where the asterisk appears, the compiler will understand whether it should interpret the asterisk as an indirection operator or as a multiplication sign.

Figure 7-2 illustrates using a pointer.

(Continued)

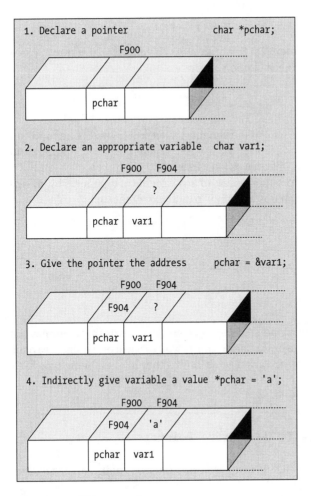

1. Declare a pointer   char *pchar;

   F900

   pchar

2. Declare an appropriate variable   char var1;

   F900   F904

   ?

   pchar | var1

3. Give the pointer the address   pchar = &var1;

   F900   F904

   F904   ?

   pchar | var1

4. Indirectly give variable a value *pchar = 'a';

   F900   F904

   F904   'a'

   pchar | var1

Figure 7-2. Using a pointer

Using Pointers

Because you can access the contents of number through the pointer pointer, you can use a dereferenced pointer in arithmetic statements, for example:

```
*pointer += 25;
```

This statement increments the value of the variable called number by 25. The * indicates you're accessing the contents of whatever the variable called pointer is pointing to. In this case, it's the contents of the variable called number.

The variable pointer can store the address of any variable of type int. This means you can change the variable that pointer points to by a statement such as this:

```
pointer = &another_number;
```

The same statement that you used previously

```
*pointer +=  25;
```

is now operating with the new variable, another_number. This means that a pointer can assume the guise of any variable of the same type, so you can use one pointer variable to change the values of many other variables, as long as they're of the same type as the pointer.

....

Try It Out: Using Pointers

Let's exercise this newfound facility in an example. You'll use pointers to increase values stored in some other variables.

```
/* Program 7.2  What's the pointer */
#include <stdio.h>

void main()
{
   long num1 = 0;
   long num2 = 0;
   long *pnum = NULL;

   pnum = &num1;                          /* Get address of num1    */
   *pnum = 2;                             /* Set num1 to 2          */
   ++num2;                                /* Increment num2         */
   num2 += *pnum;                         /* Add num1 to num2       */

   pnum = &num2;                          /* Get address of num2    */
```

(Continued)

```
    ++*pnum;                                    /* Increment num2 indirectly */

    printf ("\nnum1 = %ld   num2 = %ld   *pnum = %ld   *pnum + num2 = %ld\n",
                              num1, num2, *pnum, *pnum + num2);
}
```

When you run this program, you should get the following output:

```
num1 = 2   num2 = 4   *pnum = 4   *pnum + num2 = 8
```

The comments should make the program easy to follow up to the printf(). First, in the body of main(), you have these declarations:

```
long num1 = 0;
long num2 = 0;
long *pnum = NULL;
```

This ensures that you set out with initial values for the two variables, num1 and num2, at 0. It also declares an integer pointer, pnum, which is initialized with NULL.

 CAUTION *You should always initialize your pointers when you declare them. Using a pointer that isn't initialized to store an item of data is dangerous. Who knows what you might overwrite?*

The next statement is an assignment:

```
    pnum = &num1;                              /* Get address of num1      */
```

The pointer pnum is set to point to num1 here, because you take the address of num1 using the address of operator and store it in pnum.

The next two statements are

```
    *pnum = 2;                                 /* Set num1 to 2           */
    ++num2;                                    /* Increment num2          */
```

The first statement exploits your newfound power of the pointer, and you set the value of num1 to 2 indirectly. Then the variable num2 gets incremented by 1 in the normal way, using the increment operator.

(Continued)

The statement

```
num2 += *pnum;                          /* Add num1 to num2        */
```

adds the contents of the variable pointed to by pnum, to num2. Because pnum still points to num1, num2 is being increased by the value of num1.

The next two statements are

```
pnum = &num2;                           /* Get address of num2     */
++*pnum;                                 /* Increment num2 indirectly */
```

First, the pointer is reassigned to point to num2. The variable num2 is then incremented indirectly through the pointer. You can see that the expression ++*pnum increments the value pointed to by pnum without any problem However, if you wanted to use the postfix form, you would have to write (*pnum)++. The parentheses are essential—assuming that you want to increment the value rather than the address. If you omit them, the increment would apply to the address contained in pnum. This is because the operators ++ and unary * (and unary &, for that matter) share the same precedence level and are evaluated right to left. The compiler would apply the ++ to pnum first, incrementing the address, and only then dereference it to get the value. This is a common source of error when incrementing values through pointers, so it's probably a good idea to use parentheses in any event.

Finally, you have a printf() statement:

```
printf ("\nnum1 = %ld   num2 = %ld   *pnum = %ld   *pnum + num2 = %ld",
                         num1, num2, *pnum, *pnum + num2);
```

This displays the values of num1, num2, num2 incremented by 1 through pnum and, lastly, num2 in the guise of pnum, with the value of num2 added.

If you aren't clear on what happened in this example, go through the program again slowly. Pointers can be confusing when you encounter them for the first time. It's the multiple levels of meaning that are the source of the confusion. You can work with addresses or values, pointers, or variables, and sometimes it's hard to work out what exactly is going on. The best thing to do is keep writing short programs that use the things I've described: getting values using pointers, changing values, printing addresses, and so on. This is the only way to really get confident about using pointers.

More on Operator Precedence

I've mentioned the importance of operator precedence again in this discussion. You've accumulated a few more operators since the table back in Chapter 3; Table 7-1 shows a more complete set of operators.

Table 7-1. Operator Precedence and Associativity

Operators	Associativity
( ) [ ] postfix ++ postfix -- ->	Left to right
! ~ sizeof unary + unary - Prefix ++ prefix -- Unary * (indirection operator) & (address of)	Right to left
Type casts such as (int) and (double)	Right to left
* / %	Left to right
Binary + binary -	Left to right
<< >>	Left to right
< <= > >=	Left to right
== !=	Left to right
&	Left to right
^	Left to right
|	Left to right
&&	Left to right
||	Left to right
?: (conditional operator)	Left to right
= op= (e.g., += -= etc.)	Right to left

Table 7-1 includes all the operators you've seen up to now. There is one operator that you haven't seen yet: ->. You'll meet this operator in Chapter 11.

Let's return to using pointers and see how they work with input from the keyboard.

Try It Out: Using a Pointer with scanf()

Until now, when you've used scanf() to input values, you've used the & operator to obtain the address to be transferred to the function. When you have a pointer that already contains an address, you simply need to use the pointer name as a parameter. You can see this in the following example:

```c
/* Program 7.3  Pointer argument to scanf */
#include <stdio.h>

void main()
{
   int value = 0;
   int *pvalue = NULL;

   pvalue = &value;                    /* Set pointer to refer to value  */

   printf ("Input an integer: ");
```

(Continued)

```
    scanf(" %d", pvalue);                    /* Read into value via the pointer */

    printf("\nYou entered %d\n", value);     /* Output the value entered */
}
```

This program will just echo what you enter. How unimaginative can you get? Typical output could be something like this:

```
Input an integer: 10
You entered 10
```

HOW IT WORKS

Everything should be pretty clear up to the scanf() statement:

```
    scanf(" %d", pvalue);
```

You normally store the value entered by the user at the address of the variable. In this case, you could have used &value. But here, the pointer pvalue is used to hand over the address of value to scanf(). You already stored the address of value in pvalue with this assignment:

```
    pvalue = &value;                    /* Set pointer to refer to value   */
```

pvalue and &value are the same, so you can use either!

You then just display value:

```
    printf("\nYou entered %d", value);
```

Although this is a rather pointless example, it isn't pointerless, as it illustrates how pointers and variables can work together.

Testing for a NULL Pointer

The pointer declaration in the last example is

```
    int *pvalue = NULL;
```

Here, you initialize pvalue with the value NULL. As I said earlier, NULL is a special constant in C, and it's the pointer equivalent to 0 with ordinary numbers. The definition of NULL is contained in stdio.h, so if you use it, you must ensure that you include this header file.

When you assign 0 to a pointer, it's the equivalent of setting it to NULL, so you could write the following:

```
int *pvalue = 0;
```

However, using NULL as the initial value is preferable because it makes it clear that it's a pointer that is being initialized.

Because NULL is the equivalent of 0, if you want to test whether the pointer pvalue is NULL or not, you can write this:

```
if(!pvalue)
{
  ...
}
```

This block of statements will be executed only if pvalue isn't NULL. However, I think it's generally better to write the test as follows:

```
if(pvalue == NULL)
{
  ...
}
```

I prefer to test pointer values against NULL simply because this helps to make it clear that it's a pointer that's being checked and not a numerical value.

NOTE *It's possible to assign specific values to pointers, using numeric constants that are usually specified in hexadecimal notation. This means that you can access memory locations anywhere in the computer that may hold values of interest.*

This becomes very hazardous once you introduce the possibility of storing values in such specifically defined addresses. Unless you're absolutely sure what you're doing, the practice is best avoided.

Naming Pointers

You've already started to write some quite large programs. As you can imagine, when your programs get even bigger, it's going to get even harder to remember which variables are normal variables and which are pointers. Therefore, it's quite a good idea to use names beginning with p as pointer names. If you follow this method religiously, you'll never be in any doubt about which variables are pointers.

Where a pointer contains the address of a particular variable, the pointer is often named by prefixing the name of the variable with p. Thus, pnumber would be a pointer to a variable number. Sometimes the initial character of the variable name is capitalized when the pointer name is formed, so pNumber may also be used as the name for a pointer that contains the address of number.

Arrays and Pointers

You'll need a clear head for this bit. Let's recap for a moment and recall what an array is and what a pointer is:

- An **array** is a collection of objects of the same type that you can refer to using a single name. For example, an array called scores[50] could contain all your basketball scores for a 50-game season. You use a different index value to refer to each element in the array. scores[0] is your first score and scores[49] is your last. If you had ten games each month, you could use a multidimensional array, scores[12][10]. If you start play in January, the third game in June would be referenced by scores[5][2].

- A **pointer** is a variable that has as its value the address of another variable or constant of a given type. You can use a pointer to access different variables at different times, as long as they're all of the same type.

These seem quite different, and indeed they are, but arrays and pointers are really very closely related and they can sometimes be used interchangeably. Let's consider strings. A string is just an array of type char. If you want to input a single character with scanf(), you could use this:

```
char single;
scanf("%c", &single);
```

Here, you need the address of operator for scanf() to work because scanf() needs the address of the location where the input data is to be stored.

However, if you're reading in a string, you can write this:

```
char multiple[10];
scanf("%s", multiple);
```

Here you don't use the & operator. You're using the array name just like a pointer. If you use the array name in this way without an index value, then it refers to the address of the first element in the array.

Always keep in mind, though, that there's an important difference: arrays are *not* pointers. You can change the address contained in a pointer, but you can't change the address referenced by an array name.

Arrays and Pointers in Practice

Let's go through several examples to see how arrays and pointers work together. The following examples link together as a progression. With practical examples of how arrays and pointers can work together, you should find it fairly easy to get a grasp of the main ideas behind pointers and their relationship to arrays.

....

Try It Out: Arrays and Pointers

Just to further illustrate that an array name by itself refers to an address, try running the following program:

```
/* Program 7.4  Arrays and pointers - A simple program*/
#include <stdio.h>

void main()
{
   char multiple[] = "I am a string";

   printf("\nThe address of the first array element  : %p", &multiple[0]);
   printf("\nThe address obtained from the array name: %p\n", multiple);
}
```

On my computer, the output is as follows:

```
The address of the first array element  : 0012FED4
The address obtained from the array name: 0012FED4
```

HOW IT WORKS

You can conclude from the output of this program that the expression &multiple[0] produces the same value as multiple. So let's take this a bit further. If multiple refers to the same thing as &multiple[0], what does multiple + 1 equal? Let's try the following example.

....

....

Try It Out: Arrays and Pointers Taken Further

This program demonstrates the effect of adding an integer value to a pointer:

```
/* Program 7.5 Arrays and pointers taken further */
#include <stdio.h>

void main()
```

(Continued)

```
{
    char multiple[] = "another string";

    printf("\n          value of second element: %c\n", multiple[1]);
    printf("value of multiple after adding 1: %c\n", *(multiple + 1));
}
```

The output is

```
        value of second element: n
value of multiple after adding 1: n
```

HOW IT WORKS

You can see that multiple[1] is the same as *(multiple + 1). You can further confirm this if you display the addresses rather than the values:

```
/* Program 7.5A Arrays and pointers taken further */
#include <stdio.h>

void main()
{
    char multiple[] = "another string";

    printf("\nAddress of second element: %p", &multiple[1]);
    printf("\nValue of multiple+1       : %p\n", multiple+1);
}
```

You would get

```
Address of second element: 0012FED5
Value of multiple+1       : 0012FED5
```

Nothing unusual there, nor is there anything unusual if you display the addresses of the first, second, and third elements of the array:

```
/* Program 7.5B Arrays and pointers taken further */
#include <stdio.h>

void main()
{
    char multiple[] = "another string";

    printf(" first element: %p\n", multiple);
```

(Continued)

```
    printf("second element: %p\n", multiple + 1);
    printf(" third element: %p\n", multiple + 2);
}
```

Here's the output:

```
 first element: 0012FED4
second element: 0012FED5
 third element: 0012FED6
```

The addresses differ by 1, which is what you would expect when you add 1 to multiple and then add 2 to multiple.

Try It Out: Different Types of Arrays

That's interesting, but you already knew that the computer could add numbers together without much problem. So let's change to a different type of array and see what happens:

```
/* Program 7.6 Different types of arrays */
#include <stdio.h>

void main()
{
   long multiple[] = {1L, 2L, 3L};

   printf(" first element address: %p value: %d\n",
                                         multiple, *multiple);
   printf("second element address: %p value: %d\n", multiple + 1,
                                         *(multiple + 1));
   printf(" third element address: %p value: %d\n", multiple + 2,
                                         *(multiple + 2));
   printf("    type long occupies: %d bytes\n", sizeof(long));
}
```

If you compile and run this program, you get an entirely different result:

```
 first element address: 0012FEDC value: 1
second element address: 0012FEE0 value: 2
 third element address: 0012FEE4 value: 3
    type long occupies: 4 bytes
```

(Continued)

HOW IT WORKS

Look at the output. With this example, `multiple` is `12FEDC` and `multiple+1` is equal to `12FEE0`! You can see that `12FEE0` is 4 greater than `12FEDC`, although you only added 1. This isn't a mistake. The compiler realizes that when you add 1 to an address value, what you actually want to do is access the next variable of that type. This is why, when you declare a pointer, you have to specify the *type* of variable that's to be pointed to. Remember that `char` data is stored in 1 byte and that variables declared as `long` typically occupy 4 bytes. As you can see, on my computer variables declared as `long` are 4 bytes. Incrementing a pointer to type `long` by 1 on my computer increments the address by 4, because a value of type `long` occupies 4 bytes. On a computer that stores type `long` in 8 bytes, incrementing a pointer to `long` by 1 will increase the address value by 8.

 NOTE *Remember that although when you use an array name in this way it behaves like a pointer, an array isn't a pointer. An array has a fixed address.*

Multidimensional Arrays

So far, you've looked at one-dimensional arrays, but is it the same story with arrays that have two or more dimensions? Well, to some extent it is. However, the differences between pointers and array names start to become more apparent. Let's consider the array that you used for the tic-tac-toe program at the end of Chapter 5. You declared the array as follows:

```
char board[3][3] = {
                     {'1','2','3'},
                     {'4','5','6'},
                     {'7','8','9'}
                   };
```

You'll use this array for the examples in this section, to explore multidimensional arrays in relation to pointers.

Try It Out: Using Two-Dimensional Arrays

You'll look first at some of the addresses related to your array, board, with this example:

```c
/* Program 7.7 Two-Dimensional arrays and pointers */
#include <stdio.h>

void main()
{
   char board[3][3] = {
                        {'1','2','3'},
                        {'4','5','6'},
                        {'7','8','9'}
                      };

   printf("address of board       : %p\n", board);
   printf("address of board[0][0] : %p\n", &board[0][0]);
   printf("but what is in board[0] : %p\n", board[0]);
}
```

The output might come as a bit of a surprise to you:

```
address of board       : 0012FED8
address of board[0][0] : 0012FED8
but what is in board[0] : 0012FED8
```

HOW IT WORKS

As you can see, all three output values are the same, so what can you deduce from this? The answer is quite simple. When you declare a one-dimensional array, placing [n1] after the array name tells the compiler that it's an array with n1 elements. When you declare a two-dimensional array by placing [n2] for the second dimension after the [n1] for the first dimension, the compiler creates an array of size n1, in which each element is an array of size n2. When you declare a two-dimensional array, you're creating an array of subarrays. So when you access this two-dimensional array using the array name with a single index value, board[0] for example, you're actually referencing the address of one of the subarrays. Using the two-dimensional array name by itself references the address of the beginning of the whole array of subarrays, which is also the address of the beginning of the first subarray!

(Continued)

To summarize

```
board
board[0]
&board[0][0]
```

all have the same value, but they aren't the same thing.

This also means that the expression board[1] results in the same address as the expression board[1][0]. This should be reasonably easy to understand because the latter expression is the first element of the second subarray, board[1].

The problems start when you use pointer notation to get to the values within the array. You still have to use the indirection operator, but you must be careful. If you change the preceding example to display the value of the first element, you'll see why:

```
/* Program 7.7A Two-Dimensional arrays */
#include <stdio.h>

void main()
{
    char board[3][3] = {
                          {'1','2','3'},
                          {'4','5','6'},
                          {'7','8','9'}
                       };

    printf("value of board[0][0] : %c\n", board[0][0]);
    printf("value of board[0]    : %c\n", *board[0]);
    printf("value of board       : %c\n", **board);
}
```

The output from this program is as follows:

```
value of board[0][0] : 1
value of board[0]    : 1
value of board       : 1
```

As you can see, if you use board as a means of obtaining the value of the first element, then you need to use two indirection operators to get it: **board. You were able to use just one * in the previous program because you were dealing with a one-dimensional array. If you used only the one *, you would get the address of the first element of the array of arrays, which is the address referenced by board[0].

(Continued)

The relationship between the multidimensional array and its subarrays is shown in Figure 7-3.

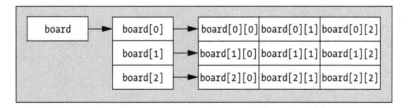

Figure 7-3. Referencing an array, its subarrays, and its elements

As Figure 7-3 shows, board refers to the address of the first element in the array of subarrays, and board[0], board[1], and board[2] refer to the addresses of the first element in the corresponding subarrays. Using two index values accesses the value stored in an element of the array. So, with this clearer picture of what's going on in your multidimensional array, let's see how you can use board to get to all the values in that array. You'll do this in the next example.

Try It Out: Getting All the Values in a Two-Dimensional Array

This example takes the previous example a bit further using a for loop:

```c
/* Program 7.8  Getting the values in a two-dimensional array */
#include <stdio.h>

void main()
{
   int i = 0;                           /* Loop counter */
   char board[3][3] = {
                        {'1','2','3'},
                        {'4','5','6'},
                        {'7','8','9'}
                      };

   /* List all elements of the array */
   for(i = 0; i < 9; i++)
     printf(" board: %c\n", *(*board + i));
}
```

(Continued)

The output from the program is as follows:

```
board: 1
board: 2
board: 3
board: 4
board: 5
board: 6
board: 7
board: 8
board: 9
```

HOW IT WORKS

The thing to notice about this program is the way you dereference board in the loop:

```
printf(" board: %c\n", *(*board + i));
```

As you can see, you use the expression *(*board + i) to get the value of an array element. The expression between the parentheses, *board+i, produces the address of the element in the array that is at offset i. Dereferencing this results in the value at this address. It's important that the brackets are included. Leaving them out would give you the value pointed to by board (i.e., the value stored in the location referenced by the address stored in board) with the value of i added to this value. So if i had the value 2, you would simply output the value of the first element of the array plus 2. What you actually want to do, and what your expression does, is add the value of i to the *address* contained in board, and then dereference this new address to obtain a value.

To make this clearer, let's see what happens if you omit the parentheses in the example. Try changing the initial values for the array so that the characters go from '9' to '1'. If you leave out the brackets in the expression in the printf() call, so that it reads like this:

```
printf(" board: %c\n", **board + i);
```

you should get output that looks something like this:

```
board: 9
board: :
board: ;
board: <
board: =
board: >
```

(Continued)

```
board: ?
board: @
board: A
```

This output results because you're adding the value of i to the contents of the first element of the array, board. The characters you get come from the ASCII table, starting at '9' and continuing to 'A'.

Also, if you used the expression **(board + i), this too would have given erroneous results. In this case, **(board + 0) points to board[0][0], whereas **(board + 1) points to board[1][0];, and **(board + 2) points to board[2][0]. If you use higher increments, you would be accessing memory locations outside the array, because there isn't a fourth element in the array of arrays.

Multidimensional Arrays and Pointers

So now that you've used the array name using pointer notation for referencing a two-dimensional array, let's use a variable that you've declared as a pointer. As I've already stated, this is where there's a significant difference. If you declare a pointer and assign the address of the array to it, then you can use that pointer to access the members of the array.

Try It Out: Multidimensional Arrays and Pointers

You can see this in action here:

```c
/* Program 7.9  Multidimensional arrays and pointers*/
#include <stdio.h>

void main()
{
    int i = 0;                          /* Loop counter     */
    char board[3][3] = {
                        {'1','2','3'},
                        {'4','5','6'},
                        {'7','8','9'}
                       };

    char *pointer = *board;             /* A pointer to char */

    for(i = 0; i < 9; i++)
      printf(" board: %c\n", *(pointer + i));
}
```

(Continued)

Here, you get the same output as before:

```
board: 1
board: 2
board: 3
board: 4
board: 5
board: 6
board: 7
board: 8
board: 9
```

HOW IT WORKS

Here, you initialize `pointer` with the address of the first element of the array, and then you just use normal pointer arithmetic to move through the array:

```
char *pointer = *board;              /* A pointer to char */

for(i = 0; i < 9; i++)
  printf(" board: %c\n", *(pointer + i));
```

Note how you dereference `board` to obtain the address you want (with *board), because `board`, by itself, is the address of the array `board[0]`, not the address of an element. You could have initialized `pointer` by using the following:

```
char pointer = &board[0][0];
```

This amounts to the same thing. You might think you could initialize `pointer` using this statement:

```
pointer = board;                    /* Wrong level of indirection! */
```

This is wrong. You should get a compiler warning if you do this. Strictly speaking, this isn't legal because `pointer` and `board` have different levels of **indirection**. That's a great jargon term that just means that `pointer` refers to an address that contains a value of type char, whereas `board` refers to an address *that refers to an address* containing a value of type char. There's an extra level with `board` compared to `pointer`. Consequently, `pointer` needs one * to get to the value, and `board` needs two. Most compilers will allow you to get away with this and just give you a warning about what you've done. However, it's very bad practice, so you shouldn't do it!

Accessing Array Elements

Now you know that, for a two-dimensional array, you have several ways of accessing the elements in that array. Table 7-2 lists these ways of accessing your board array.

Table 7-2. Pointer Expressions for Accessing Array Elements

board	0	1	2
0	board[0][0] *board[0] **board	board[0][1] *(board[0]+1) *(*board+1)	board[0][2] *(board[0]+2) *(*board+2)
1	board[1][0] *(board[0]+3) *board[1] *(*board+3)	board[1][1] *(board[0]+4) *(board[1]+1) *(*board+4)	board[1][2] *(board[0]+5) *(board[1]+2) *(*board+5)
2	board[2][0] *(board[0]+6) *(board[1]+3) *board[2] *(*board+6)	board[2][1] *(board[0]+7) *(board[1]+4) *(board[2]+1) *(*board+7)	board[2][2] *(board[0]+8) *(board[1]+5) *(board[2]+2) *(*board+8)

Try It Out: Know Your Hat Size Revisited

Here's a rewrite of the hat sizes example using pointer notation:

```
/* Program 7.10  Understand pointers to your hat size - if you dare */
#include <stdio.h>
#define TRUE  1
#define FALSE 0

void main()
{
   char size[3][12] = {              /* Hat sizes as characters */
      {'6', '6', '6', '6', '7', '7', '7', '7', '7', '7', '7', '7'},
      {'1', '5', '3', '7', ' ', '1', '1', '3', '1', '5', '3', '7'},
      {'2', '8', '4', '8', ' ', '8', '4', '8', '2', '8', '4', '8'}
                     };

   int headsize[12] =                /* Values in 1/8 inches    */
      {164,166,169,172,175,178,181,184,188,191,194,197};

   float cranium = 0.0;              /* Head circumference in decimal inches */
   int your_head = 0;                /* Headsize in whole eighths   */
   int i = 0;                        /* Loop counter                */
```

(Continued)

```
    int hat_found = FALSE;              /* Indicates when a hat is found to fit */
    int too_small = FALSE;             /* Indicates headsize is too small      */

    /* Get the circumference of the head */
    printf("\nEnter the circumference of your head above your eyebrows"
                                    " in inches as a decimal value: ");
    scanf(" %f", &cranium);
    /* Convert to whole eighths of an inch */
    your_head = (int)(8.0* cranium);
    /* Search for a hat size */
    for (i = 0 ; i < 12 ; i++)
    {
      /* Find head size in the headsize array */
      if(your_head > *(headsize+i))
        continue;

      /* If it is the first element and the head size is  */
      /* more than 1/8 smaller then the head is too small */
      /*  for a hat                                       */
      if((i == 0) && (your_head < (*headsize)-1))
      {
        printf("\nYou are the proverbial pinhead. No hat for"
                                          "you I'm afraid.\n");
        too_small = TRUE;
        break;                         /* Exit the loop */
      }

      /* If head size is more than 1/8 smaller than the current */
      /* element in headsize array, take the next element down  */
      /* as the head size                                       */
      if( your_head < *(headsize+i)-1 )
        i--;

      printf("\nYour hat size is %c %c%c%c\n",
                      *(*size + i), *(size[1] + i),
                      (i==4)?' ' : '/',  *(*size+24+i));
      hat_found=TRUE;
      break;
    }
    if(!hat_found && !too_small)
      printf("\nYou, in technical parlance, are a fathead."
                                  " No hat for you, I'm afraid.\n");
}
```

The output from this program is the same as in Chapter 5, so I won't repeat it. It's the code that's of interest, so let's look at the new elements in this program.

(Continued)

HOW IT WORKS

This program works in essentially the same way as the example from Chapter 5. The first part, in which you declare the arrays and the other variables that you need, is the same as in Program 5.6. The differences start in the for loop that searches the headsize array. The value in your_head is compared with the values in the array in the following statement:

```
if(your_head > *(headsize+i))
    continue;
```

The expression on the right side of the comparison, *(headsize+i), is equivalent to headsize[i] in array notation. The bit between the parentheses adds i to the address of the beginning of the array. Remember that adding an integer i to an address will add i times the length of each element. Therefore, the subexpression between parentheses produces the address of the element corresponding to the index value i. The dereference operator, *, then obtains the contents of this element for the comparison operation with the value in the variable your_head.

If you examine the printf() in the middle, you'll see that you mix the notation a bit, just to show you can handle it:

```
printf("\nYour hat size is %c %c%c%c\n",
                *(*size + i), *(size[1] + i),
                (i==4)?' ' : '/',  *(*size+24+i));
```

Mixing array notation with pointers as shown here isn't recommended practice at all—it's just for illustration, to show you various ways in which you can use pointer arithmetic. Let's look at how these expressions for the output values work.

The first is *(*size + i). Because size is a two-dimensional array, size by itself is a pointer to an array of pointers, each of which points to a row of the array. Therefore, *size+i gives the address of the element in the first row of the array that has the index value i. Dereferencing this in the expression *(*size + i), produces the value stored in that element. This is equivalent to size[0][i] in array notation.

The expression *(size[1] + i) is equivalent to size[1][i]. This is because size[1] is a pointer to the second row of the array, and size[1]+i is the address of the element in that row with index value i. The dereference operator obtains the value stored.

The last expression in the printf() is *(*size+24+i). This is equivalent to size[2][i]. Because *size is a pointer to the first row, adding 24 produces the address of the first element in the third row. Adding i to that gives the address of the element in the third row with index value i. This is dereferenced using * to obtain the value.

Using Memory As You Go

Pointers are an extremely flexible and powerful tool for programming over a wide range of applications. The majority of programs in C use pointers to some extent. C also has a further facility that enhances the power of pointers, in that it permits memory to be allocated dynamically when your program executes. Allocating memory dynamically is possible only because you have pointers available.

Think back to the program in Chapter 5 that calculated the average scores for a group of students. At the moment, it works for only ten students. Suppose you want to write the program so that it works without knowing the number of students in the class in advance, and so it doesn't use any more memory than necessary for the number of student scores specified. **Dynamic memory allocation** allows you to do just that. You can create arrays at runtime that are large enough to hold the precise amount of data that you require for the task.

Dynamic Memory Allocation: The malloc() Function

The standard library function to allocate memory at runtime is called malloc(), and you need to include the stdlib.h header file in your program when you use this function. When you use the malloc() function, you specify the number of bytes of memory that you want as the argument. The function returns the address of the first byte of memory allocated in response to your request. Because you get an address returned, a pointer is a useful place to put it.

A typical example of dynamic memory allocation might be this:

```
int *pNumber = (int*)malloc(100);
```

Here, you've requested 100 bytes of memory and assigned the address of this memory block to pNumber. As long as you haven't modified it, any time that you use the variable pNumber, it will point to the first int location at the beginning of the 100 bytes that were allocated. This whole block can hold 50 int values, assuming the typical int takes 2 bytes, or 25 int values on my computer, where they require 4 bytes each.

Notice the cast, (int*), that you use to convert the address returned by the function to the type "pointer to int". You've done this because malloc() is a general-purpose function that's used to allocate memory for any type of data. The function has no knowledge of what you want to use the memory for, so it actually returns a pointer of type "pointer to void", which is written as void*. The type void can best be described as an absence of type, so pointers of type void* can point to any kind of data. However, you can't dereference a pointer of type "pointer to void" because what it points to is unspecified. Many compilers will arrange for the address returned by malloc() to be automatically cast to the appropriate type, but it doesn't hurt to be specific.

You could request any number of bytes, subject only to the amount of free memory on the computer and the limit on malloc() imposed by a particular implementation. If the memory that you request can't be allocated for any reason, malloc() returns a pointer with the value NULL. Remember that this is the equivalent of 0 for pointers. It's always a good idea to check any dynamic memory request immediately using an if statement to make sure the memory is actually there before you try to use it. As with money, attempting to use memory you haven't got is generally catastrophic. For that reason, writing

```
if(pNumber == NULL)
{
  /*Code to deal with no memory allocated */
}
```

with a suitable action if the pointer is NULL is a good idea. For example, you could at least display a message "Not enough memory" and terminate the program. This would be much better than allowing the program to continue and crashing when it uses a NULL address to store something. In some instances, though, you may be able to free up a bit of memory that you've been using elsewhere, which might give you enough memory to continue.

Using the sizeof Operator in Memory Allocation

The previous example is all very well, but you don't usually deal in bytes; you deal in data of type int, type double, and so on. It would be very useful to allocate memory for 75 items of type int, for example. You can do this with the following statement:

```
pNumber = (int*) malloc(75*sizeof(int));
```

As you've seen already, sizeof is an operator that returns an unsigned integer that's the count of the number of bytes required to store its argument. It will accept a type keyword such as int or float as an argument between parentheses, in which case the value it returns will be the number of bytes required to store an item of that type. It will also accept a variable or array name as an argument. With an array name as an argument, it returns the number of bytes required to store the whole array. In the preceding example, you asked for enough memory to store 75 data items of type int. Using sizeof in this way means that you automatically accommodate the potential variability of the space required for a value of type int between one C implementation and another.

....

Try It Out: Dynamic Memory Allocation

You can put the concept of dynamic memory allocation into practice by using pointers to help calculate prime numbers. In case you've forgotten, a prime number is an integer that's exactly divisible only by 1 or by the number itself.

The process for finding a prime is quite simple. First, you know by inspection that 2, 3, and 5 are the first three prime numbers, because they aren't divisible by any lower number other than 1. Because all the other prime numbers must be

(Continued)

odd (otherwise they would be divisible by 2), you can work out the next number to check by starting at the last prime you have and adding 2. When you've checked out that number, you add another 2 to get the next to be checked, and so on.

To check whether a number is actually prime rather than just odd, you could divide by all the odd numbers less than the number that you're checking, but you don't need to do as much work as that. If a number is *not* prime, it must be divisible by one of the primes lower than the number you're checking. Because you'll obtain the primes in sequence, it will be sufficient to check a candidate by testing whether any of the primes that you've already found is an exact divisor.

You'll implement this program using pointers and dynamic memory allocation:

```c
/* Program 7.11  A dynamic prime example        */
#include <stdio.h>
#include <stdlib.h>

void main()
{
   long *primes = NULL;                /* Pointer to primes storage area   */
   long trial = 0;                     /* Integer to be tested             */

   int  i = 0;
   int found = 0;                      /* Indicates when we find a prime   */
   int total = 0;                      /* Number of primes required        */
   int count = 0;                      /* Number of primes found           */

   printf("How many primes would you like?  ");
   scanf("%d", &total);                /* Total is how many we need to find */
   total = total<4 ? 4:total;          /* Make sure it is at least 4       */

   /* Allocate sufficient memory to store the number of primes required */
   primes = (long*)malloc(total*sizeof(long));
   if (primes == NULL)
   {
      printf("\nNot enough memory. Hasta la Vista, baby.\n");
      return;
   }

   /* We know the first three primes     */
   /* so let's give the program a start. */
   *primes = 2;                        /* First prime                      */
   *(primes+1) =3;                     /* Second prime                     */
   *(primes+2) = 5;                    /* Third prime                      */
   count = 3;                          /* Number of primes stored          */
   trial = 5;                          /* Set to the last prime we have    */

   /* Find all the primes required */
   while(count<total)
```

(Continued)

```
{
  trial += 2;                        /* Next value for checking    */

  /* Try dividing by each of the primes we have      */
  /* If any divide exactly - the number is not prime */
  for(i = 0 ; i < count ; i++ )
    if(!(found = (trial % *(primes+i))))
      break;                         /* Exit if no remainder       */

  if(found)                          /* we got one - found in not 0 */
    *(primes+count++) = trial;       /* Store it and increment count */
}

/* Display primes 5-up */
for (i = 0 ; i < total ; i ++ )
{
  if(!(i%5))
    printf("\n");                    /* Newline after every 5       */
  printf ("%12ld", *(primes+i));
}
printf("\n");                        /* Newline for any stragglers  */
}
```

The output from the program looks something like this:

How many primes would you like? 25

2	3	5	7	11
13	17	19	23	29
31	37	41	43	47
53	59	61	67	71
73	79	83	89	97

HOW IT WORKS

With this example, you can enter the number of prime numbers you want the program to generate. The pointer variable, primes, refers to a memory area that will be used to store the prime numbers as they're calculated. However, no memory is defined initially in the program. The space is allocated after you've entered the number of primes that you want:

```
printf("How many primes would you like?  ");
scanf("%d", &total);                /* Total is how many we need to find */
total = total<4 ? 4:total;          /* Make sure it is at least 4        */
```

(Continued)

After the prompt, the number that you enter is stored in `total`. The next statement then ensures that `total` is at least 4. This is because you'll define and store the three primes that you know (2, 3, and 5) by default.

You then use the value in `total` to allocate the appropriate amount of memory to store the primes:

```
primes = (long*)malloc(total*sizeof(long));
if (primes == NULL)
{
    printf("\nNot enough memory. Hasta la Vista, baby.\n");
    return;
}
```

Because you're going to store each prime as type `long`, the number of bytes you require is `total*sizeof(long)`. If the `malloc()` function returns `NULL`, no memory was allocated, so you display a message and end the program.

The maximum number of primes that you can specify depends on two things: the memory available on your computer and the amount of memory that your compiler's implementation of `malloc()` can allocate at one time. The latter is probably the major constraint. You can generally rely on the `malloc()` function being able to allocate at least 32,767 bytes, but some C implementations will have a `malloc()` function supporting considerably more.

Once you have the memory allocated for the primes, you define the first three primes and store them in the first three positions in the memory area pointed to by `primes`:

```
*primes = 2;                /* First prime              */
*(primes+1) =3;             /* Second prime             */
*(primes+2) = 5;            /* Third prime              */
```

As you can see, referencing successive memory locations is simple. Because `primes` is of type "pointer to `long`", `primes+1` refers to the address of the second location—the address being `primes` plus the number of bytes required to store one data item of type `long`. To store each value, you use the indirection operator; otherwise, you would be modifying the address itself.

Now that you have three primes, you set the variable `count` to 3 and initialize the variable `trial` with the last prime you stored:

```
count = 3;                  /* Number of primes stored      */
trial = 5;                  /* Set to the last prime we have */
```

The value in `trial` will be incremented by 2 to get the next value to be tested when you start searching for the next prime.

(Continued)

All the primes are found in the while loop:

```
while(count<total)
{
  ...
}
```

The variable count is incremented within the loop as each prime is found, and when it reaches the value total, the loop ends.

Within the while loop, you first increase the value in trial by 2, and then you test whether the value is prime:

```
trial += 2;                      /* Next value for checking    */

/* Try dividing by each of the primes we have    */
/* If any divide exactly - the number is not prime */
for(i = 0 ; i < count ; i++ )
  if(!(found = (trial % *(primes+i))))
    break;                       /* Exit if no remainder       */
```

The for loop does the testing. Within this loop, the remainder after dividing trial by each of the primes that you have so far is stored in found. If the division is exact, the remainder—and therefore found—will be 0. If you find any remainder is 0, this means that the value in trial isn't a prime and you can continue with the next candidate.

The value of an assignment expression is the value that's stored in the variable on the left of the assignment operator. Thus, the value of the expression (found = (trial % *(primes+i))) will be the value that's stored in found as a result of this. This will be 0 for an exact division, so the expression !(found = (trial % *(primes+i))) will be true in this case, and the break statement will be executed. Therefore, the for loop will end if any previously stored prime divides into trial with no remainder.

If none of the primes divides into trial exactly, the for loop will end when all the primes have been tried, and found will contain the last remainder value, which will be some positive integer. If trial had a factor, the loop will have ended via the break statement and found will contain 0. Therefore, you can use the value stored in found at the completion of the for loop to determine whether you've found a new prime or not:

```
if(found)                 /* we got one - found in not 0   */
  *(primes+count++) = trial;   /* Store it and increment count  */
```

If found is positive (i.e., true), you store the value of trial in the next available slot in the memory area. The address of the next available slot is primes+count. Remember that the first slot is primes, so when you have count number of

(Continued)

primes, the last prime occupies the location primes+count-1. The statement storing the new prime also increments the value of count after the new prime has been stored.

The while loop just repeats the process until you have all the primes requested. You then output the primes five on a line:

```
for (i = 0 ; i < total ; i ++ )
{
  if(!(i%5))
    printf("\n");                    /* Newline after every 5        */
  printf ("%12ld", *(primes+i));
}
printf("\n");                        /* Newline for any stragglers   */
```

The for loop will output total number of primes. The printf() that displays each prime value just appends the output to the current line, but the if statement outputs a newline character after every fifth iteration, so there will be five primes displayed on each line. Because the number of primes may not be an exact multiple of 5, you output a newline after the loop ends to ensure that there's always at least one newline character at the end of the output.

Handling Strings Using Pointers

You've used array variables of type char to store strings up to now, but you can also use a variable of type "pointer to char" to reference a string. This approach will give you quite a lot of flexibility in handling strings, as you'll see. You can declare a variable of type "pointer to char" with a statement such as this:

```
char *pString = NULL;
```

At this point, it's worth remembering yet again that a pointer is just a variable that can store the address of another memory location. So far, you've created a pointer but not a place to store a string. To store a string, you need to allocate some memory. You can declare a block of memory that you intend to use to store string data and then use pointers to keep track of where in this block you've stored the strings.

String Input with More Control

It's often desirable to read text with more control than you get with the scanf() function. The getchar() function that's declared in stdio.h provides a much more primitive operation in that it reads only a single character at a time, but it does enable you to control when you stop reading characters. This way, you can be sure that you don't exceed the memory you have allocated to store the input.

The getchar() function reads a single character from the keyboard and returns it as type int. You can read a string terminated by '\n' into an array, buffer, like this:

```
char buffer[100];                    /* String input buffer */
char *pbuffer = buffer;              /* Pointer to buffer   */
while((*pbuffer++ = getchar()) != '\n');
*pbuffer = '\0';                     /* Add null terminator */
```

All the input is done in the while loop condition. The getchar() function reads a character and stores it in the current address in pbuffer. As long as the character stored isn't '\n', the loop will continue. After the loop ends, the '\0' character is added in the next available position. Note that this retains the '\n' character as part of the string. If you don't want to do this, then you can adjust the address where you store the '\0' to over-write the '\n'.

This doesn't prevent the possibility of exceeding the 100 bytes available in the array, so you can use this safely only when you're sure that the array is large enough. However, you could rewrite the loop to check for this:

```
while((*pbuffer++ = getchar()) != '\n')
  if(pbuffer == buffer+99)
    break;
```

Now the loop continues with another iteration as long as '\n' hasn't been read, and the address in pbuffer hasn't yet reached the last element in the buffer array. The break is executed when the last array element is reached because you have to allow for the null string terminator character to be stored. In fact, you could rewrite this statement to be independent of the size of the array:

```
while((*pbuffer++ = getchar()) != '\n')
  if(pbuffer == buffer-1+sizeof buffer)
    break;
```

This will work whatever the size of the buffer array. Don't forget that the null character still must be added to the end of the string.

....

Try It Out: Pointers to Strings

You can try the getchar() function in an example and try out working with strings through a pointer at the same time. Here's the code:

```
/* Program 7.12  Managing memory and storing strings */
#include <stdio.h>
#define BUFFER_LEN 500
void main()
{
```

(Continued)

```
    char buffer[BUFFER_LEN];                /* Store for strings        */
    char *pS1 = NULL;                       /* Pointer to first string  */
    char *pS2 = NULL;                       /* Pointer to second string */
    char *pS3 = NULL;                       /* Pointer to third string  */
    char *pbuffer = buffer;                 /* Pointer to buffer        */

    printf("\nEnter a message\n");
      pS1 = pbuffer;                                /* Store address of first message */
      while ((*pbuffer++ = getchar()) != '\n'); /* Get input until Enter pressed  */
      *(pbuffer - 1) = '\0';                        /* Add string terminator          */
    printf("\nEnter another message\n");
    pS2 = pbuffer;                              /* Store address of second message */
    while ((*pbuffer++ = getchar()) != '\n'); /* Get input until Enter pressed  */
    *(pbuffer - 1) = '\0';                      /* Add string terminator          */
    printf("\nEnter another message\n");
    pS3 = pbuffer;                              /* Store address of third message  */
    while((*pbuffer++ = getchar()) != '\n');  /* Get input till Enter pressed   */
    *(pbuffer - 1) = '\0';                      /* Add string terminator          */
    printf("\nThe strings you entered are:\n\n%s\n%s\n%s", pS1, pS2, pS3);
    printf("\nThe buffer has %d characters unused.\n",
                    &buffer[BUFFER_LEN - 1] - pbuffer + 1);
}
```

Typical output from this would be as follows:

```
Enter a message
Hello World!

Enter another message
Today is a great day for learning about pointers.

Enter another message
That's all.

The strings you entered are:
Hello World!
Today is a great day for learning about pointers.
That's all.
The buffer has 425 characters unused.
```

HOW IT WORKS

The first thing of note in this example is that you use the symbol BUFFER_LEN, specified in the #define preprocessor directive, as the dimension for the array buffer:

```
#define BUFFER_LEN 500
```

(Continued)

As you've seen before, the #define directive defines a value to be substituted for the symbol BUFFER_LEN wherever it's used in the code. This is a common technique when you want to be able to change values in a program easily.

The initial declarations for the program are as follows:

```
char buffer[BUFFER_LEN];          /* Store for strings         */
char *pS1 = NULL;                 /* Pointer to first string   */
char *pS2 = NULL;                 /* Pointer to second string  */
char *pS3 = NULL;                 /* Pointer to third string   */
char *pbuffer = buffer;           /* Pointer to Buffer         */
```

Here, you declare the string storage space as the array buffer with the length determined by the #define directive for BUFFER_LEN. You declare three pointers to keep track of where you put the strings, and a pointer, pbuffer, to keep track of the current position in buffer when working through it.

The basic operation of the program is to store messages in the array, Buffer, as they're entered. They are stored contiguously from the start of the array, and the end of each string is marked by the string terminator character, '\0'. The pointers, pS1, pS2, and pS3, keep track of the addresses of the beginning of each of the messages entered.

After outputting a prompt to the screen, you initialize pS1 to the address of the first byte in buffer:

```
printf("\nEnter a message\n");
pS1 = pbuffer;                    /* Store address of first message */
```

Because you'll read the next string into pbuffer, pS1 now records the start of the first string.

You read in the first string one character at a time with the following statements:

```
while ((*pbuffer++ = getchar()) != '\n'); /* Get input until Enter pressed  */
*(pbuffer - 1) = '\0';                     /* Add string terminator          */
```

The string is read in the while loop. The loop consists of just the condition, the loop statement itself being empty because you have just the semicolon at the end. The standard library function getchar() reads a single character from the keyboard and returns the character read. Thus, each call of the function in the loop condition reads one character.

The loop condition stores the character returned by the function getchar() at the address pointed to by pbuffer and then increments the address in pbuffer to the next byte. This incrementing occurs after the whole of the loop condition has been evaluated. The loop condition also compares the character stored at pbuffer with '\n', and when '\n' is read the loop ends. At the end of the loop, the '\n' character, which will have been the last character read, is stored at the address pbuffer-1, so you overwrite that character with the string terminator.

(Continued)

Note that you increment pbuffer to point to the next free byte as you store each character. You couldn't use the name of the array here. Although you could use it as a pointer to access elements of the array, you can't change its value. Attempting to do so would result in an error from the compiler.

Notice also how you can compute the address on the left side of an assignment using the expression (pbuffer-1). This expression computes the address in which you want to store the '\0' at the end of each string. You can use an expression on the left side of an assignment statement only when it results in an address.

By reading the string using getchar() you have a great deal of control over the input process. This approach isn't limited to just reading strings; you can use it for any input where you want to deal with it character by character. You could choose to remove spaces from the input or look for special characters such as commas that you might use to separate one input value from the next.

The subsequent strings are processed in exactly the same way as the first string. Of course, the value of pbuffer will have changed each time, so that it points to the next free element in the buffer array. The address of the first character of the second and the third strings are stored in the pointers pS2 and pS3. Managing the input in this way means that you're able to pack the strings tightly into the buffer[] array, with no wasted characters between the end of one string and the beginning of the next.

In the last printf(), you output the number of characters left in the string:

```
printf("\nThe buffer has %d characters unused.\",
                  &Buffer[BUFFER_LEN - 1] - pBuffer + 1);
```

Figure 7-4 illustrates this computation.

Figure 7-4. Determining the unused buffer space

Remember that the last index value of the array is BUFFER_LEN - 1, because array indexing starts from 0. It's a very common error, particularly when using named constants, to put BUFFER_LEN as the last index value, rather than BUFFER_LEN - 1.

(Continued)

At the outset, you initialize your pointers to NULL. You can also initialize a pointer with the address of a constant string:

```
char *pString = "To be or not to be";
```

This statement allocates sufficient memory for the string, places the constant string in the memory allocated, and after allocating space for it, sets the value of the pointer pS as the address of the first byte of the string. Contrast this with the following declaration:

```
char String[] = "To be or not to be";
```

These two statements are quite different in their effect, in spite of the apparent similarities. The first initializes the pointer, pString, to the address of a string constant. This string constant can't be changed, but the pointer can be set to point to something else. The second statement initializes the array with the character string as an initial value. This isn't a constant, and you can change the contents of the array whenever you wish. However, as I pointed out before, the address referenced by using the array name String can't be altered.

Arrays of Pointers

That last example was a bit repetitive. You used the same code for each string entered. If you could set up the pointers to the strings entered as an *array of pointers*, you could shorten the program quite a bit. Let's see how.

Try It Out: Arrays of Pointers

The following example is a rewrite of the previous program, and it demonstrates how you could use an array of pointers:

```
/* Program 7.13 Arrays of Pointers to Strings */
#include <stdio.h>
#define BUFFER_LEN 500
void main()
{
    char buffer[BUFFER_LEN];            /* Store for strings      */
    char *pS[3] = { NULL };             /* Array of string pointers */
    char *pbuffer = buffer;             /* Pointer to Buffer      */
    int i = 0;                          /* loop counter           */

    /* Read the strings from the keyboard */
    for (i=0; i<3 ; i++)
```

(Continued)

```
    {
      printf("\nEnter %s message\n", i>0 ? "another" : "a" );
      *(pS + i) = pbuffer;                    /* Save start of string      */

      while ((*pbuffer++ = getchar()) != '\n'); /* Get input till Enter pressed */
      *(pbuffer - 1) = '\0';                  /* Add terminator            */
    }

    printf("\nThe strings you entered are:\n\n");
    for(i = 0 ; i<3 ; i++)
      printf("%s\n", *(pS+i));

    printf("The buffer has %d characters unused.\n",
                  &buffer[BUFFER_LEN - 1] - pbuffer + 1);
}
```

The output from this program is the same as the previous example.

HOW IT WORKS

This is much neater, isn't it? The declarations at the beginning are now as follows:

```
char buffer[BUFFER_LEN];            /* Store for strings         */
char *pS[3] = { NULL };             /* Array of string pointers  */
char *pbuffer = buffer;             /* Pointer to Buffer         */
int i = 0;                          /* loop counter              */
```

The difference here is that you now have an array, pS, of three pointers to char, each of which is initialized with NULL. You've also declared an extra integer variable, i, which you need as an index in the for loops to iterate through the array of pointers.

The first for loop reads in three strings. The first statement in the loop is this:

```
printf("\nEnter %s message\n", i>0 ? "another" : "a" );
```

Here, you use a snappy way to alter the prompt in the printf() after the first iteration of the for loop, using your old friend the conditional operator. This outputs "a" on the first iteration, and "another" on all subsequent iterations.

The next statement saves the address currently stored in pbuffer:

```
*(pS + i) = pbuffer;                    /* Save start of  string    */
```

The expression on the left side of the assignment, *(pS + i), is equivalent to pS[i], and is a pointer, because you have an array of pointers. This assignment statement is therefore storing, in an element of the pS pointer array, the address

(Continued)

stored in the pointer pbuffer. If the left side of the expression didn't have the *, it would be referring to the *address* of one of the elements of pS, which isn't the same thing at all!

In fact, if you try leaving out the indirection operator, the program won't compile. The most likely message from the compiler is that an lvalue is required. This sounds a bit obscure, but an lvalue is just a value that can appear on the left of an assignment and so must be an address in which you can store a result.

The statements for reading the string and appending the string terminator are exactly as before:

```
while ((*pbuffer++ = getchar()) != '\n'); /* Get input till Enter pressed */
*(pbuffer - 1) = '\0';                     /* Add terminator              */
```

All the work to read each string is done in the while loop condition here. The statement to append '\0' is not in the loop: it follows it. When the loop ends, you output all three strings in another for loop, after outputting an initial message:

```
printf("\nThe strings you entered are:\n\n");
for(i = 0 ; i<3 ; i++)
  printf("%s\n", *(pS+i));
```

In the loop, you first output *pS, then *(pS+1), and finally *(pS+2). These expressions reference each of the strings in turn, and the process of outputting the characters for each string is halted by the '\0' character that you appended to them.

If you were to develop this example just a little further, you would be able to allow input of an arbitrary number of messages, limited only by the number of string pointers provided for in the array.

....

....

Try It Out: Generalizing String Input

Let's try rewriting the example to generalize string input. You can extend the program to read an arbitrary number of strings up to a given limit and ensure that you don't read strings that are longer than you've provided for. Here's the program:

```
/* Program 7.14 Generalizing string input */
#include <stdio.h>
#include <stdlib.h>
#define BUFFER_LEN 100    /* Length of input buffer          */
```

(Continued)

```
#define NUM_P 100                          /* maximum number of strings */

void main()
{
  char buffer[BUFFER_LEN];              /* Input buffer              */
  char *pS[NUM_P] = { NULL };           /* Array of string pointers  */
  char *pbuffer = buffer;               /* Pointer to buffer         */
  int i = 0;                            /* Loop counter              */
  int j = 0;                            /* Loop counter              */

  for (i = 0; i < NUM_P; i++)
  {
    pbuffer = buffer ; /* Set pointer to beginning of buffer */
    printf("\nEnter %s message, or press Enter to end\n",
                                    i>0 ? "another" : "a");

    /* Read a string of up to BUFFER_LEN characters */
    while ((pbuffer -buffer < BUFFER_LEN-1) &&
           ((*pbuffer++ = getchar()) != '\n'));

    /* check for empty line indicating end of input */
    if((pbuffer - buffer) < 2)
      break;

    /* Check for string too long */
    if((pbuffer - buffer) == BUFFER_LEN && *(pbuffer-1)!= '\n')
    {
      printf("String too long - maximum %d characters allowed.",
                                            BUFFER_LEN);
      i--;
      continue;
    }
    *(pbuffer - 1) = '\0';                /* Add terminator            */

    pS[i] = (char*)malloc(pbuffer-buffer);  /* Get memory for string   */
    if (pS[i] == NULL)                    /* Check we actually got some...*/
    {
      printf("\nOut of memory - ending program.");
      return;                            /* ...Exit if we didn't      */
    }

    /* Copy string from buffer to new memory */
    for(j = 0 ; (*(pS[i] + j) = buffer[j]) != '\0' ; j++);
  }

  /* Output all the strings */
  printf("\nIn reverse order, the strings you entered are:\n");
  while (--i >= 0 )
  {
```

(Continued)

310

```
        printf("\n%s", *(pS + i) );            /* Display strings last to first */
        free(*(pS + i));                        /* Release the memory we got      */
        *(pS + i) = NULL;                   /* Set pointer back to NULL for safety */
    }
}
```

The output is very similar to the previous two examples:

```
Enter a message, or press Enter to end
Hello

Enter another message, or press Enter to end
World!

In reverse order, the strings you entered are:
World!
Hello
```

HOW IT WORKS

This has expanded a little bit, but you've included quite a few extras compared to your original attempt at this. You now handle as many strings as you want, up to the number that you provide pointers for, in the array pS. The dimension of this array is defined at the beginning, to make it easy to change:

```
#define NUM_P 100                      /* maximum number of strings */
```

If you want to alter the maximum number of strings that the program will handle, you just need to change this directive.

At the beginning of main(), you have the declarations for the variables you need:

```
    char buffer[BUFFER_LEN];            /* Input buffer            */
    char *pS[NUM_P] = { NULL };         /* Array of string pointers */
    char *pbuffer = buffer;             /* Pointer to buffer       */
    int i = 0;                          /* Loop counter            */
    int j = 0;                          /* Loop counter            */
```

The buffer array is now just an input buffer that will contain each string as you read it. Therefore, the #define directive for BUFFER_LEN now defines the maximum length of string you can accept. You then have the declaration for your pointer array of length NUM_P, and your pointer, pbuffer, for working within buffer. Finally, you have a couple of loop control variables.

(Continued)

The first for loop reads the strings and stores them. The loop control is as follows:

```
for (i = 0; i < NUM_P; i++)
```

This ensures that you can input only as many strings as there are pointers that you've declared. Once you've entered the maximum number of strings, the loop ends and you fall through to the output section of the program.

Within the loop, a string is entered using a similar mechanism with getchar() to those that you've seen before but with an additional condition:

```
/* Read a string of up to BUFFER_LEN characters */
while ((pbuffer - buffer < BUFFER_LEN-1) &&
        ((*pbuffer++ = getchar()) != '\n'));
```

The whole process takes place in the condition for the continuation of the while loop. A character obtained by getchar() is stored at the address pointed to by pbuffer, which starts out as the address of buffer. The pbuffer pointer is then incremented to point to the next available space, and the character that was stored as a result of the assignment is compared with '\n'. If it's '\n', then the loop terminates. The loop will also end if the expression pbuffer-buffer < BUFFER_LEN-1 is false. This will occur if the next character to be stored will occupy the last position in the buffer array.

The input process is followed by the check in the following statement:

```
if((pbuffer - buffer) < 2)
  break;
```

This detects an empty line because, if you just press the Enter key, only one character will be entered: the '\n'. In this case, the break statement immediately exits the for loop and begins the output process.

The next if statement checks whether you attempted to enter a string longer than the capacity of buffer:

```
if((pbuffer – buffer) == BUFFER_LEN && *(pbuffer-1)!= '\n')
{
  printf("String too long – maximum %d characters allowed.",
                                          BUFFER_LEN);
  i--;
  continue;
}
```

Because you end the while loop when the last position in the buffer array has been used, if you attempt to enter more characters than the capacity of buffer, then the expression pbuffer-buffer will be equal to BUFFER_LEN. Of course, this will also be the case if you enter a string that fits exactly, so you must also check the last character in buffer to see if it's '\n'. If it isn't, you tried to enter too many

(Continued)

characters, so you decrement the loop counter after displaying a message and go to the next iteration.

The next statement is

```
*(pbuffer - 1) = '\0';                     /* Add terminator             */
```

This places the '\0' in the position occupied by the '\n' character, because pbuffer was left pointing to the first free element in the array buffer.

Once a string has been entered, you use the malloc() function to request sufficient memory to hold the string exactly:

```
pS[i] = (char*)malloc(pbuffer-buffer);  /* Get memory for string      */
if (pS[i] == NULL)                      /* Check we actually got some */
{
  printf("\nOut of memory – ending program.");
  return;                               /* ...Exit if we didn't       */
}
```

The number of bytes required is the difference between the address currently pointed to by pbuffer, which is the first vacant element in buffer, and the address of the first element of buffer. The pointer returned from malloc() is stored in the current element of the pS array, after casting it to type char. If you get a NULL pointer back from malloc(), you display a message and end the program.

You copy the string from the buffer to the new memory you've obtained using a for loop:

```
for(j = 0 ; (*(pS[i] + j) = buffer[j]) != '\0' ; j++);
```

The loop condition includes an assignment that stores the current element from buffer in the new memory area. You get the address to store the character from buffer[j] by adding j to the address in pS[i]. The indirection operator indicates that you're modifying the contents of the location referenced by this address. The character stored is compared with '\0', and when this was character stored, the copying process ends.

Once you exit the loop, either because you entered an empty string or because you used all the pointers in the array pS, you generate the output:

```
printf("\nIn reverse order, the strings you entered are:\n");
while (--i >= 0 )
{
   printf("\n%s", *(pS + i) );          /* Display strings last to first */
   free(*(pS + i));                     /* Release the memory we got     */
   *(pS + i) = NULL;                    /* Set pointer back to NULL for safety */
}
```

(Continued)

The index i will have a value one greater than the number of strings entered. So after the first loop condition check, you can use it to index the last string. The loop continues counting down from this value, and the last iteration will be with i at 0, which will index the first string.

The expression *(pS + i) is equivalent to pS[i] in array notation. Using pointer notation on the array of pointers here is just for exercise.

You use a new function, free(), after the last printf(). This function is complementary to malloc(), and it releases memory previously allocated by malloc(). It only requires the pointer to the memory allocated as an argument. Although memory will be freed at the end of the program automatically, it's good practice to free memory as soon as you no longer need it. Of course, once you have freed memory in this way, you can't use it, so it's a good idea to set the pointer to NULL immediately, as was done here.

 CAUTION *Errors with pointers can produce catastrophic results. If an uninitialized pointer is used to store a value before it has been assigned an address value, the address used will be whatever happens to be stored in the pointer location. This could overwrite virtually anywhere in memory.*

Try It Out: Sorting Strings Using Pointers

Using the functions declared in the string.h header file, you can demonstrate the effectiveness of using pointers through an example showing a simple method of sorting:

```
/* Program 7.15 Sorting strings */
#include <stdio.h>
#include <stdlib.h>
#include <string.h>
#define BUFFER_LEN 100              /* Length of input buffer        */
#define NUM_P 100                   /* maximum number of strings     */
#define TRUE   1
#define FALSE 0

void main()
{
    char buffer[BUFFER_LEN];        /* space to store an input string */
    char *pS[NUM_P] = { NULL };     /* Array of string pointers       */
    char *pTemp = NULL;             /* Temporary pointer              */
```

(Continued)

```c
  int i = 0;                        /* Loop counter                      */
  int sorted = FALSE;               /* Indicated when strings are sorted */
  int last_string = 0;              /* Index of last string entered      */

  printf("\nEnter successive lines, pressing Enter at the"
              " end of each line.\nJust press Enter to end.\n\n");
  while((*gets(buffer) != '\0') && (i < NUM_P))
  {
    pS[i] = (char*)malloc(strlen(buffer) + 1);
    if(pS[i]==NULL)                 /* Check for no memory allocated     */
    {
      printf(" Memory allocation failed. Program terminated.\n");
      return;
    }
    strcpy(pS[i++], buffer);
  }
  last_string = i;                  /* Save last string index            */

  /* Sort the strings in ascending order */
  while(!sorted)
  {
    sorted = TRUE;
    for (i = 0 ; i < last_string - 1 ; i++)
      if(strcmp(pS[i], pS[i + 1]) > 0)
      {
        sorted = FALSE;             /* We were out of order              */
        pTemp= pS[i];               /* Swap pointers pS[i]               */
        pS[i] = pS[i + 1];          /*         and                       */
        pS[i + 1]  = pTemp;         /*      pS[i + 1]                     */
      }
  }

  /* Displayed the sorted strings */
  printf("\nYour input sorted in order is:\n\n");
  for (i = 0 ; i < last_string ; i++)
  {
    printf("%s\n", pS[i] );
    free( pS[i] );
    pS[i] = NULL;
  }
}
```

Assuming you enter the same input data, the output from this program is as follows:

```
Enter successive lines, pressing Enter at the end of each line.
Just press Enter to end.

Many a mickle makes a muckle.
```

(Continued)

```
A fool and your money are soon partners.
Every dog has his day.
Do unto others before they do it to you.
A nod is as good as a wink to a blind horse.


Your input sorted in order is:

A fool and your money are soon partners.
A nod is as good as a wink to a blind horse.
Do unto others before they do it to you.
Every dog has his day.
Many a mickle makes a muckle.
```

HOW IT WORKS

This is quite an interesting example. It really will sort the wheat from the chaff. To simplify things a bit, you use the input function gets(), which reads a complete string up to the point you press Enter and then adds '\0' to the end. Its only argument is a pointer to the memory area where you want the string to be stored. Its return value is either the address where the input string is stored—buffer, in this case—or NULL if an error occurs. With the code as it is, though, you don't have any protection against exceeding the capacity of buffer.

The overall operation of this program is quite simple, and it involves three distinct activities:

- Read in all the input strings.

- Sort the input strings in order.

- Display the input strings in alphabetical order.

After the initial prompt lines are displayed, the input process is handled by these statements:

```
while((*gets(buffer) != '\0') && (i < NUM_P))
{
  pS[i] = (char*)malloc(strlen(buffer) + 1);
  if(pS[i]==NULL)                    /* Check for no memory allocated    */
  {
    printf(" Memory allocation failed. Program terminated.\n");
    return;
  }
  strcpy(pS[i++], buffer);
}
```

(Continued)

The input process continues until an empty line is entered or until you run out of space in the pointer array. Each line is read into buffer using the gets() function. This is inside the while loop condition, which allows the loop to continue for as long as gets() doesn't read a string containing just '\0' and the total number of lines entered doesn't exceed the pointer array dimension. The empty string with just '\0' will be a result of you pressing Enter without entering any text. You use the * to get at the contents of the pointer address return by gets(). This is the same as dereferencing buffer, of course.

As soon as you collect each input line in buffer, you allocate the correct amount of memory to accommodate the line by using the malloc() function. You get the count of the number of bytes that you need by using the strlen() function and adding 1 for the '\0' at the end. After verifying that you did get the memory allocated, you copy the string from buffer to the new memory using the library function strcpy().

You then save the index for the last string:

```
last_string = i;                      /* Save last string index            */
```

This is because you're going to reuse the loop counter, i, and you need to keep track of how many strings you have.

Once you have all your strings safely stowed away, you sort them using the simplest, and probably the most inefficient, sort going—but it's easy to follow. This takes place within these statements:

```
while(!sorted)
{
  sorted = TRUE;
  for (i = 0 ; i < last_string - 1 ; i++)
    if(strcmp(pS[i], pS[i + 1]) > 0)
    {
      sorted = FALSE;              /* We were out of order              */
      pTemp= pS[i];                /* Swap pointers pS[i]               */
      pS[i] = pS[i + 1];           /*      and                          */
      pS[i + 1]  = pTemp;          /*      pS[i + 1]                     */
    }
}
```

The sort takes place inside the while loop that continues as long as sorted is false. The sort proceeds by comparing successive pairs of strings using the strcmp() function inside the for loop. If the first string is greater than the second string, you swap pointer values. Using pointers, as you have here, is a very economical way of changing the order. The strings themselves remain undisturbed exactly where they were in memory. It's just the sequence of their addresses that changes in the pointer array, pS. This mechanism is illustrated in Figure 7-5. The time needed to swap pointers is a fraction of that required to move all the strings around.

(Continued)

Figure 7-5. Sorting using pointers

The swapping continues through all the string pointers. If you have to interchange any strings as you pass through them, you set sorted to FALSE to repeat the whole thing. It you repeat the whole thing without interchanging any, then they're in order and you've finished the sort. You track the status of this with the integer variable sorted. This is set to TRUE at the beginning of each cycle, but if any interchange occurs, then it gets set back to FALSE. If you exit a cycle with sorted still TRUE, it means that no interchanges occurred, so everything must be in order; therefore, you exit from the while loop.

The reason this sort is none too good is that each pass through all the items only moves a value by one position in the list. In the worst case, when you have the first entry in the last position, the number of times you have to repeat the process is one less than the number of entries in the list. This inefficient, but nevertheless famous, method of sorting is known as a **bubble sort**.

Handling strings and other kinds of data using pointers in this way is an extremely powerful mechanism in C. You can throw the basic data (the strings, in this case) into a bucket of memory in any old order, and then you can process them in any sequence you like without moving the data at all. You just change the pointers! You could use ideas from this example as a base for programs for sorting any text. You had better find a better sort of sort, though.

Designing a Program

Congratulations! You made it through a really tough part of the C language, and now I can show you an application using some of what you've learned. I'll follow the usual process, taking you through the analysis, design, and writing the code step by step. Let's look at the final program for this chapter.

The Problem

The problem you'll address is to rewrite the calculator program that you wrote in Chapter 3 with some new features, but this time using pointers. The main improvements that you'll make are as follows:

- Allow the use of signed decimal numbers, including a decimal point with an optional leading sign, - or +, as well as signed integers.

- Permit expressions to combine multiple operations such as `2.5+3.7-6/6`.

- Add the ^ operator, which will be raised to a power, so 2^3 will produce 8.

- Allow a line to operate on the previous result. If the previous result was 2.5, then writing

```
=*2 + 7
```

will produce the result 12. Any input line that starts with an assignment operator will automatically assume the left operand is the previous result.

You're also going to cheat a little by not taking into consideration the precedence of the operators. You'll simply evaluate the expression that's entered from left to right, applying each operator to the previous result and the right operand. This means that the expression

```
1 + 2*3 - 4*-5
```

will be evaluated as

```
((1 + 2)*3 - 4)*(-5)
```

The Analysis

You don't know in advance how long an expression is going to be or how many operands are going to be involved. You'll get a complete string from the user, and then analyze this to see what the numbers and operators are. You'll evaluate each intermediate result as soon as you have an operator with a left and a right operand.

The steps are as follows:

1. Read an input string entered by the user and exit if it is `quit`.

2. Check for an = operator, and if there is one skip looking for the first operand.

3. Search for an operator followed by an operand, executing each operator in turn until the end of the input string.

4. Display the result and go back to step 1.

The Solution

This section outlines the steps you'll take to solve the problem.

Step 1

As you saw earlier in this chapter, the scanf() function doesn't allow you to read a complete string that contains spaces, as it stops at the first whitespace character. You'll therefore read the input expression using the gets() function that's declared in the stdio.h library header file. This will read an entire line of input, including spaces. You can actually combine the input and the overall program loop together as follows:

```
/* Program 7.16 An improved calculator */
#include <stdio.h>                          /* Standard input/output */
#include <string.h>                         /* For string functions  */
void main()
{
    char input[256];                        /* Input expression      */

    while(strcmp(gets(input), "quit") != 0)
    {
      /* Code to implement the calculator */
    }
}
```

You can do this because the function strcmp() expects to receive an argument that's a pointer to a string, and the function gets() actually returns a pointer to the string that the user has typed in—&input[0] in this case. The strcmp() function will compare the string that's entered with "quit" and will return 0 if they're equal. This will end the loop.

You set the input string to a length of 256. This should be enough because most computers' keyboard buffers are 255 characters. (This refers to the maximum number of characters that you can type in before having to press Enter.)

Once you have your string, you could start analyzing it right away, but it would be better if you removed any spaces from the string. Because the input string is well defined, you don't need spaces to separate the operator from the operands. Let's add code inside the while loop to remove any spaces:

```
/* Program 7.16 An improved calculator */
#include <stdio.h>                          /* Standard input/output */
#include <string.h>                         /* For string functions  */
void main()
{
    char input[256];                        /* Input expression      */
    unsigned int index = 0; /* Index of the current a character in input */
    unsigned int to = 0;    /* To index for copying input to itself     */
    size_t input_length = 0;      /* Length of the string in input       */
    while(strcmp(gets(input), "quit") != 0)
```

```
   {
      input_length = strlen(input);        /* Get the input string length */

      /* Remove all spaces from the input by copy the string to itself */
      /* including the string terminating character                    */
      for(to = 0, index = 0 ; index<=input_length ; index++)
      if(*(input+index) != ' ')                /* If it is not a space   */
        *(input+to++) = *(input+index);        /* Copy the character     */

      input_length = strlen(input);        /* Get the new string length   */
      index = 0;                           /* Start at the first character */

      /* Code to implement the calculator */
   }
}
```

You've added declarations for the additional variables that you'll need. The variable input_length has been declared as type size_t to be compatible with the type returned by the strlen() function. This avoids possible warning messages from the compiler.

You remove spaces by copying the string stored in input to itself. You need to keep track of two indexes in the copy loop: one for the position in input where the next non-space character is to be copied to and one for the position of the next character to be copied. In the loop you don't copy spaces; you just increment index to move to the next character. The to index gets incremented only when a character is copied. After the loop is entered, you store the new string length in input_length and reset index to reference to the first character in input.

You could equally well write the loop here using array notation:

```
    for(to = 0, index = 0 ; index<=input_length ; index++)
      if(input[index] != ' ')                  /* If it is not a space */
        input[to++] = input[index];            /* Copy the character   */
```

For my taste, the code is clearer using array notation, but you'll continue using pointer notation as you need the practice.

Step 2

The input expression has two possible forms. It can start with an assignment operator, indicating that the last result is to be taken as the left operand, or it can start with a number with or without a sign. You can differentiate these two situations by looking for the '=' character first. If you find one, the left operand is the previous result.

The code you need to add next in the while loop will look for an '=', and if it doesn't find one it will look for a substring that is numeric that will be the left operand:

```
/* Program 7.16 An improved calculator */
#include <stdio.h>              /* Standard input/output    */
#include <string.h>             /* For string functions     */
```

```c
#include <ctype.h>              /* For classifying characters           */
#include <stdlib.h>             /* For converting strings to numeric values */

void main()
{
  char input[256];              /* Input expression                      */
  char number_string[30];       /* Stores a number string from input     */
  unsigned int index = 0;       /* Index of the current a character in input */
  unsigned int to = 0;          /* To index for copying input to itself  */
  size_t input_length = 0;      /* Length of the string in input         */
  unsigned int number_length = 0;   /* Length of the string in number_string */
  double result = 0.0;          /* The result of an operation            */

  while(strcmp(gets(input), "quit") != 0)
  {
    input_length = strlen(input);            /* Get the input string length */

    /* Remove all spaces from the input by copy the string to itself */
    /* including the string terminating character                 */
    for(to = 0, index = 0 ; index<=input_length ; index++)
      if(*(input+index) != ' ')              /* If it is not a space    */
        *(input+to++) = *(input+index);       /* Copy the character     */

    input_length = strlen(input);            /* Get the new string length  */
    index = 0;                               /* Start at the first character */

    if(input[index]== '=')             /* Is there =?                     */
      index++;                         /* Yes so skip over it             */
    else
    {                                  /* No - look for the left operand  */
      /* Look for a number that is the left operand for */
      /* the first operator                       */

      /* Check for sign and copy it */
      number_length = 0;                       /* Initialize length      */
      if(input[index]=='+' || input[index]=='-')     /* Is it + or -?     */
        *(number_string+number_length++) = *(input+index++)  /* Yes so copy it */

      /* Copy all following digits */
      for( ; isdigit(*(input+index)) ; index++)          /* Is it a digit? */
        *(number_string+number_length++) = *(input+index);   /* Yes - Copy it  */

      /* copy any fractional part */
      if(*(input+index)=='.')                         /* Is it decimal point? */
      { /* Yes so copy the decimal point and the following digits */
        *(number_string+number_length++) = *(input+index++);    /* Copy point */

        for( ; isdigit(*(input+index)) ; index++)             /* For each digit */
          *(number_string+number_length++) = *(input+index);     /* copy it */
```

```
    }
    *(number_string+number_length) = '\0';         /* Append string terminator */

    /* If we have a left operand, the length of number_string */
    /* will be > 0. In this case convert to a double so we    */
    /* can use it in the calculation                          */
    if(number_length>0)
      result = atof(number_string);             /* Store first number as result */
  }

  /* Code to analyze the operator and right operand */
  /* and produce the result                         */
}
```

}You include the `ctype.h` header for the character analysis functions and the `stdlib.h` header because you use the function `atof()`, which converts a string passed as an argument to a floating-point value. You've added quite a chunk of code here, but it consists of a number of straightforward steps.

The `if` statement checks for `'='` as the first character in the input:

```
if(input[index]== '=')                /* Is there =?          */
  index++;                            /* Yes so skip over it  */
```

If you find one, you increment `index` to skip over it and go straight to looking for the operand. If `'='` isn't found, you execute the `else`, which looks for a numeric left operand.

You copy all the characters that make up the number to the array `number_string`. The number may start with a unary sign, `'-'` or `'+'`, so you first check for that in the `else` block. If you find it, then you copy it to `number_string` with the following statement:

```
if(input[index]=='+' || input[index]=='-')        /* Is it + or -? */
  *(number_string+number_length++) = *(input+index++); /* Yes so copy it */
```

If a sign isn't found, then `index` value, recording the current character to be analyzed in `input`, will be left exactly where it is. If a sign is found, it will be copied to `number_string` and the value of `index` will be incremented to point to the next character.

One or more digits should be next, so you have a `for` loop that copies however many digits there are to `number_string`:

```
for( ; isdigit(*(input+index)) ; index++)          /* Is it a digit? */
  *(number_string+number_length++) = *(input+index); /* Yes - Copy it  */
```

This will copy all the digits of an integer and increment the value of `index` accordingly. Of course, if there are no digits, the value of `index` will be unchanged.

The number might not be an integer. In this case, there must be a decimal point next, which may be followed by more digits. The `if` statement checks for the decimal point. If there is one, then the decimal point and any following digits will also be copied:

```
if(*(input+index)=='.')                              /* Is it decimal point? */
{ /* Yes so copy the decimal point and the following digits */
  *(number_string+number_length++) = *(input+index++);    /* Copy point */

  for( ; isdigit(*(input+index)) ; index++)              /* For each digit */
      *(number_string+number_length++) = *(input+index);    /* copy it */
}
```

You must have finished copying the string for the first operand now, so you append a string-terminating character to number_string:

```
*(number_string+number_length) = '\0';        /* Append string terminator */
```

While there may not have been a value found, if you've copied a string representing a number to number_string, then the value of number_length must be positive because there has to be at least one digit. Therefore, you use the value of number_length as an indicator that you have a number:

```
if(number_length>0)
    result = atof(number_string);           /* Store first number as result */
```

The string is converted to a floating-point value of type double by the atof() function. Note that you store the value of the string in result. You'll use the same variable later to store the result of an operation. This will ensure that result always contains the result of an operation, including that produced at the end of an entire string. If you haven't stored a value here, because there is no left operand, result will already contain the value from the previous input string.

Step 3

At this point, what follows in the input string is very well defined. It must be an operator followed by a number. The operator will have the number that you found previously as its left operand, or the previous result. This "op-number" combination may also be followed by another, so you have a possible succession of op-number combinations through to the end of the string. You can deal with this in a loop that will look for these combinations:

```
/* Program 7.16 An improved calculator */
#include <stdio.h>              /* Standard input/output                  */
#include <string.h>             /* For string functions                   */
#include <ctype.h>              /* For classifying characters             */
#include <stdlib.h>             /* For converting strings to numeric values */

void main()
{
```

```
  char input[256];                       /* Input expression                */
  char number_string[30];                /* Stores a number string from input */
  char op = 0;                           /* Stores an operator              */

unsigned int index = 0;          /* Index of the current a character in input */
unsigned int to = 0;             /* To index for copying input to itself    */
size_t input_length = 0;         /* Length of the string in input           */
unsigned int number_length = 0;   /* Length of the string in number_string */
double result = 0.0;             /* The result of an operation              */
double number = 0.0;             /* Stores the value of number_string       */

  while(strcmp(gets(input), "quit") != 0)
  {
    input_length = strlen(input);                /* Get the input string length */

    /* Remove all spaces from the input by copy the string to itself */
    /* including the string terminating character                */
    /* Code to remove spaces as before...                        */

    /* Code to check for '=' and analyze & store the left operand as before.. */

    /* Now look for 'op number' combinations */
    for(;index < input_length;)
    {
      op = *(input+index++);                              /* Get the operator */
      /* Copy the next operand and store it in number */
      number_length = 0;                        /* Initialize the length  */

      /* Check for sign and copy it */
      if(input[index]=='+' || input[index]=='-')          /* Is it + or -? */
      *(number_string+number_length++) = *(input+index++); /* Yes - copy it. */

      /* Copy all following digits */
      for( ; isdigit(*(input+index)) ; index++)          /* For each digit */
      *(number_string+number_length++) = *(input+index);   /* copy it.      */

      /* copy any fractional part */
      if(*(input+index)=='.')                          /* Is it a decimal point? */
      { /* Copy the  decimal point and the following digits */
        *(number_string+number_length++) = *(input+index++);   /* Copy point */
        for( ; isdigit(*(input+index)) ; index++)          /* For each digit */
          *(number_string+number_length++) = *(input+index);   /* copy it.   */
      }
      *(number_string+number_length) = '\0';               /* terminate string */

      /* Convert to a double so we can use it in the calculation */
      number = atof(number_string);
    }
    /* code to produce result */
  }
}
```

In the interest of not repeating the same code ad nauseam, there are some comments indicating where the previous bits of code that you added are located in the program. I'll list the complete source code with the next addition to the program.

The for loop continues until you reach the end of the input string, which will be when you have incremented index to be equal to input_length. On each iteration of the loop, you store the operator in the variable op of type char:

```
op = *(input+index++);                          /* Get the operator */
```

With the operator out of the way, you then extract the characters that form the next number. This will be the right operand for the operator. You haven't verified that the operator is valid here, so the code won't spot an invalid operator at this point.

The extraction of the string for the number that's the right operand is exactly the same as that for the left operand. The same code is repeated. This time, though, the double value for the operand is stored in number:

```
number = atof(number_string);
```

You now have the left operand stored in result, the operator stored in op, and the right operand stored in number. Consequently, you're now prepared to execute an operation of the form

```
result=(result op number)
```

When you've added the code for this, the program will be complete.

Step 4

You can use a switch statement to select the operation to be carried out based on the operand. This is essentially the same code that you used in the previous calculator. You'll also display the output and add a prompt at the beginning of the program on how the calculator is used. Here's the complete code for the program, with the last code you're adding in bold:

```
/* Program 7.16 An improved calculator */
#include <stdio.h>              /* Standard input/output                */
#include <string.h>             /* For string functions                 */
#include <ctype.h>              /* For classifying characters           */
#include <stdlib.h>             /* For converting strings to numeric values */
#include <math.h>               /* For power() function                 */

void main()
{
    char input[256];                /* Input expression                     */
    char number_string[30];         /* Stores a number string from input    */
    char op = 0;                    /* Stores an operator                   */

    unsigned int index = 0;         /* Index of the current a character in input */
```

```
unsigned int to = 0;              /* To index for copying input to itself    */
size_t input_length = 0;          /* Length of the string in input           */
unsigned int number_length = 0;   /* Length of the string in number_string   */
double result = 0.0;              /* The result of an operation              */
double number = 0.0;              /* Stores the value of number_string       */

  printf("\nTo use this calculator, enter any expression with"
                                  " or without spaces");
  printf("\nAn expression may include the operators:");
  printf("\n               +, -, *, /, %%, or ^(raise to a power).");
  printf("\nUse = at the beginning of a line to operate on ");
  printf("\nthe result of the previous calculation.");
  printf("\nUse quit by itself to stop the calculator.\n\n");

  /* The main calculator loop */
  while(strcmp(gets(input), "quit") != 0)
  {
    input_length = strlen(input);              /* Get the input string length */

    /* Remove all spaces from the input by copy the string to itself */
    /* including the string terminating character                    */
    for(to = 0, index = 0 ; index<=input_length ; index++)
      if(*(input+index) != ' ')                    /* If it is not a space  */
        *(input+to++) = *(input+index);            /* Copy the character    */

    input_length = strlen(input);              /* Get the new string length */
    index = 0;                                 /* Start at the first character */

    if(input[index]== '=')                     /* Is there =?                  */
      index++;                                 /* Yes so skip over it          */
    else
    {                                          /* No - look for the left operand */
      /* Look for a number that is the left operand for the 1st operator */

      /* Check for sign and copy it */
      number_length = 0;                              /* Initialize length     */
      if(input[index]=='+' || input[index]=='-')             /* Is it + or -? */
        *(number_string+number_length++) = *(input+index++); /* Yes so copy it */

      /* Copy all following digits */
      for( ; isdigit(*(input+index)) ; index++)              /* Is it a digit? */
        *(number_string+number_length++) = *(input+index);   /* Yes - Copy it */

      /* copy any fractional part */
      if(*(input+index)=='.')                         /* Is it decimal point? */
      { /* Yes so copy the decimal point and the following digits */
        *(number_string+number_length++) = *(input+index++);  /* Copy point  */

        for( ; isdigit(*(input+index)) ; index++)             /* For each digit */
          *(number_string+number_length++) = *(input+index);  /* copy it       */
      }
      *(number_string+number_length) = '\0';       /* Append string terminator */
```

327

```
  /* If we have a left operand, the length of number_string */
  /* will be > 0. In this case convert to a double so we     */
  /* can use it in the calculation                           */
  if(number_length>0)
    result = atof(number_string);          /* Store first number as result */
}

/* Now look for 'op number' combinations */
for(;index < input_length;)
{
  op = *(input+index++);                            /* Get the operator */
  /* Copy the next operand and store it in number */
  number_length = 0;                       /* Initialize the length */

  /* Check for sign and copy it */
  if(input[index]=='+' || input[index]=='-')          /* Is it + or -? */
  *(number_string+number_length++) = *(input+index++); /* Yes - copy it. */

  /* Copy all following digits */
  for( ; isdigit(*(input+index)) ; index++)          /* For each digit */
  *(number_string+number_length++) = *(input+index);   /* copy it.      */

  /* copy any fractional part */
  if(*(input+index)=='.')                      /* Is it a decimal point? */
  { /* Copy the  decimal point and the following digits */
    /* Copy point      */
    *(number_string+number_length++) = *(input+index++);
    for( ; isdigit(*(input+index)) ; index++)          /* For each digit */
      *(number_string+number_length++) = *(input+index); /* copy it.      */
  }
  *(number_string+number_length) = '\0';                /* terminate string */

  /* Convert to a double so we can use it in the calculation */
  number = atof(number_string);

  /* Execute operation, as 'result op= number' */
  switch(op)
  {
    case '+':                                      /* Addition        */
      result += number;
      break;
    case '-':                                      /* Subtraction     */
      result -= number;
      break;
    case '*':                                      /* Multiplication  */
      result *= number;
      break;
    case '/':                                      /* Division        */
      /* Check second operand for zero */
      if(number == 0)
        printf("\n\n\aDivision by zero error!\n");
```

```
            else
              result /= number;
            break;
          case '%':                       /* Modulus operator - remainder */
            /* Check second operand for zero */
            if((long)number == 0)
              printf("\n\n\aDivision by zero error!\n");
            else
              result = (double)((long)result % (long)number);
            break;
          case '^':                       /* Raise to a power             */
            result = pow(result, number);
            break;
          default:                        /* Invalid operation or bad input */
            printf("\n\n\aIllegal operation!\n");
      }
    }
    printf("= %f\n", result);            /* Output the result */
  }
}
```

The switch statement is essentially the same as in the previous calculator program, but with some extra cases. Because you use the power function, pow(), to calculate resultnumber, you have to add an #include directive for the header file math.h.

Typical output from the calculator program is as follows:

```
To use this calculator, enter any expression with or without spaces
An expression may include the operators:
                  +, -, *, /, %, or ^(raise to a power).
Use = at the beginning of a line to operate on
the result of the previous calculation.
Use quit by itself to stop the calculator.

2.5+3.3/2
= 2.900000
= *3
= 8.700000
= ^4
= 5728.976100
1.3+2.4-3.5+-7.8
= -7.600000
=*-2
= 15.200000
= *-2
= -30.400000
= +2
= -28.400000
quit
```

And there you have it!

Summary

This chapter covered a lot of ground. You explored pointers in detail. You should now understand the relationship between pointers and arrays (both one-dimensional and multidimensional arrays) and have a good grasp of their uses. I introduced another function, the `malloc()` function for dynamically allocating memory, which provides the potential for your programs to use just enough memory for the data being processed in each run. You also saw the complementary function, `free()`, that you use to release memory that was previously allocated by `malloc()`. You should have a clear idea of how you can use pointers with strings and how you can use arrays of pointers.

The topics I've discussed in this chapter are fundamental to a lot of what follows in the rest of the book, and of course to writing C programs effectively, so you should make sure that you're quite comfortable with the material in this chapter before moving on to the next chapter. The next chapter is all about structuring your programs.

Exercises

The following exercises enable you to try out what you've learned in this chapter. If you get stuck, look back over the chapter for help. If you're still stuck, you can download the solutions from the Downloads area of the Apress website (`http://www.apress.com`), but that really should be a last resort.

Exercise 7-1. Write a program to calculate the average for an arbitrary number of floating-point values that are entered from the keyboard. Store all values in memory that's allocated dynamically before calculating and displaying the average. The user shouldn't be required to specify in advance how many values there will be.

Exercise 7-2. Write a program that will read an arbitrary number of proverbs from the keyboard and store them in memory that's allocated at runtime. The program should then output the proverbs ordered by their length, starting with the shortest and ending with the longest.

Exercise 7-3. Write a program that will read a string from the keyboard and display it after removing all spaces and punctuation characters. All operations should use pointers.

Exercise 7-4. Write a program that will read a series of temperature recordings as floating-point values for an arbitrary number of days, in which six recordings are made per day. The temperature readings should be stored in an array that's allocated dynamically and that's the correct dimensions for the number of temperature values that are entered. Calculate the average temperature per day, and then output the recordings for each day together, with the average on a single line with one decimal place after the point.

CHAPTER 8

Structuring Your Programs

I MENTIONED IN CHAPTER 1 THAT BREAKING UP a program into reasonably self-contained units is basic to the development of any program of a practical nature. When you're confronted with a big task, the most sensible thing to do is break it up into manageable chunks. You can then deal with each small chunk fairly easily and be reasonably sure that you've done it properly.

One of the key ideas in the C language is that every program should be segmented into functions that are relatively short. Even with the examples you've seen so far that were written as a single function, main(), other functions are also involved because you've still used a variety of standard library functions for input and output, for mathematical operations, and for handling strings.

In this chapter you'll look at how you can make your programs more effective and easier to develop by introducing more functions of your own.

In this chapter you'll learn

- More about functions

- How data is passed to a function

- How to return results from your functions

- How to define your own functions

- How pointers can be used with functions

Program Structure

As I said right at the outset, a C program consists of one or more functions, the most important of which is the function main(), where execution starts. When you used library functions such as printf() or scanf(), you saw how one function was able to call up another function to carry out a particular task and then continue execution when the task was complete. Each function in a program is a self-contained unit. When a function is called, the code within the body of that function is executed, and when the function has finished executing, control returns to the point at which that function was called. This is illustrated in Figure 8-1, where you can see an idealized representation of a C program structured as five functions. It doesn't show any details of the statements involved—just the sequence of execution.

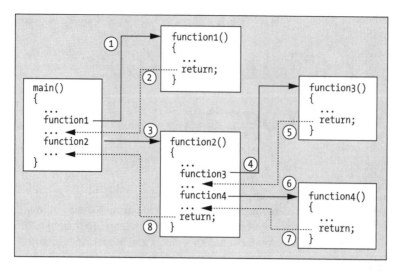

Figure 8-1. Execution of a program made up of several functions

The program steps through the statements in sequence in the normal way until it comes across a call to a particular function. At that point, execution moves to the start of that function—that is, the first statement in the body of the function. Execution of the program continues through the function statements until it hits a return statement or reaches the closing brace marking the end of the function body. This signals that execution should go back to the point immediately after where the function was originally called.

The set of functions that make up a program link together through the function calls and their return statements to perform the various tasks necessary for the program to achieve its purpose. Figure 8-1 shows each function in the program executed just once. In practice, each function can be executed many times and can be called from several points within a program. You've already seen this in the examples that called the printf() and scanf() functions several times.

Before you look in more detail at how to define your own functions, I need to explain a particular aspect of the way variables behave that I've glossed over so far.

Variable Scope

In all the examples up to now, you've declared the variables for the program at the beginning of the block that defines the body of the function main(). But you can actually define variables at the beginning of *any* block. Does this make a difference? "It most certainly does, Stanley," as Ollie would have said. Variables exist only within the block in which they're defined. They're created when they're declared, and they cease to exist at the next closing brace.

This is also true of variables that you declare within blocks that are inside other blocks. The variables declared at the beginning of an outer block also exist in the inner block. These variables are freely accessible, as long as there are no other variables with the same name in the inner block, as you'll see.

Variables that are created when they're declared and destroyed at the end of a block are called **automatic variables**, because they're automatically created and destroyed. The extent within a program where a given variable exists is called the variable's **scope**. When you use a variable within its scope, everything is OK. But if you try to reference a variable outside its scope, you'll get an error message when you compile the program because the variable doesn't exist outside of its scope. The general idea is illustrated in the following code fragment:

```
{
  int a = 0;                                  /* Create a       */
  /* Reference to a is OK here      */
  /* Reference to b is an error here */
    {
      int b = 10;                             /* Create b       */
      /* Reference to a and b is OK here */
    }                                         /* b dies here    */
  /* Reference to b is an error here */
  /* Reference to a is OK here      */
}                                             /* a dies here    */
```

All the variables that are declared within a block die and no longer exist after the closing brace of the block. Therefore, the variable a exists within both the inner and outer blocks because it's declared in the outer block. The variable b exists only within the inner block because it's declared within that block. You can understand the implications of a variable's scope through an example.

....

Try It Out: Understanding Scope

Let's take a simple example that involves a nested block that happens to be the body of a loop:

```
/* Program 8.1 A microscopic program about scope */
#include <stdio.h>
void main()
{
  int count1 = 1;                            /* Declared in outer block */

  do
  {
    int count2 = 0;                          /* Declared in inner block */
    ++count2;
    printf("\ncount1 = %d    count2 = %d", count1,count2);
```

(Continued)

```
   }while( ++count1 <= 8 );

   /* count2 no longer exists */

   printf("\ncount1 = %d\n", count1);
}
```

You will get the following output from this program:

```
count1 = 1      count2 = 1
count1 = 2      count2 = 1
count1 = 3      count2 = 1
count1 = 4      count2 = 1
count1 = 5      count2 = 1
count1 = 6      count2 = 1
count1 = 7      count2 = 1
count1 = 8      count2 = 1
count1 = 9
```

HOW IT WORKS

The block that encloses the body of main() contains an inner block that is the
do-while loop. You declare and define count2 inside the loop block:

```
   do
   {
     int count2 = 0;                              /* Declared in inner block */
     ++count2;
     printf("\ncount1 = %d     count2 = %d", count1,count2);
   }while( ++count1 <= 8 );
```

As a result, the value of count2 is never more than 1. During each iteration of the
loop, the variable count2 is created, initialized, incremented, and destroyed.
It only exists from the statement that declares it down to the closing brace for the
loop. The variable count1, on the other hand, exists at the main() block level.
It continues to exist while it's incremented, so the last printf() produces the
value 9.

Try modifying the program to make the last printf() output the value of count2. It
won't compile. You'll get an error because, at the point where the last printf() is,
count2 no longer exists. From this you may guess, correctly, that failing to initialize automatic variables before you use them can cause untold chaos, because the
memory that they occupy may be reallocated to something else at the end of
their existence. As a consequence, next time around, your uninitialized variables
may contain anything but what you expect.

Try It Out: More About Scope

Let's try a slight modification of the last example:

```
/* Program 8.2 More scope in this one */
#include <stdio.h>
void main()
{
   int count = 0;                          /* Declared in outer block */
   do
   {
     int count = 0;            /* This is another variable called count */
     ++count;                  /* this applies to inner count          */
     printf("\ncount = %d ", count);
   }
   while( ++count <= 8 );                  /* This works with outer count */

   /* Inner count is dead, this is outer */
   printf("\ncount = %d\n", count);
}
```

Now you've used the same variable name, count, at the main() block level and in the loop block. Observe what happens when you compile and run this:

```
count = 1
count = 1
count = 1
count = 1
count = 1
count = 1
count = 1
count = 1
count = 9
```

HOW IT WORKS

The output is boring, but interesting at the same time. You actually have two variables called count, but inside the loop block the local variable will "hide" the version of count that exists at the main() block level. The compiler will assume that when you use the name count, you mean the one that was declared in the current block. Inside the while loop, only the local version of count can be reached, so that is the variable being incremented. The printf() inside the loop block displays the local count value, which is always 1, for the reasons given previously. As soon as you exit from the loop, the outer count variable becomes visible, and the last printf() displays its exit value from the loop as 9.

(Continued)

Clearly, the variable that is controlling the loop is the one declared at the beginning of main(). This little example demonstrates why it isn't a good idea to use the same variable name for two different variables in a function, even though it's legal. At best, it's confusing. At worst, you'll be thinking, "That's another fine mess I've gotten myself into."

Variable Scope and Functions

The last point to note, before I get into the details of creating functions, is that the body of every function is a block (which may contain other blocks, of course). As a result, the automatic variables that you declare within a function are local to the function and don't exist elsewhere. Therefore, the variables declared within one function are quite independent of those declared in another function. There's nothing to prevent you from using the same name for variables in different functions; they'll remain quite separate.

This becomes more significant when you're dealing with large programs in which the problem of ensuring unique variables can become a little inconvenient. It's still a good idea to avoid any unnecessary or misleading overlapping of variable names in your various functions and, of course, you should try to use names that are meaningful to make your programs easy to follow. You'll see more about this as you explore functions in C more deeply.

Functions

You've already used built-in functions such as printf() or strcpy() quite extensively in your programs. You've seen how these built-in functions were executed when you referenced them by name and how you were able to transfer information to a function by means of arguments between parentheses following the function name. With the printf() function, for instance, the first argument is usually a text string in quotes, and the succeeding arguments (of which there may be none) are a series of variables or expressions whose values are to be displayed.

You've also seen how you can receive information back from a function in two ways. The first way you saw you could do this was through one of the function arguments in parentheses. You provided an address of a variable through an argument to a function, and the function placed a value in that variable. When you use scanf() to read data from the keyboard, for instance, the input is stored in an address that you supply as an argument. The second way you saw that you could receive information back from a function was as a return value. With the strlen() function, for instance, the length of the string that you supply as the argument appears in the program code in the position where the function call was made. Thus, if str is the string "example", in the expression 2*strlen(str) the value 7, which the function returns, replaces the function call in the expression. The expression will therefore amount to 2*7. Where a function returns a value of a given type, the function call can appear as part of any expression where a variable of the same type could be used.

Of necessity you've written the function main() in all your programs, so you already have basic knowledge of how a function is constructed. Let's look at what makes up a function in more detail.

Defining a Function

When you create a function, you need to specify the **function header** as the first line of the function definition, followed by the executable code for the function enclosed between braces, which is called the **function body**.

- The function header defines the name of the function, the function parameters (in other words, what values are passed to the function when it's called), and the type for the value that the function returns.

- The function body determines what calculations the function performs on the values that are passed to it.

The general form of a function is essentially the same as you've been using for main(), and it looks like this:

```
Return_type  Function_name( Parameters - separated by commas )
{
    Statements;
}
```

The statements in the function body can be absent, but the braces must be present. If there are no statements in the body of a function, the return type must be void, and the function will have no effect. You'll recall that I said that the type void means "absence of any type," so here it means that the function doesn't return a value.

Although it may not be immediately apparent, presenting a function with a content-free body is often useful during the testing phase of a complicated program. This allows you to run the program with only selected functions actually doing something; you can then add the function bodies, step by step, until the whole thing works.

The parameters between parentheses are placeholders for the argument values that you must specify when you call a function. The term **parameter** refers to a placeholder in the function definition. The term **argument** refers to a value that corresponds to a parameter when you call a function. You'll return to look at parameters in more detail a little later in this chapter.

NOTE *The statements in the body of a function can also contain nested blocks of statements. But you can't define a function inside the body of another function.*

The general form for calling a function is the expression

```
Function_name(Arguments - separated by commas)
```

You simply use the function's name followed with a list of arguments separated by commas in parentheses, just as you've been calling functions such as printf() and scanf(). A function call can appear as a statement on a line by itself, like this:

```
printf("A fool and your money are soon partners,");
```

A function that's called like this can be a function that returns a value. In this case, the value that's returned is simply discarded. A function that has been defined with a return type of void can *only* be called like this.

A function that returns a value can, and usually does, participate in an expression, for example:

```
result = 2.0*sqrt(2.0);
```

Here, the value that's returned by the sqrt() function (from math.h) is multiplied by 2.0 and the result is stored in the variable, result. Obviously, because a function with a void return type doesn't return anything, it can't possibly be part of an expression.

Naming a Function

The name of a function can be any legal name in C that isn't a reserved word (such as int, double, sizeof, and so on) and isn't the same as the name of another function in your program. You should take care not to use the same names as any of the standard library functions because this would prevent you from using the library function of the same name, and it would also be very confusing.

One way of differentiating your function names from those in the standard library is to start them with a capital letter, although some programmers find this rather restricting. A legal name has the same form as that of a variable: a sequence of letters and digits, the first of which must be a letter. As with variable names, the underline character counts as a letter. Other than that, the name of a function can be anything you like, but ideally the name that you choose should give some clue as to what the function does. Examples of valid function names that you might create are as follows:

```
cube_root    FindLast    Explosion    Back2Front
```

You'll often want to define function names (and variable names, for that matter) that consist of more than one word. There are two common approaches you can adopt that happen to be illustrated in the first two examples:

- Separate each of the words in a function name with an underline character.

- Capitalize the first letter of each word.

Both approaches work well. Which one you choose is up to you, but it's a good idea to pick an approach and stick to it. You can, of course, use one approach for functions and the other for variables. Within this book, both approaches have been sprinkled around to give you a feel for how they look. By the time you reach the end of the book, you'll probably have formed your own opinion as to which approach is best.

Function Parameters

Function parameters are defined within the function header and are placeholders for the arguments that need to be specified when the function is called. The parameters are a list of variable names and their types, with successive parameters separated by commas. The entire list of parameters is enclosed between the parentheses that follow the function name.

Parameters provide the means by which you pass information *from* the calling program *into* the function. These parameters are local to the function, and the values that are assigned to them when the function is called are referred to as **arguments**. The computation in the body of the function is then written using these parameters, which will have the values of the arguments when the function executes. Finally, when the computation has finished, the function will exit and return an appropriate value back to the original calling statement.

A typical function header is

```
int SendMessage(char* text)
```

This function has one parameter, text, which is of type "pointer to char", and it returns a value of type int.

You call a function by using the function name followed by the arguments to the function between parentheses. When you actually call the function by referencing it in some part of your program, the arguments that you specify in the call will replace the parameters in the function. As a result, when the function executes, the computation will proceed using the values that you supplied as arguments. The arguments that you specify when you call a function need to agree in type, number, and sequence with the parameters that are specified in the function header. The relationship and information passing between the calling and called function is illustrated in Figure 8-2.

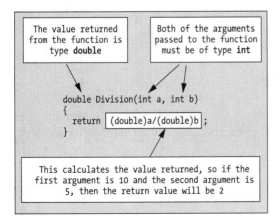

Figure 8-2. Passing arguments to a function

Specifying the Return Value Type

Let's take another look at the general form of a function:

```
Return_type  Function_name(Parameters - separated by commas)
{
    Statements;
}
```

The Return_type specifies the type of the value returned by the function. If the function is used in an expression, or as the right side of an assignment statement, the return value supplied by the function will effectively be substituted for the function in its position. The type of value to be returned by a function can be specified as any of the legal types in C, including pointers. The type can also be specified as void, meaning that no value is returned. As noted earlier, a function with a void return type can't be used in an expression or anywhere in an assignment statement.

The return type can also be type void*, which is a "pointer to void". This is an address value but with no specified type. This type is used when you want the flexibility to be able to return a pointer that may be used for a variety of purposes, as in the case of the malloc() function for allocating memory. The most common return types are shown in Table 8-1.

Table 8-1. Common Return Types

Type	Meaning	Type	Meaning
int	Integer, 2 or 4 bytes	int*	Pointer to int
short	Integer, 2 bytes	short*	Pointer to short
long	Integer, 4 bytes	long*	Pointer to long
char	Character, 1 byte	char*	Pointer to char
float	Floating-point, 4 bytes	float*	Pointer to float
double	Floating-point, 8 bytes	double*	Pointer to double
void	No value	void*	Pointer to undefined type

If a function has its return type specified as other than void, then it must return a value. This is achieved by executing a return statement to return the value.

The return Statement

The return statement provides the means of exiting from a function and resuming execution of the calling function at the point from which the call occurred. In its simplest form, the return statement is just this:

```
return;
```

In this form, the `return` statement is being used in a function where the return type has been declared as `void`. It doesn't return any value. However, the more general form of the `return` statement is this:

```
return expression;
```

This form of `return` statement must be used when the return value type for the function has been declared as some type other than `void`. The value that's returned to the calling program is the value that results when `expression` is evaluated.

 CAUTION *You'll get an error message if you compile a program that contains a function defined with a* `void` *return type that tries to return a value. You'll get an error message from the compiler if you use a bare* `return` *in a function where the return type was specified to be other than* `void`.

The return `expression` can be any expression, but it should result in a value that's the same type as that declared for the return value in the function header. If it isn't of the same type, the compiler will cast the type of the `return expression` to the one required (where this is possible) along with a warning if the cast has the potential for losing information. The compiler will produce an error message if the cast isn't possible.

There can be more than one `return` statement in a function, but each `return` statement must supply a value with the same type as that specified in the function header for the return value.

 NOTE *The calling function doesn't have to recognize or process the value returned from a called function. It's up to you how you use any values returned from function calls.*

Try It Out: Using Functions

It's always easier to understand new concepts with an example, so let's start with a trivial illustration of a program that consists of two functions. You'll write a function that will compute the average of two floating-point variables, and you'll call that function from `main()`. This is more to illustrate the mechanism of writing and calling functions than to present a good example of their practical use.

(Continued)

```
/* Program 8.3 Average of two float values */
#include <stdio.h>

/* Definition of the function to calculate an average */
float average(float x, float y)
{
   return (x + y)/2.0f;
}

/* main program - execution always starts here */
void main()
{
   float average(float x, float y);               /* Function prototype */

   float value1 = 0.0F;
   float value2 = 0.0F;
   float value3 = 0.0F;

   printf("Enter two floating-point values separated by blanks: ");
   scanf("%f %f", &value1, &value2);
   value3 = average(value1, value2);
   printf("\nThe average is: %f\n",  value3);
}
```

Typical output of this program would be

```
Enter two floating-point values separated by blanks: 2.34 4.567

The average is: 3.453500
```

HOW IT WORKS

Let's go through this example step by step. Figure 8-3 shows the order of execution in the example.

As you already know, execution begins at the first executable statement of the function main(). The first statement in the body of main() is

```
float average(float x, float y);               /* Function prototype */
```

This isn't an executable statement. All you're doing is declaring the form of the average() function that you'll be using in main(). This is called a **function prototype**.

(Continued)

Figure 8-3. Order of execution

The purpose of a function prototype is to tell the compiler the essential specifications of a function. A function prototype includes specifications for the return type and any parameter types, in addition to the name of the function itself.

Note that function prototypes require a semicolon at the end, just as the declaration of a variable does.

This function prototype includes specifications for the return type (float) and the parameter types (float and float), as well as the name of the function, average(). Compare the prototype with the function header in the actual function definition, which *doesn't* have a semicolon:

```
float average(float x, float y)
```

The compiler is able to ensure that when you use the function, you provide arguments of the appropriate type, and that the return value is handled properly in any expression in which it's used.

The variables x and y are local to the function average(), so you're free to use the same variable names in the calling function—or any other function, for that matter. Note that the prototype doesn't need to use the same parameter names as in the function definition; in fact, you can even omit them altogether in the function prototype, like this:

```
    float average(float, float);              /* Function prototype */
```

This function declaration isn't strictly necessary in this example. If you delete it, you'll see that the program will still compile and run. This is because the definition of the function average() *precedes* its use in main(), so the compiler already knows all about it. If the definition followed main(), however, then it would be essential to include the function declaration. Without it the compiler wouldn't be able to recognize average() or determine how it should be called.

(Continued)

> **NOTE** *It's good practice to always include declarations for all of the func-tions in a program, regardless of where they're called. This approach will help your programs to be more consistent in design, and it will prevent any errors occurring if, at any stage, you choose to call a function from another part of your program.*
>
> *Function declarations don't typically appear in the position shown in the preceding example. They usually appear at the beginning of a program file, preceding* main() *and the other functions in the program.*

The first executable statement that actually does something is this:

```
printf("Enter two floating point values separated by blanks: ");
```

There's nothing new here—you simply make a call to the function printf() with one argument, which happens to be a string. The actual value transferred to printf() will be a pointer containing the address of the beginning of the string that you've specified as the argument. The printf() function will then display the string that you've supplied as that argument.

The next statement is also a familiar one:

```
scanf("%f %f",&value1, &value2);
```

This calls the input function, scanf(). There are three arguments: a string, which is therefore effectively a pointer, as in your previous statement; the address of the first variable, which again is effectively a pointer; and the address of the second variable—again, effectively a pointer. As I've discussed, scanf() must have the addresses for those last two arguments to allow the input data to be stored in them. You'll see why a little later in this chapter.

Once you've read in the two values, the assignment statement is executed:

```
value3 = average(value1, value2);
```

This calls the function average(), which expects two float type values as argu-ments, and you've correctly supplied value1 and value2, which are both of type float.

There's a very important point to be made here, which is illustrated in Figure 8-4.

The important point is this: *copies* of the values of value1 and value2 are trans-ferred to the function, *not the variables themselves*. This means that the function can't change the values stored in value1 or value2. For instance, if you input the values 4.0 and 6.0 for the two variables, the compiler will create separate copies of these two values in memory, and the average() function will have access to these copies only when it's called. This mechanism is how all argument values are passed to functions in C, and it's termed the **pass-by-value** mechanism.

(Continued)

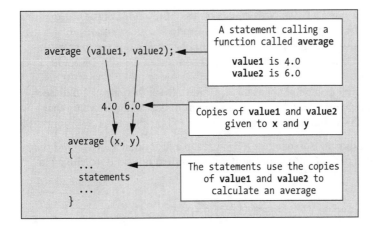

Figure 8-4. Passing arguments to a function

The only way a function can change a variable belonging to the function that called it is by receiving an argument value that's the address of the variable. When you pass an address as an argument to a function, it's still only a copy of the address that's actually passed to the function, not the original. However, the copy is still the address of the original variable. I'll come back to this point later in the chapter.

The average() function is executed with the values from value1 and value2 substituted for the parameter names in the function, which are x and y, respectively. The function is defined by the following statements:

```
float average(float x, float y)
{
  return (x + y)/2.0f;
}
```

The function body has only one statement, which is the return statement. But this return statement does all the work you need. It contains an expression for the value to be returned that works out the average of x and y. This value then appears in place of the function in the assignment statement back in main(). So, in effect, a function that returns a value acts like a variable of the same type as the return value.

Note that without the f on the constant 2.0, this number would be of type double and the whole expression would be evaluated as type double. Because the compiler would then arrange to cast this to type float for the return value, you would get a warning message during compilation because data could be lost.

Instead of assigning the result of the function to value3, you could have written the last printf() statement as follows:

```
printf("\nThe average is: %f", average(value1, value2));
```

(Continued)

Here, the function average() would receive copies of the values of the argument. The return value from the function would be supplied as an argument to printf() directly, even though you haven't explicitly created a place to store it. The compiler would take care of allocating some memory to store the value returned from average(). It would also take the trouble to make a copy of this to hand over to the function printf() as an argument. Once the printf() had been executed, however, you would have had no means of accessing the value that was returned from the function average().

Another possible option is to use explicit values in a function call. What happens then? Let's stretch the printf() statement out of context now and rewrite it like this:

```
printf("\nThe average is: %f", average(4.0, 6.0));
```

In this case, the compiler would create a memory location to store each of the constant arguments to average(), and then supply copies of those values to the function—exactly as before. A copy of the result returned from the function average() would then be passed to printf().

Figure 8-5 illustrates the process of calling a function named useful() from main() and getting a value returned.

```
void main()
{
    ...
    x = useful (y, z);
    ...
}
long useful ( int a, int b )
{
    long c; /* A local variable we are using to hold a result */
    ...            /* In here would be useful statements */
    return c:
}
```

Figure 8-5. Argument passing and the return value

The arrows in the figure show how the values correspond between main() and useful(). Notice that the value returned from useful() is finally stored in the variable x in main(). The value that's returned from useful() is stored in the variable c that is local to the useful() function. This variable ceases to exist when execution of the useful() function ends, but the returned value is still safe because a copy of the value is returned, not the original value stored in c. Thus, returning a value from a function works in the same way as passing an argument value.

Function Declarations

As you saw in the previous example, the function declaration defines the essential characteristics of a function. It defines its name, its return value type, and the type of each of its parameters. You can actually write it exactly the same as the function header and just add a semicolon at the end if you want. A function declaration is also called a **function prototype**, because it models how you use the function. A function prototype enables the compiler to generate the appropriate instructions at each point where you use the function and to check that you use it correctly in each case. When you include a header file in a program, the header file adds the function prototypes for library functions to the program. For example, the header file stdio.h contains function prototypes for printf() and scanf(), among others.

In a variation of this example, you could define the function main() first and then the function average():

```
#include <stdio.h>

void main()
{
  float average(float, float);          /* Function prototype */
  /* Rest of the code in main() ... */
}

float average(float x, float y)
{
  return (x + y)/2.0;
}
```

In this case, you must put the declaration for the function average() at the beginning of the body of main(), because main() uses that function. Without it, the code wouldn't compile.

The declaration for the function average() here is local to main() because its scope is defined by the limits of the body of main(). If you want to use the function average() in several different functions in the same program, you could put the same declaration in the body of each. However, there is another possibility, which also happens to be by far the most common method of handling function declarations in C. You could put the declaration of average() at the beginning of the file, along with the #include directives, like this:

```
#include <stdio.h>
float average(float, float);          /* Function prototype */

void main()
{
  /* Rest of the code in main() ... */
}

float average(float x, float y)
```

```
{
  return (x + y)/2.0;
}
```

The function declaration is now external to all of the functions in the source file, and its scope would extend to the end of the source file, thereby allowing any of the functions in the file to call the average() function regardless of where you've placed the definition for average() and without the need for further declarations of the function. This is the typical position for a function declaration, and you'll see this approach in the next example.

Pointers and Functions

You've already seen how it's possible to pass a pointer as an argument to a function. More than that, you've seen that this is essential if a function is to modify the value of a variable that's defined in the calling function. In fact, this is the only way it can be done. So let's explore how all this works out in practice with another example.

Try It Out: Functions Using Ordinary Variables

Let's first take an elementary example of a function that doesn't use a pointer argument. Here, you're going to try to change the contents of a variable by passing it as an argument to a function, changing it, and then returning it. You'll output its value both within the function and back in main() to see what the effect is.

```
/* Program 8.4 The change that doesn't  */
#include <stdio.h>

int change(int number);            /* Function prototype           */

void main()
{
    int number = 10;               /* Starting Value               */
    int result = 0;                /* Place to put the returned value */

    result = change(number);
    printf("\nIn main, result = %d\tnumber = %d", result, number);
}

/* Definition of the function change() */
int change(int number)
{
    number = 2 * number;
    printf("\nIn function change, number = %d\n", number);
    return number;
}
```

(Continued)

The output from this program is

```
In function change, number = 20
In main, result = 20     number = 10
```

This example demonstrates that you can't change the world without pointers. You can only change the values locally within the function.

The first thing of note in this example is that you put the prototype for the function change() outside of main() along with the #include directive:

```
#include <stdio.h>

int change(int number);              /* Function prototype           */
```

This makes it *global*, and if you had other functions in the example, they would all be able to use this function.

In main() you set up an integer variable, number, with an initial value of 10. You also have a second variable, result, which you use to store the value that you get back from the function change():

```
    int number = 10;                 /* Starting Value               */
    int result = 0;                  /* Place to put the returned value */
```

You then call the function change() and pass the value of the variable number to it:

```
    result = change(number);
```

The function change() is defined as follows:

```
int change(int number)
{
   number = 2 * number;
   printf("\nIn function change, number = %d", number);
   return number;
}
```

Within the body of the function change(), the first statement doubles the value stored in the argument that has been passed to it from main(). You even use the same variable name in the function that you used in main(), to reinforce the idea that you want to change the original value. The function change() displays the new value of number before it returns it to main() by means of the return statement.

(Continued)

In main() you also display what you got back from change() and the value of number:

```
printf("\nIn main, result = %d\tnumber = %d", result, number);
```

Look at the output, though. It demonstrates how vain and pathetic the attempt to change a variable value by passing it to a function has been. Clearly, the variable number in change() has the value 20 on return from the function. It's displayed both in the function and as a returned value in main(). In spite of our transparent subterfuge of giving them the same name, the variables with the name number in main() and change() are evidently quite separate, so modifying one has no effect on the other.

....

....

Try It Out: Using Pointers in Functions

Let's now modify the last example to use pointers, and with a following wind, you should succeed in modifying the value of a variable in main().

```
/* Program 8.5 The change that does   */
#include <stdio.h>

int change(int* pnumber);                /* Function prototype           */

void main()
{
    int number = 10;                 /* Starting Value              */
    int* pnumber = &number;          /* Pointer to starting value   */
    int result = 0;                  /* Place to put the returned value */

    result = change(pnumber);
    printf("\nIn main, result = %d\tnumber = %d", result, number);
}

/* Definition of the function change() */
int change(int* pnumber)
{
    *pnumber *= 2;
    printf("\nIn function change, *pnumber = %d\n", *pnumber );
    return *pnumber;
}
```

(Continued)

The output from this program looks like this:

```
In function change, *pnumber = 20
In main, result = 20    number = 20
```

HOW IT WORKS

There are relatively few changes to the last example. You define a pointer in main() and call pnumber, which is initialized to the address of the variable number, which holds the starting value:

```
    int* pnumber = &number;              /* Pointer to starting value    */
```

The prototype of the function change() has been modified to take account of the parameter being a pointer:

```
int change(int* pnumber);              /* Function prototype             */
```

The definition of the function change() has also been modified to use a pointer:

```
int change(int* pnumber)
{
    *pnumber *= 2;
    printf("\nIn function change, *pnumber = %d", *pnumber );
    return *pnumber;
}
```

This pointer, pnumber, has the same name as the pointer in main(), although this is of no consequence to the way the program works. You could call it anything you like, as long as it's a pointer of the correct type, because the name is local to this function.

Within the function change(), the arithmetic statement has been changed to this:

```
    *pnumber *= 2;
```

Using the *= operator isn't strictly necessary, but it makes it a lot less confusing, provided you can remember what *= does at this point. It's exactly the same as this:

```
    *pnumber = 2*(*pnumber);
```

(Continued)

The output now demonstrates that the pointer mechanism is working correctly and that the function change() is indeed modifying the value of number in main(). Of course, when you submit a pointer as an argument, it's still passed by value. Therefore, the compiler doesn't pass the original pointer; it makes a copy of the pointer to hand over to the function. Because the copy will contain the same address as the original, it still refers to the variable number, so everything works OK.

If you're unconvinced of this, you can demonstrate it for yourself quite easily by adding a statement to the function change() that modifies the pointer pnumber. You could set it to NULL, for instance. You can then check in main() that pnumber still points to number. Of course, you'll have to alter the return statement in change() to get the correct result.

....

....

Try It Out: Passing Data Using Pointers

You can exercise this method of passing data to a function using pointers in a slightly more practical way, with a revised version of the function for sorting strings from Chapter 7. You can see the complete code for the program here, and then I'll discuss it in detail. The source code defines three functions in addition to main():

```c
/* Program 8.6 The functional approach to string sorting*/
#include <stdio.h>
#include <stdlib.h>
#include <string.h>
#define TRUE  1
#define FALSE 0

int str_in(char **);            /* Function prototype for str_in   */
void str_sort(char *[], int);   /* Function prototype for str_sort */
void str_out(char *[], int);    /* Function prototype for str_out  */

#define BUFFER_LEN 240
#define NUM_P 50

/* Function main - execution starts here */
void main()
{
   char *pS[NUM_P];             /* Array of string pointers   */
   int count = 0;              /* Number of strings read     */

   printf("\nEnter successive lines, pressing Enter at the end of"
                      " each line.\nJust press Enter to end.\n");
```

(Continued)

```
        for(count = 0; count < NUM_P ; count++)        /* Max of NUM_P strings   */
          if(!str_in(&pS[count]) )                      /* Read a string          */
            break;                                      /* Stop input on 0 return */

        str_sort( pS, count );                          /* Sort strings           */
        str_out( pS, count );                           /* Output strings         */
    }


    /***************************************************
     *        String input routine                    *
     *  Argument is a pointer to a string pointer      *
     *  which is char**                                *
     *  Returns FALSE for empty string or if memory not *
     *  obtained, and returns TRUE otherwise.          *
     ***************************************************/
    int str_in(char **pString)
    {
        char buffer[BUFFER_LEN];            /* Space to store input string  */

        if(gets(buffer) == NULL )           /* NULL returned from gets()?   */
        {
            printf("\nError reading string.\n");
            return FALSE;                   /* Read error                   */
        }

        if(buffer[0] == '\0')               /* Empty string read?           */
            return FALSE;

        *pString = (char*)malloc(strlen(buffer) + 1);

        if(*pString == NULL)                /* Check memory allocation      */
        {
            printf("\nOut of memory.");
            return FALSE;                   /* No memory allocated          */
        }

        strcpy(*pString, buffer);           /* Copy string read to argument */
        return TRUE;
    }

    /***************************************************
     *        String sort routine                      *
     * First argument is array of pointers to strings  *
     * which is of type char**.                        *
     * Second argument is the number of elements in the *
     * pointer array - i.e. the number of strings      *
     ***************************************************/
    void str_sort(char *p[], int n)
    {
```

(Continued)

```
          char *pTemp = NULL;              /* Temporary pointer           */
          int i = 0;                       /* Loop counter                */
          int sorted = FALSE;              /* Strings sorted indicator    */
          while(!sorted)                   /* Loop until there are no swaps */
          {
            sorted = TRUE;                 /* Initialize to indicate no swaps */
            for( i = 0 ; i<n-1 ; i++ )
              if(strcmp(p[i], p[i + 1]) > 0)
              {
                sorted = FALSE;            /* indicate we are out of order  */
                pTemp= p[i];               /* Swap pointers p[i]            */
                p[i] = p[i + 1];           /*                and            */
                p[i + 1]  = pTemp;         /*                p[i + 1]        */
              }
          }
        }


/*****************************************************
 *        String output routine                      *
 * First argument is an array of pointers to         *
 * strings which is the same as char**               *
 * The second argument is a count of the number of   *
 * pointers in the array i.e. the number of strings  *
 *****************************************************/
void str_out(char *p[] , int n)
{
   int i = 0;                             /* Loop counter                */

   printf("\nYour input sorted in order is:\n\n");
   for (i = 0 ; i<n ; i++)
   {
     printf("%s\n", p[i]);                /* Display a string            */
     free(p[i]);                          /* Free memory for the string */
     p[i] = NULL;
   }
   return;
}
```

Typical output from this program would be

```
Enter successive lines, pressing Enter at the end of each line.
Just press Enter to end.
Mike
Adam
Mary
Steve


Your input sorted in order is:
```

(Continued)

```
Adam
Mary
Mike
Steve
```

==

HOW IT WORKS

This example works in a similar way to the sorting example in Chapter 7. It looks like a lot of code, but I've added quite a few comment lines in fancy boxes that occupy space. This is good practice for longer programs that use several functions, so that you can be sure you know what each function does.

The whole set of statements for all the functions makes up your source file. At the beginning of the program source file, before you define main(), you have your #include statements for the libraries that you're using, your constant definitions, and your function prototypes. Each of these is effective from the point of their occurrence to the end of your file, because they're defined outside of all of the functions. They are therefore effective in all of your functions.

The program consists of three functions in addition to the function main(). The prototypes of the functions defined are as follows:

```
int str_in(char **);          /* Function prototype for str_in    */
void str_sort(char *[], int);  /* Function prototype for str_sort  */
void str_out(char *[], int);   /* Function prototype for str_out   */
```

You can see that the parameter names aren't specified here. You aren't obliged to do so, but it's usually better if you do. You omit them here to show that you can leave them out. You can also use different parameter names in the function prototype from those in the function definition.

TIP *It can be useful to use longer, more explanatory names in the prototype and shorter names in the function definition to keep the code more concise.*

The prototypes in this example declare a function str_in() to read in all the strings, a function str_sort() to sort the strings, and a function str_out() to output the sorted strings in their new sequence. Each function prototype declares the types of the parameters and the return value type for that function.

The first declaration is for str_in(), and it declares the parameter as type char **, which is a "pointer to a pointer to char". Sound complicated? Well, if you take a closer look at exactly what's going on here, you'll understand how simple this really is.

(Continued)

In main(), the argument to this function is &pS[i]. This is the address of pS[i]—in other words, a pointer to pS[i]. And what is pS[i]? It's a pointer to char. Put these together and you have the type as declared: char**. You have to declare it this way because you want to modify the contents of an element in the pS array from within the function str_in. This is the only way that the str_in() function can get access to the pS array. If you used only one * in the parameter type definition and just used pS[i] as the argument, then the function would receive whatever was contained in pS[i], which isn't what you want at all! This mechanism is illustrated in Figure 8-6.

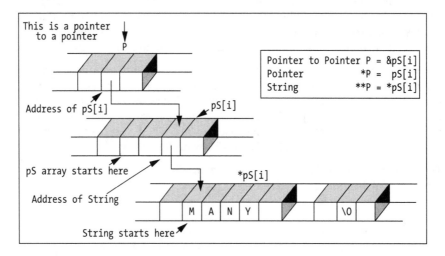

Figure 8-6. Determining the pointer type

You can now take a look at the internal working of the function.

THE STR_IN() FUNCTION

First, note the detailed comment at the beginning. This is a good way of starting out a function and highlighting its basic purpose. The function definition is as follows:

```
/****************************************************
 *       String input routine                      *
 *  Argument is a pointer to a string pointer       *
 *  which is char**                                 *
 *  Returns FALSE for empty string or if memory not *
 *  obtained, and returns TRUE otherwise.           *
 ****************************************************/
int str_in(char **pString)
{
```

(Continued)

```
    char buffer[BUFFER_LEN];              /* Space to store input string  */

    if(gets(buffer) == NULL )             /* NULL returned from gets()?   */
    {
      printf("\nError reading string.\n");
      return FALSE;                       /* Read error                   */
    }

    if(buffer[0] == '\0')                 /* Empty string read?           */
      return FALSE;

    *pString = (char*)malloc(strlen(buffer) + 1);

    if(*pString == NULL)                  /* Check memory allocation      */
    {
      printf("\nOut of memory.");
      return FALSE;                       /* No memory allocated          */
    }

    strcpy(*pString, buffer);             /* Copy string read to argument */
    return TRUE;
}
```

When the function str_in() is called from main(), the address of pS[i] is passed
as the argument. This is the address of the current free array element in which
the address of the next string that's entered should be stored. Within the function, this is referred to as the parameter pString.

The input string is stored in buffer by the function gets(). This function returns
NULL if an error occurred reading the input, so you first check for that. You check
the first character in the string obtained by gets() against '\0'. The function
replaces the newline character that results from pressing the Enter key with '\0',
so if you just press the Enter key, the first character of the string will be '\0'. If
you get an empty string entered, you return the value FALSE to main(). The symbols TRUE and FALSE are defined in preprocessor directives, after the #include
directives, so you can use these in any function within the source file.

Once you've read a string, you allocate space for it using the malloc() function
and store its address in *pString. After checking that you did actually get some
memory, you copy the contents of buffer to the memory that was allocated. If
malloc() fails to allocate memory, you simply display a message and return FALSE
to main().

The function str_in() is called in main() within this loop:

```
    for(count = 0; count < NUM_P ; count++)     /* Max of NUM_P strings   */
      if(!str_in(&pS[count]) )                   /* Read a string          */
        break;                                   /* Stop input on 0 return */
```

(Continued)

Because all the work is done in the str_in() function, all that's necessary here is to continue the loop until you get FALSE returned from the function, which will cause the break to be executed, or until you fill up the pointer array pS, which is indicated by count reaching the value NUM_P, thus ending the loop. The loop also counts how many strings are entered in count.

Having safely stored all the strings, main() then calls the function str_sort() to sort the strings with this statement:

```
    str_sort( pS, count );                       /* Sort strings          */
```

The first argument is the array name, pS, so the address of the first location of the array is transferred to the function. The second argument is the count of the number of strings so the function will know how many there are to be sorted. Let's now look at how the str_sort() function works.

THE STR_SORT() FUNCTION

The function str_sort() is defined by these statements:

```
/**************************************************
 *        String sort routine                     *
 * First argument is array of pointers to strings  *
 * which is type char**.                          *
 * Second argument is the number of elements in the *
 * pointer array – i.e. the number of strings      *
 **************************************************/
void str_sort(char *p[], int n)
{
    char *pTemp = NULL;              /* Temporary pointer         */
    int i = 0;                       /* Loop counter              */
    int sorted = FALSE;              /* Strings sorted indicator   */
    while(!sorted)                   /* Loop until there are no swaps  */
    {
        sorted = TRUE;               /* Initialize to indicate no swaps */
        for( i = 0 ; i < n - 1 ; i++ )
            if(strcmp(p[i], p[i + 1] ) > 0)
            {
                sorted = FALSE;          /* indicate we are out of order  */
                pTemp= p[i];             /* Swap pointers p[i]        */
                p[i] = p[i + 1];         /*             and           */
                p[i + 1]  = pTemp;       /*             p[i + 1]      */
            }
    }
}
```

(Continued)

Within the function, the parameter variable p has been defined as an array of pointers. This will be replaced, when the function is called, by the address for pS that's transferred as an argument. You haven't specified the dimension for p. This isn't necessary because the array is one dimensional. The address is passed to the function as the first argument, and the second argument defines the number of elements that you want to process. If the array had two or more dimensions, you would have to specify all dimensions except the first. This would be necessary to enable the compiler to know the shape of the array.

You declare the second parameter, n, in the function str_sort() as type int, and this will have the value of the argument count when the function is called. You declare a loop counter, i, and a variable named sorted that will have the value TRUE or FALSE to indicate whether or not the strings have been sorted. Remember that all the variables declared within the function body are local to that function. This means that the variable i in this function, for instance, isn't the same variable as the variable i in any other function.

The strings are sorted in the for loop. You can see how this works in Figure 8-7. Notice that only the pointers are altered. In this illustration, I used the input data you saw previously, and this input happens to be completely sorted in one pass. However, if you try this process on paper with a more disordered sequence of the same input strings, you'll see that more than one pass is often required to reach the correct sequence.

Figure 8-7. Sorting the strings

(Continued)

THE STR_OUT() FUNCTION

The last function called by main() is str_out(), which displays the sorted strings:

```
/****************************************************
*       String output routine                      *
* First argument is an array of pointers to         *
* strings which is the same as char**               *
* The second argument is a count of the number of   *
* pointers in the array i.e. the number of strings  *
****************************************************/
void str_out(char *p[] , int n)
{
    int i = 0;                         /* Loop counter                  */

    printf("\nYour input sorted in order is:\n\n");
    for (i = 0 ; i<n ; i++)
    {
      printf("%s\n", p[i]);            /* Display a string              */
      free(p[i]);                      /* Free memory for the string */
      p[i] = NULL;
    }
    return;
}
```

In this function, the parameter n receives the value of count and the strings are displayed using n as the count for the number of strings. The for loop outputs all the strings. Once a string has been displayed, the memory is no longer required, so you release the memory that it occupied by calling the library function free(). You also set the pointer to NULL to avoid any possibility of referring to that memory again by mistake.

You've used a return statement at the end of the function, but you could have left it out. Because the return type is void, reaching the end of the block enclosing the body of the function is the equivalent of return. (Remember, though, that this isn't the case for functions that return a value.)

Returning Pointer Values from a Function

You've seen how you can return numeric values from a function. You've just learned how to use pointers as arguments and how to store a pointer at an address that's passed as an argument. You can also return a pointer from a function. Let's look first at a very simple example.

Try It Out: Returning Values from a Function

You'll use increasing your salary as the basis for the example, as it's such a popular topic.

```
/* Program 8.7 A function to increase your salary */
#include <stdio.h>

long *IncomePlus(long* pPay);          /* Prototype for increase function */

void main()
{
   long your_pay = 30000L;             /* Starting salary               */
   long *pold_pay = &your_pay;         /* Pointer to pay value          */
   long *pnew_pay = NULL;              /* Pointer to hold return value  */

   pnew_pay = IncomePlus( pold_pay );
   printf("\nOld pay = $%ld", *pold_pay);
   printf("   New pay = $%ld\n", *pnew_pay);
}

/* Definition of function to increment pay */
long *IncomePlus(long *pPay)
{
   *pPay += 10000L;                    /* Increment the value for pay   */
   return pPay;                        /* Return the address            */
}
```

When you run the program, you'll get this output:

```
Old pay = $40000   New pay = $40000
```

HOW IT WORKS

In main(), you set up an initial value in the variable your_pay and define two pointers for use with the function IncomePlus(), which is going to increase your_pay. One pointer is initialized with the address of your_pay, and the other is initialized to NULL because it's going to receive the address returned by the function IncomePlus().

(Continued)

Look at the output. It looks like a satisfactory result, except that there's something not quite right. If you overlook what you started with ($30000), it looks as though you didn't get any increase at all. Because the function IncomePlus() modifies the value of your_pay through the pointer pold_pay, the original value has been changed. Clearly, both pointers, pold_pay and pnew_pay, refer to the same location: your_pay. This is a result of the statement in the function IncomePlus():

```
return pPay;
```

This returns the pointer value that the function received when it was called. This is the address contained in pold_pay. The result is that you inadvertently increase the original amount that you were paid—such is the power of pointers!

Try It Out: Using Local Storage

Let's look at what happens if you use local storage in the function IncomePlus(). After a small modification, the example becomes this:

```
/* Program 8.8 A function to increase your salary that doesn't    */
#include <stdio.h>

long *IncomePlus(long* pPay);          /* Prototype for increase function */

void main()
{
    long your_pay = 30000L;            /* Starting salary                */
    long *pold_pay = &your_pay;        /* Pointer to pay value           */
    long *pnew_pay = NULL;             /* Pointer to hold return value   */

    pnew_pay = IncomePlus(pold_pay);
    printf("\nOld pay = $%ld", *pold_pay);
    printf("   New pay = $%ld\n", *pnew_pay);
}

/* Definition of function to increment pay */
long *IncomePlus(long *pPay)
{
    long pay = 0;                      /* Local variable for the result */

    pay = *pPay + 10000;               /* Increment the value for pay   */
    return &pay;                       /* Return the address            */
}
```

(Continued)

HOW IT WORKS

When I run this I now get the following result (it's likely to be different on your machine and you may even get the correct result):

```
Old pay = $30000    New pay = $27467656
```

Numbers like $27467656 with the word "pay" in the same sentence tend to be a bit startling. You would probably hesitate before complaining about this kind of error. As I said, you may get different results on your computer, possibly the correct result this time. You should get a warning from your compiler with this version of the program. With my compiler, I get the message "Suspicious pointer conversion". This is because I'm returning the address of the variable pay, which goes out of scope on exiting the function IncomePlus(). This is the cause of the remarkable value for the new value of pay—it's junk, just a spurious value left around by something. This is an easy mistake to make, but it can be a hard one to find.

Try combining the two printf() statements in main() into one:

```
printf("\nOld pay = $%ld    New pay = $%ld\n", *pold_pay, *pnew_pay);
```

On my computer it now produces the following output:

```
Old pay = $30000    New pay = $40000
```

This actually looks right, in spite of the fact that you know there's a serious error in the program. In this case, although the variable pay is out of scope and therefore no longer exists, the memory it occupied hasn't been reused yet. In the example, evidently something uses the memory previously used by the variable pay and produces the enormous output value. Here's an absolutely 100 percent cast iron rule for avoiding this kind of problem.

 CAST-IRON RULE *Never return the address of a local variable in a function.*

So how should you implement the IncomePlus() function? Well, the first implementation was fine if you recognize that it does modify the value at the address that's passed to it. If you don't want this to happen, then you could just return the new value for the pay rather than a pointer. The calling program would then need to store the value that's returned, not an address.

(Continued)

If you wanted the new pay value to be stored in another location, the
IncomePlus() function could conceivably allocate space for it using malloc() and
then return the address of this memory. However, you should be cautious about
doing this because responsibility for freeing the memory would then be left to
the calling function. It would be better to pass two arguments to the function,
one being the address of the initial pay and the other being the address of the
location in which the new pay is to be stored. That way, the calling function has
control of the memory.

Separating the allocation of memory at runtime from the freeing of the memory
is sometimes a recipe for something called a **memory leak**. This arises when a
function that allocates memory dynamically but doesn't release it gets called
repeatedly in a loop. This results in more and more of the available memory
being occupied, until in some instances there is none left so the program crash-
es. As far as possible, you should make the function that allocates memory
responsible for releasing it.

You can look at a more practical application of returning pointers by modifying
Program 8.6. You could have written the routine str_in() in this example as follows:

```c
char *str_in(void)
{
    char buffer[BUFFER_LEN];              /* Space to store input string */
    char *pString = NULL;                 /* Pointer to string          */

    if(gets(buffer) == NULL)              /* NULL returned from gets()?  */
    {
      printf("\nError reading string.\n");
      return FALSE;                       /* Read error                  */
    }

    if(buffer[0] == '\0')                 /* Empty string read?          */
      return NULL;

    pString = (char*)malloc( strlen(buffer)  + 1);

    if(*pString == NULL)                  /* Check memory allocation     */
    {
      printf("\nOut of memory.");
      abort();                            /* No memory allocated         */
    }
    return strcpy(pString, buffer);       /* Return pString              */
}
```

Of course, you would also have to modify the function prototype to this:

```
char *str_in(void);
```

Now there are no parameters because you've declared the parameter list as void, and the return value is now a pointer to a character string rather than an integer.

You would also need to modify the for loop in main(), which invokes the function to

```
for(count=0; count < NUM_P ; count++)        /* Max of NUM_P strings    */
   if((pS[count] = str_in())== NULL)         /* Stop input on NULL return */
     break;
```

You now compare the pointer returned from str_in() and stored in pS[count] with NULL, as this would indicate that an empty string had been entered or that a string was not read because of a read error. The example would still work exactly as before, but the internal mechanism for input would be a little different. Now, the function returns the address of the allocated memory block into which the string has been copied. You might imagine that you could use the address of buffer instead, but remember that buffer is local to the function, so it goes out of scope on return from the function. You could try it if you like to see what happens.

If malloc() returns a NULL pointer, indicating that the memory for the string can't be allocated, you display a message as before, but this time you call the function abort() instead of returning from the function. This function, which is declared in stdlib.h, terminates the program immediately.

Choosing one version of the function str_in() or the other is, to some extent, a matter of taste, but on balance this latter version is probably better because it uses a simpler definition of the parameter, which makes it easier to understand. Note, however, that it does allocate memory that has to be released somewhere else in the program. When you need to do this it's best to code the function that will release the memory in tandem with coding the function that allocates it. That way, there's less risk of a memory leak.

Incrementing Pointers in a Function

When you use an array name as an argument to a function, a *copy* of the address of the beginning of the array is transferred to the function. As a result, you have the possibility of treating the value received as a pointer in the fullest sense, incrementing or decrementing the address as you wish. For example, you could rewrite the str_out() function in Program 8.6 as follows:

```
void str_out(char *p[] , int n)
{
   int i = 0;                    /* Loop counter                 */
```

```
printf("\nYour input sorted in order is:\n\n");
for (i = 0 ; i<n ; i++)
{
  printf("%s\n", *p);               /* Display a string            */
  free(*p);                         /* Free memory for the string */
  *p++ = NULL;
}
return;
}
```

You replace the array notation with pointer notation in the printf() and free() function calls. You wouldn't be able to do this with an array declared within the function body, but because you have a copy of the original array address, it's possible here. You can treat the parameter just like a regular pointer. Because the address you have at this point is a copy of the original in main(), this doesn't interfere with the original array address pS in any way. There's little to choose between this version of the function and the original. The former version, using array notation, is probably just a little easier to follow. However, operations expressed in pointer notation often execute faster than array notation.

Summary

This has been quite a long chapter because it covers a big topic. You're not done with functions yet, so I'll postpone diving into another chunky example until the end of the next chapter, which covers further aspects of using functions. So, let's pause for a moment and summarize the key points that you need to keep in mind when creating and using functions:

- C programs consist of one or more functions, one of which is called main(). The function main() is where execution always starts, and it's called by the operating system through a user command.

- A function is a self-contained, named block of code in a program. The name of a function is a unique sequence of letters and digits, the first of which must be a letter (an underline counts as a letter).

- A function definition consists of a header and a body. The header defines the name of the function, the type of the value returned from the function, and the types and names of all the parameters to the function. The body contains the executable statements for the function, which define what the function actually does.

- All the variables that are declared in a function are local to that function.

- A function prototype is a declaration statement terminated by a semicolon that defines the name, the return type, and the parameter types for a function. A function prototype is required to provide information about a function to the compiler when the definition of a function doesn't precede its use in executable code.

- Before you use a function in your source file, you should either define the function or declare the function with a function prototype.

- Arguments to a function must be of a type that's compatible with the corresponding parameters specified in its header. If you specify a parameter to be of type int, you can't then pass an argument of type float. The compiler will insert conversions to the parameter type for arguments where this is possible without loss of information.

- A function that returns a value can be used in an expression just as if it were a value of the same type as the return value.

- You can call any function other than main() as often as you need by using its name in a program.

- *Copies* of the argument values are transferred to a function, not the original values in the calling function. This is referred to as the pass-by-value mechanism for transferring data to a function.

- If you want a function to modify a variable that's declared in its calling function, the address of the variable needs to be transferred as an argument.

That covers the essentials of creating your own functions. In the next chapter, you'll add a few more techniques for using functions to those covered here. You'll also work through a more substantial example of applying functions in a practical context.

Exercises

The following exercises enable you to try out what you've learned in this chapter. If you get stuck, look back over the chapter for help. If you're still stuck, you can download the solutions from the Downloads area of the Apress website (http://www.apress.com), but that really should be a last resort.

Exercise 8-1. Define a function that will calculate the average of an arbitrary number of floating-point values that are passed to the function in an array. Demonstrate the operation of this function by implementing a program that will accept an arbitrary number of values entered from the keyboard and output the average.

Exercise 8-2. Define a function that will return a string representation of an integer that is passed as the argument. For example, if the argument is 25, then the function will return "25". If the argument is –98, then the function will return "-98". Demonstrate the operation of your function with a suitable version of main().

Exercise 8-3. Extend the function that you defined for the previous example to accept an additional argument that specifies the field width for the result, and return the string represent of the value right-justified within the field. For example, if the value to be converted is –98 and the field width argument is 5, then the string that is returned should be "   -98". Demonstrate the operation of this function with a suitable version of `main()`.

Exercise 8-4. Define a function that will return the number of words in a string that is passed as an argument. (Words are separated by spaces or punctuation characters. Assume the string doesn't contain embedded single or double quotes; that is, no words like "isn't.") Define a second function that will segment a string that's passed as the first argument to the function into words, and return the words stored in the array that's passed as the second argument. Define a third function that will return the number of letters in a string that's passed as the argument. Use these functions to implement a program that will read a string containing text from the keyboard and then output all the words from the text ordered from the shortest to the longest.

CHAPTER 9

More on Functions

NOW THAT YOU'VE COMPLETED CHAPTER 8, you have a good grounding in the essentials of creating and using functions. In this chapter you'll build on that foundation by exploring how functions can be used and manipulated; in particular, you'll investigate how you can access a function through a pointer. You'll also be working with some more flexible methods of communicating between functions.

In this chapter you'll learn

- What pointers to functions are and how you use them

- How to use static variables in functions

- How to share variables between functions

- How functions can call themselves

- How to write an Othello-type game (also known as Reversi)

Pointers to Functions

Up to now, you've considered pointers as an exceptionally useful device for manipulating data and variables that contain data. It's a bit like handling things with a pair of tongs. You can manipulate a whole range of hot items with just one pair of tongs. However, you can also use pointers to handle *functions* at a distance. Because a function has an address in memory where it starts execution (i.e., its starting address), the basic information to be stored in a pointer to a function is going to be another address.

If you think about it, though, this isn't going to be enough. If a function is going to be called through a pointer, then information also has to be available about the number and type of the arguments to be supplied, and the type of return value to be expected. The compiler can't deduce these just from the address of the function. This means that declaring a pointer to a function is going to be a little more complicated than declaring a pointer to a data type.

Declaring a Pointer to a Function

The declaration for a pointer to a function looks a little strange, and it can be confusing, so let's start with a simple example:

```
int (*pfunction) (int);
```

This declares a pointer to a function. It doesn't point to anything—yet; this statement just defines the pointer variable. The name of the pointer is pfunction, and it's intended to point to functions with one parameter of type int and that return a value of type int to the calling program. Furthermore, you can *only* use this particular pointer to point to functions with these characteristics. If you wanted a pointer to functions that accept a float argument and return float values, then you would need to declare another pointer with the required characteristics. The components of the declaration are illustrated in Figure 9-1.

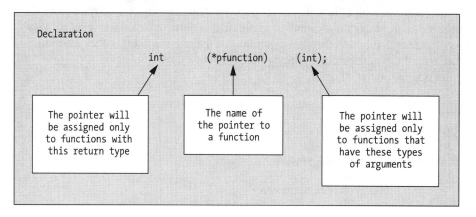

Figure 9-1. Declaring a pointer to a function

There are a lot of parentheses in a "pointer to function" declaration. In this example, the *pfunction part of the declaration must be between parentheses.

 NOTE *If you omit the parentheses, then you'll have a declaration for a function called* pfunction() *that returns a value that's a pointer to* int, *which isn't what you want.*

With "pointer to function" declarations, you must always put the * plus the pointer name between parentheses. The second pair of parentheses just encloses the parameter list in the same way as it does with a standard function declaration.

Because a pointer to a function can point only to functions with a given return type and a given number of parameters of given types, the variation in what it can point to is just the function name. Let's try a simple example and see how it works.

Try It Out: Using Pointers to Functions

In this example, you'll define three functions that have the same parameter and return types, and use a pointer to a function to call each of them in turn.

```
/* Program 9.1 Pointing to functions */
#include <stdio.h>

/* Function prototypes */
int sum(int, int);
int product(int, int);
int difference(int, int);

void main()
{
   int a = 10;                       /* Initial value for a            */
   int b = 5;                        /* Initial value for b            */
   int result = 0;                   /* Storage for results            */
   int (*pfun)(int, int);            /* Function pointer declaration    */

   pfun = sum;                       /* Points to function sum()       */
   result = pfun(a, b);              /* Call sum() through pointer      */
   printf("\npfun = sum        result = %d", result);

   pfun = product;                   /* Points to function product()   */
   result = pfun(a, b);              /* Call product() through pointer  */
   printf("\npfun = product    result = %d", result);

   pfun = difference;                /* Points to function difference() */
   result = pfun(a, b);              /* Call difference() through pointer */
   printf("\npfun = difference result = %d\n", result);
}

/* Definition of the function sum     */
int sum(int x, int y)
{
   return x + y;
}

/* Definition of the function product     */
int product(int x, int y)
{
   return x * y;
}
```

(Continued)

```
/* Definition of the function difference    */
int difference(int x, int y)
{
   return x - y;
}
```

The output from this program looks like this:

```
pfun = sum             result = 15
pfun = product         result = 50
pfun = difference      result = 5
```

HOW IT WORKS

You declare and define three different functions to return the sum, the product, and the difference between two integer arguments. Within main(), you declare a pointer to a function with this statement:

```
int (*pfun)(int, int);            /* Function pointer declaration     */
```

This pointer can be assigned to point to any function that accepts two int arguments and also returns a value of type int. Notice the way you assign a value to the pointer:

```
pfun = sum;                       /* Points to function sum()         */
```

You just use a regular assignment statement that has the name of the function, completely unadorned, on the right side! You don't need to put in the parameter list or anything. If you did, it would be wrong, because it would then be a function call, not an address, and the compiler would complain. A function is very much like an array in its usage here. If you want the address, you just use the name by itself.

In main(), you assign the address of each function, in turn, to the function pointer pfun. You then call each function using the pointer pfun and display the result. You can see how to call a function using the pointer in this statement:

```
result = pfun(a, b);              /* Call sum() through pointer       */
```

You just use the name of the pointer as though it were a function name, followed by the argument list between parentheses. Here, you're using the "pointer to function" variable name as though it were the original function name, so the argument list must correspond with the parameters in the function header for the function you're calling. This is illustrated in Figure 9-2.

(Continued)

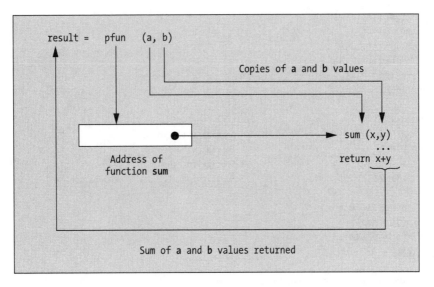

Figure 9-2. Calling a function through a pointer

Arrays of Pointers to Functions

Of course, a function pointer is a variable like any other. You can therefore create an array of pointers to functions.

To declare an array of function pointers, you just put the array dimension after the function pointer array name, for instance:

```
int (*pfunctions[10]) (int);
```

This declares an array, pfunctions, with ten elements. Each element in this array can store the address of a function with a return type of int and two parameters of type int. Let's see how this would work in practice.

Try It Out: Arrays of Pointers to Functions

You can demonstrate how you can use an array of pointers to functions with a variation on the last example:

```
/* Program 9.2 Arrays of Pointers to functions    */
#include <stdio.h>
```

(Continued)

```
/* Function prototypes    */
int sum(int, int);
int product(int, int);
int difference(int, int);

void main()
{
  int i = 0;                        /* Loop counter                     */
  int a = 10;                       /* Initial value for a              */
  int b = 5;                        /* Initial value for b              */
  int result = 0;                   /* Storage for results             */
  int (*pfun[3])(int, int);         /* Function pointer array declaration */

  /* Initialize pointers */
  pfun[0] = sum;
  pfun[1] = product;
  pfun[2] = difference;

  /* Execute each function pointed to */
  for( i = 0 ; i < 3 ; i++)
  {
    result = pfun[i](a, b);         /* Call the function through a pointer */
    printf("\nresult = %d", result);  /* Display the result              */
  }

  /* Call all three functions through pointers in an expression */
  result = pfun[1](pfun[0](a, b), pfun[2](a, b));
  printf("\n\nThe product of the sum and the difference = %d\n",
                                            result);
}

/* Definition of the function sum */
int sum(int x, int y)
{
  return x + y;
}

/* Definition of the function product */
int product(int x, int y)
{
  return x * y;
}

/* Definition of the function difference */
int difference(int x, int y)
{
  return x - y;
}
```

(Continued)

The output from this program is as follows:

```
result = 15
result = 50
result = 5

The product of the sum and the difference = 75
```

The major difference between this and the last example is the pointer array, which you declare as follows:

```
int (*pfun[3])(int, int);          /* Function pointer array declaration */
```

This is similar to the previous declaration for a single pointer variable, but with the addition of the array dimension in square brackets following the pointer name. If you wanted a two-dimensional array, two sets of square brackets would have to appear here, just like declarations for ordinary array types. You still enclose the parameter list between parentheses, as you did in the declaration of a single pointer. Again, in parallel with what happens for ordinary arrays, all the elements of the array of "pointers to functions" are of the same type and will accept only the argument list specified. So, in this example, they can all only point to functions that take two arguments of type int and return an int value.

When you want to assign a value to a pointer within the array, you write it in the same way as an element of any other array:

```
pfun[0] = sum;
```

Apart from the function name on the right of the equal sign, this could be a normal data array. It's used in exactly the same way. You could have chosen to initialize all the elements of the array of pointers within the declaration itself:

```
int (*pfun[3])(int, int) = { sum, product, difference };
```

This would have initialized all three elements and would have eliminated the need for the assignment statements that perform the initialization. In fact, you could have left out the array dimension, too, and gotten it by default:

```
int (*pfun[])(int, int) = { sum, product, difference };
```

The number of initializing values between the braces would determine the number of elements in the array.

(Continued)

When it comes to calling a function that an array element points to, you write it as follows:

```
result = pfun[i](a, b);   /* Call the function through a pointer */
```

This, again, is much like the previous example, with just the addition of the index value in square brackets that follow the pointer name. You index this array with the loop variable, i, as you've done many times before with ordinary data arrays.

Look at the output. The first three lines are generated in the for loop, where the functions sum(), product(), and difference() are each called in turn through the corresponding element of the pointer array. The last line of output is produced using the value result from the following statement:

```
result = pfun[1](pfun[0](a, b), pfun[2](a, b));
```

This statement shows that you can incorporate function calls through pointers into expressions, in the same way that you might use a normal function call. Here, you call two of the functions through pointers, and their results are used as arguments to a third function that's called through a pointer. Because the elements of the array correspond to the functions sum(), product(), and difference() in sequence, this statement is equivalent to the following:

```
result = product(sum(a, b), difference(a, b));
```

The sequence of events in this statement is as follows:

1. Execute sum(a,b) and difference(a, b) and save the return values.

2. Execute the function product() with the returned values from step 1 as arguments, and save the value returned.

3. Store the value obtained from step 2 in the variable result.

Pointers to Functions As Arguments

You can also pass a pointer to a function as an argument. This allows a different function to be called, depending on which function is addressed by the pointer that's passed as the argument.

Try It Out: Pointers to Functions As Arguments

You could produce a variant of the last example that will pass a pointer to a function as an argument to a function:

```
/* Program 9.3 Passing a Pointer to a function     */
#include <stdio.h>

/* Function prototypes */
int sum(int,int);
int product(int,int);
int difference(int,int);
int any_function(int(*pfun)(int, int), int x, int y);

void main()
{
   int a = 10;                    /* Initial value for a */
   int b = 5;                     /* Initial value for b */
   int result = 0;                /* Storage for results */
   int (*pf)(int, int) = sum;     /* Pointer to function */

   /* Passing a pointer to a function */
   result = any_function(pf, a, b);

   printf("\nresult = %d", result );

   /* Passing the address of a function      */
   result = any_function(product,a, b);

   printf("\nresult = %d", result );

   printf("\nresult = %d\n", any_function(difference, a, b));
}

/* Definition of a function to call a function */
int any_function(int(*pfun)(int, int), int x, int y)
{
   return pfun(x, y);
}

/* Definition of the function sum      */
int sum(int x, int y)
{
   return x + y;
}

/* Definition of the function product     */
int product(int x, int y)
```

(Continued)

```
{
   return x * y;
}

/* Definition of the function difference */
int difference(int x, int y)
{
   return x - y;
}
```

The output looks like this:

```
result = 15
result = 50
result = 5
```

HOW IT WORKS

The function that will accept a "pointer to a function" as an argument is
any_function(). The prototype for this function is as follows:

```
int any_function(int(*pfun)(int, int), int x, int y);
```

The function named any_function() has three parameters. The first parameter
type is a pointer to a function that accepts two integer arguments and returns an
integer. The last two parameters are integers that will be used in the call of the
function specified by the first parameter. The function any_function() itself
returns an integer value that will be the value obtained by calling the function
indicated by the first argument.

Within the definition of any_function(), the function specified by the pointer
argument is called in the return statement:

```
int any_function(int(*pfun)(int, int), int x, int y)
{
   return pfun(x, y);
}
```

The name of the pointer pfun is used, followed by the other two parameters as
arguments to the function to be called. The value of pfun and the values of the
other two parameters, x and y, all originate in main().

Notice how you initialize the function pointer pf that you declared in main():

```
   int (*pf)(int, int) = sum;   /* Pointer to function */
```

(Continued)

You place the name of the function sum() as the initializer after the equal sign. As you saw earlier, you can initialize function pointers to the addresses of specific functions just by putting the function name as an initializing value.

The first call to any_function() involves passing the value of the pointer pf and the values of the variables a and b to any_function():

```
result = any_function(pf, a, b);
```

The pointer is used as an argument in the usual way, and the value returned by any_function() is stored in the variable result. Because of the initial value of pf, the function sum() will be called in any_function(), so the returned value will be the sum of the values of a and b.

The next call to any_function() is in this statement:

```
result = any_function(product,a, b);
```

Here, you explicitly enter the name of a function, product, as the first argument, so within any_function() the function product will be called with the values of a and b as arguments. In this case, you're effectively persuading the compiler to create an internal pointer to the function product and passing it to any_function().

The final call of any_function() takes place in the argument to the printf() function call:

```
printf("\nresult = %d\n", any_function(difference, a, b));
```

In this case, you're also explicitly specifying the name of a function, difference, as an argument to any_function(). The compiler knows from the prototype of any_function() that the first argument should be a pointer to a function. Because you specify the function name, difference, explicitly as an argument, the compiler will generate a pointer to this function for you and pass that pointer to any_function(). Lastly, the value returned by any_function() is passed as an argument to the function printf(). When all this unwinds, you eventually get the difference between the values of a and b displayed.

Take care not to confuse the idea of passing an address of a function to a function, such as in this expression:

```
any_function(product, a, b)
```

with the idea of passing a value returned from a function, as in this statement:

```
printf("\n%d", product(a, b));
```

(Continued)

In the former case, you're passing the address of the function product() as an argument, and if and when it gets called depends on what goes on inside the body of the function any_function(). In the latter case, however, you're calling the function product() before you call printf() and passing the result obtained as an argument to printf().

Variables in Functions

Structuring a program into functions not only simplifies the process of developing the program, but also extends the power of the language to solve problems. The power of the language is further enhanced by the properties of variables within a function and some extra capabilities that C provides in declaring variables. Let's take a look at some of these now.

Static Variables: Keeping Track Within a Function

So far, all the variables you've used have gone out of scope at the end of the block in which they were defined, and their memory has then become free for reallocation. These are called **automatic variables** because they're automatically created at the point where they're declared, and they're automatically destroyed when program execution leaves the block in which they were declared. This is a very efficient process because the memory containing data in a function is retained only for as long as you're executing statements within the function in which the variable was declared.

However, there are some circumstances in which you might want to retain information from one function call to the next within a program. You may wish to maintain a count of something within a function, such as the number of times the function has been called or the number of lines of output that have been written. With just automatic variables you have no way of doing this.

However, C does provide you with a way to do this with **static variables**. You could declare a static variable count, for example, with this declaration:

```
static int count = 0;
```

The word static in this statement is a keyword in C. The variable declared in this statement differs from an automatic variable in two ways. First of all, despite the fact that it may be defined within the scope of a function, this static variable doesn't get destroyed when execution leaves the function. Second, whereas an automatic variable is initialized each time its scope is entered, the initialization of a variable declared as static occurs only once, right at the beginning of the program.

NOTE *You can make any type of variable within a function a* static *variable.*

Try It Out: Using Static Variables

You can see static variables in action in the following very simple example:

```c
/* Program 9.4 Static versus automatic variables */
#include <stdio.h>

/* Function prototypes */
void test1(void);
void test2(void);

void main()
{
   int i = 0;

   for( i = 0; i < 5; i++ )
   {
     test1();
     test2();
   }
}

/* Function test1 with an automatic variable */
void test1(void)
{
   int count = 0;
   printf("\ntest1   count = %d ", ++count );
}

/* Function test2 with a static variable */
void test2(void)
{
   static int count = 0;
   printf("\ntest2   count = %d ", ++count );
}
```

This produces the following output:

```
test1   count = 1
test2   count = 1
test1   count = 1
test2   count = 2
test1   count = 1
test2   count = 3
test1   count = 1
test2   count = 4
test1   count = 1
test2   count = 5
```

(Continued)

HOW IT WORKS

As you can see, the two variables called count are quite separate. The changes in the values of each show clearly that they're independent of one another. The static variable count is declared in the function test2():

```
static int count = 0;
```

Although you specify an initial value, here the variable would have been initialized to 0 anyway because you declared it as static.

NOTE *All static variables are initialized to 0 unless you initialize them with some other value.*

The static variable count is used to count the number of times the function is called. This is initialized when program execution starts, and its current value when the function is exited is maintained. It isn't reinitialized on subsequent calls to the function. Because the variable has been declared as static, the compiler arranges things so that the variable will be initialized only once, when program execution starts.

The automatic variable count in the function test1() is declared as follows:

```
int count = 0;
```

Because this is an automatic variable, it isn't initialized by default, and if you don't specify an initial value, it will contain a junk value. This variable gets reinitialized to 0 at each entry to the function, and it's discarded on exit from test1(); therefore, it never reaches a value higher than 1.

Although a static variable will persist for as long as the program is running, it will be visible only within the scope in which it was declared, and it can't be referenced outside that original scope.

Sharing Variables Between Functions

You also have a way of sharing variables between all your functions. In the same way that you can declare constants at the beginning of a program file, so that they're outside the scope of the functions that make up the program, you can also declare variables like this. These are called **global variables** because they're accessible anywhere. Global variables are declared in the normal way; it's the position of the declaration that's significant and determines whether or not they're global.

Try It Out: Using Global Variables

By way of a demonstration, you can modify the previous example to share the count variable between the functions as follows:

```
/* Program 9.5 Global variables */
#include <stdio.h>

int count = 0;                          /* Declare a global variable   */

/* Function prototypes */
void test1(void);
void test2(void);

void main()
{
   int count = 0;                       /* This hides the global count */

   for( ; count < 5; count++)
   {
     test1();
     test2();
   }
}

/* Function test1 using the global variable   */
void test1(void)
{
   printf("\ntest1   count = %d ", ++count);
}

/* Function test2 using a static variable */
void test2(void)
{
   static int count;                    /* This hides the global count */
   printf("\ntest2   count = %d ", ++count);
}
```

The output will be this:

```
test1   count = 1
test2   count = 1
test1   count = 2
test2   count = 2
test1   count = 3
test2   count = 3
test1   count = 4
```

(Continued)

```
test2    count = 4
test1    count = 5
test2    count = 5
```

HOW IT WORKS

In this example you have three separate variables called count! The first of these is the global variable count that's declared at the beginning of the file:

```
#include <stdio.h>

int count = 0;
```

This isn't a static variable (although you could make it static if you wanted to), so you must initialize it. It's potentially accessible in any function from the point where it's declared to the end of the file, so it's accessible in any of the functions here.

The second variable is an automatic variable count that's declared in main():

```
int count = 0;                          /* This hides the global count */
```

Because it has the same name as the global variable, the global variable count can't be accessed from main(). Any use of the name count in main() will refer to the variable declared within the body of main(). The local variable count *hides* the global variable.

The third variable is a static variable count that's declared in the function test2():

```
static int count;                       /* This hides the global count */
```

Because this is a static variable, it will be initialized to 0 by default. This variable also hides the global variable of the same name, so only the static variable count is accessible in test2().

The function test1() works using the global count. The functions main() and test2() use their local versions of count, because the local declaration hides the global variable of the same name.

Clearly, the count variable in main() is incremented from 0 to 4, because you have five calls to each of the functions test1() and test2(). This has to be different from the count variables in either of the called functions; otherwise, they couldn't have the values 1 to 5 that are displayed in the output.

(Continued)

You can further demonstrate that this is indeed the case by simply removing the declaration for count in test2() as a static variable. You'll then have made test1() and test2() share the global count, and the values displayed will run from 1 to 10. If you then put a declaration back in test2() for count as an initialized automatic variable with the statement

```
int count = 0;
```

the output from test1() will run from 1 to 5, and the output from test2() will remain at 1, because the variable is now automatic and will be reinitialized on each entry to the function.

Global variables can replace the need for function arguments and return values. They look very tempting as the complete alternative to automatic variables. However, you should use global variables sparingly. They can be a major asset in simplifying and shortening some programs, but using them excessively will make your programs prone to errors. It's very easy to modify a global variable and forget what consequences it might have throughout your program. The bigger the program, the more difficult it becomes to avoid erroneous references to global variables. The use of local variables provides very effective insulation for each function against the possibility of interference from the activities of other functions. You could try removing the local variable count from main() in Program 9.5 to see the effect of such an oversight on the output.

 CAUTION *As a rule, it's unwise to use the same names in C for local and global variables. There's no particular advantage to be gained, other than to demonstrate the effect, as you saw in the example. Using local and global variables with the same name also makes programs error-prone and difficult to follow.*

Functions That Call Themselves: Recursion

It's possible for a function to call itself. This is termed **recursion**. You're unlikely to come across a need for recursion very often, so we won't dwell on it, but it can be a very effective technique in some contexts. There are a few bad jokes based on the notion of recursion, but we won't dwell on those either.

Obviously, when a function calls itself there's the immediate problem of how the process stops. This is similar to the problem with an indefinite loop, and the answer is similar too: a function that calls itself must also contain the means of stopping the process. Let's see how it works.

Try It Out: Recursion

The primary uses of recursion tend to arise in complicated problems, so it's hard to come up with original but simple examples to show how it works. Therefore, I'll follow the crowd and use the standard illustration: the calculation of the factorial of an integer. A factorial of any integer is the product of all the integers from 1 up to the integer itself. So here you go:

```
/* Program 9.6 Calculating factorials using recursion */
#include <stdio.h>

long factorial(long);

void main()
{
   long number = 0;
   printf("\nEnter an integer value: ");
   scanf(" %ld", &number);
   printf("\nThe factorial of %ld is %ld\n", number, factorial(number));
}

/* Our recursive factorial function */
long factorial(long n)
{
   if(n < 2)
     return n;
   else
     return n*factorial(n - 1);
}
```

Typical output from the program looks like this:

```
Enter an integer value: 4

The factorial of 4 is 24
```

HOW IT WORKS

This is very simple once you get your mind around what's happening. Let's go through a concrete example of how it works. Assume you enter the value **4**. Figure 9-3 shows the sequence of events.

(Continued)

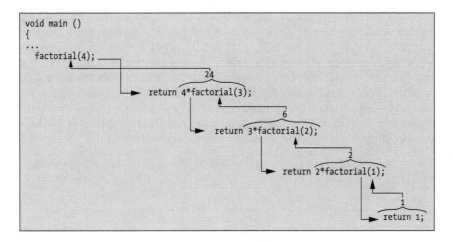

Figure 9-3. Recursive function calls

Within the statement

```
printf("\nThe factorial of %ld is %ld", number, factorial(number));
```

the function factorial() gets called from main() with number having the value 4 as the argument.

Within the factorial() function itself, because the argument is greater than 1, the statement executed is

```
return n*factorial(n - 1);
```

This is the second return statement in the function, and it calls factorial() again with the argument value 3 from within the arithmetic expression. This expression can't be evaluated and the return can't be completed until the value is returned from this call to the function factorial() with the argument 3.

This continues, as shown in Figure 9-3, until the argument in the last call of the factorial() function is 1. In this case, the first return statement

```
return n;
```

is executed and the value 1 is returned to the previous call point. This call point is, in fact, inside the second return in the factorial() function, which can now calculate 2 * 1 and return to the previous call.

(Continued)

In this way, the whole process unwinds, ending up with the value required being returned to main() where it's displayed. So for any given number n, you'll have n calls to the function factorial(). For each call, a copy of the argument is created, and the location to be returned to is stored. This can get expensive as far as memory is concerned if there are many levels of recursion. A loop to do the same thing would be cheaper and faster. If you do need or want to use recursion, the most important thing to remember is that there has to be a way to end the process. In other words, there must be a mechanism for *not* repeating the recursive call. In this example, you use a check for the argument supplied being 1.

Notice how factorial values grow very quickly. With quite modest input values, you'll exceed the capacity of a long integer and start getting the wrong results.

Functions with a Variable Number of Arguments

It can't have escaped your notice that some functions in the standard libraries accept a variable number of arguments. The functions printf() and scanf() are obvious examples. You may come up with a need to do this yourself from time to time, so the standard library stdarg.h provides you with routines to write some of your own.

The immediately obvious problem with writing a function with a variable number of parameters is how to specify its prototype. Suppose you're going to produce a function to calculate the average of two or more values of type double. Clearly, calculating the average of fewer than two values wouldn't make much sense. The prototype would be written as follows:

```
double average(double v1, double v2, ...);
```

The **ellipses** (that's the fancy name for the three periods after the second parameter type) indicate that a variable number of arguments may follow the first two fixed arguments. You must have at least one fixed argument. The remaining specifications are as you would usually find with a function prototype. The first two arguments are of type double, and the function returns a double result.

The second problem with variable argument lists that hits you between the eyes next is how you reference them when writing the function. Because you don't know how many there are, you can't possibly give them names. The only conceivable way to do this is indirectly, through pointers. The stdarg.h library header provides you with three routines that are usually implemented as macros, but they look and operate like functions so I'll discuss them as though they were. You need to use all three when implementing your own function with a variable number of arguments. They are called va_start(), va_arg(), and va_end(). The first of these has the following form:

```
void va_start(va_list parg, last_fixed_arg);
```

The name of the function is obtained from **variable argument start**. This function accepts two arguments: a pointer parg of type va_list and the name of the last fixed parameter that you've specified for the function you're writing. So using the function average() as an illustration, you can start to write the function as follows:

```
double average( double v1, double v2,...)
{
  va_list parg;                 /* Pointer for variable argument list */
  /* More code to go here... */
  va_start( parg, v2);
  /* More code to go here... */
}
```

You first declare the variable parg of type va_list. You then call va_start() with this as the first argument and specify the last fixed parameter v2 as the second argument. The effect of the call to va_start() is to set the variable parg to point to the first variable argument that was passed to the function when it was called. You still don't know what type of value this represents, and the standard library is no further help in this context. You must determine the type of each variable argument, either implicitly—all variable arguments assumed to be of a given type, for instance—or by deducing the type of each argument from information contained within one of the fixed arguments.

The average() function deals with arguments of type double, so the type isn't a problem. You now need to know how to access the value of each of the variable arguments, so let's see how this is done by completing the function average():

```
/* Function to calculate the average of a variable number of arguments */
double average( double v1, double v2,...)
{
  va_list parg;              /* Pointer for variable argument list */
  double sum = v1+v2;        /* Accumulate sum of the arguments    */
  double value = 0;          /* Argument value                     */
  int count = 2;             /* Count of number of arguments       */

  va_start(parg,v2);         /* Initialize argument pointer        */
  while((value = va_arg(parg, double)) != 0.0)
  {
    sum += value;
    count++;
  }
  va_end(parg);              /* End variable argument process      */
  return sum/count;
}
```

You can work your way through this step by step. After declaring parg, you declare the variable sum as double and as being initialized with the sum of the first two fixed arguments, v1 and v2. You'll accumulate the sum of all the argument values in sum. The next variable, value, declared as double will be used to store the values of the variable arguments as you obtain them one by one. You then declare a counter, count, for the total number of arguments and initialize this with the value 2 because you know you have at least that many values from the fixed arguments. After you call va_start() to initialize parg, most of the action takes place within the while loop. Look at the loop condition:

```
while((value = va_arg(parg, double)) != 0.0)
```

The loop condition calls another function from stdarg.h, va_arg(). The first argument to va_arg() is the variable parg you initialized through the call to va_start(). The second argument is a specification of the type of the argument you expect to find. The function va_arg() returns the value of the current argument specified by parg, and this is stored in value. It also updates the pointer parg to point to the next argument in the list, based on the type you specified in the call. It's essential to have some means of determining the types of the variable arguments. If you don't specify the correct type, you won't be able to obtain the next argument correctly. In this case, the function is written assuming the arguments are all double. Another assumption you're making is that all the arguments will be nonzero except for the last. This is reflected in the condition for continuing the loop being that value isn't equal to 0. Within the loop, you have familiar statements for accumulating the sum in sum and for incrementing count.

When an argument value obtained is 0, the loop ends and you execute the statement

```
va_end(parg);                    /* End variable argument process     */
```

The call to va_end() is essential to tie up loose ends left by the process. It resets the parg point to NULL. If you omit this call, your program may not work properly. Once the tidying up is complete, you can return the required result with the statement

```
return sum/count;
```

....

Try It Out: Using Variable Argument Lists

After you've written the function average(), it would be a good idea to exercise it in a little program to make sure it works:

```
/* Program 9.7 Calculating an average using variable argument lists */
#include <stdio.h>
#include <stdarg.h>

double average(double v1 , double v2,...);        /* Function prototype */
```

(Continued)

```
void main()
{
  double Val1 = 10.5, Val2 = 2.5;
  int num1 = 6, num2 = 5;
  long num3 = 12, num4 = 20;

  printf("\n Average = %lf", average(Val1, 3.5, Val2, 4.5, 0.0));
  printf("\n Average = %lf", average(1.0, 2.0, 0.0));
  printf("\n Average = %lf\n", average( (double)num2, Val2,(double)num1,
                             (double)num4,(double)num3, 0.0));
}


/* Function to calculate the average of a variable number of arguments */
double average( double v1, double v2,...)
{
  va_list parg;              /* Pointer for variable argument list */
  double sum = v1+v2;        /* Accumulate sum of the arguments    */
  double value = 0;          /* Argument value                     */
  int count = 2;             /* Count of number of arguments       */

  va_start(parg,v2);         /* Initialize argument pointer        */

  while((value = va_arg(parg, double)) != 0.0)
  {
    sum += value;
    count++;
  }
  va_end(parg);              /* End variable argument process      */
  return sum/count;
}
```

If you compile and run this, you should get the following output:

```
Average = 5.250000
Average = 1.500000
Average = 9.100000
```

HOW IT WORKS

This output is a result of three calls to average with different numbers of arguments. Remember, you need to ensure that you cast the variable arguments to the type double, because this is the argument type assumed by the function average(). You can call the average() function with as many arguments as you like as long as the last one is 0.

(Continued)

You might be wondering how `printf()` manages to handle a mix of types. Well, remember the first argument is a control string with format specifiers. This supplies the information necessary to determine the types of the arguments that follow as well as how many there are. The number of arguments following the first must match the number of format specifiers in the control string. The type of each argument after the first must match the type implied by the corresponding format specifier. You've seen how things don't work out right if you specify the wrong format for the type of variable you want to output.

....

Basic Rules for Variable-Length Argument Lists

Here's a summary of the basic rules and requirements for writing functions to be called with a variable number of arguments:

- There needs to be at least one fixed argument in a function that accepts a variable number of arguments.

- You must call `va_start()` to initialize the value of the variable argument list pointer in your function. This pointer also needs to be declared as type `va_list`.

- There needs to be a mechanism to determine the type of each argument. Either there can be a default type assumed or there can be a parameter that allows the argument type to be determined. For example, in the function `average()`, you could have an extra fixed argument that would have the value 0 if the variable arguments were `double` and 1 if they were `long`. If the argument type specified in the call to `va_arg()` isn't correct for the argument value specified when your function is called, your function won't work properly.

- You have to arrange for there to be some way to determine when the list of arguments is exhausted. For example, the last argument in the variable argument list could have a fixed value that can be detected because it's different from all the others, or a fixed argument could contain a count of the number of arguments in total or in the variable part of the argument list.

- There are restrictions on the types of variable arguments you're allowed to use. You can't use `char`, `unsigned char`, or `float` types with `va_arg()`. You should use `int` instead of `char` types and `double` rather than `float`. Check the documentation for your compiler for full details.

- You must call `va_end()` before you exit a function with a variable number of arguments. If you fail to do so, the function won't work properly.

Note that the process described for handling variable argument lists is for ANSI C. The UNIX implementation differs quite significantly from this, so if this is what you're using, you need to check your compiler documentation.

You could try a few variations in Program 9.7 to understand this process better. Put some output in the function average() and see what happens if you change a few things. For example, you could display value and count in the loop in the function average(). You could then modify main() to use an argument that isn't double, or you could introduce a function call in which the last argument isn't 0.

The main() Function

You already know that the main() function is where execution starts. What I haven't discussed up to now is that main() can have a parameter list so that you can pass arguments to main() when you execute a program from the command line. You can write the main() function either with no parameters or with two parameters.

When you write main() with parameters, the first parameter is of type int and represents a count of the number of arguments in the command that was entered to execute main(), including the name of the program itself. Thus, if you added two arguments following the name of the program on the command line, the value of the first argument to main() will be 3. The second parameter to main() is an array of pointers to strings. The argument that will be passed when you write two arguments following the name of the program at the command line will be an array of three pointers. The first will point to the name of the program, and the second and third will point to the two arguments that you entered at the command line.

```
/* Program 9.8 A program to list the command line arguments */
#include <stdio.h>
void main(int argc, char *argv[])
{
  int i = 0;
  printf("Program name: %s\n", argv[0]);
  for(i = 1 ; i<argc ; i++)
    printf("\nArgument %d: %s", i, argv[i]);
}
```

The value of argc must be at least 1 because you can't execute a program without entering the program name. You therefore output argv[0] as the program name. Subsequent elements in the argv array will be the arguments that were entered at the command line, so you output these in sequence within the for loop.

I entered the following command to execute this program as the source file had the name BeginningC.c:

```
BeginningC   first   second_arg   "Third is this"
```

Note the use of double quotes to enclose an argument that includes spaces. This is because spaces are normally treated as delimiters. You can always enclose an argument between double quotes to ensure it will be treated as a single argument.

The program then produced the following output as a result of the preceding command:

```
Program name: BegC

Argument 1: first
Argument 2: second_arg
Argument 3: Third is this
```

As you can see, putting double quotes around the last argument ensured that it was read as a single argument and not as three arguments.

All command-line arguments will be read as strings, so when numerical values are entered at the command line, you'll need to convert the string containing the value to the appropriate numerical type. You can use one of the functions shown in Table 9-1 that are declared in stdlib.h to do this.

Table 9-1. Functions That Convert Strings to Numerical Values

Function	Description
atof()	Converts the string passed as an argument to type double
atoi()	Converts the string passed as an argument to type int
atol()	Converts the string passed as an argument to type long

For example, if you're expecting a command-line argument to be an integer, you might process it like this:

```
int arg_value = 0;        /* Stores value of command line argument */
if(argc>1)                /* Verify we have at least one argument  */
  arg_value = argv[1];
else
{
  printf("Command line argument missing.");
  return;
}
```

Note the check on the number of arguments. It's particularly important to include this before processing command-line arguments, as it's very easy to forget to enter them.

Ending a Program

There are several ways of ending a program. Falling off the end of the body of main() is equivalent to executing a return statement in main(), which will end the program. There are two standard library functions that you can call to end a program, both of which are declared in the stdlib.h header. Calling the abort() function terminates the program immediately and represents an abnormal end to program operations, so you shouldn't use this for a normal end to a program. You would call abort() to end a program like this:

```
abort();                    /* Abnormal program termination */
```

This statement can appear anywhere in your program.

Calling the exit() function results in a normal end to a program. The function requires an integer argument that will be returned to the operating system. A value of 0 usually represents a completely normal program end. You may use other values to indicate the status of the program in some way. What happens to the value returned by exit() is determined by your operating system. You could call the exit() function like this:

```
exit(1);                    /* Normal program end - status is 1 */
```

You can call exit() to terminate execution from anywhere in your program.

You can also end a program by executing a return statement with an integer value in main(), for example:

```
return 1;
```

When you want to do this, you should specify the return type to main() as type int. This has a special meaning in main() (and *only* in main(), not in any other function), and it's the equivalent of calling exit() with the value specified in the return statement as the argument. Thus, the value in the return statement will be passed back to the operating system.

Libraries of Functions: Header Files

I've already mentioned that your compiler comes with a wide range of standard functions that are declared in **header files**, sometimes called **include files**. These represent a rich source of help for you when you're developing your own applications. You've already come across some of these because header files are such a fundamental component of programming in C. So far, you've used functions of the header files listed in Table 9-2.

Table 9-2. Standard Header Files You Have Used

Header File	Functions
stdio.h	Input/output functions
stdarg.h	Macros supporting a variable number of arguments to a function
math.h	Mathematical floating-point functions
stdlib.h	Memory allocation functions
string.h	String-handling functions
ctype.h	Character-conversion functions

All the header files in Table 9-2 contain declarations for a range of functions, as well as definitions for various constants. They're all ANSI standard libraries, so all ANSI- standard conforming compilers will support them and provide at least the basic set of functions, but typically they'll supply much more. To comprehensively discuss the contents of even the ANSI standard library header files and functions could double the size of this book, so I'll mention just the most important aspects of the ANSI header files and leave it you to browse the documentation that came with your compiler.

The header file stdio.h contains declarations for quite a large range of high-level input/output functions, so I'll devote the whole of Chapter 10 to exploring some of these.

As well as memory allocation functions, stdlib.h provides facilities for converting character strings to their numerical equivalents from the ASCII table. There are also functions for sorting and searching. In addition, functions that generate random numbers are available through stdlib.h.

You used the string.h file in Chapter 6. With some compilers, this header file also declares functions for managing buffers, as there's a strong affinity between these functions and the general process of handling strings. They generally compare, copy, and move fixed-length blocks of memory, whereas the functions discussed in Chapter 6 are oriented toward variable-length strings.

A header file providing a very useful range of functions also related to string processing is ctype.h, which you saw in Chapter 6. The ctype.h header includes functions to convert characters from uppercase to lowercase (and vice versa) and a number of functions checking for alphabetic characters, numeric digits, and so on. These provide an extensive toolkit for you to do your own detailed analysis of the contents of a string, which is particularly useful for dealing with user input.

I strongly recommend that you invest some time in becoming familiar with the contents of these header files and the libraries that are supplied with your compiler. This familiarity will greatly increase the ease with which you can develop applications in C.

Designing a Program

At this point, you've finished with functions, and because you're more than halfway through the capabilities of C, an example of reasonable complexity wouldn't come amiss. In this program, you're going to put to practical use the various elements of C that you've covered so far in the book.

The Problem

The problem that you're going to solve is to write another game. There are several reasons for choosing to write a game. First, games tend to be just as complex, if not more so, than other types of programs, even when the game is simple. And second, games are more fun!

The game is in the same vein as Othello or, if you remember Microsoft Windows 3.0, Reversi. The game is played by two players who take turns placing a colored counter on a square board. One player has black counters and the other has white counters. The board has an even number of squares along a side. The starting position, followed by five successive moves, is shown in Figure 9-4.

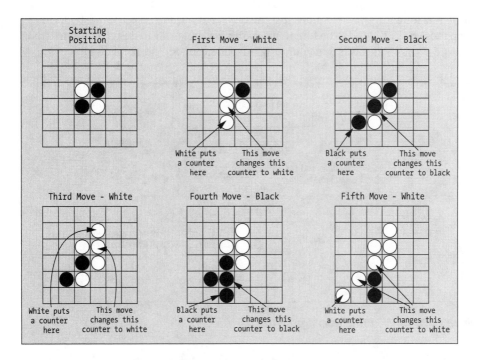

Figure 9-4. Starting position and initial moves in Reversi

You can only place a counter adjacent to an opponent's counter, such that one or more of your opponent's counters—in a line diagonally, horizontally, or vertically—are enclosed between two of your own counters. The opponent's counters are then changed to counters of your own color. The person with the most counters on the board at the end of the game wins. The game ends when all the squares are occupied by counters. The game can also end if neither player can place a counter legally, which can occur if you or your opponent manage to convert all the counters to the same color.

The game can be played with any size of board, but you'll implement it here on a 6×6 board. You'll also implement it as a game that you play against the computer.

The Analysis

This problem's analysis is a little different from those you've seen up to now. The whole point of this chapter is to introduce the concept of **structured programming**—in other words, breaking a problem into small pieces—which is why you've spent so long looking at functions.

A good way to start is with a diagram. You'll start with a single box, which represents the whole program or the main() function, if you like. Developing from this, on the next level down you'll show the functions that will need to be directly called by the main() function, and you'll indicate what these functions have to do. Below that, you'll show the functions that those functions, in turn, have to use. You don't have to show the actual functions; you can show just the tasks that need to be accomplished. However, these tasks *do* tend to be functions, so this is a great way to design your program. Figure 9-5 shows the tasks that your program will need to perform.

Figure 9-5. Tasks in the Reversi program

You can now go a step further than this and begin to think about the actual sequence of actions, or functions, that the program is going to perform. Figure 9-6 is a flowchart that describes the same set of functions but in a manner that shows the sequence in which they're executed and the logic involved in deciding that. You're moving closer now to a more precise specification of how the program will work.

This isn't absolutely fixed, of course. There's a lot of detail that you'll need to fill in. This sort of diagram can help you get the logic of the program clear in your mind, and from there you can progress to a more detailed definition of how the program will work.

The Solution

This section outlines the steps you'll take to solve the problem.

Step 1

The first thing to do is set up and display the initial board. You'll use a smaller-than-normal board (6×6), as this makes the games shorter, but you'll implement the program with the board size as a symbol defined by a preprocessor directive. You'll then be able to change the size later if you want. You'll display the board using a separate function, as this is a self-contained activity.

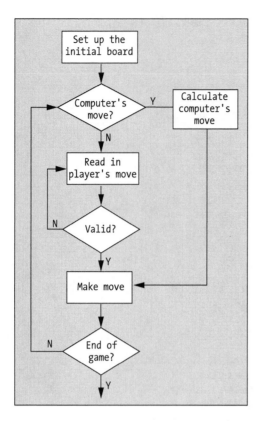

Figure 9-6. The basic logic of the Reversi program

Let's start with the code to declare, initialize, and display the grid. The computer will use '@' as its counter, and the player will have 'O' for his counter:

```c
/* Program 9.9 REVERSI An Othello-type game */
#include <stdio.h>

#define SIZE 6                    /* Board size - must be even */

/* Function prototypes */
void display(char board[][SIZE]);

void main()
{
   char board [SIZE][SIZE] = { 0 };    /* The board            */
   int row = 0;                        /* Board row index      */
   int col = 0;                        /* Board column index   */

   printf("\nREVERSI\n\n");
   printf("You can go first on the first game, then we will take turns.\n");
   printf("   You will be white - (O)\n   I will be black   - (@).\n");
   printf("Select a square for your move by typing a digit for the row\n "
```

```
                    "and a letter for the column with no spaces between.\n");
        printf("\nGood luck!  Press Enter to start.\n");
        scanf("%c", &again);

        /* Blank all the board squares */
        for(row = 0; row < SIZE; row++)
          for(col = 0; col < SIZE; col++)
            board[row][col] = ' ';

        /* Place the initial four counters in the center */
        board[SIZE/2 - 1][SIZE/2 - 1] = board[SIZE/2][SIZE/2] = '0';
        board[SIZE/2 - 1][SIZE/2] = board[SIZE/2][SIZE/2 - 1] = '@';

        display(board);                        /* Display the board  */
      }


      /*********************************************
       * Function to display the board in its      *
       * current state with row numbers and column *
       * letters to identify squares.              *
       * Parameter is the board array.             *
       *********************************************/
      void display(char board[][SIZE])
      {
        int row  = 0;                    /* Row index      */
        int col = 0;                     /* Column index   */
        char col_label = 'a';            /* Column label   */

        printf("\n ");                   /* Start top line */
        for(col = 0 ; col<SIZE ;col++)
          printf("   %c", col_label+col); /* Display the top line */
        printf("\n");                    /* End the top line      */

        /* Display the intermediate rows */
        for(row = 0; row < SIZE; row++)
        {
          printf("  +");
          for(col = 0; col<SIZE; col++)
            printf("---+");
          printf("\n%2d|",row + 1);

          for(col = 0; col<SIZE; col++)
            printf(" %c |", board[row][col]);  /* Display counters in row */
          printf("\n");
        }

        printf("  +");                         /* Start the bottom line   */
        for(col = 0 ; col<SIZE ;col++)
          printf("---+");                      /* Display the bottom line */
        printf("\n");                          /* End the bottom  line    */
      }
```

The function display() outputs the board with row numbers to identify the rows and the letters from 'a' onward to identify each column. This will be the reference system by which the user will select a square to place his counter.

The code looks complicated, but it's quite straightforward. The first loop outputs the top line with the column label, from 'a' to 'f' with the board size. The next loop outputs the squares that can contain counters, a row at a time, with a row number at the start of each row. The last loop outputs the bottom of the last row. Notice how you've passed the board array as an argument to the display() function rather than making board a global variable. This is to prevent other functions from modifying the contents of board accidentally. The function will display a board of any size.

Step 2

You need a function to generate all the possible moves that can be made for the current player. This function will have two uses: first, it will allow you to check that the move that the player enters is valid, and second, it will help you to determine what moves the computer can make. But first you must decide how you're going to represent and store this list of moves.

So what information do you need to store, and what options do you have? Well, you've defined the grid in such a way that any cell can be referenced by a row number and a column letter. You could therefore store a move as a string consisting of a number and a letter. You would then need to accommodate a list of moves of varying length, to allow for the possibility that the dimensions of the board might change to 10×10 or greater.

There's an easier option. You can create a second array with the same dimensions as the board, and store a 1 for positions where there is a valid move and a 0 otherwise. You can store values of type int in this array. The function will need three parameters: the board array, so that it can check for vacant squares; the moves array, in which the valid moves are to be recorded; and the identity of the current player, which will be the character used as a counter for the player.

The strategy will be this: for each a blank square, search the squares around that square for an opponent's counter. If you find an opponent's counter, then follow a line of opponent counters (horizontal, vertical, and diagonal) until you find a player counter. If you do in fact find a player counter along that line, then you know that the original blank square is a valid move for the current player.

You can add the function definition to the file following the definition of the display() function:

```
/* Program 9.9 REVERSI An Othello-type game */
#include <stdio.h>

#define SIZE 6                      /* Board size - must be even */

/* Function prototypes */
void display(char board[][SIZE]);
int valid_moves(char board[][SIZE], int moves[][SIZE], char player);
```

```
void main()
{
   char board [SIZE][SIZE] = { 0 };    /* The board           */
   int moves[SIZE][SIZE] = { 0 };      /* Valid moves         */
   int row = 0;                        /* Board row index     */
   int col = 0;                        /* Board column index  */

   /* Other code for main as before... */
}

/* Code for definition of display() as before... */

/*********************************************
 * Calculates which squares are valid moves  *
 * for player. Valid moves are recorded in the *
 * moves array - 1 indicates a valid move,    *
 * 0 indicates an invalid move.               *
 * First parameter is the board array         *
 * Second parameter is the moves array        *
 * Third parameter identifies the player      *
 * to make the move.                          *
 * Returns valid move count.                  *
 *********************************************/
int valid_moves(char board[][SIZE], int moves[][SIZE], char player)
{
   int rowdelta = 0;                 /* Row increment around a square    */
   int coldelta = 0;                 /* Column increment around a square */
   int row = 0;                      /* Row index                        */
   int col = 0;                      /* Column index                     */
   int x = 0;                        /* Row index when searching         */
   int y = 0;                        /* Column index when searching      */
   int no_of_moves = 0;              /* Number of valid moves            */
   /* Set the opponent           */
   char opponent = (player == '0')? '@' : '0';

   /* Initialize moves array to zero */
   for(row = 0; row < SIZE; row++)
     for(col = 0; col < SIZE; col++)
       moves[row][col] = 0;

   /* Find squares for valid moves.                           */
   /* A valid move must be on a blank square and must enclose */
   /* at least one opponent square between two player squares */
   for(row = 0; row < SIZE; row++)
     for(col = 0; col < SIZE; col++)
     {
       if(board[row][col] != ' ')     /* Is it a blank square? */
         continue;                     /* No - so on to the next */

       /* Check all the squares around the blank square  */
       /* for the opponent's counter                     */
```

```
      for(rowdelta = -1; rowdelta <= 1; rowdelta++)
        for(coldelta = -1; coldelta <= 1; coldelta++)
        {
          /* Don't check outside the array, or the current square */
          if(row + rowdelta < 0 || row + rowdelta >= SIZE ||
             col + coldelta < 0 || col + coldelta >= SIZE ||
                                  (rowdelta==0 && coldelta==0))
            continue;

          /* Now check the square */
          if(board[row + rowdelta][col + coldelta] == opponent)
          {
            /* If we find the opponent, move in the delta direction  */
            /* over opponent counters searching for a player counter */
            x = row + rowdelta;        /* Move to           */
            y = col + coldelta;        /* opponent square   */

            /* Look for a player square in the delta direction */
            for(;;)
            {
              x += rowdelta;           /* Go to next square */
              y += coldelta;           /* in delta direction*/

              /* If we move outside the array, give up */
              if(x < 0 || x >= SIZE || y < 0 || y >= SIZE)
                break;

              /* If we find a blank square, give up */
              if(board[x][y] == ' ')
                break;
               /*  If the square has a player counter */
               /*  then we have a valid move          */
              if(board[x][y] == player)
              {
                moves[row][col] = 1;   /* Mark as valid */
                no_of_moves++;         /* Increase valid moves count */
                break;                 /* Go check another square     */
              }
            }
          }
        }
    }
    return no_of_moves;
}
```

You have added a prototype for the valid_moves() function and a declaration for the array moves in main().

Because the counters are either '0' or '@', you can set the opponent counter in the valid_moves() function as the one that isn't the player counter that's passed as an argument. You do this with the conditional operator. You then zero the moves array in the first nested loop, so you only have to set valid positions to 1. The second nested loop iterates through all the squares on the board, looking for those that are blank. When you find a blank square, you search for an opponent counter in the inner loop:

```
/* Check all the squares around the blank square  */
/* for the opponent's counter                     */
for(rowdelta = -1; rowdelta <= 1; rowdelta++)
  for(coldelta = -1; coldelta <= 1; coldelta++)

    ...
```

This will iterate over all the squares that surround the blank square and will include the blank square itself, so you skip the blank square or any squares that are off the board with this if statement:

```
/* Don't check outside the array, or the current square */
if(row + rowdelta < 0 || row + rowdelta >= SIZE ||
   col + coldelta < 0 || col + coldelta >= SIZE ||
                         (rowdelta==0 && coldelta==0))
  continue;
```

If you get past this point, you've found a nonblank square that's on the board. If it contains the opponent's counter, then you move in the same direction, looking for either more opponent counters or a player counter. If you find a player counter, the original blank square was a valid move, so you record it. If you find a blank or run of the board, then it isn't a valid move, so you look for another blank square.

The function returns a count of the number of valid moves, so you can use this value to indicate whether or not the function returns any valid moves. Remember, any positive integer is true and 0 is false.

Step 3

Now that you can produce an array that contains all the valid moves, you can fill in the game loop in main(). You'll base this on the flowchart that you saw earlier. You can start by adding two nested do-while loops: the outer one will initialize each game, and the inner one will iterate over player and computer turns.

```
/* Program 9.9 REVERSI An Othello-type game */
#include <stdio.h>

#define SIZE 6   /* Board size - must be even */

/* Function prototypes */
void display(char board[][SIZE]);
int valid_moves(char board[][SIZE], int moves[][SIZE], char player);

void main()
{
  char board [SIZE][SIZE] = { 0 };    /* The board              */
```

```
int moves[SIZE][SIZE] = { 0 };       /* Valid moves          */
int row = 0;                         /* Board row index      */
int col = 0;                         /* Board column index   */
int no_of_games = 0;                 /* Number of games      */
int no_of_moves = 0;                 /* Count of moves       */
int invalid_moves = 0;               /* Invalid move count   */
int comp_score = 0;                  /* Computer score       */
int user_score = 0;                  /* Player score         */
char again = 0;                      /* Replay choice input  */
int player = 0;                      /* Player indicator     */

/* Prompt for how to play - as before */

/* The main game loop */
do
{
  /* On even games the player starts; */
  /* on odd games the computer starts */
  player = ++no_of_games % 2;
  no_of_moves = 4;                   /* Starts with four counters */

  /* Blank all the board squares */
  for(row = 0; row < SIZE; row++)
    for(col = 0; col < SIZE; col++)
      board[row][col] = ' ';

  /* Place the initial four counters in the center */
  board[SIZE/2 - 1][SIZE/2 - 1] = board[SIZE/2][SIZE/2] = 'O';
  board[SIZE/2 - 1][SIZE/2] = board[SIZE/2][SIZE/2 - 1] = '@';

  /* The game play loop */
  do
  {
    display(board);                  /* Display the board  */
    if(player++ % 2)
    { /*   It is the player's turn                 */
      /* Code to get the player's move and execute it */
    }
    else
    { /* It is the computer's turn                 */
      /* Code to make the computer's move          */
    }
  }while(no_of_moves < SIZE*SIZE && invalid_moves<2);

  /* Game is over */
  display(board);                    /* Show final board  */

  /* Get final scores and display them */
  comp_score = user_score = 0;
  for(row = 0; row < SIZE; row++)
    for(col = 0; col < SIZE; col++)
```

```
        {
          comp_score += board[row][col] == '@';
          user_score += board[row][col] == 'O';
        }
      printf("The final score is:\n");
      printf("Computer %d\n    User %d\n\n", comp_score, user_score);

      fflush(stdin);                        /* Flush the input buffer */
      printf("Do you want to play again (y/n): ");
      scanf("%c", &again);                  /* Get y or n            */
    }while(tolower(again) == 'y');          /* Go again on y         */

    printf("\nGoodbye\n");
}


/* Code for definition of display() */

/* Code for definition of valid_moves() */
```

I recommend that you don't run this program yet because you haven't written the code to handle input from the user or moves from the computer. At the moment, it will just loop indefinitely, printing a board with no new moves being made. You'll sort out those parts of the program next.

The variable player determines whose turn it is. When player is 0, it's the computer's turn, and when player is 1, it's the player's turn. This is set initially to the remainder when the game count is divided by 2, so that the computer and the player will take the first turn on alternate games. To determine who takes the next turn, you increment the variable player and take the remainder modulo 2, and then test the result in the if statement, which will allow you to alternate between the computer and the player automatically.

The game ends when the count of the number of counters in no-of_moves reaches SIZE*SIZE, the number of squares on the board. It will also end if invalid_moves reaches 2. You set invalid_moves to 0 when a valid move is made and increment it each time no valid move is possible. Thus, it will reach 2 if for two successive moves there's no valid option, which means that neither player can go. At the end of a game, you output the final board and the results, and offer the option of another game.

You can now add the code to main() that will make the player and computer moves:

```
/* Program 9.9 REVERSI An Othello-type game */
#include <stdio.h>
#include <ctype.h>

#define SIZE 6                          /* Board size - must be even */

/* Function prototypes */
void display(char board[][SIZE]);
int valid_moves(char board[][SIZE], int moves[][SIZE], char player);
void make_move(char board[][SIZE], int row, int col, char player);
```

```
void computer_move(char board[][SIZE], int moves[][SIZE], char player);

void main()
{
   char board [SIZE][SIZE] = { 0 };     /* The board            */
   int moves[SIZE][SIZE] = { 0 };       /* Valid moves          */
   int row = 0;                         /* Board row index      */
   int col = 0;                         /* Board column index   */
   int no_of_games = 0;                 /* Number of games      */
   int no_of_moves = 0;                 /* Count of moves       */
   int invalid_moves = 0;               /* Invalid move count   */
   int comp_score = 0;                  /* Computer score       */
   int user_score = 0;                  /* Player score         */
   char y = 0;                          /* Column letter        */
   int x = 0;                           /* Row number           */
   char again = 0;                      /* Replay choice input  */
   int player = 0;                      /* Player indicator     */

   /* Prompt for how to play - as before */

   /* The main game loop */
   do
   {
      /* On even games the player starts; */
      /* on odd games the computer starts */
      player = ++no_of_games % 2;
      no_of_moves = 4;                  /* Starts with four counters */

      /* Blank all the board squares */
      for(row = 0; row < SIZE; row++)
        for(col = 0; col < SIZE; col++)
          board[row][col] = ' ';

      /* Place the initial four counters in the center */
      board[SIZE/2 - 1][SIZE/2 - 1] = board[SIZE/2][SIZE/2] = 'O';
      board[SIZE/2 - 1][SIZE/2] = board[SIZE/2][SIZE/2 - 1] = '@';

      /* The game play loop */
      do
      {
        display(board);               /* Display the board  */
        if(player++ % 2)
        { /*   It is the player's turn                    */
          if(valid_moves(board, moves, 'O'))
          {
            /* Read player moves until a valid move is entered */
            for(;;)
            {
              fflush(stdin);          /* Flush the keyboard buffer */
              printf("Please enter your move (row column): ");
              scanf("%d%c", &x, &y);  /* Read input         */
```

```
          y = tolower(y) - 'a';      /* Convert to column index */
          x--;                       /* Convert to row index    */
          if( x>=0 && y>=0 && x<SIZE && y<SIZE && moves[x][y])
          {
            make_move(board, x, y, 'O');
            no_of_moves++;           /* Increment move count */
            break;
          }
          else
            printf("Not a valid move, try again.\n");
        }
      }
      else                           /* No valid moves */
        if(++invalid_moves<2)
        {
          fflush(stdin);
          printf("\nYou have to pass, press return");
          scanf("%c", &again);
        }
        else
          printf("\nNeither of us can go, so the game is over.\n");
    }
    else
    { /* It is the computer's turn                    */
      if(valid_moves(board, moves, '@')) /* Check for valid moves */
      {
        invalid_moves = 0;               /* Reset invalid count    */
        computer_move(board, moves, '@');
        no_of_moves++;                   /* Increment move count   */
      }
      else
      {
        if(++invalid_moves<2)
          printf("\nI have to pass, your go\n"); /* No valid move */
        else
          printf("\nNeither of us can go, so the game is over.\n");
      }
    }
  }while(no_of_moves < SIZE*SIZE && invalid_moves<2);

  /* Game is over */
  display(board);                    /* Show final board */

  /* Get final scores and display them */
  comp_score = user_score = 0;
  for(row = 0; row < SIZE; row++)
    for(col = 0; col < SIZE; col++)
    {
      comp_score += board[row][col] == '@';
      user_score += board[row][col] == 'O';
    }
```

```
    printf("The final score is:\n");
    printf("Computer %d\n    User %d\n\n", comp_score, user_score);

    fflush(stdin);                  /* Flush the input buffer */
    printf("Do you want to play again (y/n): ");
    scanf("%c", &again);            /* Get y or n              */
  }while(tolower(again) == 'y');    /* Go again on y           */

    printf("\nGoodbye\n");
}


/* Code for definition of display() */

/* Code for definition of valid_moves() */
```

The code to deal with game moves uses two new functions, for which you add prototypes. The function make_move() will execute a move, and the computer_move() function will calculate the computer's move. For the player, you calculate the moves array for the valid moves in the if statement:

```
    if(valid_moves(board, moves, 'O'))
    ...
```

If the return value is positive, then there are valid moves, so you read the row number and column letter for the square selected:

```
        printf("Please enter your move: "); /* Prompt for entry */
        scanf("%d%c", &x, &y);              /* Read input       */
```

You convert the row number to an index by subtracting 1 and the letter to an index by subtracting 'a'. You call tolower() just to be sure the value in y is lowercase. Of course, you must include the ctype.h header for this function. For a valid move, the index values must be within the bounds of the array and moves[x][y] must be 1:

```
        if( x>=0 && y>=0 && x<SIZE && y<SIZE && moves[x][y])
        ...
```

If you have a valid move, then you execute it by calling the function make_move(), which you'll write in a moment (notice that the code won't compile yet, because you make a call to this function without having defined it in the program).

If there are no valid moves for the player, you increment invalid_moves. If this is still less than 2, then you output a message that the player can't go and go to the next iteration for the computer's move. If invalid_moves isn't less than 2, however, you output a message that the game is over, and the do-while loop condition controlling game moves will be false.

For the computer's move, if there are valid moves, you call the computer_move() function to make the move and increment the move count. The circumstances in which there are no valid moves are handled in the same way as for the player.

Let's add the definition of the make_move() function next. To make a move, you must place the appropriate counter on the selected square and flip any adjacent rows of opponent counters that are bounded at the opposite end by a player counter. You can add the code for this function at the end of the source file (I won't repeat all the other code):

```
/*******************************************************************
 * Makes a move. This places the counter on a square and reverses  *
 * all the opponent's counters affected by the move.               *
 * First parameter is the board array.                             *
 * Second and third parameters are the row and column indices.     *
 * Fourth parameter identifies the player.                         *
 *******************************************************************/
void make_move(char board[][SIZE], int row, int col, char player)
{
  int rowdelta = 0;                  /* Row increment              */
  int coldelta = 0;                  /* Column increment           */
  int x = 0;                         /* Row index for searching    */
  int y = 0;                         /* Column index for searching */
  char opponent = (player == 'O')? '@' : 'O';  /* Identify opponent */

  board[row][col] = player;          /* Place the player counter   */

  /* Check all the squares around this square */
  /* for the opponent's counter              */
  for(rowdelta = -1; rowdelta <= 1; rowdelta++)
    for(coldelta = -1; coldelta <= 1; coldelta++)
    {
      /* Don't check off the board, or the current square */
      if(row + rowdelta < 0 || row + rowdelta >= SIZE ||
         col + coldelta < 0 || col + coldelta >= SIZE ||
                           (rowdelta==0 && coldelta== 0))
        continue;

      /* Now check the square */
      if(board[row + rowdelta][col + coldelta] == opponent)
      {
        /* If we find the opponent, search in the same direction */
        /* for a player counter                                  */
        x = row + rowdelta;          /* Move to opponent */
        y = col + coldelta;          /* square           */

        for(;;)
        {
          x += rowdelta;             /* Move to the      */
          y += coldelta;             /* next square      */

          /* If we are off the board give up */
          if(x < 0 || x >= SIZE || y < 0 || y >= SIZE)
            break;
```

```
         /* If the square is blank give up */
         if(board[x][y] == ' ')
           break;

         /* If we find the player counter, go backward from here  */
         /* changing all the opponent's counters to player         */
         if(board[x][y] == player)
         {
           while(board[x-=rowdelta][y-=coldelta]==opponent) /* Opponent? */
             board[x][y] = player;    /* Yes, change it */
           break;                     /* We are done     */
         }
       }
     }
   }
 }
}
```

The logic here is similar to that in the valid_moves() function for checking that a square is a valid move. The first step is to search the squares around the square indexed by the parameters row and col for an opponent counter. This is done in the nested loops:

```
for(rowdelta = -1; rowdelta <= 1; rowdelta++)
  for(coldelta = -1; coldelta <= 1; coldelta++)
  {
    ...
  }
```

When you find an opponent counter, you head off in the same direction looking for a player counter in the indefinite for loop. If you fall off the edge of the board or find a blank square, you break out of the for loop and continue the outer loop to move to the next square around the selected square. If you do find a player counter, however, you back up, changing all the opponent counters to player counters.

```
         /* If we find the player counter, go backward from here  */
         /* changing all the opponent's counters to player         */
         if(board[x][y] == player)
         {
           while(board[x-=rowdelta][y-=coldelta]==opponent) /* Opponent? */
             board[x][y] = player;    /* Yes, change it */
           break;                     /* We are done     */
         }
```

The break here breaks out of the indefinite for loop.

Now that you have this function, you can move on to the trickiest part of the program, which is implementing the function to make the computer's move. You'll adopt a relatively simple strategy for determining the computer's move. You'll evaluate each of the possible valid moves for the computer. For each valid computer move, you'll determine what the best move is that the player could make and determine a score for that. You'll then choose the computer move for which the player's best move produces the lowest score.

Before you get to write computer_move(), you'll implement a couple of helper functions. The first will be the function get_score() that will calculate the score for a given board position. You can add the following code to the end of the source file for this:

```
/******************************************************************
 * Calculates the score for the current board position for the    *
 * player. player counters score +1, opponent counters score -1   *
 * First parameter is the board array                             *
 * Second parameter identifies the player                         *
 * Return value is the score.                                     *
 ******************************************************************/
int get_score(char board[][SIZE], char player)
{
    int score = 0;                      /* Score for current position */
    int row = 0;                        /* Row index                  */
    int col = 0;                        /* Column index               */
    char opponent = player == 'O' ? '@' : 'O';   /* Identify opponent */

    /* Check all board squares */
    for(row = 0; row < SIZE; row++)
      for(col = 0; col < SIZE; col++)
    {
      score -= board[row][col] == opponent; /* Decrement for opponent */
      score += board[row][col] == player;   /* Increment for player   */
    }
    return score;
}
```

This is quite simple. The score is calculated by adding 1 for every player counter on the board and subtracting 1 for each opponent count on the board.

The next helper function is best_move(), which will calculate and return the score for the best move of the current set of valid moves for a player. The code for this is as follows:

```
/******************************************************************
 * Calculates the score for the best move out of the valid moves  *
 * for player in the current position.                            *
 * First parameter is the board array                             *
 * Second parameter is the moves array defining valid moves.      *
 * Third parameter identifies the player                          *
 * The score for the best move is returned                        *
 ******************************************************************/
int best_move(char board[][SIZE], int moves[][SIZE], char player)
```

```
{
  int row = 0;                          /* Row index     */
  int col = 0;                          /* Column index */
  int i = 0;                            /* Loop index    */
  int j = 0;                            /* Loop index    */

  char opponent = player=='O'?'@':'O'; /* Identify opponent */

  char new_board[SIZE][SIZE] = { 0 }; /* Local copy of board    */
  int score = 0;                        /* Best score             */
  int new_score = 0;                    /* Score for current move */

  /* Check all valid moves to find the best */
  for(row = 0 ; row<SIZE ; row++)
    for(col = 0 ; col<SIZE ; col++)
    {
      if(!moves[row][col])              /* Not a valid move?  */
        continue;                       /* Go to the next     */

      /* Copy the board */
      for(i = 0 ; i<SIZE ; i++)
        for(j = 0 ; j<SIZE ; j++)
          new_board[i][j] = board[i][j];

      /* Make move on the board copy */
      make_move(new_board, row, col, player);

      /* Get score for move */
      new_score = get_score(new_board, player);

      if(score<new_score)               /* Is it better?            */
              score = new_score;        /* Yes, save it as best score */
    }
  return score;                         /* Return best score        */
}
```

Remember that you must add function prototypes for both of these helper functions to the other function prototypes in main():

```
/* Function prototypes */
void display(char board[][SIZE]);
int valid_moves(char board[][SIZE], int moves[][SIZE], char player);
void make_move(char board[][SIZE], int row, int col, char player);
void computer_move(char board[][SIZE], int moves[][SIZE], char player);
int best_move(char board[][SIZE], int moves[][SIZE], char player);
int get_score(char board[][SIZE], char player);
```

Step 4

The last piece to complete the program is the implementation of the `computer_move()` function. The code for this is as follows:

```
/*******************************************************************
 * Finds the best move for the computer. This is the move for      *
 * which the opponent's best possible move score is a minimum.     *
 * First parameter is the board array.                             *
 * Second parameter is the moves array containing valid moves.     *
 * Third parameter identifies the computer.                        *
 *******************************************************************/
void computer_move(char board[][SIZE], int moves[][SIZE], char player)
{
    int row = 0;                    /* Row index               */
    int col = 0;                    /* Column index            */
    int best_row = 0;               /* Best row index          */
    int best_col = 0;               /* Best column index       */
    int i = 0;                      /* Loop index              */
    int j = 0;                      /* Loop index              */
    int new_score = 0;              /* Score for current move  */
    int score = 100;                /* Minimum opponent score  */
    char temp_board[SIZE][SIZE];    /* Local copy of board     */
    int temp_moves[SIZE][SIZE];     /* Local valid moves array */
    char opponent = (player == 'O')? '@' : 'O'; /* Identify opponent */

    /* Go through all valid moves */
    for(row = 0; row < SIZE; row++)
      for(col = 0; col < SIZE; col++)
      {
        if(moves[row][col] == 0)
          continue;

        /* First make copies of the board and moves arrays */
        for(i = 0; i < SIZE; i++)
          for(j = 0; j < SIZE; j++)
            temp_board[i][j] = board[i][j];

        /* Now make this move on the temporary board */
        make_move(temp_board, row, col, player);

        /* find valid moves for the opponent after this move */
        valid_moves(temp_board, temp_moves, opponent);

        /* Now find the score for the opponent's best move */
        new_score = best_move(temp_board, temp_moves, opponent);
```

```
      if(new_score<score)          /* Is it worse?                    */
      {                            /* Yes, so save this move          */
        score = new_score;         /* Record new lowest opponent score */
        best_row = row;            /* Record best move row            */
        best_col = col;            /* and column                      */
      }
    }
  }
  /* Make the best move */
  make_move(board, best_row, best_col, player);
}
```

This isn't difficult with the two helper functions. Remember that you're going to choose the move for which the opponent's subsequent best move is a minimum.

In the main loop that is controlled by the counters row and col, you make each valid move, in turn, on the copy of the current board that's stored in the local array temp_board. After each move, you call the valid_moves() function to calculate the valid moves for the opponent in that position and store the results in the temp_moves array. You then call the best_move() function to get the score for the best opponent move from the valid set stored in the array temp_moves. If that score is less than any previous score, you save the score, the row, and the column index for that computer move, as a possible best move.

The variable score is initialized with a value that's higher than any possible score, and you go about trying to minimize this (because it's the strength of the opponent's next move) to find the best possible move for the computer. After all of the valid computer moves have been tried, best_row and best_col contain the row and column index for the move that minimizes the opponent's next move. You then call make_move() to make the best move for the computer.

You can now compile and execute the game. The game starts something like this:

```
    a   b   c   d   e   f
  +---+---+---+---+---+---+
1|   |   |   |   |   |   |
  +---+---+---+---+---+---+
2|   |   |   |   |   |   |
  +---+---+---+---+---+---+
3|   |   | O | @ |   |   |
  +---+---+---+---+---+---+
4|   |   | @ | O |   |   |
  +---+---+---+---+---+---+
5|   |   |   |   |   |   |
  +---+---+---+---+---+---+
6|   |   |   |   |   |   |
  +---+---+---+---+---+---+
```

```
Please enter your move: 3e
     a   b   c   d   e   f
   +---+---+---+---+---+---+
 1| |   |   |   |   |   |   |
   +---+---+---+---+---+---+
 2| |   |   |   |   |   |   |
   +---+---+---+---+---+---+
 3| |   |   | 0 | 0 | 0 |   |
   +---+---+---+---+---+---+
 4| |   |   | @ | 0 |   |   |
   +---+---+---+---+---+---+
 5| |   |   |   |   |   |   |
   +---+---+---+---+---+---+
 6| |   |   |   |   |   |   |
   +---+---+---+---+---+---+
```

The computer doesn't play too well because it looks only one move ahead, and it doesn't have any favoritism for edge and corner cells.

Also, the board is only 6×6. If you want to change the board size, then just change the value of SIZE to another even number. The program will work just as well.

Summary

If you've arrived at this point without too much trouble, you're well on your way to becoming a competent C programmer. This chapter and the previous one have covered all you really need to write well-structured C programs. A functional structure is inherent to the C language, and you should keep your functions short, with a well-defined purpose. This is the essence of good C code. You should now be able to approach your own programming problems with a functional structure in mind right from the outset.

Don't forget the flexible power that pointers give you as a C programmer. They can greatly simplify many programming problems, and you should frequently find yourself using them as function arguments and return values. After a while, it will be a natural inclination. The real teacher is experience, so going over the programs in this chapter again will be extremely useful if you don't feel completely confident. And once you feel confident with what's in this book, you should be raring to have a go at some problems of your own.

There's still one major new piece of language territory in C that you have yet to deal with so far, and that's all about data and how to structure it. You'll look at data in Chapter 11. But before you do that, you need to examine input/output in more detail than you have so far. Handling input and output is an important and fascinating aspect of programming, so that's where you're headed next.

Exercises

The following exercises enable you to try out what you've learned in this chapter. If you get stuck, look back over the chapter for help. If you're still stuck, you can download the solutions from the Downloads area of the Apress website (http://www.apress.com), but that really should be a last resort.

Exercise 9-1. A function with the prototype

```
double power(double x, int n);
```

should calculate and return the value of x^n. That is, the expression power(5.0, 4) will evaluate to 5.0 * 5.0 * 5.0 * 5.0, which will result in the value 625.0.

Implement the power() function as a recursive function (so it should call itself) and demonstrate its operation with a suitable version of main().

Exercise 9-2. Implement functions with the prototypes

```
double add(double a, double b);        /* Returns a+b */
double subtract(double a, double b);   /* Returns a-b */
double multiply(double a, double b);   /* Returns a*b */
double array_op(double array[], int size, double (*pfun)(double,double));
```

The parameters for the array_op() function are the array to be operated on, the number of elements in the array, and a pointer to a function defining the operation to be applied between successive elements. The array_op() function should be implemented so that when the subtract() function is passed as the third argument, the function combines the elements with alternating signs. So for an array with four elements, x1, x2, x3, and x4, it computes the value of

```
x1-x2+x3-x4
```

Demonstrate the operation of these functions with a suitable version of main().

Exercise 9-3. Define a function that will accept an array of pointers to strings as an argument and return a pointer to a string that contains all the strings joined into a single string, each terminated by a newline character. If an original string in the input array has newline as its last character, the function shouldn't add another to the string. Write a program to demonstrate this function in operation by reading a number of strings from the keyboard and outputting the resultant combined string.

Exercise 9-4. Implement a function that has the prototype

```
char* to_string(int count, double first, ...);
```

This function should return a string that contains string representations of the second and subsequent arguments, each to two decimal places and separated by commas. The first argument is a count of the number of arguments that follow. Write a suitable version of main() to demonstrate the operation of your function.

CHAPTER 10

Essential Input and Output Operations

IN THIS CHAPTER YOU'RE GOING TO LOOK in more detail at input from the keyboard, output to the screen, and output to a printer. The good news is that everything in this chapter is fairly easy, although there may be moments when you feel it's all becoming a bit of a memory test. Treat this as a breather from the last two chapters. After all, you don't have to memorize everything you see here; you can always come back to it when you need it.

The C language has no input or output capability within the language. All operations of this kind are provided by functions from standard libraries. You've been using many of these functions to provide input from the keyboard and output to the screen in all the preceding chapters.

This chapter will miraculously put all the pieces together into some semblance of order and round it out with the aspects I haven't explained so far. I'll also add a bit about printing because it's usually a fairly essential facility for a program. You don't have a final program with this chapter for the simple reason that I don't really cover anything that requires any practice on a substantial example (it's that easy).

In this chapter you'll learn

- How to read data from the keyboard

- How to format data for output on the screen

- How to deal with character output

- How to output data to a printer

Input and Output Streams

Up to now you've primarily used scanf() for keyboard input and printf() for output to the screen. Actually, there has been nothing in particular about the way you've used these functions to specify where the input came from or where the output went. The information that scanf() received could have come from anywhere, as long as it was a suitable stream of characters. Similarly, the output from printf() could have been going anywhere that could accept a stream of characters. This is no accident: the standard input/output functions in C have been designed to be device independent, so that the transfer of data to or from a specific device isn't a concern of the programmer.

The C library functions and the operating system make sure that operations with a specific device are executed correctly.

Each input source and output destination in C is called a **stream**. An **input stream** is a source of a sequence of characters or bytes, and an **output stream** is a destination for a sequence of characters or bytes that originate in your program. A stream is independent of the physical piece of equipment involved, such as the display or the keyboard. Each device that a program uses will usually have one or more streams associated with it, depending on whether it's simply an input device or an output device such as a printer or a keyboard, or a device that can have both input and output operations, such as a disk drive. This is illustrated in Figure 10-1.

Figure 10-1. Standard and nonstandard streams

A disk drive can have multiple input and output streams because it can contain multiple files. The correspondence is between a stream and a file, not between a stream and the device. A stream can be associated with a specific file on the disk. The stream that you associate with a particular file could be an **input stream**, so you could only read from the file; it could be an **output stream**, in which case you could only write to the file; or the stream might allow **input** and **output**, so reading and writing the file would both be possible. Obviously, if the stream that is associated with a file is an input stream, the file must have been written at some time so it contained some data. You could also associate a stream with a file on a CD-ROM drive. Because this device is typically read-only, the stream would, of necessity, be an input stream.

There are two further kinds of streams: **character streams** and **binary streams**. The main difference between these is that data transferred to or from character streams is treated as a sequence of characters and may be modified by the library routine concerned, according to a format specification. Data that's transferred to or from binary streams is just a sequence of bytes that isn't modified in any way. I'll discuss binary streams in Chapter 12 when I cover reading and writing disk files.

Standard Streams

C has three predefined **standard streams** that are automatically available in any program, provided, of course, that you've included the stdio.h header file, which contains their definitions, into your program. These standard streams are stdin, stdout, and stderr. Two other streams that are supported by many systems are stdprn and stdaux.

No initialization or preparation is necessary to use these streams. You just have to apply the appropriate library function that sends data to them. They are each preassigned to a specific physical device, as shown in Table 10-1.

Table 10-1. Standard Streams

Stream	Device
stdin	Keyboard
stdout	Display screen
stderr	Display screen
stdprn	Printer
stdaux	Serial port

You'll concentrate on the standard input stream, stdin; the standard output stream, stdout; and the printer stream, stdprn.

The stderr stream is simply the stream to which error messages from the C library are sent, and you can direct your own error messages to stderr if you wish. The main difference between stdout and stderr is that output to stdout is buffered in memory, so the data that you write to it won't necessarily be transferred immediately to the device, whereas stderr is unbuffered, so any data you write to it is always transferred immediately to the device. I won't discuss this further, other than to say that stderr points to the display screen and can't be redirected to another device. Output to the stream stdaux is directed to the serial port and is outside the scope of this book for reasons of space rather than complexity.

Both stdin and stdout can be reassigned to files, instead of the default of keyboard and screen, by using operating system commands. When you do this, however, error conditions can arise that wouldn't normally with the default devices, and that's a pretty good reason not to do it for the moment.

Input from the Keyboard

There are two forms of input from the keyboard on stdin that you've already seen in previous chapters: **formatted input**, which is provided principally by scanf(), and **unformatted input**, in which you receive the raw character data from a function such as getchar(). There's rather more to both of these possibilities, so let's look at them in detail.

Formatted Keyboard Input

As you know, the function scanf() reads characters from the stream stdin and converts them to one or more values according to the format specifiers in a format control string. The prototype of the scanf() function is as follows:

```
int scanf(char *format, ... );
```

The format control string parameter is of type char *, a pointer to a character string as shown here. However, this usually appears as an explicit argument in the function call, such as

```
scanf("%lf", &variable);
```

But there's nothing to prevent you from writing this:

```
char str[] = "%lf";
scanf(str, &variable);
```

The format control string is basically a coded description of how scanf() should convert the incoming character stream to the values required. Following the format control string, you can have one or more optional arguments, each of which is an address in which a corresponding converted input value is to be stored. As you've seen, this implies that each of these arguments must be a pointer or a variable name preceded by & to define the address of the variable rather than its value.

The scanf() function reads from stdin until it comes to the end of the format control string, or until an error condition stops the input process. This sort of error would occur as the result of input that didn't correspond to what was expected with the current format specifier, as you'll see. Something that I haven't previously noted is that scanf() returns a value that is the count of the number of input values read.

Input Format Control Strings

The format control string used with scanf() isn't precisely the same as that used with printf(). For one thing, whitespace characters—blank ' ', tab '\t', or newline '\n'—in the format control string cause scanf() to read and ignore whitespace characters up to the next nonwhitespace character in the input. A single whitespace character in the format control string causes any number of consecutive whitespace characters to be ignored. You can therefore include as many whitespace characters as you wish in the format string to make it more readable. Any nonwhitespace character other than % will cause scanf() to read but not store successive occurrences of the character. If you want scanf() to ignore commas separating values in the input for instance, just separate the format specifiers by commas. There are other differences too, as you'll see when I discuss formatted output a bit later in this chapter.

The most general form of a format specifier is shown in Figure 10-2.

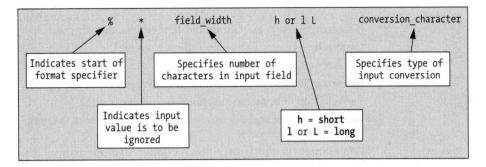

Figure 10-2. The general form of an output specifier

Let's take a look at what the various parts of this general form mean:

- The % simply indicates the start of the format specifier. It must always be present.

- The next * is optional. If you include it, it indicates that the next input value is to be ignored. This isn't normally used with input from the keyboard. It does become useful, however, when stdin has been reassigned to a file and you don't want to process all the values that appear within the file in your program.

- The field width is optional. It's an integer specifying the number of characters that scanf() should assume makes up the current value being input. This allows you to input a sequence of values without spaces between them. This is also often quite useful when reading files.

- The next character is also optional, and it can be h, L or l (lowercase letter L). If it's h, it can only be included with an integer conversion specifier (d, I, o, u, or x) and indicates that the input is to be converted as short. If it's l, then it indicates long when preceding an int conversion specifier and double when preceding a float conversion specifier. The prefix L applied to e, E, f, g, or G specifies the value is of type long double.

- The conversion character specifies the type of conversion to be carried out on the input stream and therefore must be included. The possible characters and their meanings are shown in Table 10-2.

Table 10-2. Conversion Characters and Their Meanings

Conversion Character	Meaning
d	Convert input to int.
i	Convert input to int. If preceded by 0, then assume octal digits input. If preceded by 0x or 0X, then assume hexadecimal digits input.
o	Convert input to int and assume all digits are octal.
u	Convert input to unsigned int.
x	Convert to int and assume all digits are hexadecimal.
c	Read the next character as char (including whitespace).
s	Input the string of nonwhitespace characters, starting with the next nonwhitespace character.
e, f, or g	Convert input to type float. A decimal point and an exponent in the input are optional.

You can also read a string that consists of specific characters by placing all the possible characters between square brackets in the specification. For example, the specification %[0123456789.-] will read a numerical value as a string, so if the input is –1.25 it will be read as "-1.25". To read a string consisting of the lowercase letters a to z, you could use the specification %[abcdefghijklmnopqrstuvwxyz]. This will read any sequence of the characters that appear between the square brackets as a string, and the first character in the input that isn't in the set between the square brackets marks the end of the input. Although it isn't required by the ANSI standard, many C library implementations support the form %[a-z] to read a string consisting of any lowercase letters.

A specification using square brackets is also very useful for reading strings that are delimited by characters other than whitespace. In this case, you can specify the characters that are *not* in the string by using the ^ character as the first character in the set. Thus, the specification %[^,] will include everything in the string except a comma, so this form will enable you to read a series of strings separated by commas.

Table 10-3 shows a few examples of applying the various options.

Table 10-3. Examples of Options in Conversion Specifications

Specification	Description
%lf	Read the next value as type double
%*d	Read the next integer value but don't store it
%5d	Read the next five characters as an integer
%Lf	Read the next value as a floating-point value of type long double
%hu	Read the next value as type unsigned short

Let's exercise some of these format control strings with practical examples.

....

Try It Out: Exercising Formatted Input

To start, let's read a variety of data and then output the result:

```
/* Program 10.1        Exercising formatted input */
#include <stdio.h>

void main()
{
   int i = 0;
   int j = 0;
   int k = 0;
   float fp1 = 0.0;
   char word1[20] = " ";
   char word2[20] = " ";

   k = scanf("%f %d %d %[abcdefghijklmnopqrstuvwxyz] %*1d %s",
      &fp1, &i , &j, word1, word2);
   printf("\nCount of values read = %d\n", k);
   printf("\nfp1 = %f    i = %d    j = %d", fp1, i, j);
   printf("\nword1 = %s    word2 = %s\n", word1, word2);
}
```

Here's an example of the output from this program:

```
-2.35 15 25 ready2go

Count of values read = 5

fp1 = -2.350000    i = 15    j = 25
word1 = ready    word2 = go
```

HOW IT WORKS

The first three input values are read in a straightforward way. The fourth input value is read using the specifier "%[abcdefghijklmnopqrstuvwxyz]", which will read a sequence of lowercase letters as a string. This reads the string "ready" because the character that follows, '2', isn't in the set between the square brackets. The '2' in the input is read using the specifier "%*1d". The * in the specification causes the input to be read but not stored, and the field width is one character. The word "go" is read and stored in word2 using the "%s" specifier.

The value of k is the count of the number of values processed. As you can see, the value reflects the number of values stored and doesn't include the value read by the "%*1d" specification.

(Continued)

It isn't essential that you enter all the data on a single line. If you key in the first two values and press Enter, the scanf() function will wait for you to enter the next value on the next line.

Now let's change the program a little bit by altering one statement. Replace the input statement with

```
k = scanf("%4f %d %d %*d %[abcdefghijklmnopqrstuvwxyz] %*1d %[^o]",
                                    &fp1, &i , &j, word1, word2);
```

Now run the program with exactly the same input line as before. You should get the following output:

```
-2.35 15 25 ready2go

Count of values read = 5

fp1 = -2.300000   i = 5   j = 15
word1 = ready   word2 = g
```

Because you specified a field width of 4 for the floating-point value, the first four characters are taken as defining the value of the first input variable. The following integer value to be input is read as 5, the last digit following the value read as –2.3. The integer that's stored in j is 15, and the value 25 is read and ignored by the "%*d" specification. The last string is read now as just "g" because the specification "%[^o]" accepts any character in the string except the letter 'o'.

Let's try another variation. Change the input statement to this:

```
k = scanf("%4f %4d %d %*d %[abcdefghijklmnopqrstuvwxyz] %*1d %[^o]",
                                    &fp1, &i , &j, word1, word2);
```

With exactly the same input line as before, you should now get the following output:

```
-2.35 15 25 ready2go

Count of values read = 5

fp1 = -2.300000   i = 5   j = 15
word1 = ready   word2 = g
```

So what can you conclude from this case? The first floating-point value has clearly been defined by the first four characters of input. The next two values result in the integers 5 and 15. This shows that in spite of the fact that you specified a field width of 4 for the second integer, it appears to have been overridden.

(Continued)

This is a consequence of the blank following digit 5, which terminates the input scanning for the value being read. So whatever value you put as a field width, the scanning of the input line for a given value stops as soon as you meet the first blank. You could change the specifiers for the integer values to %12d and the result would still be the same for the given input.

You can demonstrate one further aspect of numerical input processing by running the last version of the previous example with a slightly different input line:

```
-2.3A 15 25 ready2go

Count of values read = 1

fp1 = -2.300000   i = 0   j = 0
word1 =      word2 =
```

The count of the number of input values is 1, corresponding to a value for the variable fp1 being read. The A in the input stream is invalid in numerical input, and so the whole process stops dead. No values for variables i and j, word1 and word2, are processed. This demonstrates how unforgiving scanf() really is. A single invalid character in the input stream will stop your program in its tracks. If you want to be able to recover from the situation in which invalid input is entered, you can use the return value from scanf() as a measure of whether all the necessary input has been processed correctly and include some code to retrieve the situation when necessary.

The simplest approach would perhaps be to print an irritable message and then demand the whole input be repeated. But beware of errors in your code getting you into a permanent loop in this circumstance. You'll need to think through all of the possible ways that things might go wrong if you're going to produce a robust program.

Characters in the Input Format String

You can include a sequence of one or more characters that isn't a format conversion specifier within the input format string. If you do this, you're indicating that you expect the same characters to appear in the input and that the scanf() function should read them but not store them. These have to be matched exactly, character for character, by the data in the input stream. Any variation will terminate the input scanning process in scanf().

Try It Out: Including Characters in the Input Format String

You can illustrate the effect of including characters in the input format string with the following example:

```
/* Program 10.2 Characters in the format control string */
#include <stdio.h>

void main()
{
   int i = 0;
   int j = 0;
   int k = 0;
   float fp1 = 0.0;

   k = scanf("fp1 = %f i = %d %d", &fp1, &i , &j);
   printf("\nCount of values read = %d", k);
   printf("\nfp1 = %f\ti = %d\tj = %d\n", fp1, i, j);
}
```

Here's an example of the output:

```
fp1 = 3.14159 i = 7 8

Count of values read = 3
fp1 = 3.141590  i = 7   j = 8
```

HOW IT WORKS

It doesn't matter whether or not the blanks before and after the = are included in the input—they're whitespace characters and are therefore ignored. The important thing is to include the same characters that appear in the format control string, in the correct sequence and at the correct place in the input. Try an input line in which this isn't the case:

```
fp1 = 3.14159 i = 7 j = 8

Count of values read = 2
fp1 = 3.141590  i = 7   j = 0
```

(Continued)

Now only two values are read. This is because the character j in the input stops processing immediately, and no value is received by the variable j. The input processing of characters by scanf() is also case sensitive. If you input Fp1= instead of fp1=, no values will be processed at all, because the mismatch with the capital F will stop scanning before any values are entered.

....

Variations on Floating-Point Input

When you're reading floating-point values formatted using scanf(), you not only have a choice of specification that you use, but also you can enter the values in a variety of forms. You can see this with a simple example.

....

Try It Out: Floating-Point Input

With this example you can try various forms of specifier and various ways in which you can enter the input values:

```
/* Program 10.3 Floating-Point Input */
#include <stdio.h>

void main()
{
  float fp1 = 0.0f;
  float fp2 = 0.0f;
  float fp3 = 0.0f;
  int k = 0;
  k = scanf("%f %f %f", &fp1, &fp2, &fp3);
  printf("\nReturn value = %d", k);
  printf("\nfp1 = %f  fp2 = %f  fp3 = %f\n", fp1, fp2, fp3);
}
```

Here's an example of output from this program with the same input value written three different ways:

```
3.14 .314E1 .0314e+02

Return value = 3
fp1 = 3.140000  fp2 = 3.140000  fp3 = 3.140000
```

(Continued)

HOW IT WORKS

This example demonstrates three different ways of entering the same value. The first way is a straightforward decimal value, the second has an exponent value defined by the E1 that indicates that the value is to be multiplied by 10, and the third has an exponent value of e+02 and therefore is to be multiplied by 100. As you can see, when you're reading a floating-point value with the "%f" specification, you have the option of whether or not to include an exponent. If you do include an exponent, you can define it beginning with either an e or an E. You also have the option to include a sign for the exponent value, + or -, and, of course, the value can be signed too. There are countless variations possible here.

You could try changing the printf() statement to the following:

```
k = scanf("%e %g %f", &fp1, &fp2, &fp3);
```

Here's the output with this statement in the program:

```
3.14 .314e1 .0314E2

Return value = 3
fp1 = 3.140000  fp2 = 3.140000  fp3 = 3.140000
```

Clearly all three format specifications work equally well with the various input forms. The variation between these is only when you use them for output with the printf() function.

I recommend that you experiment with the various possibilities here. In particular, try experimenting with floating-point numbers and the field-width specifiers that you used for reading integers.

Note that you could dispense with the variable k, and put the scanf() call as the argument to the first printf():

```
printf("\nReturn value = %d\n", scanf("%f %f %f", &fp1, &fp2, &fp3));
```

This is just to show that it can be done, but because it makes the code rather inelegant and harder to follow, I don't recommend it as a rule!

Reading Hexadecimal and Octal Values

As you saw earlier, you can read hexadecimal values from the input stream using the format specifier %x. For octal values you use %o. These are very straightforward, but let's see them working in an example.

Try It Out: Reading Hexadecimal and Octal Values

Try the following example:

```
/* Program 10.4 Reading hexadecimal and octal values */
#include <stdio.h>

void main()
{
   int i = 0;
   int j = 0;
   int k = 0;
   int n = 0;

   n = scanf(" %d %x %o", &i , &j, &k );
   printf("\n%d values read.", n);
   printf("\ni = %d   j = %d   k = %d\n", i, j, k );
}
```

Here's some sample output:

```
12 12 12

3 values read.
i = 12   j = 18   k = 10
```

HOW IT WORKS

You read the three values entered as 12. The first is read with a decimal format specifier %d, the second using a hexadecimal format specifier %x, and the third using an octal format specifier %o. The output shows that 12 in hexadecimal is 18 in decimal notation, whereas 12 in octal is 10 in decimal notation.

Hexadecimal data entry can be useful when you want to enter bit patterns (sequences of 1s and 0s), as they're easier to specify in hexadecimal than in decimal. Each hexadecimal digit corresponds to 4 bits, so you can specify a 16-bit word as four hexadecimal digits. Octal is hardly ever used, and it appears here mainly for historical reasons.

Note the following example of output:

```
18 18 18

3 values read.
i = 18   j = 24   k = 1
```

(Continued)

Here, the first two values are read correctly as 18, as a hexadecimal value is indeed 24 in decimal notation. However, the third value is read as 1. This is because 8 isn't a legal octal digit. Octal digits are 0 to 7.

You can enter hexadecimal values using A to F or a to f, or even a mixture if you're so inclined. Here's another example of output:

```
12 aA 17

3 values read.
i = 12   j = 170   k = 15
```

The value aA is $10 \times 16 + 10$, which is 170 as a decimal value. The octal value 17 is $1 \times 8 + 7$, which is 15 as a decimal value.

There's no difference between using "%x" and "%X" with scanf(), but they'll have a different effect when you use them with printf() for output. You can demonstrate this by changing the last printf() statement to the following:

```
printf("\ni = %x   j = %X   k = %d\n", i, j, k );
```

This now outputs the first two values in hexadecimal notation. You can get the following output with the input shown:

```
26 AE 77

3 values read.
i = 1a   j = AE   k = 63
```

So "%x" produces hexadecimal output using hexadecimal digits a to e, and "%X" produces output using hexadecimal digits A to E.

Reading Characters Using scanf()

You tried reading strings in the first example, but there are more possibilities. You know that there are three format specifiers for reading one or more characters. You can read a single character and store it as type char using the format specifier %c. For a string of characters, you use either the specifier %s or the specifier %[ ]. In this case, the string is stored as a null-terminated string with '\0' as the last character. With %[ ] format specification, the string to be read must include only the characters between the square brackets, or if the first character between the square brackets is ^, the string must contain only characters that are *not* among those following the ^ characters. Thus, %[aeiou] will read a string that consists only of vowels. The first character that isn't a vowel will signal the end of the string. The specification %[^aeiou] reads a string that contains any character that isn't a vowel. The first vowel will signal the end of the string.

Note that one interesting aspect of the %[ ] specification is it enables you to read a string containing spaces, something that the %s specification can't do.

Try It Out: Reading Characters and Strings

You can see these character-reading capabilities in operation with the following example:

```
/* Program 10.5 Reading characters with scanf() */
#include <stdio.h>

void main()
{
  char initial = ' ';
  char name[80] = { 0 };
  char age[4] = { 0 };
  printf("Enter your first initial: ");
  scanf("%c", &initial );
  printf("Enter your first name:" );
  scanf("%s", name );

  if(initial != name[0])
    printf("\n%s,you got your initial wrong.", name);
  else
    printf("\nHi, %s. Your initial is correct. Well done!", name );
  printf("\nEnter your full name and your age separated by a comma:\n" );
  scanf("%[^,] , %[0123456789]", name, age );
  printf("\nYour name is %s and you are %s years old\n", name, age );
}
```

Here's some output from this program:

```
Enter your first initial: I
Enter your first name:Ivor

Hi, Ivor. Your initial is correct. Well done!
Enter your full name and your age separated by a comma:
Ivor Horton    , 99

Your name is
Ivor Horton     and you are 99 years old
```

(Continued)

HOW IT WORKS

This program first expects you to enter your first initial and then your first name.
It checks that the first letter of your name is the same as the initial you entered.
This works in a straightforward way, as you can see from the output.

Next, you're asked to enter your full name followed by your age, separated by a
comma. The read operation is carried out by the following statement:

```
scanf("%[^,] , %[0123456789]", name, age );
```

I deliberately spaced out the input data so you could see that the first input
specification, %[^,], reads any character as part of the string that isn't a comma,
including spaces. You then have a comma in the control string that will cause
scanf() to read the comma (or several commas in succession) and not store it.
The input for age is read as a string with the specifier %[0123456789]. This will
read any sequence of consecutive digits as a string.

Note that the comma in the input string is essential for the input to be read
properly. If you leave it out, scanf() will attempt to read the comma as part of
the input for age. Because a comma is evidently not a digit, this will stop input
for age so it will just consist of an empty string.

If you try entering a space and then your initial as the first input, the program
will treat the blank as the value for initial and the single character you entered
as your name. With the way the control string is defined, the first character that
you enter when using the %c specifier is taken to be the character, whatever it is.
If you don't want a space to be accepted as the initial, you can fix this by writing
the input statement as follows:

```
scanf(" %c", &initial );
```

Now the first character in the control string is a space, so scanf() will read and
ignore any number of spaces and read the first character that isn't a space into
initial.

Pitfalls with scanf()

There are two very common mistakes people make when using scanf() that you should
keep in mind:

- Don't forget that the arguments must be pointers. Perhaps the most common
  error is to forget the ampersand (&) when specifying single variables as arguments to scanf(), particularly because you don't need it with printf(). Of course,
  the & isn't necessary if the argument is an array name or a pointer variable.

- When reading a string, remember to ensure that there's enough space for the string to be read in, *plus* the terminating '\0'. If you don't do this, you'll overwrite something in memory, possibly even some of your program code.

String Input from the Keyboard

As you've seen, the gets() function in stdio.h will read a complete line of text as a string. The prototype of the function is as follows:

```
char *gets(char *str);
```

This function reads successive characters into the memory pointed to by str until you press the Enter key. It appends the terminating null, '\0', in place of the newline character that is read when you press the Enter key. The return value is identical to the argument, which is the address where the string has been stored. The following example provides a reminder of how it works.

Try It Out: Reading a String with gets()

Here's a simple program using gets():

```
/* Program 10.6 Reading a string with gets() */
#include <stdio.h>

void main()
{
  char initial[2] = {0};
  char name[80] = {0};

  printf("Enter your first initial: ");
  gets(initial);
  printf("Enter your name: " );
  gets(name);
  if(initial[0] != name[0])
    printf("\n%s,you got your initial wrong.\n", name);
  else
    printf("\nHi, %s. Your initial is correct. Well done!\n", name);
}
```

Here's some output from this program:

```
Enter your first initial: M
Enter your name: Mephistopheles

Hi, Mephistopheles. Your initial is correct. Well done!
```

(Continued)

```
                        HOW IT WORKS
```

You read the initial and the name as strings using gets(). The function is very easy to use because there's no format specification involved. Because gets() will read characters until you press Enter, you can now enter your full name if you wish.

For string input, using gets() is usually the preferred approach unless you want to control the content of the string, in which case you can use %[]. The %[] specification is more convenient to use when the nonstandard %[a-z] form is supported, but remember, because this is nonstandard, your code is no longer as portable as it is if you use the standard form for reading a string of lowercase letters, %[abcdefghijklmnopqrstuvwxyz].

Unformatted Input from the Keyboard

The getchar()function reads one character at a time from stdin. getchar() is defined in stdio.h, and its general syntax is as follows:

```
int getchar(void);
```

The getchar() function requires no arguments, and it returns the character read from the input stream. Note that this character is returned as int, and the character is displayed on the screen as it is entered.

With many implementations of C, the header file conio.h is often provided. This provides additional functions for character input and output. One of the most useful of these is getch(), which reads a character from the keyboard without displaying it on the screen. This is particularly useful when you need to prevent others from being able to see what's being keyed in—for example, when a password is being entered.

Output to the Screen

Writing data to the screen is much easier than reading input from the keyboard. You know what data you're writing, whereas with input you have all the vagaries of possible incorrect entry of the data. The primary function for formatted output to the stdout stream is printf().

Fortunately—or unfortunately, depending how you view the chore of getting familiar with this stuff—printf() provides myriad possible variations for the output you can obtain, much more than the scope of the format specifiers associated with scanf().

Formatted Output to the Screen Using printf()

The printf() function is defined in the header file stdio.h, and its general form is as follows:

```
int printf(char *format, ...);
```

The first parameter is the format control string. The argument for this parameter is usually passed to the function as an explicit string constant, as you've seen in all the examples, but it can be a pointer to a string that you specify elsewhere. The optional arguments to the function are the values to be output in sequence, and they must correspond in number and type with the format conversion specifiers that appear in the string that is passed as the first argument.

Of course, as you've also seen in earlier examples, if the output is simply the text that appears in the control string, then there are no additional arguments after the first. But where there are argument values to be output, there must be *at least* as many arguments as there are format specifiers. If not, the results are unpredictable. If there are *more* arguments than specifiers, then the excess is ignored. This is because the function uses the format string as the determinant of how many arguments follow and what type they have.

NOTE *The fact that the format string alone determines how the data is interpreted is the reason why you get the wrong result with a* %d *specifier combined with a* long *argument on systems on which* int *is 2 bytes rather than 4.*

The format conversion specifiers for printf() are a little more complicated than those used for input with scanf(). The general form of the format specifier is shown in Figure 10-3.

Figure 10-3. Format specifications for the printf() *function*

You've seen most of the details before, but let's take a quick pass through the elements of this general format specifier:

- The % sign indicates the start of the specifier, as it does for output.

- The optional flag characters are +, -, #, and blank. These affect the output, as shown in Table 10-4.

Table 10-4. Effects of the Optional Flag Characters in an Output Specification

Character	Use
+	Ensures that, for signed output values, there's always a sign preceding the output value—either a plus or a minus sign.
-	Specifies that the output value is left-justified in the output field and padded with blanks on the right. The default positioning of the output is right-justified.
#	Specifies that 0 is to precede an octal output value, 0x; or 0X is to precede a hexadecimal output value; or a floating-point output value will contain a decimal point. For the g or G floating-point conversion characters, trailing zeroes will also be omitted.
Blank	Specifies that positive or zero output values are preceded by a blank rather than a plus sign.

- The optional field_width specifies the minimum number of characters for the output value. If the value requires more characters, the field is simply expanded. If it requires less than the minimum specified, then it is padded with blanks, unless the field width is specified with a leading zero, as in 09, for example, where it would be filled on the left with zeroes.

- The precision specifier is also optional and is generally used with floating-point output values. A specifier of .n indicates that n decimal places are to be output. If the value to be output has more than n significant digits, it's rounded or truncated.

- You use the h, l (lowercase letter L), or L specification to specify that the output conversion is being applied to short, long, or long double values, respectively.

- The conversion character that you use defines how the output is to be converted for a particular type of value to be output. Conversion characters are defined in Table 10-5.

Believe it or not, this set of output options includes only the most important ones. If you consult the documentation accompanying your compiler, you'll find a few more.

Table 10-5. Conversion Characters in an Output Specification

Conversion Character	Output Produced
Applicable to Integers	
d	Signed decimal integer value
o	Unsigned octal integer value
u	Unsigned decimal integer value
x	Unsigned hexadecimal integer value with lowercase hexadecimal digits a, b, c, d, e, f
X	As x but with uppercase hexadecimal digits A, B, C, D, E, F
Applicable to Floating-Point	
f	Signed decimal value
e	Signed decimal value with exponent
E	As e but with E for exponent instead of e
g	As e or f depending on size of value and precision
G	As g but with E for exponent values
Applicable to Characters	
c	Single character
s	All characters until '\0' is reached or precision characters have been output

Escape Sequences

You can include whitespace characters in the format control string for printf(). The characters that are referred to as whitespace are the newline, carriage return, and form-feed characters; blank (a space); and tab. Some of these are represented by escape sequences that begin with \. Table 10-6 shows the most common escape sequences.

Table 10-6. Common Escape Sequences

Escape Sequence	Description
\a	Bell sound (a beep on your computer)
\b	Backspace
\f	Form-feed or page eject
\n	Newline
\r	Carriage return (for printers) or move to the beginning of the current line for output to the screen
\t	Horizontal tab

You use the escape sequence, \\, in format control strings when you want to output the backslash character \. If this weren't the case, it would be impossible to output a backslash, because it would always be assumed that a backslash was the start of an escape sequence.

NOTE *Of course, you can use escape sequences within any string, not just in the context of the format string for the* printf() *function.*

Different Output

Let's take a look at some of the variations that you haven't made much use of so far. Those with field width and precision specifiers are probably the most interesting.

Try It Out: Outputting Integers

Let's try a sample of integer output formats first:

```
/* Program 10.7 Integer output variations */
#include <stdio.h>

void main()
{
   int i = 15;
   int j = 345;
   int k = 4567;
   long li = 56789L;
   long lj = 678912L;
   long lk = 23456789L;

   printf("\ni = %d    j = %d    k = %d    i = %6.3d    j = %6.3d    k = %6.3d\n",
                                            i ,j, k, i, j, k);
   printf("\ni = %-d    j = %+d    k = %-d    i = %-6.3d    j = %-6.3d    k ="
                            " %-6.3d\n",i ,j, k, i, j, k);
   printf("\nli = %d    lj = %d    lk = %d\n", li, lj, lk);
   printf("\nli = %ld    lj = %ld    lk = %ld\n", li, lj, lk);
}
```

(Continued)

When you execute this example, you should see something like this:

```
i = 15   j = 345    k = 4567   i =    015   j =     345   k =    4567

i = 15   j = +345   k = 4567   i = 015      j = 345      k = 4567

li = -8747    lj = 23552    lk = -5099

li = 56789    lj = 678912    lk = 23456789
```

HOW IT WORKS

This example illustrates a miscellany of options for integer output. You can see the effects of the - flag by comparing the first two lines produced by these statements:

```
printf("\ni = %d   j = %d    k = %d   i = %6.3d   j = %6.3d   k = %6.3d\n",
                                      i ,j, k, i, j, k);
printf("\ni = %-d   j = %+d   k = %-d   i = %-6.3d   j = %-6.3d   k ="
                        " %-6.3d\n",i ,j, k, i, j, k);
```

The - flag causes the output to be left-justified. The effect of the field width specifier is also apparent from the spacing of the last three outputs in each group of six. Note that the default width provides just enough output positions to accommodate the number of digits to be output, so the - flag has no effect.

You get a leading plus in the output of j on the second line because of the flag modifier. You can use more than one flag modifier if you want. With the second output of the value of i, you have a leading zero inserted due to the minimum precision being specified as 3. You could also have obtained leading zeroes by preceding the minimum width value with a 0 in the format specification.

The third output line is produced by the following statement:

```
printf("\nli = %d   lj = %d   lk = %d\n", li, lj, lk);
```

Here, you can see that failure to insert the 1 (lowercase letter L) modifier when outputting integers of type long results in apparent garbage, because the output value is assumed to be a 2-byte integer. Of course, if your system implements type int as a 4-byte integer, the values will be correct here. The problem arises only if long and int are differentiated.

(Continued)

You get the correct values from this statement:

```
printf("\nli = %ld   lj = %ld   lk = %ld\n", li, lj, lk);
```

It's unwise to specify inadequate values for the width and the precision of the values to be displayed. Weird and wonderful results may be produced if you do. Try experimenting with this example to see just how much variation you can get.

Try It Out: Variations on a Single Integer

You'll try one more integer example to run the gamut of possibilities with a single integer value:

```
/* Program 10.8 Variations on a single integer */
#include <stdio.h>
void main()
{
   int k = 678;

   printf("%%d   %%o   %%x   %%X");  /* Display format as heading */
   printf("\n%d %o %x %X", k, k, k, k );      /* Display values */

   /* Display format as heading then display the values */
   printf("\n\n%%8d      %%-8d      %%+8d      %%08d      %%-+8d");
   printf("\n%8d  %-8d  %-+8d  %08d  %-+8d\n", k, k, k, k, k );
}
```

HOW IT WORKS

This program may look a little confusing at first because the first of each pair of printf() statements displays the format used to output the number appearing immediately below. The %% specifier simply outputs the % character.

When you execute this example, you should get something like this:

```
%d   %o   %x   %X
678  1246  2a6  2A6

%8d       %-8d      %+8d      %08d      %-+8d
     678  678       +678      00000678  +678
```

(Continued)

The first row of output values is produced by this statement:

```
printf("\n%d  %o  %x  %X", k, k, k, k );      /* Display values */
```

The outputs are decimal, octal, and two varieties of hexadecimal for the value 678, with the default width specification. The corresponding format appears above each value in the output.

The next row of output values is produced by this:

```
printf("\n%8d  %-8d  %-+8d  %08d  %-+8d\n", k, k, k, k, k );
```

This statement includes a variety of flag settings with a width specification of 8. The first is the default right-justification in the field. The second is left-justified because of the - flag. The third has a sign because of the + flag. The fourth has leading zeroes because the width is specified as 08 instead of 8, and it also has a sign because of the + flag. The last output value uses a specifier with all the trimmings, %-+8d, so the output is left-justified in the field and also has a leading sign.

NOTE *When you're outputting multiple rows of values on the screen, using a width specification—possibly with tabs—will enable you to line them up in columns.*

Outputting Floating-Point Values

If plowing through the integer options hasn't started you nodding off, then take a quick look at the floating-point output options through working examples.

Try It Out: Outputting Floating-Point Values

Look at the following example:

```
/* Program 10.9 Outputting floating-point values */
#include <stdio.h>

void main()
{
   float fp1 = 345.678f;
```

(Continued)

```
    float fp2 = 1.234E6f;
    double fp3 = 234567898.0;
    double fp4 = 11.22334455e-6;

    printf("\n%f  %+f  %-10.4f  %6.4f\n", fp1, fp2, fp1, fp2);
    printf("\n%e  %+E\n", fp1, fp2);
    printf("\n%f  %g  %#+f  %8.4f  %10.4g\n", fp3,fp3, fp3, fp3, fp4);
}
```

HOW IT WORKS

With my compiler, I get this output:

```
345.678009       +1234000.000000 345.6780        1234000.0000

3.456780e+002    +1.234000E+006

234567898.000000       2.34568e+008   +234567898.000000    234567898.0000
1.122e-005
```

It's possible that you may not get exactly the same output, but it should be close. You may have only two-digit exponent values, for example. Most of the output is a straightforward demonstration of the effects of the format conversion specifiers that I've discussed, but a few points are noteworthy.

The value of the first output for fp1 differs slightly from the value that you assigned to the variable. This is typical of the kind of small difference that can creep in when floating-point numbers are converted from decimal to binary. With fractional decimal values, there isn't always an exact equivalent in binary floating-point.

In the output generated by the statement

```
    printf("\n%f  %+f  %-10.4f  %6.4f\n", fp1, fp2, fp1, fp2);
```

the second output value for fp1 shows how the number of decimal places after the point can be constrained. The output in this case is left-justified in the field. The second output of fp2 has a field width specified that is too small for the number of decimal places required and is therefore overridden.

The second printf() statement is as follows:

```
    printf("\n%e  %+E\n", fp1, fp2);
```

This outputs the same values in floating-point format with an exponent. Whether you get an uppercase E or a lowercase e for the exponent indicator depends on how you write the format specifier.

(Continued)

In the last line, you can see how the g-specified output of fp3 has been rounded up compared to the f specified output.

> **NOTE** *There are a huge number of possible variations for the output obtainable with* printf()*. It would be very educational for you to play around with the options, trying various ways of outputting the same information.*

Character Output

Now that you've looked at the various possibilities for outputting numbers, let's have a look at outputting characters.

Outputting Strings

In addition to the string output capabilities of printf(), you have the puts() function declared in stdio.h, which complements the gets() function. The general form of puts() is as follows:

```
int puts(char *string);
```

The puts() function accepts a pointer to a string as an argument and displays the string on stdout. The string must be terminated by '\0'. It returns a non-negative value if no errors occur on output. The puts() function is very useful for outputting single-line messages, for example:

```
puts("Is there no end to input and output?");
```

This will output the string that is passed as the argument and then move the cursor to the next line. The function printf() requires an explicit '\n' to be included at the end of the string to do the same thing.

> **NOTE** *The function* puts() *will, of course, also process embedded* '\n' *characters to generate new lines.*

Unformatted Output to the Screen

Also included in stdio.h, and complementing the function getchar(), is the function putchar(). This has the following general form:

```
int putchar(int c);
```

The putchar() function outputs a single character, c, to stdout and returns the character that was displayed. This allows you to output a message one character at a time, which can make your programs a bit bigger. For example, you could write

```
char string[] = "Jabberwocky!\n";
puts(string);
```

or you could write

```
char string[] = "Jabberwocky!\n";
int i = 0;
while( string[i] != '\0')
  putchar(string[i++]);
```

Both of these code fragments will output the same thought-provoking message. Of course, the real purpose of these functions is to give you complete control of input and output operations, if and when you need it. With putchar(), for instance, you could choose to output a selected sequence of characters from the middle of a string. You wouldn't be able to do this very easily with just puts(). You could also selectively transform certain characters within a string before output.

Sending Output to the Printer

To print, you just need to use a more generalized form of the printf() function called fprintf(). This is actually designed to send formatted output to *any* stream, but you'll stick to printing for now. For the purpose of printing, the general form for using fprintf() is as follows:

```
fprintf(stdprn, format_string, argument1, argument2, ..., argumentn);
```

The function will return a value of type int that is a count of the number of values that were sent to stdprn. With the exception of the first argument and the extra f in the function name, fprintf() looks exactly like printf(). And so it is. If you don't have stdprn defined with your compiler and library, you'll need to consult your documentation to see how to handle printing, but most systems do support stdprn. You can use the same format string with the same set of specifiers to output data to your printer, in exactly the same way that you display results with printf(). However, there are a couple of minor variations you need to be aware of. I'll illustrate these in the next example.

Try It Out: Printing on a Printer

This program shows how you can get programs to output to a printer:

```
/* Program 10.10 Printing on a printer - where else? */
#include <stdio.h>
void main()
{
   fprintf( stdprn, "The barber shaves all those who do not"
                                    " shave themselves.");
   fprintf(stdprn, "\n\rQuestion: Who shaves the barber?\n\r");
   fprintf(stdprn, "\n\rAnswer: She doesn't need to shave.\f");
}
```

HOW IT WORKS

The only oddities here are the new escape sequences \r and \f. The sequence \n\r is equivalent to a newline/carriage return on a printer, and the \f is a form-feed character, which produces a page eject on printers where this is necessary.

Summary

Although I chose the various specifications for formatting that you've seen in this chapter with the idea of them being as meaningful as possible, there are a lot of them. The only way you're going to become comfortable with them is through practice. This practice generally needs to take place in a practical context. Understanding the various codes is one thing, but they'll probably become really familiar to you only once you've used them a few times in real programs. Naturally, then, I recommend that you go and find practical uses for these formatting codes. In the meantime, you can always look them up here!

Exercises

The following exercises enable you to try out what you've learned in this chapter. If you get stuck, look back over the chapter for help. If you're still stuck, you can download the solutions from the Downloads area of the Apress website (http://www.apress.com), but that really should be a last resort.

Exercise 10-1. Write a program that will read, store, and output the following five types of strings on separate lines, when one of each type of string are entered on a single line without spaces between them:

- Type 1: A sequence of lowercase letters followed by a digit (e.g., number1)

- Type 2: Two words that both begin with a capital letter and have a hyphen between them (e.g., Seven-Up)

- Type 3: A decimal value (e.g., 7.35)

- Type 4: A sequence of upper- and lowercase letters and spaces (e.g., Oliver Hardy)

- Type 5: A sequence of any characters except spaces and digits (e.g., floating-point)

A sample of input that should be read as five separate strings is

babylon5John-Boy3.14159Stan Laurel'Winner!'

Exercise 10-2. Write a program that will read the numerical values in the following line of input and output the total:

$3.50 , $4.75 , $9.95 , $2.50

Exercise 10-3. Define a function that will output an array of values of type double that is passed as an argument along with the number of elements in the array. The prototype of the function will be

void show(double array[], int array_size, int field_width);

The values should be output five to a line, each with two decimal places after the decimal point and in a field width of 12. Use the function in a program that will output the values from 1.5 to 4.5 in steps of 0.3 (i.e., 1.5, 1.8, 2.1, and so on, up to 4.5).

Exercise 10-4. Define a function using the getchar() function that will read a string from stdin terminated by a character that is passed as the second argument to the function. Thus the prototype will be:

char *getString(char *buffer, char end_char);

The return value is the pointer that is passed as the first argument. Write a program to demonstrate the use of the function to read and output five strings that are from the keyboard, each terminated by a colon.

CHAPTER 11

Structuring Data

SO FAR, YOU'VE LEARNED HOW TO DECLARE and define variables that can hold various types of data, including integers, floating-point values, and characters. You also have the means to create arrays of any of these types and arrays of pointers to memory locations containing data of the types available to you. Although these have proved very useful, there are many applications in which you need even more flexibility.

For instance, suppose you want to write a program that processes data about breeding horses. You need information about each horse such as its name, its date of birth, its coloring, its height, its parentage, and so on. Some items are strings and some are numeric. Clearly, you could set up arrays for each data type and store them quite easily. However, this has limitations—for example, it doesn't allow you to refer to Dobbin's date of birth or Trigger's height particularly easily. You would need to synchronize your arrays by relating data items through a common index. Amazingly, C provides you with a better way of doing this, and that's what I'll discuss in this chapter.

In this chapter you'll learn

- What structures are

- How to declare and define data structures

- How to use structures and pointers to structures

- How you can use pointers as structure members

- How to share memory between variables

- How to define your own data types

- How to write a program that produces bar charts from your data

Data Structures: Using struct

The keyword struct enables you to define a collection of variables of various types called a **structure** that you can treat as a single unit. This will be clearer if you see a simple example of a structure declaration:

```
struct horse
{
    int age;
    int height;
} Silver;
```

This example declares a **structure** type called horse. This isn't a variable name; it's a new type. This type name is usually referred to as a **structure tag**, or a **tag name**. The naming of the structure tag follows the same rules as for a variable name, which you should be familiar with by now.

NOTE *It's legal to use the same name for a structure tag name and another variable. However, I don't recommend that you do this because it will make your code confusing and difficult to understand.*

The variable names within the structure, age and height, are called **structure members**. In this case, they're both of type int. The members of the structure appear between the braces that follow the struct tag name horse.

In the example, an instance of the structure, called Silver, is declared at the same time that the structure is defined. Silver is a variable of type horse. Now, whenever you use the variable name Silver, it includes both members of the structure: the member age and the member height.

Let's look at the declaration of a slightly more complicated version of the structure type horse:

```
struct horse
{
    int age;
    int height;
    char name[20];
    char father[20];
    char mother[20];
} Dobbin = {
            24, 17, "Dobbin", "Trigger", "Flossie"
          };
```

Any type of variable can appear as a member of a structure, including arrays. As you can see, there are five members to this version of the structure type called horse: the integer members age and height, and the arrays name, father, and mother. Each member declaration is essentially the same as a normal variable declaration, with the type followed by the name and terminated by a semicolon. Note that initialization values can't be placed here because you aren't declaring variables; you're defining members of a type called horse. A structure type is a kind of specification or blueprint that can then be used to define variables of that type—in this example, of type horse.

You define an instance of the structure horse after the closing brace of the structure definition. This is the variable Dobbin. Initial values are also assigned to the member variables of Dobbin, in a manner similar to that used to initialize arrays, so initial values *can* be assigned when you define instances of the type horse.

In the declaration of the variable Dobbin, the values that appear between the final pair of braces apply, in sequence, to the member variable age (24), height (17), name ("Dobbin"), father ("Trigger"), and mother ("Flossie"). The statement is finally terminated with a semicolon. The variable Dobbin now refers to the complete collection of members included in the structure. The memory occupied by the structure Dobbin is shown in Figure 11-1. You can always find out the amount of memory that's occupied by a structure using the sizeof operator.

Figure 11-1. Memory occupied by Dobbin

Defining Structure Types and Structure Variables

You could have separated the declaration of the structure from the declaration of the structure variable. Instead of the statements you saw previously, you could have written the following:

```
struct horse
{
   int age;
   int height;
   char name[20];
   char father[20];
   char mother[20];
};

struct horse Dobbin = {
                  24, 17,"Dobbin", "Trigger", "Flossie"
               };
```

You now have two separate statements. The first is the definition of the structure tag horse, and the second is a declaration of one variable of that type, Dobbin. Both the structure definition and the structure variable declaration statements end with a semicolon. The initial values for the members of the Dobbin structure tell you that the father of Dobbin is Trigger and his mother is called Flossie.

You could also add a third statement to the previous two examples that would define another variable of type horse:

```
struct horse Trigger = {
                  30, 15, "Trigger", "Smith", "Wesson"
               };
```

Now you have a variable Trigger that holds the details of the father of Dobbin, where it's clear that the ancestors of Trigger are "Smith" and "Wesson".

Of course, you can also declare multiple structure variables in a single statement. This is almost as easy as declaring variables of one of the standard C types, for example:

```
struct horse Piebald, Bandy;
```

This declares two variables of type horse. The only additional item in the declaration, compared with standard types, is the keyword struct. I haven't initialized the values—to keep the statement simple—but in general it's wise to do so.

Accessing Structure Members

Now that you know how to define a structure and declare structure variables, you need to be able to refer to the members of a structure. A structure variable name is *not* a pointer. You need a special syntax to access the members.

You refer to a member of a structure by writing the structure variable name followed by a period, followed by the member variable name. For example, if you found that Dobbin had lied about his age and was actually much younger than the initializing value would suggest, you could amend the value by writing this:

```
Dobbin.age = 12;
```

The period between the structure variable name and the member name is actually an operator called the **member selection operator**. This statement sets the age member of the structure Dobbin to 12. Structure members are just the same as variables of the same type. You can set their values and use them in expressions in the same way as ordinary variables.

....

Try It Out: Using Structures

You can try out what you've learned so far about structures in a simple example that's designed to appeal to horse enthusiasts:

```
/* Program 11.1 Exercising the horse */
#include <stdio.h>

void main()
{
  /* Structure declaration */
  struct horse
  {
    int age;
    int height;
    char name[20];
    char father[20];
    char mother[20];
```

(Continued)

```
    };

    struct horse My_first_horse;           /* Structure variable declaration   */

    /* Initialize  the structure variable from input data */
    printf("Enter the name of the horse: " );
    scanf("%s", My_first_horse.name );              /* Read the horse's name    */

    printf("How old is %s? ", My_first_horse.name );
    scanf("%d", &My_first_horse.age );              /* Read the horse's age     */

    printf("How high is %s ( in hands )? ", My_first_horse.name );
    scanf("%d", &My_first_horse.height );           /* Read the horse's height */

    printf("Who is %s's father? ", My_first_horse.name );
    scanf("%s", My_first_horse.father );            /* Get the father's name    */

    printf("Who is %s's mother? ", My_first_horse.name );
    scanf("%s", My_first_horse.mother );            /* Get the mother's name    */

    /* Now tell them what we know */
    printf("\n%s is %d years old, %d hands high,",
        My_first_horse.name, My_first_horse.age, My_first_horse.height);
    printf(" and has %s and %s as parents.\n", My_first_horse.father,
                                        My_first_horse.mother );
}
```

Depending on what data you key in, you should get output approximating the following:

```
Enter the name of the horse: Neddy
How old is Neddy? 12
How high is Neddy ( in hands )? 14
Who is Neddy's father? Bertie
Who is Neddy's mother? Nellie

Neddy is 12 years old, 14 hands high, and has Bertie and Nellie as parents.
```

HOW IT WORKS

The way you reference members of a structure makes it very easy to follow what is going on in this example. You define the structure horse with this statement:

```
struct horse
{
    int age;
    int height;
```

(Continued)

```
    char name[20];
    char father[20];
    char mother[20];
};
```

The structure has two integer members, age and height, and three char array members, name, father, and mother. Because there's just a semicolon following the closing brace, no variables of type horse are declared here.

After defining the structure horse, you have the following statement:

```
struct horse My_first_horse;        /* Structure variable declaration   */
```

This declares one variable of type horse, which is My_first_horse. This variable has no initial values assigned in the declaration.

You then read in the data for the name member of the structure My_first_horse with this statement:

```
scanf("%s", My_first_horse.name );            /* Read the horse's name   */
```

No address of operator (&) is necessary here, because the name member of the structure is an array, so you implicitly transfer the address of the first array element to the function scanf(). You reference the member by writing the structure name, My_first_horse, followed by a period, followed by the name of the member, which is name. Other than the notation used to access it, using a structure member is the same as using any other variable.

The next value you read in is for the age of the horse:

```
scanf("%d", &My_first_horse.age );            /* Read the horse's age    */
```

This member is a variable of type int, so here you must use the & to pass the address of the structure member.

 NOTE *When you use the address of operator (&) for a member name, you place the & in front of the whole reference to the member, not in front of the member name.*

The following statements read the data for each of the other members of the structure in exactly the same manner, prompting for the input in each case. Once input is complete, the values read are output to the display as a single line using these statements:

(Continued)

```
printf("\n\n%s is %d years old, %d hands high,",
    My_first_horse.name, My_first_horse.age, My_first_horse.height);
printf(" and has %s and %s as parents.", My_first_horse.father,
                                    My_first_horse.mother );
```

The long names that are necessary to refer to the members of the structure tend to make this statement appear complicated, but it's quite straightforward. You have the names of the member variables as the arguments to the function following the first argument, which is the standard sort of format control string that you've seen many times before.

Unnamed Structures

You don't have to give a structure a tag name. When you declare a structure and any instances of that structure in a single statement, you can omit the tag name. In the last example, instead of the structure declaration for type horse, followed by the instance declaration for My_first_horse, you could have written this statement:

```
struct
{                                       /* Structure declaration and... */
   int age;
   int height;
   char name[20];
   char father[20];
   char mother[20];
} My_first_horse;            /* ...structure variable declaration combined */
```

A serious disadvantage with this approach is that you can no longer define further instances of the structure in another statement. All the variables of this structure type that you want in your program must be defined in the one statement.

Arrays of Structures

The basic approach to keeping horse data is fine as far as it goes. But it will probably begin to be a bit cumbersome by the time you've accumulated 50 or 100 horses. You need a more stable method for handling a lot of horses. It's exactly the same problem that you had with variables, which you solved using an array. And you can do the same here: you can declare a horse array.

....

Try It Out: Using Arrays of Structures

Let's saddle up and extend the previous example to handle several horses:

```
/* Program 11.2    Exercising the horses */
#include <stdio.h>
#include <ctype.h>
void main()
{
   struct horse                      /* Structure declaration */
   {
     int age;
     int height;
     char name[20];
     char father[20];
     char mother[20];
   };

   struct horse My_horses[50];       /* Structure array declaration   */
   int hcount = 0;                   /* Count of the number of horses */
   int i = 0;                        /* Loop counter                  */
   char test = '\0';                 /* Test value for ending         */

   for(hcount = 0; hcount < 50 ; hcount++ )
   {
     printf("\nDo you want to enter details of a%s horse (Y or N)? ",
                                     hcount?"nother " : "" );
     scanf(" %c", &test );
     if(tolower(test) == 'n')
        break;

     printf("\nEnter the name of the horse: " );
     scanf("%s", My_horses[hcount].name );  /* Read the horse's name */

     printf("\nHow old is %s? ", My_horses[hcount].name );
     scanf("%d", &My_horses[hcount].age );  /* Read the horse's age  */

     printf("\nHow high is %s ( in hands )? ", My_horses[hcount].name );
     /* Read the horse's height*/
     scanf("%d", &My_horses[hcount].height );

     printf("\nWho is %s's father? ", My_horses[hcount].name );
     /* Get the father's name */
     scanf("%s", My_horses[hcount].father );

     printf("\nWho is %s's mother? ", My_horses[hcount].name );

     /* Get the mother's name  */
```

(Continued)

```
        scanf("%s", My_horses[hcount].mother );
    }

    /* Now tell them what we know. */
    for (i = 0 ; i < hcount ; i++ )
    {
      printf("\n\n%s is %d years old, %d hands high,",
              My_horses[i].name, My_horses[i].age, My_horses[i].height);
      printf(" and has %s and %s as parents.", My_horses[i].father,
                                        My_horses[i].mother );
    }
}
```

The output from this program is little different from the previous example you saw that dealt with a single horse. The main addition is the prompt for input data for each horse. Once all the data for a few horses has been entered, or if you have the stamina, the data on 50 horses has been entered, the program outputs a summary of all the data entered, one line per horse. The whole mechanism works very well in the mane (almost an unbridled success, you might say).

HOW IT WORKS

In this version of equine data processing, you first declare the horse structure, and this is followed by the declaration

```
    struct horse My_horses[50]; /* Structure array declaration   */
```

This declares the variable My_horses, which is an array of 50 horse structures. Apart from the keyword struct, it's just like any other array declaration.

You then have a for loop controlled by the variable hcount:

```
    for(hcount = 0; hcount < 50 ; hcount++ )
    {
      ...
    }
```

This creates the potential for the program to read in data for up to 50 horses. The loop control variable hcount is used to accumulate the total number of horse structures entered. The first action in the loop is in these statements:

```
    printf("\nDo you want to enter details of a%s horse (Y or N)? ",
                                        hcount?"nother " : "" );
    scanf(" %c", &test );
    if(tolower(test) == 'n')
      break;
```

(Continued)

457

On each iteration, the user is prompted to indicate if he or she wants to enter data for another horse by entering **Y** or **N**. The printf() statement for this uses the conditional operator to insert "nother" into the output on every iteration after the first. After reading the character that the user enters, using scanf(), the if statement executes a break, which immediately exits from the loop if the response is negative.

The succeeding sequence of printf() and scanf() statements are much the same as before, but there are two points to note in these. Look at this statement:

```
scanf("%s", My_horses[hcount].name ); /* Read the horse's name */
```

You can see that the method for referencing the member of one element of an array of structures is easier to write than to say! The structure array name has an index in square brackets, to which a period and the member name are appended. If you wanted to reference the third element of the name array for the fourth structure element, then you would write My_horses[3].name[2].

 NOTE *Of course, the index values start from 0, as with arrays of other types, so the fourth element of the structure array has the index value 3, and the third element of the member array is accessed by the index value 2.*

Now look at this statement from the example:

```
scanf("%d", &My_horses[hcount].age ); /* Read the horse's age */
```

Notice that the arguments to scanf() don't need the & for the string array variables, such as My_horses[hcount].name, but they *do* require them for the integer arguments My_horses[hcount].age and My_horses[hcount].height. It's very easy to forget the address of operator when reading values for variables like these.

Don't be misled at this point and think that these techniques are limited to equine applications. They can perfectly well be applied to porcine problems and also to asinine exercises.

Structures in Expressions

A member of a structure that's one of the built-in types can be used as any other variable in an expression. Using the structure from Program 11.2, you could write this rather meaningless computation:

```
My_horses[1].height = (My_horses[2].height + My_horses[3].height)/2;
```

I can think of no good reason why the height of one horse should be the average of two other horses' heights (unless there's some Frankenstein-like assembly going on) but it's a legal statement.

You can also use a complete structure element in an assignment statement:

```
My_horses[1] = My_horses[2];
```

This statement causes *all* the members of the structure My_horses[2] to be copied to the structure My_horses[1], which means that the two structures become identical. The only other operation that's possible with a whole structure is to take its address using the & operator. You can't add, compare, or perform any other operations with a complete structure. To do those kinds of things, you must write your own functions.

Pointers to Structures

The ability to obtain the address of a structure raises the question of whether you can have pointers to a structure. Because you can take the address of a structure, the possibility of declaring a pointer to a structure does, indeed, naturally follow. You use the notation that you've already seen with other types of variables:

```
struct horse *phorse;
```

This declares a pointer, phorse, that can store the address of a structure of type horse.

You can now set phorse to have the value of the address of a particular structure, using exactly the same kind of statement that you've been using for other pointer types, for example:

```
phorse = &My_horses[1];
```

Now phorse points to the structure My_horses[1]. You can immediately reference elements of this structure through your pointer. So if you wanted to display the name member of this structure, you could write this:

```
printf("\nThe name is %s.", (*phorse).name);
```

The parentheses around the dereferenced pointer are essential, because the precedence of the member selection operator (the period) is higher than that of the pointer-dereferencing operator, *.

However, there's another way of doing this, and it's much more readable and intuitive. You could write the previous statement as follows:

```
printf("\nThe name is %s.", phorse->name );
```

So you don't need parentheses or an asterisk. You construct the operator -> from a minus sign immediately followed by the greater than symbol. The operator is sometimes called the **pointer to member** operator for obvious reasons. This notation is almost invariably used in preference to the usual pointer-dereferencing notation you used at first, because it makes your programs so much easier to read.

Dynamic Memory Allocation for Structures

You have virtually all the tools you need to rewrite Program 11.2 with much a more economical use of memory. In the original version, you allocated the memory for an array of 50 horse structures, even when in practice you probably didn't need anything like that amount.

To create dynamically allocated memory for structures, the only tool that's missing is an array of pointers to structures, which is declared very easily, as you can see in this statement:

```
struct horse *phorse[50];
```

This statement declares an array of 50 pointers to structures of type horse. Only memory for the pointers has been allocated by this statement. You must still allocate the memory necessary to store the actual members of each structure that you need.

....

Try It Out: Using Pointers with Structures

You can see the dynamic allocation of memory for structures at work in the following example:

```
/* Program 11.3 Pointing out the horses */
#include <stdio.h>
#include <ctype.h>
#include <stdlib.h>            /* For malloc() */

void main()
{
   struct horse              /* Structure declaration */
   {
     int age;
     int height;
     char name[20];
     char father[20];
     char mother[20];
   };

   struct horse *phorse[50]; /* pointer to structure array declaration */
   int hcount = 0;           /* Count of the number of horses         */
   int i = 0;                /* Loop counter                          */
   char test = '\0';         /* Test value for ending input           */
```

(Continued)

```
      for(hcount = 0; hcount < 50 ; hcount++ )
      {
        printf("\nDo you want to enter details of a%s horse (Y or N)? ",
                                          hcount?"nother " : "" );
        scanf(" %c", &test );
        if(tolower(test) == 'n')
          break;

        /* allocate memory to hold a structure    */
        phorse[hcount] = (struct horse*) malloc(sizeof(struct horse));

        printf("\nEnter the name of the horse: " );
        scanf("%s", phorse[hcount]->name );  /* Read the horse's name */

        printf("\nHow old is %s? ", phorse[hcount]->name );
        scanf("%d", &phorse[hcount]->age );  /* Read the horse's age  */

        printf("\nHow high is %s ( in hands )? ", phorse[hcount]->name );
        scanf("%d", &phorse[hcount]->height ); /* Read the horse's height */

        printf("\nWho is %s's father? ", phorse[hcount]->name );
        scanf("%s", phorse[hcount]->father );  /* Get the father's name */

        printf("\nWho is %s's mother? ", phorse[hcount]->name );
        scanf("%s", phorse[hcount]->mother );  /* Get the mother's name */
      }

      /* Now tell them what we know. */
      for (i = 0 ; i < hcount ; i++ )
      {
        printf("\n\n%s is %d years old, %d hands high,",
                    phorse[i]->name, phorse[i]->age, phorse[i]->height);
        printf(" and has %s and %s as parents.",
                             phorse[i]->father, phorse[i]->mother);
        free(phorse[i]);
      }
    }
```

The output should be exactly the same as that from Program 11.2, given the same input.

HOW IT WORKS

This looks very similar to the previous version, but it operates differently. Initially, you don't have any memory allocated for any structures. The declaration

```
    struct horse *phorse[50]; /* pointer to structure array declaration */
```

(Continued)

defines only 50 pointers to structures of type horse. You still have to find some-where to put the structures to which these pointers are going to point:

```
phorse[hcount] = (struct horse*) malloc(sizeof(struct horse));
```

In this statement, you allocate the space for each structure as it's required. Let's have a quick reminder of how the malloc() function works. The malloc() function allocates the number of bytes specified by its argument and returns the address of the block of memory allocated as a pointer to type void. In this case, you use the sizeof operator to provide the value required.

It's very important to use sizeof when you need the number of bytes occupied by a structure. It doesn't necessarily correspond to the sum of the bytes occupied by each of its individual members, so you're likely to get it wrong if you try to work it out yourself.

Variables other than type char are often stored beginning at an address that's a multiple of 2 for 2-byte variables, a multiple of 4 for 4-byte variables, and so on. This is called **boundary alignment**, and it has nothing to do with C but is a hardware requirement where it applies. Arranging variables to be stored in memory like this makes the transfer of data between the processor and memory faster. This arrangement can result in unused bytes occurring between member variables of different types, though, depending on their sequence. These have to be accounted for in the number of bytes allocated for a structure. Figure 11-2 presents an illustration of how this can occur.

Figure 11-2. The effect of boundary alignment on memory allocation

As the value returned by malloc() is a pointer to void, you then cast this to the type you require with the expression (struct horse*). This enables the pointer to be incremented or decremented correctly, if required.

```
scanf("%s", phorse[hcount]->name );  /* Read the horse's name    */
```

(Continued)

In this statement, you use the new notation for selecting members of a structure through a pointer. It's much clearer than `(*phorse[hcount]).name`. All subsequent references to members of a specific `horse` structure use this new notation.

Lastly in this program, you display a summary of all the data entered for each horse, freeing the memory as you go along.

··

More on Structure Members

So far, you've seen that any of the basic data types, including arrays, can be members of a structure. But there's more. You can also make a structure a member of a structure. Furthermore, not only can pointers be members of a structure, but also a pointer to a structure can be a member of a structure.

This opens up a whole new range of possibilities in programming with structures and, at the same time, increases the potential for confusion. Let's look at each of these possibilities in sequence and see what they have to offer. Maybe it won't be a can of worms after all.

Structures As Members of a Structure

At the start of this chapter, you examined the needs of horse breeders and, in particular, the necessity to manage a variety of details about each horse, including its name, height, date of birth, and so on. You then went on to look at Program 11.1, which carefully avoided date of birth and substituted age instead. This was partly because dates are messy things to deal with, as they're represented by three numbers and hold all the complications of leap years. However, you're now ready to tackle dates, using a structure that's a member of another structure.

You can define a structure type designed to hold dates. You can specify a suitable structure with the tag name `Date` with this statement:

```
struct Date
{
   int day;
   int month;
   int year;
};
```

You can define the structure `horse`, including a date-of-birth variable, like this:

```
struct horse
{
   struct Date dob;
   int height;
   char name[20];
   char father[20];
```

```
    char mother[20];
};
```

Now you have a single variable member within the structure that represents the date of birth of a horse, and this member is itself a structure. Next, you can define an instance of the structure horse with the usual statement:

```
struct horse Dobbin;
```

You can define the value of the member height with the same sort of statement that you've already seen:

```
Dobbin.height = 14;
```

If you want to set the date of birth in a series of assignment statements, then you can use the logical extension of this notation:

```
Dobbin.dob.day = 5;
Dobbin.dob.month = 12;
Dobbin.dob.year = 1962;
```

You have a very old horse. The expression Dobbin.dob.day is referencing a variable of type int, so you can happily use it in arithmetic or comparative expressions. But if you were going to use the expression Dobbin.dob, then you would be referring to a struct variable of type date. Because this is clearly not a basic type but a structure, you can use it only in an assignment such as this:

```
Trigger.dob = Dobbin.dob;
```

This *could* mean that they're twins, but it doesn't guarantee it!

If you can find a good reason to do it, you can extend the notion of structures that are members of a structure to a structure that's a member of a structure that's a member of a structure. In fact, if you can make sense of it, you can continue with further levels of structure. Your C system is likely to provide for at least 15 levels of such convolution. But beware: if you reach this depth of structure nesting, you're likely to be in for a bout of repetitive strain injury just typing the references to members.

Declaring a Structure Within a Structure

You could have declared the Date structure within the horse structure definition, as in the following code:

```
struct horse
{
    struct Date
    {
```

```
      int day;
      int month;
      int year;
   } dob;

   int height;
   char name[20];
   char father[20];
   char mother[20];
};
```

This has an interesting effect. Because the declaration is enclosed within the scope of the horse structure definition, it doesn't exist outside it, and so it becomes impossible to declare a Date variable external to the horse structure. Of course, each instance of a horse type variable would contain the Date type member, dob. But a statement such as this:

```
struct Date my_date;
```

would cause a compiler error. The message generated will say that the structure type date is undefined. If you need to use Date outside the structure horse, then its definition must be placed outside of the horse structure.

Pointers to Structures As Structure Members

Any pointer can be a member of a structure. This includes a pointer that points to a structure. A pointer structure member that points to the same type of structure is also permitted. For example, the horse type structure could contain a pointer to a horse type structure. Interesting, but is it of any use? Well, as it happens, yes.

Try It Out: Pointers to Structures As Structure Members

You can demonstrate a structure containing a pointer to a structure of the same type with a modification of the last example:

```
/* Program 11.4   Daisy chaining the horses */
#include <stdio.h>
#include <ctype.h>
#include <stdlib.h>

void main()
{
   struct horse                    /* Structure declaration    */
   {
      int age;
```
(Continued)

```
   int height;
   char name[20];
   char father[20];
   char mother[20];
   struct horse *next;                /* Pointer to next structure   */
};

struct horse *first = NULL;          /* Pointer to first horse      */
struct horse *current = NULL;        /* Pointer to current horse    */
struct horse *previous = NULL;       /* Pointer to previous horse   */

char test = '\0';                    /* Test value for ending input */

for( ; ; )
{
  printf("\nDo you want to enter details of a%s horse (Y or N)? ",
                                  first != NULL?"nother " : "" );
  scanf(" %c", &test );
  if(tolower(test) == 'n')
    break;

  /* Allocate memory for a structure */
  current = (struct horse*) malloc(sizeof(struct horse));

  if(first == NULL)
    first = current;                 /* Set pointer to first horse  */

  if(previous != NULL)

    previous -> next = current; /* Set next pointer for previous horse */

  printf("\nEnter the name of the horse: ");
  scanf("%s", current -> name);      /* Read the horse's name       */

  printf("\nHow old is %s? ", current -> name);
  scanf("%d", &current -> age);      /* Read the horse's age        */

  printf("\nHow high is %s ( in hands )? ", current -> name );
  scanf("%d", &current -> height);   /* Read the horse's height     */

  printf("\nWho is %s's father? ", current -> name);
  scanf("%s", current -> father);    /* Get the father's name       */

  printf("\nWho is %s's mother? ", current -> name);
  scanf("%s", current -> mother);    /* Get the mother's name       */
```

(Continued)

```
    current->next = NULL;              /* In case it's the last...  */
    previous = current;               /* Save address of last horse */
  }


  /* Now tell them what we know. */
  current = first;                    /* Start at the beginning      */

  while (current != NULL)      /* As long as we have a valid pointer */
  { /* Output the data*/
    printf("\n\n%s is %d years old, %d hands high,",
                    current->name, current->age, current->height);
    printf(" and has %s and %s as parents.", current->father,
                                      current->mother);
    previous = current;      /* Save the pointer so we can free memory */
    current = current->next;         /* Get the pointer to the next */
    free(previous);                  /* Free memory for the old one */
  }
}
```

This example should produce the same output as Program 11.3 (given the same input), but here you have yet another mode of operation.

HOW IT WORKS

This time, not only do you have no space for structures allocated, but also you have only three pointers defined initially. These pointers are declared and initialized in these statements:

```
    struct horse *first = NULL;       /* Pointer to first horse      */
    struct horse *current = NULL;     /* Pointer to current horse    */
    struct horse *previous = NULL;    /* Pointer to previous horse   */
```

Each of these pointers has been defined as a pointer to a horse structure. The pointer first is used solely to store the address of the first structure. The second and third pointers are working storage: current holds the address of the current horse structure that you're dealing with, and previous keeps track of the address of the previous structure that was processed.

You've added a member to the structure horse with the name next, which is a pointer to a horse type structure. This will be used to link together all the horses you have, where each horse structure will have a pointer containing the address of the next. The last structure will be an exception, of course: its next pointer will be NULL. The structure is otherwise exactly as you had previously. It's shown in Figure 11-3.

(Continued)

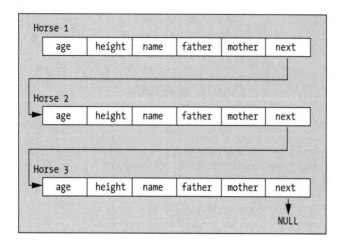

Figure 11-3. A sequence of linked horses

The input loop is

```
for( ; ; )
{
  ...
}
```

The input loop is now an indefinite loop, because you don't have an array to worry about. You don't need to mess around with indexes. It's also unnecessary to keep count of how many sets of data are read in, so you don't need the variable hcount or the loop variable i. Because you allocate memory for each horse, you can just take them as they come.

The initial statements in the loop are

```
printf("\nDo you want to enter details of a%s horse (Y or N)? ",
                          first != NULL?"nother " : "" );
scanf(" %c", &test );
if(tolower(test) == 'n')
  break;
```

After the prompt, you exit from the loop if the response 'N' or 'n' is detected. Otherwise, you expect another set of structure members to be entered. You use the pointer first to get a slightly different prompt on the second and subsequent iterations, because the only time it will be NULL is on the first loop iteration.

Assuming you get past the initial question in the loop, you execute these statements:

(Continued)

```
current = (struct horse*) malloc(sizeof(struct horse));

if(first == NULL)
  first = current;                    /* Set pointer to first horse  */

if(previous != NULL)
  previous -> next = current; /* Set next pointer for previous horse */
```

On each iteration, you allocate the memory necessary for the current structure. To keep things short, you don't check for a NULL return from malloc(), although you ought to do this in practice.

If the pointer first is NULL, you must be on the first loop iteration, and this must be the first structure about to be entered. Consequently, you set the pointer first to the pointer value that you've just obtained from malloc(), which was stored in the variable current. The address in first is the key to accessing the first horse in the chain. You can get to any of the others by starting with the address in first and then looking in the member pointer next to obtain the address of the next structure. You can step from there to the next structure and so on to any horse in the sequence.

The next pointer always needs to point to the next structure if there is one, but the address of the next structure can be determined only once you actually have the next structure. Therefore, on the second and subsequent iterations, you store the address of the current structure in the next member of the previous structure, whose address you'll have saved in previous. On the first iteration, the pointer previous will be NULL at this point, so of course you do nothing.

At the end of the loop, following all the input statements, you have these statements:

```
current->next = NULL;        /* In case it's the last...   */
previous = current;          /* Save address of last horse */
```

The pointer next in the structure pointed to by current, which you're presently working with, is set to NULL in case this is the last structure and there's no next structure. If there is a next structure, this pointer next will be filled in on the next iteration. The pointer previous is set to current and is ready for the next iteration, when the current structure will indeed be the previous structure.

The strategy of the program is to generate a daisy chain of horse structures, in which the next member of each structure points to the next structure in the chain. The last is an exception because there's no next horse, so the next pointer contains NULL. This arrangement is called a **linked list**.

Once you have the horse data in a linked list, you process it by starting with the first structure and then getting the next structure through the pointer member next. When the pointer next is NULL, you know that you've reached the end of the list. This is how you generate the output list of all the input.

(Continued)

Linked lists are invaluable in applications in which you need to process an unknown number of structures, such as you have here. The main advantages of a linked list relate to memory usage and ease of handling. You occupy only the minimum memory necessary to store and process the list. Even though the memory used may be fragmented, you have no problem progressing from one structure to the next. As a consequence, in a practical situation in which you may need to deal with several different types of objects simultaneously, each can be handled using its own linked list, with the result that memory use is optimized. There is one small cloud associated with this—as there is with any silver lining—and it's that you pay a penalty in slower access to the data.

The output process shows how a linked list is accessed as it steps through the linked list you've created with these statements:

```
current = first;                    /* Start at the beginning    */

while (current != NULL)     /* As long as we have a valid pointer */
{ /* Output the data*/
  printf("\n\n%s is %d years old, %d hands high,",
                  current->name, current->age, current->height);
  printf(" and has %s and %s as parents.", current->father,
                                        current->mother);
  previous = current;    /* Save the pointer so we can free memory */
  current = current->next;       /* Get the pointer to the next */
  free(previous);                /* Free memory for the old one */
}
```

The current pointer controls the output loop, and it's set to first at the outset. Remember that the first pointer contains the address of the first structure in the list. The loop steps through the list, and as the members of each structure are displayed, the address stored in the member next, which points to the next structure, is assigned to current.

The memory for the structure that was displayed is then freed. It's obviously fairly essential that you free the memory for a structure only once you have no further need to reference it. It's easy to fall into the trap of putting the call of the function free() straight after you've output all of the member values for the current structure. This would create some problems, because then you couldn't legally reference the current structure's next member to get the pointer to the next horse structure.

For the last structure in the linked list, the pointer next will contain NULL and the loop will terminate.

Doubly Linked Lists

A disadvantage of the linked list that you created in the previous example is that you can only go forward. However, a small modification of the idea gives you the **doubly linked list**, which will allow you to go through a list in either direction. The trick is to include an extra pointer in each structure to store the address of the previous structure in addition to the pointer to the next structure.

....

Try It Out: Doubly Linked Lists

You can see a doubly linked list in action in a modified version of Program 11.4:

```
/* Program 11.5 Daisy chaining the horses both ways */
#include <stdio.h>
#include <ctype.h>
#include <stdlib.h>

void main()
{
  struct horse                        /* Structure declaration        */
  {
    int age;
    int height;
    char name[20];
    char father[20];
    char mother[20];
    struct horse *next;               /* Pointer to next structure     */
    struct horse *previous;           /* Pointer to previous structure */
  };

  struct horse *first = NULL;         /* Pointer to first horse        */
  struct horse *current = NULL;       /* Pointer to current horse      */
  struct horse *last = NULL;          /* Pointer to previous horse     */

  char test = '\0';                   /* Test value for ending input */

  for( ; ; )
  {
    printf("\nDo you want to enter details of a%s horse (Y or N)? ",
                              first == NULL?"nother " : "");
    scanf(" %c", &test );
    if(tolower(test) == 'n')
      break;

    /* Allocate memory for each new horse structure */
    current = (struct horse*)malloc(sizeof(struct horse));
```

(Continued)

```
      if( first == NULL )
      {
        first = current;                    /* Set pointer to first horse  */
       current->previous = NULL;
      }
      else
      {
        last->next = current;    /* Set next address for previous horse */
        current->previous = last; /* Previous address for current horse */
      }

      printf("\nEnter the name of the horse: ");
      scanf("%s", current -> name );     /* Read the horse's name   */

      printf("\nHow old is %s? ", current -> name);
      scanf("%d", &current -> age);       /* Read the horse's age    */

      printf("\nHow high is %s ( in hands )? ", current -> name);
      scanf("%d", &current -> height);   /* Read the horse's height */

      printf("\nWho is %s's father? ", current -> name);
      scanf("%s", current -> father);    /* Get the father's name   */

      printf("\nWho is %s's mother? ", current -> name);
      scanf("%s", current -> mother);    /* Get the mother's name   */

      current -> next = NULL;      /* In case it's the last horse..*/
      last = current;              /* Save address of last horse   */
    }

    /* Now tell them what we know. */
    while(current != NULL)          /* Output horse data in reverse order */
    {
      printf("\n\n%s is %d years old, %d hands high,",
               current->name, current->age, current->height);
      printf(" and has %s and %s as parents.", current->father,
                                        current->mother);
      last = current;        /* Save pointer to enable memory to be freed */
      current = current->previous; /* current points to previous in list */
      free(last);                  /* Free memory for the horse we output */
    }
  }
```

For the same input, this program should produce the same output as before,
except that the data on horses entered is displayed in reverse order to that of
entry—just to show that you can do it.

(Continued)

HOW IT WORKS

The initial pointer declarations are now as follows:

```
struct horse *first = NULL;       /* Pointer to first horse    */
struct horse *current = NULL;     /* Pointer to current horse  */
struct horse *last = NULL;        /* Pointer to previous horse */
```

You change the name of the pointer recording the horse structure entered on the previous iteration of the loop to last. This name change isn't strictly necessary, but it does help to avoid confusion with the structure member previous.

The structure horse is declared as follows:

```
struct horse                      /* Structure declaration      */
{
  int age;
  int height;
  char name[20];
  char father[20];
  char mother[20];
  struct horse *next;             /* Pointer to next structure     */
  struct horse *previous;         /* Pointer to previous structure */
};
```

The horse structure now contains two pointers: one to point forward in the list, called next, the other to point backward to the preceding structure, called previous. This allows the list to be traversed in either direction, as you demonstrate by the fact that you output the data at the end of the program in reverse order.

Aside from the output, the only changes to the program are to add the statements that take care of the entries for the pointer structure member previous. In the beginning of the input loop you have

```
if( first == NULL )
{
  first = current;                /* Set pointer to first horse   */
  current->previous = NULL;
}
else
{
  last->next = current;     /* Set next address for previous horse */
  current->previous = last; /* Previous address for current horse */
}
```

(Continued)

Here, you take the option of writing an `if` with an `else`, rather than the two `if`s you had in the previous version. The only material difference is setting the value of the structure member `previous`. For the first structure `previous` is set to `NULL`, and for all subsequent structures it's set to the pointer `last`, whose value was saved on the preceding iteration.

The other change is at the end of the input loop:

```
last = current;                         /* Save address of last horse  */
```

This statement is added to allow the pointer `previous` in the next structure to be set to the appropriate value, which is the `current` structure that you're recording in the variable `last`.

The output process is virtually the same as in the previous example, except that you start from the last structure in the list and work back to the first.

Bit-Fields in a Structure

Bit-fields provide a mechanism that allows you to define variables that are each one or more binary bits within a single integer word, which you can nevertheless refer to explicitly with an individual member name for each one.

NOTE *Bit-fields are used most frequently when memory is at a premium and you're in a situation in which you must use it as sparingly as possible.*

Bit-fields will slow your program down appreciably compared to using standard variable types. You must therefore assess each situation upon its merits to decide whether the memory savings offered by bit-fields are worth this price in execution speed for your programs. In most instances, bit-fields won't be necessary or even desirable, but you need to know about them.

An example of declaring a bit-field is shown here:

```
struct
{
    unsigned int flag1 : 1;
    unsigned int flag2 : 1;
    unsigned int flag3 : 2;
    unsigned int flag4 : 3;
} indicators;
```

This defines a variable with the name `indicators` that's an instance of an anonymous structure containing four bit-fields with the names `flag1` through `flag4`. These will all be stored in a single word, as illustrated in Figure 11-4.

Figure 11-4. Bit-fields in a structure

The first two bit-fields, being a single bit specified by the 1 in their definition, can only assume the values 0 or 1. The third bit-field, `flag3`, has 2 bits and so it can have a value from 0 to 3. The last bit-field, `flag4`, can have values from 0 to 7, because it has 3 bits. These bit-fields are referenced in the same manner as other structure members, for example:

```
indicators.flag4 = 5;
indicators.flag3 = indicators.flag1 = 1;
```

You'll rarely, if ever, have any need for this facility. I've included bit-fields here for the sake of completeness and for that strange off chance that, one day, bit-fields will be just what you need in a particularly tight memory situation.

Structures and Functions

Because structures represent such a powerful feature of the C language, their use with functions is very important. You'll now look at how you can pass structures as arguments to a function and how you can return a structure from a function.

Structures As Arguments to Functions

There's nothing unusual in the method for passing a structure as an argument to a function. It's exactly the same as passing any other variable. Analogous to the `horse` structure, you could create this structure:

```
struct family
{
   char name[20];
```

```
    int age;
    char father[20];
    char mother[20];
};
```

You could then construct a function to test whether two members of the type family are siblings:

```
int siblings(struct family member1, struct family member2)
{
    if(strcmp(member1.mother, member2.mother) == 0)
      return 1;
    else
      return 0;
}
```

This function has two arguments, each of which is a structure. It simply compares the strings corresponding to the member mother for each structure. If they're the same, they are siblings and 1 is returned. Otherwise, they can't be siblings so 0 is returned. You're ignoring the effects of divorce, in-vitro fertilization, cloning, and any other possibilities that may make this test inadequate.

Pointers to Structures As Function Arguments

Remember that a copy of the value of an argument is transferred to a function when it's called. If the argument is a large structure, this can take quite a bit of time, as well as occupying whatever additional memory the copy of the structure requires. Under these circumstances, you should use a pointer to a structure as an argument. This avoids the memory consumption and the copying time, because now only a copy of the pointer is made. The function will access the original structure directly through the pointer. More often than not, structures are passed to a function using a pointer, just for these reasons of efficiency. You could rewrite the siblings() function like this:

```
int siblings(struct family *member1, struct family *member2)
{
    if(strcmp(member1->mother, member2->mother) == 0)
      return 1;
    else
      return 0;
}
```

Now, there is a downside to this. The pass-by-value mechanism provides good protection against accidental modification of values from within a called function. You lose this if you pass a pointer to a function. On the upside, if you don't need to modify the values pointed to by a pointer argument (you just want to access and use them, for instance), then there's a technique for getting a degree of protection, even though you're passing pointers to a function.

Have another look at the last siblings() function. It doesn't need to modify the structures passed to it—in fact, it only needs to compare members. You could therefore rewrite it like this:

```
int siblings(struct family const *pmember1, struct family const *pmember2)
{
    if(strcmp(pmember1->mother, pmember2->mother) == 0)
      return 1;
    else
      return 0;
}
```

You'll recall the const modifier from earlier in the book, where you used it to make a variable effectively a constant. This function declaration specifies the parameters as type "pointers to constant family structures". This implies that the structures pointed to by the pointers transferred to the function will be treated as constants within the function. Any attempt to change those structures will cause an error message during compilation. Of course, this doesn't affect their status as variables in the calling program, because the const keyword applies only to the values while the function is executing.

Note the difference between the previous definition of the function and this one:

```
int siblings(struct family *const pmember1, struct family *const pmember2)
{
    if(strcmp(pmember1->mother, pmember2->mother) == 0)
      return 1;
    else
      return 0;
}
```

The indirection operator in each parameter definition is now in front of the keyword const, rather than in front of the pointer name as it was before. Does this make a difference? You bet it does. The parameters here are "constant pointers to structures of type family", not "pointers to constant structures". Now you're free to alter the structures themselves in the function, but you must not modify the addresses stored in the pointers. It's the pointers that are protected here, not the structures to which they point.

A Structure As a Function Return Value

There's nothing unusual about returning a structure from a function, either. The function prototype merely has to indicate this return value in the normal way, for example:

```
struct horse my_fun(void);
```

This is a prototype for a function taking no arguments that returns a structure of type horse.

Although you can return a structure from a function like this, it's often more convenient to return a pointer to a structure. Let's explore this in more detail through a working example.

Try It Out: Returning a Pointer to a Structure

To demonstrate how returning a pointer to a structure works, you can rewrite the previous horse example in terms of humans and perform the input in a separate function:

```c
/* Program 11.6 Basics of a family tree */
#include <stdio.h>
#include <ctype.h>
#include <stdlib.h>

struct Family *get_person(void);        /* Prototype for input function */

struct Date
{
   int day;
   int month;
   int year;
};

struct Family                           /* Family structure declaration */
{
   struct Date dob;
   char name[20];
   char father[20];
   char mother[20];
   struct Family *next;                 /* Pointer to next structure     */
   struct Family *previous;             /* Pointer to previous structure */
};

void main()
{
   struct Family *first = NULL;         /* Pointer to first person    */
   struct Family *current = NULL;       /* Pointer to current person  */
   struct Family *last = NULL;          /* Pointer to previous person */
   char more = '\0';                    /* Test value for ending input */

   for( ; ; )
   {
     printf("\nDo you want to enter details of a%s person (Y or N)? ",
                                     first != NULL?"nother " : "" );
     scanf(" %c", &more);
     if(tolower(more) == 'n')
```

(Continued)

```
      break;

    current = get_person();

    if(first == NULL)
    {
      first = current;                /* Set pointer to first Family  */
      last = current;                 /* Remember for next iteration  */
    }
    else
    {
      last->next = current;   /* Set next address for previous Family */
      current->previous = last;   /* Set previous address for current */
      last = current;                 /* Remember for next iteration     */
    }
  }

  /* Now tell them what we know */

  /* Output Family data in reverse order */
  while (current  != NULL)
  {
    printf("\n%s was born %d/%d/%d, and has %s and %s as parents.",
           current->name, current->dob.day, current->dob.month,
           current->dob. year, current->father,  current->mother );

    last = current;      /* Save pointer to enable memory to be freed */
    current = current->previous;   /* current points to previous list */
    free(last);           /* Free memory for the Family we output      */
  }
}

/*   Function to input data on Family members    */
struct Family *get_person(void)
{
  struct Family *temp;          /* Define temporary structure pointer */

  /* Allocate memory for a structure */
  temp = (struct Family*) malloc(sizeof(struct Family));

  printf("\nEnter the name of the person: ");
  scanf("%s", temp -> name );         /* Read the Family's name       */

  printf("\nEnter %s's date of birth (day month year); ", temp->name);
  scanf("%d %d %d", &temp->dob.day, &temp->dob.month, &temp->dob.year);

  printf("\nWho is %s's father? ", temp->name );
  scanf("%s", temp->father );         /* Get the father's name        */

  printf("\nWho is %s's mother? ", temp->name );
```

(Continued)

```
    scanf("%s", temp -> mother );        /* Get the mother's name      */

    temp->next = temp->previous = NULL; /* Set pointers to NULL        */

    return temp;                    /* Return address of Family structure */
}
```

HOW IT WORKS

Although this looks like a lot of code, you should find this example quite straightforward. It operates similarly to the previous example, but it's organized as two functions instead of one.

The structure declaration

```
struct Date
{
   int day;
   int month;
   int year;
};
```

defines a structure type Date with three members, day, month, and year, which are all declared as integers. No instances of the structure are declared at this point.

The next structure declaration is

```
struct Family                       /* Family structure declaration   */
{
   struct Date dob;
   char name[20];
   char father[20];
   char mother[20];
   struct Family *next;               /* Pointer to next structure      */
   struct Family *previous;           /* Pointer to previous structure */
};
```

This defines a structure type Family, which has a Date type structure as its first member. It then has three conventional char arrays as members. The last two members are pointers to structures. They're intended to allow a doubly linked list to be constructed, being pointers to the next and previous structures in the list, respectively.

An important difference between this and the previous examples is that both structure declarations are external to all the functions and are therefore available globally. This is necessary because you want to define Family structure variables in both the functions main() and get_person().

(Continued)

NOTE *Only the specification of the structure type is accessible globally. All the variables of type* Family *declared within each function are local in scope to the function in which they're declared.*

The function get_person() has this prototype:

```
struct Family *get_person(void);  /* Prototype for input function   */
```

This indicates that the function accepts no arguments but returns a pointer to a Family structure.

The process parallels the operation of Program 11.5, with the differences that you have global structure type declarations and you input a structure within a separate function.

After verifying that the user wants to enter data by checking his or her response in more, the function main() calls the function get_person(). Within the function get_person(), you declare this pointer:

```
struct Family *temp;        /* Define temporary structure pointer */
```

This is a "pointer to a Family type structure" and it has local scope. The fact that the declaration of the structure type is global has no bearing on the scope of actual instances of the structure. The scope of each instance that you declare will depend on where the declaration is placed in the program.

The first action within the function get_person() is

```
temp = (struct Family*) malloc(sizeof(struct Family));
```

This call to malloc() obtains sufficient memory to store a structure of type Family and stores the address that's returned in the pointer variable, temp. Although temp is local and will go out of scope at the end of the function get_person(), the memory allocated by malloc() is more permanent. It remains until you free it yourself within the program somewhere, or until you exit from the program completely.

The function get_person() reads in all the basic data for a person and stores that data in the structure pointed to by temp. As it stands, the function will accept any values for the date, but in a real situation you would include code for data validity checking. You could verify that the month value is from 1 to 12 and the day value is valid for the month entered. Because a birth date is being entered, you might verify that it isn't in the future.

(Continued)

The last statement in the function get_person() is

```
return temp;                /* Return address of Family structure */
```

This returns a copy of the pointer to the structure that it has created. Even though temp will no longer exist after the return, the address that it contained that points to the memory block obtained from malloc() is still valid.

Back in main(), the pointer that's returned is stored in the variable current and is also saved in the variable first if this is the first iteration. You do this because you don't want to lose track of the first structure in the list. You also save the pointer current in the variable last, so that on the next iteration you can fill in the backward pointer member, previous, for the current person whose data you've just obtained.

After all the input data has been read, the program outputs a summary to the screen in reverse order, in a similar fashion to the previous examples.

An Exercise in Program Modification

Perhaps we ought to produce an example combining both the use of pointers to structures as arguments and the use of pointers to structures as return values. You can declare some additional pointers, p_to_pa and p_to_ma, in the structure type Family in the previous example by changing that structure declaration as follows:

```
struct Family                          /* Family structure declaration  */
{
  struct Date dob;
  char name[20];
  char father[20];
  char mother[20];
  struct Family *next;                 /* Pointer to next structure     */
  struct Family *previous;             /* Pointer to previous structure */
  struct Family *p_to_pa;              /* Pointer to father structure    */
  struct Family *p_to_ma;              /* Pointer to mother structure    */
};
```

Now you can record the addresses of related structures in the pointer members p_to_pa and p_to_ma. You'll need to set them to NULL in the get_person() function by adding the following statement just before the return statement:

```
temp->p_to_pa = temp->p_to_ma = NULL;      /* Set pointers to NULL  */
```

You can now augment the program with some additional functions that will fill in your new pointers p_to_pa and p_to_ma once data for everybody has been entered. You could code this by adding two functions. The first function, set_ancestry(), will accept pointers to Family structures as arguments and check whether the structure pointed to by the second argument is the father or mother of the structure pointed to by the first argument. If it is, the appropriate pointer will be updated to reflect this, and 1 will be returned; otherwise 0 will be returned. Here's the code:

```
char set_ancestry(struct Family *pmember1, struct Family *pmember2)
{
    if(strcmp(pmember1->father, pmember2->name) == 0)
    {
        pmember1->p_to_pa = pmember2;
        return 1;
    }

    if( strcmp(pmember1->mother, pmember2->name) == 0)
    {
        pmember1->p_to_ma = pmember2;
        return 1;
    }
    else
        return 0;
}
```

The second function will test all possible relationships between two Family structures:

```
/* Fill in pointers for mother or father relationships */
char related (struct Family *pmember1, struct Family *pmember2)
{
    return set_ancestry(pmember1, pmember2) ||
                        set_ancestry(pmember2, pmember1);
}
```

The related() function calls set_ancestry() twice in the return statement to test all possibilities of relationship. The return value will be 1 if either of the calls to set_ancestry() returns the value 1. A calling program can use the return value from related() to determine whether or not a pointer has been filled in.

NOTE *Because you use the library function* strcmp() *here, you must add an* #include *directive for* string.h *at the beginning of the program.*

You now need to add some code to the main() function that you created in Program 11.6 to use the function related() to fill in all the pointers in all the structures where valid addresses can be found. You can insert the following code into main() directly after the loop that inputs all the initial data:

```
current = first;

while(current->next != NULL) /* Check for relation for each person in */
{                            /* the list up to second to last          */
  int parents = 0;        /* Declare parent count local to this block */
  last = current->next;   /* Get the pointer to the next              */

  while(last != NULL)     /* This loop tests current person           */
  {                       /* against all the remainder in the list    */
    if(related(current, last))        /* Found a parent ?             */
      if(++parents == 2)    /* Yes, update count and check it         */
        break;              /* Exit inner loop if both parents found  */

    last = last->next;      /* Get the address of the next            */
  }
  current = current->next;  /* Next in the list to check              */
}

/* Now tell them what we know etc. */
/* rest of output code etc.  ...   */
```

This is a relatively self-contained block of code to fill in the parent pointers where possible. Starting with the first structure, a check is made with each of the succeeding structures to see if a parent relationship exists. The checking stops for a given structure if two parents have been found (which would have filled in both pointers) or the end of the list is reached.

Of necessity, some structures will have pointers where the values can't be updated. Because you don't have an infinite list, and barring some very strange family history, there will always be someone whose parent records aren't included. The process will take each of the structures in the list and check it against all the following structures to see if they're related, at least up to the point where the two parents have been discovered.

Of course, you also need to insert prototypes for the functions related() and test() at the beginning of the program, immediately after the prototype for the function get_person(). These prototypes would look like this:

```
char related(struct Family *pmember1, struct Family *pmember2);
char set_ancestry(struct Family *pmember1, struct Family *pmember2);
```

To show that the pointers have been successfully inserted, you can extend the final output to display information about the parents of each person by adding some additional statements immediately after the last printf(). You can also amend the output loop to start from `first` in a similar manner to that employed in Program 11.4; the output loop will thus be as follows:

```
/* Output Family data in correct order */
current = first;

while (current != NULL)              /* Output Family data in correct order */
{
  printf("\n%s was born %d/%d/%d, and has %s and %s as parents.",
            current->name, current->dob.day, current->dob.month,
          current->dob. year, current->father,  current->mother);
  if(current->p_to_pa != NULL )
    printf("\n\t%s's birth date is %d/%d/%d  ",
            current->father, current->p_to_pa->dob.day,
                      current->p_to_pa->dob.month,
                      current->p_to_pa->dob.year);
  if(current->p_to_ma != NULL)
    printf("and %s's birth date is %d/%d/%d.\n  ",
            current->mother, current->p_to_ma->dob.day,
                      current->p_to_ma->dob.month,
                      current->p_to_ma->dob.year);

  current = current->next;           /* current points to next in list     */
}
```

This should then produce the dates of birth of both parents for each person using the pointers to the parents' structures, but only if the pointers have been set to valid addresses. Note that you don't free the memory in the loop. If you did this, the additional statements to output the parents' dates of birth would produce junk output when the parent structure appeared earlier in the list. So finally, you must add a separate loop at the end of `main()` to delete the memory when the output is complete:

```
/* Now free the memory */
current = first;
while(current != NULL)
{
  last = current;     /* Save pointer to enable memory to be freed */
  current = current->next; /* current points to next in list       */
  free(last);         /* Free memory for last                    */
}
```

If you've assembled all the pieces into a new example, you should have a sizeable new program to play with. Here's the sort of output that you should get:

```
Do you want to enter details of a  person (Y or N)? y

Enter the name of the person: Jack

Enter Jack's date of birth (day month year); 1 1 65
```

```
Who is Jack's father? Bill

Who is Jack's mother? Nell

Do you want to enter details of another  person (Y or N)? y

Enter the name of the person: Mary

Enter Mary's date of birth (day month year); 3 3 67

Who is Mary's father? Bert

Who is Mary's mother? Moll

Do you want to enter details of another  person (Y or N)? y

Enter the name of the person: Ben

Enter Ben's date of birth (day month year); 2 2 89

Who is Ben's father? Jack

Who is Ben's mother? Mary

Do you want to enter details of another  person (Y or N)? n

Jack was born 1/1/65, and has Bill and Nell as parents.
Mary was born 3/3/67, and has Bert and Moll as parents.
Ben was born 2/2/89, and has Jack and Mary as parents.
     Jack's birth date is 1/1/65  and Mary's birth date is 3/3/67.
```

You could try to modify the program to output everybody in chronological order or possibly work out how many offspring each person has.

Sharing Memory

You've already seen how you can save memory through the use of bit-fields, which are typically applied to logical variables. C has a further capability that allows you to place several variables in the same memory area. This can be applied somewhat more widely than bit-fields when memory is short, because circumstances frequently arise in practice in which you're working with several variables, but only one of them holds a valid value at any given moment.

Another instance in which you can share memory between a number of variables to some advantage is when your program processes a number of different kinds of data record, but only one kind at a time, and the kind to be processed is determined at execution time. A third possibility is that you want to access the same data at different times, and assume it's of a different type on different occasions. You might have a group of variables of numeric data types, for instance, that you want to treat as simply an array of type char so that you can move them about as a single chunk of data.

Unions

The facility in C that allows the same memory area to be shared by a number of different variables is called a **union**. The syntax for declaring a union is similar to that used for structures, and a union is usually given a tag name in the same way. You use the keyword union to define a union. For example, the following statement declares a union to be shared by three variables:

```
union u_example
{
   float decval;
   int *pnum;
   double my_value;
} U1;
```

This statement declares a union with the tag name u_example, which shares memory between a floating-point value decval, a pointer to an integer pnum, and a double precision floating-point variable my_value. The statement also defines one instance of the union with a variable name of U1. You can declare further instances of this union with a statement such as this:

```
union u_example U2, U3;
```

Members of a union are accessed in exactly the same way as members of a structure. For example, to assign values to members of U1 and U2, you can write this:

```
U1.decval = 2.5;
U2.decval = 3.5 * U1.decval;
```

....

Try It Out: Using Unions

Here's a simple example that makes use of a union:

```
/* Program 11.7 The operation of a union */
#include <stdio.h>

void main()
{
   union u_example
   {
```

(Continued)

```
        float decval;
        int pnum;
        double my_value;
    } U1;

    U1.my_value = 125.5;
    U1.pnum = 10;
    U1.decval = 1000.5f;
    printf("\ndecval = %f   pnum = %d   my_value = %lf",
                    U1.decval, U1.pnum, U1.my_value );

    printf("\nU1 size = %d\ndecval size = %d   pnum size = %d   my_value"
                        " size = %d",sizeof U1, sizeof U1.decval,
                            sizeof U1.pnum, sizeof U1.my_value);
}
```

HOW IT WORKS

This example demonstrates the structure and operation of a union. You declare the union U1 as follows:

```
union u_example
{
    float decval;
    int pnum;
    double my_value;
} U1;
```

The three members of the union are of different types and they each require a different amount of storage (assuming your compiler assigns 2 bytes to variables of type int).

With the assignment statements, you assign a value to each of the members of the union instance U1 in turn:

```
    U1.my_value = 125.5;
    U1.pnum = 10;
    U1.decval = 1000.5f;
```

Notice that you reference each member of the union in the same way as you do members of a structure.

The next two statements output each of the three member values, the size of the union U1, and the size of each of its members. You get this output (or something close if your machine assigns 4 bytes to variables of type int):

(Continued)

```
decval = 1000.500000    pnum = 8192    my_value = 125.50016
U1 size = 8
decval size = 4    pnum size = 2    my_value size = 8
```

The first thing to note is that the last variable that was assigned a value is correct, and the other two have been corrupted. This is to be expected, because they all share the same memory space. The second thing to notice is how little the member my_value has been corrupted. This is because only the least significant part of my_value is being modified. In a practical situation, such a small error could easily be overlooked, but the ultimate consequences could be dire. You need to take great care when using unions that you aren't using invalid data.

 NOTE *You can see from the output of the sizes of the union and its members that the size of the union is the same as the size of the largest member.*

Pointers to Unions

You can also define a pointer to a union with a statement such as this:

```
union u_example *pU;
```

Once the pointer has been defined, you can modify members of the union, via the pointer, with these statements:

```
pU = &U2;
U1.decval = pU->decval;
```

The expression on the right of the second assignment is equivalent to U2.decval.

Initializing Unions

If you wish to initialize an instance of a union when you declare it, you can initialize it only with a constant of the same type as the first variable in the union. The union just declared, u_example, can be initialized only with a float constant, as in the following:

```
union u_example U4 = 3.14f;
```

You can always rearrange the sequence of members in a definition of a union so that the member that you want to initialize occurs first. The sequence of members has no other significance, because all members overlap in the same memory area.

Structures As Union Members

Structures and arrays can be members of a union. It's also possible for a union to be a member of a structure. To illustrate this, you could write

```
struct my_structure
{
    int num1;
    float num2;
    union
    {
      int *pnum;
      float *pfnum;
    } my_U;
} samples[5];
```

Here, you declare a structure type, `my_structure`, that contains a union without a tag name, so instances of the union can exist only within instances of the structure. You also define an array of five instances of the structure, referenced by the variable name `samples`. The union within the structure shares memory between two pointers.

To reference members of the union, you use the same notation that you used for nested structures. For example, to access the pointer to `int` in the third element of the structure array, you use the expression appearing on the left in the following statement:

```
samples[2].my_U.pnum = &my_num;
```

You're assuming here that the variable `my_num` has been declared as type `int`.

It's important to realize that when you're using a value stored in a union, you always retrieve the last value assigned. This may seem obvious, but in practice it's all too easy to use a value as `float` that has most recently been stored as an integer, and sometimes the error can be quite subtle, as shown by the curious output of `my_value` in Program 11.7. Naturally, you'll usually end up with garbage if you do this.

Defining Your Own Data Types

With structures you've come pretty close to defining your own data types. It doesn't look quite right because you must use the keyword `struct` in your declarations of structure variables. Declaration of a variable for a built-in type is simpler. However, there's a feature of the C language that permits you to get over this and make the declaration of variables of structure types you've defined follow exactly the same syntax as for the built-in types. You've already seen this in Chapter 4, but here, with structures, it really comes into its own.

Structures and the typedef Facility

Suppose you have a structure for geometric points with three coordinates, x, y, and z, that you define with the following statement:

```
struct pts
{
   int x;
   int y;
   int z;
};
```

You can now define an alternative name for declaring such structures using the keyword typedef. The following statement shows how you might do this:

```
typedef struct pts Point;
```

This statement specifies that the name Point is a synonym for struct pts.

When you want to declare some instances of the structure pts, you can use a statement such as this:

```
Point start_pt;
Point end_pt;
```

Here, you declare the two structure variables start_pt and end_pt. The struct keyword isn't necessary, and you have a very natural way of declaring structure variables. The appearance of the statement is exactly the same form as a declaration for a float or an int.

You could have combined the typedef and the structure declaration as follows:

```
typedef struct pts
{
   int x;
   int y;
   int z;
} Point;
```

Don't confuse this with a basic struct declaration. Here, Point isn't a structure variable name—this is a type name you're defining. When you need to declare structure variables, as you've just seen, you can use a statement such as this:

```
Point my_pt;
```

There's nothing to prevent you from having several types defined that pertain to a single structure type, or any other type for that matter, although this can be confusing in some situations. One application of this that can help to make your program more understandable is where you're using a basic type for a specific kind of value and you would like to use a type name to reflect the kind of variable you're creating. For example, suppose your application involves weights of different kinds—weights of components and weights of assembly, for instance. You might find it useful to define a type name, weight, as a synonym for type double. You could do this with the following statement:

```
typedef double weight;
```

You can now declare variables of type weight:

```
weight piston = 6.5;
weight valve = 0.35;
```

Of course, these variables are all of type double because weight is just a synonym for double, and you can still declare variables of type double in the usual way.

Simplifying Code Using typedef

Another useful application of typedef is to simplify complicated types that can arise. Suppose you had occasion to frequently define pointers to the structure pts. You could define a type to do this for you with this statement:

```
typedef struct pts *pPoint;
```

Now, when you want to declare some pointers, you could just write this:

```
pPoint pfirst;
pPoint plast;
```

The two variables declared here are both pointers to structures of type pts. The declarations are less error-prone to write and they're also easier to understand.

In Chapter 9 I discussed pointers to functions, which are declared with an even more complicated notation. One of the examples had the pointer declaration

```
int(*pfun)(int, int);                    /* Function pointer declaration */
```

If you were expecting to use several pointers to functions of this kind in a program, you could use typedef to declare a generic type for such declarations with this statement:

```
typedef int (*function_pointer)(int, int);    /* Function pointer type */
```

This doesn't declare a variable of type "pointer to a function". This declares function_pointer as a type name that you can use to declare a "pointer to function", so you could replace the original declaration of pfun with this statement:

```
function_pointer pfun;
```

This is evidently much simpler than what you started with. The benefit in simplicity is even more marked if you have several such pointers to declare, because you can declare three pointers to functions with the following statements:

```
function_pointer pfun1;
function_pointer pfun2;
function_pointer pfun3;
```

Of course, you can also initialize them, so if you assume you have the functions `sum()`, `difference()`, and `product()`, you can declare and initialize your pointers with

```
function_pointer pfun1 = sum;
function_pointer pfun2 = difference;
function_pointer pfun3 = product;
```

The type name that you've defined naturally only applies to "pointers to functions" with the arguments and return type that you specified in the `typedef` statement. If you want something different, then you can simply define another type.

Designing a Program

You've reached the end of another long chapter, and it's time to see how you can put what you've learned into practice in the context of a more substantial example.

The Problem

Numerical data is almost always easier and faster to understand when it's presented graphically. The problem that you're going tackle is to write a program that produces a vertical bar chart from a set of data values. This is an interesting problem for a couple of reasons. It will enable you to make use of structures in a practical context. The problem also involves working out how to place and present the bar chart within the space available, which is the kind of messy manipulation that comes up quite often in real-world applications.

The Analysis

You won't be making any assumptions about the size of the "page" that you're going to output to, or the number of columns, or even the scale of the chart. Instead, you'll just write a function that accepts a dimension for the output page and then makes the set of bars fit the page if possible. This will make the function useful in virtually any situation. You'll store the values in a sequence of structures in a linked list. In this way, you'll just need to pass the first structure to the function, and the function will be able to get at them all. You'll keep the structure very simple, but you can embellish it later with other information of your own design.

Assume that the order in which the bars are to appear in the chart is going to be the same as the order in which the data values were entered, so you won't need to sort them. There will be two functions in your program: a function that generates the bar chart and a function main() that exercises the bar chart generation process.

These are the steps required:

1. Write the bar-chart function.

2. Write a main() function to test the bar-chart function once you've written it.

The Solution

This section outlines the steps you'll take to solve the problem.

Step 1

Obviously, you're going to use a structure in this program because that's what this chapter has been about. The first stage is to design the structure that you'll use throughout the program. You'll use a typedef so that you don't have to keep reusing the keyword struct:

```
/* Program 11.8 Generating a bar chart */
#include <stdio.h>

typedef struct barTAG
{
   double value;
   struct barTAG *pnextbar;
}bar;

void main()
{
   /* Code for main */
}

/* Definition of the bar-chart function */
```

The barTAG structure will define a bar simply by its value. Notice how you define the pointer in the structure to the next structure. This will enable you to store the bars as a linked list, which has the benefit that you can allocate memory as you go so none will be wasted. This suits this situation because you'll only ever want to step through the bars from the first to the last. You'll create them in sequence from the input values and append each new bar to the tail of the previous one. You'll then create the visual representation of the bar chart by stepping through the structures in the linked list. You may have thought that the typedef statement would mean that you could use the bar type name that you're defining here. However, you have to use struct barTAG here because at this point the compiler hasn't finished processing the typedef yet, so bar isn't defined. In other words, the barTAG structure is analyzed first by the compiler, after which the typedef can be expedited to define the meaning of bar.

Now you can specify the function prototype for the bar-chart function and use the skeleton of the definition for the function. It will need to have parameters for a pointer to the first bar in the linked list, the page height and width, and the title for the chart to be produced:

```
/* Program 11.8 Generating a bar chart */
#include <stdio.h>

#define PAGE_HEIGHT  20
#define PAGE_WIDTH   40

typedef struct barTAG
{
   double value;
   struct barTAG *pnextbar;
}bar;

typedef unsigned int uint;      /* Type definition */

/* Function prototype */
int bar_chart(bar *pfirstbar, uint page_width, uint page_height, char *title);

void main()
{
   /* Code for main */
}

int bar_chart(bar *pfirstbar, uint page_width, uint page_height,
                                              char *title)
{
   /* Code for function... */
   return 0;
}
```

You've added a typedef to define uint as an alternative to unsigned int. This will shorten statements that declare variables of type unsigned int.

Next, you can add some declarations and code for the basic data that you need for the bar chart. You'll need the maximum and minimum values for the bars and the vertical height of the chart, which will be determined by the difference between the maximum and minimum values. You also need to calculate the width of a bar, given the page width and the number of bars, and you must adjust the height to accommodate a horizontal axis and the title:

```
/* Program 11.8 Generating a bar chart */
#include <stdio.h>

#define PAGE_HEIGHT  20
#define PAGE_WIDTH   40
```

```
typedef struct barTAG
{
   double value;
   struct barTAG *pnextbar;
}bar;

typedef unsigned int uint;     /* Type definition */

/* Function prototype */
int bar_chart(bar *pfirstbar, uint page_width, uint page_height,
                                             char *title);

void main()
{
   /* Code for main */
}

int bar_chart(bar *pfirstbar, uint page_width, uint page_height,
                                             char *title)
{
   bar *plastbar = pfirstbar;   /* Pointer to previous bar        */
   double max = 0.0;            /* Maximum bar value              */
   double min = 0.0;            /* Minimum bar value              */
   double vert_scale = 0.0;     /* Unit step in vertical direction */
   uint bar_count = 1;          /* Number of bars - at least 1    */
   uint barwidth = 0;           /* Width of a bar                 */
   uint space = 2;              /* spaces between bars            */

   /* Find maximum and minimum of all bar values */

   /* Set max and min to first bar value */
   max = min = plastbar->value;

   while((plastbar = plastbar->pnextbar) != NULL)
   {
     bar_count++;                /* Increment bar count */
     max = (max < plastbar->value)? plastbar->value : max;
     min = (min > plastbar->value)? plastbar->value : min;
   }
   vert_scale = (max - min)/page_height; /* Calculate step length */

   /* Check bar width */
   if((barwidth = page_width/bar_count - space) < 1)
   {
     printf("\nPage width too narrow.\n");
     return -1;
   }

   /* Code for rest of the function...  */
   return 0;
}
```

The space variable stores the number of spaces separating one bar from the next, and you arbitrarily assign the value 2 for this.

You will, of necessity, be outputting the chart a row at a time. Therefore, you'll need a string that corresponds to a section across a bar that you can use to draw that bar row by row and a string of the same length that contains spaces to use when there's no bar at a particular position across the page. Let's add the code to create these:

```c
/* Program 11.8 Generating a bar chart */
#include <stdio.h>
#include <stdlib.h>

#define PAGE_HEIGHT  20
#define PAGE_WIDTH   40

typedef struct barTAG
{
   double value;
   struct barTAG *pnextbar;
}bar;

typedef unsigned int uint;      /* Type definition */

/* Function prototype */
int bar_chart(bar *pfirstbar, uint page_width, uint page_height,
                                       char *title);

void main()
{
   /* Code for main */
}

int bar_chart(bar *pfirstbar, uint page_width, uint page_height,
                                       char *title)
{
   bar *plastbar = pfirstbar;  /* Pointer to previous bar         */
   double max = 0.0;           /* Maximum bar value               */
   double min = 0.0;           /* Minimum bar value               */
   double vert_scale = 0.0;    /* Unit step in vertical direction */
   uint bar_count = 1;         /* Number of bars - at least 1     */
   uint barwidth = 0;          /* Width of a bar                  */
   uint space = 2;             /* spaces between bars             */
   uint i = 0;                 /* Loop counter                    */
   char *column = NULL;        /* Pointer to bar column section   */
   char *blank = NULL;         /* Blank string for bar+space      */

   /* Find maximum and minimum of all bar values */

   /* Set max and min to first bar value */
   max = min = plastbar->value;
```

```
    while((plastbar = plastbar->pnextbar) != NULL)
    {
      bar_count++;                 /* Increment bar count */
      max = (max < plastbar->value)? plastbar->value : max;
      min = (min > plastbar->value)? plastbar->value : min;
    }
    vert_scale = (max - min)/page_height; /* Calculate step length */

    /* Check bar width */
    if((barwidth = page_width/bar_count - space) < 1)
    {
      printf("\nPage width too narrow.\n");
      return -1;
    }

    /* Set up a string that will be used to build the columns */

    /* Get the memory */
    if((column = malloc(barwidth + space + 1)) == NULL)
    {
      printf("\nFailed to allocate memory in barchart()"
                          " - terminating program.\n");
      abort();
    }
    for(i = 0 ; i < space ; i++)
      *(column+i)=' ';           /* Blank the space between bars */
    for( ; i < space+barwidth ; i++)
      *(column+i)='#';           /* Enter the bar characters    */
    *(column+i) = '\0';          /* Add string terminator       */

    /* Set up a string that will be used as a blank column */

    /* Get the memory */
    if((blank = malloc(barwidth + space + 1)) == NULL)
    {
      printf("\nFailed to allocate memory in barchart()"
                          " - terminating program.\n");
      abort();
    }

    for(i = 0 ; i < space+barwidth ; i++)
      *(blank+i) = ' ';          /* Blank total width of bar+space */
    *(blank+i) = '\0';           /* Add string terminator          */

    /* Code for rest of the function... */
    free(blank);                 /* Free memory for blank string  */
    free(column);                /* Free memory for column string */
    return 0;
}
```

You'll draw a bar using '#' characters. When you draw a bar, you'll write a string containing space spaces and barwidth '#' characters. You allocate the memory for this dynamically using the library function malloc(), so you must add an #include directive for the header file stdlib.h. The string that you'll use to draw a bar is column, and blank is a string of the same length containing spaces. After the bar chart has been drawn and just before you exit, you free the memory occupied by column and blank.

Next, you can add the final piece of code that draws the chart:

```
/* Program 11.8 Generating a bar chart */
#include <stdio.h>
#include <stdlib.h>

#define PAGE_HEIGHT  20
#define PAGE_WIDTH   40
#define TRUE  1
#define FALSE 0

typedef struct barTAG
{
   double value;
   struct barTAG *pnextbar;
}bar;

typedef unsigned int uint;     /* Type definition */

/* Function prototype */
int bar_chart(bar *pfirstbar, uint page_width, uint page_height,
                                            char *title);

void main()
{
   /* Code for main */
}

int bar_chart(bar *pfirstbar, uint page_width, uint page_height,
                                            char *title)
{
   bar *plastbar = pfirstbar;   /* Pointer to previous bar            */
   double max = 0.0;            /* Maximum bar value                  */
   double min = 0.0;            /* Minimum bar value                  */
   double vert_scale = 0.0;     /* Unit step in vertical direction    */
   double position = 0.0;       /* Current vertical position on chart */
   uint bar_count = 1;          /* Number of bars - at least 1        */
   uint barwidth = 0;           /* Width of a bar                     */
   uint space = 2;              /* spaces between bars                */
   uint i = 0;                  /* Loop counter                       */
   uint bars = 0;               /* Loop counter through bars          */
   char *column = NULL;         /* Pointer to bar column section      */
   char *blank = NULL;          /* Blank string for bar+space         */
   int axis = FALSE;            /* Indicates axis drawn               */
```

```
/* Find maximum and minimum of all bar values */

/* Set max and min to first bar value */
max = min = plastbar->value;

while((plastbar = plastbar->pnextbar) != NULL)
{
  bar_count++;                    /* Increment bar count */
  max = (max < plastbar->value)? plastbar->value : max;
  min = (min > plastbar->value)? plastbar->value : min;
}
vert_scale = (max - min)/page_height; /* Calculate step length */

/* Check bar width */
if((barwidth = page_width/bar_count - space) < 1)
{
  printf("\nPage width too narrow.\n");
  return -1;
}

/* Set up a string that will be used to build the columns */

/* Get the memory */
if((column = malloc(barwidth + space + 1)) == NULL)
{
  printf("\nFailed to allocate memory in barchart()"
                       " - terminating program.\n");
  abort();
}
for(i = 0 ; i < space ; i++)
  *(column+i)=' ';          /* Blank the space between bars */
for( ; i < space+barwidth ; i++)
  *(column+i)='#';          /* Enter the bar characters      */
*(column+i) = '\0';         /* Add string terminator         */

/* Set up a string that will be used as a blank column */

/* Get the memory */
if((blank = malloc(barwidth + space + 1)) == NULL)
{
  printf("\nFailed to allocate memory in barchart()"
                       " - terminating program.\n");
  abort();
}

for(i = 0 ; i < space+barwidth ; i++)
  *(blank+i) = ' ';         /* Blank total width of bar+space */
*(blank+i) = '\0';          /* Add string terminator          */

printf("^ %s\n", title);    /* Output the chart title         */
```

```
/* Draw the bar chart */
position = max;
for(i = 0 ; i <= page_height ; i++)
{
  /* Check if we need to output the horizontal axis */
  if(position <= 0.0 && !axis)
  {
    printf("+");              /* Start of horizontal axis    */
    for(bars = 0; bars < bar_count*(barwidth+space); bars++)
      printf("-");            /* Output horizontal axis      */
    printf(">\n");
    axis = TRUE;              /* Axis was drawn              */
    position -= vert_scale;/* Decrement position          */
    continue;
  }
  printf("|");               /* Output vertical axis        */
  plastbar = pfirstbar;      /* start with the first bar    */

  /* For each bar... */
  for(bars = 1; bars <= bar_count; bars++)
  {
    /* If position is between axis and value, output column */
    /* otherwise output blank                               */
    printf("%s", position <= plastbar->value &&
                 plastbar->value >= 0.0 && position > 0.0 ||
                 position >= plastbar->value &&
                 plastbar->value <= 0.0 &&
                 position <= 0.0 ? column: blank);
    plastbar = plastbar->pnextbar;
  }
  printf("\n");              /* End the line of output      */
  position -= vert_scale;   /* Decrement position          */
}
if(!axis)                   /* Have we output the horizontal axis? */
{                           /* No, so do it now            */
  printf("+");
  for(bars = 0; bars < bar_count*(barwidth+space); bars++)
    printf("-");
  printf(">\n");
}

free(blank);               /* Free memory for blank string   */
free(column);              /* Free memory for column string  */
return 0;
}
```

The for loop outputs page_height lines of characters. Each line will represent a distance of vert_scale on the vertical axis. You get this value by dividing page_height by the difference between the maximum and minimum values. Therefore, the first line of output corresponds to position having the value max, and it's decremented by vert_scale on each iteration until it reaches min.

On each line, you must decide first if you need to output the horizontal axis. This will be necessary when position is less than or equal to 0 and you haven't already displayed the axis.

On lines other than the horizontal axis, you must decide what to display for each bar position. This is done in the inner for loop that repeats for each bar. The conditional operator in the printf() call outputs either column or blank. You output column if position is between the value of the bar and 0, and you output blank otherwise. Having output a complete row of bar segments, you output '\n' to end the line and decrement the value of position.

It's possible that all the bars could be positive, in which case you need to make sure that the horizontal axis is output after the loop is complete, because it won't be output from within the loop.

Step 2

Now you just need to implement main() to exercise the bar_chart() function:

```
/* Program 11.8 Generating a bar chart */
#include <stdio.h>
#include <string.h>
#include <stdlib.h>

#define PAGE_HEIGHT  20
#define PAGE_WIDTH   40
#define TRUE   1
#define FALSE  0

typedef struct barTAG        /* Bar structure       */
{
    double value;            /* Value of bar        */
    struct barTAG *pnextbar; /* Pointer to next bar */
}bar;                        /* Type for a bar      */

typedef unsigned int uint;   /* Type definition     */

/* Function prototype */
int bar_chart(bar *pfirstbar, uint page_width, uint page_height, char *title);

int main()
{
    bar firstbar;            /* First bar structure */
    bar *plastbar = NULL;    /* Pointer to last bar */
    char value[80];          /* Input buffer        */
    char title[80];          /* Chart title         */

    printf("\nEnter the chart title: ");
    gets(title);             /* Read chart title    */
```

```
  for( ;; )                              /* Loop for bar input  */
  {
    printf("Enter the value of the bar, or use quit to end: ");
    gets(value);

    if(strcmp(value, "quit") == 0)       /* quit entered?      */
     break;                              /* then input finished */

    /* Store in next bar */
    if(plastbar == NULL)                 /* First time?        */
    {
      firstbar.pnextbar = NULL;          /* Initialize next pointer */
      plastbar = &firstbar;              /* Use the first          */
    }
    else
    {
      /* Get memory */
      if((plastbar->pnextbar = malloc(sizeof(bar))) == NULL)
      {
        printf("Oops! Couldn't allocate memory\n");
        return -1;
      }
      plastbar = plastbar->pnextbar;     /* Old next is new bar  */
      plastbar->pnextbar = NULL;         /* New bar next is NULL */
    }
    plastbar->value = atof(value);       /* Store the value      */
  }

  /* Create bar-chart */
  bar_chart(&firstbar, PAGE_WIDTH, PAGE_HEIGHT, title);

  /* We are done, so release all the memory we allocated */
  while(firstbar.pnextbar != NULL)
  {
    plastbar = firstbar.pnextbar;           /* Save pointer to next */
    firstbar.pnextbar = plastbar->pnextbar; /* Get one after next   */
    free(plastbar);                         /* Free next memory     */
  }
  return 0;
}

int bar_chart(bar *pfirstbar, uint page_width, uint page_height, char *title)
{
  /* Implementation of function as before... */
}
```

After reading the chart title using gets(), you read successive values in the for loop. For each value other than the first, you allocate the memory for a new bar structure before storing the value. Of course, you keep track of the first structure, firstbar, because this is the link to all the others, and you track the pointer to the last structure you added so that you can update its pnextbar pointer when you add another. Once you have all the values, you call bar_chart() to produce the chart. Finally, you delete the memory for the bars. Note that you need to take care to not delete firstbar, as you didn't allocate the memory for this dynamically. You need an #include directive for string.h because you use the gets() function.

All you do then is add a line to main() that actually prints the chart from the values typed in. Typical output from the example is shown here:

```
Enter the chart title: Trial Bar Chart
Enter the value of the bar, or use quit to end: 6
Enter the value of the bar, or use quit to end: 3
Enter the value of the bar, or use quit to end: -5
Enter the value of the bar, or use quit to end: -7
Enter the value of the bar, or use quit to end: 9
Enter the value of the bar, or use quit to end: 4
Enter the value of the bar, or use quit to end: quit


^ Trial Bar Chart
|                     ####
|                     ####
|                     ####
|                     ####
|    ####             ####
|    ####             ####
|    ####             ####
|    ####             ####  ####
|    ####  ####       ####  ####
|    ####  ####       ####  ####
|    ####  ####       ####  ####
|    ####  ####       ####  ####
+-----------------------------------> 
|          ####  ####
|          ####  ####
|          ####  ####
|          ####  ####
|          ####  ####
|                ####
|                ####
|                ####
```

Summary

This has been something of a marathon chapter, but its topic is extremely important. Having a good grasp of structures rates alongside understanding pointers and functions in importance if you want to use C effectively.

Most real-world applications deal with things such as people, cars, or materials, which require several different values to represent them. Structures in C provide a ready tool for dealing with these sorts of complex objects. Although some of the operations may seem a little complicated, remember that you're dealing with complicated entities, so the complexity isn't implicit in the programming capability; rather, it's built into the problem you're tackling.

In the next chapter, you'll look at how you can store data in external files. This will, of course, include the ability to store structures.

Exercises

The following exercises enable you to try out what you've learned in this chapter. If you get stuck, look back over the chapter for help. If you're still stuck, you can download the solutions from the Downloads area of the Apress website (http://www.apress.com), but that really should be a last resort.

Exercise 11-1. Define a struct type with the name Length that represents a length in yards, feet, and inches. Define an add() function that will add two Length arguments and return the sum as type Length. Define a second function, show(), that will display the value of its Length argument. Write a program that will use the Length type and the add() and show() functions to sum an arbitrary number of lengths in yards, feet, and inches that are entered from the keyboard and output the total length.

Exercise 11-2. Define a struct type that contains a person's name consisting of a first name and a last name, plus the person's phone number. Use this struct in a program that will allow one or more names and corresponding numbers to be entered and will store the entries in an array of structures. The program should allow a second name to be entered and output all the numbers corresponding to the name, and optionally output all the names with their corresponding numbers.

Exercise 11-3. Modify or reimplement the program from the previous exercise to store the structures in a linked list in ascending alphabetical order of the names.

Exercise 11-4. Write a program to use a struct to count the number of occurrences of each different word in a paragraph of text that's entered from the keyboard.

Managing Large Amounts of Data

IF YOUR COMPUTER COULD ONLY EVER PROCESS data stored within the main memory of the machine, the scope and variety of applications that you could deal with would be severely limited. Virtually all serious business applications require more data than would fit into main memory and depend on the ability to process data that's stored on an external device, such as a fixed disk drive. In this chapter you'll explore how you can process data stored on an external device.

C provides a range of functions in the header file stdio.h for writing to and reading from an external device. The external device is typically a fixed disk drive or a floppy disk, but not exclusively. Because, consistent with the philosophy of the C language, the facilities that you'll use are device independent, they apply to virtually any external storage device. However, you'll assume in this chapter's examples that you're dealing with disk files.

In this chapter you'll learn

- What a file is in C

- How files are processed

- How to write and read formatted files and binary files

- How to retrieve data from a file by direct random access to the information

- How to use temporary work files in a program

- How to write a file viewer program

The Concept of a File

With all the examples you've seen up to now, any data that the user entered when the program was executed was lost once the program finished running. At the moment, if the user wants to run the program with the same data, he or she must enter it again each time. There are lots of occasions when this is not only inconvenient, but also makes the programming task impossible.

If you want to maintain a directory of names, addresses, and telephone numbers, for instance, a program in which you have to enter all the names, addresses, and telephone numbers each time you run it is worse than useless! The answer is to store data on permanent storage that continues to be maintained after your computer is switched off. As I'm sure you know, this storage technique is called a **file**, and it's usually stored on a hard disk.

You're probably familiar with the basic mechanics of how a disk works. If so, this can help you recognize when a particular approach to file usage is efficient and when it isn't. On the other hand, if you know nothing about disk file mechanics, don't worry at this point. There's nothing in the concept of file processing in C that depends on any knowledge of physical storage devices.

A file is essentially a serial sequence of bytes, as illustrated in Figure 12-1.

Figure 12-1. Structure of a file

A file has a beginning and an end, and it has a **current position**, typically defined as so many bytes from the beginning. The current position is where any file action (a read from the file or a write to the file) will take place. You can move the current position to any other point in the file. A new current position can be specified as an offset from the beginning of the file or, in some circumstances, as a positive or negative offset from the previous current position.

Of course, you can write any data you like to a file. As you'll see, there are various ways that you can write data to a file, but it ultimately ends up as just a series of bytes, whatever the data is. This means that when the file is read, the program must know what sort of data the file represents. You've seen many times now that exactly what a series of bytes represents is dependent upon how you interpret it. A sequence of 12 bytes could be twelve characters, twelve 8-bit signed integers, twelve 8-bit unsigned integers, six 16-bit signed integers, a 32-bit integer followed by an 8-byte floating-point value, and so on. All of these will be perfectly valid interpretations of the data, so it's important that a program reading a file has the correct assumptions about how it was written.

Processing Files

The files that are resident on your disk drive each have a name, and the rules for naming files will be determined by your operating system.

When you write a program to process a file, it wouldn't be particularly convenient if the program would only work with a specific file with a particular name. If it did, you would need to produce a different program for each file you might want to process. For this reason, when you process a file in C, your program references a file through a **file pointer**. A file pointer is associated with a particular file when the program is run so that, on different occasions, the program can work with different files. In the examples in this chapter, I'll use Microsoft Windows file names. If you're using a different operating system environment, such as UNIX, you'll need to adjust the names of the files appropriately.

If you want to use several files simultaneously, you need a separate file pointer for each file, although as soon as you've finished using a file, you can associate the file pointer with another file. So if you need to process several files, but you'll be working with them one at a time, then you need only the one file pointer.

Opening a File

You associate a specific external file name with an internal file pointer variable through a process referred to as **opening** a file. This is achieved through the standard library function fopen(), which returns the file pointer for a specific external file. The function fopen() is defined in stdio.h, and it has this prototype:

```
FILE *fopen(char *name, char* mode);
```

The first argument to the function is a pointer to the name of the external file that you want to process, stored as a text string. You can specify the name explicitly as an argument, or you can use an array, or a pointer to a char variable in which you've stored the character string that defines the file name. You would typically obtain the file name through some external means, such as from the command line when the program was started, or you could arrange to read it in from the keyboard. You could also define the file name as a constant at the beginning of the program when the program always works with the same file.

The second argument to the function fopen() is a character string that specifies what you want to do with the file. This is called the **file mode**. As you'll see, this spans a whole range of possibilities, but for the moment you'll look at just three file modes (which nonetheless comprise the basic set of operations on a file). Table 12-1 lists these three file modes.

Table 12-1. File Modes

Mode	Description
"w"	Open a file for **w**rite operations
"a"	Open a file for **a**ppend operations (adding to the end of the file, for example)
"r"	Open a file for **r**ead operations

 NOTE *Notice that the mode specifiers are character strings defined between double quotes, not single characters between single quotes.*

Assuming the call to fopen() is successful, it returns a pointer that you can now use to reference the file in further input/output operations, using other functions in the library.

 NOTE *The pointer returned by* fopen() *is referred to as a **file pointer**, or a **stream pointer**.*

So, a call to fopen() does two things for you: it creates a file pointer indicating the specific file that your program is going to operate on, and it determines what you can do with that file within your program.

The pointer that's returned by fopen() is of type "pointer to FILE", where FILE specifies a structure that has been predefined in the header file stdio.h through a typedef. Because it has been defined using a typedef, a declaration of a file pointer only requires the use of the word FILE. The structure associated with a file pointer will contain information about the file. This could be the mode specified, the address of the buffer in memory to be used, and a pointer to the current position in the file for the next operation. You don't need to worry about the contents of this structure in practice. It's all taken care of by the input/output functions. However, if you really want to know about the FILE structure, you can browse through the library header file.

As you've seen, when you want to have several files open at once, they must each have their own file pointer variable declared, and they're each opened with a separate call to fopen() with the value returned stored in a separate file pointer. There's a limit to the number of files you can have open at one time that will be specified by the value FOPEN_MAX that's defined in stdio.h, but it won't normally be a real constraint.

If you wanted to write to an existing file with the name myfile.txt, you would use these statements:

```
FILE *pfile = NULL;              /* Declaration of file pointer      */
pfile = fopen("myfile.txt", "w");  /* Open file myfile.txt to write it */
```

The first statement is a declaration for your file pointer of type FILE. You've initialized the pointer to NULL to be on the safe side. The second statement opens the file and associates the physical file specified by the file name myfile.txt with your internal pointer pfile. Because you've specified the mode as "w", you can only write to the file; you can't read from it. The string that you supply as the first argument is limited to a maximum of FILENAME_MAX characters, where FILENAME_MAX is defined in the stdio.h header file. This value is usually sufficiently large that it isn't a real restriction.

If the file name myfile.txt doesn't already exist, the function fopen() will create it. Because you've just provided the file name as the first argument to the fopen() function, the file is assumed to be in the current directory, and if it's absent, that's where it will be created. You can also specify a string that is the full path for the file, in which case the file will be assumed to be at that location and will be created there if necessary. Note that if the directory that's supposed to contain the file doesn't exist when you specify the file path, it won't be created and the fopen() call will fail. If the call to fopen() does fail for any reason, NULL will be returned. If you then attempt further operations with a NULL file pointer, this will crash your program.

 NOTE *So here you have the facility to create a new file. Simply call* fopen() *with mode* "w" *and the first argument specifying the name you want to assign to the new file.*

On opening a file for writing, the file is positioned at the beginning of any existing data for the first operation. This means that any data previously written to the file will be overwritten when you initiate any write operations.

If you want to add to an existing file rather than overwrite it, you specify mode "a", which is the append mode of operation. This positions the file at the end of any previously written data. If the file specified doesn't exist, as in the case of mode "w", a new file will be created. Using the file pointer that you declared previously, to open the file to add data to the end you would use the following statement:

```
pfile = fopen("myfile.txt", "a");      /* Open file myfile.txt to add to it */
```

If you want to read a file, once you've declared your file pointer, you would open it using this statement:

```
pfile = fopen("myfile.txt", "r");
```

Because you've specified the mode argument as "r", indicating that you want to read the file, you can't write to this file. The file position will be set to the beginning of the data in the file.

Clearly, if you're going to read the file, it must already exist. If you inadvertently try to open a file for reading that doesn't exist, fopen() will return NULL. It's therefore a good idea to check the value returned from fopen() in an if statement, to make sure that you really are accessing the file you want.

Deleting a File

Because you have the ability to create a file, at some point you'll need to know how to delete a file programmatically, too. The remove() function that's declared in stdio.h does this. You use it like this:

```
remove("pfile.txt");
```

This will delete the file from the current directory that has the name pfile.txt.

You need to double-check any operations on files, but in particular you need to check operations that delete files.

Renaming a File

There are many circumstances in which you'll want to rename a file. You might be updating the contents of a file by writing a new, updated file, for instance. You'll probably want to assign a temporary name to the new file while you're creating it, and then change the name to that of the old file once you've deleted it. Renaming a file is very easy. You just use the rename() function, which has the prototype

```
int rename(const char *oldname, const char *newname);
```

The integer that's returned will be 0 if the name change was successful and nonzero otherwise. Here's an example of using the rename() function:

```
if(rename( "C:\\temp\\myfile.txt", "C:\\temp\\myfile_copy.txt"))
  printf("Failed to rename file.");
else
  printf("File renamed successfully.");
```

The preceding code fragment will change the name of the myfile.txt file in the temp directory on drive C: to myfile_copy.text. A message will be produced that indicates if the name change succeeded. Obviously, if the file path is incorrect or the file doesn't exist, the renaming operation will fail.

Writing to a File

Once you've opened a file for writing, you can write to it any time from anywhere in your program, provided you have access to the pointer for the file that has been set by fopen(). So, if you want to be able to access a file from anywhere in a program that contains multiple functions, you need to ensure the file pointer has global scope.

NOTE *As you'll recall, to ensure the file pointer has global scope you place the declaration for it outside of all of the functions, usually at the beginning of the program code.*

The simplest write operation is provided by the function fputc(), which writes a single character to a file. It has the following prototype:

```
int fputc(int c, FILE *pfile);
```

The fputc() function writes the character specified by the first argument to the file defined by the second argument, which is a file pointer. If the write is successful, it returns the character that was written. Otherwise it returns EOF.

NOTE EOF *is a special character called the **end-of-file character**. In fact, the symbol* EOF *is defined in* stdio.h *and usually has the value –1. However, this isn't necessarily always the case, so you should use* EOF *in your programs rather than an explicit value.*

In practice, characters aren't written to the physical file one by one. This would be extremely inefficient. Hidden from your program and managed by the output routine, output characters are written to an area of memory called a **buffer** until a reasonable number have been accumulated, whereupon they're written to the file in one go. This mechanism is illustrated in Figure 12-2.

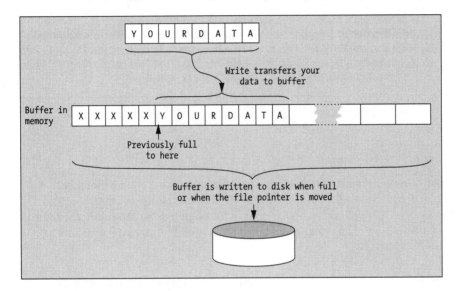

Figure 12-2. Writing a file

Note that the function putc() is equivalent to fputc(). It requires the same arguments and the return type is the same. The difference between them is that putc() may be implemented in the standard library as a macro, whereas fputc() is definitely a function.

Reading from a File

The fgetc() function is complementary to fputc() and reads a character from a file that has been opened for reading. It takes the file pointer as its only argument and returns the character read as type int if the read is successful; otherwise, it returns EOF. The typical use of fgetc() is illustrated by the following statement:

```
mchar = fgetc(pfile);            /* Reads a character into mchar */
```

You're assuming here that the variable mchar has been declared to be of type int.

Behind the scenes, the actual mechanism for reading a file is the inverse of writing to a file. A whole block of characters is read into a buffer. The characters are then handed over to your program one at a time as you request them, until the buffer is empty, whereupon another block is read. This makes the process very fast, because most fgetc() operations won't involve reading the disk but simply moving a character from the buffer in main memory to the place where you want to store it.

Note that the function getc() that's equivalent to fgetc() is also available. It requires an argument of type FILE* and returns the character read as type int, so it's virtually identical to fgetc(). The only difference between them is that getc() may be implemented as a macro, whereas fgetc() is a function.

CAUTION *Don't confuse the function* getc() *with the function* gets()*. They're quite different in operation:* getc() *reads a single character from the stream specified by its argument, whereas* gets() *reads a whole line of input from the standard input stream, which is the keyboard. You've already used the* gets() *function in previous chapters for reading a string from the keyboard.*

Closing a File

When you've finished with a file, you need to tell the operating system that this is the case and free up your file pointer. This is referred to as **closing** a file. You do this through the function fclose(), which accepts a file pointer as an argument and returns an int value set to EOF if an error occurs and 0 otherwise. Typical usage would be as follows:

```
fclose(pfile);                    /* Close the file associated with pfile */
```

The result of executing this statement is that the connection between the pointer, pfile, and the physical file name is broken, so pfile can no longer be used to access the physical file it represented. If the file was being written, then the contents of the output buffer are written to the file to ensure that data isn't lost.

It's good programming practice to close a file as soon as you've finished with it. This protects against output data loss, which could occur if an error in another part of your program caused the execution to be stopped in an abnormal fashion. This could result in the contents of the output buffer being lost, as the file wouldn't be closed properly.

NOTE *Another reason for closing files as soon as you've finished with them is that the operating system will usually limit the number of files you may have open at one time. Closing files as soon as you've finished with them minimizes the chances of you falling afoul of the operating system in this respect.*

There is a function in stdio.h that will force any unwritten data left in a buffer to be written to a file. This is the function fflush(), which you've already used in previous chapters to flush the input buffer. With your file pointer pfile, you could force any data left in the output buffer to be written to the file by using this statement:

```
fflush(pfile);
```

The fflush() function returns a value of type int, which is normally 0 but will be set to EOF if an error occurs.

....

Try It Out: Using a Simple File

You now have enough knowledge of the file input/output capabilities in C to write a simple program that writes a file and then reads it. So let's do just that:

```c
/* Program 12.1 Writing a file a character at a time */
#include <stdio.h>
#include <string.h>

void main()
{
  char mystr[80];                  /* Input string           */
  int i = 0;                       /* Loop counter           */
  int lstr = 0;                    /* Length of input string */
  int mychar = 0;                  /* Character for output   */
  FILE *pfile = NULL;              /* File pointer           */
  char *filename = "C:\\myfile.txt";

  printf("\nEnter an interesting string.\n");
  gets(mystr);                     /* Read in a string       */

  /* Create a new file we can write */
  pfile = fopen(filename, "w");
  if(pfile == NULL)
  {
    printf("Error opening %s for writing. Program terminated.", filename);
    abort();
  }

  lstr = strlen( mystr );
  for(i = lstr-1 ; i >= 0 ; i--)
    fputc(mystr[i], pfile);        /* Write string to file backward  */

  fclose(pfile);                   /* Close the file                 */

  /* Open the file for reading */
  pfile = fopen(filename, "r");
```

(Continued)

```
    if(pfile == NULL)
    {
      printf("Error opening %s for reading. Program terminated.", filename);
      abort();
    }

    /* Read a character from the file and display it */
    while((mychar = fgetc(pfile)) != EOF)
      putchar(mychar);                    /* Output character from the file */
    putchar('\n');                        /* Write newline                  */

    fclose(pfile);                        /* Close the file                 */
    remove(filename);                     /* Delete the physical file       */
}
```

Here's an example of some output from this program:

```
Enter an interesting string.
Too many cooks spoil the broth.
.htorb eht liops skooc ynam ooT
```

HOW IT WORKS

The name of the file that you're going to work with is defined by this statement:

```
char *filename = "C:\\myfile.txt";
```

This statement defines the file with the name myfile.txt on drive C: with the Microsoft Windows notation for file names. Note that you must use the escape sequence '\\' to get a backslash character. If you forget to do this and just use a single backslash, the compiler will think that you're writing an escape sequence '\m', which it won't recognize as valid.

Before running this program—or indeed any of the examples working with files—make sure you don't have an existing file with the same name and path. If you do, you should change the initial value for filename in the example; otherwise, your existing file will be overwritten.

After displaying a prompt, the program reads a string from the keyboard. It then executes the following statement:

```
pfile = fopen(filename, "w");
```

This statement calls fopen() to create the new file myfile.txt on drive C: and opens it for writing. The second argument to fopen() determines the mode as writing the file.

(Continued)

Next, you verify that the file was opened successfully:

```
if(pfile == NULL)
{
  printf("Error opening %s for writing. Program terminated.", filename);
  abort();
}
```

Without these statements, you run the risk of attempting operations with `pfile` as `NULL`, which would surely crash the program. If you discover that `pfile` is `NULL`, you output a message and call `abort()` for an abnormal end to the program.

After determining the `length` of the string using `strlen()` and storing the result in `lstr`, you have a loop defined by these statements:

```
for(i = lstr-1 ; i >= 0 ; i--)
  fputc(mystr[i], pfile);      /* Write string to file backward  */
```

The loop index is varied from a value corresponding to the last character in the string `lstr-1` back to 0. Therefore, the `putc()` function call within the loop writes to the new file character by character, in reverse order. The particular file you're writing is specified by the pointer `pfile` as the second argument to the function call.

After the file is closed with a call to `fclose()`, it's reopened in reading mode by this statement:

```
pfile = fopen(filename, "r");
```

The mode specification `"r"` indicates that you intend to read the file, so the file position will be set to the beginning of the file. This statement is also followed by essentially the same check for a `NULL` return value as when you wrote the file.

Next, you use the `getc()` function to read characters from the file within the `while` loop condition:

```
while((mychar = fgetc(pfile)) != EOF)
  putchar(mychar);             /* Output character from the file */
```

The file is read character by character. The read operation actually takes place within the loop continuation condition. As each character is read, it's displayed on the screen using the function `putc()` within the loop. The process stops when `EOF` is returned by `getc()` at the end of the file.

The last two statements in the program are

```
fclose(pfile);          /* Close the file            */
remove(filename);       /* Delete the physical file  */
```

(Continued)

517

These statements provide the necessary final tidying up, now that you've finished with the file. After closing the file, the program calls the remove() function, which will delete the file identified by the argument. This avoids cluttering up the disk with stray files. If you want to check the contents of the file that was written using a text editor, just remove or comment out the call to remove().

Writing a String to a File

Analogous to the puts() function for writing a string to stdout, you have the fputs() function for writing a string to a file. Its prototype is as follows:

```
int fputs(char *pstr, FILE *pfile);
```

The first argument is a pointer to the character string that's to be written to the file, and the second argument is a file pointer. The operation of the function is slightly odd, in that it continues to write characters from a string until it reaches a '\0' character, which it doesn't write to the file. This can complicate reading back variable-length strings from a file that have been written by fputs(). It works this way because it's a character write operation, not a binary write operation, so it's expecting to write a line of text that has a newline character at the end. A newline character isn't required by the operation of the function, but it's very helpful when you want to read the file back (using the complementary fgets() function, as you'll see).

The fputs() function returns EOF if an error occurs and 0 under normal circumstances. You use it in the same way as puts(), for example:

```
fputs("The higher the fewer", pfile);
```

This will output the string appearing as the first argument to the file pointed to by pfile.

Reading a String from a File

Complementing fputs() is the function fgets() for reading a string from a file. It has the prototype

```
char *fgets(char *pstr, int nchars, FILE *pfile);
```

The fgets() function has three parameters. The function will read a string into the memory area pointed to by pstr, from the file specified by pfile. Characters are read from the file until either a '\n' is read or nchars-1 characters have been read from the file, whichever occurs first.

If a newline character is read, it's retained in the string. A '\0' will be appended to the end of the string in any event. If there is no error, fgets() will return the pointer, pstr; otherwise, NULL is returned. The second argument to this function enables you to ensure that you don't overrun the memory area that you've assigned for input in your program. To prevent the capacity of your data input area from being exceeded, just specify the length of the area or the array that will receive the input data as the second argument to the function.

··

Try It Out: Transferring Strings to and from a File

You can exercise the functions to transfer strings to and from a file in an example that also uses the append mode for writing a file:

```
/* Program 12.2  As the saying goes...it comes back! */
#include <stdio.h>

void main()
{
   char *proverbs[] =
           { "Many a mickle makes a muckle.\n",
             "Too many cooks spoil the broth.\n",
             "He who laughs last didn't get the joke in"
                                  " the first place.\n"
           };

   char more[60] = "A nod is a good as a wink to a blind horse.\n";
   FILE *pfile = NULL;                /* File pointer */
   int i = 0;                         /* Loop counter */
   char *filename = "C:\\myfile.txt";

   /* Create a new file( if myfile.txt does not exist */
   pfile = fopen(filename, "w");
   if(pfile == NULL)
   {
     printf("Error opening %s for writing. Program terminated.", filename);
     abort();
   }

   /* Write our first three sayings. */
   for(i = 0 ; i < sizeof proverbs/sizeof proverbs[0] ; i++)
     fputs(proverbs[i], pfile);
   fclose(pfile);                     /* Close the file */

   pfile = fopen(filename, "a");      /* Open it again to append data */
   if(pfile == NULL)
   {
     printf("Error opening %s for writing. Program terminated.", filename);
     abort();
   }
```

(Continued)

```
    fputs(more, pfile);                 /* Write another proverb    */
    fclose(pfile);                      /* Close the file           */

    pfile = fopen(filename, "r");       /* Open the file to read it */
    if(pfile == NULL)
    {
      printf("Error opening %s for writing. Program terminated.", filename);
      abort();
    }
    while(fgets(more, 60, pfile) != NULL)   /* Read a proverb */
      printf("\n%s", more);                 /* and display it */

    fclose(pfile);                      /* Close the file */
    remove(filename);                   /* and remove it  */
}
```

HOW IT WORKS

You initialize the array of pointers, proverbs[], in the following statement:

```
char *proverbs[] =
          { "Many a mickle makes a muckle.\n",
            "Too many cooks spoil the broth.\n",
            "He who laughs last didn't get the joke in"
                                " the first place.\n"
          };
```

You specify the three sayings as initial values, which causes the compiler to allocate the space necessary to store each string, and then you put the address of the space allocated for each in the appropriate element of the pointer array. The compiler will automatically fill in the dimension for the array to provide sufficient pointers for the number of strings specified as initializing values. Each string has '\n' as the last character, so the fgets() function will be able to recognize the end of each string when you read it back.

You have a further declaration of a string:

```
char more[60] = "A nod is a good as a wink to a blind horse.\n";
```

This initializes a conventional char array with another proverb. You also include '\n' at the end for the same reason as before.

After creating and opening a file on drive C: for writing, the program executes the loop:

```
for(i = 0 ; i < sizeof proverbs/sizeof proverbs[0] ; i++)
  fputs(proverbs[i], pfile);
```

(Continued)

The contents of each of the memory areas pointed to by elements of the proverbs[] array are written to the file in the for loop using the function fputs(). This function is extremely easy to use; it just requires a pointer to the string as the first argument and a pointer to the file as the second.

The number of iterations is set with the following expression:

```
sizeof proverbs/sizeof proverbs[0]
```

The expression size of proverbs will evaluate to the total number of bytes occupied by the complete array, and sizeof proverbs[0] will result in the number of bytes required to store a single pointer in one element of the array. Therefore, the whole expression will evaluate to the number of elements in the pointer array. You could have manually counted how many initializing strings you supplied, of course, but doing it this way means that the correct number of iterations is determined automatically, and this expression will still be correct even if the array dimension is changed by adding more initializing strings.

Once the first set of proverbs has been written, the file is closed and then reopened with this statement:

```
pfile = fopen(filename, "a");
```

Because you have the mode specified as "a", the file is opened in append mode. Note that the current position for the file is automatically set to the end of the file in this mode, so that subsequent write operations will be appended to the end of the existing data in the file.

You then write to the file with the following statement:

```
fputs(more, pfile);
```

The additional proverb that's stored in the character more array is then written to the file using fputs(). As you can see, the function fputs() is just as easy to use with an array as it is with a pointer. Because you're in append mode, the new proverb will be added at the end of the existing data in the file.

Having written the file, you close it and then reopen it for reading using the mode specifier "r". You then have the following loop:

```
while(fgets(more, 60, pfile) != NULL)    /* Read a proverb */
  printf("\n%s", more);                  /* and display it */
```

You read strings successively from the file into the more array within the loop continuation condition. After each string is read, you display it on the screen by the call to printf() within the loop. The reading of each proverb by fgets() is terminated by detecting the '\n' character at the end of each string. The loop terminates when the function fgets() returns NULL.

(Continued)

An alternative to reusing the more array for input would be to allocate an area dynamically. Here, you could obtain the maximum length of a string by checking the length of the proverbs that you wrote to the file. In general, though, this won't be possible, so it's worth considering whether the length of each string should be recorded in the file. This would then enable a program that was reading the file to allocate space for whatever was coming next.

Finally, the file is closed and then deleted using the function remove() in the same fashion as the previous example.

Formatted File Input and Output

Writing characters and strings to a file is all very well as far as it goes, but you normally have many other types of data in your programs. To write numerical data to a file, you need something more than you've seen so far, and where the contents of a file are to be human readable, you need a character representation of the numerical data. The mechanism for doing just this is provided by the functions for formatted file input and output.

Formatted Output to a File

You've already encountered the function for formatted output to a file when I discussed standard streams back in Chapter 10. It's virtually the same as the printf() statement, except that there's one extra parameter and a slight name change. Its typical usage is

```
fprintf(pfile, "%12d%12d%14f", num1, num2, fnum1);
```

As you can see, the function name has an additional f (for file), compared with printf(), and the first argument is a file pointer specifying the destination of the output. The file pointer obviously needs to be set through a call to fopen() first. The remaining arguments are identical to that of printf(). This example writes the values of the three variables num1, num2, and num3 to the file specified by the file pointer pfile, under control of the format string specified as the second argument. Therefore, the first two variables are of type int and are to be written with a field width of 12, and the third variable is of type float and is to be written to the file with a field width of 14.

Formatted Input from a File

You get formatted input from a file by using the function fscanf(). To read three variable values from a file pfile you would write this:

```
fscanf(pfile, "%12d%12d%14f", &num1, &num2, &fnum1);
```

This function works in exactly the same way as scanf() does with stdin, except that here you're obtaining input from a file specified by the first argument. The same rules govern the specification of the format string and the operation of the function as apply to scanf(). The function returns EOF if an error occurs such that no input is read; otherwise, it returns the number of values read as a value of type int.

....

Try It Out: Using Formatted Input and Output Functions

You can demonstrate the formatted input and output functions with an example that will also show what's happening to the data in these operations:

```
/* Program 12.3 Messing about with formatted file I/O */
#include <stdio.h>

void main()
{
    long num1 = 234567L;                   /* Input values...           */
    long num2 = 345123L;
    long num3 = 789234L;

    long num4 = 0L;                        /* Values read from the file... */
    long num5 = 0L;
    long num6 = 0L;

    float fnum = 0.0f;                     /* Value read from the file  */
    int   ival[6] = { 0 };                 /* Values read from the file */
    int i = 0;                             /* Loop counter              */
    FILE *pfile = NULL;                    /* File pointer              */
    char *filename = "C:\\myfile.txt";

    pfile = fopen(filename, "w");               /* Create file to be written */
    if(pfile == NULL)
    {
      printf("Error opening %s for writing. Program terminated.", filename);
      abort();
    }
    fprintf(pfile, "%6ld%6ld%6ld", num1, num2, num3);   /* Write file        */
    fclose(pfile);                              /* Close file        */
    printf("\n %6ld %6ld %6ld", num1, num2, num3);   /* Display values written */

    pfile = fopen(filename, "r");               /* Open file to read   */
    fscanf(pfile, "%6ld%6ld%6ld", &num4, &num5 ,&num6); /* Read back        */
    printf("\n %6ld %6ld %6ld", num4, num5, num6);     /* Display what we got */

    rewind(pfile);                              /* Go to the beginning of the file */
    fscanf(pfile, "%2d%3d%3d%3d%2d%2d%3f", &ival[0], &ival[1], /* Read it again */
```

(Continued)

```
                           &ival[2], &ival[3], &ival[4] , &ival[5], &fnum);
    fclose(pfile);                              /* Close the file and   */
    remove(filename);                           /* delete physical file. */

    /* Output the results */
    printf("\n");
    for( i = 0 ; i < 6 ; i++ )
      printf("%sival[i] = %d", i == 4 ? "\n\t" : "\t", i, ival[i]);
    printf("\nfnum = %f\n", fnum);
}
```

The output from this example will be

```
234567 345123 789234
234567 345123 789234
        ival[i] = 0    ival[i] = 1    ival[i] = 2    ival[i] =3
        ival[i] = 4    ival[i] = 5
fnum = 234.000000
```

HOW IT WORKS

This example writes the values of num1, num2, and num3, which are defined and assigned values in their declaration, to the file myfile.txt on drive C:. This is referenced through the pointer pfile. The file is closed and reopened for reading, and the values are read from the file in the same format as they were written. You then have the following statement:

```
    rewind(pfile);
```

This statement calls the rewind() function, which simply moves the current position back to the beginning of the file so that you can read it again. You could have achieved the same thing by closing the file, then reopening it again, but with rewind() you do it with one function call and the operation will be a lot faster.

Having repositioned the file, you read the file again with this statement:

```
    fscanf(pfile, "%2d%3d%3d%3d%2d%2d%3f", &ival[0], &ival[1], /* Read it again */
                        &ival[2], &ival[3], &ival[4] , &ival[5], &fnum);
```

This statement reads the same data into the array ival[] and the variable fnum, but with different formats from those that you used for writing the file. You can see from the effects of this that the file consists of just a string of characters once it has been written, exactly the same as the output to the screen from printf().

(Continued)

> **NOTE** *You can lose information if you choose a format specifier that outputs fewer digits precision than the stored value holds.*

You can see that the values you get back from the file when you read it will depend on both the format string that you use and upon the variable list that you specify in the fscanf() function.

None of the intrinsic source information that existed when you wrote the file is necessarily maintained. Once the data is in the file, it's just a sequence of bytes in which the meaning is determined by how you interpret them. This is demonstrated quite clearly by this example, in which you've converted the original three values into eight new values.

Lastly, you leave everything neat and tidy in this program by closing the file and using the function remove() to delete it.

Dealing with Errors

The examples in this book have included minimal error checking and reporting because the code for error checking tends to take up a lot of space in the book and make the programs look rather complicated. In real-world programs, however, it's essential that you do as much error checking and reporting as you can.

Generally, you should write your error messages to stderr, which is automatically available to your program and always points to your display screen. Even though stdout may be redirected to a file by an operating system command, stderr continues to be assigned to the screen. It's important to check that a file you want to read does in fact exist, and you've been doing this in the examples, but there's more that you can do. First of all, you can write error messages to stderr rather than stdin, for example:

```
char *filename = "C:\\MYFILE.TXT";    /* File name    */
FILE *pfile = NULL;                    /* File pointer */
    ....
if(pfile = fopen(myfile, "r") == NULL)
{
  fprintf(stderr, "\nCannot open %s to read it.", filename);
  abort();
}
```

The merit of writing to stderr is that the output will always be directed to the display and it will always be written immediately to the display device. The stream stdin is buffered and can be redirected to a file, but stderr can't be redirected.

TIP *It's always a good idea to use a string variable to store your file names, as then you can refer to them in your error output.*

Knowing that some kind of error occurred is useful, but you can do more than this. The perror() function outputs a string that you pass as an argument plus an implementation-defined error message corresponding to the error that occurred. You could therefore rewrite the previous fragment as follows:

```
if(pfile = fopen(myfile, "r") == NULL)
{
  perror(strcat("Error opening ", filename));
  abort();
}
```

This will output your message consisting of the file name appended to the first argument to strcat(), plus a system-generated message relating to the error. The output will be written to stderr.

If an error occurs when you're reading a file, you can check whether the error was due to reaching the end of file or some other reason. The feof() function will return a nonzero integer if the end of file has been reached, so you can check for this with statements such as these:

```
if(feof(pfile))
  printf("End of file reached");
```

Note that I didn't write the message to stderr, because reaching the end of the file isn't necessarily an error.

The ferror() function returns a nonzero integer if an error occurred with an operation on the stream that's identified by the file pointer that you pass as the argument. Calling this function enables you to establish positively that an error did occur. The errno.h header file defines a value, errno, that may indicate what kind of file error has occurred. You need to read the documentation for your C implementation to find out the specifics of this. The value of errno may be set for errors other than just file operations.

It's wise to include some basic error checking and reporting code in all of your programs. Once you've written a few programs, you'll find that including some standard bits of code for each type of operation warranting error checks is no hardship. With a standard approach, you can copy most of what you need from one program to another.

Further File Operation Modes

You've processed files only as text files so far, where information is written as strings of characters. Text mode is generally the default mode of operation, but you can specify explicitly that file operations are in text mode if you want to be sure about it. You do this by adding t to the end of the existing specifiers. This gives you the mode specifiers "wt", "rt", and "at" in addition to the original three.

You can also open a file for update—that is, for both reading and writing—using the specifier "r+". If you want the mode to be specified explicitly as a text operation, it will become "r+t" or "rt+". Either specification for the file mode is perfectly acceptable. You can also specify the mode "w+" if you want to both read and write a new file, or when you want to discard the original contents of an existing file before you start. To specify text mode explicitly, this would become "wt+" or "w+t".

As I've said, in update mode you can both read and write the file. However, you can't write to the file immediately after reading it or read from the file immediately after writing it, unless EOF has been reached or the position in the file has been changed by some means. (This involves calling a function such as rewind() or some other functions that you'll see later in this chapter.) The reason for this is that writing to a file doesn't necessarily write the data to the external device. It simply transfers it to a buffer in memory that's written to the file once it's full or when some other event causes it to be written. Similarly, the first read from a file will fill a buffer area in memory and subsequent reads will transfer data from the buffer until it's empty, whereupon another file read to fill the buffer will be initiated. This is illustrated in Figure 12-3.

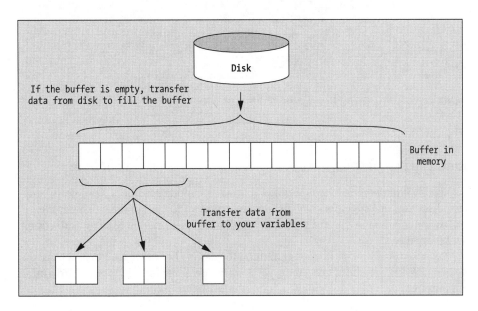

Figure 12-3. Buffered input operations

This means that if you switch immediately from write mode to read mode, data will be lost because it will be left in the buffer. In the case of switching from read mode to write mode, the current position in the file may be different from what you imagine it to be, and you may inadvertently overwrite data on the file. A switch from read to write or vice versa, therefore, requires an intervening event that implicitly flushes the buffers. The fflush() function I mentioned earlier in this chapter will cause bytes remaining in an output buffer to be written to an output file.

Unformatted File Input/Output

The alternative to text mode operations on a file is **binary mode**. In this mode, no transformation of the data takes place, and there's no need for a format string to control input or output, so it's much simpler than text mode. The binary data as it appears in memory is transferred directly to the file. Characters such as '\n' and '\0' that have specific significance in text mode are of no consequence in binary mode.

Binary mode has the advantage that no data is transformed or precision lost, as can happen with text mode due to the formatting process. It's also somewhat faster than text mode because no transformation operations are performed. The two modes are contrasted in Figure 12-4.

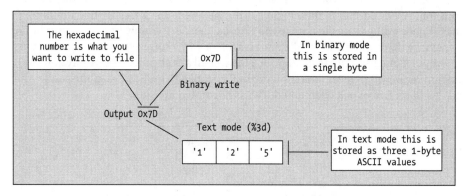

Figure 12-4. Contrasting binary mode and text mode

Specifying Binary Mode

You specify binary mode by appending b to the basic mode specifiers. Therefore, you have the additional specifiers "wb" for writing a binary file, "rb" to read a binary file, "ab" to append data to the end of a binary file, and "rb+" to enable reading and writing of a binary file.

Because binary mode involves handling the data to be transferred to and from the file in a different way from text mode, you have a new set of functions to perform input and output.

Writing a Binary File

You use the fwrite() function to write a binary file. This is best explained with an example of its use. Assuming you open the file to be written with the statement

```
pfile = fopen(filename, "wb");
```

the variable `filename` points to the string defining the name of the file, and `pfile` has been declared as a pointer to an object of type `FILE` as before.

You can write to the file with this statement:

```
wcount = fwrite(pdata, size, num_items, pfile);
```

The `fwrite()` function operates on the principle of writing a specified number of data items to a file, where each item is a given number of bytes long. The first argument, `pdata`, is a pointer containing the starting address in memory of where the data items to be written are stored. The second argument, `size`, specifies the size in bytes of each item to be written. The third argument, `num_items`, defines a count of the number of items to be written to the file. The file to which the data is to be transferred is identified by the last argument, `pfile`. The function `fwrite()` returns the count of the number of items actually written. If the operation was unsuccessful for some reason, this value will be less than `num_items`.

The return value and the arguments `size` and `num_items` are all of the same type as that returned by the `sizeof` operator. This is defined as type `size_t`, which is an unsigned integer type.

Let's assume that you want to write data stored in an array `data`, where `data` has been defined as

```
double data[] = { 2.5, 3.5. 5.5, 6.75, 9.5 };
```

You can write the contents of the `data` array to the file with the following statement:

```
wcount = fwrite(data, sizeof data[0], sizeof data/sizeof data[0], pfile);
```

Here you use the `sizeof` operator to specify the size in bytes of the objects to be transferred and the number of items to be transferred. This is a good way of specifying these values when this is possible, because it reduces the likelihood of error. Of course, in a real context, you should also check the return value in `wcount` to be sure the write was successful.

This means that your function for binary writes to a file is geared to writing a number of objects of any length. You can write in units of your own structures as easily as you can write `int` values, values of type `double`, or sequences of individual bytes. This doesn't mean that the values you write in any given output operation all have to be of the same type. You might allocate some memory using `malloc()`, for instance, into which you assemble a sequence of data items of different types and lengths. You could then write the whole block of memory in one go as a sequence of bytes. Of course, when you come to read them back, you need to know the precise sequence and types for the values in the file if you are to make sense of them.

Reading a Binary File

You use the fread() function to read a binary file, once it has been opened in read mode. Using the same variables as in the example of writing a binary file, to read the file you would use a statement such as this:

```
wcount = fread( data, sizeof(double), num_items, pfile);
```

This operates exactly as the inverse of the write operation. Starting at the address specified by data, the function reads num_items objects, each of the number of bytes specified by the second argument. The function returns the count of the number of items that were read. If the read isn't completely successful, the count will be less than the number of objects requested.

....

Try It Out: Reading a Binary File

You can apply the binary file operations to a version of the program you first saw in Chapter 7 for calculating primes. This time, you'll use a disk file as a buffer to calculate a larger number of primes. You can make the program automatically spill primes on to a disk file if the array assigned to store the primes is insufficient for the number of primes requested. In this version of the program to find primes, you'll use array notation throughout and improve the checking process a little.

In addition to the function main() that will contain the prime finding loop, you'll write a function to test whether a value is prime called test_prime(), a helper function that will check a given value against a block of primes called check(), and a function called put_primes(), which will retrieve the primes from the file and display them.

As this program consists of several functions, let's take a look at main() first:

```
/* Program 12.4  A prime example using binary files */
#include <stdio.h>
#include <stdlib.h>
#include <math.h >                         /* For square root function sqrt() */

#define MEM_PRIMES 100               /* Count of number of primes in memory */

/* Function prototypes */
int test_prime(unsigned long N);
void put_primes(void);
int check(unsigned long buffer[], int count, unsigned long N);

/* Global variables */
char myfile[] = "C:\\myfile.bin";                  /* Physical file name   */
FILE *pfile = NULL;                                /* File pointer         */
```

(Continued)

```
  unsigned long primes[MEM_PRIMES] = { 2UL,3UL,5UL }; /* Array to store primes */
  int index = 3;                     /* Index of free location in array primes */
  int nrec = 0;                              /* Number of file records */

  void main()
  {
    unsigned long trial = 5UL;                      /* Prime candidate */
    long num_primes = 3L;                           /* Prime count     */
    long total = 0L;                                /* Total required  */
    int i = 0;                                      /* Loop counter    */

    printf("How many primes would you like?  ");
    scanf("%d", &total);               /* Total is how many we need to find */
    total = total<4 ? 4:total;         /* Make sure it is at least 4        */

    /* Prime finding and storing loop */
    while(num_primes < total)          /* Loop until we get total required  */
    {
      trial += 2;                      /* Next value for checking          */
      if(test_prime(trial))            /* Check if trial is prime          */
      {                                /* Positive value means prime       */
        primes[index++] = trial;       /* so store it                      */
        num_primes++;                  /* Increment total number of primes */

        if(index == MEM_PRIMES)        /* Check if array is full           */
        {
          /* File opened OK?   */
          if((pfile = fopen(myfile, "ab")) == NULL)
          { /* No, so explain and end the program */
            printf("\nUnable to open %s to append\n", myfile);
            abort();
          }
          /* Write the array   */
          fwrite(primes, sizeof(long), MEM_PRIMES, pfile);

          fclose(pfile);                            /* Close the file */
          index = 0;                     /* Reset count of primes in memory */
          nrec++;                        /* Increment file record count     */
        }
      }
    }

    if(total>MEM_PRIMES)               /* If we wrote some to file         */
      put_primes();                    /* Display the contents of the file */
    if(index)                          /* Display any left in memory       */
      for(i = 0; i<index ; i++)
      {
        if(i%5 == 0)
          printf("\n");                           /* Newline after five    */
        printf("%12lu", primes[i]);               /* Output a prime        */
```

(Continued)

```
        }

     if(total>MEM_PRIMES)                              /* Did we need a file?  */
       if(remove(myfile))                              /* then delete it.      */
         printf("\nFailed to delete %s\n", myfile);    /* Delete failed        */
       else
         printf("\nFile %s deleted.\n",myfile);        /* Delete OK            */
   }
```

![HOW IT WORKS]

After the usual #include statements, you have the definition for MEM_PRIMES, which is the maximum number of primes to be held in memory. Once more than this number of primes has been computed, the primes in memory will be written to a disk file automatically by the program. If you request less than this number, none will be written to disk.

The prototypes for four functions used in the program are

```
int test_prime(unsigned long N);
void put_primes(void);
int check(unsigned long buffer[], int count, unsigned long N);
```

You write just the parameter types within the prototypes without using a parameter name. Function prototypes can be written either with or without parameter names, but the parameter types must be specified. Generally, it's better to include names, because they give a clue to the purpose of the parameter. The names in the prototype can be different from the names used in the definition of the function, but you should only do this if it helps to make the code more readable.

The following statements are the declarations for the global variables:

```
char myfile[] = "C:\\myfile.bin";               /* Physical file name    */
FILE *pfile = NULL;                             /* File pointer          */
unsigned long primes[MEM_PRIMES] = { 2UL,3UL,5UL }; /* Array to store primes */
int index = 3;                      /* Index of free location in array primes */
int nrec = 0;                                   /* Number of file records */
```

These can all be accessed by any function in the program. The first declaration defines a char array containing the name of the external file to be used. You need the double backslash to get a backslash character in the string. You should change this file name to suit your environment.

(Continued)

You include the file pointer pfile and the character array myfile, which holds the external file name, as global variables so that you can use input and output operations on the file from anywhere in the program. This allows the function put_primes() to be defined without parameters. You also define the array to hold primes in memory as global, and you insert the first three primes as initial values.

The definition of the function main() follows the global declarations. When the program executes, you enter the number of primes you want to find, and this value controls the loop for testing prime candidates. Checking for a prime is performed by the function test_prime(), which is called in the if statement condition within the loop. The function returns 1 if the value tested is prime and 0 otherwise. If a prime is found, then you execute these statements:

```
primes[index++] = trial;      /* so store it                        */
num_primes++;                 /* Increment total number of primes   */
```

The first statement stores the prime that you've found in the primes[] array. You keep track of how many primes you have in total with the variable num_primes, and the variable index records how many you have in memory at any given time.

Every time you find a prime and add it to the primes[] array, you perform the following check:

```
if(index == MEM_PRIMES)                    /* Check if array is full */
{
  /* File opened OK?    */
  if((pfile = fopen(myfile, "ab")) == NULL)
  { /* No, so explain and end the program */
    printf("\nUnable to open %s to append\n", myfile);
    abort();
  }
  /* Write the array    */
  fwrite(primes, sizeof(long), MEM_PRIMES, pfile);

  fclose(pfile);                             /* Close the file */
  index = 0;                        /* Reset count of primes in memory */
  nrec++;                           /* Increment file record count    */
}
```

If you've filled the primes array, the if condition will be true and you'll execute the associated statement block. In this case, the file is opened in binary mode to append data. The first time this occurs, a new file will be created. On subsequent calls of the fopen() function file, the existing file will be opened with the current position set at the end of any existing data in the file, ready for the next block to be written. Once a block is written, the file is closed, as it will be necessary to reopen it for reading in the function that performs the checking of prime candidates.

(Continued)

Finally in this group of statements, the count of the number of primes in memory is reset to 0 because they've all been safely stowed away, and the count of the number of blocks of primes written to the file is incremented.

When sufficient primes have been found to fulfill the number requested, you display the primes with the following statements:

```
if(total>MEM_PRIMES)              /* If we wrote some to file         */
  put_primes();                   /* Display the contents of the file */
if(index)                         /* Display any left in memory       */
  for(i = 0; i<index ; i++)
  {
    if(i%5 == 0)
      printf("\n");               /* Newline after five    */
    printf("%12lu", primes[i]);   /* Output a prime        */
  }
```

It's quite possible that the number of primes requested could be accommodated in memory, in which case you won't write to a file at all. You must therefore check whether total exceeded MEM_PRIMES before calling the function put_primes() that outputs the primes in the file. If the value of index is positive, then there are primes in the primes array that haven't been written to the file. In this case, you display these in the for loop, five to a line.

Finally in main(), you remove the file from the disk with the following statements:

```
if(total>MEM_PRIMES)                               /* Did we need a file? */
  if(remove(myfile))                               /* then delete it.     */
    printf("\nFailed to delete %s\n", myfile);     /* Delete failed       */
  else
    printf("\nFile %s deleted.\n",myfile);         /* Delete OK           */
```

The first if ensures that you don't attempt to delete the file if you didn't create one.

The function to check whether or not a value is prime is as follows:

```
/******************************************************************
 * Function to test if a number, N, is prime using primes in      *
 * memory and on file                                             *
 * First parameter N - value to be tested                         *
 * Return value - a positive value for a prime, zero otherwise    *
 ******************************************************************/
int test_prime(unsigned long N)
{
  unsigned long buffer[MEM_PRIMES]; /* local buffer for primes from the file */

  int i = 0;                                          /* Loop counter */
  int k = 0;
```

(Continued)

```
  if(nrec > 0)                                   /* Have we written records? */
  {
    if((pfile = fopen(myfile, "rb")) == NULL)    /* Then open the file      */
    {
      printf("\nUnable to open %s to read\n", myfile);
      abort();
    }

    for(i = 0; i < nrec ; i++)
    { /* Check against primes in the file first */
      /* Read primes */
      fread(buffer, sizeof(long), MEM_PRIMES, pfile);
      if((k = check(buffer, MEM_PRIMES, N)) >= 0)  /* Prime or not?          */
      {
        fclose(pfile);                             /* Yes, so close the file */
        return k;                                  /* 1 for prime, 0 for not */
      }
    }
    fclose(pfile);                                 /* Close the file         */
  }

  return check(primes, index, N);          /* Check against primes in memory */
}
```

The test_prime() function accepts a candidate value as an argument and returns 1 if it's prime and 0 if it isn't.

If you've written anything to the file, this will be indicated by a positive value of nrec. In this case, the primes in the file need to be used as divisors first, because they are lower than those currently in memory as you compute them in sequence.

NOTE *As you may remember, a prime is a number with no factors other than 1 and itself. It's sufficient to check whether a number is divisible by any of the primes less than the square root of the number to verify that it's prime. This follows from the simple logic that any exact divisor greater than the square root must have an associated factor (the result of the division) that's less than the square root.*

To read the file, the function executes this statement:

```
fread(buffer, sizeof(long), MEM_PRIMES, pfile);
```

This reads one block of primes from the file into the array buffer. The second argument defines the size of each object to be read, and MEM_PRIMES defines the number of objects of the specified size to be read.

(Continued)

Once the block is read, the following check is executed:

```
if((k = check(buffer, MEM_PRIMES, N)) >= 0)  /* Prime or not?          */
{
  fclose(pfile);                             /* Yes, so close the file */
  return k;                                  /* 1 for prime, 0 for not */
}
```

Within the `if` condition, the `check()` function is called to determine if any of the array elements divide into the prime candidate with no remainder. This function returns 0 if an exact division is found, indicating the candidate isn't prime. If no exact division is found with primes up to the square root of the candidate value, 1 is returned, indicating that the candidate must be prime. Whatever value is returned from `check()`, in both cases you've finished checking so the file is closed and the same value is returned to `main()`.

The value –1 is returned from `check()` if no exact division has been found, but the square root of the test value hasn't been exceeded. You don't need to check for the –1 return explicitly, because it's the only possibility left if the value returned from `check()` isn't 0 or 1. In this case, the next block, if there is one, is read from the file in the next iteration of the `for` loop.

If the contents of the file have been exhausted without determining whether or not N is prime, the `for` loop will end, and you'll close the file and execute the following statement:

```
return check(primes, index, N);              /* Check against primes in memory */
```

Here, the test value is tried against any primes in the `primes` array in memory by the function `check()`. If a prime is found, the `check()` function will return 1; otherwise, the function will return 0. The value that's returned by the `check()` function will be returned to `main()`.

The code for the `check()` function is as follows:

```
/*******************************************************************
 * Function to check whether an integer, N, is divisible by any    *
 * of the elements in the array pbuffer up to the square root of N.*
 * First parameter buffer - an array of primes                     *
 * second parameter count - number of elements in pbuffer          *
 * Third parameter N - the value to be checked                     *
 * Return value - 1 if N is prime, zero if N is not a prime,       *
 *                -1 for more checks                               *
 *******************************************************************/
int check(unsigned long buffer[], int count, unsigned long N)
{
  int i = 0;                                 /* Loop counter              */
  /* Upper limit */
  unsigned long root_N = (unsigned long)(1.0 + sqrt((double)N));
```

(Continued)

```
     for(i = 0 ; i<count ; i++)
     {
       if(N % buffer[i] == OUL )        /* Exact division?           */
         return 0;                      /* Then not a prime          */

       if(buffer[i] > root_N)           /* Divisor exceeds square root? */
         return 1;                      /* Then must be a prime       */
     }
     return -1;                         /* More checks necessary...   */
}
```

The role of this function is to check if any of the primes contained in the buffer array that's passed as the first argument divide exactly into the test value supplied as the second argument. The local variables in the function are declared in these statements:

```
     int i = 0;                         /* Loop counter              */
     /* Upper limit */
     unsigned long root_N = (unsigned long)(1.0 + sqrt((double)N));
```

The integer variable, root_N, will hold the upper limit for divisors to be checked against the trial value. Only divisors less than the square root of the test value N are tried.

The checking is done in the for loop:

```
     for(i = 0 ; i<count ; i++)
     {
       if(N % buffer[i] == OUL )        /* Exact division?           */
         return 0;                      /* Then not a prime          */

       if(buffer[i] > root_N)           /* Divisor exceeds square root? */
         return 1;                      /* Then must be a prime       */
     }
```

This steps through each of the divisors in the buffer array. If a divisor is found, the function will end and return 0 to indicate that the value isn't prime. If you arrive at a divisor that's greater than root_N, you've tried all those lower than this value, so N must be prime and the function returns 1. If the loop ends, you haven't found an exact divisor, but you haven't tried all values up to root_N, so the function returns –1 to indicate there's more checking to be done.

The last function that you need to define is designed to output all the primes written to the file:

```
/* Function to output primes from the file */
void put_primes(void)
{
    unsigned long buffer[MEM_PRIMES];     /* Buffer for a block of primes */
    int i = 0;                            /* Loop counter              */
```

(Continued)

```
    int j = 0;                              /* Loop counter           */

    if((pfile = fopen( myfile, "rb"))==NULL)   /* Open the file        */
    {
      printf("\nUnable to open %s to read primes for output\n", myfile);
      abort();
    }

    for (i = 0 ; i< nrec ; i++)
    {
      /* Read a block of primes   */
      fread(buffer, sizeof(long), MEM_PRIMES, pfile);

      for(j = 0 ; j<MEM_PRIMES ; j++)                /* Display the primes */
      {
        if(j%5 == 0)                                 /* Five to a line     */
          printf("\n");
        printf("%12lu", buffer[j]);                  /* Output a prime     */
      }
    }
    fclose(pfile);                                   /* Close the file     */
}
```

The operation of the put_primes() function is very simple. Once the file is opened, blocks of primes are read into the buffer array and as each is read, the for loop outputs the values to the screen, five to a line with a field width of 12. After all records have been read, the file is closed.

To run the program, you need to assemble all the functions that you've described into a single file and compile it. You'll be able to get as many primes as your computer and your patience permit.

A disadvantage of this program is that when you have a large number of primes, the output whizzes by on the screen before you can inspect it. You can do several things to fix this. You can write the output to the printer for a permanent record, instead of writing it to the screen. Or perhaps you can arrange for the program to display a prompt and wait for the user to press a key, between the output of one block and the next.

....

Moving Around in a File

For many applications, you need to be able to access data in a file other than in the sequential order you've used up to now. You can always find some information that's stored in the middle of a file by reading from the beginning and continuing in sequence until you find what you want. But if you've written a few million items to the file, this may take some time.

Of course, to access data in random sequence requires that you have some means of knowing where the data that you would like to retrieve is stored in the file. Arranging for this is a complicated topic in general. There are many different ways of constructing pointers or indexes to make direct access to the data in a file faster and easier. The basic idea is similar to that of an index to a book. You have a table of keys that identify the contents of each record in the file you might want, and each key has an associated position in the file defined that records where the data is stored.

Let's look at the basic tools in the library that you need to enable you to deal with this kind of file input/output.

File Positioning Operations

There are two aspects to file positioning: finding out where you are at a given point in a file and moving to a given point in a file. The former is basic to the latter: if you never know where you are, you can never decide how to get to where you want to go.

A random position in a file can be accessed regardless of whether the file concerned was written in binary or text mode. However, working with text mode files can get rather complicated in some environments. This results from the fact that the number of characters recorded in the file can be greater than the number you actually wrote. This is due to a '\n' character in memory translating into two characters when written to a file in text mode (carriage return, CR, and linefeed, LF). Of course, your C library sorts everything out when you read the data back. The problem arises when you think a point in the file is 100 bytes from the beginning. If you subsequently write some different data that's the same length in memory, it will only be the same length on the file if it contains the same number of '\n' characters. For this reason, you'll sidestep the complications of moving about in text files and concentrate the examples on the much more useful—and easier—context of binary files.

Finding Out Where You Are

You have two functions to tell you where you are in a file, both of which are very similar but not identical. They each complement a different positioning function. The first is the function ftell(), which has the prototype

```
long ftell(FILE *pfile);
```

This function accepts a file pointer as an argument and returns a long integer value that specifies the current position in the file. This could be used with the file that's referenced by the pointer pfile that you've used previously, as in the following statement:

```
fpos = ftell(pfile);
```

The variable fops of type long now holds the current position in the file and, as you'll see, you can use this in a function call to return to this position at any subsequent time. The value is actually the offset in bytes from the beginning of the file.

The second function providing information on the current file position is a little more complicated. The prototype of the function is

```
int fgetpos(FILE *pfile, fpos_t *position);
```

The first parameter is your old friend the file pointer. The second parameter is a pointer to a type that's defined in stdio.h called fpos_t. If you're curious about fpos_t, then have a look at it in stdio.h; otherwise, don't worry too much about it.

This function is designed to be used with the positioning function fsetpos(), which you'll come to very shortly. The function fgetpos() returns 0 if the operation was successful; otherwise, it returns a nonzero integer value. You could declare a variable here to be of type fpos_t with a statement such as this:

```
fpos_t here = 0;
```

You could now record the current position in the file with the statement

```
fgetpos(pfile, &here);
```

This records the current file position in the variable here.

 CAUTION *Note that you must declare a variable of type* fpos_t. *It's no good just declaring a pointer of type* fpos_t*, *as there won't be any memory allocated to store the position data.*

Setting a Position in a File

As a complement to ftell(), you have the function fseek(), which has the prototype

```
int fseek(FILE *pfile, long offset, int origin);
```

The first parameter is a pointer to the file you're repositioning. The second and third parameters define where you want to go. The second parameter is an offset from a reference point specified by the third parameter. The reference point can be one of three values that are specified by the predefined names SEEK_SET, which defines the beginning of the file; SEEK_CUR, which defines the current position in the file; and SEEK_END, which, as you might guess, defines the end of the file. Of course, all three values are defined in the header file stdio.h. For a text mode file, the second argument must be a value that was returned by ftell() if you're to avoid getting lost. The third argument for text mode files must be SEEK_SET. So for text mode files, all operations with fseek() are performed with reference to the beginning of the file.

For binary files, the offset argument is simply a relative byte count. You can therefore supply positive or negative values for the offset when the reference point is specified as SEEK_CUR.

You have the fsetpos() function to go with fgetpos(). This has the rather straightforward prototype

```
int fsetpos(FILE *pfile, fpos_t *position);
```

The first parameter is a pointer to the file that was opened with fopen(), and the second is a pointer of the type you can see, where the value was obtained by calling fsetpos().

You can't go far wrong with this one really. You could use it with a statement such as this:

```
fsetpos(pfile, &here);
```

The variable here was previously set by a call to fgetpos(). As with fgetpos(), a nonzero value is returned on error. Because this function is designed to work with a value that was returned by fgetpos(), you can only use it to get to a place in a file that you've been to before, whereas fseek() allows you to go to any specific position.

Note that the verb "seek" is used to refer to operations of moving the read/write heads of a disk drive directly to a specific position in the file. This is why the function fseek() is so named.

With a file that you've opened for update by specifying the mode as "rb+" or "wb+", for example, either a read or a write may be safely carried out on the file after executing either of the file positioning functions, fsetpos() or fseek(). This is regardless of what the previous operation on the file was.

....

Try It Out: Random Access to a File

To exercise your newfound skills with files, you can modify a program from the previous chapter to allow you to keep a dossier on family members. In this case, you'll create a file containing data on all family members, and then you'll process the file to output data on each member and that member's parents. This example has been coded to illustrate aspects of using the C language, rather than elegance or consistency in usage. The structures used only extend to a minimum range of members in each case. You can, of course, embellish these to hold any kind of scuttlebutt you like on your relatives.

Let's look at the function main() first:

```
/* Program 12.5 Investigating the family.*/
#include <stdio.h>
#include <ctype.h>
#include <stdlib.h>
```

(Continued)

```
#include <string.h>

char myfile[] = "C:\\myfile.bin";              /* Physical file name    */
FILE *pfile = NULL;                             /* File pointer          */

struct Date                                     /* Structure for a date  */
{
   int day;
   int month;
   int year;
};

typedef struct family                  /* Family structure declaration */
{
   struct Date dob;
   char name[20];
   char pa_name[20];
   char ma_name[20];
}Family;

/* Function prototypes */
int get_person(Family *pfamily);         /* Input function            */
void show_person_data(void);             /* Output function           */
void get_parent_dob(Family *pfamily);    /* Function to find pa & ma */

void main()
{
   Family member;                          /* Stores a family structure */
   Family *pmember = &member;              /* Points to the family structure */

   if((pfile = fopen(myfile, "wb")) == NULL)
   {
     printf("\nUnable to open %s for writing.\n", myfile);
     abort();
   }

   while(get_person(pmember))              /* As long as we have input */
     fwrite(pmember, sizeof member, 1, pfile);   /*   write it away     */

   fclose(pfile);                   /* Close the file now that it's written */

   show_person_data();                     /* Show what we can find out    */

   if(remove(myfile))
     printf("\nUnable to delete %s.\n", myfile);
   else
     printf("\nDeleted %s OK.\n", myfile);
}
```

(Continued)

HOW IT WORKS

After the #include statements, you have the global variables and structure defini-tions. You've seen all of these in previous examples. Family isn't a variable, but it has been declared as a type name for the structure family. This will allow you to declare Family type objects without having to use the keyword struct. Following the structure declarations, you have the prototypes for the three functions that you're using in addition to main().

Because you want to try out the file-positioning functions in addition to the basic file read and write operations, the example has been designed to exercise these as well. You get the input on one person at a time in the get_person() func-tion, where the data is stored in the structure pointed to by pmember. You write each structure to the file as soon as it is received, and the input process ceases when the function get_person() returns 0.

When the while loop ends, the input file is closed and the function show_person_data() is called. You use the file position getting and setting func-tions within this function. Lastly, the file is deleted from the disk by the function remove().

The code for the input function, get_person(), is as follows:

```
/* Function to input data on Family members */
int get_person( Family *temp)
{
    static char more = '\0';                      /* Test value for ending input */

    printf("\nDo you want to enter details of a%s person (Y or N)? ",
                                 more != '\0'?"nother " : "" );
    scanf(" %c", &more);

    if(tolower(more) == 'n')
          return 0;

    printf("\nEnter the name of the person: ");
    scanf("%s", temp->name);                      /* Read the Family's name */

    printf("\nEnter %s's date of birth (day month year); ", temp->name);
    scanf("%d %d %d", &temp->dob.day, &temp->dob.month, &temp->dob.year);

    printf("\nWho is %s's father? ", temp->name);
    scanf("%s", temp->pa_name);                   /* Get the father's name  */

    printf("\nWho is %s's mother? ", temp->name);
    scanf("%s", temp->ma_name);                   /* Get the mother's name  */

    return 1;
}
```

(Continued)

This function is fairly self-explanatory. None of the mechanisms involved in this function is new to you. An indicator, more, controls whether or not reading data continues, and it's set by the input following the first prompt. It's defined as static so the variable and its value persists in the program from one call of get_person() to the next. This allows the prompt to work correctly in selecting a slightly different message for the second and subsequent iterations.

If no data input takes place, which is triggered when **N** or **n** is entered in response to the initial prompt in the function, 0 is returned. If more data entry occurs, it's entered into the appropriate structure members and 1 is returned.

The next function generates the output for each person, including the date of birth of both parents, if they've been recorded. The code for this function is as follows:

```
/* Function to output data on people on file   */
void show_person_data(void)
{
    Family member;                      /* Structure to hold data from file  */
    Family *pmember = &member;          /* Pointer to Family structure        */
    fpos_t current = 0;                 /* File position                      */

    pfile = fopen(myfile, "rb");        /* Open file for binary read          */

    /* Read data on person */
    while(fread(pmember, sizeof member, 1, pfile))
    {
      fgetpos(pfile, &current);         /* Save current position              */
      printf("\n\n%s's father is %s, and mother is %s.",
              pmember->name, pmember->pa_name, pmember->ma_name);
      get_parent_dob(pmember);          /* Get parent data                    */
      fsetpos(pfile, &current);         /* Position file to read next         */
    }
      fclose(pfile);                    /* Close the file                     */
}
```

This function processes each structure in sequence from the file. At the outset, an object of type Family and a pointer to it are declared in the following statements:

```
    Family member;                      /* Structure to hold data from file  */
    Family *pmember = &member;          /* Pointer to Family structure        */
```

The first variable declared is member of type Family, and the second is of type "pointer to Family" and is initialized with the address of the first variable declared, member. The variable member has space allocated for the structure type, and pmember provides a convenient working pointer.

(Continued)

Next, a local variable, current, is declared with the following statement:

```
fpos_t current = 0;                    /* File position              */
```

This statement declares current as type fpos_t. This variable will be used to remember the current position in the file. The get_parent_dob() function is called later in this function, which also accesses the file. It's therefore necessary to remember the file position of the next structure to be read on each iteration before calling get_parent_dob().

After opening the file for binary read operations, all of the processing takes place in a loop controlled by

```
while(fread(pmember, sizeof member, 1, pfile))
```

This uses the technique of reading the file within the loop condition and using the value returned by the function fread() as the determinant of whether or not the loop continues. If the function returns 1, the loop continues, and when 0 is returned, the loop is terminated.

Within the loop you have these statements:

```
fgetpos(pfile, &current);          /* Save current position      */
printf("\n\n%s's father is %s, and mother is %s.",
        pmember->name, pmember->pa_name, pmember->ma_name);
get_parent_dob(pmember);           /* Get parent data            */
fsetpos(pfile, &current);          /* Position file to read next */
```

First, the current position in the file is saved, and the parents of the current person pointed to by pmember are displayed. You then call the function get_parent_dob(), which will search the file for parent entries. On returning after the call to this function, the file position is unknown, so a call to fsetpos() is made to restore it to the position required for the next structure to be read. After all the structures have been processed, the while loop terminates and the file is closed.

The function to find the dates of birth for the parents of an individual is as follows:

```
/* Function to find parents' dates of birth. */
void get_parent_dob(Family *pmember)
{
    Family testmem;                      /* Stores a relative       */
    Family *ptestmem = &testmem;         /* Pointer to the relative */
    int num_found = 0;                   /* Count of relatives found */

    rewind(pfile);                       /* Set file to the beginning */

    /* Get the stuff on a relative */
```

(Continued)

```
        while(fread(ptestmem, sizeof(Family), 1, pfile))
        {
          if(strcmp(pmember->pa_name, ptestmem->name) == 0)    /*Is it pa?        */
          { /* We have found dear old dad */
            printf("\n Pa was born on %d/%d/%d.",
                  ptestmem->dob.day, ptestmem->dob.month, ptestmem->dob.year);

            if(++num_found == 2)                    /* Increment parent count    */
              return;                               /* We got both so go home     */
          }
          else
            if(strcmp(pmember->ma_name, ptestmem->name) == 0) /*Is it ma?        */
            { /* We have found dear old ma */
              printf("\n Ma was born on %d/%d/%d.",
                    ptestmem->dob.day, ptestmem->dob.month, ptestmem->dob.year);

              if(++num_found == 2)                    /* Increment parent count    */
                  return;                             /* We got both so go home     */
            }
        }
      }
```

As the file has already been opened by the calling program, it's only necessary to set it back to the beginning with the rewind() function before beginning processing. The file is then read sequentially, searching each structure that's read for a match with either parent name. The search mechanism for the father is contained in the following statements:

```
        if(strcmp(pmember->pa_name, ptestmem->name) == 0)    /*Is it pa?        */
        { /* We have found dear old dad */
          printf("\n Pa was born on %d/%d/%d.",
                ptestmem->dob.day, ptestmem->dob.month, ptestmem->dob.year);

          if(++num_found == 2)                    /* Increment parent count    */
            return;                               /* We got both so go home     */
        }
```

The name entry for the father of the person indicated by pmember is compared with the name member in the structure indicated by ptestmem. The pointer, ptestmem, has the address of the family structure that was last read as a candidate parent. If the father check fails, the function continues with an identical mother check.

If a parent is found, the date of birth information is displayed. A count is kept in num_found of the number of parents discovered in the file, and the function is exited if both have been found. The function ends in any event after all structures have been read from the file.

(Continued)

To run this program, you need to assemble the code for main() and the other functions into a single file. You can then compile and execute it. Of course, the example could have been written equally well using ftell() and fseek() as positioning functions.

As in the previous examples in this chapter, the program uses a specific file name, on the assumption that the file doesn't already exist when the program is run. There's a way in C to create temporary files that get around this.

....

Using Temporary Work Files

Very often you need a work file just for the duration of a program. You use it only to store intermediate results and you can throw it away when the program is finished. The program that calculates primes in this chapter is a good example. You really only need the file during the calculation.

You have a choice of two functions to help with temporary file usage, and each has advantages and disadvantages.

Creating a Temporary Work File

The first function will create a temporary file automatically. Its prototype is

```
FILE *tmpfile(void);
```

The function takes no arguments and returns a pointer to the temporary file. If the file can't be created for any reason—for example, if the disk is full—the function returns NULL. The file is created and opened for update, so it can be written and read, but obviously it needs to be in that order. You can only ever get out what you have put in. The file is automatically deleted on exit from your program, so there's no need to worry about any mess left behind. You'll never know what the file is called, and because it doesn't last this doesn't matter.

The disadvantage of this function is that the file will be deleted as soon as you close it. This means you can't close the file, having written it in one part of the program, and then reopen it in another part of the program to read the data. You must keep the file open for as long as you need access to the data. A simple illustration of creating a temporary file is provided by these statements:

```
FILE pfile;                        /* File pointer                 */
pfile = tmpfile();                 /* Get pointer to temporary file */
```

Creating a Unique File Name

The second possibility is to use a function that provides you with a unique file name. Whether or not this ends up as the name of a temporary file is up to you. The prototype for this function is

```
char *tmpnam(char *filename);
```

If the argument to the function is NULL, the file name is generated in an internal static object, and a pointer to that object is returned. If you want the name stored in a char array that you declare yourself, it must be at least L_tmpnam characters long, where L_tmpnam is a constant predefined in stdio.h. In this case, the file name is stored in the array that you specify as an argument, and a pointer to your array is also returned.

So, to take the first possibility, you can create a unique file with the following statements:

```
FILE *pfile = NULL;
char *filename = NULL;
pfile = fopen(filename = tmpnam(NULL), "wb+");
```

Here, you declare your file pointer pfile and your pointer filename that will contain the address of the temporary file name. You combine the call to tmpnam() with the call to open the file by putting the assignment as the first argument to fopen(). Because the argument to tmpnam() is NULL, the file name will be generated as an internal static object whose address will be placed in the pointer filename.

Don't be tempted to write this:

```
pfile = fopen(tmpnam(NULL), "wb+");    /* Wrong!! */
```

If you do, you no longer have access to the file name, so you can't use remove() to delete the file.

If you want to create the array to hold the file name yourself, you could write this:

```
FILE *pfile = NULL;
char filename[L_tmpnam];
pfile = fopen(tmpnam(filename), "wb+");
```

Remember, the assistance that you've obtained from the standard library is just to provide a unique name. It's your responsibility to delete any files created.

NOTE *You should note that you'll be limited to a maximum number of unique names from this function in your program, but it will be at least 25, and with some implementations a great deal more.*

Designing a Program

Now that you've come to the end of this chapter, you can put what you've learned into practice with a final program.

The Problem

The problem you're going to solve is to write a file viewer program. This will display any file in hexadecimal representation and as characters.

The Analysis

The program will open the file as binary read-only and then display the information in two columns, the first being the hexadecimal representation of the bytes in the file, and the second being the bytes represented as characters. The file name will be supplied as a command-line argument or, if that isn't supplied, the program will ask for the file name.

The stages are as follows:

1. If the file name isn't supplied, get it from the user.

2. Open the file.

3. Read and display the contents of the file.

The Solution

This section outlines the steps you'll take to solve the problem.

Step 1

You can easily check to see if the file name appears at the command line by specifying that the function main() has parameters. Up until now, you've chosen to ignore the possibility of parameters being passed to main() that I introduced in Chapter 9, but here you can use it as the means of identifying the file that's to be displayed. You'll recall that when main() is called, two parameters are passed to it. The first parameter is an integer indicating the number of words in the command line, and the second is an array of pointers to strings. The first string contains the name that you used to start the program at the command line, and the remaining strings represent the arguments that follow at the command line. Of course, this mechanism allows an arbitrary number of values to be entered at the command line and passed to main().

If the value of the first argument to main() is 1, then there's only the program name on the command line, so in this case you'll have to prompt for the file name to be entered:

```c
/* Program 12.6 Viewing the contents of a file */
#include <stdio.h>

int main(int argc, char *argv[])
{
  char filename[80];                   /* Stores the file name         */

  if(argc == 1)                        /* No file name on command line? */
  {
    printf("Please enter a filename: "); /* Prompt for input           */
    gets(filename);                    /* Get the file name entered    */
  }
  return 0;
}
```

Note that you also have the return type for main() specified as type int. The value returned from main() is passed to the operating system, and it can be used as an indicator of whether or not the program ran successfully.

Step 2

If the first argument to main() isn't 1, then you have at least one more argument, which you assume is the file name. You therefore copy the string pointed to by argv[1] to the variable openfile. Assuming that you have a valid file name, you can open the file and start reading it:

```c
/* Program 12.6 Viewing the contents of a file */
#include <stdio.h>

int main(int argc, char *argv[])
{
  char filename[80];                   /* Stores the file name         */
  FILE *pfile;                         /* File pointer                 */

  if(argc == 1)                        /* No file name on command line? */
  {
    printf("Please enter a filename: "); /* Prompt for input           */
    gets(filename);                    /* Get the file name entered    */
  }
  else
    strcpy(filename, argv[1]);         /* Get 2nd command line string   */

  /* File can be opened OK? */
  if((pfile = fopen(filename, "rb")) == NULL)
  {
```

```
    printf("Sorry, can't open %s", filename);
    return -1;
  }
  fclose(pfile);                        /* Close the file             */
  return 0;
}
```

You put the call to the fclose() function to close the file at the end of the program so that you don't forget about it later. Also, you use a return value of –1 for the program to indicate when an error has occurred.

Step 3

You can now output the file contents. You do this by reading the file 1 byte at a time and saving this data in a buffer. Once the buffer is full or the end of file has been reached, you output the buffer in the format you want. When you output the data as characters, you must first check that the character is printable; otherwise strange things may start happening on the screen. You use the function isprint(), declared in ctype.h, for this. If the character isn't printable, you'll print a period instead.

Here's the complete code for the program:

```
/* Program 12.6 Viewing the contents of a file */
#include <stdio.h>
#include <ctype.h>
#include <string.h>

#define DISPLAY 80                      /* Length of display line     */
#define PAGE_LENGTH 20                  /* Lines per page             */

int main(int argc, char *argv[])
{
  char filename[80];                    /* Stores the file name       */
  FILE *pfile;                          /* File pointer               */
  unsigned char buffer[DISPLAY/4 - 1];  /* File input buffer          */
  int count = 0;                        /* Count of characters in buffer */
  int lines = 0;                        /* Number of lines displayed  */
  int i = 0;                            /* Loop counter               */

  if(argc == 1)                         /* No file name on command line? */
  {
    printf("Please enter a filename: "); /* Prompt for input          */
    gets(filename);                     /* Get the file name entered  */
  }
  else
    strcpy(filename, argv[1]);          /* Get 2nd command line string */

    /* File can be opened OK?        */
    if((pfile = fopen(filename, "rb")) == NULL)
    {
```

```
            printf("Sorry, can't open %s", filename);
            return -1;
          }
       while(!feof(pfile))                      /* Continue until end of file   */
       {
         if(count < sizeof buffer)              /* If the buffer is not full    */
           buffer[count++] = (unsigned char)fgetc(pfile);    /* Read a character */
         else
         { /* Output the buffer contents, first as hexadecimal */
           for(count = 0; count < sizeof buffer; count++)
             printf("%02X ", buffer[count]);
           printf("| ");                        /* Output separator             */

           /* Now display buffer contents as characters */
           for(count = 0; count < sizeof buffer; count++)
             printf("%c", isprint(buffer[count]) ? buffer[count]:'.');
           printf("\n");                         /* End the line                 */
           count = 0;                            /* Reset count                  */

           if(!(++lines%PAGE_LENGTH))            /* End of page?                 */
            if(getchar()=='E')                   /* Wait for Enter               */
              return 0;                          /* E pressed                    */
         }
       }

       /* Display the last line, first as hexadecimal */
       for(i = 0; i < sizeof buffer; i++)
         if(i < count)
           printf("%02X ", buffer[i]);          /* Output hexadecimal           */
         else
           printf("   ");                        /* Output spaces                */
       printf("| ");                             /* Output separator             */

       /* Display last line as characters */
       for(i = 0; i < count; i++)
         /* Output character     */
         printf("%c",isprint(buffer[i]) ? buffer[i]:'.');
       /* End the line          */
       printf("\n");
       fclose(pfile);                            /* Close the file               */
       return 0;
     }
```

The symbol DISPLAY specifies the width of a line on the screen for output, and the symbol PAGE_LENGTH specifies the number of lines per page. You arrange to display a page, and then wait for Enter to be pressed before displaying the next page, thus avoiding the whole file whizzing by before you can read it.

You declare the buffer to hold input from the file as

```
unsigned char buffer[DISPLAY/4 - 1];     /* File input buffer              */
```

The expression for the array dimension arises from the fact that you'll need four characters on the screen to display each character from the file, plus one separator. Each character will be displayed as two hexadecimal digits plus a space, and as a single character, making four characters in all.

You continue reading as long as the `while` loop condition is true:

```
while(!feof(pfile))                     /* Continue until end of file   */
```

The library function, `feof()`, returns true if `EOF` was read from the file specified by the argument; otherwise, it returns false.

You fill the `buffer` array with characters from the file in the `if` statement:

```
if(count < sizeof buffer)               /* If the buffer is not full    */
  buffer[count++] = (unsigned char)fgetc(pfile);   /* Read a character  */
```

When `count` exceeds the capacity of `buffer`, the `else` clause will be executed to output the contents of the buffer:

```
else
{ /* Output the buffer contents, first as hexadecimal */
  for(count = 0; count < sizeof buffer; count++)
    printf("%02X ", buffer[count]);
  printf("| ");                         /* Output separator             */

  /* Now display buffer contents as characters */
  for(count = 0; count < sizeof buffer; count++)
    printf("%c", isprint(buffer[count]) ? buffer[count]:'.');
  printf("\n");                         /* End the line                 */
  count = 0;                            /* Reset count                  */

  if(!(++lines%PAGE_LENGTH))            /* End of page?                 */
    if(getchar()=='E')                  /* Wait for Enter               */
      return 0;                         /* E pressed                    */
}
```

The first `for` loop outputs the contents of `buffer` as hexadecimal characters. You then output a separator character and execute the next `for` loop to output the same data as characters. The conditional operator in the second argument to `printf()` ensures that nonprinting characters are output as a period.

The `if` statement increments the line count, `lines`, and for every `PAGE_LENGTH` number of lines, waits for a character to be entered. If you press Enter, the next pageful will be displayed, but if you press **E** and then Enter, the program will end. This provides you with an opportunity to escape from continuing to output the contents of a file that's larger than you thought.

The final couple of `for` loops are similar to those you've just seen. The only difference is that spaces are output for array elements that don't contain file characters. An example of the output is as follows. It shows part of the source file for the self-same program.

```
Please enter a filename: E:\Prog12_06.c
2F 2A 20 50 72 6F 67 72 61 6D 20 31 32 2E 36 20 56 69 65 | /* Program 12.6 Vie
77 69 6E 67 20 74 68 65 20 63 6F 6E 74 65 6E 74 73 20 6F | wing the contents o
66 20 61 20 66 69 6C 65 20 2A 2F 0D 0A 23 69 6E 63 6C 75 | f a file */..#inclu
64 65 20 3C 73 74 64 69 6F 2E 68 3E 0D 0A 23 69 6E 63 6C | de <stdio.h>..#incl
75 64 65 20 3C 63 74 79 70 65 2E 68 3E 20 0D 0A 23 69 6E | ude <ctype.h> ..#in
63 6C 75 64 65 20 3C 73 74 72 69 6E 67 2E 68 3E 20 0D 0A | clude <string.h> ..
0D 0A 23 64 65 66 69 6E 65 20 44 49 53 50 4C 41 59 20 38 | ..#define DISPLAY 8
30 20 20 20 20 20 20 20 20 20 2F 2A 20 4C 65 6E 67 74 68 20 6F | 0       /* Length o
66 20 64 69 73 70 6C 61 79 20 6C 69 6E 65 20 2A 2F 0D 0A | f display line */..
23 64 65 66 69 6E 65 20 50 41 47 45 5F 4C 45 4E 47 54 48 | #define PAGE_LENGTH
20 32 30 20 20 20 2F 2A 20 4C 69 6E 65 73 20 70 65 72 20 | 20   /* Lines per
70 61 67 65 20 20 20 20 20 20 20 20 20 2A 2F 0D 0A 0D 0A 20 | page         */....
69 6E 74 20 6D 61 69 6E 28 69 6E 74 20 61 72 67 63 2C 20 | int main(int argc,
63 68 61 72 20 2A 61 72 67 76 5B 5D 29 0D 0A 7B 0D 0A 20 | char *argv[])..{..
20 20 63 68 61 72 20 66 69 6C 65 6E 61 6D 65 5B 38 30 5D | char filename[80]
3B 20 20 2F 2A 20 53 74 6F 72 65 73 20 74 68 65 20 66 69 | ;  /* Stores the fi
6C 65 20 6E 61 6D 65 20 2A 2F 0D 0A 20 20 20 46 49 4C 45 | le name */..   FILE
20 2A 70 66 69 6C 65 3B 20 20 20 20 20 20 20 20 2F 2A 20 | *pfile;        /*
46 69 6C 65 20 70 6F 69 6E 74 65 72 20 20 20 20 20 20 20 | File pointer
20 20 2A 2F 0D 0A 20 20 20 75 6E 73 69 67 6E 65 64 20 63 | */..   unsigned c
```

Summary

Within this chapter I've covered all of the basic tools necessary to provide you with the ability to program the complete spectrum of file functions. The degree to which these have been demonstrated in examples has been, of necessity, relatively limited. There are many ways of applying these tools to provide more sophisticated ways of managing and retrieving information in a file. For example, it's possible to write index information into the file, either as a specific index at a known place in the file, often the beginning, or as position pointers within the blocks of data, rather like the pointers in a linked list. You should experiment with file operations until you feel confident that you understand the mechanisms involved.

Although the functions I discussed in this chapter cover most of the abilities you're likely to need, you'll find that the input/output library provided with your compiler offers quite a few additional functions that give you even more options for handling your file operations.

Exercises

The following exercises enable you to try out what you've learned in this chapter. If you get stuck, look back over the chapter for help. If you're still stuck, you can download the solutions from the Downloads area of the Apress website (http://www.apress.com), but that really should be a last resort.

Exercise 12-1. Write a program that will write an arbitrary number of strings to a file. The strings should be entered from the keyboard and the program shouldn't delete the file, as it will be used in the next exercise.

Exercise 12-2. Write a program that will read the file that was created by the previous exercise, and retrieve the strings one at a time in reverse sequence and write them to a new file in the sequence in which they were retrieved. For example, the program will retrieve the last string and write that to the new file, then retrieve the second to last and retrieve that from the file, and so on for each string in the original file.

Exercise 12-3. Write a program that will read names and telephone numbers from the keyboard and write them to a new file if a file doesn't already exist and add them if the file does exist. The program should optionally list all the entries.

Exercise 12-4. Extend the program from the previous exercise to implement retrieval of all the numbers corresponding to a given second name. The program should allow further inquiries, adding new name/number entries and deleting existing entries.

CHAPTER 13

Supporting Facilities

AT THIS POINT YOU'VE COVERED THE COMPLETE C language, as well as the important library functions. You should be reasonably confident in programming all aspects of the language. If you aren't, that's simply because you need more practice. Once you've learned the elements of the language, competence comes down to practice, practice, practice.

In this final chapter I'll tie up a few loose ends. You'll delve deeper into the capabilities you have available through the preprocessor, and you'll look at a few more library functions that you're sure to find useful.

In this chapter you'll learn

- More about the preprocessor and its operation

- How to write preprocessor macros

- What logical preprocessor directives are and how you can use them

- What conditional compilation is and how you can apply it

- More about the debugging methods that are available to you

- How you use some of the additional available library functions

Preprocessing

As you are certainly aware of by now, preprocessing of your source code occurs before it's compiled to machine instructions. The preprocessing phase can execute a range of service operations specified by preprocessor directives, which are identified by the # symbol as the first character. The preprocessing phase provides an opportunity for manipulating and modifying your C source code prior to compilation. Once the preprocessing phase is completed, and all directives have been analyzed and executed, the compiler begins the compile phase proper, which generates the machine code equivalent of your program.

You've already used preprocessor directives in all the examples, and you're familiar with both the #include and #define directives. There are a number of other directives that add considerable flexibility to the way in which you specify your programs. Keep in mind, as you proceed, that all these are preprocessing operations that occur before your program is compiled. They modify the set of statements that constitute your program. They aren't involved in the execution of your program at all.

Including Header Files in Your Programs

A header file is any external file, usually stored on disk, whose contents are included into your program by use of the #include preprocessor directive. You're completely familiar with statements such as this:

```
#include <stdio.h>
```

This fetches the standard library header file supporting input/output operations into your program.

This is a particular case of the general statement for including standard libraries into your program:

```
#include <standard_library_file_name>
```

Any library header file name can appear between the angled brackets. If you include a header file that you don't use, the only effect, apart from slightly confusing anyone reading the program, is to extend the compilation time.

You can include your own source files into your program with a slightly different #include statement. Here's a typical example:

```
#include "MYFILE.H"
```

This statement will introduce the contents of the file named between double quotes into the program in place of the #include directive. The contents of any file can be included into your program by this means. You simply specify the name of the file between quotes as shown in the example. With the majority of compilers, you can specify the file name with either upper- or lowercase characters.

You can also give the file whatever name you like. You don't have to use the extension .H, although it's a convention commonly adhered to by most programmers in C. The difference between using this form and using angled brackets lies in the source assumed for the required file. The precise operation is compiler dependent and will be described in the compiler documentation, but usually the first form will search the default header file directory for the required file, whereas the second form will search the source directory followed by the default header file directory.

You can use this mechanism for dividing your program into several files and, of course, for managing the declarations for any library functions of your own. A very common use of this facility is to create a header file containing all the function prototypes and global variables. These can then be managed as a separate unit and included at the beginning of the program. You need to avoid duplicating information if you include more than one file into your program. Duplicate code will often cause compilation errors. You'll see later in this chapter how you can ensure that any given block of code will appear only once in your program, even if you inadvertently include it several times.

NOTE *A file introduced into your program by an* #include *directive may also contain another* #include *directive. If so, preprocessing will deal with the second* #include *in the same way as the first and continue replacing such directives with the contents of the corresponding file until there are no more* #include *directives in the program.*

External Variables and Functions

With a program that's made up of several files, you'll frequently find that you want to use a global variable that's defined in another file. You can do this by declaring the variable as external to the current file using the extern keyword. For example, if you have variables defined in another file as global (which means outside of any of the functions) using the statements

```
int number = 0;
long array[20] = { 0L };
```

then in a function in which you want to access these, you can specify that these variable names are external by using the statements

```
extern int number;
extern long array[20];
```

These statements don't create these variables—they just identify to the compiler that these names are defined elsewhere for the rest of this source file. The variable must be declared somewhere else in the program, usually in another source file. If you want to make these external variables accessible to all functions within the current file, then you should declare them as external at the very beginning of the file, prior to any of the functions' definitions. With programs consisting of several files, it's common practice to place all global variables at the beginning of one file and all the extern statements in a header file. The extern statements can then be incorporated into any program file that needs access to these variables by using an include statement for the header file.

NOTE *Only one **declaration** of each global variable is allowed in a file. Of course, the global variables may be declared as external in as many files as necessary.*

Substitutions in Your Program Code

There are preprocessor directives for replacing symbols in your source code before it's compiled. The simplest kind of symbol substitution you can make is one you've already seen. For example, the preprocessor directive to substitute the specified numeric value, wherever the character string PI occurs, is as follows:

```
#define PI 3.14159265
```

Apart from the fact that PI *looks* like a variable, this has nothing to do with variables. Here the identifier PI is a token, rather like a voucher, that is exchanged for the sequence of digits specified in the #define directive. When your program is ready to be compiled after preprocessing has been completed, the string PI will no longer appear, having been replaced by its definition wherever it occurs in the source file. The general form of this sort of preprocessor directive is

```
#define identifier sequence_of_characters
```

Here, identifier conforms to the usual definition of an identifier in C, as any sequence of letters and digits, the first of which is a letter and where the underline character counts as a letter. Note that the replacement for identifier is any sequence of characters, not just digits.

A very common use of the #define directive is to define array dimensions by way of a substitution, to allow a number of array dimensions to be determined by a single token. Only one directive in the program then needs to be modified to alter the dimensions of a number of arrays in the program. This helps considerably in minimizing errors when such changes are necessary, for example:

```
#define DIMENSION 50
int array1[DIMENSION] = { 0 };
int array2[DIMENSION] = { 0 };
int array3[DIMENSION] = { 0 };
```

Here, the dimensions of all three arrays can be changed by modifying the single #define directive, and of course the array declarations that are affected can be anywhere in the program file. The advantages of this approach in a large program involving dozens or even hundreds of functions should be obvious. Not only is it easy to make a change, but also using this approach ensures that the same value is being used through a program. This is especially important with large projects involving several programmers working together to produce the final product.

You've used numerical substitution in the last two examples, but as I said, you're in no way limited to this. You could, for example, write

```
#define Black White
```

This will cause any occurrence of `Black` in your program to be replaced with `White`. The sequence of characters that is to replace the token identifier can be anything at all.

Macro Substitutions

A **macro** is based on the ideas implicit in the `#define` directive examples you've seen so far, but it provides a greater range of possible results by allowing what might be called multiple parameterized substitutions. This not only involves substitution of a fixed sequence of characters for a token identifier, but also allows parameters to be specified, which may themselves be replaced by argument values, wherever the parameter appears in the substitution sequence.

Let's look at an example:

```
#define Print(My_var) printf("%d", My_var)
```

This directive provides for two levels of substitution. There is the substitution for `Print(My_var)` by the string immediately following it in the `#define` statement, and there is the possible substitution of alternatives for `My_var`. You could, for example, write

```
Print(ival);
```

This will be converted during preprocessing to the statement

```
printf("%d", ival);
```

You could use this directive to specify a `printf()` statement for an integer variable at various points in your program. A common use for this kind of macro is to allow a simple representation of a complicated function call in order to enhance the readability of a program.

Macros That Look Like Functions

The general form of the kind of substitution directive just discussed is

```
#define macro_name( list_of_identifiers ) substitution_string
```

This shows that in the general case, multiple parameters are permitted, so you're able to define more complex substitutions.

 CAUTION *You must not leave a space between the macro name and the left parenthesis enclosing the substitution arguments.*

To illustrate how you use this, you can define a macro for producing a maximum of two values with the following directive:

```
#define max(x, y) x>y ? x : y
```

You can then put the statement in the program:

```
result = max(myval, 99);
```

This will be expanded during preprocessing to produce the following code:

```
result = myval>99 ? myval : 99;
```

It's important to be conscious of the substitution that is taking place, and not to assume that this is a function. You can get some strange results otherwise, particularly if your substitution identifiers include an explicit or implicit assignment. For example, the following modest extension of the last example can produce an erroneous result:

```
result = max(myval++, 99);
```

The substitution process will generate this statement:

```
result = myval++>99 ? myval++ : 99;
```

The consequence of this is that if the value of myval is larger than 99, myval will be incremented twice. Note that it does *not* help to use parentheses in this situation. If you write the statement as

```
result = max((myval++), 99);
```

preprocessing will convert this to

```
result = (myval++>99) ? (myval++) : 99;
```

You need to be very cautious if you're writing macros that generate expressions of any kind. In addition to the multiple substitution trap you've just seen, precedence rules can also catch you out. A simple example will illustrate this. Suppose you write a macro for the product of two parameters:

```
#define product(m, n)  m*n
```

You then try to use this macro with the statement

```
result = product(x, y + 1);
```

Of course, everything works fine, but you don't get the result you want, as the macro expands to

```
result = x*y + 1;
```

It could take a long time to discover that you aren't getting the product of the two parameters at all in this case, as there's no external indication of what's going on. There's just a more or less erroneous value propagating through the program. The solution is very simple. If you use macros to generate expressions, put parentheses around everything. So you should rewrite the example as follows:

```
#define product(m, n)  ((m)*(n))
```

Now everything will work as it should. The inclusion of the outer parentheses may seem excessive, but because you don't know the context in which the macro expansion will be placed, it's better to include them. If you write a macro to sum its parameters, you will easily see that without the outer parentheses, there are many contexts in which you will get a result that's different from what you expect. Even with parentheses, expanded expressions that repeat a parameter, such as the one you saw earlier that used the conditional operator, will still not work properly when the argument involves the increment or decrement operators.

Preprocessor Directives on Multiple Lines

A preprocessor directive must be a single logical line, but this doesn't prevent you from using the statement continuation character, \, that you've already seen in the context of spreading a C language statement over several lines.

You could write

```
#define min(x, y) \
             ((x)<(y) ? (x) : (y))
```

Here, the directive definition continues on the second line with the first nonblank character found, so you can position the text on the second line wherever you feel looks like the nicest arrangement. Note that the \ must be the last character on the line, immediately before you press Enter.

Strings As Macro Arguments

String constants are a potential source of confusion when used with macros. The simplest string substitution is a single-level definition such as

```
#define MYSTR "This string"
```

Suppose you now write the statement

```
printf("%s", MYSTR);
```

This will be converted during preprocessing into the statement

```
printf("%s", "This string");
```

This should be what you are expecting. You couldn't use the #define directive without the quotes in the substitution sequence and expect to be able to put the quotes in your program text instead. For example, suppose you write

```
#define  MYSTR  This string
  ...
printf("%s", "MYSTR" );
```

There will be no substitution for MYSTR in the printf() function in this case. Anything in quotes in your program is assumed to be a literal string, so it won't be analyzed during preprocessing.

There's a special way of specifying that the substitution for a macro argument is to be implemented as a string. For example, you could specify a macro to display a string using the function printf() as follows:

```
#define PrintStr(arg) printf("%s", #arg)
```

The # character preceding the appearance of the arg parameter in the macro expansion indicates that the argument is to be surrounded by double quotes when the substitution is generated. Therefore, if you write the following statement in your program:

```
PrintStr(Output);
```

this will be converted during preprocessing to

```
printf("%s", "Output");
```

You may be wondering why this apparent complication has been introduced into preprocessing. Well, without this facility you wouldn't be able to include a variable string in a macro definition at all. If you were to put the double quotes around the macro parameter, it wouldn't be interpreted as a variable; it would be merely a string with quotes around it. On the other hand, if you put the quotes in the macro expansion, the string between the quotes wouldn't be interpreted as an identifier for a parameter; it would be just a string constant. So what might appear to be an unnecessary complication at first sight is actually an essential tool for creating macros that allow strings between quotes to be created.

A common use of this mechanism is for converting a variable name to a string, such as in the directive

```
#define show(var) printf("\n%s = %d", #var, var);
```

If you now write

```
show(number);
```

this will generate the statement

```
printf("\n%s = %d", "number", number);
```

You can also generate a substitution that would allow you to display a string with double quotes included. Assuming you've defined the macro PrintStr as shown previously and you write the statement

```
PrintStr("Output");
```

it will be preprocessed into the statement

```
printf("%s", "\"Output\"");
```

This is possible because the preprocessing phase is clever enough to recognize the need to put \" at each end to get a string that includes double quotes to be displayed correctly.

Joining Two Results of a Macro Expansion

There are times when you may wish to generate two results in a macro and join them together with no spaces between them. Suppose you try to define a macro to do this as follows:

```
#define join(a, b) ab
```

This can't work in the way you need it to. The definition of the expansion will be interpreted as ab, not as the parameter a followed by the parameter b. If you separate them with a blank, the result will be separated with a blank, which isn't what you want either. The preprocessing phase provides you with another operator to solve this problem. The solution is to specify the macro as follows:

```
#define join(a, b) a##b
```

The presence of the operator consisting of the two characters ## serves to separate the parameters and to indicate that the result of the two substitutions are to be joined. For example, writing the statement

```
strlen(join(var, 123));
```

will result in the statement

```
strlen(var123);
```

This might be applied to synthesizing a variable name for some reason, or generating a format control string from two or more macro parameters.

Logical Preprocessor Directives

The last example you looked at appears to be of limited value, because it's hard to envision when you would want to simply join var to 123. After all, you could always use one parameter and write var123 as the argument. One aspect of preprocessing that adds considerably more potential to the previous example is the possibility for multiple macro substitutions where the arguments for one macro are derived from substitutions defined in another. In the last example, both arguments to the join() macro could have been generated by other #define substitutions or macros. Preprocessing also supports directives that provide a logical if capability, which vastly expands the scope of what you can do during the preprocessing phase.

Conditional Compilation

The first logical directive I'll discuss allows you to test whether an identifier exists as a result of having been created in a previous #define directive. It takes the following form:

```
#if defined identifier
```

If the specified identifier has been defined, then statements that follow the #if are included in the program code until the directive

```
#endif
```

is reached. If the identifier hasn't been defined, the statements between the #if and the #endif will be skipped. This is the same logical process you use in C programming, except that here you're applying it to the inclusion or exclusion of program statements in the source file.

You can also test for the absence of an identifier. In fact, this tends to be used more frequently than the form you've just seen. The general form of this directive is

```
#if !defined identifier
```

Here, the statements following the #if down to the #endif will be included if the identifier hasn't previously been defined. This provides you with a method of avoiding duplicating functions, or other blocks of code and directives, in a program consisting of several files, or to ensure bits of code that may occur repeatedly in different libraries aren't repeated when the #include statements in your program are processed.

The mechanism is simply to top and tail the block of code you want to avoid duplicating as follows:

```
#if !defined block1
  #define block1
  /* Block of code you do not */
  /* want to be repeated.     */
#endif
```

If the identifier block1 hasn't been defined, the block following the #if will be included and processed and block1 will be defined. The following block of code down to the #endif will also be included in your program. Any subsequent occurrence of the same group of statements won't be included because the identifier block1 now exists.

The #define directive doesn't need to specify a substitution value in this case. For the conditional directives to operate, it's sufficient for block1 to appear in a #define directive. You can now include this block of code anywhere you think you might need it, with the assurance that it will never be duplicated within a program. The preprocessing directives ensure this can't happen.

 NOTE *It's a good idea to get into the habit of always protecting code in your own libraries in this fashion. You'll be surprised how easy it is to end up duplicating blocks of code accidentally, once you've collected a few libraries of your own functions.*

You aren't limited to testing just one value with the #if preprocessor directive. You can use logical operators to test if multiple identifiers have been defined. For example, the statement

```
#if defined block1 && defined block2
```

will evaluate to true if both block1 and block2 have previously been defined, and so the code that follows such a directive won't be included unless this is the case.

A further extension of the flexibility in applying the conditional preprocessor directives is the ability to undefine an identifier you've previously defined. This is achieved using a directive such as this:

```
#undef block1
```

Now, if `block1` had previously been defined, after this directive it's no longer defined. The ways in which these directives can all be combined to useful effect is only limited by your own ingenuity.

There are alternative ways of writing these directives that are slightly more concise. You can use whichever of the following forms you prefer. The directive

```
#ifdef block
```

is the same as

```
#if defined block
```

And the directive

```
#ifndef block
```

is the same as

```
#if !defined block
```

Directives Testing for Specific Values

You can also use a form of the `#if` directive to test the value of a constant expression. If the value of the constant expression is nonzero, the following statements down to the next `#endif` are included in the program code. If the constant expression evaluates to 0, the following statements down to the next #endif are skipped. The general form of the #if directive is

```
#if constant_expression
```

This is most frequently applied to test for a specific value being assigned to an identifier by a previous preprocessing directive. You might have the following sequence of statements, for example:

```
#if CPU == Pentium4
  printf("\nPerformance should be good." );
#endif
```

The `printf()` statement will be included in the program here only if the identifier `CPU` has been defined as `Pentium4` in a previous `#define` directive.

Multiple-Choice Selections

To complement the `#if` directives, you have the `#else` directive. This works in exactly the same way as the `else` statement does, in that it identifies a group of directives to be executed or statements to be included if the `#if` condition fails, for example:

```
#if CPU == Pentium4
  printf("\nPerformance should be good." );
#else
  printf("\nPerformance may not be so good." );
#endif
```

In this case, one or the other of the `printf()` statements will be included, depending on whether or not `CPU` has been defined as `Pentium4`.

The preprocessing phase also supports a special form of the `#if` for multiple-choice selections, in which only one of several choices of statements for inclusion in the program is required. This is the `#elif` directive, which has the general form

```
#elif constant_expression
```

An example of using this would be as follows:

```
#define US 0
#define UK 1
#define Australia 2
#define Country US
#if Country == US
  #define Greeting "Howdy, stranger."
#elif Country == UK
  #define Greeting "Wotcher, mate."
#elif Country == Australia
  #define Greeting "G'day, sport."
#endif
printf("\n%s", Greeting );
```

With this sequence of directives, the output of the `printf()` statement will depend on the value assigned to the identifier `Country`, in this case `US`.

Standard Preprocessing Macros

There are usually a considerable number of standard preprocessing macros defined, which you'll find described in your compiler documentation. I'll just mention two that are of general interest and that are available to you.

The _DATE_ macro provides a string representation of the date in the form Mmm dd yyyy when it's invoked in your program. Here Mmm is the month in characters, such as Jan, Feb, and so on. The pair of characters dd is the day in the form of a pair of digits 1 to 31, where single-digit days are preceded by a blank. Finally, yyyy is the year as four digits—1994, for example.

A similar macro, _TIME_, provides a string containing the value of the time when it's invoked, in the form hh:mm:ss, which is evidently a string containing pairs of digits for hours, minutes, and seconds, separated by colons. Note that the time is when the compiler is executed, not when the program is run.

You could use this macro to record when your program was last compiled with a statement such as this:

```
printf("\nProgram last compiled at %s on %s", __TIME__, __DATE__ );
```

Note that both _DATE_ and _TIME_ have two underscore characters at the beginning and the end. Once the program containing this statement has been compiled, the values that will be output by the printf() statement are fixed until you compile it again. On subsequent executions of the program, the then current time and date will be output. Don't confuse these macros with the time function I'll discuss later in this chapter.

Debugging Methods

Most of your programs will contain errors, or bugs, when you first complete them. Removing such bugs from a program can represent a substantial proportion of the time required to write the program. The larger and more complex the program, the more bugs it's likely to contain and the more time it will take to get the program to run properly. Very large programs, such as those typified by operating systems or complex applications such as word processing systems or even C program development systems, can be so complex that all the bugs can never be eliminated. You may already have experience of this in practice with some of the systems on your own computer. Usually these kinds of residual bugs are relatively minor, with ways in the system to work around them.

Your approach to writing a program can significantly affect how difficult it will be to test. A well-structured program consisting of compact functions, each with a well-defined purpose, is much easier to test than one without these attributes. Finding bugs will also be easier in a program that has extensive comments documenting the operation and purpose of its component functions, and that has well-chosen variable and function names. Good use of indentation and statement layout can also make testing and fault-finding simpler.

It's beyond the scope of this book to deal with debugging comprehensively, but in this section I'll introduce the basic ideas that you need to be aware of. Then when it comes to debugging, you'll know which direction you're heading in and what tools are available to assist you.

Integrated Debuggers

Many compilers are supplied with extensive debugging tools built into the program development environment. These can be very powerful facilities that can dramatically reduce the time required to get a program working. They typically provide a varied range of aids to testing a program that include the following:

- *Tracing program flow*: This capability allows you to execute your program one source statement at a time. It operates by pausing execution after each statement is executed and continuing with the next statement after you press a designated key. Other provisions of the debug environment will usually allow you to display information easily, pausing to show you what's happening to the data in your program.

- *Setting breakpoints*: Executing a large or complex program one statement at a time can be very tedious. It may even be impossible in a reasonable period of time. All you need is a loop that executes 10,000 times to make it an unrealistic proposition. Breakpoints provide an excellent alternative. With breakpoints, you define specific selected statements in your program at which a pause should occur to allow you to check what's happening. Execution continues to the next breakpoint when you press a specified key.

- *Setting watches*: This sort of facility allows you to identify variables that you want to track the value of as execution progresses. The values of the variables that you select are displayed at each pause point in your program. If you step through your program statement by statement, you can see the exact point at which values are changed or perhaps not changed when you expect them to be.

- *Inspecting program elements*: It may also be possible to examine a wide variety of program components. For example, at breakpoints, the inspection can show details of a function such as its return type and its arguments. You can also see details of a pointer in terms of its address, the address it contains, and the data stored at the address contained in the pointer. Seeing the values of expressions and modifying variables may also be provided for. Modifying variables can help to bypass problem areas to allow other areas to be executed with correct data, even though an earlier part of the program may not be working properly.

The Preprocessor in Debugging

By using conditional preprocessor directives, you can arrange for blocks of code to be included in your program to assist in testing. In spite of the power of the debug facilities included with many C development systems, the addition of tracing code of your own can still be useful. You have complete control of the formatting of data to be displayed for debugging purposes, and you can even arrange for the kind of output to vary according to conditions or relationships within the program.

....

Try It Out: Debugging Using Preprocessor Directives

You can illustrate how this can be done using a slightly modified version of a previous program that calls functions through an array of function pointers:

```
/* Program 13.1 Debugging using preprocessor directives */
#include <stdio.h>
#include <stdlib.h>

#define random(NumValues) ((int)(((double)(rand())*(NumValues))/(RAND_MAX+1.0)))
#define test
#define testf

/* Function prototypes   */
int sum(int, int);
int product(int, int);
int difference(int, int);

void main()
{
  int i = 0;                          /* Loop counter                      */
  int j = 0;                          /* Index for function selection       */
  int a = 10, b = 5;                  /* Starting values                    */
  int result = 0;                     /* Storage for results                */
  int (*pfun[3])(int, int);           /* Function pointer array declaration */

  /* Initialize pointers */
  pfun[0] = sum;
  pfun[1] = product;
  pfun[2] = difference;

#ifdef notrandom
  srand((unsigned int)time(NULL));    /* Seed random number generation      */
#endif

  /* Execute each function pointed to */
  for(i = 0 ; i < 10 ; i++)
  {
    j = random(3);                    /* Generate random index 0 to 2       */

    #ifdef test
    printf("\nRandom number = %d", j );
    if( j>2 )
    {
      printf("\nInvalid array index = %d", j);
      break;
    }
```

(Continued)

```
      #endif

    result = pfun[j](a , b);              /* Call random function         */
    printf("\nresult = %d", result );
  }
  result = pfun[1](pfun[0](a , b), pfun[2](a , b));
  printf("\n\nThe product of the sum and the difference = %d\n", result);
}

/* Definition of the function sum */
int sum(int x, int y)
{
  #ifdef testf
  printf("\nFunction sum called.");
  #endif

  return x + y;
}

/* Definition of the function product      */
int product( int x, int y )
{
  #ifdef testf
  printf("\nFunction product called.");
  #endif

  return x * y;
}

/* Definition of the function difference */
int difference(int x, int y)
{
  #ifdef testf
  printf("\nFunction difference called.");
  #endif

  return x - y;
}
```

HOW IT WORKS

You have a macro defined at the beginning of the program:

```
#define random(NumValues) ((int)(((double)(rand())*(NumValues))/(RAND_MAX+1.0)))
```

This defines the macro random() in terms of the function rand() that's declared in stdlib.h. The function rand() generates random numbers in the range 0 to RAND_MAX, which is a constant defined in stdlib.h.

(Continued)

The macro maps values from this range to produce values from 0 to NumValues-1. You cast the value from rand() to double to ensure that computation will be carried out as type double, and you cast the result overall back to int because that's what you want in the program. It's quite possible that your version of stdlib.h may already contain a macro for random() that does essentially the same thing. If so, you'll get an error message as the compiler won't allow two different definitions of the same macro. In this case, just delete the definition from the program.

After initializing the function pointers, you have the following code:

```
#ifndef notrandom
srand((unsigned int)time(NULL));      /* Seed random number generation      */
#endif
```

This code allows the possibility of defining the symbol notrandom, in which case the statement that seeds the random number generation process with the time value won't be included in the code. This will have the effect of making the results repeatable because the default seed is a constant. If you add a directive to define notrandom, every time you run the program you should get the same sequence of results. This can be very helpful when the program isn't working properly.

Look at the loop in main() that follows:

```
for(i = 0 ; i < 10 ; i++)
{
  j = random(3);                      /* Generate random index 0 to 2      */

  #ifdef test
  printf("\nRandom number = %d", j );
  if( j>2 )
  {
    printf("\nInvalid array index = %d", j);
    break;
  }
  #endif

  result = pfun[j](a , b);            /* Call random function              */
  printf("\nresult = %d", result );
}
```

This has been modified, compared to the previous version, by indexing the function pointer array using the variable j, which has its value generated by the macro call random(3).This will generate a random value between 0 and 2. This makes the example more interesting because you now don't know beforehand what the sequence of function calls is going to be. It depends on what sequence of random index values is generated.

(Continued)

Within the loop, you have two statements that will be included if the symbol test is defined. The first displays the value of the index j. You might well want to see this value when the program is being tested. The second statement, the if, is just a precaution. If by some means, you obtained a value for j that was outside the range of valid indexes for the array pfun, who knows what might happen.

Let's look at one of the functions that may be called, product() for example:

```
int product( int x, int y )
{
  #ifdef testf
  printf("\nFunction product called.");
  #endif

  return x * y;
}
```

This also has some code included if testf is defined. You can therefore control whether the statements in the #ifdef block are included here independently from the block in main(). With the program as written with both test and testf defined, you'll get trace output for the random index values generated and a message from each function as it's called, so you can follow the sequence of calls in the program exactly.

You can have as many different symbolic constants defined as you wish. As you've seen previously in this chapter, you can combine them into logical expressions using the #if defined form of the conditional directive.

Using the assert() Macro

The assert() macro is defined in the standard library header file assert.h. This macro enables you to insert tests of arbitrary expressions in your program that will cause the program to be terminated with a diagnostic message if a specified expression is 0. The argument to the assert() macro is an expression that results in a integer value, for example:

```
assert(a == b);
```

The expression will be true (nonzero) if a is equal to b. If a and b are unequal, then the argument to the macro will be false and the program will be terminated with a message relating to the assertion. Termination is achieved by calling abort(), so it's an abnormal end to the program—as it should be.

The assertion facility allowing assertions to occur can be switched off by defining the symbol NDEBUG before the #include directive for assert.h, like this:

```
#define NDEBUG            /* Switch off assertions */
#include <assert.h>
```

This will cause all assertions to be ignored.

With some systems, assertions are disabled by default, in which case you can enable them by undefining NDEBUG:

```
#undef NDEBUG                          /* Switch on assertions */
#include <assert.h>
```

By including the directive to undefine NDEBUG, you ensure that assertions are enabled for your source file. The #undef directive must appear before the #include directive for assert.h to be effective.

You can demonstrate this in operation with a simple example.

....

Try It Out: Demonstrating the assert() Macro

Here's the code for a program that uses the assert() macro:

```
/* Program 13.2 Demonstrating assertions */
#undef NDEBUG                          /* Switch on assertions */
#include <stdio.h>
#include <assert.h>

void main()
{
  int x = 0;
  int y = 5;
  for(x = 0 ; x < 20 ; x++)
  {
    printf("\nx = %d    y = %d", x, y);
    assert(x<y);
  }
}
```

Compiling and executing this with my compiler produces the following output:

```
x = 0   y = 5
x = 1   y = 5
x = 2   y = 5
x = 3   y = 5
x = 4   y = 5
x = 5   y = 5
Assertion failed: x<y , file Prog13_02.C, line 13
```

(Continued)

HOW IT WORKS

At this point, apart from the assert() statement, the program shouldn't need much explanation as it simply displays the values of x and y in the for loop.

The program is terminated by the assert() macro as soon as the condition x<y becomes false. As you can see from the output, this is when x reaches the value 5. The macro displays the output on stderr, which is always the display screen. Not only do you get the condition that failed displayed, but you also get the file name and line number in the file where the failure occurred. This is particularly useful with multifile programs in which the source of the error is pinpointed exactly.

Assertions are often used for critical conditions in a program in which, if certain conditions aren't met, disaster will surely ensue. You would want to be sure that the program wouldn't continue if such errors arise. Program 13.1 contains exactly this kind of situation, in which you're generating index values using a random number generator. With this sort of technique, there's always the possibility of a bug somewhere resulting in an invalid index value. If the index is outside the limits of the array pfun, the result is pretty much guaranteed to be catastrophic, as you'll be trying to execute a nonexistent function at a spurious address. Instead of the #ifdef block, you could simply have written this:

```
assert(j <= 2);
```

It's very simple and effective, and provides sufficient information to pin down where the program is terminated if an error occurs.

You could switch off the assertion mechanism in the example by replacing the #undef directive with

```
#define NDEBUG
```

This must be placed before the #include statement for assert.h to be effective, although assertions may be disabled by default. With this #define at the beginning of Program 13.2, you'll see that you get output for all the values of x from 0 to 19, and no diagnostic message.

Additional Library Functions

The library functions are basic to the power of the C language. Although I've covered quite a range of standard library functions so far, it's beyond the scope of this book to discuss all the standard libraries. However, I can introduce a few more of the most commonly used functions I haven't dealt with in detail up to now.

The Date and Time Function Library

Because time is an important parameter to measure, C includes a standard library of functions called `time.h` that deal with time and dates. They provide output in various forms from the hardware timer in your PC.

The simplest function has the prototype

```
clock_t clock(void);
```

This function returns the processor time (not the elapsed time) used by the program since execution began, as a value of type `clock_t`. The type `clock_t` is defined in `time.h` and is usually equivalent to `long`. The value is measured in clock ticks. To convert the value returned by the function `clock()` to seconds, you divide it by the constant `CLOCKS_PER_SEC`, which is also defined in the library `time.h`. The function returns –1 if an error occurs.

As you've seen, the `time()` function returns the calendar time as a value of type `time_t`. The current calendar time is the time in seconds since a fixed time and date. The fixed time and date is 00:00:00GMT on January 1, 1970, in Borland libraries, for example, and this is typical of how time values are defined.

The prototype of the `time()` function is

```
time_t time(time_t *);
```

If the argument isn't `NULL`, the current calendar time is also stored in the location pointed to by the pointer to the `time_t` argument. The type `time_t` is defined in the header file and is equivalent to `long`.

To calculate elapsed time in seconds between two successive `time_t` values returned by `time()`, you can use the function `difftime()`, which has the prototype

```
double difftime(time_t T2, time_t T1);
```

The function will return the value T2 - T1 expressed in seconds as a value of type `double`.

....

Try It Out: Using Time Functions

You could define a function to log the elapsed time and processor time used between successive calls, by using functions from `time.h` as follows:

```
/* Program 13.3 Test our timer function */
#include <stdio.h>
#include <time.h>

void main()
```

(Continued)

```
{
  long count = 100000000;              /* Number of loop iterations */
  long i = 0;                          /* Loop counter              */
  time_t calendar = 0;                 /* Holds calendar time       */
  clock_t now = 0;                     /* Holds initial clock time  */
  int interval = 3;                    /* Seconds interval for o/p  */
  int elapsed = 0;                     /* Elapsed clock time secs.  */

  calendar = time(NULL);               /* Get current calendar time */
  now = clock();                       /* Get current clock time    */
  printf("Initial clock time = %d Initial calendar time = %d\n",
                                                  now, calendar);


    for(i = 0L ; i<count ; i++)
    {
      elapsed = (clock()-now)/CLOCKS_PER_SEC;
      if(elapsed>=interval)
      {
        interval += 3;
        printf("\nElapsed = %ld seconds   iterations = %ld", elapsed, i);
      }
    }

  printf("\nCPU time for %ld iterations is %.2lf seconds\n",
                          count, (double)(clock()-now)/CLOCKS_PER_SEC );
  printf("\Final clock time = %d Final calendar time = %d\n",
                                              clock(), time(NULL));
  printf("\nElapsed calendar time to execute the program is %lf\n",
                              difftime(time(NULL), calendar));
}
```

On a relatively slow machine by current standards, I get the following output:

```
Initial clock time = 0 Initial calendar time = 1061812672

Elapsed = 3 seconds   iterations = 15913359
Elapsed = 6 seconds   iterations = 31958533
Elapsed = 9 seconds   iterations = 47991900
Elapsed = 12 seconds   iterations = 64031562
Elapsed = 15 seconds   iterations = 80075097
Elapsed = 18 seconds   iterations = 96121005
CPU time for 100000000 iterations is 18.72 seconds
Final clock time = 18718 Final calendar time = 1061812691

Elapsed calendar time to execute the program is 19.000000
```

(Continued)

HOW IT WORKS

This program illustrates the use of the functions clock(), time(), and difftime(). The time() function returns the current time in seconds, so you won't get values less than 1 second. Depending on the speed of your machine, you may want to adjust the number of iterations in the loop to reduce or increase the time required to execute this program.

You record and display the initial values for the clock time and the calendar time with these statements:

```
now = clock();                          /* Get current clock time   */
calendar = time(NULL);                  /* Get current calendar time */
printf("\nInitial clock time = %ld Initial calendar time = %ld\n",
                                                    now, calendar);
```

You then have a loop that will execute count times:

```
for(i = 0L ; i<count ; i++)
{
  elapsed = (clock()-now)/CLOCKS_PER_SEC;
  if(elapsed>=interval)
  {
    interval += 3;
    printf("\nElapsed = %ld seconds  iterations = %ld", elapsed, i);
  }
}
```

To give you some indication that something is happening, the statements in the loop will output the elapsed clock time and the current iteration count every 3 seconds.

Finally, you output the values returned by clock() and time(), and calculate the clock and calendar time intervals:

```
printf("\nCPU time for %ld iterations is %.2lf seconds\n",
                          count, (double)(clock()-now)/CLOCKS_PER_SEC );
printf("\Final clock time = %d Final calendar time = %d\n",
                                              clock(), time(NULL));
printf("\nElapsed calendar time to execute the program is %lf\n",
                                  difftime(time(NULL), calendar));
```

Generally, you would use clock() to calculate time intervals during execution of a program, as this produces a value with 1 millisecond precision.

Getting the Date

Having the time in seconds since a date over thirty years ago is interesting, but it's often more convenient to get today's date. You can do this with the function ctime(), which has the prototype

```
char *ctime(time_t *);
```

The function accepts a pointer to a time_t variable as an argument that contains a calendar time value that was returned by the time() function. It returns a pointer to a 26-character string containing the day, the date, the time, and the year, that is terminated by a newline and a '\0'.

A typical string returned might be

```
"Mon Aug 25  10:45:56 2003\n\0"
```

You might use the ctime() function like this:

```
time_t calendar = 0;
calendar = time(NULL);                  /* Store calendar time            */
printf("\n%s", ctime(&calendar));       /* Output calendar time as date string */
```

You can also get at the various components of the time and date from a calendar time value by using the library function localtime(). This function has the prototype

```
struct tm *localtime(time_t *);
```

This function accepts a pointer to a time_t value and returns a pointer to a structure type tm, which is defined in the time.h header file. The structure contains the members listed in Table 13-1.

Table 13-1. Members of the tm Structure

Member	Description
tm_sec	Seconds on 24-hour clock
tm_min	Minutes on 24-hour clock
tm_hour	Hours on 24-hour clock
tm_mday	Day of the month (1 to 31)
tm_mon	Month (0 to 11)
tm_year	Year (current year minus 1900)
tm_wday	Weekday (Sunday is 0; Saturday is 6)
tm_yday	Day of year (0 to 365)
tm_isdst	Daylight saving flag (0 for daylight saving time)

All these structure members are of type int. This structure is a static structure, so the values of its members are overwritten with each call to the function. If you want to keep any of the member values, you need to copy them elsewhere before the next call to localtime(), or you could create your own tm structure and save the whole lot if you really need to.

Here's a code fragment that will output the day and the date from the members of the tm structure:

```
time_t calendar = 0;                    /* Holds calendar time        */
struct tm *time_data;                   /* Holds address of tm struct */
char *days[] = {"Sunday",    "Monday", "Tuesday", "Wednesday",
                "Thursday", "Friday", "Saturday"             };
char *months[] = {"January", "February", "March",
                  "April",    "May",      "June",
                  "July",    "August",   "September",
                  "October", "November", "December"  };

calendar = time(NULL);                  /* Get current calendar time */
printf("\n%s", ctime(&calendar));
time_data = localtime(&calendar);
printf("Today is %s %s %d %d\n",
                  days[time_data->tm_wday], months[time_data->tm_mon],
                  time_data->tm_mday,       time_data->tm_year+1900);
```

You've defined arrays of strings to hold the days of the week and the months. You use the appropriate member of the structure that has been set up by the call to the localtime() function. You use the day in the month and the year values from the structure directly. You can easily extend this to output the time.

Try It Out: Getting the Date

It's very easy to pick out the members you want from the structure of type tm returned from the function localtime(). You can demonstrate this with the following example:

```
/* Program 13.4        Getting date data with ease */
#include <stdio.h>
#include <time.h>
void main()
{
  char *Day[7] = {
                  "Sunday"    , "Monday", "Tuesday", "Wednesday",
                  "Thursday", "Friday", "Saturday"
               };
  char *Month[12] = {
                  "January",    "February", "March",    "April",
```

(Continued)

```
                   "May",        "June",      "July",      "August",
                   "September", "October",  "November", "December"
                };
  char *Suffix[] = { "st", "nd", "rd", "th" };


  int i = 3;                          /* Day suffix index             */
  struct tm *OurT = NULL;             /* Pointer for the time structure */
  time_t Tval = 0;                    /* Calendar time                */

  Tval = time(NULL);                  /* Get calendar time            */
  OurT = localtime(&Tval);            /* Generate time structure      */

  switch( OurT->tm_mday )
  {
    case 1: case 21: case 31:
      i= 0;                           /* Select "st" */
      break;
    case 2: case 22:
      i = 1;                          /* Select "nd" */
      break;
    case 3: case 23:
      i = 2;                          /* Select "rd" */
      break;
    default:
      i = 3;                          /* Select "th" */
      break;
  }

  printf("\nToday is %s the %d%s %s %d", Day[OurT->tm_wday],
    OurT->tm_mday, Suffix[i], Month[OurT->tm_mon], 1900 + OurT->tm_year);
  printf("\nThe time is %d : %d : %d",
    OurT->tm_hour, OurT->tm_min, OurT->tm_sec );
}
```

HOW IT WORKS

In this example, the first declarations in main() are as follows:

```
  char *Day[7] = {
                  "Sunday"   , "Monday", "Tuesday", "Wednesday",
                  "Thursday", "Friday", "Saturday"
              };
  char *Month[12] = {
                   "January",   "February", "March",     "April",
                   "May",       "June",     "July",      "August",
                   "September", "October",  "November", "December"
                };
  char *Suffix[] = { "st", "nd", "rd", "th" };
```

(Continued)

Each defines an array of pointers to char. The first holds the days of the week, the second contains the months in the year, and the third holds the suffixes to numerical values for the day in the month when representing dates. You could have left out the array dimensions in the first two declarations and the compiler would have computed them for you, but in this case you're reasonably confident about both these numbers, so this is an instance in which putting them in helps to avoid an error.

You also declare a structure variable in the following declaration:

```
struct tm *OurT = NULL;                 /* Pointer for the time structure */
```

This provides space to store the pointer to the structure returned by the function local_time().

You first obtain the current time in Tval using the function time(). You then use this value to generate the values of the members of the structure returned by the function localtime(). If you wanted to keep the data in the structure, you would need to copy it before calling the localtime() function again, as it would be over-written. Once you have the structure from localtime(), you execute the switch:

```
switch( OurT->tm_mday )
{
  case 1: case 21: case 31:
    i= 0;                             /* Select "st" */
    break;
  case 2: case 22:
    i = 1;                            /* Select "nd" */
    break;
  case 3: case 23:
    i = 2;                            /* Select "rd" */
    break;
  default:
    i = 3;                            /* Select "th" */
    break;
}
```

The sole purpose of this is to select what to append to the date value. Based on the member tm_mday, the switch selects an index to the array Suffix[] for use when outputting the date.

The day, the date, and the time are displayed, with the day and month strings obtained by indexing the appropriate array with the corresponding structure member value. The addition of 1900 to the value of the member tm_year is because this value is measured relative to the year 1900.

Summary

Your standard library header files are an excellent source of examples of coding preprocessing directives. You can view these examples with any text editor. Virtually all of the
capabilities of the preprocessor are used in the libraries, and you'll find lots of C source
code there too. It's also useful to familiarize yourself with the contents of the libraries,
as you can find there many things not necessarily described in the library documentation. If you aren't sure what the type clock_t is, for example, just look in the library
time.h, where you'll find the definition.

If you've reached this point and are confident that you've understood and can
apply what you've read, you should now be a full-fledged C programmer. C program
code will be meat and drink to you by this stage. All you need now is more practice. To
get better at programming, there's no alternative to practice, and the more varied the
types of programs you write, the better. You can always improve your skills, but fortunately—or unfortunately, depending on your point of view—it's unlikely that you'll
ever reach perfection in programming. However, every time you get a new piece of
code to work as it should, it will always generate a thrill and a feeling of satisfaction.
Enjoy your programming!

Exercises

The following exercises enable you to try out what you've learned in this chapter. If you
get stuck, look back over the chapter for help. If you're still stuck, you can download the
solutions from the Downloads area of the Apress website (http://www.apress.com), but
that really should be a last resort.

Exercise 13-1. Define a macro, COMPARE(x,y), that will result in the value −1 if x<y, 0
if x==y, and 1 if x>y. Write an example to demonstrate that your macro works as it
should. Can you see any advantage that your macro has over a function that does
the same thing?

Exercise 13-2. Define a function that will return a string containing the current
time in 12-hour format (am/pm) if the argument is 0 and in 24-hour format if the
argument is 1. Demonstrate that your function works with a suitable program.

Exercise 13-3. Define a macro, print_value(expr), that will output on a new line:

```
exp = result
```

where result is the value that results from evaluating expr. Demonstrate the operation of your macro with a suitable program.

APPENDIX A

Computer Arithmetic

IN THE CHAPTERS OF THIS BOOK, I've deliberately kept discussion of arithmetic to a minimum. However, it's important, so I'm going to quickly go over the subject in this appendix. If you feel confident in your math skills, this review will be old hat to you. If you find the math parts tough, then this section should show you how easy it really is.

Binary Numbers

First, let's consider exactly what you intend when you write a common, everyday decimal number, such as 324 or 911. Obviously, what you mean is "three hundred and twenty-four" or "nine hundred and eleven." Put more precisely, you mean

324 is $3 \times 10^2 + 2 \times 10^1 + 4 \times 10^0$, which is $3 \times 10 \times 10 + 2 \times 10 + 4$

911 is $9 \times 10^2 + 1 \times 10^1 + 1 \times 10^0$, which is $9 \times 10 \times 10 + 1 \times 10 + 1$

We call this decimal notation because it's built around powers of 10. (This is derived from the Latin *decimalis* meaning "of tithes," which was a tax of 10 percent. Ah, those were the days. . . .)

Representing numbers in this way is very handy for people with ten fingers and/or ten toes, or indeed ten of any kind of appendage. However, your PC is rather less handy, being built mainly of switches that are either on or off. It's OK for counting up to two, but not spectacular at counting to ten. I'm sure you're aware that this is the primary reason why your computer represents numbers using base 2 rather than base 10. Representing numbers using base 2 is called the **binary** system of counting. With numbers expressed using base 10, digits can be from 0 to 9 inclusive, whereas with binary numbers digits can only be 0 or 1, which is ideal when you only have on/off switches to represent them. In an exact analogy to the system of counting in base 10, the binary number 1101, for example, breaks down like this:

$1 \times 2^3 + 1 \times 2^2 + 0 \times 2^1 + 1 \times 2^0$, which is $1 \times 2 \times 2 \times 2 + 1 \times 2 \times 2 + 0 \times 2 + 1$

This amounts to 13 in the decimal system. In Table A-1, you can see the decimal equivalents of all the possible numbers you can represent using eight binary digits (a **bi**nary dig**it** is more commonly known as a **bit**).

Table A-1. Decimal Equivalents of 8-Bit Binary Values

Binary	Decimal	Binary	Decimal
0000 0000	0	1000 0000	128
0000 0001	1	1000 0001	129
0000 0010	2	1000 0010	130
. . .	. . .	. . .	. . .
0001 0000	16	1001 0000	144
0001 0001	17	1001 0001	145
. . .	. . .	. . .	. . .
0111 1100	124	1111 1100	252
0111 1101	125	1111 1101	253
0111 1110	126	1111 1110	254
0111 1111	127	1111 1111	255

Notice that using the first seven bits, you can represent numbers from 0 to 127, which is a total of 2^7 numbers, and that using all eight bits, you get 256 or 2^8 numbers. In general, if you have n bits, you can represent 2^n integers, with values from 0 to 2^n-1.

Adding binary numbers inside your computer is a piece of cake, because the "carry" from adding corresponding digits can only be 0 or 1, and very simple circuitry can handle the process. Figure A-1 shows how the addition of two 8-bit binary values would work.

```
       Binary          Decimal

     0001 1101             29
  +  0010 1011          +  43
     ----------          ------
     0100 1000             72
     ΛΛΛΛΛΛ/             ------
     Carries
```

Figure A-1. Adding binary values

Hexadecimal Numbers

When you start dealing with larger binary numbers, a small problem arises. Look at this one:

1111 0101 1011 1001 1110 0001

Binary notation here starts to be more than a little cumbersome for practical use, particularly when you consider that if you work out what this is in decimal, it's only

16,103,905—a miserable eight decimal digits. You can sit more angels on the head of a pin than that! Clearly, we need a more economical way of writing this, but decimal isn't always appropriate. Sometimes (as you saw in Chapter 3) you might need to be able to specify that the tenth and twenty-fourth bits from the right are set to 1, but without the overhead of writing out all the bits in binary notation. To figure out the decimal integer required to do this sort of thing is hard work, and there's a good chance you'll get it wrong anyway. A much easier solution is to use hexadecimal notation, in which the numbers are represented using base 16.

Arithmetic to base 16 is a much more convenient option, and it fits rather well with binary. Each hexadecimal digit can have values from 0 to 15 (the digits from 10 to 15 being represented by letters A to F, as shown in Table A-2), and values from 0 to 15 correspond nicely with the range of values that four binary digits can represent.

Table A-2. Hexadecimal Digits and Their Values in Decimal and Binary

Hexadecimal	Decimal	Binary
0	0	0000
1	1	0001
2	2	0010
3	3	0011
4	4	0100
5	5	0101
6	6	0110
7	7	0111
8	8	1000
9	9	1001
A	10	1010
B	11	1011
C	12	1100
D	13	1101
E	14	1110
F	15	1111

Because a hexadecimal digit corresponds to four binary digits, you can represent a large binary number as a hexadecimal number simply by taking groups of four binary digits, starting from the right, and writing the equivalent hexadecimal digit for each group. Look at the following binary number:

1111 0101 1011 1001 1110 0001

Taking each group of four bits in turn and replacing it with the corresponding hexadecimal digit from the table, this number expressed in hexadecimal notation will come out as follows:

F   5   B   9   E   1

You have six hexadecimal digits corresponding to the six groups of four binary digits. Just to prove that it all works out with no cheating, you can convert this number directly from hexadecimal to decimal by again using the analogy with the meaning of a decimal number. The value of this hexadecimal number therefore works out as follows.

F5B9E1 as a decimal value is given by

$$15\times16^5 + 5\times16^4 + 11\times16^3 + 9\times16^2 + 14\times16^1 + 1\times16^0$$

This turns out to be

$$15{,}728{,}640 + 327{,}680 + 45{,}056 + 2{,}304 + 224 + 1$$

Thankfully, this adds up to the same number you got when converting the equivalent binary number to a decimal value: 16,103,905.

Negative Binary Numbers

There's another aspect to binary arithmetic that you need to understand: negative numbers. So far, you've assumed that everything is positive—the optimist's view, if you will—and so the glass is still half full. But you can't avoid the negative side of life—the pessimist's perspective—that the glass is already half empty. How can a negative number be represented inside a computer? Well, you have only binary digits at your disposal, so the solution has to be to use one of those to indicate whether the number is negative or positive.

For numbers that you want to allow to have negative values (referred to as **signed numbers**), you must first decide on a fixed length (in other words, the number of binary digits) and then designate the leftmost binary digit as a **sign bit**. You have to fix the length to avoid any confusion about which bit is the sign bit.

Because your computer's memory consists of 8-bit bytes, the binary numbers are going to be stored in some multiple (usually a power of 2) of 8 bits. Thus, you can have some numbers with 8 bits, some with 16 bits, and some with 32 bits (or whatever), and as long as you know what the length is in each case, you can find the sign bit—it's just the leftmost bit. If the sign bit is 0, the number is positive, and if it's 1, the number is negative.

This seems to solve the problem, and in some computers it does. Each number consists of a sign bit that is 0 for positive values and 1 for negative values, plus a given number of bits that specify the absolute value of the number—unsigned, in other words. Changing +6 to –6 then just involves flipping the sign bit from 0 to 1. Unfortunately, this representation carries a lot of overhead with it in terms of the complexity of the circuits that are needed to perform arithmetic with this number representation. For this reason, most computers take a different approach.

Ideally, when two integers are added, you don't want the computer to be messing about, checking whether either or both of the numbers are negative. You just want to use simple "add" circuitry regardless of the signs of the operands. The add operation will combine corresponding binary digits to produce the appropriate bit as a result, with a carry to the next digit along where this is necessary. If you add –8 in binary to

+12, you would really like to get the answer +4 using the same circuitry that would apply if you were adding +3 and +8.

If you try this with your simplistic solution, which is just to set the sign bit of the positive value to 1 to make it negative, and then perform the arithmetic with conventional carries, it doesn't quite work:

12 in binary is	0000 1100
–8 in binary (you suppose) is	1000 1000
If you now add these together, you get	1001 0100

This seems to be –20, which isn't what you wanted at all. It's definitely not +4, which you know is 0000 0100. "Ah," I hear you say, "you can't treat a sign just like another digit." But that is just what you *do* want to do.

Let's see how the computer would like you to represent –8 by trying to subtract +12 from +4, as that should give you the right answer:

+4 in binary is	0000 0100
+12 in binary is	0000 1100
Subtract the latter from the former and you get	1111 1000

For each digit from the fourth from the right onward, you had to "borrow" 1 to do the subtraction, just as you would when performing ordinary decimal arithmetic. This result is supposed to be –8, and even though it doesn't look like it, that's exactly what it is. Just try adding it to +12 or +15 in binary, and you'll see that it works!

Of course, if you want to produce –8 you can always do so by subtracting +8 from 0.

What *exactly* did you get when you subtracted 12 from 4 or +8 from 0, for that matter? It turns out that what you have here is called the **2's complement** representation of a negative binary number, and you can produce this from any positive binary number by a simple procedure that you can perform in your head. At this point, I need to ask a little faith on your part and avoid getting into explanations of *why* it works. I'll just show you how the 2's complement form of a negative number can be constructed from a positive value, and you can prove to yourself that it does work. Let's return to the previous example, in which you need the 2's complement representation of –8.

You start with +8 in binary:

0000 1000

You now "flip" each binary digit, changing 0s to 1s and vice versa:

1111 0111

This is called the **1's complement** form, and if you now add 1 to this, you'll get the 2's complement form:

1111 1000

This is exactly the same as the representation of –8 you got by subtracting +12 from +4. Just to make absolutely sure, let's try the original sum of adding –8 to +12:

+12 in binary is	0000 1100
Your version of –8 is	1111 1000
If you add *these* together, you get	0000 0100

The answer is 4—magic. It works! The "carry" propagates through all the leftmost 1s, setting them back to 0. One fell off the end, but you shouldn't worry about that—it's probably compensating for the one you borrowed from off the end in the subtraction sum you did to get –8. In fact, what's happening is that you're making an assumption that the sign bit, 1 or 0, repeats forever to the left. Try a few examples of your own; you'll find it always works, automatically. The really great thing about using 2's complement representation of negative numbers is that it makes arithmetic very easy (and fast) for your computer.

Big-Endian and Little-Endian Systems

As I've discussed, integers generally are stored in memory as binary values in a contiguous sequence of bytes, commonly groups of 2, 4, or 8 bytes. The question of the sequence in which the bytes appear can be very important—it's one of those things that doesn't matter until it matters, and then it *really* matters!

Let's consider the decimal value 262,657 stored as a 4-byte binary value. I chose this value because in binary it happens to be

0000 0000 0000 0100 0000 0010 0000 0001

so each byte has a pattern of bits that is easily distinguished from the others.

If you're using an Intel PC, the number will be stored as follows:

Byte address:	00	01	02	03
Data bits:	0000 0001	0000 0010	0000 0100	0000 0000

As you can see, the most significant eight bits of the value—the one that's all 0s—are stored in the byte with the highest address (last, in other words), and the least significant eight bits are stored in the byte with the lowest address, which is the leftmost byte. This arrangement is described as **little-endian**.

If you're using a mainframe computer, a RISC workstation, or a Mac machine based on a Motorola processor, the same data is likely to be arranged in memory like this:

Byte address:	00	01	02	03
Data bits:	0000 0000	0000 0100	0000 0010	0000 0001

Now the bytes are in reverse sequence with the most significant eight bits stored in the leftmost byte, which is the one with the lowest address. This arrangement is described as **big-endian**.

 NOTE *Regardless of whether the byte order is big-endian or little-endian, within each byte the bits are arranged with the most significant bit on the left and the least significant bit on the right.*

This is all very interesting, you may say, but why should it matter? Most of the time, it doesn't. More often than not, you can happily write your C program without knowing whether the computer on which the code will execute is big-endian or little-endian. It *does* matter, however, when you're processing binary data that comes from another machine. Binary data will be written to a file or transmitted over a network as a sequence of bytes. It's up to you how you interpret it. If the source of the data is a machine with a different endian-ness from the machine on which your code is running, you must reverse the order of the bytes in each binary value. If you don't, you have garbage.

For those who collect curious background information, the terms "big-endian" and "little-endian" are drawn from the book *Gulliver's Travels* by Jonathan Swift. In the story, the emperor of Lilliput commanded all his subjects to always crack their eggs at the smaller end. This was a consequence of the emperor's son having cut his finger following the traditional approach of cracking his egg at the big end. Ordinary, law-abiding Lilliputian subjects who cracked their eggs at the smaller end were described as Little Endians. The Big Endians were a rebellious group of traditionalists in the Lilliputian kingdom who insisted on continuing to crack their eggs at the big end. Many were put to death as a result.

Floating-Point Numbers

We often have to deal with very large numbers—the number of protons in the universe, for example—which need around 79 decimal digits. Clearly there are lots of situations in which you'll need more than the ten decimal digits you get from a 4-byte binary number. Equally, there are lots of very small numbers, for example, the amount of time in minutes it takes the typical car salesperson to accept your offer on a 1982 Ford LTD (and it's covered only 380,000 miles . . .). A mechanism for handling both these kinds of numbers is, as you may have guessed, **floating-point** numbers.

A floating-point representation of a number in decimal notation is a decimal value 0 with a fixed number of digits multiplied by a power of 10 to produce the number you want. It's easier to demonstrate than to explain, so let's look at some examples. The number 365 in normal decimal notation could be written in floating-point form as follows:

0.3650000E03

The E stands for "exponent" and precedes the power of 10 that the 0.3650000 (the mantissa) part is multiplied by to get the required value. That is

$$0.3650000 \times 10 \times 10 \times 10$$

which is clearly 365.

The mantissa in the number here has seven decimal digits. The number of digits of precision in a floating-point number will depend on how much memory it is allocated. A single precision floating-point value occupying 4 bytes will provide approximately seven decimal digits accuracy. I say "approximately" because inside your computer these numbers are in binary floating-point form, and a binary fraction with 23 bits doesn't exactly correspond to a decimal fraction with seven decimal digits.

Now let's look at a small number:

0.3650000E-04

This is evaluated as $.365 \times 10^{-4}$, which is .0000365—exactly the time in minutes required by the car salesperson to accept your cash.

Suppose you have a large number such as 2,134,311,179. How does this look as a floating-point number? Well, it looks like this:

0.2134311E10

It's not quite the same. You've lost three low-order digits and you've approximated your original value as 2,134,311,000. This is a small price to pay for being able to handle such a vast range of numbers, typically from 10^{-38} to 10^{+38} either positive or negative, as well having an extended representation that goes from a minute 10^{-308} to a mighty 10^{+308}. They're called floating-point numbers for the fairly obvious reason that the decimal point "floats" and its position depends on the exponent value.

Aside from the fixed precision limitation in terms of accuracy, there's another aspect you may need to be conscious of. You need to take great care when adding or subtracting numbers of significantly different magnitudes. A simple example will demonstrate this kind of problem. You can first consider adding .365E-3 to .365E+7. You can write this as a decimal sum:

$$0.000365 + 3,650,000.0$$

This produces the result

3,650,000.000365

When converted back to floating-point with seven digits of precision, this becomes

0.3650000E+7

So you might as well not have bothered. The problem lies directly with the fact that you carry only seven digits precision. The seven digits of the larger number aren't affected by any of the digits of the smaller number because they're all further to the right. Funnily enough, you must also take care when the numbers are nearly equal. If you compute the difference between such numbers, you may end up with a result that has only one or two digits precision. It's quite easy in such circumstances to end up computing with numbers that are totally garbage.

APPENDIX B

ASCII Character Code Definitions

THE FIRST 32 AMERICAN STANDARD CODE for Information Interchange (ASCII) characters provide control functions. Many of these haven't been referenced in this book but are included here for completeness. In Table B-1, only the first 128 characters are included. The remaining 128 characters include further special symbols and letters for national character sets.

Table B-1. ASCII Character Code Values

Decimal	Hexadecimal	Character	Control
000	00	Null	NUL
001	01	--	SOH
002	02	--	STX
003	03	--	ETX
004	04	--	EOT
005	05	--	ENQ
006	06	--	ACK
007	07	--	BEL (audible bell)
008	08	--	Backspace
009	09	--	HT
010	0A	--	LF (linefeed)
011	0B	--	VT (vertical tab)
012	0C	--	FF (form feed)
013	0D	--	CR (carriage return)
014	0E	--	SO
015	0F	--	SI
016	10	--	DLE
017	11	--	DC1
018	12	--	DC2
019	13	--	DC3
020	14	--	DC4
021	15	--	NAK
022	16	--	SYN

(Continued)

Table B-1. ASCII Character Code Values (Continued)

Decimal	Hexadecimal	Character	Control
023	17	--	ETB
024	18	--	CAN
025	19	--	EM
026	1A	--	SUB
027	1B	--	ESC (escape)
028	1C	--	FS
029	1D	--	GS
030	1E	--	RS
031	1F	--	US
032	20	--	Space
033	21	!	--
034	22	"	--
035	23	#	--
036	24	$	--
037	25	%	--
038	26	&	--
039	27	'	--
040	28	(	--
041	29	)	--
042	2A	*	--
043	2B	+	--
044	2C	,	--
045	2D	-	--
046	2E	.	--
047	2F	/	--
048	30	0	--
049	31	1	--
050	32	2	--
051	33	3	--
052	34	4	--
053	35	5	--
054	36	6	--
055	37	7	--
056	38	8	--
057	39	9	--
058	3A	:	--
059	3B	;	--
060	3C	<	--

(Continued)

Table B-1. ASCII Character Code Values (Continued)

Decimal	Hexadecimal	Character	Control
061	3D	=	--
062	3E	>	--
063	3F	?	--
064	40	@	--
065	41	A	--
066	42	B	--
067	43	C	--
068	44	D	--
069	45	E	--
070	46	F	--
071	47	G	--
072	48	H	--
073	49	I	--
074	4A	J	--
075	4B	K	--
076	4C	L	--
077	4D	M	--
078	4E	N	--
079	4F	O	--
080	50	P	--
081	51	Q	--
082	52	R	--
083	53	S	--
084	54	T	--
085	55	U	--
086	56	V	--
087	57	W	--
088	58	X	--
089	59	Y	--
090	5A	Z	--
091	5B	[	--
092	5C	\	--
093	5D	]	--
094	5E	^	--
095	5F	_	--
096	60	'	--
097	61	a	--
098	62	b	--

(Continued)

Table B-1. ASCII Character Code Values (Continued)

Decimal	Hexadecimal	Character	Control
099	63	c	--
100	64	d	--
101	65	e	--
102	66	f	--
103	67	g	--
104	68	h	--
105	69	i	--
106	6A	j	--
107	6B	k	--
108	6C	l	--
109	6D	m	--
110	6E	n	--
111	6F	o	--
112	70	p	--
113	71	q	--
114	72	r	--
115	73	s	--
116	74	t	--
117	75	u	--
118	76	v	--
119	77	w	--
120	78	x	--
121	79	y	--
122	7A	z	--
123	7B	{	--
124	7C	|	--
125	7D	}	--
126	7E	~	--
127	7F	Delete	--

Reserved Words in C

THE WORDS IN THE FOLLOWING LIST are **keywords** in C, so you must not use them for other purposes such as variable names or function names.

auto	for	struct
break	goto	switch
case	if	typedef
char	inline	union
const	int	unsigned
continue	long	void
default	register	volatile
do	restrict	while
double	return	_Bool
else	short	_Complex
enum	signed	_Imaginary
extern	sizeof	
float	static	

Index

G

forums.apress.com

FOR PROFESSIONALS BY PROFESSIONALS™

JOIN THE APRESS FORUMS AND BE PART OF OUR COMMUNITY. You'll find discussions that cover topics of interest to IT professionals, programmers, and enthusiasts just like you. If you post a query to one of our forums, you can expect that some of the best minds in the business—especially Apress authors, who all write with *The Expert's Voice*™—will chime in to help you. Why not aim to become one of our most valuable participants (MVPs) and win cool stuff? Here's a sampling of what you'll find:

DATABASES
Data drives everything.

Share information, exchange ideas, and discuss any database programming or administration issues.

INTERNET TECHNOLOGIES AND NETWORKING
Try living without plumbing (and eventually IPv6).

Talk about networking topics including protocols, design, administration, wireless, wired, storage, backup, certifications, trends, and new technologies.

JAVA
We've come a long way from the old Oak tree.

Hang out and discuss Java in whatever flavor you choose: J2SE, J2EE, J2ME, Jakarta, and so on.

MAC OS X
All about the Zen of OS X.

OS X is both the present and the future for Mac apps. Make suggestions, offer up ideas, or boast about your new hardware.

OPEN SOURCE
Source code is good; understanding (open) source is better.

Discuss open source technologies and related topics such as PHP, MySQL, Linux, Perl, Apache, Python, and more.

PROGRAMMING/BUSINESS
Unfortunately, it is.

Talk about the Apress line of books that cover software methodology, best practices, and how programmers interact with the "suits."

WEB DEVELOPMENT/DESIGN
Ugly doesn't cut it anymore, and CGI is absurd.

Help is in sight for your site. Find design solutions for your projects and get ideas for building an interactive Web site.

SECURITY
Lots of bad guys out there—the good guys need help.

Discuss computer and network security issues here. Just don't let anyone else know the answers!

TECHNOLOGY IN ACTION
Cool things. Fun things.

It's after hours. It's time to play. Whether you're into LEGO® MINDSTORMS™ or turning an old PC into a DVR, this is where technology turns into fun.

WINDOWS
No defenestration here.

Ask questions about all aspects of Windows programming, get help on Microsoft technologies covered in Apress books, or provide feedback on any Apress Windows book.

HOW TO PARTICIPATE:

Go to the Apress Forums site at **http://forums.apress.com/**.

Click the New User link.